NAPOLEON

NAPOLEON

THE PATH TO POWER, 1769–1799

PHILIP DWYER

B L O O M S B U R Y
LONDON · NEW DELHI · NEW YORK · SYDNEY

First published in Great Britain 2007
This paperback edition published 2008

Copyright © 2007 by Philip Dwyer

Maps by John Gilkes

The moral right of the author has been asserted

Bloomsbury Publishing Plc
50 Bedford Square
London WC1B 3DP

www.bloomsbury.com

Bloomsbury Publishing, London, New Delhi, New York and Sydney

A CIP catalogue record for this book is available from the British Library

ISBN 13: 978 0 7475 6677 9

Typeset by Hewer Text UK Ltd, Edinburgh
Printed and bound in Great Britain by CPI (UK) Ltd, Croydon CR0 4YY

For my father,
Francis Matthew Dwyer

Contents

Maps

A Note on the Use of Names

Napoleon Bonaparte was christened Napoleone di Buonaparte and was known by that name for the first two decades of his life; his first name was also sometimes spelled Nabulio, Nabulione, Napulione or Napolionne. The name is unusual and its origins are obscure, although he was probably named after his father's uncle, who died a year before Napoleone's birth. For the purposes of this book, I have used 'Napoleone' in the passages dealing with his youth, and then 'Buonaparte' once he graduates from the military academy in Paris. Similarly, I have kept the Corsican versions of the names of the Buonaparte family for the early stages. For example, Joseph – the future King of Spain – is referred to as Giuseppe, Louis – the future King of Holland – as Luigi, and so on. It was only after the Buonaparte family was definitively installed in France in 1793 that they began to adopt French versions of their names. After marrying Josephine in 1796, Napoleone di Buonaparte changed the spelling of his name to Napoleon Bonaparte, and, therefore, from that moment on, I refer to him as simply 'Bonaparte' (which Josephine called him all her life). Where he is referred to as 'Napoleon', it is generally a reference to the period after 1804.

Prologue: The Bridge at Arcola

Napoleon is one of those figures whose legend is so persistent that it often confounds historical reality, especially in the popular imagination. Indeed, Napoleon contributed much towards constructing his own myth, from his youth even until after he fell from power, when, while in exile, he dictated his memoirs to a group of disciples who took down his every word in the hope that his version of history would prevail. Such were Napoleon's skills as a chronicler that much of the legend is still unquestioningly accepted.

One of the most blatant examples of the legend of Napoleon prevailing is in the account we have of the battle to take Arcola, a nondescript northern Italian village in a desolate setting about thirty-two kilometres east of Verona. On a bleak winter's day in November 1796, French and Austrian imperial forces confronted each other, separated by the river Alpone and a small wooden bridge that was about thirty paces long and set on three stone piles. The unimposing bridge, still in its original place, is now made of concrete and metal. The road leading up to it is built up above the surrounding fields; there is a dyke on either side of the road, and also on either side of the river bank, in order to prevent the village and the surrounding fields from flooding. Crossing this bridge at the earliest possible moment was crucial to Bonaparte's plan.

On the opposite side of the Alpone facing the French were two battalions of Croatians, part of the Austrian imperial army, and several cannon placed in such a way that they could fire on anyone approaching the bridge along the exposed roadway for hundreds of metres. Rather than advance, the French troops took cover behind the dykes. Some of Bonaparte's leading generals – Lannes, Bon, Verdier and Verne – were wounded trying to lead their men forward. 'At that disheartening sight, [General Pierre-François] Augereau [who would go on to become a marshal of the Empire], the intrepid Augereau, rushed forward, went through the ranks of frightened soldiers, tore the flag from the flag bearer and advanced towards the enemy; a courageous few followed him, the others hesitated; but vile shots having killed five or six, they retreated and again took refuge behind the embankment.'[1] Augereau, although abandoned by his men, escaped without injury and returned to his starting point.

According to one of his aides-de-camp, Captain Joseph Sulkowski, Bonaparte decided to repeat the same heroic gesture, flag in hand:

> We suddenly saw him appear on the embankment, surrounded by his general staff and followed by his guides, he dismounted, drew his sword, took the flag and rushed onto the middle of the bridge amid a rain of fire. The troops saw him but none of them imitated him. I was present at that incredible cowardice and can hardly believe it . . . The moment was brief, but fatal for all those who surrounded Bonaparte, his aide-de-camp Muiron, general Vignolle, the lieutenant of the guides, and two of Belliard's adjutants fell by his side. I myself was hit by shot, right in the chest, the rolled up coat I was carrying around my neck saved my life; but at the same time a shell exploded at my feet and hit me in the head with the earth it threw up; the blow was so violent that I lost consciousness, and when I came to I was already far from the scene, carried by troops.[2]

Jean-Baptiste Muiron did indeed die on the bridge that day, but whether he threw himself in front of his commander to protect him from Austrian bullets is another matter. A number of other officers were killed or wounded in the attempt to take the bridge. It is remarkable that Bonaparte was not among them, and this may very well have been because the Austrians ceased fire believing that an officer was approaching them for talks.[3]

When the Austrians opened up again, probably realizing their mistake, Bonaparte withdrew. This time everybody rushed to follow his example. The soldiers only stopped when they were out of range of the cannon. The throng was so great that, in the confusion that followed, Bonaparte was pushed into a ditch full of water and would have drowned had not several men dragged their commander to safety while under an Austrian counter-attack. Two more days of bitter fighting followed until, on the third day, Bonaparte sent General Masséna, another future marshal of the Empire and one of the most competent French generals, to cross the Alpone further north to attack the Austrian troops, while Augereau was sent south to cross the river at Albaredo to take Arcola at the rear. The French troops' performance had been disappointing; Bonaparte complained about their behaviour in a letter to the French government. 'You know the character of the French,' he wrote, 'a little unpredictable.'[4] General Joubert, who had fought in Italy since 1794, described Arcola in similar terms: 'Never have we fought so badly,' he wrote, 'never have the Austrians fought so well.'[5] Except for a few elite troops, cowardice, war-weariness and lack of morale were prevalent, even after the victories that had been won thus far during the early stages of the campaign. 'We fight nonchalantly, and almost with repugnance,' wrote Pierre Garrau, one of the civilian commissaries attached to the army. 'Even the leaders are disgusted.'[6] While Bonaparte's trusted chief of staff, General Louis-Alexandre Berthier, reported: 'Our corps are not what they used to be . . . Our heroes are exhausted from being always under fire . . . We are losing all our heroes through fighting.'[7]

This is not how the battle, described by Bonaparte as having decided the fate of Italy, or the behaviour of the French troops, was presented to the public back home.[8] 'Too much courage was harmful,' Bonaparte wrote of the officers who had followed him onto the bridge. 'They were almost all wounded: Generals Verdier, Bon, Verne, Lannes were put out of action. Augereau seized a flag and carried it to the end of the bridge; he stayed there several minutes without producing the slightest impact. Nevertheless, the bridge had to be crossed . . . I proceeded there myself. I asked the troops if they were still the victors of Lodi [a battle fought six months previously]; my presence produced a movement among the troops that decided me to tempt the passage.'[9] Augereau is not placed on an equal footing with Bonaparte, but neither is he completely ignored. Within a short time, however, the roles of Augereau and Bonaparte were quickly reversed so that, 'Augereau, following Bonaparte's lead, took up the flag in order to throw himself among the combatants and bring about victory.'[10] The cowardice, or common sense, depending on one's point of view, of the troops was expunged entirely from the official report. Indeed, the fact that the attempted crossing failed was discreetly forgotten.

To some extent, the narrative depends as much on what is not said as what is exaggerated. An aide-de-camp, Jean Lemarois, later repeated the official version on a visit to Paris, where he was sent by Bonaparte with the enemy flags taken at Arcola: 'Bonaparte was there, he gave the signal to attack and tracing out himself, with flag in hand, the path to victory to his brave companions in arms, he shook and then dispersed the fourth enemy army.'[11] The suggestion that Bonaparte took the bridge and defeated the enemy is implicit. A week later, once again so as not to let the public forget the battle, a letter from Bonaparte to the wife of Muiron, the officer who died at Bonaparte's side during the battle, was published in a Paris newspaper. It went, 'You have lost a husband who was dear to you, I have lost a friend to whom I have been attached for a long time; but the *patrie* [motherland] has lost more than both of us.' On Bonaparte's request, the poet and playwright Marie-Joseph Chénier composed the 'Mort de Muiron' (Death of Muiron): 'Arcola, in your glens made famous by our warriors, / The tears of the victor have dampened his laurels.'[12]

The heroic image of Bonaparte successfully charging the bridge was transformed, within a short space of time, into a propaganda cornerstone, represented in countless engravings and paintings. One of the most celebrated representations of that day, the first iconic painting of Bonaparte, is by Antoine-Jean Gros, *Bonaparte at the Bridge of Arcola* (see frontispiece).[13] Gros, one of Jacques-Louis David's favourite pupils, was a young, struggling artist living in Genoa. He was introduced to Bonaparte's wife, Josephine, by the French consul in Genoa, Guillaume Faipoult. Gros later boasted to his mother that he had manoeuvred his way into a meeting with Josephine with the intention of executing a portrait of Bonaparte, 'whose glory and the details I was given of his physiognomy only inflamed the desire.'[14] Josephine took Gros with her to Milan, where she introduced him to her husband. Flattered that a student of David wanted to meet him, Bonaparte, whom Gros described as 'cold and severe', agreed to pose for the young artist, although 'pose' is hardly the word for what happened. 'One cannot give the name of sitting to the little time that he gives me,' Gros complained to his mother. 'I cannot therefore choose my colours; I have to resign myself to only painting the nature of his physiognomy, and after that, as best I can, to give the portrait its form.'[15] There is a story that Josephine forced an impatient Bonaparte to sit on her knees over breakfast while Gros made the sketches he needed.

As incongruous as this image may be, and in such trying circumstances, Gros is said to have achieved an amazing likeness of Bonaparte, at least according to one of his aides-de-camp, Antoine Lavalette, who was witness to three of the 'sittings'.[16] It was painted twice and then copied ad infinitum from engravings originally ordered by Bonaparte himself. The portrait was considered an 'innovation' by contemporaries because of the feeling of movement conveyed by the body and the face.[17] It is a deeply masculine image: Bonaparte is perfectly calm and resolute, manly, advancing towards an unseen enemy with sword in one hand, staff in the other, as the flag unfurls in the wind behind. Bonaparte does not look at the enemy, though; he looks at his own men, unseen, who, the onlooker must assume, have followed him on to the bridge. His hair, blowing in the wind, merges with the folds of the flag in the background, blurred in cannon smoke.

For Gros, it was a question of representing a particular moment and, in some ways, this painting is the eighteenth-century equivalent of a cinematic close-up in which the part explains the whole.[18] French artists, both before and after Arcola, often drew on antiquity and often depicted battle scenes as a type of scenic panorama.[19] Heroic courage and self-sacrifice could be seen in these paintings, but the individual's story was always subsumed within the whole. This painting represented the hero rather than merely the concept of heroism. It portrayed the Republican hero, a general who led his troops into battle, thus epitomizing the citizen-soldier.[20] Historical accuracy aside, it not only allowed people to recognize Bonaparte, but also to identify with him.

The French had been accustomed to worshipping a canon of 'great men', including *philosophes* and generals, celebrated in paintings and statues commissioned by the state, and who were increasingly taking the place previously occupied by kings and saints.[21] This led, among other things, to an increase in the number of relatively cheap busts in bourgeois households. A man of great acts, indeed just about anyone of notoriety, could aspire to public recognition in the form of a statue, whether in a public square and for which sub-scriptions had been carried out, or miniature clay representations for private use. Even full-scale statues, once reserved for monarchs, represented important civic and military figures by the late eight-eenth century.[22]

The 'democratization' of paintings, statues and other artistic representations of public figures increased with the fall of the monarchy in 1792. Just who was represented would largely be determined by political vicissitudes or expediency. The *philosophes* Voltaire and Rousseau became favourites in the early stages of the Revolution and so, too, were the hero of the American Revolution, the Marquis de Lafayette, the finance minister, Jacques Necker – very popular with the people of Paris and whose dismissal by Louis XVI contributed to tensions that led to the storming of the Bastille – and the Comte de Mirabeau, a recalcitrant noble with a scandalous lifestyle who was one of the leading lights of the opening phases of the Revolution. Later there would be representations of radical republicans and popular demagogues, such as Jean-Paul Marat (whose newspaper, the rabid *Ami du peuple*, would make him the darling of the people of Paris) and the nominal head of the Committee of Public Safety, Maximilien Robespierre. These figures were still part of a political elite, but the Revolution also made heroes of unknown individuals ready to sacrifice their lives for the sake of the *patrie*, 'martyrs of liberty', victims of internal as well as external enemies. Indeed, the Committee of Public Safety, the governmental body that ran France at war during the Terror, had established a cult to honour all those who sacrificed their lives for the *patrie* and, for a time, the cult of the martyr dominated revolutionary iconography.

After the fall of Robespierre in July 1794, and with the corre-sponding decline in revolutionary zeal, the cult of the martyr gradually gave way to the cult of the military hero, mainly ex-pressed through depictions of victorious generals.[23] It was hoped that the elevation of such figures would bolster public support for the new regime, which was at war with the rest of Europe, and connect the individual to the nation. But that was unlikely to be enough. Conscription, introduced in 1792, changed the nature of warfare. It was no longer uniquely an affair of kings with standing armies; it now became an affair of nations that involved the people. And the people had to have their heroes. The hero was fundamentally different from the 'great man'. The hero was capable of performing quasi-miraculous feats, possessed extraordinary abilities and always came at the right time to save the moment.[24] Between 1793 and 1794, when the cult of the hero reached its peak, a series of pamphlets dealt specifically with the actions of the common soldier, who nevertheless often remained anonymous. They were often read by teachers to their students. Whether these so-called 'heroic actions' actually occurred or whether, as in the case of the Bridge at Arcola, they were exaggerated, they nonetheless extolled the virtues of the common republican soldier, and portrayed him fighting a numerically superior enemy to the death.

The tradition of romanticizing and idealizing the wars was continued by Bonaparte during the first Italian campaign. Many of the stories recounted by common soldiers were reprinted in his newspaper, the *Courrier de l'armée* (The Army Courier). For example, in October 1797 one can read: 'A sergeant of the 5th company of the 3rd battalion, Citizen Moreau, rushed at the enemy in a sortie at the head of a few chasseurs, took from him an entrenchment by bayonet, and killed two men with his own hands.'[25] Such accounts, in which non-commissioned and junior officers featured heavily, were a reward for having done one's duty and an incentive for others to do so in the future. However, the idea of a collective fraternity of soldiers, stressed at the beginning of the war, was slowly yielding to the ideal of the heroic individual.

Bonaparte was instinctively able to exploit this need for the hero. He was not the only person to promote and dramatize his own role in the wars, but by the end of 1797, if Bonaparte was not yet a household name he was at least known to many people throughout France and Europe. 'People were already speaking a great deal in Paris about General Bonaparte,' wrote the contemporary author Madame de Staël of this period, 'the superiority of his mind, together with the brilliance of his talents as general gave his name an importance that no other individual had acquired since the beginning of the Revolution.'[26] The following pages are about understanding how Napoleon went about constructing his life, and how he constructed his own legend.

THE OUTSIDER, 1769–1792

1

The Pleasure of Recognition

Imaginary Landscapes

As Corsica comes into view, first the mountains, their peaks covered by the clouds, become clearer in the distance. Then, if the wind is blowing in the right direction and it is the right time of the year, you become aware of the smell; it is the smell of the *maquis*, the thick undergrowth that still covers large parts of the island. It was a smell the eighteenth-century Scottish tourist and travel writer, James Boswell, who visited the island in October and November 1765, described as penetrating and fresh. But that hardly does justice to its distinctive, unique odour of wild rosemary, thyme, myrtle, pine, juniper, lavender, marjoram, mimosa and wild olive. It is so strong that it sometimes wafts over you out at sea, even before land can clearly be seen, overpowering the salt spray the ship throws up.

That sight, and perhaps that smell, accompanied by the screeching of seagulls and the flapping of sails, would have greeted the young Buonaparte when, on 15 September 1786, after an absence of almost eight years, he stood on the deck of a ship watching the island and his hometown, Ajaccio, come into view. The closer the date for leaving France came, the more he had looked forward to seeing his family, his town, his house, his street, all those places associated with his childhood that had evoked in him such fond and vivid memories while he was away. A few months previously, while on garrison duty in Valence, he wondered about the satisfaction he would 'find in seeing my compatriots and my relatives . . . Tender sensations that the memory of my childhood allows me to experience, should I not conclude that my happiness will be complete?'[1]

Buonaparte associated happiness with his homeland. His father had died about eighteen months previously of either cancer of the stomach or possibly a perforated ulcer. His brothers and sisters, some of whom he had never met before, were all waiting on the quay at Ajaccio.* So, too, were his Aunt Gertura Paravicini; his Uncle Nicolino; Camilla Ilari, the woman who had nursed him as a child; his grandmother, Maria-Saveria Buonaparte, affectionately known as 'minanna'; the shepherd Bagalino, a loyal servant of the family; and some of the friends he used to play with as a boy. His mother, Letizia, known, perhaps unfairly, as a rather stern, devout woman, had chosen to remain at home. The group then headed back to the family home, a simple two-storied building not far from the 'cathedral', the principal church in the heart of Ajaccio. The population of the town was about 4,700 inhabitants and it was, according to the reports, insalubrious. People apparently avoided the cathedral in summer because of the local custom of burying the dead under the church floor; incense would have been used to hide the foul odour. Animals were often slaughtered in the streets and their hides hung out to dry in full view.[2] None of this, however, would have struck the young Buonaparte as odd as he walked through the streets to meet his mother, whom he had only seen once in all the years he had been away from home.

Once back among his people, the seventeen-year-old Buonaparte, still at heart a boy in a man's uniform, must have been faced with a number of significant problems, such as forming new emotional bonds with his family and re-learning the language of his childhood. In the years he had been away he had virtually forgotten his Corsican patois, a mixture of the Genoese and Tuscan dialects. Most of his relatives would not have spoken French or, like his mother, would have spoken it poorly. He would have appeared to both the family and neighbours as a stranger, as a *francisé*, someone who had adopted French manners and the French language. He was not to become familiarized again with his mother tongue until much later, after longer stays on the island. Even so, in

---

* Between 1765 and 1786, Letizia Buonaparte gave birth to twelve children, eight of whom survived (infant mortality in the middle of the eighteenth century was high; half of all children died before the age of ten). Three children had been born since Napoleone had left; Luigi had just been born when he left Ajaccio for Brienne.

Léonard-Alexis Daligé de Fontenay, *Maison natale de Napoléon Ier à Ajaccio* (The House Where Napoleon I was Born in Ajaccio), 1849. The Buonapartes occupied the first and second floors. The house was extended in 1797. In 1805, Napoleon had the houses across the street destroyed and a little square constructed in which trees were planted. (*Courtesy of Photo RMN* – © *Jean Schormans*)

France, every time Buonaparte opened his mouth to speak, he reminded his listeners that he was not French. He was afflicted with a heavy Corsican accent all his life. He was teased about it during his schooldays in France and, even after he assumed command of the Army of Italy, his soldiers used to make fun of him, exaggerating his accent. His writing style was also full of 'Italianisms' or phrases that smacked of Corsica. Buonaparte had adopted the veneer of Frenchness, but he was never able to shake off his cultural origins. Back on his island home, caught between two cultures, he seems to have, at first, spent more time with the French than he did with his own people, dining often with fellow officers in the artillery stationed there.[3]

Buonaparte alluded to his thoughts and feelings in an essay on happiness a few years later, which was revealing about his state of mind and his views of his homeland. 'You return . . . after an absence of four years: you wander around the sites, the places where you played in those first tender years, witness to the restlessness man's first hint of consciousness and the dawn of passions awakens in our senses. You live a moment of your childhood, you enjoy its pleasures . . . You have, you say to yourself, a father and a dear mother, sisters still at the age of innocence, brothers who are also friends; too happy, run, fly, do not lose a moment.'[4] He enjoyed what he referred to as the sweet pleasures of recognition, tender respect and sincere friendship. He felt, he admitted, all the fire of love for the motherland; it seemed to him to be the most precious of all joys because it was not associated with regret or rejection or fatigue, or any other kind of weakness. He would while away the time dreaming, reading, jotting down notes either in the garden of one of his family's country properties, under the grotto in the woods thick with olive trees near his home, or in the shade of a big oak that marked the woods from the groves around it. During his second visit to the island in 1788, he would go for daily walks, sometimes accompanied by his older brother, Giuseppe (Joseph), or he would go and sit on the beach and watch the sun set. Everywhere he went, he was welcomed with a friendly greeting by peasants who made him feel even more at home, or at least that is what he preferred to remember. 'Our daily walks continued along the coast,' his older brother recalled, 'well beyond the Chapelle des Grecs, bordering a gulf as beautiful as that of Naples, in a country heavy with the scent of myrtle and oranges. Sometimes we did not get back until nightfall.'[5] At other times, returning home in the light of the moon, the beauty of the night and its silence enraptured him. The Corsica he had longed for all those years in France, the Corsica he had imagined and which he was now rediscovering as a young man, seemed to have been one and the same. He felt more at home on the island than anywhere else.

Carlo and Paoli

The enforced absence from his home and his family had been brought about by Buonaparte's father, Carlo, when he decided to send Napoleone to France to be educated. Napoleone had been nine years of age. This decision had largely been the result of Carlo's collaboration with the French authorities who occupied the island in 1768.

This had not always been the case. Carlo had once been a rebel who had taken an active part in the Corsican revolt against the Genoese, who had held the island for the last 400 years, and the French, who had come to their aid. This in itself was a turn-around for the young man. A few months after his arranged 'marriage' – there does not seem to have been a Church wedding[6] – with the fourteen- or fifteen-year-old Letizia Ramolino in 1764, Carlo, eighteen, was off to Rome, leaving his pregnant wife behind.[7] (In fact, the couple do not seem to have kept house together until 1767, two children and three years after signing the dotal settlement.) The voyage was organized and financed by Carlo's uncle, Luciano, with the aim of giving him an education that would bring both an income and social prestige back home. Carlo was supposed to pursue studies in law, but records show that he was not enrolled at university; dancing and flute playing were the only lessons he seems to have taken. What is more, he got into trouble by passing himself off as a noble from Florence, single at that, leading a life well beyond his means, and getting involved with a married woman who seems to have kept him for a while. It was even rumoured that he had seduced a virgin and made her pregnant with the promise of marriage, a report that is impossible to confirm.[8] Given Carlo's lack of haste in leaving Rome after having told his friends that he was being pursued by the pregnant girl's family, the story may have been no more than a ploy on his part to extort money from acquaintances to finance further his philandering lifestyle. In short, this was a period of indulgence for Carlo. Eighteen months or so after he left Corsica, Carlo returned home penniless. And yet, six months later, he was established in the new rebel capital, Corte, in the heart of the island, at the new university founded by the head of the Corsican independence movement, Pasquale Paoli, and was on his way to becoming a lawyer and an intimate associate of the rebel leader. What had happened to bring about this transformation?

Carlo's 'memoirs' suggest that he left Rome 'inflamed with the love of the nation, then labouring to throw off the Genoese yoke'.[9] It is possible. The Corsican nationalist movement was originally given its impetus by students living outside the island and he may have run into some who had stirred his imagination with visions of a bright new future. However, Carlo was ambitious, driven by a desire to get ahead socially, which may account for why he passed himself off as a noble in Italy. It is not difficult to imagine, therefore, that Carlo was more interested in advancing his own cause than that of Corsica. It is even possible that he approached both the French and the Corsican authorities to see which side was more amenable to his advances. We know, for example, that his first contact with the French military commander the Comte de Marbeuf, who resided in the official capital, Bastia, consisted of a letter, since lost, and whose content remains unknown. We do know, however, that Marbeuf replied on 5 November 1765 to say that whatever subject Carlo had brought up did not concern him, but rather the Genoese Republic. Carlo may have been trying to ingratiate himself with the French authorities by supplying them with information he had gleaned from a journey he had recently made into the interior of the island. In any event, Carlo's advances were curtly dismissed by the French commander, while his attempts to get an introduction to Paoli fared no better. He had been attempting to do so for a month when, on 11 December 1765, the nineteen-year-old wrote a fawning letter to Paoli beginning: 'To write to your Excellency is the greatest pleasure and the greatest honour that I could have on this earth,' and ending, 'If it is true that your Excellency judges the most secret sentiments of the heart according to a person's appearance, I can be reassured and hope that he will recognize in me the attachment and the sincerity which is the duty of a subject and with which, bowing humbly before your Excellency, I kiss his hand.'[10]

Much later, when Carlo came to visit him in school in France, Napoleone was to sense an obsequiousness in his father towards people in authority.[11] But it was, nevertheless, ambition, not sycophancy that Carlo passed on to his sons; they would never hesitate to approach the great and powerful to solicit favours. Since Carlo made no headway with the French, it is more than likely that he decided to transform himself into a servant of the Corsican motherland.

Artist unknown, *Carlo Maria Bonaparte*, last quarter of the eighteenth century. (*Courtesy of Photo RMN – © Gérard Blot*)

To be fair to Carlo, the transformation may not have been entirely opportunistic, and may have been inspired by Paoli, who was perfectly capable of bringing out the best in young Corsicans. Carlo would certainly not have been the first person to have succumbed to the aura of 'greatness' surrounding the man. Boswell confessed that 'from having known intimately so exalted a character, my sentiments of human nature were raised, while, by a sort of contagion, I felt an honest ardour to distinguish myself.'[12] Boswell described Paoli as 'tall, strong, well made; of a fair complexion, a sensible, free, and open countenance, and a manly, and noble carriage.' His writing about their encounter helped transform Paoli into a sort of living hero of antiquity.[13] 'My ideas of him had been greatly heightened by the conversation I had held with all sorts of people in the island, they having represented him to me as something above humanity. I had the strongest desire to see so exalted a character; but I feared that I should be unable to give a proper account why I had presumed to trouble him with a visit, and that I should sink to nothing before him.'[14] Paoli was treated with enormous reverence on the island.

Pasquale Paoli, the son of a prominent leader of the Corsican independence movement, Giacinto Paoli, was elected the leader of the revolt on 15 July 1754.[15] He was just thirty years of age and was, at the time, serving as a captain in the army of Naples. He had spent the last fifteen years in exile, but Corsica was never far from his thoughts. The return of Paoli to the island represents a decisive phase in the Corsican struggle for independence. Not only was he able to give the movement an ideological grounding through the adoption of a 'constitution' based on a number of 'universal principles',[16] but he was also able to gain international recognition for Corsica's standing. As a result, Paoli became by far the most prestigious leader of the movement.

Politically astute, eloquent, charming, widely read, of distinguished appearance and possessing a serenity that impressed contemporaries, he had a natural talent for the administration, and succeeded in transforming old Corsican institutions into an assembly of elected deputies that met at regular intervals. He was also able to inspire in some of his countrymen a religious devotion bordering on the fanatical. His regime may not have been a democracy in the sense that we know it, but its mixture of liberal ideals and Corsican traditions ensured that the island was governed with a firm but humane hand. The problem, for Paoli, was the notables of the island. To govern effectively, he had to have them on side, but they were a difficult lot to control and could always rally a part of the peasantry to their families.

This may have been one of the reasons why Paoli courted Carlo. Whatever Carlo's motives for joining the struggle, he moved from Ajaccio to the rebel capital, Corte, and somehow became Paoli's unofficial personal secretary and a member of his bodyguard. In other words, Carlo had managed to obtain, in a very short space of time and by means that remain unclear, Paoli's confidence. This helps explain why, when Paoli decided to resist the French occupation in May 1768, Carlo followed Paoli 'into the heart of the storm',[17] probably acting as his aide-de-camp.

'A Violent Enthusiasm for Liberty'

The Genoese had ruled over the island of Corsica since the fifteenth century, although they never really extended their influence beyond the coastal towns. Friction between the Genoese rulers and their Corsican subjects remained a constant, so that peasant uprisings, and the inevitable bloody and brutal reprisals, occurred throughout the course of Genoese rule. In the eighteenth century, between 1729 and 1755, four revolts under different leaders developed into a movement for national liberation that culminated in the formation of an independent Corsican government. During this period, Genoa lost effective control of the island, and was never able to re-establish it for any great length of time after that. Genoa's military ineffectualness was, in part, a result of the disastrous financial circumstances in which the republic found itself in the second half of the eighteenth century, but the poor quality of the Genoese troops also helps account for it.

As far as France was concerned, this left Corsica vulnerable to foreign occupation. Corsica lay in the path of French grain convoys from Italy, Africa and the Levant (the eastern Mediterranean) and was, therefore, of enormous strategic concern for France. French forces were consequently dispatched to the island on three occasions – in 1738–41, in 1748–53 and again in 1764–8 – at times when there seemed a real danger that the island might fall into the hostile hands of Spain, Sardinia or Austria. The French were clearly motivated not by a desire to implant themselves on the island, but to resolve the Genoese-Corsican conflict and to prevent the island from falling under the control of a power that might be hostile to France. The outcome of the French presence was that, in January 1768, Genoa signed a treaty at Versailles allowing the French to militarily occupy the island and exercise sovereign power over its people. In return, France was to pay Genoa the annual sum of 200,000 livres for ten years. The shame felt by the Italian republic

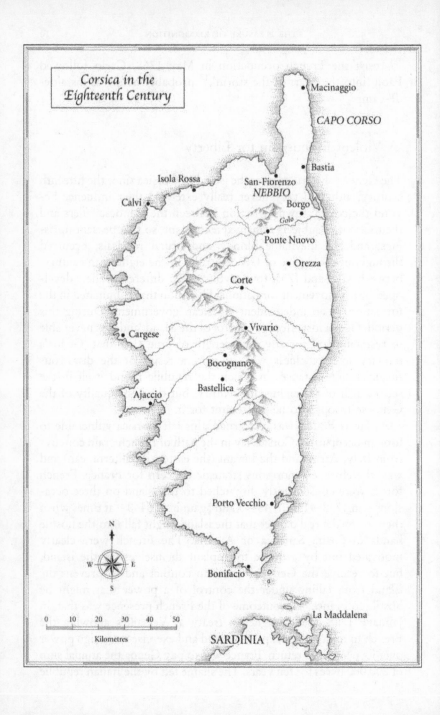

Corsica in the
Eighteenth Century

Macinaggio

CAPO CORSO

Bastia

Isola Rossa

San-Fiorenzo
NEBBIO

Calvi

Borgo

Golo

Ponte Nuovo

Orezza

Corte

Vivario

Cargese

Bocognano

Bastellica

Ajaccio

Porto Vecchio

N

W   E

S

Bonifacio

0   10   20   30   40   50

Kilometres

La Maddalena

SARDINIA

in renouncing its right to the island was covered by a clause in the treaty that gave Genoa the opportunity to take the island back at some later stage after recompensing France for the cost of the operation. Given the state of Genoese finances, however, there could be no mistake – France had bought Corsica outright and no one, especially Paoli, was fooled.

The French military establishment did not have a particularly high regard for Corsicans. One officer considered them 'the most vicious and the most corrupt [people] that exist on the planet'.[18] In fact, there seems to have been a consensus among the French that Corsicans were 'wretched and lazy' and that they waited around all day smoking their pipes, working only occasionally.[19] The Corsican propensity to fight, however, motivated by 'a violent enthusiasm for liberty', was well regarded.[20] General Dumouriez, a future revolutionary who served in Corsica, recognized that 'Corsicans loved liberty'.[21]

No matter how motivated, the poorly equipped, undisciplined Corsican militia was no match for the well-trained and well-supplied French army. Despite some initial setbacks (in early November 1768, for example, the French garrison in the northeast of the island was defeated at Borgo), the arrival of reinforcements under the command of the energetic and decisive Noël Jourda, Comte de Vaux, made the outcome of the struggle inevitable. The sixty-four-year-old de Vaux was not only an experienced soldier, but he had also been stationed on the island between January 1738 and April 1741. During that time he had become familiar with the terrain as well as the attitudes and customs of its people.

On 5 May 1769, de Vaux set out with an army of about 3,500 men from the north coast of Corsica, where they had landed during the preceding weeks. He headed for the centre of the island through rugged, mountainous terrain, passing through villages deserted by their inhabitants along the way. The decisive clash took place on 8 May on a bridge over the Golo river at the village of Ponte Nuovo. About 1,000 rebels attacked the French troops in an attempt to stop their advance. The attack failed. The outnumbered rebels were either cut down on the bridge or drowned in the Golo, which was swollen by the melting snow and the spring rains. In the confusion of battle, Swiss and Prussian mercenaries hired by Paoli also opened fire on the Corsicans trying to get across the bridge. Nightfall brought a halt to the fighting and saved, according to one French witness, 300 to 400 rebels who would not have managed to escape in daylight. French losses were estimated at between fifty and ninety killed, while rebel losses were anywhere between 500 and 600, relatively high by Corsican standards.[22]

The political and psychological consequences of the defeat for the Corsican independence movement were considerable; morale collapsed overnight and organized resistance virtually came to an end. Paoli, too, was thoroughly discredited by the defeat while the desertions and defections, already taking place before the battle, began to multiply; allegiance proved to be capricious in the face of adversity. With the French gaining their ultimate objective, Corte, Paoli was reduced to proposing an armistice to de Vaux on 14 May. Within a week, most of the island was in French hands and, even though sporadic fighting continued for a number of years to come, effective resistance was over.

The Choice

It is possible that Carlo was at Ponte Nuovo. Afterwards, along with the remnants of the Corsican troops, he retreated to Corte but, since the rebels could do nothing to defend the town against the French, they soon dispersed. Carlo may have taken his wife and his first born, Giuseppe, then only five months old, on the long journey over the mountains to Porto Vecchio on the south-east coast of the island. He was also probably among the volunteers who joined Paoli at Vivario, carrying out the last skirmishes of the war in the gorges of Vecchio (5 and 6 June 1769). When the group reached the town of Porto Vecchio on 13 June, more than a month after the battle, the decision was taken to flee the island. Paoli and some 300 followers boarded two British ships (placed at Paoli's disposal, probably by the English Consul in Livorno, sympathetic to Paoli and the Corsican cause) and sailed for Italy.[23] Carlo was not one of them. For reasons unknown, he stayed behind. He later stated that he did so on Paoli's injunction to look after his family, but, in the

Henry Benbridge, *Pascal Paoli à la bataille de Ponte Novo, 1769* (Pascal Paoli at the Battle of Ponte Nuovo, 1769), 1769. A messenger arrives to tell Paoli that the battle is lost. The bridge of Ponte Nuovo is in the background, where one can also see the town of Corte in flames. The painting was probably commissioned for the English Consulate in Livorno. (*Courtesy of Photo RMN – © Michéle Bellot*)

light of Paoli's subsequent attitude towards the Buonapartes on his return to the island from exile in England twenty years later, this explanation is not entirely convincing. Nor is Napoleon's assertion that his father remained behind on Uncle Luciano's insistence.[24] Either Paoli used the occasion as a pretext to see the last of him, or the prospect of going into exile with little or no hope of furthering his own ambitions may have been the decisive factor in Carlo's decision to remain.

Either way, Carlo made a conscious choice not to get on one of those ships and sail into exile. Others, as we have seen, preferred to leave, while hundreds more took to the *maquis* and continued their armed resistance against the French invaders, whose military detachments regularly fell into ambushes. Guerrilla leaders, supported by exiles living in Tuscany, galvanized the independence movement so that armed clashes between the rebels and the French army were to continue on a regular basis right up to the outbreak of the French Revolution in 1789 and were to cause hundreds of deaths on both sides.[25] One of the guerrilla leaders, Angelo Matteo Bonelli, nicknamed 'Zampaglino' (which roughly means 'little paw'), a relative of the Buonapartes, was at the head of a band of about twenty or so men. The repression that inevitably followed the Corsicans' hit-and-run tactics – rebels hung, women raped, suspects deported, houses burnt down, livestock slaughtered – inflamed the hatred of certain sections of Corsican society towards the French. On the other hand, the continual skirmishes increased the contempt of the French soldier and his officers towards the locals since, as is the nature of guerrilla warfare, every islander was potentially an enemy. Many years would pass before the French were able to venture into the interior of the island without an armed escort, although, judging by the letters of the Comte de Roux, a French officer stationed on the island, the guerrilla activity seems to have subsided by the beginning of 1776, eight years after Ponte Nuovo.[26]

These clashes initially hampered the new French regime in Corsica in establishing itself, but establish itself it inevitably did, largely as a result of the Comte de Marbeuf, a governor with a forceful enough personality to give his office a certain standing. Marbeuf appreciated both the country and its inhabitants, and made an effort to avoid bullying and to remain accessible to those whom he governed, even though there were lapses in this policy from time to time; he was known to have violently dispossessed proprietors who refused to cede him their lands. On one occasion, he gave the town of Bonifacio a portrait of himself with the inscription, 'Nature made Marbeuf and then broke the mould'. The painting was solemnly paraded in a procession to the church by the clergy, displayed opposite the pulpit, and then escorted by the garrison, in great pomp, back to the town hall.[27]

Carlo was astute enough not to resist the French once they occupied the island. On the contrary, he did his best to ingratiate himself with them and especially with Marbeuf. We do not know when exactly the relationship was formed, but we do know that they were close enough for Carlo to invite Marbeuf to be Napoleone's godfather in July 1771.[28] Marbeuf, who resided in the capital, Bastia, the largest town, with a population of about 8,000 people, could not appear for the baptism, and sent Lorenzo Giubega, one of the richest and most influential personalities on the island, in his stead. Marbeuf nevertheless visited the Buonaparte household on 15 August (Napoleone's second birthday) of that same year, where he met Letizia for the first time. He was, by all accounts, taken with her.

Other influential families derived little benefit from the French and preferred to give their children an Italian education.[29] Not Carlo. His co-operation, or collaboration, was to be rewarded materially in a number of different ways – he was, for example, able to obtain subsidies to drain swampland in Corsica – but perhaps the most important gain was accession to the French aristocracy (after supplying somewhat dubious documents proving four generations of nobility), which, in turn, opened up the possibility of educating his children at the expense of the French state. To obtain scholarships for his children, Carlo had to supply paperwork to certify that, despite being a *gentilhomme*, he was not a man of substance and that he was, therefore, unable to give his children the benefit of an education appropriate to their rank in life. The certificate was not enough, however. It had to be supported by an influential member of the French court. This is, undoubtedly, why Carlo's initial demands for scholarships were unsuccessful.[30] It was only after subsequent demands were made through the intermediary of Marbeuf that Carlo finally succeeded in securing places in French schools for his children. As the oldest, Giuseppe went to the seminary of Autun, one of the most prestigious colleges in the kingdom (in France, as first born, he would have been destined for the military, but in Corsica the Church took precedence over the state); Napoleone was sent to the military college at Brienne, in the north of France; Maria-Anna (Elisa) was sent to Saint-Cyr, a select girls' school outside of Paris that had been established by Madame de Maintenon, Louis XIV's morganatic wife; and Luciano (Lucien) was to eventually follow Napoleone to Brienne. Personal inclination had absolutely nothing to do with the choice of careers: tradition, family contacts and lack of suitable alternatives did. This is how Napoleone came to leave home at the age of nine to pursue an education in a foreign land and in a foreign language.

A 'Vigorous and Rude' Education

The morning of the departure (probably 15 December 1778) was undoubtedly a hectic one in the Buonaparte household. The two boys, Giuseppe and Napoleone, were to leave the space that made up their world and all that they felt comfortable with, and were not to see it again before they were young men. Letizia insisted on accompanying her children to Bastia, where they were to be taken by boat to Italy; the rest of the journey would be made overland to France. To reach Bastia they would have to cross most of the island; the first leg of the trip, between Ajaccio and Corte, would have been made on horse or mule, since the road leading to the Corsican capital was not able to sustain a carriage. Along the way, they would have spent a night at a village called Bocognano, about halfway between Ajaccio and Corte, where they had relatives. At Corte, however, Marbeuf kindly put transport at the family's disposal, another indication of the close relationship between the governor and the Buonapartes. Letizia (and probably Carlo) took the first carriage, while the two children and their fifteen-year-old uncle, Letizia's half-brother, the young Giuseppe Fesch, who would go on to become a cardinal and who was accompanying them as far as the seminary at Aix-en-Provence in France, got into the second. The whole journey would have taken about three days, but once at Bastia, Marbeuf also put apartments at their disposal. The next morning, the small group boarded the ship that was to take them to Italy. About a half-hour later, Letizia embraced her family one last time before going back to the quay. The sails were let out, the anchor was raised, and the ship slowly put to sea. Letizia decided to stay on for a few days in Marbeuf's apartments; it led to all sorts of gossip around the town.[31]

The college at Brienne was a small school that housed only about 110 students, of which about fifty were *élèves du roi*, that is, the sons of poor nobles who were educated at the expense of the state. It was one of twelve schools that had been designated by the king for the education of noble children destined for the armed services, although we do not know why Brienne was chosen for Napoleone over the other schools: perhaps it was simply because there was a vacancy. This particular school was run by monks from the Franciscan order of Minim, a comparatively small teaching order.[32] It was so small, in fact, that they had to bring in outside help to teach mathematics, languages, writing, drawing, fencing and dancing. And since it was run by monks, a monastic style of life was imposed. Students entered the school at the age of eight or nine.[33] Once they were admitted, they stayed for at least six years, during which time they were not allowed, under any pretext whatsoever, to return home, even if home was in the vicinity. In other words, students did not leave until their education was complete or their parents took them away. Brienne was not, for all that, a prison. During the holidays, two weeks starting on 15 September, they were allowed to go on 'great walks' that could last from morning until evening. The rules, moreover, were not inflexible. In extreme cases, or on the recommendation of influential people, the minister of war could grant leave. In June 1783, for example, the minister allowed one of Napoleone's comrades, a boy by the name of Rigollot, whose father was dying, to leave the establishment. Further permissions were granted for children who were sick and who needed to breathe the 'country air' or to take the waters. But, as a general rule, students were granted leave only in exceptional circumstances.

The headmasters of the twelve colleges were given instructions on how to educate their boys. The students were to learn how to dress themselves, how to keep their belongings in order and to go without any kind of domestic servant. They had to go with their heads shaven until the age of twelve, when they were allowed to grow their hair long and to wear it in a ponytail. Hair was to be powdered only on Sundays and Feast days. They slept off two corridors that each contained seventy rooms or cells. The cells were less than two square metres in size and contained no other furniture than a camp bed, a water jug and a basin. Each boy had only a single straw mattress and one blanket, even in winter (and it snowed in Brienne), unless the boy was of feeble constitution. In the evening, the students were locked in their rooms, which were only used for sleeping, and let out again once they had woken up. Since most of the boys were destined for the military where they would pass through the lower ranks before obtaining any creature comforts, they were meant to be given a 'vigorous and rude' education that would make the rest of their lives appear easy in comparison.[34] This kind of upbringing was meant to produce tough boys. They were encouraged to play sports, early variations of tennis (*la paume*), badminton (*le volant*) and ball games.[35] They were to be punished at times, but they were not to be hit. It was thought, rather progressively, that striking 'deranged the health, harmed the spirit and corrupted the character'.[36] Instead, punishment was meted out in other ways, through deprivation – of playing, walking and eating with classmates. Physical or psychological humiliation was not considered acceptable for the sons of the nobility.

Teaching was centred on the 'heroes of Antiquity'. The school's prospectus states that 'history could become for a young man the school of morality and virtue.'[37] This probably bore little resemblance to what actually went on in the college, but there was a definite relationship between ancient history as a model for the contemporary period and what was taught at the school. As for the syllabus, Napoleone's day was divided into blocks: from six to eight in the morning – toilet, prayers, reading on good manners or the laws of the state, mass, breakfast; from eight to ten o'clock – mathematics, Latin, history, geography and physics; from ten to twelve – drawing fortifications, maps and landscapes; from twelve to two – lunch and recreation; from two to four – Latin, geography, history, physics and mathematics; from four to six – weapons,

dancing, music, study or writing; from six to eight
from eight to ten – dinner, recreation, prayers
objective was to produce 'robust bodies, enlightened
honest hearts'.[39]

The school was, by any standards, a difficult physical environment, but it was also to prove a harsh psychological environment
for Napoleone. If on Corsica he had been near the top of the social
ladder, at Brienne he was nearer the bottom. Most of the boys
present were his social superiors.[40] Some of their mothers and
fathers attended court at Versailles, and some could even trace their
names back centuries in history. But that was the whole point; by
bringing together children from different social strata, and by
placing them in a situation where they learned the same subjects
while wearing the same uniform, the monarchy was attempting to
develop a level playing field within the nobility.[41] This does not
negate the fact that boys like Napoleone would have faced enormous cultural and linguistic barriers as well as an ethnic divide (he
had a crash course in French at Autun a couple of months before
arriving at Brienne). As a consequence, historians generally agree
that Napoleone had a rough time of it.[42] Examples are often cited of
Napoleone quarrelling and coming to blows with other children
almost every day, of living in relative isolation, and making very
few friends. Stories are told about his days at Brienne that reinforce
the image of a wilful loner: Napoleone finding solace and refuge in a
garden he cultivated with the greatest care, around which he had
erected a palisade, where he spent his time reading or dreaming, and
reacting violently when that territory was accidentally transgressed;
Napoleone refusing to bend to the will of a monk who wanted to
punish him by making him kneel at the door of the refectory – he
ended up having a fit and vomiting; Napoleone leading a group of
boys to victory in a snow fight; Napoleone egging on his fellow
students to throw their mattresses out of a window to provoke a
monk.[43] Napoleon himself later spoke of being teased (his name,
pronounced with an Italian lilt, was transformed into *paille au nez*,
a silly rib that can be translated as 'straw in the nose'), and mocked
because of his accent.[44] He tells of being morose and sombre as an
adolescent and taking refuge in reading. Even though there is
nothing to suggest that Napoleone was treated any differently to

ny other new boy at school, he appears to have suffered more than most, and consequently had some trouble adapting to his surroundings.

The point is not whether these and other stories are true – the sources are unreliable, written many years after the event – nor so much what they may or may not tell us about Napoleone as a child, but rather what they tell us about the way Bonaparte, as adult, wanted to be seen, and how Bonaparte's childhood was mythologized over the years. During the first Italian campaign, for example, Bonaparte allowed an extract from an anonymous English pamphlet, supposedly written by someone who knew him at Brienne, to be printed in one of the army newspapers he created. In his youth, we can read, Bonaparte was 'sombre and even shy. Constantly alone, he was the enemy of every game and every amusement . . . he seemed to know that destiny would call upon him one day . . . it was as though he was practising in advance a role he was to play.' Bonaparte then took on a taste for solitude. 'It was in that inaccessible retreat that Bonaparte's soul, avid for glory, slowly fertilized the seeds of a noble ambition.'[45] The only amusement that Bonaparte shared with his fellow students was playing war games. 'It was during these adolescent games that he took the first lessons of victory.' We find a similar image in an anonymous pamphlet published in 1802, also supposedly by a former schoolmate. 'Cold, reserved, taciturn, almost always alone, replying only in monosyllables, for a long time he retained among us the nickname of *Spartiate*. Rarely taking part in our games and our amusements, he preferred to be alone to read a serious but instructive book. For a long time he was without any trustworthy friend: he studied a student for a long time before forming the slightest liaison with him; he appeared to be looking in his fellow schoolmates for a soul of his own calibre.'[46]

These stories – these myths – gained credence for being in print and were then simply repeated by others, thereby assuming the weight of authority.[47] Louis-Antoine Fauvelet de Bourrienne, for example, one of Napoleone's classmates, who later became his secretary, and whose memoirs are notoriously unreliable and possibly even ghost-written from a collection of disparate notes and documents, was one of the first to mention the 'snow fight' story.[48] The image of the child Napoleon as an asocial loner, picked on by his fellow students, who displayed a strong desire for liberty, and who already displayed martial virtues – including stoicism and selflessness – is, in some respects, a political image that needs, accordingly, to be treated with a certain amount of scepticism. If not Bonaparte, then others were fabricating the image of an outsider who had been chosen by destiny in childhood to play a great role, and whose heroic potential was evident even as a boy. It fits the classical mould of the hero: alienated from his surroundings because misunderstood, he finds inner strength to continue on his path towards greatness.

Napoleone probably was a loner, a marginal figure. There is nothing to indicate the contrary, including the report from the inspector general for military schools, the Chevalier de Keralio, who supposedly noticed Napoleone at Brienne in 1781 and who wrote of him as being in 'excellent health, docile expression, mild, straightforward, thoughtful. Conduct most satisfactory.'[49] The report, completely out of character with everything we know about this period of his life, is from Bourrienne's memoirs and is, therefore, more than likely apocryphal. It is, nevertheless, possible that Napoleone did not have as much trouble getting on with other boys as has sometimes been made out: we know that he made friends and that he got on well with some of the teaching staff. There is, however, little doubt that Brienne was a watershed in the young boy's life, and it probably marked him for years to come. This is not to say that, for his age, his social background, and the society in which he lived, Napoleone didn't have a relatively normal childhood. What it does show is that, in the face of tremendous difficulties, Napoleone could adapt and flourish.

By the time his parents had come to visit Napoleone in 1782 – Letizia was supposedly shocked by his thinness and the physical change in Napoleone's appearance[50] – he had decided which branch of the armed services he wanted to enter: the navy, whose performance against England during the American War of Independence made it a sought-after posting.[51] It would have meant a period of training with the fleet at Toulon, close to home. He was supposedly encouraged along this path by Chevalier de Keralio, but the inspector soon retired and his recommendations were not followed by his successor. The problem was that Napoleone had only done four years and four months at Brienne, when the regulations for entry into the navy required a minimum of six years' study. Instead, Napoleone opted for the artillery, which was fashionable and was similar to the navy in so far as promotions were based on merit alone (unlike the army). The administration was, in fact, already complaining about the number of candidates seeking entry into what passed for the best-armed service in the world. In effect, it was difficult to get in to the artillery. The student had to be good in mathematics and study three or four years more than other officers, and then he could still fail the qualifying exam. Boys from the lower ranks of the nobility thus preferred to be assigned to either the navy or the artillery, where an individual was valued for his skill and where promotion was gained through experience, not birth and money. The artillery became both one of the most highly professional branches of the armed forces in the late eighteenth century and the one in which noble dominance was least marked.[52] On 17 October 1784, the fifteen-year-old Buonaparte left Brienne in the company of four classmates and a Minim monk, and headed for Paris.

2

'You Will Be My Avenger'

'A Sombre and Cantankerous Youth'

The eighteenth-century tourist to Paris seeing it for the first time may have expected an 'incomparable town'. Instead, he would have found a 'mixture of palaces and dumps, . . . a succession of interminable beautiful streets and a great many more others that were sordid', a sky that was always 'covered with clouds', and the streets soiled by 'the foul black mud maintained by constant rain'.[1] It was a constant complaint among travellers. 'Walking,' wrote the English tourist, Arthur Young, about the narrow, crowded Parisian streets, 'which in London is so pleasant and so clean, that ladies do it every day, is here a toil and fatigue to a man, and an impossibility to a well-dressed woman. The coaches are numerous, and, what are much worse, there are an infinity of one-horse cabriolets, which are driven by young men of fashion and their imitators, alike fools, with such rapidity as to be real nuisances . . . I saw a poor child run over and probably killed, and have been myself many times blackened with the mud of the kennels.'[2] Rats were another problem. The number, according to one contemporary chronicler, defied the imagination.[3]

The Paris in which Buonaparte arrived in the autumn of 1784 was still largely a medieval city with no sewerage and no footpaths, not that he would have experienced all that much of it. Much like at Brienne, as a student of the *Ecole militaire*, he was virtually cut off from the rest of society, and on the rare occasions when he was allowed out into the streets of Paris, he would have been accompanied. The building itself was an imposing, relatively new edifice at one end of the Champ de Mars, housing over a thousand people, and was no more a military school than its sister schools in the provinces. The ostensible purpose was to prepare young noblemen in the art of war. They did practise firearms twice a week and learned about fortifications, but no history of warfare and no strategy were taught. Indeed, very little prepared them for life in the regiments to which they would be assigned. Furthermore, although the system sought to promote greater equality within the officer corps by easing the divide between the haves and have-nots, it, in fact, gave a distinct advantage to those with money.[4]

In many respects, however, life for Buonaparte at the *Ecole militaire* was a considerable improvement over Brienne.[5] On St Helena, he later related how the cadets were fed and treated like affluent officers.[6] That may have been the case for Buonaparte, impressed by his new surroundings: the magnificent buildings; the staff, who outnumbered the students; the fact that he had his own room; and the food served on china. Most contemporaries, however, complained about both the quantity and the quality of the food that was served.[7] Moreover, cadets, who were between thirteen and fifteen, were submitted to a regime in which they were overworked: rising at half past five in the morning, between exercises, study and classes, they had very little time to themselves. It placed an even greater strain on students who arrived at the *Ecole* in a mediocre physical state.[8]

The fifteen-year-old Buonaparte negotiated this new environment with the only resources at his disposal – introversion and hostility. It is probable that he was just as taciturn as at Brienne, and that he dealt with any feelings of inferiority (social status and ethnicity would have remained issues) by working hard and, so it is said, by joining minor nobles in fist fights with the boys of high birth.[9] Once again, we are bereft of verifiable information, even though the reports we have from this period are a little more reliable than those for Brienne. We are told, for example, that Buonaparte was 'morose' and that on a number of occasions he declaimed 'strongly against the luxury of the young men at the Ecole militaire . . . He did not suffer observations, even those made in his interest, and I am persuaded that it was a result of this excessive irritability that he could not constrain to which he owes his reputation, which he kept for a long time, of a sombre and cantankerous youth.'[10] The memoirs of the Duchesse d'Abrantès, possibly ghost-written by Balzac, are particularly untrustworthy in places, but her description here is consistent with the little we know about Buonaparte from this period. Luciano, who eventually joined his brother at the *Ecole militaire*, remembered how he 'welcomed me without the least demonstration of tenderness, which made me force mine back into my heart . . . there was nothing likeable in his manners, either for me or the other classmates of his age, who did not like him, probably because, like me, they feared him because of his temperament, which was completely different to theirs.'[11] Admittedly, Luciano did not get on particularly well with his brother, especially in later years, but it was just like Buonaparte to hide what he really felt. Joseph (Giuseppe) recalled years later that when Buonaparte left him at Autun, on his way to Brienne, he 'only shed one tear which he tried in vain to conceal'.[12]

One of the reasons Buonaparte was still unable to integrate successfully at the *Ecole militaire* was his overt espousal of everything Corsican. It found expression in an idolization of the man who best represented the Corsican struggle for independence, Pasquale Paoli, who, in Buonaparte's febrile mind, was transformed into an idealized and idolized hero.[13] His interest in Corsican history was developed at Brienne – we know, for example, that he wrote to his father in 1784 asking for James Boswell's *An Account of Corsica*, available in French and Italian translations[14] – and it seems to have been more keenly honed with his arrival in Paris. Boswell's account, which rapidly became a success when it appeared in 1768, helped create the image of Paoli as champion of liberty against tyranny and slavery.[15]

Buonaparte took this image on board and, in some respects, modelled himself on his hero.[16] Young boys were, after all, expected to emulate heroic characters from the past.[17] What is distinctive about Buonaparte, however, is that he chose a living heroic character. Just about everything he wrote during this period of his life has as its subject either Corsica or Paoli. In a number of these notes and essays, Paoli, 'one of the bravest men in modern Italy',[18] is represented with two characteristics: he was a patriot, animated uniquely by love of the mother country; and he was an able legislator,[19] the Corsican Washington,[20] the new Lycurgus, the new Solon.[21] Indeed, Buonaparte fantasized about doing one day what Paoli, and for that matter his father, were never able to accomplish – to liberate Corsica from the French. He even considered writing a poem on Corsican liberty. The work was to start with a dream. While he was asleep in a cavern, the Corsican motherland appeared before him; she put a knife in his hand, saying: 'You will be my avenger.' He supposedly recited this passage to a friend, Laugier de Bellecour, with great enthusiasm, brandishing an old rusty blade. Like much of what we hear of Buonaparte's youth, both the poem and the rusty blade are more than likely apocryphal.[22] But what is in no doubt is that Paoli represented both a role model for Buonaparte and someone whose work he could fulfil and accomplish.[23] Inspired by Paoli and the independence fighters, Buonaparte thus dreamed about throwing off the French yoke.[24]

One of the most revealing elements of Buonaparte's idealization of Paoli is the light it throws on his relationship with his own father.[25] It is no coincidence that Paoli represented just about everything that Buonaparte's father did not. As we have seen, both fought the French, but, after the collapse of the independence movement at the battle of Ponte Nuovo in 1768, Paoli chose exile, while Buonaparte's father remained behind and collaborated. Carlo had, in Buonaparte's eyes at least, betrayed the Corsican cause.[26] Seen from this perspective, Buonaparte's obsession with Corsica in his youth becomes clearer. It was not only a case of using his cultural heritage to reassert his identity in the face of a hostile environment (largely at school), but also a muted revolt against his father. To identify with Paoli and the Corsican independence movement was to identify with everything his father had rejected, and, hence, was a rejection of everything that his father stood for. Paoli had virtually usurped the place of Carlo to become an 'idealized' father figure,[27] a theme that is omnipresent in Buonaparte's writing.

Buonaparte's enthusiastic espousal of the Corsican cause and his hatred of the French did not go unnoticed.[28] A caricature that was sketched by one of his classmates on the white pages of his atlas gives us an idea of the extent to which Buonaparte talked about Paoli, and also just how ridiculous his schoolmates thought his behaviour was.[29] In the sketch, Buonaparte is represented marching to help Paoli. An old teacher tries to hold him back by grabbing his wig. But the young man, resolute, his two hands holding on to a baton, walks decisively on. Underneath, the artist wrote the words: 'Buonaparte, runs, flies to help Paoli to rescue him from his enemies.' The administrators of the school were also alarmed by his behaviour. One of the principal aims of the school was to make 'subjects who are capable, docile, devoted, filled with zeal; above all, grateful subjects who dedicate themselves entirely to His Majesty's service'.[30] Buonaparte seemed determined not to conform even though, as a scholarship holder of the king, he was asked to moderate his love of Corsica, which, after all, was part of France.[31] One can imagine the reprimand having the opposite effect; there is no indication that Buonaparte's enthusiasm for Paoli during these years ever waned. It is obvious that Buonaparte was using his Corsican heritage, in part thrust upon him by his fellow students,[32] as a means of asserting himself.

Caricature of Paoli and Bonaparte taken from the atlas of a student by the name of Vaugoudy, circa 1785. (*Archives nationales, Paris*)

Death of the Father

When Carlo came to Paris on business in the summer of 1784, he was increasingly suffering from stomach aches, nausea and vomiting. He consulted Marie-Antoinette's doctor, M. de Lassonne, who, given the state of eighteenth-century medicine, could suggest nothing better than taking the waters in Corsica. Naturally, Carlo's suffering grew worse and, in the month of November 1784, he once more took the road to France, not only to conduct his eldest son, Giuseppe, to Metz, where he was to take an exam to enter the artillery (he had left the seminary at Autun, probably in 1782, and was bent on a career in the military), but to consult with the Faculty of Medicine.

They reached the French coast with difficulty, and only after having been driven back by bad weather to Calvi, on the Corsican coast, before they could re-embark for the mainland. The second crossing also took place in a storm, but this time they managed to reach Toulon successfully. Carlo wanted once again to consult the Queen's doctor in Paris but, on the advice of an eminent doctor in the region, he went to Montpellier, where he submitted himself to the treatment of a number of specialists. Their recommendation – to eat pears. His case was hopeless. In the face of death, he turned to religion. Giuseppe, who was with him to the last, wrote that 'my father's long and cruel sickness had singularly weakened his organs and his faculties to the point where, a few days before his death, in a fever, he cried out that any outside help could not save him, *since Napoleon, whose sword would one day triumph over Europe*, would in vain attempt to deliver his father from the dragon of death that obsessed him'.[33] Nineteenth-century historians sympathetic to Napoleon saw this as a premonition. In fact, Joseph (Giuseppe), whose memoirs are not always reliable, probably made this up; there is nothing about it in the extremely detailed account of Carlo's death left behind by Giuseppe Fesch, Letizia's half-brother, who was present during the ordeal. Carlo passed away early in the morning of 24 February 1785 at the age of thirty-nine.[34]

Given Buonaparte's melancholic state of mind, one would expect the death of his father to have thrown him further into depression. There is no indication of this, though. Indeed, there is little to go on in the two letters he wrote – one to his great-uncle and one to his mother –

a month later. Admittedly, he speaks of his suffering – in the letter to his great-uncle, the archdeacon Luciano, he wrote that 'it is pointless telling you how much I am aware of the misfortune that has just occurred', while in the letter to his mother he begins by saying, 'now that time has calmed a little the first transports of my pain' – but it is possible that he did not feel any great sadness for a father he had only seen twice in the last six years. Oddly, he used the letter to his great-uncle to lament about being away from his homeland. 'Where did his father die?' he rhetorically asks, 'one hundred leagues from his home, in a foreign country indifferent to his existence, far from all that was most precious to him.'[35] The letter to his mother is more detached (he refers to his father as 'that darling husband'); he asks her to submit to destiny, reminds her that the circumstances demand resignation, thanks her for her generosity and, ending on a more filial if somewhat forced note, promises that he will double his care and gratitude to compensate her a little for the loss.[36] He added a postscript, telling her the queen had just given birth to a prince, the Duke of Normandy, on 27 March at seven o'clock in the evening. If Buonaparte meant to make the point that death is replaced by birth and that life thus goes on, it was an awkward way of doing so.

'Resignation' is the key word here. Buonaparte's reaction can, up to a point, be accounted for by what appears to have been the cultural norm of the day, that is, a general indifference towards death, and its acceptance as an act of God.[37] But if there was no external outpouring of grief – and this is speculative – there may have been deeper, underlying reasons. It is possible Buonaparte resented his father, even if unconsciously, for having sent him away from a warm family environment so many years ago. An indication of the son's attitude towards the father can be seen in his reaction to a request, in 1802, from the municipal council of Montpellier for permission to build a monument to Carlo. Bonaparte, then first consul of France, rejected the request on the grounds that he should be left in peace. It was his brother, Louis (Luigi), who exhumed his father's body, had it transported to the village of Saint-Leu and had a monument erected in his honour. This does not mean that Buonaparte did not love his father, but it safe is to say his feelings towards him were ambivalent. Another indication of what Napoleon really thought of his father can be gleaned from the references noted by his disciples many years later on St Helena. Napoleon remembered him as a 'good' man, but also as 'a man of pleasure', who had dissipated the family fortune (which was patently not the case), and who 'played' at being the *grand seigneur* and went on costly voyages to Paris.[38] In fact, it is possible Buonaparte was embarrassed by his father's social position, or rather his lack of it. This is evident from an anecdote, which we can take to be true, about his father when he visited Brienne in 1782. Napoleon recalled how he embarrassed him with his affected and far too affable behaviour towards the monks.[39] He did not actually admit that he felt liberated by his father's death, but he did go so far as to state that, without it, he would have followed in his father's footsteps as a noble and, consequently, would have been lost during the Revolution.[40] In short, Napoleon never acknowledged the efforts or the

Artist unknown, *Letizia Bonaparte*, beginning of the nineteenth century. Judging from the bees on her gown, this portrait must have been done after the foundation of the Empire. (*Courtesy of Photo RMN – © Gérard Blot*)

sacrifices his father made to give his children an education that would enable them to advance in society. Napoleon's view of his father, which bordered on the disdainful, starkly contrasted with what he felt for his mother.

Napoleon's relationship with his mother was just as complex and ambivalent as his relationship with his father. At St Helena, Napoleon portrayed Letizia as the source of all his good habits and, by extension, of his rise to power.[41] In Napoleon's eyes, she was devout, austere, pious and irreproachable. In reality, she liked spending money on clothes, was known to flirt on occasion, and may possibly have had an extra-marital relationship with the French governor of the island, Marbeuf.[42] She was a strict disciplinarian, and in many respects the relationship between mother and son was defined by a constant battle of wills. During the first nine years of his life, Letizia did not hesitate to slap and hit Napoleone into a semblance of obedience. While in exile, Napoleon once told a companion, General Bertrand, of an incident that had occurred when he was an altar boy in Ajaccio. Acting like a spoiled brat, he affected to speak very loudly and to serve the priest badly during mass. Letizia said nothing, but the next day tricked Napoleone into letting his guard down by telling him he had been invited to lunch with his uncle in the country. When he went to his room to change, and as soon as his pants were down, Letizia sprang on him and gave him a hiding.[43] Napoleon complained to his mother about it years later at Elba – the humiliation must have run deep – outraged that she could deceive a child like that. Her formidable nature nevertheless earned his respect. It is telling that Buonaparte reproached his father, who had successfully provided for the family while alive, while it was difficult for him to fault his mother.

When Carlo was dying, he made Giuseppe promise to give up any thoughts of following a career in the army, and to return to Corsica to devote himself to his family duties. It would have been impossible for Giuseppe to refuse or to go back on his promise. Indeed, he held good to his word by returning to Corsica, re-learning the language, which he had largely forgotten, and by building up contacts with friends, such as the young and able lawyer, Carlo Andrea Pozzo di Borgo, who helped him in business matters. As time went on, Giuseppe became accustomed to his new role, fitted in to Corsican society, and forgot about joining the army. But he needed a career, so, on the advice of his great-uncle, Luciano, he left for Tuscany to enrol at the University of Pisa, where he managed to obtain qualifications that would enable him to acquire a place in the French-Corsican judicial system.

This is perhaps why Buonaparte took an active role in family affairs. It was Buonaparte, for example, on leaving the *Ecole militaire* in Paris in 1785, who asked the Bishop of Autun, the nephew of Marbeuf, whether it would be possible to give his little brother, Luciano, a scholarship for the seminary at Aix. It was granted. It was also Buonaparte who made requests on behalf of his mother, and who wrote petitions and reports to various government offices concerning the family's financial affairs. He was also thinking about getting his other brother, Luigi, who turned eight in September 1785, registered as a poor noble so that he would be eligible for a scholarship at one of the military colleges. Gradually, Buonaparte seemed to be usurping his brother's position as head of the family. Later, as his power increased, the role that he played in the family correspondingly increased or, rather, his dictatorial nature prevailed. Luciano once remarked, 'One did not discuss with him [Buonaparte], he got angry at the least observation, and flew into a rage at the smallest resistance.'[44]

With the death of his father, Buonaparte needed to leave college as early as possible in order to help the family financially. He therefore graduated after only one year of training in the artillery: forty-second out of a class of fifty-eight. It was not a particularly brilliant start to his career, but most of those who finished had already had two to four years of schooling. Furthermore, he had the privilege of being the first Corsican to graduate from the *Ecole militaire*. His commission was antedated to 1 September 1785, so that he became an officer at the age of sixteen.

A Corsican in France, a Frenchman in Corsica

Valence, Buonaparte's first posting, was a pleasant town of about 5,000 people on the Rhône river. He went there – officers could, up to a point, choose where they wanted to be posted – because it was closer to the island where he soon hoped to be detached (the regiment at Valence always supplied the two companies that were stationed in Corsica), but probably also because the La Fère regiment stationed in the town was meant to be one of the best in the artillery. Buonaparte was fortunate enough to know one other person in Valence.[45] The paternal administration of the French royal artillery had decided that Alexandre Des Mazis, whom Buonaparte had befriended at the *Ecole militaire*, would be placed in the same regiment as his older brother, a first lieutenant in the garrison at Valence, who subsequently became a kind of mentor.

At this time, Buonaparte made his debut in society. Like most of his fellow officers, he took a sparsely furnished room – a bed, a table and an armchair – at an inn (now on the corner of Grand'rue and Croissant). He took dancing lessons but was, generally speaking, socially awkward (this is certainly the impression one gets from reading the memoirs of the Duchesse d'Abrantès), not knowing how to enter a room or how to leave it, how to greet people, or even how to get up or how to sit down with any grace. He was shy and, as a result, incapable of putting others at their ease. At sixteen going on seventeen, he was, nevertheless, able to meet women in society and had a few innocent flutters of the heart. The first was with a girl by the name of Ema, whom he saw in the midst of a group of young people at Nice or perhaps Valence. 'Mademoiselle,' he wrote after first setting eyes on her, 'I need to see you without your friends . . . Tell me that you will do justice to sentiments that are worthy of you. Tell me that your heart responds to mine, that it fights for me and that it is not indifferent to me.' No reply was forthcoming, but Buonaparte was persistent; another letter was sent off. 'Whatever the disposition of your heart, mine will always be happy to serve you, even if it has to renounce pleasing you. The idea that you are unhappy, troubled, tired of reverences so flattering and so pure hurts me. Love a little the one who loves you too much. Let me read your soul.' Still no reply. Eventually, Buonaparte got the message. He sent her a last note that read, 'Goodbye, Mademoiselle! Note that it is in nobody's power, not even yours, to prevent me from looking upon all that could be agreeable to you as a happy thing.'[46] Such excessiveness was typical of how Buonaparte approached sentiments of the heart. Women were, in his eyes, fortresses to be stormed with all the vigour and enthusiasm that could be mustered, and were all the more desirable for being unobtainable. Buonaparte did not obsess too long about Ema, though; his mind was soon filled with thoughts of another girl, Caroline du Colombier. Her mother, Anne du Colombier, used to invite Buonaparte to her country house, where they met. Caroline was not yet seventeen, and their relationship was completely innocent. They used to arrange to meet, on one occasion to see the sunrise while they ate cherries together, an idea he may have got from reading Rousseau's *Confessions*.[47] But that is about as far as it went; he may never have even held Caroline's hand.

Apart from these flirtations with the opposite sex, we know that he walked a great deal in his time off and undertook a few excursions in the Dauphine. With a guide and a comrade from the regiment, he climbed Mount Roche-Colombe in June 1786. Buonaparte seems to have adjusted reasonably well to garrison life and to have made, if not friends, then close acquaintances with whom he could talk. Apart from the Des Mazis brothers, we know that he was in contact with an officer by the name of Charles-Théodore Damoiseau. We also know that he took his meals, along with the other officers of the regiment, at Chez Géry at the Hôtel des Trois Pigeons, rue Pérollerie; that he took part in a ball organized by the officers; that he remained in contact with his captain, M. Masson d'Autume, whom he visited in retirement in 1790 at his château near Auxonne; and that he also kept up good relations with his first lieutenant, M. de Courcy, whom he visited each time he passed through Valence.

It was while he was on garrison duty that Buonaparte developed his literary tastes, preferring to read in the evening rather than drink or gamble at cards. Indeed, he seems to have taken on a programme of reading and note-taking that would help him fill the lacunas in education left within him from his schooling.[48] He learned by heart the verses of Corneille, Racine and Voltaire and, during his first stay in Corsica, he liked to recite them aloud with his brother, Giuseppe, imitating the great tragedians of his age.[49] Corneille's *Cinna* was Buonaparte's favourite play during this period, but he also read the plays of Racine – *Andromaque, Phèdre, Iphigénie, Britannicus* – and novels that were the best-sellers of his day – the *Contemporaines* by

Restif de la Bretonne, the *Comte de Cominges* by François Arnaud. Voltaire he liked less, read him anyway, as did many educated people of the day, but said of him later, on St Helena, that Voltaire did not know men, nor greatness, nor the truth of passion. He admired Montesquieu and read the *Spirit of the Laws* with a friend, Carlo Andrea Pozzo di Borgo, while he was in Corsica. He was passionate about Jacques-Henri-Bernardin de Saint Pierre's *Paul et Virginie* and still liked to read it out aloud when he was in exile. As a young man, he believed Rousseau to be the most profound, the most penetrating of all the *philosophes*, even if in his later years he was to disown him, blaming him, quite unjustly, for the Revolution. He was a 'fervent disciple' of Rousseau, with whom he may have identified; Rousseau was also a 'foreigner' among the French (he was born in Geneva), a prophet for the persecuted and misunderstood.[51] It was only much later that, like most of his youthful enthusiasms, Napoleon tried to deny his fondness for Rousseau. Buonaparte also read history, such as Jean-Charles Laveaux's *Vie de Frédéric II*, even if his reading was relatively superficial and without any great insights into military strategy or tactics. It is perhaps from books like these that Buonaparte first gleaned the idea that it was possible for an individual, as soldier, to make something of his life. 'The reading of history,' he later admitted to his master of the horse, General Armand de Caulaincourt, 'very soon made me feel that I was capable of achieving as much as men who are placed in the highest ranks of our annals, though I had no goal before me, and though my hopes went no farther than my promotion to General.'[52]

One other author was widely read by Buonaparte during this period, the Abbé Raynal, a former Jesuit and a contributor to the *Encyclopédie*. Even if he is forgotten today, his name was on every patriot's lips at the beginning of the Revolution, and he was considered the precursor of a new political system. Buonaparte read especially, several times, Raynal's six-volume *Histoire philosophiques et politiques des établissements et du commerce dans les deux Indes*, one of the most powerful anti-colonial and anti-slavery documents of the period. Even though it had been officially suppressed two years after its first appearance in 1770, and publicly burnt by the royal executioner, it was still widely available. It is

possible that Buonaparte identified with the anti-colonial theme
running through the book. Raynal, therefore, may have provided
Buonaparte with the intellectual ammunition he needed to help
formulate his own ideas about France and Corsica. Buonaparte was
hoping to find an intellectual mentor, or perhaps simply approval,
when he wrote to Raynal, 'I am not yet eighteen, but I am already a
writer'. Not much of one, though. Raynal was used to disciples and
treated them with benevolence and even flattery. 'Every beginner',
he wrote back, undoubtedly thinking of himself, 'must attach
himself to an established celebrity.'[53] Buonaparte may even have
dropped in on Raynal at Marseilles (where he lived in internal exile)
on his way either to or from Corsica, but we do not know this for
sure. We do know, however, that Buonaparte submitted his *Corsican Letters*, a kind of history of Corsica he had been working on,
to Raynal for commentary.

Whatever his distractions may have been at Valence, it is clear
that he never really stopped thinking about his homeland. Understandably, he longed to see his family and his island again, but
was obliged by army regulations to stay one year with his
regiment before he could take advantage of any leave. This is
the moment when, in September 1786, Buonaparte arrived in
Corsica after an absence of almost eight years. He did not spend
all his time reading 'sheltered by the tree of peace and the orange
tree', as he put it, or with walks across the country during which
he re-discovered the beauty of his homeland. He was also
concerned about more mundane matters. Chief among them
was the poor state of the family finances and his desire to help
the family out of an embarrassing situation. The Buonapartes had
fallen on hard times. Not only had the family lost its father, but it
had also lost its two most influential patrons, the two people who
had protected them most on the island: the Comte de Marbeuf
died in 1786, five days after Buonaparte landed in Ajaccio, and
the patriarch of the family, the archdeacon Luciano, was sixty-
eight years old and suffering from gout that laid him up in bed.
As soon as Buonaparte was home, therefore, he set about trying
to put the family finances in order by sending off letters to
various authorities in France, reclaiming what the Buonaparte
family considered its rightful due.

Since nothing came of the written reclamations, Buonaparte decided to go to Paris in person to try to sort matters out. Before doing so, however, he had to prolong his leave. On 21 April, he sent his colonel a certificate signed by a doctor demanding an extension of five and a half months as of 16 May, with pay, on the pretext of ill health; he had been suffering from a minor fever ever since the month of March. Leave was granted, quite normal in an army where no more than a third of infantry and only a quarter of the cavalry officers remained with their regiments in winter,[54] and on 12 September, almost a year after he had arrived in Corsica, he set out for France.

It was in the months of October to December 1787 that Buonaparte really got to know Paris, staying at the Hôtel de Cherbourg in the rue Four-Saint-Honoré (today 33 rue Vauvilliers). He went to Versailles in a moderately priced coach called 'coaches for the court', the eighteenth-century equivalent of a tourist bus. They were comfortable but not particularly rapid, and took five hours to reach Versailles. He went to the theatre, especially the Théâtre des Italiens. It has been suggested that Buonaparte lost his virginity during this stay in Paris, at least if one of his written 'sketches' is to be believed. One cold November evening, after he came out of the Italiens, he took one of the passages along the Palais Royal where prostitutes used to linger waiting for customers.[55] It was there that a young woman with a pale complexion, frail physique and, as he was to discover, a sweet voice, caught his eye. Painfully conscious 'of the unpleasantness of her profession', he nevertheless found the courage to speak to her. She was from Nantes in Brittany, and had been a soldier's woman before being abandoned in Paris.

> 'Let's go to your place,' she said to him after recounting her life. 'But what will we do there?' Buonaparte supposedly replied. 'Let's go. We can warm up and you can have your pleasure.' I had no intention of becoming over-scrupulous at this stage. I had already tempted her [an interesting use of the word], so that she would not consider running away when pressed by the argument I had prepared for her, and I did not want her to start feigning an honesty that I wished she did not possess.[56]

This encounter with a prostitute is taken by most historians at face value, but it is entirely possible that the account is fictional, nothing more than a fanciful exercise of the pen.[57]

The reason Buonaparte came to Paris in the first place was to sort out the family's business affairs. In spite of the steps he took, he received no official reply and his leave had almost run out; he asked for a second prolongation so that he could take part in the meeting of the Corsican Estates back home to discuss family matters. His presence was a necessity, he argued. A second prolongation of six months was granted (1 December 1787–1 June 1788). He spent that time in Corsica, where he arrived on 1 January 1788. Little is known about this second stay on the island, except that he went to Bastia a number of times.[58] Buonaparte nevertheless had to start thinking about returning to his regiment, from which he had been absent for about eighteen months. He left the island towards the end of May, after having briefly seen Giuseppe, who returned from Pisa armed with a doctorate, to go to his regiment at Auxonne, where it had been stationed since the month of December 1787.

Buonaparte arrived at Auxonne in the first days of June 1788, and was to spend the next fourteen months in the region. There is little that we know for sure about his stay there. His health was not the best, since he had come down with a 'fever', which kept him laid up for long periods of time.[59] According to Buonaparte's own letters, he had little money, ate only once a day, slept badly and changed his clothes only once every eight days.[60] This may have been the origin of his scruffy looks during this period, but it would, nevertheless, be a mistake to think that he lived in penury. This depiction of his life probably reflects, if anything, Buonaparte's penchant for the romantic. Admittedly, he was sending money back to the family in Corsica, but he still had enough to spend on books, an expensive item at the time.

There was little else to do at Auxonne but work, go to bed at ten o'clock in the evening and get up at four o'clock in the morning. He does, however, seem to have made some 'intimate acquaintances', to use his expression, in the regiment; Alexandre Des Mazis was there once again, but he also befriended Le Lieur de Ville-sur-Arcis, Rolland de Villarceaux and Jullien de Bidon.[61] Buonaparte was becoming much more communicative, much more confident, and it was undoubtedly this confidence that made him amenable to chatter. This character trait was to last right up to the first Italian campaign in 1796, when he was described as amiable, talkative, gladly joking around, sometimes taking part in the games his staff played, or making fun of the older officers. At Brienne and the *Ecole militaire*, his manner was more forced: he was a foreigner; under pressure to succeed in his exams; deprived of both leave and liberty for years at a time. He also learned to shut himself away for long periods. At Valence and Auxonne, he seems to have been happier, perhaps not as hard on himself. He was proud to be wearing a uniform and to be counted as an officer in the Royal Artillery, despite his continuing inherent dislike of the French occupier. He also enjoyed the independence of a rank that was won by hard work and sacrifice, the self-confidence that came with it, and the warmth of relations between officers of the same rank who used the informal 'tu' among themselves. He was, in short, enjoying his youth for the first time, and taking part in life's distractions. He was also arguing politics to the point where, if Buonaparte himself is to be believed, he gained a bit of a reputation in town.[62]

Nevertheless, his mind never wandered very far from Corsica. In letters home, he plied his great-uncle, Luciano, with questions about all those in the extended family, and it is obvious from the way he put pen to paper that he had a great deal of affection for those he asked after: 'Is Minanna just as restless? Does Mammucia Catherine still go to the vines and does she still argue with Nuranea? Is Fesch still arguing with Marcariotto, with the canons, with the bishop? . . . Does he still infuriate him? . . . What is Aunt Antonietta doing? Is she still with her daughter Marcariota? Is Francesca still as lazy? What has become of the wife of Pietro Paolo? . . . Who is teaching philosophy to Luciano? Some monk? [he used the Italian word *frate*] Are you happy with him? He should read ancient history. So Jérôme is doing well. All the better. Are they good? I doubt it.'[63]

While at Auxonne, Buonaparte completed his military education. The garrison was considered one of the best, if not *the* best military establishment in France. Even in September 1789, at a time when

many officers had started to emigrate because of events in Paris, all
the officers of La Fère were accounted for. The garrison was under
the command of Baron Jean-Pierre du Teil, who applied the
principles taught by Jacques-Antoine-Hippolyte, Comte de
Guibert, whose writings – *Essai général de tactique* (1772) and
the *Défense du système de guerre moderne* (1779) – caused a
sensation when they appeared. They went a long way towards
revolutionizing French military thought and were to lay the foundations of the French army that would conquer Europe.[64] Buonaparte continued to take classes in theory from nine until twelve
o'clock in the morning, two or three times a week. In the afternoon,
from two until four o'clock, he took drawing lessons, important for
any artillery officer. Tuesday was dedicated to mathematics, and
three times a week, at least from the months of May to October,
there was artillery practice. Given Buonaparte's intractable nature,
it is quite surprising how well he fitted in with his military unit; he
seems to have emulated the ideal officer, described at the time as
someone who was 'studious', 'filled with ambition' and 'ardent for
work'.[65]

It was also during this period that Buonaparte encountered the
French people in revolution. The first was at Seurre, a little town
about thirty kilometres south-west of Auxonne, which rioted in
April 1789 after a barge loaded with wheat was about to be shipped
out. The mob murdered two grain merchants in the process. In a
time of scarcity, this type of event occurred throughout France in
the spring and summer of 1789: peasants were particularly sensitive
to seeing grain destined for the towns being taken away from their
region. The commandant of the Duchy of Bourgogne, the Marquis
de Gouvernet, immediately sent three companies from the La Fère
regiment to Seurre, in all about 100 men under the orders of
Lieutenant du Manoir. Buonaparte was second in command,
but, by the time they reached Seurre, the disturbance was over
and there was no longer any need to intervene.[66] We can discount
the anecdote reported by some historians about the energetic
summation Buonaparte was meant to have yelled out in the streets
of Seurre: 'Let honest people go home, I only shoot rabble.' The
troops, nevertheless, stayed in the town two months, during which
time they were obliged to intervene at the nearby Citeaux Abbey,

where the monks were in open rebellion. Here, too, we can probably discount the anecdote where Buonaparte took it upon himself to lock up a few of the ringleaders. At least, there is no mention of it in his correspondence. On the contrary, he talks of the delicious wine the abbey served him during the course of a dinner.[67]

Another encounter occurred at Auxonne on 19 July 1789, at three o'clock in the afternoon. About fifty boatmen and porters gathered in the town, rang the church bells and badly treated a deputy mayor who made the mistake of arguing with them. The people of the town were soon on the march, and the troops looked like going over to them. Buonaparte apparently harangued the troops for three-quarters of an hour, although we do not know with what success. 'I spent the night on a chair,' he later wrote, 'in the salon of the general. Every now and then, we would receive news that [something] was being pillaged, and I do not know how many times I had to carry orders to deploy detachments. There were 450 men under arms all night. We did not want to shoot or hurt people. That is what was embarrassing. At dawn, one of the gates of the town was broken down and the rumours started all over again.'[68] About fifty people were arrested, a few of whom were later hung as an example.

In spite of the unrest, family affairs were still uppermost in his mind. Buonaparte thought of returning to Paris and staying a few weeks to knock on all the appropriate doors in order to expedite matters. 'Send me three hundred francs to go to Paris,' he pleaded with his uncle, Luciano. 'There at least things can happen, I can make contacts, overcome obstacles. Everything tells me that I will succeed this time. Would you prevent me from trying for the sake of a hundred ecus?' Luciano refused – he was miserly but perhaps also realized the futility of Buonaparte's promised representations – and replied that he should try to get a loan in Auxonne. 'The sad state of my family afflicts me,' Buonaparte replied to this suggestion, 'all the more so because I cannot see any solution. You are mistaken in hoping that I could find money here to borrow. Auxonne is a very small town; I have not been here long enough moreover to have made any serious contacts.'[69] So many setbacks upset Letizia; Buonaparte tried to console his mother. She was, perhaps, never so badly off as at that moment. Obliged to raise four children – Luigi (Louis), ten, Carlotta-Maria (Pauline), eight, Maria-Annunziata (Caroline), seven, and Gerolamo (Jérôme), four – she also had to pay Luciano's board at the seminary in Aix, and she had supported Giuseppe while he was at university in Pisa. The family's financial straits were undoubtedly the reason Buonaparte asked for another leave of absence.

He was lucky to get it under the circumstances. The commander of the La Fère regiment, du Teil, wrote to the commandant of the Duchy of Burgundy complaining about the lack of officers, stating that he wanted to cancel all leave because of the 'popular brigandage and the regrettable circumstances on the part of the troops' (he was referring to the mutinous behaviour of some of the troops in August).[70] He made it clear that he was already lacking officers and that, in the coming winter of 1789, he would have no more than two or three captains instead of the usual ten in the regiment. The Marquis de Gouvernet replied saying that he should accord only a small number of leaves, not to those who said they were sick, because the abuse was too great, but to those who could prove that they had important business to attend to. Buonaparte had obviously made a case, and du Teil did not persist. He had to take leave himself; his château in the Dauphine had been sacked and he had to repair the damage.

So, Buonaparte was granted leave once again. He set off for Corsica, full of ideas for writing a history of the island.

3

Corsica in Revolution

An Island in Turmoil

A French officer who returned to Corsica in 1789 after an absence of one year found that the island and its people had undergone a profound transformation: 'I found the same individuals I had left behind, but their tone and attitude had changed considerably . . . everybody, the young as well as the old, had become serious. Eyes were constantly fixed on the sea in the hope of seeing arrive a vessel carrying dispatches from France. Each day people expected to hear of a revolution; everything that happened over the last few months forecast great changes in the administration of the kingdom.'[1]

Even if we allow for some exaggeration, politics seems to have become the main topic of conversation for the people of Corsica in 1789: animated discussions could break out at any time in public squares; popular societies and clubs of various political colourings were formed in imitation of what was taking place on the main-land.[2] The excitement was caused by Louis XVI convoking the Estates-General for May 1789 in an attempt to resolve the king-dom's financial crisis. The inability to sort out the monarchy's financial problems had led to a succession of ministers and the meeting of an Assembly of Notables in February 1787 to try and push through tax reforms. When that failed, and persistent attempts by the monarchy to introduce wide-ranging reforms were stymied by the nobility and the legal establishment, the king had little choice but to call for an Estates-General, an advisory body of representa-tives that had last met in 1614. The Estates was based on the three orders that made up the social structure of the kingdom: the First

Estate represented the Church; the Second Estate represented the nobility; and the Third Estate represented everyone else. Deputies were to be elected to each Estate.

In Corsica, Louis XVI had decided that the island was to be represented by four deputies (one each for the nobility and the clergy, two for the Third Estate). The elections for those deputies, as in much of the rest of France, took place in an atmosphere that was tense and expectant but, in Corsica, they resulted in tumultuous scenes in some electoral assemblies, riots and even deaths in others. Thus, on 31 April, during the electoral assembly for the Third Estate at the Church of the Conception in Bastia, a bloody riot broke out when the mayor, a man by the name of Rigo, was insulted and manhandled by people who wanted to prevent him from taking part in the assembly. The incident turned ugly when one of his relatives, an officer in the corps of the King of Naples, hit a worker with his sword and had to take refuge in a nearby printer's, where the crowd caught up with him and killed him. In the meantime, the mayor had managed to escape, but the intervention of troops was needed to put an end to the riot, which resulted in two killed and seven wounded. The electoral assembly was able to proceed the next day, but the French administration had to be protected by the army, and although it re-established calm in Bastia, it inevitably increased the hatred felt against the king's administrators on the island.[3]

Once the elections to the Estates-General had taken place, the situation remained relatively calm in Corsica until news of the storming of the Bastille (14 July 1789) reached the island in the first days of August. The Bastille fortress, on the eastern outskirts of Paris, had been demonized in the latter part of the eighteenth century and had become a symbol of monarchical despotism. It was there that the king could imprison anyone he chose with what was called a *lettre de cachet*, a simple piece of paper that detained an individual without any kind of legal process. Towards the end of the eighteenth century, those people were often either political dissenters, or at least writers whose works were deemed seditious, or young and often noble delinquents whose families thought it best that their sons be locked up for a while for their own good, and who petitioned the king to do so. It was the arbitrary nature of this act that was objected to and which became the focus of discussion about absolutism and the nature of the monarchy. Although the people involved in the event did not attack the Bastille as a political symbol – the fortress was also an arsenal and they were looking for weapons with which they could arm themselves – it certainly became one in the weeks and months that followed.

The political implications of the fall of the Bastille were clear and immediate. It meant that power had shifted out of the hands of the king, and for that matter the Estates-General, which had since declared itself the National Assembly, and into the hands of the people.* All over France, royal authority began to collapse as the people – represented by popular militias and town councils – assumed local authority. This local revolt, this municipal revolution on mainland France, was mirrored in Corsica in the weeks that followed. On 14 August, the electoral assembly of Bastia, which had not dispersed since it had met in April to vote for its representative to the Third Estate, proceeded to choose a 'revolutionary municipality'. It immediately set to work by forcing the governor and his troops to wear the red, white and blue revolutionary cockade.[4] The cockade was adopted from about July 1789 onwards by 'patriots' to clearly distinguish themselves from royalists (who often wore a white cockade), and later from counter-revolutionaries (who wore black cockades). Made of paper, but sometimes of cloth rosettes or ribbons, they were generally worn on hats, coat lapels and as scarves. In the summer of 1789, the Marquis de Lafayette, commander of the Parisian National Guard, had combined the red and blue (the colours of the city of Paris) with the colour of the uniform of the French Guards (white)[5] and so the tricolour cockade became a patriotic symbol par excellence and went on to become the French national colours.

The example of the 'revolution' in Bastia was followed in the rest of the island. At Corte, peasants invaded the record office of the court, took the register of fines and burnt it. The royal army, which should have repressed the riot, locked itself in the citadel, abandoning the streets to the peasants. At Ajaccio, the electoral assembly started calmly electing a 'revolutionary municipality' but soon the

* The Estates-General, which began life in May 1789, declared itself the National Constituent Assembly in June, and is generally referred to as the National Assembly.

town's population, swelled by people from the surrounding region who had come to celebrate the Feast of the Assumption (15 August) and to take part in the religious procession, rose in revolt. A large crowd, sporting the Corsican national flag (the head of a Moor, black, on a white background) and wearing the French cockade, turned against the bishop of Ajaccio, Monsignor Benoît-André Doria.[6] He had made the mistake of closing the cathedral doors to the town on the pretext that work was in progress. This was in part true, but Doria had dithered about carrying out necessary repairs on the seminary and the cathedral ever since 1777. To cries of 'Long live the Madonna', the crowd, in spite of the presence of troops, dragged him from his home to the nearby cathedral, made him wear a cobbler's bonnet decked with the tricolour cockade, and obliged him to part with 4,000 livres on the spot. The unrest, however, seems to have been motivated more by a desire to obtain work than by politics, although there was an element of discontent as a result of the lack of changes on the island despite the reforms introduced by the National Assembly in Paris. Once again, as in the rest of Corsica, the riot led to the formation of a revolutionary municipal committee, a *comité patriotique*, of thirty-six members, which included Giuseppe Buonaparte as secretary and which, in turn, decided on the formation of a local militia.

In the course of the month of August, the urban movement spread to the countryside and the mountains, where rural communities were soon caught up in the general unrest. Six hundred inhabitants of mountain communities in the province of Ajaccio turned against the large estates, burning harvests, pulling out vines, cutting down olive trees and setting houses on fire. One thousand, five hundred people turned on the Greek community of Cargese, which was saved from destruction by the timely intervention of royal troops. Assemblies were convoked without the permission of the municipal authorities, committees were named that took over their business, unpopular priests were chased from their parishes and vicars were named to replace them.

As in France, effective municipal power was rapidly passing from the hands of 'legal' institutions into those of self-appointed local assemblies. Twenty years after the establishment of French rule on the island, Corsican hatred and resentment was still running high.

To that extent, the revolution in Corsica was certainly a revolt against the abuse, perceived or otherwise, of monarchical institutions, but its ultimate objective was to establish a 'national', that is a regional, government of its own. There was, nevertheless, a profound sentiment that this change could only take place with, rather than without, the French people. Corsicans were, therefore, fighting to become an integral part of France and to break any obstacles that prevented this from happening.

Initially, revolutionary politics in Corsica was determined by the clash between two groups whose interests were specifically Corsican; it had little or nothing to do with the events on the mainland. On the one side was a pro-French faction made up of people who had most benefited from the royal administration, who supported the monarchy and who sought to maintain their pre-eminent position on the island. Made up, for the most part, of nobles and notables who had gained materially from the *ancien régime*, they were probably no more than a few hundred strong but had, up until then, occupied the most influential positions on the island. The other faction comprised young, ambitious, talented men who had found little outlet within the French administrative system. They included the Buonapartes, but also more prominent Corsican families like the Pozzo di Borgos, the Salicetis, the Arenas and the Colonna-Cesaris. They were perhaps more representative of the Corsican elite population as a whole, and most of them were later to support the returned leader, Paoli, from exile. They quickly adopted the name 'patriots' to distinguish themselves from those who sided with the royalists. The patriots looked favourably on the revolution in France and regarded it as an extension of their own, and, as such, were bound to clash with the conservatives on the island who sought to maintain the status quo. If a conflict between the two parties was inevitable, the pro-French party, for the moment at least, could rely on the regular French troops stationed in Corsica for support.

This picture was complicated enormously by family ties and rivalries. The clan, and not class or one's place in the social order, was the most important social grouping on the island.[7] Clan leaders, called *capi di partito*, competed with one another for positions of power. A victory for the head of the clan meant that all the clan members shared in the spoils. This meant that individual personal and familial ambitions were often subordinated to the clan's influence and prestige. It also meant that ideology played a secondary role in Corsican politics, so that even though lines would eventually be drawn up between royalists (following the French and the king), nationalists (following Paoli) and popular republicans (revolutionaries disgruntled with Paoli), they were always subordinated to the struggle between clans for political pre-eminence. There was, therefore, no traditional partition of the Corsican population into the First, Second and Third Estates – 'those who prayed, those who fought and those who worked' – as in the rest of France.

A more important element in Corsican society, one that often underlined clan rivalry, was the 'vendetta', whose origins are dubious and are sometimes attributed to the Moors who occupied the island between 850 and 1034.[8] There was no code of conduct; killing an opponent by a shot in the back was just as honourable as facing one's enemy and killing him. Once begun, the vendetta could spread to whole families, and in this women played an important role in keeping alive the flame of revenge, which could last for a century and more. Rather than curb this widespread practice, the Genoese had actually encouraged it in order to keep clans divided, thereby reducing the prospect of a united opposition to their rule. If peace on the island reigned, it was largely due to the draconian measures introduced under French rule directed against anyone carrying arms; anyone found guilty of pursuing a vendetta had his house burnt to the ground.

Working towards the Revolution

When Buonaparte arrived in Corsica for the third time in three years at the end of September 1789, the island was therefore in upheaval. Of course, he delighted in seeing his mother again and, according to the expression used in another essay he was yet to write, the *Discours de Lyons*, his still innocent sisters and his brothers, whom he treated like friends; he had, after all, been away for about fifteen months. The only member of the family not present on this third visit was his sister Maria-Anna (Elisa), still in France completing her education at Saint-Cyr.

Once back on the island, Buonaparte quickly got caught up in events, even if, along with his brother, Giuseppe, he had much more ambition than political experience or common sense. Giuseppe had a taste for politics, a flair for revolutionary factionalising and had welcomed the Revolution with enthusiasm. In their attempts to climb the political ladder, the brothers were soon going to run up against those who had returned from twenty years' exile and who had no intention of letting their influence or authority be usurped by inexperienced upstarts. Nor was the Buonaparte clan as numerous or as rich as other competing clans on the island.[9] They may not have gone unnoticed, but the Buonapartes did not have the political versatility, the capacity for intrigue or the connections to succeed. That did not stop them from trying. Shortly after his arrival, Buonaparte entered the political arena by becoming a member of a local political club of which his brother, Giuseppe, was already secretary. Along with his friend, Carlo Andrea Pozzo di Borgo, Buonaparte started distributing the tricolour cockade, forbidden by the governor of the island, the Vicomte de Barrin, to fellow citizens, as well as getting involved in the formation of a local militia.[10]

Buonaparte was encouraged in this choice by developments in Versailles. On 17 June, a deadlock over voting procedures between the Third Estate, on the one hand, and the First and Second Estates on the other, was broken when the Third Estate declared itself a National Assembly. It thereby effectively brought about a rupture with the monarchy and instituted a revolution. Two of the Corsican deputies to the National Assembly – Cristoforo Saliceti and Pietro Paolo Colonna de Cesari-Rocca – had proposed that a Central Committee and a militia be set up in Corsica. The minister of war ordered twelve magistrates on the island to form a commission to deliberate on the proposal. When the commission's official findings were finally delivered in the form of a manifesto (17 October), it actually came out against the creation of a Central Committee, concluding that it would not only cost large amounts of money, but that it would also provoke troubles and rumours in what was essentially a peaceful island. As for the creation of a Corsican National Guard, it would cost even more.

The decision proved to be unpopular. Disturbances broke out in Bastia and Ajaccio. Buonaparte seems to have taken a part in channelling this discontent. At Ajaccio, at a meeting convoked by patriots in the Church of Saint Francis (31 October), he used the occasion to read out a petition, which he had probably written, and which he proposed sending to the National Assembly in Paris in order to help 're-establish Corsica within the rights that nature had given the country'.[11] It was, in fact, an attack against the commission and was immediately covered in signatures, Buonaparte's at the top, followed by Pozzo di Borgo's.[12] It was a fine gesture on the part of Buonaparte and the Corsican patriots, but perfectly futile. The National Assembly, which had recently moved from Versailles to Paris, was snowed under with this type of appeal from the provinces.

In the meantime, Buonaparte left for Bastia, the centre of revolutionary activity on the island. As soon as he arrived on Saturday, 4 November, he began distributing two trunks of trico-lour cockades he had had made in Livorno.[13] According to one historian, Buonaparte also asked permission of the French governor of the island to enlist men in a Corsican National Guard and, when that was refused, called a meeting of the citizens of Bastia, which took place the next day, 5 November. When the governor ordered his troops to disperse it, a serious riot took place in which two soldiers and two children were killed. Buonaparte may have been actively involved in the rioting itself; both the cockade and the question of a National Guard were at the centre of the troubles directed against the Vicomte de Barrin.[14]

In some respects, Buonaparte's actions exacerbated the situation. In others, though, the insurrection was the logical consequence of the revolutionary process that had begun in Corsica with the convocation of the Estates-General, and which was to reverberate in the weeks and months ahead. All the revolts from the end of October 1789 onwards contain the demand for the application of the French revolutionary decrees in Corsica, notably those concerning the suppression of the political and administrative structures of the *ancien régime*, which patriots wanted to replace with elected, decentralized and democratic institutions. Bastia took the lead but the movement was general. In other words, the insurrection in Corsica did not have as its objective the overthrow of French domination, but the elimination of those obstacles that prevented

Corsica from fully benefiting from the reforms being pushed through in Paris. The Corsican peasantry, for example, was attached to both France and the Revolution because of the limited but real gains it acquired as a result of the revolutionary movement.[15] The most important repercussion of the Corsican unrest, however, was to take place in Paris.

On 30 November 1789, a letter drawn up in Ajaccio, probably inspired by Buonaparte, stating that the troubles in Corsica stemmed from the uncertainty about the island's future, was read to the Assembly by the Comte de Volney (whom we will come across again during the preparations for the expedition to Egypt).[16] What did the Assembly want to do with Corsica? the missive asked. Keep it under a military regime, give it back to the Republic of Genoa or declare it an integral part of the French monarchy? Volney was followed to the rostrum by Saliceti, who proposed that indeed Corsica should be declared an integral part of the French empire, and that the same laws and conditions should apply there as in the rest of France.[17] If this had not been done in the past, it was more as a concession to Genoese pride than anything else. France had absolutely no intention of handing over Corsica, despite a clause in the treaty dating back to 1768 stipulating that the island would revert back to Genoa if Genoa ever approached France, but then only after it had paid for the expenses the French had incurred during the occupation. Given the state of Genoese finances, there was never any question of that happening. It had, nevertheless, been a sore point for Corsicans, who feared that one day France would return the island.[18] It was in virtue of an article in the Declaration of the Rights of Man (introduced in August 1789), namely, the right of peoples to dispose of themselves, that Corsica was integrated into the French kingdom. Corsica, it should be noted, was not the only foreign region in France to take advantage of this right. The most remarkable example was probably that of Strasbourg, where, on 13 June 1790, delegates from the National Guard of Alsace, Lorraine and Franche-Comté – that is, from territories annexed by France about a century previously – asserted they were French, not because of any treaty that had united them to France, but because of their desire to be French.[19]

As was sometimes the case in the heady early days of the Revolution, Saliceti's motion started an avalanche. The Comte de Mirabeau – a renegade noble who got himself elected to the Third Estate and who was one of the leading lights of the revolutionary movement – presented a second decree proposing an amnesty to all Corsicans who had taken part in the struggle for liberty in 1768-9 and had been forced to flee into exile.[20] The proposal was accepted even though it meant, as the Corsican deputies for the nobility and the clergy, Matteo Buttafuoco and the Abbé Peretti della Rocca, were at pains to point out, that the return of Paoli and his supporters to Corsica might lead to the independence movement being re-ignited (Buttafuoco was marked as a reactionary by Corsican patriots for raising this point).

When news of the decree reached the island some weeks later, there was a general outburst of joy. On 27 December, a Te Deum was celebrated in every Corsican church. In Ajaccio, a bonfire was lit in the public square where people danced around it crying out 'Vive la France', 'Vive le roi'.[21] Buonaparte had a banner hung out of the house in the rue Saint Charles painted with the words 'Vive la nation, vive Paoli, vive Mirabeau'.

This is an apparent evolution in Buonaparte's thinking on France and Corsica. If outwardly he had integrated into French society, inwardly he still defined himself in opposition to the French.[22] 'Frenchmen,' he wrote in an essay in 1786, 'not content with having stolen all that we [Corsicans] cherish, you have also corrupted our morals. The actual state of my homeland and the impotence to do anything about it is just another reason to flee a country [France] where I am obliged by duty to command men I must, by virtue, hate.'[23] This is the only indication we have that Buonaparte was torn between love of his motherland, which at this stage he always associated with his island homeland, and the duties he felt obliged to fulfil as a French officer, but it is also an unambiguous expression of the French as the ethnic enemy, as the hated 'other'. It is a theme found constantly in Buonaparte's writings during this period. Thus, in a letter to Paoli written in June 1789, he complained that 'slavery was the price of our submission: burdened by the triple chain of the soldier, the jurist, and the tax collector, our fellow countrymen live despised . . . by those who hold the administration in hand. Is it not the most cruel of tortures a person with feeling can experience?'[24]

This hostility is best illustrated by a Gothic short story written by Buonaparte in the summer of 1789 called *Nouvelle Corse* (which could be translated as either 'Corsican novella' or 'New Corsica').[25] The protagonist, a young Englishman, is on his way to Spain from Livorno, Italy, when his ship is forced by bad weather to drop anchor at a rocky island called Gorgona, about half a league in circumference. (There is, in fact, an island called Gorgona situated between Corsica and Livorno, which Buonaparte may have sailed past on his way to Italy.) There he meets an old man who relates how, in fighting the French on Corsica, he saw the lives of forty of his companions end by torture. One day he and his band resolved to avenge their deaths and took 100 Frenchmen prisoner (one assumes to kill them). On their way back to their mountain retreat, however, some friends warn him that the 'tyrants' – that is, the French – have taken his house:

> I left my men to fly to the help of my unfortunate father who I found drowning in his own blood. He only had the force to tell me: 'My son, avenge me. It is the first law of nature. Die like me if you have to, but never recognize the French as your master.' I continued on my way to find out what had happened to my mother when I came across her naked body, covered in wounds and in the most obscene posture. My wife and three of my brothers had been hung in the same place. Seven of my sons, of whom three were under the age of five, had met the same fate. Our cabin had been burnt, the blood of our goats was confounded with that of my relatives. I looked for my daughter everywhere but could not find her: furious, distraught, transported by rage, I wanted to die at the hands of those brigands who had killed my people.[26]

He then went on to recount how he came to the island and how any Frenchmen who had the misfortune of being shipwrecked were first given aid as men, and then killed as Frenchmen.

The violence running through this and other stories is particularly noticeable. There are any number of ways of explaining this: as a literary artifice to heighten sympathy for the victims; as a normal outpouring of aggression on the part of a young man; as a cultural expression of revenge (the Corsican vendetta); or as a comparatively simple expression of rage against all those whom he felt had hurt him (his parents, the French). However, while Buonaparte held Corsicans who collaborated with the French in contempt, there is a certain ambiguity in the Gorgona story in particular that reflects Buonaparte's own confusion about his identity. Those against whom the violence is directed are not always French. His victims are also Corsican (*Nouvelle Corse*), or in the case of other short stories like the *Comte d'Essex* and the *Masque Prophète*, the oppressed, or those who struggle against a corrupt tyrant.[27] Buonaparte identified with the victims of these violent scenarios, thus aligning himself with the oppressed, whose sole object becomes revenge. At the same time, however, Buonaparte placed himself in the position of the aggressor, since he imagined the acts of violence committed against the oppressed Corsicans. There are evident textual switches between the narrator of these stories and the perpetrators who commit the outrages against Corsicans. In other words, Buonaparte identified with the victims, but at the same time imagined acts of violence against them.

At this stage of his life, hatred of his opponents, that is the French, seems to have been even stronger than love of his own people. One should consider the possibility that this hatred, a self-centred emotion, may have been a reflection of what Buonaparte most disliked in himself, namely, the fact that he (unconsciously) identified with the French as the oppressor, the conqueror of his people. What is more certain is that with Buonaparte's participation in the Revolution in Corsica, his outlook towards France became more ambivalent. For the moment, Corsicans had seemingly achieved what they had so long desired, a semblance of independence, the right to govern themselves and recognition of their identity, all the while belonging to a larger national entity, the French nation. When Buonaparte now cried 'Vive Mirabeau' alongside his customary 'Vive Paoli', it was the first instance of his identifying with the French, rather than rejecting them as he had done so emphatically up until now. This does not mean that he had become

French – he was still Corsican above all else – but he was now identifying for the first time with Corsica *and* France. 'From now on,' wrote Buonaparte to the Abbé Raynal, 'we [the Corsicans and the French] have the same interests, the same concerns. The sea no longer separates us.'[28] He was eventually to renounce publishing his history of Corsica in the form of the *Corsican Letters*, and focused instead on local politics. It was inadvertently going to push him further along the path towards adopting a French identity.

Buonaparte became deeply involved in Corsican politics throughout 1790 and 1791, working within the framework of the Revolution and at the same time working constantly for the advancement of the Buonaparte clan. He took an active part in the campaign leading up to the municipal elections at Ajaccio, in which a relative, a man by the name of Jean-Jérôme Levie, became mayor in March 1790. That same month, he also helped his brother get elected to the municipality of Ajaccio, despite the fact that Giuseppe was twenty-two instead of the mandatory twenty-five. In vain, his opponents had brandished his birth certificate in public, but Giuseppe's success in spite of not meeting the age requirements was not unusual.[29] The Revolution was also an explosion of youth and many held public office before reaching the official age limits imposed by the government in Paris. To those who challenged the election, Giuseppe's partisans argued that the mayor knew only Corsican and that Giuseppe possessed an uncommon knowledge of both French and Italian. More importantly, Buonaparte worked towards getting Giuseppe elected to the new Corsican general assembly that was planned to meet at the convent of Orezza, in the northeast of the island, in April. Buonaparte, who had not yet come into his own and who was at this stage playing a supporting role to Giuseppe, accompanied his brother to Orezza.

The first Congress of Orezza (12–20 April 1790) was held in the Convent of Saint François, today a ruin. Apart from bringing about the administrative unity of the island by electing the administrators of the Department of Corsica, it was mainly concerned with restoring law and order. The Buonapartes arrived on 14 April only to find that most of the people there had either fought with Paoli and had recently returned to the island, or were the sons of martyrs to the cause. The Buonapartes, it has to be remembered, had benefited from the French occupation and may have been looked upon with some suspicion by the others. It is perhaps to prove his patriotic fervour that Buonaparte wrote an inflammatory letter to the municipality of Ajaccio inviting its members to chase the 'foreigner' – the French – from town.[30]

As a result, once back in Ajaccio in the first days of May, while Napoleone, Giuseppe and a number of other friends were walking in the Piazza del Olmo, they were attacked by a group of about forty or fifty royalists for writing such an incendiary letter. An armed supporter of the Buonapartes was able to hold the mob off long enough for Napoleone to calm them down.[31] It was the first, but not the last time that he would have to face an angry mob. It is clear, however, that Buonaparte did want to chase all the French administrators from the island, and he may even have been one of the key players in a movement that ended in the expulsion of all French employees from Ajaccio on 25 June.[32] Buonaparte is supposed to have given the movement its ideological justification by publishing an account on behalf of the municipality of Ajaccio explaining the events that had taken place over the last year, essentially laying the blame for the unrest on the French administration. In doing so, Buonaparte once again portrayed his people as victims. 'Cast a glance', he pleads, 'on our unfortunate country. Alas, naked, despoiled, depopulated, awash in the blood of its martyrs, we see it strewn with men who, in their enthusiasm, have sacrificed everything for the price of freedom.'[33]

The Return of the *Babbo*

This kind of emotional outpouring was to pale in comparison with the principal event of 1790, in Corsica at least, namely, the return of Paoli to the island. For the past twenty years, since the failed rebellion in 1768, Paoli had been living on a pension from the British government in a house in Old Bond Street in London, where he was able to renew his friendship with James Boswell.

Despite his sixty-four years of age, and despite having lived in exile for over twenty years, the prestige and fame of the independence leader was such that many Corsicans believed he would solve all their problems. His political objective was Corsican autonomy under French protection, something that was feasible during the early stages of the Revolution. As early as 1789, he had dispatched agents to Paris to negotiate his return to Corsica, although there seems to have been some hesitancy on his part about resuming public life. On 23 December 1789, he wrote to a friend, 'From the moment that the *patrie* obtained its liberty, all solicitude ceases; and if my stay here were to give offence, I would retire to a place where you would no longer hear talk of me. I have to renounce seeing my *patrie*, because I can see that I would only add useless jealousies and pretexts to those with bad intentions who will badly interpret all my words and actions to the prejudice of the nation.'[34]

Paoli had not entirely given up his dream of playing a role, if not the leading role, in a new Corsica but, at this stage, he did not know what kind of administration would take shape and whether he would be involved in it. If the administration were to be centralized and emanate from Paris, there would be little or no place for him. If, on the other hand, Corsica were to have a more autonomous administration, the path would be open for his return. As far as the French revolutionaries were concerned, it was politically expedient to give Paoli a general amnesty at this time. It was hoped that he might use his influence in Corsica to keep it under French rule. Paoli was thus given permission to return, and Boswell gave Paoli a farewell dinner before he left. Arriving in Paris on 3 April 1789, he was feted and celebrated as a revolutionary martyr, introduced to Parisian society by the Marquis de Lafayette, praised by Maximilien Robespierre[35] and even presented to Louis XVI. On 22 April 1790, he appeared before the National Assembly and swore obedience and fidelity to the French people.

The municipality of Ajaccio decided, therefore, to send a deputation (Giuseppe was one of them) to meet the great man in France.[36] After landing in Marseilles, it finally caught up with Paoli at Lyons, although, delayed by bad weather, a rival delegation from Bastia had reached him first.[37] As Paoli travelled through France on his way to Corsica, he received a hero's welcome: Lyons, Tournon,

Valence, Aix, Marseilles and Toulon all turned out to see him. It was no doubt with bitter irony that Paoli saw how he was now welcomed as a hero by the very same people responsible for dashing his dreams of an independent Corsica. It was, however, merely a taste of what awaited him on the island.

One year after the fall of the Bastille, on 14 July 1790, Paoli landed at Macinaggio, in the northernmost tip of the island in the district of Capo Corso. It was a strategic move designed to avoid favouritism towards either Bastia or Ajaccio, although he first entered Bastia three days later to the sound of church bells and cannon, and to cries of 'Long live the father of the *patrie*'. Indeed, the popular enthusiasm bordered on the delirious by those wanting to see, hear or touch Paoli; he still benefited from an impressive physique, with long white hair and clear blue eyes. The enthusiasm was encouraging but, given the nature of Corsican politics, combined with the volatile situation in France, that kind of unanimity could not last.

The next day revealed just how difficult Paoli's situation was. Despite insisting that he was no more than a simple citizen working for the good of his country, Paoli's intention was to rule over all Corsica. In many respects, he was already the uncontested master of the situation: royal authority had all but disappeared along with many of the French administrators who had fled the island, while the enemies of Paoli who had not already left Corsica on his arrival were soon banished. Indeed, his very first act as nominal head of the island was to exile his adversaries: Matteo Buttafuoco, Ugo Peretti and François Gaffori and his clan, that is, the 'aristocratic party', partisans of the *ancien régime*. His second act was to issue a decree (20 July) proclaiming his attachment to France. It was important to allay fears the French might have had about Paoli's intentions and, at this stage at least, he had no plans to break away. Changes, however, were inevitable and, indeed, one could say that his return was to inaugurate a new phase in Corsican politics. The void left by the monarchy had allowed young revolutionaries to take a lead in Corsica. Indeed, they had been united in their common struggle against the conservative monarchical forces on the island. However, given Paoli's reputation and his popularity, along with the exiled independence fighters who returned with him, his arrival was to throw these young revolutionaries back into the shadow where they found themselves in the unenviable position of having to vie with one another for the favour of the *babbo*, or father, as Paoli was called, in the hope of becoming his assistant, and possibly succeeding him as the first man in Corsica. This rivalry was to be the leitmotiv of politics on the island for the next few years.

No doubt inspired by what was taking place there, and wanting to continue his involvement in politics on the island, Buonaparte had written to his colonel in Auxonne on 16 April 1790, asking for a four-and-a-half-month extension of his leave.* He again used the pretext of poor health, something that was not *entirely* untrue since he had been suffering from a mild fever. A medical certificate accompanied the letter. Buonaparte's commander, M. de Lance, had little choice but to grant the leave. So Buonaparte was still in Corsica for the return of his idol. He was part of the delegation sent from Ajaccio to greet Paoli – they met at Bastia on 4 August 1790 – and we know that he accompanied Paoli when he left that town on 30 August in a very festive atmosphere. Triumphal arches had been erected at the entry to the villages along the way, while the militia marched in front of the procession shouting and discharging their muskets.[38] It may have been in the course of this victory parade through the northern half of the island, on its way to Orezza and passing through Ponte Nuovo, that Buonaparte and Paoli exchanged views on the conflict. The story, however, falls within the logic of the legend – Buonaparte, who would have just turned twenty-one, telling his idol how he would have fought the battle – and cannot be given much credence. Moreover, Paoli was accompanied by more than five hundred followers, so there was probably little chance of Buonaparte getting close to the man. The important thing to note, however, is that he was in Paoli's entourage, welcomed or not, and was evidently trying to ingratiate himself with the returned leader. It was, of course, politically expedient to do so

---

* In the spring and summer of 1790, a critical period for the Revolution, about half the officers of the line army, and slightly less for the cavalry and artillery, were on leave. Samuel F. Scott, *The Response of the Royal Army to the French Revolution: The Role and Development of the Line Army, 1787–93* (Oxford, 1978), p. 83.

– anyone who hoped to get ahead in Corsica from now on would have to obtain Paoli's favour – but one should not underestimate the extent to which all three Buonaparte brothers, Napoleone, Giuseppe and Luigi, held Paoli in awe. Buonaparte, especially, not only looked up to him as a hero, but wanted the *babbo*'s approval.

Paoli undoubtedly hoped to resolve many of the island's problems by convoking a second Congress at Orezza from 8–27 September 1790. In many respects it was a turning point in Corsican history, since it marked the emergence of a purely Corsican local government.[39] Paoli presided, and opened the proceedings with a speech that outlined his conception of what the Revolution meant for Corsica. He wanted union with France, but, in becoming French, he wanted Corsica to continue to be itself, with its past, its martyrs and heroes, and he wanted France to let Corsica alone to establish its own administration and commercial relations with its neighbours without being too dependent on the French. He acknowledged that it was necessary for France to have free access to Corsican ports for reasons of security, and that it even be allowed the right to raise troops on the island. In short, Paoli was advocating a type of federation, or rather confederation. When he spoke of the *patrie* he did so in reference to Corsica, not to France, which he referred to as the empire.

The congress was an enormous success for Paoli. Four extraordinary deputies were elected and were to be sent to Paris, either relatives of Paoli or supporters who owed him their election. Paoli was accorded a pension of 50,000 livres per year, an enormous sum of money, and was confirmed in his election as commander of the Corsican National Guard. Finally, despite protests from Paoli, a statue was to be erected to him in Corte. In short, Paoli held in his hands both military and civil power, something that was incompatible with the spirit of the new constitution being drawn up in Paris by the National Assembly. It led to a number of French eyebrows being raised. In fact, most of the decisions of the Corsican electoral assembly were, strictly speaking, illegal. Paoli's appointment as head of the National Guard throughout the island, for example, went against the Constitution, which stipulated that no one person should command the National Guard of more than one district. So, too, was the election of functionaries at the district level, and a host of other decisions adopted by the Congress (principal among them the decree annulling the laws passed during the regimes of the previous French governors of the island), all of which would have grated with even the most radical of the French revolutionaries at this stage of the game.

For Giuseppe and the Buonapartes, however, the second Congress of Orezza was a disappointment. Giuseppe did not get elected to the island's departmental administrative body, as he had hoped. In fact, the role of the Buonapartes at Orezza was limited, a measure of the family's lack of influence. Paoli did, however, arrange for the elections to the local district administrations (there were nine in all) also to take place at Orezza and not, as required by law, in the principal towns. Paoli could therefore dominate the proceedings, a step that favoured Giuseppe, who was not only elected to the district of Ajaccio, but was also named its president.[40] This was quite an achievement for a young man of twenty-two (once again, he did not even have the required minimum age to stand for public office), and certainly a sign of some trust on the part of Paoli.

As for Buonaparte, this was an induction into political life. Paoli was a hands-on clan chieftain who had to control everything, and from the first he acted as master; the assembly at Orezza simply approved. Positions were granted as a reward for services rendered and for loyalty to Paoli. If Buonaparte later became a despot it was partly because he lived in an era of despots, sometimes enlightened, often not, who had total control over the machinery of government. But nor should one underestimate his first learning experiences in politics on Corsica. He was to see Paoli and his followers use violence and intrigue to get rid of opponents, he was to see Paoli break the law on any number of occasions in order to get his way, and he was to see Paoli welcomed as a charismatic hero, cheered and fêted wherever he went. Given what we know about how Bonaparte attempted to construct a charismatic authority even before he came to power, perhaps Paoli really did serve as the model he would emulate and surpass?

Denunciations

On 11 October 1790, Carlo Andrea Pozzo di Borgo, a deputy to the National Assembly in Paris, received a letter from Buonaparte denouncing the citizens of Ajaccio – 'this town is filled with bad citizens; you have no idea how mad and how malicious they are' – for anti-Paolist intrigue.[41] This outburst may have been brought on by a recent, if unsuccessful, attempt to have Giuseppe's election to the district administration annulled, for Buonaparte proposed that three of its members be dismissed and that three others be appointed by the departmental administration. He closed with the following words: 'This measure is violent, perhaps illegal, but indispensable, because three bad and feeble and ignorant [men have this position] and all is lost.'[42]

It was the first but certainly not the last time Buonaparte was to denounce a political opponent. Buonaparte was willing, even at this young age, to bypass the law if it were in his own interests to do so, always invoking some higher good. Denunciation, it has to be said, was part of the revolutionary process,[43] but it was also a habit consistent with Buonaparte's overt political expediency. Buonaparte's youth, and the fact that he often spoke in favour of his clan, can partly explain his behaviour, but one should also note a ruthless determination to advance, first within Paolist circles, and when that was no longer possible, within the pro-French anti-Paolist clique on the island.

Buonaparte's leave had run out. He had to return to France, and was waiting for favourable winds before embarking. He made sure that he came away with certificates of patriotism attesting to the good nature of his revolutionary fervour, to the fact that he possessed the character and the qualities of an honest citizen, which assured any reader that he was animated by the purest patriotism, and that he had given indubitable proof of his attachment to the National Assembly and the Revolution from the beginning.[44] These certificates had become necessary in order to travel. They were passports of a kind that showed that the bearer was a trusted revolutionary.

Buonaparte, nevertheless, had difficulty physically leaving the island. His ship was twice thrown back on to the coast of Corsica by unfavourable winds in the months of October and November, and was still in Ajaccio at the beginning of 1791, where he continued his political activities while waiting for more clement weather. We know that he was present at the opening of the Globo Patriottico (Patriotic Club), affiliated with the Jacobin Club in Paris, on 6 January.[45] The Jacobin Club (or the Society of the Friends of the Constitution) had been founded by a group of radical deputies from the National Assembly (its name came from the Jacobin convent at which it met), and was one of the many popular societies that sprang up at the outset of the Revolution. Within a short time, affiliated branches opened in the provinces, often corresponding with the mother club in Paris, or provincial centres formed their own clubs and popular societies. This was also the case for the Patriotic Club in Corsica. To start with, it had about sixty members and was meant to diminish the factionalism among the clans. One of its first rules was that members had to leave their pistols and daggers with the police. In order to swell its ranks, they were admitting people as young as fourteen and fifteen; Luciano was among them.

Buonaparte attended every session of the club while he was still on the island. His last act before leaving was to attack the leader of the pro-French party, Matteo Buttafuoco, who had stood up in the National Assembly in Paris and accused Paoli of trying to establish a dictatorship on the island (October and November 1790). Buonaparte withdrew to one of the family properties in the country, at Milelli, to think about what he wanted to write. The result was the *Letter to Buttafuoco*.[46] On 23 January 1791, the Patriotic Club voted to have the speech published in pamphlet form, as a service to the public, and sent to the National Assembly in Paris. Buttafuoco, it should be pointed out, was considered a traitor by most Corsicans because he had not only collaborated with the French during the years of occupation, but had been in command of the Royal Corsican Regiment that helped defeat Paoli at Ponte Nuovo. Filippo Masseria, president of the Patriotic Club, urged Buonaparte to write a letter of denunciation as an expression of the members' feelings. One can see the same themes in Buonaparte's preceding unpublished *Letters* – namely, the cruelties of the French victors and the oppression of the royal government that had reduced Corsica to a miserable state:

Fear, the remorse of the avenger! The goods, the pensions, the fruit of your treason will be taken away from you! In the decrepitude of old age and poverty, in the terrible solitude of your crime, you will live long enough to be tormented by your conscience . . . Dripping with the blood of his brothers, sullied by crimes of every nature, he confidently presents himself in the guise of a general, iniquitous recompense for his heinous crimes! He dares think of himself as a representative of the nation, he who betrayed it, and you tolerate him!

The pamphlet attempts but fails to be ironic, and is full of inaccurate and exaggerated accusations, most of which Buttafuoco did not deserve. Ten years later, it should be noted, Buonaparte asked for copies of this letter to be burned (Napoleon attempted to destroy much of his early writing).[47] What it demonstrates is the deterioration of royal authority, not only on the island but within France: an officer in the king's army was publicly attacking one of the representatives of the nobility to the National Assembly. On a more personal note, Buonaparte's pamphlet, like most of his other writings, is full of anger directed not only against the French but also against an aristocrat who was evidently a traitor in his eyes. It is also a diatribe against an anti-Paolist and this, perhaps more than anything else, helps explains the virulence of the attack. Buonaparte was defending his hero, championing not only the Corsican underdog but especially of Paoli, and at the same time Buonaparte may have been washing away the sins of his own collaborationist family. In this, as in just about everything Buonaparte did and thought during this period, his underlying motive was to please the *babbo*, or at least to try and direct the *babbo*'s gaze towards him.

He did not entirely succeed. Interestingly, although Pozzo di Borgo, who had already attacked Buttafuoco in the National Assembly (6 November 1790), met with the total approval of Paoli, Buonaparte's address – probably an imitation of Pozzo di Borgo's – met with a chilly reception. Paoli found the whole thing excessive. 'I received your brother's pamphlet,' he wrote to Giuseppe. 'It would have made a greater impression on me if it had said less and if it had shown less partiality.'[48] It may very well be that Pozzo di Borgo's speech in Paris had finished off Buttafuoco as a force on the island

and that Buonaparte had been flogging a dead political horse, but Paoli's cool reaction is nevertheless significant. He obviously thought the Buonapartes' enthusiasm and initiative needed to be reined in. The difference between Pozzo di Borgo and Buonaparte at this stage was that Pozzo was acting with Paoli's approval – that is, obeying his orders and enjoying his favour as a result – whereas Buonaparte was acting on his own initiative.[49] Besides, there is an implicit criticism of Paoli in the pamphlet in phrases like 'Paoli dreamed of becoming Solon, but copied the original badly', or 'Paoli, constantly surrounded by enthusiasts and hotheads, was unable to imagine that one could have any other passion than that of fanaticism for liberty and independence'. The implication was that Paoli was not a particularly good judge of men. Buonaparte's feelings, even towards those for whom he professed admiration, were always complex and often ambivalent. We may, in fact, be seeing the first crack in the idealized Paolian edifice. Paoli's reaction to this letter is, therefore, understandable, but probably came as a disappointment to Buonaparte. His attempts to insinuate himself into Paoli's entourage had been gauche and naïve. For the moment, what is clear is that, deprived of his full support, the Buonapartes' success in Corsican politics would be extremely limited. The relationship between the two clans was soon to sour and would have far-reaching consequences for the Buonaparte family.

4

Ambition Awakened

The Republican

Buonaparte finally succeeded in leaving Corsica, accompanied by the twelve-year-old Luigi, in the last week of January. He had decided to take Luigi's education personally in hand. On 6 February 1791, they were at Valence, where Buonaparte attended a session of the local club. Two days later, they were on the road to Lyons, having left Valence on foot without waiting for the coach, despite the cold weather. Buonaparte stopped along the way at a 'poor man's cabin' at the village of Serve for a rest, spoke with the locals at length and then wrote to his Uncle Fesch. In his letter he described the patriotic club at Valence, and the peasants in the region – 'I have seen a resolute people at Valence, the troops are patriots and the officers aristocrats . . . the women are everywhere royalist' – a clear indication that he had become politicized over the previous year or so, along with the rest of the French nation: he was now aware of the mood of the people in a way that he had not been previously.[1]

That evening they slept at Saint-Valliers and, in the room of the inn, Buonaparte wrote down a few thoughts about love. 'When man is in a foreign country, without relatives and far from his house, do not be mistaken, he needs a link, support, a feeling that takes the place of a brother, of a father . . . Love comes to his rescue and offers him all these advantages.'[2] If there is one thing that we can learn from this, apart from the fact that Buonaparte was probably already feeling wistful after having just left behind a hectic life in Corsica, and that he somehow confuses love of the *patrie* with romantic love – something he had done earlier on in an essay known as the *Dialogue sur l'amour* – it is that love was thought of as a way of filling the void, of lending meaning to his life.

The next day they crossed the town of Châlons, and then walked on to Auxonne, where, as soon as he arrived, Buonaparte went to see his commanding officer.[3] After all, his leave had expired three months previously, so there would have been some explaining to do. He produced his certificates of patriotism that explained his delay in leaving Corsica. The colonel took it all in without too much fuss, probably glad to see an officer return to the ranks, and agreed that Buonaparte had been detained in Corsica for good reasons. Some of his fellow officers in the regiment, royalists, supposedly offered a less friendly welcome, accusing him of having an 'insurrectional manner', that is, of having led Corsicans against the governor of the island.[4] Although the artillery was one of the more radicalized branches of the armed forces, the officers did not, on the whole, share the political opinions of their troops. Many of them left the service, despising the Revolution, and emigrated. There were, however, officers who were proclaimed revolutionaries, either out of self-interest, because there was now a chance for rapid promotion, or because they placed the service of their country before all else.[5]

In many respects, though, life at Auxonne in 1791 was no different from his previous stay in 1788–9. Buonaparte worked fifteen- and sixteen-hour days. Auguste Marmont, who was later to become one of Napoleon's marshals, wrote that Buonaparte would often go to Dijon and Nuits, undoubtedly on his days off, although we do not know what he did there. For the rest, he lived in a small house in Auxonne, rue Vauban, with two rooms. Buonaparte kept the bedroom for himself and put Luigi in the other room. He gave his brother daily lessons in mathematics, history and geography. His treatment of Luigi was sometimes harsh: he dished out corporal punishment whenever he thought it necessary to 'correct' him. But Luigi was a hard worker and a fast learner, and made rapid progress. There is no doubt that he was his brother's favourite and that Buonaparte held an affection for him that can only be described as paternal: 'He is studying hard,' he wrote to Giuseppe, 'and is learning to write in French ... All the women here are in love

with him. He has taken on a little French tone, proper, agile.'[6] It
would seem that Buonaparte enjoyed teaching his brother, shaping
him, but probably only because Luigi was submissive at this stage
of his life: he admired his two older brothers. 'You only have to say
one word and I will stay,' Luigi wrote to Giuseppe. 'You only have
to say the opposite and I will come. You should know that after
Napolione you are the one that I love and cherish the most.'[7]

Luigi was not Buonaparte's only concern, however. He was still
preoccupied with Corsica and with his own political future there.
To this end, accompanied by his brother, he went to Dôle on foot,
about thirty-two kilometres there and back, to read the proofs of
his *Letter to Buttafuoco*, printed at 100 copies. In the hope of
finding a publisher, Buonaparte even walked as far as Besançon,
over forty kilometres away, to ask a printer if he would be
interested in his planned history of Corsica.[8] We do not know
what the reply was, but, in any case, the history was never
completed. He also contacted Paoli, sent him several examples of
his *Letter to Buttafuoco*, and asked him for copies of documents
that would allow him to complete his history. Paoli's response,
written at the beginning of April 1791, was less than encouraging.
Not only (as we have seen) did he indirectly criticize Buonaparte
for his letter against Buttafuoco – 'Do not go to the trouble to
contradict the falsehoods of Buttafuoco; such a man as this cannot
enjoy any credit with a people who have always esteemed honour
and who have now recovered their liberty' – but he also refused
access to the documents Buonaparte asked for, remarking that,
'History is not written in one's youth'.[9]

Buonaparte's second stay at Auxonne did not last very long; he was
to leave on 14 June 1791. In the process of the democratization of
the army, the La Fère regiment lost its name and, along with other
regiments, received a simple numerical nomination, in this case the
1st artillery regiment. In addition, men were being transferred from
one regiment to the other. Buonaparte was made first lieutenant of
the 4th artillery regiment stationed at Valence, where he arrived on
16 June, taking a room with Mlle Bou. (Although we know that he
tried to get out of this posting by writing to a friend of his father's in
Paris.[10]) Luigi occupied a room on the first floor, where there was

also a little dark room that sometimes served as a punishment cell for the boy who would one day become King of Holland.

Two clubs had been formed at Valence in the image of their parent clubs in Paris. One was called the Société des Surveillants (Society of Overseers) and professed religious toleration. The other was the Society of the Friends of the Constitution (or Jacobin Club); Buonaparte joined the latter as soon as he arrived in Valence and rose, within a very short space of time, to become its secretary. It held its public meetings in the Church of St Apollinaris. The club had over 200 members, many of whom were recruited from the 4th artillery regiment, which meant that a certain amount of rivalry existed between Buonaparte and other officers of the regiment as to who was the most assiduous and the most fervent in their civic loyalty.

It was here that Buonaparte continued his political apprenticeship. The club was, for example, responsible for the funeral services held for the victims of Nancy (three regiments stationed there rebelled in July and August 1790. Twenty-three mutineers were executed to set an example), by having a mass to 'change the hearts of its enemies and to bring them back to the principles of the holy Constitution'.[11] It sent a letter of congratulations to the first purchaser of nationalized Church property at Drôme. On 7 June, it asked the municipality to draw up a list of émigrés from Valence, that is, people who had fled France because they were disgusted with the Revolution. It also ordered the municipality to prepare a cannon and to have it always ready to fire so that it could be used as an alarm signal for the town and its environs (presumably if the town were ever attacked, but by whom it was not clear). But, apart from his political activity at the local level, both in Corsica and now in France, two further important developments were going to help Buonaparte decide where he actually stood on the question of political loyalty.

The first was the king's attempted flight from Paris in June 1791. It was one of the turning points in the Revolution and deepened the growing chasm between royalists and revolutionaries.[12] In October 1789, a large mob of Parisian women (and some men) went to Versailles demanding bread and decided that the royal family would be better off in Paris. Compelled to move to Paris and installed in the Tuileries Palace, Louis XVI felt as though he was being held a prisoner, and that he was being forced against his will to work with a constitution he did not want. By the summer of 1791, exasperated with the limits placed on his own power, fearing for his family's safety after he and the queen were maltreated by the Paris mob (18 April), and outraged at the changes being forced on the Catholic Church by the revolutionaries, he decided to secretly flee the capital. During the night of 20 June, the royal family and a few loyal servants successfully managed to sneak past the guards and out of the Tuileries Palace, and headed towards the Luxembourg border. However, Louis was recognized en route by a local post-master by the name of Drouet. The party was stopped on the evening of 21 June at a little town called Varennes and brought back to Paris in humiliating circumstances.

When news of his flight reached the provinces – and it would have reached Valence by 24 June – it provoked spontaneous manifestations of loyalty to the nation and the Constitution all over the country.[13] On 3 July 1791, twenty-three popular clubs from the departments of the Drôme, Isère and Ardèche met at Valence to discuss the king's flight. Emotions were running high. People ranted against aristocrats; spoke of imminent war; and the Society of Overseers demanded the removal of all coats of arms from public façades. At seven o'clock in the morning, members of the club met on a field that was renamed for the occasion the 'Champs de l'Union' (Field of Union). After having heard a mass celebrated by the bishop in the cathedral, they went on to the Church of St Ruf, decked out in patriotic guise, where the president of the Society of the Friends of the Constitution read out an oath. Everyone swore to remain loyal to the nation and the law, to maintain the Constitution at the risk of their lives, to rally around the flag of liberty, and to watch out for the enemies of the public good.

Three days later, the army was required to swear another oath of loyalty.[14] They had done so once before, two years previously, on 23 August 1789, in the middle of Auxonne, when Buonaparte and his fellow officers, right hand raised, left hand on the pommel of their swords, had sworn to remain loyal to the nation, the king and the law. In the new oath, officers promised loyalty not to the king, whose name was not even mentioned, but to the National Assembly, which thereby became the only recognized authority in France and which was to serve as the rallying point of the nation. There was a problem, however. In the world of eighteenth-century noble officers, the king was officially seen as the incarnation of the nation.[15] Total obedience to the king was a concept that nobles were reared on. Their function in society, especially if they were of the nobility of the sword (those who had received their titles in the service of the king's armies), was to die protecting the 'throne of the state'. Those two words – throne and state – were inseparable. Service rendered to the king was service rendered to the state.[16] Thus a number of officers in the regiment of Valence refused to take the oath. The great majority, did, however, including Buonaparte who disapproved of the emigration of his comrades, would have felt no loyalty to the king, and would not have had a problem writing and signing the oath.

About a week later, Buonaparte found himself raising his hand to swear another oath, this time a civic one, on the anniversary of the fall of the Bastille.[17] On 14 July, the civic oath took place with the administrative body and the judiciary escorted by the National Guard and the gendarmerie arriving at ten o'clock in the morning on the Champs de l'Union to the sound of cannon fire. A large crowd had gathered to watch; the 4th artillery regiment formed a guard of honour around the Constitutional altar. After the speeches and the mass were over, the officers of the regiment approached the altar. In the presence of the communal authorities and the assembled crowd, the army units solemnly promised, again, to remain loyal to the nation and the law. Cries of 'Je le jure' (I swear) broke out mixed with the sound of cannon fire and a band that had struck up the revolutionary song, the 'Ça Ira' (It will be all right). At midday, a Te Deum was said and the official ceremonies were concluded. That evening, Buonaparte attended a banquet in the town at which he made a toast to the patriots of Auxonne who had come to Valence for the occasion.

These feast days designed to celebrate the Revolution and unify the people around the Assembly and the Constitution made a profound impression on Buonaparte. He was swept along with the enthusiasm these types of revolutionary ceremonies were designed to create; he spoke of how touched he had been by the people he had met in a letter to a friend.[18] They must also have had some impact on his position towards France and Corsica. Even though local loyalties and local patriotism took precedence over France – when Buonaparte spoke of the nation he was still speaking of Corsica[19] – these ceremonies must have obliged Buonaparte to think outside of his island home, perhaps seriously for the first time, and to decide where he stood on important political issues, such as loyalty to the monarchy versus loyalty to the elected Assembly. This, of course, is speculative, but what is clear is that Buonaparte made a choice and came down heavily on the side of the Constitution against the king.

Buonaparte's radical republican tendencies – or rather his anti-monarchism – have led some historians to compare him to revolutionaries who abandoned the monarchy when it became obvious they could no longer work with Louis XVI.[20] Buonaparte's republicanism, however, was far less practical and can be associated with his dislike of France as the conqueror and oppressor of his people. It is, moreover, consistent with his expressions of love for Corsica during his time at the Ecole militaire. Despite having benefited from an education in France on a royal scholarship and despite being an officer in the Royal Artillery, Buonaparte felt no great loyalty towards the monarchy. It was, therefore, not difficult to abandon the king and to adopt the mantle of republicanism, something that he was to do with characteristic verve. Buonaparte was now being drawn into the debates about the political future of the nation and, in this context, the nation was something much larger than Corsica. It was preparing the way for the rift that was soon to divide the Buonapartes and the Paolist faction back home.

By August 1791, Buonaparte was already thinking of taking a fourth extended leave. The circumstances that called him back to Corsica were, this time, clearly political. The National Assembly was about to dissolve itself and he wanted to return to help Giuseppe stand for the new Assembly. He was also thinking of his own active involvement in the Corsican revolution. The minister of war had just called for volunteer battalions of National Guard to be formed in each department, and Buonaparte hoped to get elected to one of those battalions in Corsica. He consequently asked for leave to go back home. According to one source, impossible to verify, his commander, a royalist by the name of Campagnol, did not want to grant it, so Buonaparte supposedly went over his head and approached his former commander, the Baron du Teil, who had been promoted inspector general of the artillery in the 6th Department, which included Valence.[21] Du Teil granted him a leave of three months as of 1 September. His timing could not have been better. Buonaparte had already left France and was in Corsica when an order to suspend all leave for 1791 – war between France and Austria seemed imminent – issued on 8 September, arrived in Valence. The minister of war, with whom the order originated, especially warned the commanders of the artillery regiments to be very circumspect about granting leave.

'I Wanted You to Be Free'

Buonaparte's hopes of seeing his brother elected to the new Legislative Assembly* were to be disappointed. Giuseppe's name was not even put forward for consideration. His two rivals in influence – Carlo Andrea Pozzo di Borgo and Marius Peraldi – triumphed over him. It is commonly argued that Paoli kept Giuseppe out of the running because he found the Buonaparte brothers too young and too ambitious (true on both counts), because he associated the Buonaparte family with Carlo's volte-face, or because he realized they would never entirely belong to him.[22] Instead, Paoli had Giuseppe elected to the departmental administration to fill one of the vacancies left by the resignations of Pozzo di Borgo and Peraldi. It obliged Giuseppe to move to Corte, now the capital of the department, away from his native town and power base, Ajaccio. It is possible that Paoli hoped, in this way, to isolate Giuseppe from his political stamping ground in Ajaccio.[23]

* The National Assembly dissolved itself in September 1791. A new parliament, the National Legislative Assembly, referred to simply as the Legislative Assembly, met in October of that year.

If Giuseppe's political ambitions were cut down to size, his younger brother fared better, perhaps because his objectives were less ambitious and hence more attainable. Buonaparte had set his sights on becoming a high-ranking officer in the Corsican National Guard and had thus set down the path of his own political career. Up until then he had always acted in a supporting role to his brother, concerned more about Giuseppe's success than his own. In the summer of 1790, for example, when Buonaparte was in Bastia, he had written to his brother shortly before Giuseppe's election to the Congress at Orezza to say how worried he was by it.[24] He had been afraid that Giuseppe would not succeed. A position in the National Guard, he hoped, would enable him to continue on in Corsica without losing his commission in the army. According to a law passed on 12 August 1791, all ranks in the volunteer battalions were to be obtained through election: only staff officers and sergeant-majors were to be taken from the regular troops of the line and were to be named by the general commanding the military division where the battalion was in service.[25] Buonaparte was helped in his objective by the fact that the new commanding general of the island, Biron, did not want to come to Corsica before order had been completely restored in the border region of the Alps where he was stationed. This made the second in charge, Antoine Rossi, the actual commander-in-chief on the island. Rossi was a distant relative of the Buonapartes and was having difficulty finding staff officers for his battalions; most of the French officers in Corsica did not know enough Italian to be of any use in training volunteers. He gratefully received Buonaparte's request to become a staff officer and, as early as 1 November 1791, asked Narbonne, the minister of war, if he could give Lieutenant Buonaparte a place.

Buonaparte's plans to stay on in Corsica were soon frustrated by developments in Paris. On 3 February 1792, about three weeks after Narbonne gave his initial assent to Buonaparte's placement, the Legislative Assembly voted a law ordering all regular officers to return to their units by 1 April, forbidding them to hold appointments in the National Guard, except those with the rank of lieutenant colonel. The only way for Buonaparte to remain in Corsica was to be elected lieutenant colonel in the Corsican National Guard. It seems Buonaparte made the decision to do so around the beginning of March.

There were four Corsican battalions in all. They had been a little slow to organize and not without some scandal; their formation had been accompanied by some glaring illegalities. Some departmental members had abused their privileges to get themselves elected lieutenant colonels, arbitrarily excluding their competitors or those who were not related. Paoli himself admitted that the battalions were composed of rejects from the villages.[26] They had no officers they would obey, and were considered to be corrupt. Buonaparte knew all this but did not really care as long as he was able to stay on his beloved island. Moreover, getting Buonaparte elected to one of these battalions would be a tremendous coup for the Buonaparte clan.

It happened that two positions were vacant in the second battalion of the National Guard of Ajaccio. The election was to take place at the end of March 1792.[27] Buonaparte had to compete with five other people, all of them belonging to clans richer and more influential than his own. Failure was a real risk. Two people in particular were a threat – Giovani Peraldi and Matteo Pozzo di Borgo. The Pozzo di Borgos were incontestably the most influential family in Ajaccio and one of the most well-established families on the island. They were not only rich in land, which automatically carried with it a certain amount of political influence, but also had succeeded to all the offices the town of Ajaccio had to offer. Matteo Pozzo di Borgo, who was linked to Buonaparte by education, friendship and politics, was the younger brother of Carlo Andrea, the deputy to the Legislative Assembly, elected largely as a result of Paoli's favour and influence.

The Peraldis were from Cauro, a small locality near Ajaccio, and had gathered around them a vast number of followers. Marius Peraldi, the head of the family, had also been elected a member of the Legislative Assembly and was a personal friend of Paoli. The candidate Giovani was his brother. There was already a certain amount of rivalry between the Peraldis and the Buonapartes over Giuseppe's failure to get elected to the Legislative Assembly. Since the Peraldi clan was already powerful in the district of Ajaccio, it did not intend to let the Buonapartes get the upper hand. It did its best, therefore, to discredit the young Buonaparte, publicly making fun of his ambition, his petulance and his lack of wealth in epigrams, songs and insults.[28] At one point, around the middle of March, Buonaparte got so angry that he supposedly challenged Marius Peraldi to a duel. Peraldi, however, simply failed to turn up at the appointed time, and was able to do so without losing face or honour because the duel was not part of Corsican custom.

Not all the odds were against Buonaparte, however. As we have seen, the mayor of Ajaccio, Jean-Jérôme Levie, was a Buonaparte man. The Buonapartes were also much more influential outside the town, where they had managed to form alliances with inland families, notably at Bastelica, at the foot of the Mount d'Or, and Bocognano. This was going to prove *the* decisive factor in the events that followed, since the National Guard were mostly re-cruited from the countryside. The Buonapartes had one other important advantage: the support of Cristoforo Saliceti, who would help sway the elections in their favour. Saliceti took some religious troubles that had occurred in Ajaccio as a pretext to call four companies of volunteers into the town, companies that were willing to do his bidding. They arrived on 1 April in time for the elections, and took up positions in the town. Much to the chagrin of Letizia, her son decided to foot the bill for lodging them, and made sure they received plenty to eat and drink.[29] This was a common practice in local elections, and a means of controlling, not always success-fully, the results.[30] Letizia's house on rue St Charles was thus always full of volunteers.

Getting the National Guard into Ajaccio was only part of the battle. Everything depended on the three commissaries charged with presiding over the elections – Quenza, Morati (sometimes written Murati) and Grimaldi. The commissaries arrived in Ajaccio on 30 March, two days before the election. The choice of their lodgings, according to Corsican custom, would have an enormous impact on the way the voting took place, since they were indirectly indicating to everyone where their preferences lay. Quenza stayed with the Ramolinos (Letizia was a Ramolino). Grimaldi was a friend of the Buonapartes; on arriving in Ajaccio he paid his respects to Letizia and stayed with them. In other words, two of the three commissaries could be relied upon, but the third, Morati, went to the house of a family backing Buonaparte's chief rival, Peraldi. Throughout 31 March, the eve of the election, Buonaparte agonised over what to do until, finally, he decided in favour of abduction. He ordered one of his most active partisans, Angelo Matteo Bonelli, a coarse authoritarian highlander, the very same 'Zampaglino' who had continued to fight against the French after Paoli had left the island (and who would later fight the British when they occupied the island briefly in 1794–5), to kidnap Morati. It is claimed that, when Morati was dragged before Buonaparte, Buonaparte told him: 'I wanted you to be free; you were not at the Peraldis; here you are at home.'[31]

This violent action could have led to fighting between the two clans the next day, the day of the election. On 1 April, 521 National Guards, mostly sympathetic to Buonaparte, trooped into the Church of St Francis, where the election was to take place. The volunteers had received orders not to appear armed, but most had a concealed pistol or a dagger. This was another commonly practised means of preventing one's adversary from getting elected, that is, it was usual to intimidate one's opponents.[32] As soon as the session opened, Matteo Pozzo di Borgo made a speech protesting against the kidnapping and violation of Peraldi's home, trying to make his voice heard over the booing and jeering from the Buonaparte supporters. He was pulled off the rostrum by his legs and probably would have been killed if, according to one historian at least, it were not for Buonaparte and a certain Captain Casanova de Sartène, who intervened to protect him.[33]

How much of this entire episode is true is difficult to establish.[34] Since Buonaparte had two out of the three commissaries under control, it does not seem necessary for him to have abducted the third, all the more so since such an action was likely to provoke a violent reprisal. Certainly it would have worsened the already bad blood between the Peraldis and the Buonapartes. On the other hand, much of what happened seems consistent with local practices in other parts of France, where violence and intimidation were frequently used to influence election results. Important is the outcome: Giovan Battisa Quenza was elected first in command; Buonaparte polled second. The Buonaparte clan was delighted; that evening their friends and supporters came to congratulate the new second in command of the volunteers. Luciano wrote to Giuseppe, 'Buonaparte is lieutenant colonel with Quenza; at the moment the house is full of people and the music of the regiment'.[35] This new position would soon throw him into the thick of Corsican politics.

The Easter Sunday Murders

One week later, on Easter Sunday, a quarrel over a game of skittles degenerated into a gunfight that was to see Buonaparte and his battalion of National Guard pitted against the town of Ajaccio.[36]

Around five o'clock in the evening of Easter Sunday, 8 April, in the rue de la Cathédrale, some girls playing skittles started to argue among themselves. Two sailors – cousins – got involved and, in turn, started arguing between themselves. Insults were exchanged – *porco* (pig), *cuglione* (dickhead) – and a dagger was drawn. The noise alerted a company of twelve volunteers in the National Guard. On their way they stopped a man carrying a pistol; he resisted and was arrested. A master mason, who also happened to be passing by, was stopped and searched. A scuffle ensued, others came running to help, shots were fired, one man fell badly wounded, while the National Guard, harassed by gunfire from neighbouring windows, were forced to beat a hasty retreat to their quarters.

While all this was happening, Buonaparte was in the Grande Rue. On hearing the shots, he hurried towards the cathedral, gathering with him six or seven officers from the volunteer battalion along the way. When he arrived in front of the cathedral, Buonaparte and his officers confronted an armed group of men coming out of the church. He tried to argue his way out of the standoff, but soon shots were fired and an officer of the National Guard was killed on the spot. Buonaparte and his group had time enough to flee, rushing into a nearby house and, from there, escaping through the back to a nearby seminary. One of the officers used a woman as a shield while he made his retreat. At the seminary, the two lieutenant colonels, Quenza and Buonaparte, declared that, since the town was blatantly in insurrection, the battalion had the right to protect itself by shooting back. The next day, Monday 9 April, after occupying various strategic positions, and after receiving reinforcements from about one hundred National Guard outside of Ajaccio, they started, in effect, laying siege to the town, firing, for example, on people coming out of the cathedral from mass: a widow and a girl of thirteen were mortally wounded.

Over the next few days, with hundreds more National Guard from the surrounding districts arriving to reinforce their comrades, Buonaparte and the town were at a standoff. Negotiators went back and forth, conferences were held, ceasefires were arranged and broken, shots continued to ring out during most of the siege, although there were no more killed or wounded, while the National Guard prevented anybody from entering or leaving the town, and prohibited access to the town fountains. At one stage, Buonaparte, on horseback, went from one advanced post to another haranguing his troops. He is even supposed to have given a speech in front of a group of about three hundred National Guards in the Capuchin convent to the effect that the whole nation had been outraged by the offences heaped on them, but that they would know how to avenge the insult. This was the language of the blood feuds for which Corsica was renowned. There was talk of kidnapping the French commandant of the citadel, Maillard, as well as attempts to convince the grenadiers from the 42nd regiment to defect. The troops, however, were loyal to their commanding officers and treated these attempts with scorn. Nevertheless, both bread and wood were starting to run short and no one could leave to work the fields. Moreover, many of the inhabitants did not dare go out into the streets during the day for fear of being shot at by the volunteers.

Even so, it was probably with a great deal of relief that Buonaparte heard of the arrival of two commissaries, appointed by the Directory at Corte, with instructions to sort out the mess. Buonaparte even went to meet them at Bocognano, about thirty-two kilometres from Ajaccio, to tell them his version of events. They entered Ajaccio on Monday, 16 April, a week after the troubles had begun. (On the way, they met peasants carrying empty sacks heading for town where they hoped to get a share of the loot.) The first thing the commissaries did was to prohibit everyone from carrying arms, volunteers and townspeople alike. They then ordered the volunteer battalions back to their villages. They ordered Quenza and Buonaparte to Corte, in spite of Buonaparte's pleas that it was a humiliation for the National Guard. It took some time to convince Buonaparte, and it was only after Giuseppe had advised him, and the commissaries had reiterated their summons and threatened him with force, that he finally gave in. The two commissaries nevertheless blamed the town for the unrest and had thirty-four of its citizens imprisoned.

Almost as soon as the shooting had finished, Buonaparte wrote his version of events, in Italian, to the Directory of the department.[37] In a long statement, Buonaparte accused the population of Ajaccio, which was made up of 'cannibals', of having mistreated, insulted and assassinated the volunteers. He assured the Directory that the National Guard were forced to defend themselves against people who had long premeditated a plot and that, on 9 April, it was the Ajacciens who had opened fire. He failed to mention the dead and wounded caused by the volunteers. The people of Ajaccio had not obeyed the local municipality because it was full of brigands. 'In the terrible crisis in which we found ourselves, energy and audacity were called for; a man was needed who, if he were asked, after his mission, would swear to having transgressed no law and would be in the position to reply, like Cicero or Mirabeau: I swear that I have saved the Republic.'[38]

That man, of course, was Buonaparte. The arrogance of his report is telling; some of the more imperious traits that would later characterise Napoleon were already present. He was daring enough to incite regular French troops to revolt; he was bold enough to use the local authorities in his cause; and he was callous enough to open fire on a civilian population, and to lay siege to his home town by depriving it of flour, wood and water. And for what? To avenge the death of an officer shot in cold blood before the cathedral, or to avenge the insults he and his men had suffered? These are certainly factors that help explain the behaviour of the volunteers. Buonaparte's first instinct, despite being an officer in the royal army and a commander in the National Guard, was to think of revenge, to punish his adversaries. But it would be unwise to simply reduce his actions to the Corsican 'vendetta' by focusing too much on the violence or Buonaparte's impetuous nature. This episode has to be seen as part of a local political struggle in which two factions, for want of a better word, were vying with each other for dominance. Buonaparte, who represented pro-revolutionary Corsicans, was attempting to use his power to neutralize the adversary, conservative Corsicans who remained loyal to the Catholic Church and the French monarchy. One indication of this is Buonaparte's effort to get troops into the citadel, which would not only have allowed him to dominate the whole town, but would also would have pleased Paoli.

When the commissaries carried out their inquiry, they were not ill-disposed towards Buonaparte. True, one of them was a relative, but they nevertheless decided on the dispersal of the battalions, which were sent out of Ajaccio to Corte and Bonifacio. Buonaparte was obliged to follow. On the way to Corte, he went to see Paoli, no doubt to give his version of events. We do not know what was

Jean-Baptiste Greuze, *Le capitaine Bonaparte à l'âge de vingt-deux ans* (Captain Bonaparte at the age of twenty-two), 1792. The earliest known portrait of Bonaparte in the uniform of artillery captain. (*Courtesy of RMN – © Yann Martin*)

actually said during this interview, but soon afterwards Giuseppe wrote to Buonaparte to say that it would be better if he went to France for a while.[39] Buonaparte had already made the decision to do so; the affair would be judged in Paris, so Buonaparte had to go there to defend himself. Armed with certificates of good citizenship, and attestations from the municipality of Ajaccio and the Directory of Corsica – both pre-dating the Easter insurrection – he set off for Paris around the end of April or the beginning of May.

Buonaparte, Paris and the Revolution

Buonaparte arrived in Paris on 28 May 1792, on the eve of a new revolutionary uprising, and took a room in the same hotel as the Corsican deputies, the Hôtel des Patriotes Hollandais in the rue Saint-Roch (today the rue des Moulins).[40] It had taken him almost a month to reach his destination, although it is not known what caused this delay. On the way to Paris, Buonaparte learned what he and so many of his contemporaries thought was impossible – France had declared war against Austria.*

The outbreak of war between France and its eastern neighbours on 20 April, which would eventually engulf all the European monarchies and would not end until the battle of Waterloo twenty-three years later, is a remarkable example of how just about everybody involved in foreign relations misinterpreted the intentions of everyone else.[41] Up until this time, the Great Powers (Britain, Austria, Russia and Prussia) had taken no particular interest in the Revolution. On the contrary, they were quite content to see a great power rival in political turmoil and to see the French presence and influence in Europe consequently diminish. Besides, at the beginning of the Revolution, Austria, Russia and Prussia were occupied elsewhere: Russia and Austria were at war with the

---

* In fact, the Legislative Assembly declared war on 'the king of Hungary and Bohemia'. This was a technicality and was, in effect, a declaration of war against Austria. The Hapsburg ruler, Leopold II, Archduke of Austria, King of Hungary and Bohemia, Holy Roman Emperor, died on 1 March 1792. He was succeeded by his son, Francis, who had not yet been formally elected Holy Roman Emperor. There was also the hope entertained by the revolutionaries of avoiding war with Prussia and with the Holy Roman Empire.

Ottoman Empire until July 1790, when Austria had to abandon this fight to concentrate on suppressing a revolt in the Austrian Netherlands. When this was crushed in the winter of 1790, Vienna then turned its attention to the ill-fated kingdom of Poland, where Russia and Prussia were also seeking to gain territory (Poland eventually disappeared from the map, swallowed up by its neighbours in three consecutive partitions). At this particular point in time, all three eastern European powers were far more interested in what was happening in their own backyards than what was going on in France.

Louis XVI's attempted flight from Paris changed all this. Leopold II of Austria, who was, after all, Marie-Antoinette's brother, felt he had to make some sort of gesture in support of the French monarchy. In August 1791, Leopold, in association with Frederick William II of Prussia, issued the Declaration of Pillnitz. They were ready, the two monarchs declared, to restore the king of France to a position from which he could strengthen the foundations of monarchical government. The declaration, at first, went unnoticed in France, but after the election of the Legislative Assembly, which met for the first time at the beginning of October, the deputies increasingly turned their attention to events in the German states. Ever since the fall of the Bastille, people who were unprepared to work with the National Assembly, who were disgusted by the spectacle of the mob and the consequent diminution in monarchical power, had been leaving France in their thousands. Many such opponents of the Revolution – termed the émigrés – had gathered in the town of Koblenz, at the confluence of the Rhine and Moselle, where both of the king's brothers, the Comte d'Artois and the Comte de Provence, had emigrated in the summer of 1789. There they prepared for war, subsidized by large grants from the courts of Vienna, Berlin, Petersburg and from a number of German princes.

The formation of a counter-revolutionary army on France's borders could hardly be tolerated by the revolutionaries; it acted as a magnet for those opposed to the Revolution, who emigrated in a number of waves, usually after events that marked a radicalization of the Revolution (such as the fall of the Bastille and the flight to Varennes). More than 6,000 French officers emigrated in 1791 alone.[42] Indeed, the 'émigrés problem' was becoming so serious that the Legislative Assembly passed a law in November 1791 declaring 'suspect' of plotting against the government all those who had left the country, and all those who did not return by 1 January 1792 outlaws. Increasingly, the émigrés gathering on the eastern borders of France came to be seen as a threat by revolutionaries keen to blame the problems they were experiencing inside France on 'traitors', both within and without the country. This took place in an atmosphere of fear and suspicion that was heightened after the king's flight. Much of this suspicion was directed at the monarchy. Rumours were rife that the country's foreign policy was being run by an 'Austrian committee' headed by Marie-Antoinette and that secret agents were being sent to Koblenz and Vienna to plot a counter-revolution. The revolutionaries' suspicions were not entirely unfounded, as they later learned. Marie-Antoinette was indeed writing both to her brother, Leopold II, and to the Austrian ambassador in Paris asking for help, claiming that only an armed demonstration from a concert of European powers could save the monarchy from total ruin.

The Revolution and the monarchy were in conflict, a conflict that could only be resolved with the elimination of one of the adverse parties. But, for the monarchy to be destroyed, the revolutionaries would have to prove that the king was working against them. One way of doing that, or at least so thought a minority of radical deputies in the Legislative Assembly, would be to go to war against Austria, which was responsible for the Declaration of Pillniz. Austria, it has to be pointed out, had been the traditional enemy of France for many years and was loathed by most French. The Declaration of Pillnitz, the revolutionaries objected, was a blatant attempt by Austria to intervene in France's domestic affairs (they spoke of *lèse-nation*). It was not too difficult, therefore, for the small number of radical revolutionaries in the Legislative Assembly, whose ultimate goal was the overthrow of the monarchy, to convince the vast majority of moderate deputies to vote for war. The process, nevertheless, took a number of months and was made easier by Austria, when, increasingly alarmed by the turn of events in France and sympathetic to Marie-Antoinette's appeals for intervention, it threatened the Legislative Assembly in December 1791 and again in February 1792. If a French army took action against the émigrés in Germany, Vienna warned, it would be forced to intervene. Under the circumstances, it was easy to sweep the majority of moderate deputies along in the wave of nationalist rhetoric that followed these threats. When it came to it, only seven deputies voted against war. They all expected it to be a short conflict, which is one of the reasons the French entered into it so enthusiastically. They did not count on Prussia, and eventually every other European monarchy, joining the fray, so that what started out as a limited Austro-French war expanded into the largest conflict the world had yet seen.[43]

There is nothing to indicate that Buonaparte was keen to take part in this war, or that he even followed it with much interest.[44] His mind was preoccupied with other matters. It would also be a mistake to think, given his revolutionary activity in Corsica, that Buonaparte had any enthusiasm for the Revolution in Paris. He discovered that Paris, to use his expression, was suffering from the greatest 'convulsions', which is a little ironic considering that he had largely been the cause of one such 'convulsion' in his home town. At the time, various factions were pulling people, and the Revolution, in different directions. Royalists despised the Constitution and hated the manner in which the king had been treated. Moderates had been desperately trying to stem the tide of radicalism and republicanism ever since the attempted flight of the king and, although they had initially consolidated their hold on power, they soon lost the initiative to more radical deputies in the Legislative Assembly and the popular societies of Paris. Indeed, it was this group of radical deputies who had pushed for war, and who were now preaching the necessity of replacing the king with a Republic. It was within this context of heightened tensions between radicals and royalists that Buonaparte arrived in Paris at the end of May 1792. It was no doubt because of the violent street scenes that he was soon to witness that he learned contempt for both the workings of the Legislative Assembly and the people of Paris. After his experiences there, Buonaparte came down decidedly in favour of law and order and against the mob, an opinion that was reinforced by the events of 20 June.

That same day, Buonaparte and an old school acquaintance from Brienne, Bourrienne, whom he had met the day after his arrival in

Paris, had a rendezvous for lunch in the rue Saint-Honoré, near the Palais Royal. On their way, a group of 'seven or eight thousand men, armed with pikes, axes, swords, muskets, skewers [*broches*], and pointed sticks', whose behaviour and clothes represented the worst dregs of society, passed by.[45] This huge crowd was heading for the Tuileries where, they said, they wanted to plant a Tree of Liberty, a symbol of adherence to the Revolution, in the middle of the royal palace. The demonstration was, in fact, a popular protest against Louis' refusal to approve a number of laws recently passed by the Legislative Assembly, and his abrupt dismissal of all his ministers one week previously. On the terrace of the Café Bord de l'Eau, Buonaparte watched the demonstration get out of control as the crowd poured into the undefended palace and forced their way into the king's apartments. The king was alone and for almost two hours he was subjected, once again, to the threats of the people of Paris shouting, 'Down with the veto' and 'To the devil with the veto.' In the face of this, Louis showed enormous courage. 'The men of the *faubourgs* [suburbs of Paris]', Buonaparte wrote to his brother, 'presented the king with two cockades, one white and the other tricolour. They gave him a choice, Choose, they said to him, to reign here or at Koblenz. The king behaved well. He put on the red bonnet.'[46] The *bonnet rouge*, also known as the Phrygian bonnet or liberty cap, was another symbol, along with the tricolour cockade, of approval for the Revolution. Borrowed from classical Rome – the bonnet was sported by former slaves who had been freed by their masters – it began to be worn in Paris in the spring of 1792 by people who wanted to trumpet their affiliation with the Revolution.[47] The king's decision to borrow a liberty cap and to drink to the health of the nation was an evident attempt to appease the mob, but he did not, for all that, change his policies.

While Paris was in turmoil, Buonaparte was attempting to reintegrate into his artillery regiment. Before doing so, however, he had to face an inquiry, of sorts, in Paris. Colonel Maillard, the commandant of Ajaccio, sent a report back to Paris in which he did little more than summarize events.[48] He did not blame either Quenza or Buonaparte for inciting the non-commissioned officers of the 42nd regiment to revolt and did not demand, as he had every

Artist unknown, *Journée des sans culottes* (The *journée* of the *sans-culottes*), 1792. (*Bibliothèque nationale, Paris*)

right to, that they be tried by court martial. As well, there was the report from the royal commissary, Grandin, who had been wounded by the National Guard while coming out of church on Monday, the report from the Directory of the Department, and the manifesto of the town of Ajaccio.[49] All of these documents were damning for the Corsican battalion and its two lieutenant colonels. They proved that Buonaparte and Quenza had committed an obvious act of rebellion by refusing to obey orders from Maillard. On 8 July, the minister of war, Pierre Auguste Lajard, wrote to Maillard that, having examined the dossier carefully, he found that Quenza and Buonaparte had promoted the unrest and the excesses of the troops they commanded.[50] Both, he concluded, were 'infinitely reprehensible' and, if their crimes had been military, they would have been instantly court-martialled. But, Lajard added, both civilian and military personnel were implicated in the affair and, in the interests of maintaining order, it had to be referred to the Ministry of Justice. The Ministry, undoubtedly preoccupied by more pressing matters, simply did not follow the matter up.

The affair was, in fact, conveniently forgotten by a government in short supply of trained officers and, two days after being blamed for the disturbance, Buonaparte was promoted to captain (10 July). It was not unusual for officers who displayed an appropriate amount of political loyalty to have charges against them overlooked.[51] He was even awarded back pay, as though his service in the army had never been interrupted. To be promoted to captain at the age of twenty-two without ever having seen action in the field was indeed good fortune. And yet, Buonaparte hesitated before rejoining his artillery regiment, for this would have meant renouncing his command as lieutenant colonel in the National Guard and giving up an environment he knew how to negotiate. It took him almost a month to make up his mind, but he did so by 7 August, writing to Giuseppe to tell him that he was rejoining his regiment. 'As such, no matter what happens, I will have established myself in France.'[52]

This is another development in the evolution of Buonaparte's political character. The Easter Sunday 'insurrection' obviously brought home the difficulty of getting ahead in a country in which the Paolist clientele system left the Buonaparte clan in a marginalised position. For the first time, Buonaparte considered living in France and making the best of what the Revolution had to offer. His attitude, however, was ambivalent. He still wanted to be known as a faithful and sincere adherent of Paoli, and wrote to Giuseppe the day after his arrival in Paris to say that Paoli 'was everything and could do everything. He will be everything in the future which no one can foresee.'[53] He was advising Giuseppe to tread carefully and to cover his bases. He was doing everything possible to remain on good terms with both Paoli and Pozzo di Borgo for the future advancement of his family.

Three days after he had announced his decision to join the troops of the line, Buonaparte witnessed another attack on the Tuileries. After the declaration of war the previous April, the commander of the Austro-Prussian forces, the Duke of Brunswick, issued a declaration from Koblenz on 25 July, threatening to punish anyone who defended themselves against the allied army 'according to the severity of the law of war'. He further declared that if the Tuileries were attacked again, or if the king and his family were harmed in any way, then Paris would be delivered up to 'a military execution and total destruction'. Designed to intimidate the people of Paris, it had the opposite effect. It galvanized the people of Paris, who turned their anger against the monarchy.

On 10 August 1792, Buonaparte saw a crowd of people heading towards the Tuileries; he ran to the house of Bourrienne's brother, Fauvelet, who had a furniture shop near the Carousel looking over the Tuileries gardens, where from a window he was able to observe what took place. On the way, he met a crowd of men parading a pike on top of which was the head of some hapless individual who had displeased the crowd. They stopped to question him, forcing him to shout, 'Vive la nation'. It was a time when the mob ruled, and it was not uncommon for it to turn on people they considered suspect or 'aristocratic', which could simply mean being well dressed. They were still hunting down aristocrats after the Tuileries had been stormed in June.[54] This time, the Tuileries Palace was attacked by about 20,000 people, a mixture of National Guard, many of whom had come from the provinces to celebrate the fall of the Bastille, and the people of Paris – shopkeepers, artisans and tradesmen – armed with knives, pikes and hatchets. Its defenders, about 900 Swiss Guard and between 100 and 200 courtiers and former officers, were quickly overcome and at least 600 butchered. The king and his family were forced to flee and seek protection from the Legislative Assembly, which was housed nearby.

Afterwards, Buonaparte 'wandered through the cafés near the Assembly: the anger was extreme everywhere one went; hatred was in their hearts and could be seen on their faces, even though they were not at all from the lower classes. Those places must have filled daily with regulars because, even though there was nothing particular about my clothes, or perhaps it was because the expression on my face was calmer, it was easy to see that I was producing many hostile and distrustful looks, as though I were a stranger or a suspect.' Buonaparte, undoubtedly drawn by curiosity to contemplate the aftermath of the massacre, walked through the Tuileries where the victims of the attack lay strewn across the pavement. It was the first time he had seen the bloody consequences of battle, and he later wrote that no other battlefield made such an impression on him as this one.[55] Walking among the bodies, he claimed he saved a Swiss Guard about to be killed by a Marseillais by simply saying, 'Man of the South, save this poor wretch.' 'Are you from the South?' the other replied. 'Yes.' 'Well then, let's save him.'[56]

Buonaparte was shocked to see well-dressed people flocking to the scene as though it were some bizarre spectacle that both repulsed and attracted them at the same time. The artist, the Comte de Paroy, passing by the Tuileries in the early evening, 'was stopped by a horrible spectacle: the naked bodies of the unfortunate Swiss and of others who had been massacred at the château were being brought in chariots. Almost all of them had their heads cut off. The bodies were piled one on top of the other near a fountain at the end of the

Artist unknown, *La Fondation de la République, 10 août 1792* (The Foundation of the Republic, 10 August 1792). (*Bibliothèque nationale, Paris*)

street. The heat had already brought about a decomposition that infected the air. I was pushed by the crowd eager to see the scene, whatever it brought. Women wanted to see everything, especially out of curiosity, for this horrible scene snatched from them cries of repugnance and reprobation.'[57]

That day, the monarchy and the Constitution were suspended, and the Legislative Assembly decreed that the electors would assemble on 2 September to vote a new parliament, the National Convention, to meet in Paris on 20 September. In effect, the monarchy had been overthrown and a Republic was about to be instituted. If Buonaparte did not change his mind on the spot about joining his regiment, as some historians have suggested, more pressing family matters probably contributed to what seems like an impulsive decision to return once again to Corsica, probably with the idea of helping Giuseppe in the elections to the Convention (despite accepting the commission, Buonaparte never joined his regiment). In addition, decrees handed down in August by the Legislative Assembly closing certain religious establishments obliged Buonaparte to go and get his sister, Maria-Anna (Elisa), out of the school of Saint-Louis at Saint-Cyr near Versailles and to escort her back to Corsica. It was as good an excuse as any to leave France.[58] By the time they left Paris on 9 September, and finally managed to get a boat to Corsica from Toulon, probably on 10 October, the elections were over. Once again, Giuseppe had failed to become a candidate. Buonaparte was not the only member of the family whose ambitions were about to be frustrated.

THE REVOLUTIONARY, 1792–1796

5

Disillusion

Increasing Tensions

Not only had Giuseppe not been elected to the Convention, he had also lost his position in the departmental administration. Paoli had withdrawn his support and, as a result, the two were no longer on speaking terms. About a week after landing in Ajaccio, on 15 October, Buonaparte went to Corte, where his volunteer battalion was now stationed, and immediately sought out Paoli to resolve the situation.[1] We do not know what happened when Buonaparte finally met with him (probably on 22 October), but it does not appear that he was successful in defending his brother. This is not surprising: Buonaparte's impetuous behaviour at Ajaccio had no doubt given Paoli cause for reflection. We know that, in private, Paoli blamed the departmental administration for the whole fiasco, referring to the *giovani inesperti* (inexperienced young men) in the Directory and holding them responsible for the *ragazzoni inesperti* (inexperienced boys) placed in command of the National Guard.[2] It was a blatant dig at both brothers. There was also Paoli's refusal to take on Luciano as his secretary. 'Luciano can have no hope at all that the General [Paoli] would want him with him. He has stated this openly. He recognizes his talents, but he does not want to merge with us. This is the basis of the affair.'[3]

This development and the resultant cooling between the two parties was a blow to the Buonapartes' plans. The brothers, despite doing their utmost to please the *babbo*, had put their relationship with him in jeopardy by thinking only of their own advancement. Paoli was understandably wary. Not only were they young, ambitious and pushy, but the family had, after all, collaborated while he had suffered exile. Paoli is supposed to have referred to the brothers disdainfully as *i figli di Carlo* (Carlo's sons).[4] However, at this stage, even though relations were tense, there was no question of a complete falling out. Still, Paoli's attitude towards the Buonaparte clan would grow increasingly distant as the Buonaparte brothers drew closer to the Jacobin faction in Corsica, whose allegiance to Paris and the Revolution strengthened as relations between Paoli and the Convention soured. The brothers had no choice in the matter; if they wanted to satisfy their ambitions they had to ally themselves with another powerful faction. Relations between the Buonaparte clan and Paoli would worsen with the aborted expedition to invade and annex the island of Sardinia, a hiccup on the revolutionary scene that would have received little attention from historians if it were not for the fact that it was Buonaparte's first experience of battle.

The Expedition to Sardinia

The idea for an invasion of Sardinia had been mooted as early as February 1791, when the Corsican deputy, Buttafuoco, proposed a diversion against the King of Piedmont, whose policies had aroused suspicion in Corsica.[5] Nothing would be easier, he wrote, than taking the island. It was simply a question of forming detachments composed of volunteers and troops of the line. The only unanswered question concerned choosing a leader for the expedition.[6] Buttafuoco, in good Corsican style, then went on to propose his father-in-law, Maréchal de Camp Gaffori, who had the advantage of having lived in Sardinia for a number of years.[7] When France declared war on Austria, another Corsican, Antoine Constantini, a member of the Jacobin club, addressed a report to the military committee of the Legislative Assembly assuring them that the conquest of Sardinia would be very easy. The inhabitants of the islands would, he believed, help them achieve this goal. Like most invasions undertaken by the revolutionaries, it was believed that the peoples about to be conquered were longing to overthrow their masters and welcome the French.

The proximity of Sardinia helps explain in part why the project was born in Corsica, but there were other considerations. Economic – Sardinia was called the island of wheat, and it was hoped that it would be able to supply the Midi with badly needed grain as well as the beef and horses necessary to furnish the Army of the Midi and to help the operations in Piedmont and the Alps. Military – the invasion would divert enemy forces away from the mainland and relieve pressure on the French army. Political – an expedition against Sardinia, like an invasion of Britain, managed to fire the imagination of some French revolutionaries, although the island itself was of no great military or strategic importance and the decision to go ahead with the invasion was made simply because the opportunity presented itself. Diplomatic – the invasion was meant to intimidate Florence and Naples who, although officially neutral, were decidedly hostile towards the revolutionary government. Ideological considerations do not seem to have played a role. More persuasive was the argument that Sardinia could later be used as a chip at the bargaining table in return for which France would receive compensation elsewhere.

These, at least, were the arguments developed by the minister of war, Lazare Carnot, in a report that was approved by the Executive Council of the Convention. It consequently ordered (16 September 1792) four vessels, six frigates and a number of transport troops to concentrate at the port of Villefranche in the south of France, ready for a general attack against the possessions of the King of Piedmont. Two commissaries, Barthélemy Arena and Marius Peraldi, were nominated to follow the invasion and negotiate with the principal Sardinian leaders. The command of the expedition was given to General Jacques Bernard Modeste d'Anselme. His plan was to sail with the French fleet under Rear Admiral Laurent Truguet with volunteers from Marseilles and battalions of regular troops from the Army of the Midi. They would pick up troops at Bastia and Calvi before landing at Ajaccio, where they would be joined by 3,000 men from both the regular regiments and the volunteer battalions. The fact that the volunteer battalions had absolutely no combat experience and, as we have seen with the Easter Sunday troubles, even less discipline, does not seem to have been a consideration, but then the expedition was meant to be uncomplicated and straightforward.

The problem was that it was so badly prepared that its failure was almost a foregone conclusion. Corsican administrators were soon involved in misappropriating funds destined for the expedition (whether with or without the knowledge of Paoli is not clear). Truguet was such a useless addition to the expedition that he did not even think of blockading the Sardinian ports; he was too busy having a good time in Genoa, where he stayed for almost a month. General Anselme was probably the only person to have a realistic assessment of the difficulties involved in the invasion and was, in fact, so much against the project that he was soon relieved of his command and replaced by General Brunet. Brunet also came out against the expedition and designated as his replacement Raphaël Casabianca. The expected 6,000 National Guard from Marseilles and the Bouches-du-Rhône turned out to be 4,500 at the time of their embarkation, but only 1,000 were actually armed. The Phalange Marseillais (Phalanx of Marseilles), as it was called, was that in name only. Most of the volunteers seem to have joined up at the prospect of loot and pillage, and the expedition appears to have been used by both Anselme and the government in Paris as an opportunity to get rid of these undesirable elements.

Apart from a few interested parties, there does not seem to be any indication that the expedition aroused any enthusiasm whatsoever among Corsicans. Except for Buonaparte. He saw an opportunity to participate in a military campaign where there was a possibility of distinguishing himself. Perhaps it was the cooling of relations with Paoli, or perhaps it was simply that Buonaparte was starting to find the Corsican scene too small, but he had already been thinking of opportunities outside Corsica. We know, for example, that it was during this period that he played with the idea of going to India. He spoke about it in front of Letizia and Giuseppe, thinking the English would pay well for someone with his qualifications.[8] But, for the time being, the chance for glory offered itself in the ill-conceived expedition against Sardinia.

When Rear Admiral Truguet landed at Ajaccio towards the end of October 1792 to the welcoming sounds of music and gun shots fired in the air,[9] he soon formed a relationship with the Buonapartes, who often came across him at the numerous balls to which he was invited. It seems that the forty-year-old Truguet was taken with the young Maria-Anna (Elisa), but she was only sixteen and apparently incapable of recognizing a good match when she saw one.[10] In the midst of the balls and the various diversions that were planned for the invading army, the military expedition was more or less organized. Truguet soon found out, however, that Paoli had no intention of releasing the four volunteer battalions and the three army regiments that had been designated for the expedition. Paoli complained of the 'thinness' of his forces and insisted that he could not release more than 1,800 men. Moreover, the expedition suffered from considerable delays and, as the date of the planned invasion drew closer, the number and value of the troops diminished. By the time the lack of discipline that reigned among both French volunteers and sailors from the mainland made itself felt, relations between the French and Corsicans would be strained to breaking point.

The situation came to a head when, on 18 December, French sailors from the expedition, together with soldiers of the 42nd regiment, wandered through the town of Ajaccio singing revolutionary songs – the 'Carmagnole' and the 'Ça Ira' – and crying out, *A bas les aristos!* (Down with the aristocrats!) and *A la lanterne!* (String them up!).[11] They paraded around with rope, which they said they were going to use to hang the aforementioned aristocrats. Inevitably, the French did kill and hang from a mast in sight of the whole town a Corsican National Guard, before taking down the body, hacking it to pieces, and throwing it into the ocean. The carnage did not stop there. They then entered the prison, where they found under lock and key an artisan accused of having wounded a soldier from the 42nd the previous night, and they also captured two Corsican volunteers from the Quenza-Buonaparte battalion. The three men were hung and their bodies cut up and paraded in the streets before finally also being thrown into the sea, all to the tune of the 'Ça Ira'. A procurator of the commune of Ajaccio, Antonio Peraldi, tried to intervene at one stage. It was an act of courage that almost cost him his life. They had already placed a rope around his neck when soldiers from a Corsican regiment came to his aid and, with some difficulty, cut him down just in time; Peraldi had already lost consciousness and was making gurgling noises. One can easily imagine the reaction of the Corsican volunteers when news of this barbarous behaviour reached them. It was only the presence of mind of their commanders, Quenza and Buonaparte, perhaps having learned their lesson from the 'Ajaccio affair', that prevented further bloodshed from occurring. They managed to get the volunteers back into their barracks and then further away from the town by billeting them in nearby villages.

Tensions were exacerbated even further when the volunteers from Marseilles arrived on the island in January. When one of their officers was jailed for bad behaviour, a group of armed Marseillais killed a Corsican National Guard for refusing to set him free. On another occasion, a lieutenant colonel of the Marseilles volunteers pillaged a goldsmith's and abducted a woman, whom he took on board the ship that was to take them to Sardinia. Buonaparte himself barely escaped being lynched by a mob of Marseillais volunteers. He was about to be set upon when a sergeant from his battalion came to his aid, drew his dagger and struck dead the Marseillais that happened to be holding Buonaparte. Other Corsican soldiers arrived and the Marseillais beat a retreat.[12]

These incidents necessarily obliged Truguet to change his plans; he could no longer consider bringing angry Corsican volunteers bent on revenge on board his ships. However, as he was also obliged to use the Corsican volunteers, he decided to use them separately in an attack on the island of La Maddalena, while the bulk of the fleet and the troops of the line, commanded by General Casabianca, were directed against the capital of Sardinia, Cagliari, which was on the opposite end of the island from La Maddalena.[13] Truguet believed that such a plan of attack would have the advantage of dividing the Sardinian forces in two. It was to forget that the Sardinians did not have a plan of defence and that La Maddalena was too far from Cagliari for the one to have any bearing on the outcome of the other.

The day after setting sail from Bonifacio on 18 February, the Corsican volunteers were within sight of the island of La Maddalena, but a calm obliged the ships to stop for a few hours and, when night fell, the wind came up in a violent storm. They were forced to sail back to Bonifacio, where they stayed for two days.[14] On 22 February, at nine in the morning, they left again. However, the convoy containing the troops in sixteen small vessels refused to follow. The volunteers were afraid of the Sardinian half-galleys. There were, in fact, only two of them, and their sole advantage was their lightness; they had three cannon apiece. *La Fauvette*, the French corvette that was to escort the convoy, had twenty-four cannons and easily out-gunned anything the Sardinians might have thrown against them. This was hardly an encouraging beginning to the expedition and should have warned those in charge of the volunteers' lack of suitability. Colonna-Cesari, former deputy to the Estates-General, second-in-command of the Corsican volunteers earmarked for the expedition, headed for La Maddalena all the same. He was hoping to arouse their honour and, revitalized by the reproaches made by the people of Bonifacio, the battalions consented to follow. The fleet was eventually able to cast anchor south-west of La Maddalena without any mishaps.

At four in the afternoon, under the cover of fire from *La Fauvette*, the Corsican volunteers landed on the beach of Santo Stefano, the principal town on the island. The Sardinian garrison had placed itself behind the rocks to oppose the landing and, after firing several salvos, withdrew to the large square tower at the extreme end of the island. The Corsicans had only suffered one casualty and were able to occupy the town. The following days, 24 and 25 February, in pouring rain and in freezing weather, Buonaparte bombarded the town, succeeded in setting fire to it on four occasions, destroyed eighty houses, set alight the timber yard, and silenced the batteries of the two small forts.

Then everything went wrong. The French sailors on board *La Fauvette* decided of their own accord to leave. The news spread rapidly to the rest of the convoy and to the volunteers on the island. They feared that *La Fauvette* was going to sail off without them, so a retreat was carried out in the greatest disorder. Nobody even bothered to inform Lieutenant Colonel Buonaparte and his little battery of three guns of what was going on. It was only later in the evening that he learned of the evacuation, by which time most of the troops had embarked. He could either cut his losses and make a run for it or try to recover his cannon. He decided on the latter, forcing his men to drag the cannon across the island to the point of embarkation. All was in vain, however, for by the time they reached the landing place there were not enough boats to transport them from shore to ship. Buonaparte had to spike and then leave the cannon behind.

All those who had advocated the expedition now sought to exculpate themselves by putting the blame on Colonna-Cesari, who had by no means distinguished himself, and on Paoli who had, it was claimed, told Colonna-Cesari to sabotage the expedition. Although grossly unjust, the story was widespread at the time. Paoli had been sceptical about the success of the expedition from the very start and Colonna-Cesari had agreed with him. If they chose to participate in it, they did so reluctantly, but they did, nevertheless, put funding and troops at the disposal of the French. This did not prevent the loss of credit associated with the failure of the expedition, something Colonna-Cesari was unable to overcome. In vain he argued in an essay published in both French and Italian that the insurrection of the sailors was to blame for the lack of victory. In vain he described how he alone confronted the mutinous crew.[15] The sailors recited their version of events and highlighted especially Colonna-Cesari's tears as he tried to convince them to change their minds; they nicknamed him *pleureur* (whimperer), while in Paris, Saliceti ungraciously referred to him as the 'hero of the Maddalena'.[16]

Once Buonaparte was back at Bonifacio (28 February), he busied himself writing up two plans of attack and a report on the necessity of occupying La Maddalena, as well as justifying his role in the failed expedition. He also signed, along with his comrades, an attestation to the zeal and patriotism of Colonna-Cesari.[17] That same day, however, Buonaparte wrote a report on the attack which intimated that Colonna-Cesari was responsible for its failure, and which was sent in triplicate to the minister of war, to Paoli, and to the general commanding the army of the Alps.[18] One historian has cast doubt on the authenticity of this document,[19] but it is likely that Buonaparte was covering his back. In any event, a few days later, in a public square called Dorian, a second attempt was made on Buonaparte's life. Sailors from *La Fauvette* set on him, yelling

'String up the aristocrat', but Corsican volunteers came to Buonaparte's rescue, slitting open the stomach of one the attackers in the process.[20]

In this unhealthy atmosphere, Buonaparte thought it best not to stay around. On 14 March, Buonaparte wrote to Colonna-Cesari a note that reads, 'I am leaving this night for Ajaccio because my presence here is useless and because I want to be as close as possible to have news from the commissaries in order to counsel my comrades about the direction they should take.'[21] Buonaparte, in other words, simply informed his superior that he was leaving his post to go to Ajaccio. He had undoubtedly heard that the Convention had decided to send three commissaries with large powers to investigate conditions in Corsica. The Convention had also decreed the suppression of the four volunteer battalions, which were to be replaced by four battalions of chasseurs, whose officers were to be named by the French government. This was evidently bad news for Buonaparte – it was, after all, the original pretext that had enabled him to stay on the island and away from France – the more so since, as things turned out, his name was not on the list of designated officers.[22]

The Rupture

That is why, at the beginning of March 1793, Buonaparte went to Corte where, according to popular accounts, he had a stormy interview with Paoli. What exactly happened, though, is difficult to determine. According to some, Paoli expressed his hostility towards France and even asserted that he was determined to secede, at which Buonaparte supposedly turned on Paoli with such vehemence that the *babbo* brusquely left the room. It is from this moment, note these historians, that a falling-out between the two men was inevitable.[23] There is, however, nothing in the documents that supports this version of events. It is more likely that Buonaparte went to Corte to complain of the injustice with which he had been treated in having his command taken away from him. Paoli was apparently sympathetic and may have done his best to placate the young man.[24]

But the fact remains that the Buonapartes' situation was decidedly fragile – within the space of about two years they had gone
from a position of relative strength to having lost all their
administrative and military offices – and over the next few
months a rift was to take place. The break nevertheless took
time in coming, and it was not so much the *babbo*'s politics that
were going to bring things to a head as a decision on the part of
the Buonaparte clan to form a new alliance with an opposing
faction on the island.

This decision was made because Paoli was clearly falling out of
favour with the revolutionaries in Paris. For some time now, Paoli
had found that the French government was treating him too
flippantly and with suspicion. Truguet, for example, had asked
for Paoli's help to invade Sardinia without, however, going into the
details of the expedition and without any instructions from the
minister of war or the Executive Council. Barthélemy Arena, a
former ally of Paoli, openly attacked him over the failed expedition
in the clubs and newspapers of Marseilles and Avignon. Paoli, he
never tired of repeating, resembled more a pasha than a constitutional general.[25] These criticisms spread discord, according to Paoli,
between the Corsican people and the people of Provence and the
department of the Bouches-du-Rhône. When the French volunteers
were let loose on Corsica before going off on the Sardinian
expedition, Paoli was justifiably outraged and complained to the
minister of the interior.[26] The Marseillais, moreover, were telling
everybody that Paoli had betrayed them, thereby increasing the
hostility of the people of Provence against him. The Jacobin club of
Toulon invited the club at Bastia to watch the behaviour of the
babbo. On 13 March, the Jacobin club of Marseilles reported that
Paoli had been arrested by patriots, which was not true, and had
embarked on a ship for France, where he would receive his due
punishment. The club broke into an uproar and the portrait of the
babbo, which was still hanging above the rostrum, was torn down
and burnt amid loud applause.

Paoli's suspicions of French intentions only increased when the
three special commissaries arrived on the island, sent by the Convention on the pretext of examining the defences of Corsica. The
commissaries – Saliceti, Joseph-Etienne Delcher (a lawyer and a

member of the Committee of General Defence) and Jean-Pierre
Lacombe-Saint-Michel (a former artillery officer) – were appointed
on 5 February 1793 and were invested with unlimited powers. It
took two months for the commissaries to arrive and open negotiations, by which time the Convention had already decided, on 2
April, that it was going to outlaw Paoli. News of the decree,
however, did not reach Corsica until 18 April. This put Saliceti
and the other commissaries in an extremely difficult position.
Indeed, Saliceti seems to have been horrified at the Convention's
decree; it spoilt any chances of an accommodation with Paoli.[27] The
very day he received news of the decree, however, Saliceti decided
to carry it out and ordered the municipality of Corte to arrest Paoli
and Carlo Andrea Pozzo di Borgo. The municipality did not even
bother replying. It considered the order absurd; the gendarmes sent
to carry out the order came back saying that the people had wanted
to hang them.

Corsican patriots were naturally indignant. Over a period of
several days, peasants from all over the island assembled in Corte
– to where Paoli and his entourage had withdrawn – threatened
to chop down the Tree of Liberty that had been planted in the
public square to celebrate the Revolution, and forced the citizens
of Corte to throw away their tricolour cockades. The administrators of the town were obliged to break into the stockpiles of
flour to feed them. Similar scenes were played out in other
towns in Corsica. The commissaries managed to hang on to
Calvi, San-Fiorenzo and Bastia but, at Ajaccio, a lieutenant
colonel of the 4th Corsican battalion took hold of the citadel,
locked himself in and swore that he would remain faithful to
Paoli. At Bonifacio, Quenza seized the munitions and declared
that he would only follow Paoli's orders.[28]

Buonaparte was at Ajaccio when news of the decree reached the
island; he was surprised and troubled by it. He understood immediately that war would break out between the French Republic
and Corsica, which Paoli would win at least at the beginning of the
struggle, and that Paoli's enemies, who would probably include the
Buonapartes, would be banished and deprived of their belongings.
According to Lucien's (Luciano) memoirs, a family meeting was
held to discuss the issue.

I found mama as she usually is, surrounded by my younger brothers and sisters. Napoleon, sitting in the window recess where I saw him before entering the door, impatient as he undoubtedly was to see me arrive with Joseph . . . And so Napoleon, in his grand uniform of commander of the National Guard, held between his legs our youngest sister, Caroline [who would later become the wife of Joachim Murat], whom he let play with the chain of his watch. Louis painted puppets, alone in the corner of the room. Paulette and Jérôme were playing together and Elisa, the grand lady of the house who was not yet fourteen, was also working at the side of our mother, preoccupied with her work.[29]

This idyllic portrayal of the Buonaparte family should be taken with a pinch of salt: it presents the reader with a unified front when the discussions between the brothers may very well have been heated and divisive. According to Lucien, his two older brothers were incensed by Paoli's behaviour, and Buonaparte's decision to take the side of the French. This is possible, although Buonaparte's actions in the weeks that followed suggest that he was doing everything in his power to heal the rift between the Paolists and the pro-French faction. He spoke in the Jacobin club of Ajaccio to propose a union with the Société des Amis Incorruptibles du Peuple (Society of the Incorruptible Friends of the People), a club that had originally been founded by the adversaries of the Buonapartes, the Peraldis, to counter the Jacobins. He even decided to write to the Convention in the name of the local club (the Société Populaire), asking the deputies to rescind the decree of 2 April.[30] The letter is nothing less than a plea in favour of Paoli. It was claimed by some contemporaries that he even pasted on the walls of Ajaccio the response of the municipality refuting the Convention's accusation against Paoli.[31] He also wrote to the municipal council of Ajaccio, stating that the circumstances were critical, and that war between France and Corsica would break out unless the municipality was able to rise to the occasion and convoke an assembly of citizens who would take a solemn oath to die French and republican.[32] His plea fell on deaf ears. The Easter Sunday debacle was still fresh in people's minds and, besides, the Buonapartes no longer had as much influence in a town where a Paolist municipality had been elected in December 1792. In a last attempt, Buonaparte had a friend, Masseria, write a letter to Paoli on his behalf, but his overtures were left unanswered.[33] Buonaparte, in fact, seems to have been the only person in the family trying to come to some sort of resolution with Paoli. His brothers had realized long ago that there could be no compromise.

Luciano, for example, had been leading a campaign against Paoli in concert with the Italian revolutionary, Filippo Buonarroti. Only eighteen years old and as passionate as his older brother, Luciano was eloquent and arrogant, but lacked discipline. Moroever, there was little substance behind the articulate façade. He was also a fervent Jacobin, and vigorously proclaimed his hatred of kings. As secretary of the Patriotic Club of Ajaccio, he translated into Italian the speeches of Charles de Sémonville, a deputy of the Convention who was sent as ambassador to the Sublime Porte,* but who had stopped off at Corsica on the way to try to counter Paoli's influence. Initially an enthusiastic advocate of Paoli, Luciano had also associated with the Society which formed in Corte under the name of the Société des Amis du Peuple (Society of the Friends of the People, deeply Paolist and formed around the *babbo*), where he played a considerable role despite his age. When he did move against Paoli, it may have been out of anger at not being accepted as his secretary. Because he was so young and politically naïve, he was probably being used by one Corsican faction, in this case in the person of Arena, in its fight against Paoli.

The event that brought matters between the Buonapartes and the Paolists to a head was a speech delivered by Luciano in March 1793 at the Jacobin Club of Toulon (Luciano was meant to accompany Sémonville to Constantinople, but they were caught up in the English blockade at Toulon and could not proceed). In it he painted a very dark portrait of the Corsican leader. Paoli, he told the members, was a tyrant who wanted to reign over the island, exercise the despotism of a sovereign, and who committed arbitrary and barbaric acts.[34] He also connected the failure of the Sardinian

---

* The Ottoman Empire was often referred to as the 'Sublime Porte', or just the 'Porte', a reference to one of the gates in the imperial palace in Constantinople through which ambassadors and foreign dignitaries passed on their way to see the Sultan.

expedition with the treacherous behaviour of Paoli. The fact that Paoli had spent so many years in exile in Britain was now interpreted in a new and suspicious light (France declared war on Britain on 1 February 1793).

Luciano, no doubt feeling that the time to abandon Paoli had come, acted on his own initiative without consulting his brothers.[35] The club welcomed the denunciation with great enthusiasm and it was immediately transformed into an address to the Convention, where it was read on 2 April in front of an Assembly that increasingly had a tendency to see traitors everywhere.[36] The deputies did not even wait for the report of the three commissaries they had only just sent to the island. On a motion put forward by a deputy by the name of Pierre Joseph Cambon, the Convention decreed that Paoli and Pozzo di Borgo were to be arrested. One should not think that Luciano's address was entirely responsible for the Convention's decree against Paoli; however, it probably tipped the balance in a relationship that had been on the decline for many months previously.

Luciano was exultant at his little triumph in Toulon and wrote to his brothers to say that he had 'struck a mortal blow at my enemies', although it is not clear who exactly his enemies were.[37] This letter was supposedly intercepted by Paoli's man, Pozzo di Borgo, and was soon known about all over the island. Consequently, one can assert with a reasonable amount of confidence that it was this step that finally broke the tenuous chain still linking the Buonapartes to Paoli. The Buonapartes, who had been educated by the French with French money, were now considered the principal actors in a plot against the Corsican people. At about the same time that news of Luciano's attack arrived on the island, Buonaparte approached Colonna Leca, commander of the National Guard of Ajaccio, on behalf of the French commissaries on the island, to offer him the rank of general if he co-operated with France and opened the doors of the citadel. Colonna Leca, however, refused and instead induced Geronimo Pozzo di Borgo and his men to disarm and expel the regular troops.[38] Now the citadel was firmly in the hands of the Paolists whose guns dominated the town.

Buonaparte had obviously taken sides by this stage. Not only was it a long time since he had believed in Corsican independence, he was now actively working on behalf of the French authorities to secure strongholds on the island. There was also a regular correspondence between Saliceti and Buonaparte during this period that was intercepted by the administration at Corte; Buonaparte had been ordered to assume the military command of Ajaccio. In the light of this, Pozzo di Borgo ordered the mayor of Ajaccio, Vincenzo Guitera, and Colonna Leca to arrest Buonaparte,[39] so he decided to leave Ajaccio and try to join the commissaries in Bastia. On the evening of 2 May, a faithful supporter from Bocognano, Santo Bonelli, arrived in Ajaccio with weapons and horses; they set out the next day at dawn. On the road between Ajaccio and Corte, Buonaparte met a cousin who advised them to flee the island: Luciano's letter to his brothers, in which he boasted of being responsible for the Convention's decree against Paoli, had been intercepted by the Directory of the island. Buonaparte and his family, therefore, were now considered the enemies of Paoli and he would be arrested if he reached Corte. Nothing more could be done to save the situation, so he turned around.

On 6 May, Buonaparte secretly re-entered Ajaccio; he was not out of danger but at least he had friends there who could help him. He went first to his uncle Paravicini and then to his cousin Ramolino. Paravicini eventually hid him in a grotto in his garden. When night fell, Buonaparte took refuge at the house of his old friend, the mayor, where armed men loyal to him had gathered. He spent the evening and the two following days hiding, reading and talking to Levie's wife, Mamminina. On the third evening, a gendarme knocked on the door with orders to search the house. Levie managed to put him off, but there was always the risk that the house would be searched at some future date, and more thoroughly the next time. It was decided, therefore, that Buonaparte had to leave immediately, first by boat and then overland by horse. It seems that he had great trouble finding a horse and a man who would guide him across the steep mountain paths, but he eventually found both, although the horse was apparently skeletal and had trouble standing.

'Perpetual Infamy'

Buonaparte arrived in Bastia three days later on 11 May, and had no difficulty in convincing the commissaries that Ajaccio had to be retaken. If the French remained masters of the port towns – Calvi, Bastia, Ajaccio – they would have nothing to fear from Paoli receiving outside help from the British. Bonifacio, where Quenza with his battalion of volunteers had declared themselves in favour of Paoli, also had to be taken. Buonaparte assured the commissaries that he could retake Ajaccio and that, with the exception of the Peraldi clan, the whole city was pro-French. After a long conversation with Buonaparte, Lacombe-Saint-Michel wrote to the newly elected minister of war, Jean-Baptiste Bouchotte, 'The people of Ajaccio are with us, but it is oppressed by the Corsican garrison'.[40] Nothing could have been further from the truth, but Buonaparte was obviously telling the commissaries what they wanted to hear and, to add weight to his arguments, presented them with a plan of attack. Detachments from the Swiss regiments stationed on the island would enter the town of Ajaccio on the pretext that they had been ordered to the mainland. Once there, they would join up with detachments of troops from the 52nd that would be dispatched by sea and take the town.

Preparations for this planned assault took place over the next week (11–22 May). During the night of 23 May, Lacombe-Saint-Michel, Saliceti, Buonaparte and Giuseppe left the bay of San Fiorenzo with 400 regular French troops of the line plus a handful of gendarmes, light infantry and artillerymen on board the corvette *Belette*, the brig *Hasard*, and a few sailing barges. They knew that they were short of troops but the decision had been made to stun the Corsicans with an audacious strike. Bad weather kept them at sea for seven days, however, and it was not until 31 May that they reached the gulf of Ajaccio, by which time Paoli had had time to secure the town against an attack.[41]

Tradition has it that Buonaparte, who had set sail before the main convoy and disembarked at Provenzale on 29 May, was able to get a note to his mother days before which said, *Preparatevi, questo paese non è per noi* (Prepare [to leave], this country is not for us).[42] It is recognition that any hope of playing an important part in Corsican politics was definitively dashed. Letizia managed to get out of Ajaccio with Fesch, Luigi, Maria-Anna (Elisa) and Carlotta-Maria (Pauline) – she left Maria-Annunziata (Caroline) and Gerolamo (Jérôme) with her mother – before their house, mill and three farmhouses were sacked by Paolist supporters (23 May), a relatively common occurrence in conflicts between clans.[43] They travelled overnight along the narrow paths through the *maquis*, and at sunrise hid next to the coast.[44] On 31 May, Buonaparte, who had regained the corvette that had just landed in the gulf of Ajaccio, probably near what is known as the Capitello tower, saw people making signs to the vessel and recognized his mother. He and Giuseppe rowed out to them and brought them back on board, setting them down that same night at Giraglia, from where the family headed overland for Calvi.

On 1 June, the French troops disembarked in the gulf of Ajaccio announcing their presence, as pre-arranged, by loud shouts and cannon shot. Only twenty-three Swiss guards, six regular troops of the line, plus a few individuals went over to them. It was evident from the start that they could expect no help from the inhabitants of the town. Besides, most of the Ajacciens had been disarmed and reinforcements of volunteer battalions were pouring in from the surrounding region. As a result, the invasion party did not even bother probing the town's defences; they simply bivouacked near the Capitello tower, where they spent the whole day of 2 June, and then peacefully re-embarked that evening and headed back to Calvi. They had captured one prisoner, who had a tattoo of the name 'Paoli' with a cross on his arm.

Buonaparte did not join them; he rode to Calvi by horse, where he arrived the next day. A little later, the family learned of the decision made by an assembly that had met in Corte, where Paoli had convened a council between 27 and 29 May: the Buonapartes 'born in the mud of despotism and elevated under the gaze of a luxurious pasha' (a reference to Marbeuf) were condemned to 'perpetual infamy'.[45] The rupture was official. Buonaparte and his family sailed from Calvi on 11 June. Before doing so, however, Buonaparte wrote a violent memorandum against Paoli, accusing his former idol of effrontery, of having an unlimited desire for power, and of being disloyal to France. 'Paoli,' he wrote, 'has the appearance of goodness and gentleness, but he has hatred and vengeance in his heart.'[46] The memorandum was accompanied by a plan of operations to retake Corsica.

'It Is Better to Eat Than Be Eaten'

Six weeks previously, Buonaparte had praised Paoli as the 'patriarch of liberty'. Up to this point, Buonaparte had used his Corsican heritage to assert his own identity, not only because he was a patriot (of that there is no doubt), but also because it was a means of overcoming the isolation he felt as a youth in France. He identified all the more readily with his persecuted and oppressed countrymen, and initially rejected the French, because he felt browbeaten at school. At that time, Buonaparte perceived Paoli as an ideal leader with pure motives, his government the expression of the general will of the people, respected and obeyed by all. In this idealized world, all Corsican men were courageous and all Corsican women were chaste. As long as the dream did not come face to face with the reality, Buonaparte was able to preserve his illusions, making France and the French responsible for all his country's problems. Once he was obliged to deal with the practicalities of Corsican politics, however, his idealism was bound to fail him.

Revolutionary Corsica must have been an enormous disappointment for Buonaparte with its petty factional politicking, personal jealousies, family hatreds, intrigues, corruption and nepotism. Since they could not gain what they desired from the Paolists, or rather, because they were excluded by the Paolists, the Buonaparte family, along with many other disaffected Corsican families, found itself turning towards the pro-French Jacobin faction, represented by men like Saliceti. The role played by Saliceti in influencing the Buonaparte family's political options is fundamental. Saliceti, second only in popularity on Corsica to Paoli, was about the same height, build and complexion as Buonaparte, that is, pale, to the extent that the Duchesse d'Abrantès wrote how much he reminded her of a vampire.[47] The political destiny of these two men was entwined from this period, with Buonaparte very much playing a subordinate role in the early stages. When, for example, Saliceti wrote a pamphlet directed against Buttafuoco and in defence of Paoli, Buonaparte devoured it.[48] He had it with him when he wrote his own *Letter to Buttafuoco* (23 January 1791), which bears some resemblance to it, as does the *Discours de Lyons* (August 1791). The two men had met in March 1792 and used to see each other either at Ajaccio, where Saliceti had a company of volunteers, or at Corte. When Saliceti went back to the mainland to take up his seat on the Convention at the end of 1792, their relationship was cemented by a correspondence. Saliceti apparently persuaded Buonaparte that Corsica should not become independent. It was from this time on (from the beginning of 1792) that Buonaparte turned to France.[49] Saliceti voted for the death of Louis XVI in January 1793. On hearing of the execution, Buonaparte wrote to another deputy, Charles de Sémonville, 'I have thought long and hard on our situation; the Convention has undoubtedly committed a great crime and I deplore it more than anyone, but, whatever happens, Corsica must always remain united to France; it cannot have an existence except on that condition. My family and I, I must warn you, will defend the cause of union.'[50] This shift in Buonaparte's thinking, from supporting Corsican independence to a desire to work with France, was completed by the end of 1792 and the beginning of 1793.

If there was already a tendency to lean towards France, it was strengthened by Paoli's attitude towards the Buonapartes. For Paoli, the Buonaparte clan had been sullied by collaboration. Moreover, there was no shortage of families in Ajaccio who were not only better off financially but whose loyalty was unquestionable. This fact eventually dawned on the young Buonaparte, although he, more than any other member of the family, did everything in his power to delay the inevitable. Luciano's condemnation of Paoli had done nothing more than precipitate a process that was already well under way. When the break did come, Buonaparte quickly joined in military action against the Paolists. As we have already seen, though, the French attempt to capture Ajaccio was a disaster. Only three places on the island remained in pro-French hands – Calvi, Bastia and San Lorenzo – and they were sure to come under siege from the Paolists.

Buonaparte and his family were now outlaws, and were financially ruined. The family's best chances were on the mainland
with all the opportunities that France and the Revolution presented.

Once Buonaparte accepted the French cause, he turned his back
on Paoli and Corsica. This meant rejecting a good deal of what
Buonaparte had stood for when he was younger. Corsica no longer
represented liberty and Corsicans no longer stood for all that was
good in the struggle for that liberty. Paoli made that transformation
easy for him. Moreover, he was to turn on Paoli and Corsica with
the same depth of hatred that he once reserved for France. About a
month after fleeing to France, Buonaparte wrote a political pamphlet, about fifteen pages long, known as the *Souper de Beaucaire*. It
was at first printed at his own expense, but was later published by
the army – on the orders of Saliceti, it should be noted – and can be
seen in the context of the intense propaganda campaign conducted
from Paris to politically educate and galvanize the troops at the
front; by the summer of 1794, millions of copies of newspapers,
songbooks and pamphlets had been distributed free of charge.[51]
Buonaparte's pamphlet is not only a piece of revolutionary propaganda, and a blatant attempt to ingratiate himself with the regime
in Paris, but also an invective against Paoli, who is accused of having
deceived the people:

> Paoli also raised it [the tricolour flag] in Corsica long enough to
> deceive the people, to crush the true friends of liberty, to lead his
> compatriots into his criminal and ambitious projects. He raised the
> tricolour flag and had vessels of the Republic shot at . . . he
> devastated and confiscated the goods of the most well off families
> because they were attached to the unity of the Republic [like the
> Buonapartes]; and he declared enemy of the *patrie* all those who
> remained in our armies . . .[52]

The pamphlet, in other words, is an intellectual exercise in which
Buonaparte attempts to justify his falling-out with Paoli, first of
all to himself, and also to distance himself publicly from a man
now held in abhorrence by the Republic. By holding Paoli
responsible for the rupture between France and Corsica, Buona-

parte was also reproaching him for the rift between the Paolists and his own family. He had not rejected Paoli; Paoli had rejected him. He could, therefore, turn to his new masters with a clear conscience. In the account he wrote of the situation in Corsica in June, the *Position politique*, he bluntly stated: 'One has to choose sides; it may as well be with the side that triumphs, with the side that devastates, pillages, burns. The alternative, it is better to eat than be eaten.'[53]

Therefore, the flight from Corsica was fundamental in the process of his becoming French.[54] To be Corsican *and* French was never really a possibility for Buonaparte, except perhaps for a brief period between 1790 and 1792 when it seemed that Corsica could become an integral part of France. Now he was obliged to turn his back on Corsica in response to the way that Corsica had turned its back on him. The Duchesse d'Abrantès later recounted a suggestive anecdote in this respect. Her family was also from Corsica and her mother knew Letizia when she was first married. Later, at court in Paris, the Duchesse d'Abrantès's mother used to speak Corsican to Napoleon, who used to reply that he had forgotten it and that, besides, he was French. 'Come along, Napoleon! Don't say such a ridiculous thing . . . What do you mean by that: *I am French*? . . . Although you are French, you were born in a province of France called Corsica. If a man is from Auvergne, is he any the less French?'[55] The answer should have been 'no', but Buonaparte was unable to reconcile one sentiment with the other.

Buonaparte thus fled Corsica disgusted and disenchanted, but having gained some valuable experience at intrigue and politicking. Indeed, Corsica had been a formative experience for Buonaparte as politician. He had taken part in two minor coups (the election to the Corsican National Guard and the Ajaccio affair), had either observed or taken part in at least three revolutionary *journées* (insurrections), and had assisted at a number of 'elections'. He had taken part in the revolutionary movement, had dirtied his hands both in street fighting and in the corruption of the democratic process, and, in the end, he had come away a good deal more cynical about men and politics. The idealism that was once so apparent in his writings was replaced by a more calculating attitude. The

Corsican experience had taught Buonaparte to become more politically savvy, more determined and more focused in his ambitions. In some respects he had grown up. His political apprenticeship was by no means over, but he had certainly come a long way since the first months of the Revolution.

6

The Jacobin

Refugees

The town of Toulon was on the verge of revolt. In the summer of 1792, the Jacobin club of Toulon had gained control of the municipality through violence and intimidation.[1] One year later, however, the tide had turned. In what amounted to a bloodless coup, disaffected bourgeois, riding on the wave of discontent caused by Jacobin policies, won a popular majority in the district sections* and welcomed 'persecuted patriots' from the rest of the region. It was part of a tide of reaction sweeping the Midi. People had not only lost all faith in the Convention in Paris, but also in the dominant Jacobin faction. Once the sections had been won over, the moderates extended their control over other areas of the town, like the National Guard. They eventually closed down the Jacobin club and began to settle old scores, arresting former Jacobin officials and many simple sailors and dockyard workers, who would later wreak vengeance on the town. Furthermore, the crews of the frigates *La Melpomène* and *La Minerve* mutinied in April 1793 against their officers, a sign, if one was needed, that the crews had become highly politicized.[2] In June, a purge of the Convention in Paris saw twenty-nine republican deputies, sometimes known as the 'Brissotins' (named after the leading figure in the group, Jacques-Pierre Brissot) and sometimes as the 'Girondins' (named

---

* 'Sections' were electoral districts that had been created in the major French cities in 1790. In Paris, for example, there were forty-eight sections; in Marseilles and Lyons, thirty-two. Citizens met there on a regular basis so that they became permanent centres of political agitation. They disappeared in 1795.

after the department from which many of them came) – the very same people responsible for initiating war – arrested and imprisoned by even more radical republicans, known as the 'Mountain' or the 'Montagnards'. The Girondins lost control of the Convention largely because they had been unable to prosecute the war effectively and to resolve the enormous problems facing the country – civil war, religious conflict, and serious financial and economic difficulties – but also because they did not know how to keep the people of Paris on their side.

The arrest of the Girondin deputies was considered by many in the provinces an affront to the principle of national sovereignty. Many departments and some of the major urban centres in the provinces reacted against this excessive radicalism by attempting to break away from Paris. It was part of a movement against the Convention commonly referred to as the Federalist Revolt. In the south of France, both Marseilles and Toulon were caught up in this revolt. The municipality of Toulon, for example, cancelled the decrees emanating from the Convention, and declared any law passed since the arrest of the Girondins in June illegal. As Toulon was also an important port, and home to a large proportion of the French navy, it prohibited the fleet from sailing out. Further measures included the rationing of bread and price fixing, and the door of each house had to display the name of the inhabitants and their means of making a living.

The Buonapartes landed in the middle of this struggle between Paris and the provinces, on 13 June 1793, having evaded British and Spanish ships of war, one family among the hundreds forced to flee Corsica as political refugees in the wake of the conflict between the pro-Paolist and pro-French factions on the island.[3] They quickly became disgusted by the spectacle the town offered: they may have been Jacobins on Corsica, but French Jacobins were infinitely more radical.[4] By the time they arrived, about 100 notables had been arrested without due process. Each day massacres were both expected and feared. After only a week they decided to settle in the nearby village of La Valette, where they were to have a month of relative tranquillity, living off money borrowed from friends, from the local commune, and from Buonaparte, who had managed to receive back pay as an officer in the army. In their hasty flight from

Ajaccio, they had been unable to take any of their belongings. Luciano later alluded to the distress into which they were forced, arriving at Toulon with nothing and having to live off the rations obtained as 'patriotic refugees'.[5]

The first task was to get the family established with the help of the few political contacts they had, and by cultivating other contacts wherever possible. It was, essentially, as a result of their contacts with Saliceti that the family was able to get a good start. Saliceti had become one of the most important representatives-on-mission in the region of Marseilles and was able to use his influence to help fellow Corsicans in exile. Luciano was made quartermaster at Saint-Maximin (re-baptised Marathon by the local revolutionaries, partly at the insistence of Luciano), a little village near Toulon.[6] He became president of the revolutionary committee in the town and, in an excess of zeal, changed his name to that of a self-sacrificing heroic character of ancient Roman history, Junius Brutus, who is said to have executed his own sons for failing in their duty. Giuseppe accompanied Saliceti to Paris where, with the help of friends, they were able to persuade the Convention to allocate 600,000 livres to help Corsican patriots in exile. He was later made commissary of war in the army. Uncle Fesch, who had left the priesthood after fleeing Corsica, was also made quartermaster at Chauvet. In fact, the role played by Saliceti in getting the family established was fundamental.

Buonaparte would be appointed to command the artillery at the siege of Toulon as a direct consequence of his relations with Saliceti. Saliceti, however, was not the only contact they used. The Buonaparte sons had adopted much the same approach that allowed their father to get ahead: they did not hesitate to solicit help from anybody with any influence – ministers, deputies to the Convention, famous writers and famous doctors.[7] Indeed, obtaining patronage from influential personalities was not only common practice at the time, but was essential to getting ahead. The Buonapartes were no more or less 'pushy' in this respect than many other families. Certainly, when Buonaparte was later in Paris, he earned the reputation of someone who 'knocked on all the doors', who told everyone who cared to listen about his projects, and who complained of the injustices of which he was supposedly a victim,[8] but how else was one to gain the ear of important people?

One of the contacts Buonaparte was able to count on was the family du Teil. Around the end of June or the beginning of July 1793, Buonaparte went to Nice, where a number of companies from his regiment were stationed. There he encountered the brother of his former commander and mentor, Jean du Teil, in command of the artillery of the Army of Italy and charged with drawing up a plan for the defence of the Mediterranean coast. He attached Buonaparte as captain to one of the coastal batteries.

The Situation in the Midi

There is some doubt about where Buonaparte was between the beginning of July and the end of August of that year. Alternative itineraries have been suggested. The first has Buonaparte at Valence from 23–28 August and at Auxonne for the rest of the month up until the beginning of September. The second, more likely account has him travelling from Nice to Avignon.

According to this second version of events, du Teil ordered Buonaparte on 8 July to go to Avignon to collect a convoy of powder being sent to the Army of Italy. Buonaparte, however, was unaware that the Federalists – those in the provinces who had revolted against Paris – were already in control of Avignon; contradictory rumours were flying about. When news of the fall of the town was confirmed, Buonaparte nevertheless decided to press on. The decision was undoubtedly a difficult one. If he continued, he risked falling into the hands of the rebels; if he returned to Nice he would not fulfil his mission. He was helped in his decision by news that the Convention was forming an army of about 2,000 men under the command of Jean-Baptiste Carteaux, who had only recently been made a general, to fight the rebels. Buonaparte arrived at Carteaux's headquarters at Pontet at dusk on 14 July.

We can discount the historians who give Buonaparte a preponderant role during the siege of Avignon.[9] We can also discount Napoleon's remarkable version of events as related at St Helena, which suggests that he was already in the town when the Federalists arrived: 'They wanted to use me, I who did not care to get involved in civil war. I refused, saying that it was difficult, and that the ramparts were too narrow, and encouraged them to take up a position in the rear. The Federalists withdrew, and Carteaux entered.'[10] Napoleon was either lying, perpetuating the myth that he did not get involved in civil wars, or he somehow got the facts mixed up and really believed that he had been at Avignon before Carteaux entered the town. In fact, Buonaparte did not join Carteaux at Avignon until 27 July, where he was immediately treated as a suspect, that is, as an aristocrat and an officer of the royal army.[11]

The commissaries of war in Avignon at the time vouched for him. Buonaparte was ordered to descend the Rhône and to requisition the carriages and horses necessary to transport the munitions destined for the Army of Italy. When he did not receive any of the wagons he had reclaimed a few days before from the district of Tarascon,[12] he decided to go there in person. Buonaparte arrived in Beaucaire, an important commercial town situated on the Rhône, not far from Avignon, on the last day of the annual fair of Sainte-Madeleine, which was held in spite of the political turmoil in the region. It was there, on the evening of 28 July, that he dined at a tavern in the rue des Bains (today rue A. Méric) with four merchants who had come for the local fair, an experience he used a little later as the basis of a political pamphlet on the situation in the Midi, the *Souper de Beaucaire*. He probably wrote the pamphlet in order to dispel any doubts about his presence in Avignon during the Federalist occupation,[13] but as we have seen it was also a denunciation of Paoli; Buonaparte was demonstrating his loyalty to the Convention.

On the evening of the 24 August 1793, Carteaux's troops succeeded in retaking Marseilles, an important port of over 100,000 people. As soon as they entered the town, what was left of the revolt was drowned in blood. About 500 people, some only suspected of being rebels, some entirely innocent but who had the misfortune of being in the wrong place at the wrong time, were executed on the spot without so much as the pretence of a trial. At least one historian argues that Buonaparte was present in the town during the massacres.[14] This is unlikely, although he no doubt believed the rebels got what was coming to them. In a passage in the *Souper de*

Beaucaire, Buonaparte argues that no mercy should be shown to those who commit a sacrilege against the Holy Republic: 'If you are capable of such baseness, no stone should be left unturned in your city; in one month's time a traveller, passing by your ruins, should believe that you were destroyed one hundred years ago!' Certainly, this violent political rhetoric, a common occurrence in the media of the time, was meant to demonstrate just how fervent a revolutionary Bonaparte was, but once in a position of authority he would show few qualms about putting civilian populations to the sword.

The fall of Marseilles and the ensuing massacres only served to strengthen the resolution of the people of Toulon. The representative-on-mission, Paul Barras, a man who was going to play a decisive role in Buonaparte's later career, only added to their determination when he launched a proclamation threatening to raze the city.[15] The citizens of Toulon, who knew what to expect at the hands of the Jacobins, decided to open negotiations with Admiral Hood, who was commanding the British fleet in the Mediterranean, seeking military aid and assistance. This was an unexpected opportunity; Lord Hood offered to defend the town on the condition that they renounce the Republic in favour of the French monarchy and hand over all military installations to him.[16] The Toulonnais clutched at the safety Hood's presence seemed to offer.

Britain was the last of the Great Powers to enter the war against France, and only did so after the French invaded the Low Countries at the end of 1792.[17] Until then the British government, under William Pitt, had hoped to remain neutral in the struggle between Revolutionary France and the rest of Europe. Even if the vast majority of British politicians did not approve of what was going on in France, especially the way the revolutionaries treated the French monarchy, they were happy to stand on the sidelines and watch a powerful rival implode. All that changed, however, when first Belgium (then known as the Austrian Netherlands) and then the Dutch Republic were threatened by a French army. French domination of that region was something the British could not allow. The Low Countries were primordial to British national interests, not least because of their still considerable navy, their proximity to the Channel, and their overseas possessions (especially the Dutch possessions at the Cape of Good Hope and Ceylon, from which British sea routes to India could be threatened).

The French threat to the Low Countries would inevitably have pushed Britain into the arms of the Austro-Prussian coalition – Britain had shown itself remarkably cordial to both powers towards the end of 1792 – but the French revolutionaries left Britain no choice. At first, the French had been hopeful that Britain would join France in an alliance. They even sent a renegade bishop, Charles-Maurice de Talleyrand, on two diplomatic missions to London at the beginning of 1792 with that end in mind. By the end of the year, though, French attitudes towards Britain had changed dramatically. In the Convention, Britain was now accused of inciting insurrection in France and of preparing for war. The revolutionaries decided, therefore, to pre-empt affairs. On 1 February 1793, the Convention voted, unanimously, to declare war on Britain. The British government, it has to be said, left the French little choice: shipments of grain and raw material to France had been halted the previous December; and in January 1793, Pitt expelled the French envoy to London. The British responded in the only way they could to a declaration of war: by mobilizing the Royal Navy, and by putting its considerable financial resources behind the Continental coalition. From this time on until Waterloo and the end of the conflict with France – a period sometimes referred to as the final phase in the second Hundred Years' War – Britain bankrolled all the anti-French coalitions, providing considerable subsidies to all its allies to keep their armies in the field. As for the navy, it attacked French merchantmen on the high seas, blockaded French ports, and seized a number of French colonies.

The Siege of Toulon

All of this explains what the British were doing in Toulon, but Buonaparte's presence was due more to one of those chance occurrences that would later convince him that Fate had reserved a special place for him.

The revolutionary army commanded by Carteaux had received the order to reduce the rebel city of Toulon. Carteaux was the son of a sergeant major who had lost his leg during the Seven Years' War in Hanover and who died of his wounds at the hospital of the Invalides in Paris. Carteaux had donned the military uniform at the age of nine. He was first a dragoon, then a foot soldier, but he turned to portrait painting when he left the army in 1779. One of his paintings, which represents Louis XVI on a horse, earned him the sum of 6,000 livres.

With the outbreak of Revolution, though, he sided not with the monarchy but with the revolutionaries. He was named lieutenant in the national gendarmerie, storming the Tuileries with his men on 10 August 1792 in defence of the popular cause. He was eventually sent to the Army of the Alps, and was later used against the Federalists, whom he easily defeated, claiming that he had prevented the Federalists from Lyons and Marseilles from joining up.

Jean-Baptiste François Carteaux, *Louis XVI (1754–1793) Roi constitutionnel, il porte la cocarde tricolore* (Louis XVI, constitutional king, wearing the tricolour cockade), 1791. (*Courtesy of Photo RMN – © Droits réservés*)

It was this feat that gave him an unwarranted reputation. He was, in fact, a vain, proud man with little military competence.

On 7 September, Carteaux's army managed to take a village called Ollioules, a few kilometres from Toulon. In the process, however, a man was killed and two others were wounded, including the commander of the artillery, Captain Dommartin. Dommartin had to be replaced, and by a man who, according to the expression used by the representatives-on-mission, was distinguished and full of talent. At that time (16 September), Buonaparte was in Nice, where he paid a visit to his friend, compatriot and protector, Saliceti. Saliceti, convinced that Buonaparte was the man for the job, offered him the position without even bothering to consult the generals in command. Buonaparte accepted on the spot. 'Chance has been wonderful to us,' wrote Saliceti. 'We stopped Citizen Buonaparte, a learned captain who was on his way to the Army of Italy, and we ordered him to replace Dommartin.'[18] Saliceti knew what he was talking about. He had been present during Carteaux's initial attack on Toulon and complained that neither the general nor his entourage had 'the least understanding of either the men they led, or of military machines, or of their effects.' It was great good luck that one of the two representatives keeping watch over operations at Toulon was Corsican and knew Buonaparte.

Toulon was considered to be one of the most impregnable fortified cities in the world. When the British arrived at the end of August, they augmented the system of defence around the port by attempting to render inaccessible any point that might be used to attack their fleet. Despite a few minor victories at the beginning of the siege, the revolutionaries' efforts had pretty much petered out by the time Buonaparte arrived.[19] Carteaux was a good choice when it came to brutal reprisals against local populations in revolt, such as at Avignon, but he was incompetent in matters of siege warfare. He especially came under attack in the letters of the representatives-on-mission to the Committee of Public Safety. In one letter, for example, after complaining about Carteaux's incompetence, Saliceti and another representative-on-mission, Thomas Gasparin, extolled the virtues of 'Buona-Parte', the only artillery captain, they believed, able to plan operations, and suggested that he be promoted. This was about two weeks after he had first arrived and it was undoubtedly part of a concerted effort by the representatives-on-mission to move competent people into positions of authority. The reports they sent back to Paris tell of the incredible disorder that existed in the army, composed for the most part of recruits from Marseilles who, according to the representatives-on-mission, had only enlisted in order to avoid suspicion of being counter-revolutionaries.[20] The lack of available experienced officers was undoubtedly the main reason the Committee of Public Safety took note of Saliceti's request and promoted Buonaparte on 18 October to the rank of *chef de bataillon* (major). In short, Buonaparte was not only technically competent – he obviously knew a great deal more about siege warfare than Carteaux – but he also had political support. It was this combination of political connections, ability and luck that allowed Buonaparte to advance as quickly as he did.

Buonaparte's first task when he arrived at Toulon was to organize the artillery. It was less than impressive, made up of four cannon, two mortars and only a few companies of volunteers to man them. There was also a total lack of command; everyone from the general-in-chief down to his lowliest aide-de-camp gave orders and changed siege dispositions at will. Buonaparte established an artillery park, put some order into the service, and employed all the non-commissioned officers he could get his hands on. Three days after he arrived, as a result of his own zeal and organizational skills, the army had an adequate artillery – fourteen cannon pieces and four mortars with all the necessary equipment. He produced a stream of orders for the cannon, horses, draught-oxen and stores necessary for the effective prosecution of the siege.[21] He ordered 5,000 sacks of earth a day from Marseilles to build ramparts. He created an arsenal at Ollioules where eighty blacksmiths, cartwrights and carpenters worked, manufacturing and repairing muskets and incendiary cannon balls. He requisitioned skilled workers from Marseilles to make equipment for the artillery and took over a foundry in the region so that he could produce case shot, cannon balls and shells for his mortars. He reorganized the artillery company, obtained powder that was sadly lacking on his arrival, fought with suppliers, and scrounged more cannon from the surrounding region. Within a relatively short space of time, he

Paul Grégoire, *Siège de Toulon* (Siege of Toulon), between 1793 and 1799.
(*Bibliothèque nationale, Paris*)

had managed to gather almost one hundred guns and mortars,
which worked twenty hours a day.

After having established two batteries – they were given good
revolutionary names like *La Montagne* and the *Sans-Culottes* –
Buonaparte persuaded Carteaux to attack a position known as
Mount Caire. By taking Mount Caire, Fort Eguilette would fall.
The plan made perfect sense but Carteaux only designated a small
number of troops and cannon to the task. As a result, the attack
(launched on 22 September) failed miserably. Worse, the English
realized the strategic importance of Mount Caire and immediately
set about building an impressive earthwork, equipping it with
twenty heavy cannon and four mortars. Once this was complete,
Fort Mulgrave, as it was baptized by the English, would be very
difficult to take.

Driven to despair by the incompetence of his superior
officers, Buonaparte reported them to the Committee of Public
Safety. 'The first measure I propose,' he wrote on 25 October,
'is that you send to the army, to command the artillery, a

general of artillery who will be able, if only because of his rank, to command respect and impose himself on the bunch of fools on the general staff, with whom one has constantly to argue and lay down the law in order to overcome their prejudices and make them take steps which theory and experience have shown to be axiomatic to any trained officer of this corps.' Another denunciation; this time he included a plan to take Toulon by attacking Fort Eguilette.[22] Topographically, Toulon and the surrounding countryside bear a remarkable resemblance to Ajaccio, something that Buonaparte would have realized shortly after arriving. The key to controlling Toulon was Fort Eguilette; it dominates both the Inner Road and the Outer Road. From there, the French could bombard Toulon as well as the fleet in the harbour. With the fleet gone, Toulon, cut off from the outside world, would fall. Buonaparte did not originally think up this plan – it had been discussed and decided on by other generals and the representatives-on-mission well before he arrived at Toulon[23] – but he, quite sensibly under the circumstances, adopted it and passed it off as his own.

Carteaux's lack of willingness to support Buonaparte's efforts resulted in Saliceti making the artillery independent of the army.[24] Buonaparte was thus able to continue making his own preparations, with the support of the representatives-on-mission.[25] His letters from this period are authoritative, not to say haughty, which suggests that he did not consider himself subordinate to Carteaux.[26] Over a period of about six weeks (between 15 October and 30 November), he spent his time trying to counter the two most important British emplacements – Forts Mulgrave and Malbousquet – by setting up eleven new batteries to bombard them and Toulon itself. By this stage, Hood had a combined force of about 17,000 troops (British, Spanish, Piedmontese, Neapolitan and French émigrés) at his disposal under the command of Major General O'Hara. When the new commander-in-chief of the French siege forces, François-Amédée Doppet, a doctor by profession, did arrive, he proved even more unfit for command than Carteaux. It was, in part, because of Buonaparte's intriguing behind the scenes, along with Saliceti, that Doppet was replaced

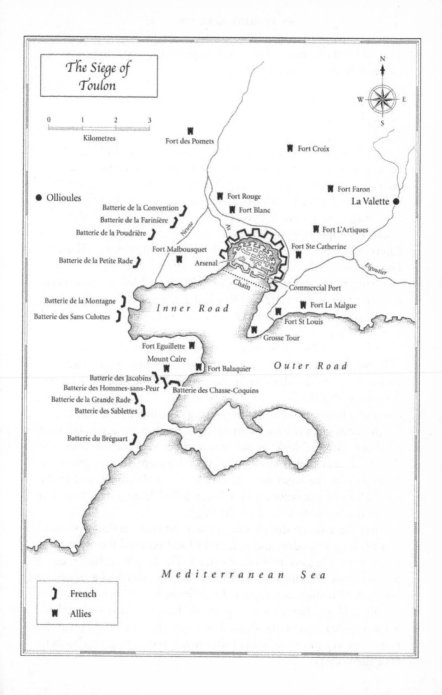

The Siege of
Toulon

0   1   2   3
Kilometres

● Ollioules

Fort des Pomets

Fort Croix

Batterie de la Convention
Batterie de la Farinière
Batterie de la Poudrière

Fort Rouge

Fort Faron
La Valette ●

Fort Blanc

Fort L'Artiques

Fort Malbousquet

Fort Ste Catherine

Batterie de la Petite Rade

Arsenal

Chain

Commercial Port

Batterie de la Montagne

Inner Road

Fort La Malgue

Batterie des Sans Culottes

Fort St Louis

Grosse Tour

Fort Eguillette
Mount Caire

Fort Balaquier

Outer Road

Batterie des Jacobins
Batterie des Hommes-sans-Peur

Batterie des Chasse-Coquins

Batterie de la Grande Rade
Batterie des Sablettes

Batterie du Bréguart

Mediterranean Sea

〕 French

Ⓦ Allies

Neune

Ay

Egoutier

after only three weeks by a real soldier, the sixty-five-year-old General Jacques Dugommier.

'Ville Infame'

On 25 November, Dugommier summoned a council of war; Buonaparte was present as secretary. Three plans were presented for consideration, but Saliceti's arguments convinced the others that Buonaparte's plan to take Fort Eguilette was the best.[27] Indeed, Dugommier may have left everything up to Buonaparte.[28] Before it could be implemented, however, the Allies made a sudden and determined sortie from Fort Malbousquet, threatening Ollioules. Dugommier, Saliceti and Buonaparte all led the counter-attack, incurring heavy casualties on both sides; it had led to the capture of Major General O'Hara.[29] (Decades later, on St Helena, Napoleon would claim that he captured O'Hara himself, but it is more likely that two volunteers from the Isère and two soldiers from the 59th captured him.) Two more weeks of preparations under the direction of Buonaparte went by, including the arrival of new forces under the command of André Masséna (future marshal of the Empire, who met Buonaparte for the first time at Toulon). On 17 December, under the cover of a bombardment and in pouring rain, the final assault began. Six thousand men stormed Fort Mulgrave and succeeded in taking it at about three o'clock in the morning, at the cost of over one thousand casualties. During this time, Buonaparte was given the order to take the lesser forts of Eguilette and Balaquier, and in the course of the operation, had a horse killed from under him and received a bayonet wound to the thigh.

After these successful attacks, it was clear that the fleet's position was no longer tenable, and Admiral Hood ordered the evacuation of the port. He gave two other orders. The first was that those in fear of reprisals and wishing to flee Toulon should be taken on board British ships as refugees. An estimated 7,500 people took up the offer. Many more, it was said, would have liked to flee, but there was no more room on the ships. There were harrowing scenes at the quaysides as panic took hold of the crowds trying to get on boats to take them away:

The rafts that had been placed around the boats and vessels that had served as barracks sank under the weight of the masses crowded on them. In a moment the harbour was covered with the ill-fated struggling against death. Hearts were closed to pity: those still swimming and who asked to be received into the boats were pushed away with blows from oars or swords. Fear took hold of the Neapolitan soldiers who . . . waiting to be transported onto their vessels, opened fire on those coming out of the port, to force them to give way.[30]

The second order was given to Captain William Sydney Smith, whom Buonaparte would meet again in Syria. He was instructed to destroy as much of the French navy as possible. Preparations took place all day on 18 December, but the work was bungled by some Spaniards who prematurely set fire to a gunpowder-packed frigate, the *Iris*, making it difficult to fire the other ships. The action was further hampered by French prisoners, loyal to the Republic, who prevented the English from blowing up the arsenal. The loss was nevertheless substantial: nine French ships of the line and three frigates were destroyed, while another twelve vessels were towed away. Just as importantly, the timber stocks built up over the years, so necessary for the continued construction of vessels, also went up in flames. To put the magnitude of this naval disaster in perspective – it has been described as the single most crippling blow to the French navy in the second half of the eighteenth century[31] – as many ships again were destroyed during the Battle of the Nile by Nelson a few years later, while only three vessels were destroyed and eighteen captured during the Battle of Trafalgar.

When the republicans entered Toulon on the morning of 19 December, the reprisals began. Escaped convicts, avenging themselves on a city that had punished them, added to the general carnage. Buonaparte did not take part in the massacres in the town, although he was probably responsible for sinking four ships of fleeing women and children.[33] Was it for that reason, perhaps suffering from a twinge of guilt, that he used his influence to rescue some people in danger of being massacred? He was not the only officer to do so.[34] Most of the officers of the regular army were disgusted by what they saw and attempted to limit the carnage whenever they could.

Artist unknown, *Prise de Toulon par l'armée républicaine le 29 frimaire an II*
(Taking of Toulon by the Republican Army, 19 December 1793),
circa 1793. The image represents a despicable and cowardly enemy,
carrying off its booty and, as such, deserving no mercy from the Republican
troops.[32] (*Bibliothèque nationale, Paris*)

The representatives-on-mission, however, were inflexible; they
had come not to conquer but to terrify. Indeed, revolutionary
publicists during this period generally justified terror as a means of
defending the nation against its internal enemies. Joseph Fouché, a
former Oratorian and the future minister of police during the
Consulate and the Empire, wrote to his friend on the Committee
of Public Safety, Collot d'Herbois, after taking the town of Lyons
in December 1794. At the end of the short missive he wrote:
'Goodbye, my friends, tears of joy are running from my eyes
and inundating my soul. – P.S. There is only one way to celebrate
this victory; two hundred and thirteen rebels are being struck down
this evening by a thunderbolt.'[35]

The representatives-on-mission at Toulon were just as blood-
thirsty. In a letter signed by all five representatives present
(Barras, Saliceti, Jean-François Ricord, Augustin Robespierre

and Fréron) there is the following passage: 'The national vengeance has been unfurled. The shooting is constant. All the naval officers have been exterminated. The Republic will be avenged in a manner that it deserves. The spirit of the patriots will be appeased.'[36] According to his own account, Pierre-Marie-Stanislas Fréron, the corrupt son of a *philosophe*, toyed with the idea of razing Toulon from the map, and boasted that they would kill two hundred a day until there were no more traitors left.[37] Barras, who wrote that, 'We shoot conspirators every day,' would have preferred to 'take from Toulon the small number of patriots and to shoot all the rest; we would have been finished in a day.'[38] The rhetoric may have been worse than the reality, although the reality was bad enough. The following account describes events over a period of two days:

In the afternoon of 19, a proclamation enjoined all citizens, without distinction, to go to the [place] known as the Champ de Mars. Patrols were meant to scour the town, visiting houses, immediately shooting all those who had not obeyed the order. [Since nightfall was approaching and 'patriots' were mixed in with the crowd, everyone was sent home and told to reassemble the next day.] When they reassembled on the Champ de Mars, representatives chose a certain number of jurors from among the prisoners of the *Themistocles* [republicans who had been imprisoned for months on the ship during the siege]. Embittered by their long imprisonment, furious that their most implacable enemies had eluded them by a prompt flight, they were delighted to be the judges, better yet, the executioners of those who remained behind. Wearing the red bonnet, and holding a stick at the end of which was a sign with the words, *oppressed patriot*, they walked through the silent and trembling crowd. They chose the guilty according to their own interests, their hatred or their caprice. *To one side*, they would tell those destined for death ... Those who had not been chosen received once again the order to return to town. They had hardly gone a few steps when the signal was given and a thunderbolt struck down the ill fated, to the number of two hundred, who had been crowded along the wall of the enclosure of the Champ de Mars. Several volleys were fired. However, not all had been mortally wounded. A voice was then heard, promising, in the name of the Republic, mercy to anyone who was still alive. A few got up, and were cut down again.[39]

Pons' memoirs, from which this extract is taken, need to be read with a degree of caution. They were written during the Restoration at the instigation of the municipality of Toulon, which wanted to assure the 'good graces of the king'.[40] But even if the details are questionable, there is no doubt that a massacre took place. It is estimated that firing squads and the guillotine executed around 1,000 people, far fewer than has sometimes been made out, but hundreds more died trying to get to vessels as the town was evacuated, and hundreds more drowned in ships that were sunk.[41] For some time after, Toulon was known as *ville infame* (vile town) until being re-baptized Port-la-Montagne, and all public buildings and monuments were destroyed by the revolutionaries in an act of revenge.

According to tradition, Buonaparte's military reputation was seen to have begun with the siege of Toulon. Indeed, some histories emphasize his role to the extent that the reader could be mistaken for thinking he was in charge of operations: the assumption is that Buonaparte thought up the plan of attack when, as we have seen, he did not.[42] It should also be noted, despite his almost feverish activity during this period, that there was almost no mention made of his name in the dispatches sent from Toulon and that he was given only a brief mention in the official newspaper, the *Moniteur universel*, along with two other Corsicans, Barthélemy Arena and Jean-Baptiste Cervoni.[43] Dugommier, justly or otherwise, was hailed as the hero of the siege of Toulon. Buonaparte did, however, play a key role, and his talent as a soldier and fledgling commander stands out here. According to a number of memoirs he, more than anybody else, was responsible for the disposition of the artillery.[44]

It gives me great pleasure [wrote François Doppet, whose memoirs, written in 1797, have a tendency to marginalize everyone but himself] to say that this young officer, who has since become the hero of Italy, combined a lot of talent and rare degree of courage, and the most indefatigable activity. Whenever I visited the positions held by this army, either before or after my trip to Lyons, I always found him at his post. If he needed a moment's rest, he took it on the ground wrapped in his cloak. He never left the batteries.[45]

As a result of Toulon, Buonaparte was noticed by powerful men and promoted to brigadier general. But all this could have led to nothing. High military rank was notoriously perilous during this period: literally dozens of generals, and hundreds of general officers, were executed or sent to the guillotine for failing to perform according to the requirements of their revolutionary masters – seventeen generals in 1793 and sixty-seven the following year.[46] All would depend on what Buonaparte did next, and on how well he could politically exploit his position.

Italy – the First Plans

Shortly after Toulon, Buonaparte was able to obtain from influential friends a position in charge of the inspection of the Mediterranean coast from the Var to the Bouches-du-Rhône. It was hardly the behaviour of a man burning with ambition, especially since the war was being fought actively elsewhere, but, to be near his family, the posting was convenient; the headquarters for the inspection was based in Marseilles, where his mother and siblings had eventually found lodgings. The period of penury suffered after fleeing Corsica seems to have lasted no longer than three months, after which the three eldest sons – Giuseppe, Napoleone and Brutus-Luciano – were employed and were able to send money to their mother. Moreover, Letizia continued to receive financial assistance as a refugee.[47]

From December 1793 to March 1794, Buonaparte kept busy, travelling up and down the coast inspecting the coastal batteries and forts, and setting up new batteries where necessary, including on the island of Hyères, not far from the port of Toulon.[48] By providing for the defence of Provence in this manner, Buonaparte was helping to secure the communications of the army between the

Rhône valley and the Italian front. At the beginning of January he was busy inspecting the forts of Marseilles and writing to the minister of war, without asking the advice or the permission of his superiors, imploring him to refurbish the Fort Saint-Nicolas, just in case it was necessary to 'control' or 'subdue' (*maîtriser*) the town.[49]

It was an unfortunate phrase; word of the letter got out. Only a few months before, the town of Marseilles had been besieged by revolutionary troops and, after it fell, subjected to the usual excesses. Why it might have been necessary to 'subdue' Marseilles again is not clear, but it is emblematic of the tensions that existed between civilian and military authorities in the Midi.[50] Marseilles' inhabitants were exasperated by this display of revolutionary zeal; the local deputies were contacted and alerted. A representative from the department, Granet, stood up in the Convention to inform his fellow deputies that they were 'proposing to repair the Bastille of Marseilles that Louis XIV built in order to tyrannize the Midi', and that the commander of the artillery (Buonaparte's name was not mentioned) was responsible for this suggestion. He demanded, as a consequence, that 'General Lapoype and his general of the artillery be summoned to the bar to give an account of their conduct'.[51] This was a serious development. In the past, men who had been summoned to the Convention invariably found themselves fighting for their lives. Fortunately for Buonaparte, he had protectors in Paris.

To be on the safe side, Buonaparte gave himself a mission to inspect the forts along the coast, without ever notifying the authorities of his exact position. In this manner, he had an official excuse for not knowing that he had been summoned by the Committee of Public Safety while his friends in Paris did their best to overcome any difficulties. Moreover, the population of Marseilles, seeing that the project to reinforce the Fort Saint-Nicolas had been abandoned, calmed down. The only person to go through the ordeal of confronting the Convention was General Lapoype, who had nothing to do with the affair except that his name had been mentioned in the assembly. He was a 'ci-devant', that is, a former noble, and had no contacts in Paris to help him. On 13 March, he appeared before the Convention, where he was able to demonstrate that Buonaparte had gone over his head. Buonaparte was, therefore, the only person responsible. The accusation was lost in the general indifference of the Convention; by this time, the incident had been forgotten and no one had insisted on pursuing it further.

The episode illustrates that Buonaparte had allied himself, perhaps unwittingly, with the extremist faction in the Convention. In particular, Augustin Robespierre, the brother of Maximilien, unofficial head of the Committee of Public Safety, looked after Buonaparte's interests in Paris. Augustin seems to have been so impressed with Buonaparte – in a letter to his brother he described him as having 'transcendental merit'[52] – that, at one stage, he considered bringing him to Paris to take charge of the armed forces in the capital city, thereby replacing the *sans-culotte** drunkard François Hanriot. This did not come about, but both Saliceti and Augustin were prepared to support the dynamic officer – his enthusiasm and competency were a refreshing contrast to many others – and used Buonaparte's evident talent for planning operations to the fullest. Based in Nice at the end of March and the beginning of April, he was given the task of organizing an expedition to Corsica.

In addition, Buonaparte devised two plans in the spring of 1794 to drive the well-entrenched Piedmontese from their positions in northern Italy.[53] When the campaign season began in the spring of 1793, France was faced with a formidable European coalition (the first of seven coalitions over the next twenty-three years), comprising Austria, Prussia, Britain, Spain, the Holy Roman Empire, the Dutch Republic, the Kingdom of Sardinia-Piedmont, the Kingdom of the Two Sicilies and a number of other lesser Italian states (but not the Republics of Genoa and Venice). Some of these countries had joined the coalition after the execution of Louis XVI in January 1793. The French, therefore, were obliged to fight on five separate fronts: in the south-east against Piedmont, in the south-west against Spain, in the east against Prussia, in the north against Austria and Holland, and against the British navy everywhere at sea. In addition, the revolutionary government in Paris also had to deal with the

---

* *Sans-culottes* were part of a popular movement in Paris (and, to a lesser extent, in the provinces), made up of people who asserted their working class origins by, among other things, wearing trousers rather than *culottes* (knee-breeches), which were worn by the bourgeoisie and aristocrats.

Federalist revolts, as well as a number of counter-revolutionary uprisings at home. The French response to this threat was partly ideological: in November 1792, the Convention voted to assist all peoples who wanted to 'recover their liberty', that is, it was going to bring the French Revolution to the rest of Europe. It was this decree that helped convince the British government that war with France was inevitable. The other response was practical: it introduced conscription in February 1793 (known as the *levée en masse*). This injection of hundreds of thousands of conscripts – an event sometimes referred to as the 'birth-cry of total war'[54] – allowed the revolutionary government to form a number of separate armies (fourteen in all at the height of the Terror) to cope with each of these fronts, placed under the overall direction of the minister of war, Lazare Carnot. It was largely through his efforts – he was dubbed the 'organizer of victory' – that a potentially disastrous military and political situation was turned around in 1794, and real gains were made on a number of fronts.

The front that would most directly concern Buonaparte was in Italy. There, on the border with France, the King of Piedmont, Victor Amadeus III, a mild man, if not perhaps a little indecisive, ruled over one of the oldest and possibly one of the most successful royal houses in Europe.[55] It was a centralized, absolutist system that had a large and reasonably effective army, but which was by no means as sclerotic as many other *ancien régime* monarchies. The king was also related through marriage alliances to Louis XVI: two of his daughters were married to the king's brothers, the Comte d'Artois and the Comte de Provence, both of whom were to become kings of France, while his eldest son, Charles Emmanuel, who would later become King of Piedmont, was married to one of Louis XVI's sisters. Needless to say, French influence over Piedmont was predominant, at least in some circles, to the point where the Piedmontese nobility, perfectly bilingual as many European nobles were, drew heavily on French style, customs and tradition.

Victor Amadeus did not approve of the Revolution, but nor did he want to get involved in French domestic affairs. Unfortunately for Piedmont, two of its territories – Savoy and the county of Nice – lay on the French side of the Alps and had, as a result, been coveted by various French governments for generations. In the context of the Revolution, these regions were first 'liberated' and then 'reunited' to France at the end of 1792 and the beginning of 1793. Piedmont was, in effect, too small a power to defend itself against France, so Victor Amadeus was obliged to turn to Austria, which possessed the neighbouring Duchy of Milan, covering most of Lombardy, for support, and consequently joined the coalition against France. After some initial successes in Savoy, the Piedmontese army was pushed back over the Alps as the French advanced towards the Republic of Genoa. The Italian front soon petered out, though, and, with the onset of winter, ground to a halt. All of these events took place while Buonaparte was occupied with affairs in Corsica, but the resumption of the campaign in the summer of 1794 did not see any significant movement take place; the French were distracted in suppressing the Federalist revolts in the south of France. The stalemate on the Italian front was at the origins of Buonaparte's plans to drive the Piedmontese from their positions.

The first plan was centred on the small port town of Oneglia on the Italian Riviera, halfway between Nice and Genoa, that, despite being surrounded by the Republic of Genoa, actually belonged to Piedmont. It was important to break the stranglehold on the port being exerted by the British navy and Piedmontese privateers based there in order to free it for the Genoese grain trade. Buonaparte's plans for the offensive were 'inspired' by Pierre-Joseph de Bourcet, a military theorist he had read as an officer in training, whose *Principes de la guerre de montagnes* (Principles of mountain warfare) (1775) had imagined a campaign in precisely this region.[56] Buonaparte, with Luigi in tow, accompanied the French forces led by General Masséna that moved up the coast from Nice in late April and early May when a number of towns fell in quick succession: the operation would have been a useful introduction to an army on campaign.[57]

Towards the end of June, Buonaparte presented a second 'Plan for the Preparatory Operation at the Opening of the Campaign in Piedmont', once again based on the work by Bourcet.[58] It was designed to exploit the successes of the first plan, and to break through into the plains around Mondovi to relieve the Army of Italy of supply shortages. Like the first plan, it too was signed by Buonaparte's supporters, the representatives-on-mission, Augustin

Robespierre, Jean-François Ricord and Armand de Laporte, and, like the first, it had to be approved by Carnot, as minister of war, and by the Committee of Public Safety. Approval came and a new offensive was launched. Once again, everything went according to plan, and then Carnot put a halt to the operation after some initial gains. He did not want a major offensive in Italy at a time when he was about to launch one on the Rhine, nor did he want the army travelling too far from the still unstable region of the Midi. Carnot was more interested in an all-out offensive against Spain than in Italy at this stage.

Augustin Robespierre travelled to Paris to get Carnot to change his mind. He had brought with him a memorandum, probably written by Buonaparte, which stressed the need for a concerted effort against Austria.[59] 'The principles of war,' it reads, 'are the same as those of a siege. Fire must be concentrated on a single point, and as soon as the breach is made the equilibrium is broken and the rest is nothing – the place is taken.' Buonaparte was suggesting a diversionary attack against Piedmont; it would compel Austria to weaken its forces on the Rhine and thus create favourable conditions for a French breakthrough there. It is this same plan that Buonaparte would implement as commander of the Army of Italy in 1796.

7

Shifting Political Sands

Arrest

While the younger Robespierre waited for a reply from the Committee of Public Safety, Buonaparte was sent on a mission to Genoa.

At the beginning of the summer of 1794, with its armies in northern Italy engaged in a war against Piedmont and Austria, the French revolutionary government wanted to establish the attitudes and intentions of the Republic of Genoa. The Committee of Public Safety knew that two Austrian generals were in Genoa at that time, and Carnot was unconvinced by the reassurances of neutrality given by the Genoese envoy in Paris, Boccardi. The Committee, therefore, decided to send someone to Genoa on a mission to try to uncover the real intentions of the government. At the same time, he was to find out what the enemies of France were planning. The man chosen for this task was Buonaparte, partly because he understood Italian. On 11 July, he was ordered by Augustin Robespierre and Ricord to go to Genoa, ostensibly to confer with the government on the defence of the coast and to make a number of inquiries on the subject of neutrality violated by the Genoese.

The letter was accompanied by secret instructions. Buonaparte was to go over the Fort of Savone, the fortress of Genoa; gather information on Genoese artillery capacity; and 'study the civic and political conduct' of the ambassador of the French Republic, Jean Tilly, whose maladroit initiatives had, on a number of occasions, compromised French propaganda and alarmed the Genoese government.[1] He had also been the object of complaints from the English and Austrian envoys in Genoa. Finally, there was probably a third objective to the mission. With an expedition to Corsica in mind, Buonaparte made contact with Corsican refugees in Genoa.

On 11 July 1794, Buonaparte left Nice in the company of the deputy, Jean-François Ricord, one of the habitual companions of the younger Robespierre, with a suite of officers among whom were Andoche Junot, Marmont and his own brother, Luigi.[2] The 'mission' stopped first at San Remo and only reached Genoa late in the evening of 15 July. For the last several months, the authors of a plot against the oligarchic regime had been locked up in the infamous 'Tour' in Genoa. All, without exception, were enthusiastic friends of France and zealous revolutionaries. Tilly had been unable to obtain their release, as a result of which, it was believed, the prestige of revolutionary France had been damaged. It is probable that the Committee of Public Safety was counting on Buonaparte's local knowledge to persuade the Genoese government to change its mind on this point (as on others), but it would appear that Buonaparte did not pursue this aspect of his mission with any particular vigour. The diplomatic aspects of the voyage took second place in his mind to the military ones. Indeed, he used much of the information he gathered in 1794 during his first campaign in Italy two years later.

We do not have the report that Buonaparte wrote back to Paris. We do know, however, that shortly after his return to Nice on 28 July, Tilly was recalled and arrested. It is possible that Buonaparte denounced him. More importantly, however, Buonaparte was able to make a number of observations about the Italian countryside and on the ease of a future military operation directed against the Piedmontese and Genoese forces. He came away convinced, on the whole correctly, that the majority of Genoese nobles were against France and the Revolution. It partly explains why he was prepared to eradicate the Genoese Republic a few years later.

One week after his return from Italy, on 4 August, news reached the south of France about the events that had taken place in Paris. After the fall of the monarchy on 10 August 1792, and the execution of the king the following January, the Revolution entered into its most radical phase. The dire threat to the Republic that resulted from foreign invasion, and the initial defeats suffered by the revolutionary armies, called for drastic measures. A Committee of Public Safety was created in April 1793 to successfully prosecute and co-ordinate the war effort. It did so by making terror 'the order of the day', and by ruthlessly eliminating anybody it considered a threat to the Revolution – suspect aristocrats, refractory priests, but also many workers whose frustration with the Revolution may have found expression in a disparaging remark after one too many drinks, or those who did not perform to expectations at the front. The Terror also devoured its own, as factions within the Republic vied for power in a deadly game of politics. This was the period (from about March 1793 to June 1794) during which the guillotine was at its busiest – not only in Paris where, at the height of the Terror, twenty to thirty people a day would be driven from their prison through the streets of Paris to 'kiss the blade' – but also in the provinces where more expeditious methods of dispatching people were used. At Nantes, in November 1793, for example, up to 1,800 people were drowned after being stripped naked, tied together in batches and sent to the middle of the Loire in holed barges. When Lyons, the second largest city in France and which had also revolted against Paris, was taken by revolutionary troops in October 1793, the guillotine proved too slow; over 1,800 rebels were executed by cannon-fire and grapeshot beside previously dug mass graves.

Maximilien Robespierre, the nominal head of the Committee of Public Safety, the man most associated with the Terror – a cold idealist, an ascetic, a zealot who did not hesitate to send his own friends to the guillotine – was arrested on 27 July 1794. The previous day, he had appeared before the Convention to deliver a speech that vaguely threatened a number of unnamed deputies. It was enough to stir the deputies of the Convention into action, fearful for their own lives. After unsuccessfully trying to commit suicide by blowing his brains out (all he succeeded in doing was shooting his lower jaw off), he was carted off in a bloody mess to the spot where so many of his victims had passed before him, at what is today the Place de la Concorde, and summarily dispatched along with a number of his supporters. His younger brother, Augustin, out of a sense of (perhaps mistaken) loyalty, volunteered to follow his brother to the scaffold the same day. This event, known as Thermidor after the revolutionary month in which it took place, was a coup of sorts, made up of those who were unhappy with the Terror, and those, like Barras, Fouché and Fréron, republican zealots who were afraid that Robespierre would bring them to account for their own past excesses in dealing with the counter-revolution.

The news of events that filtered through to the south of France was incomplete and too vague for people to realize what had actually happened, but, within a week, it had become clear that a dramatic change had occurred and that it was now politically expedient to distance oneself from Robespierre and even to turn on those who had supported him. The representatives-on-mission in the south of France lost no time in so doing. They were positioning themselves so as not to be compromised by those wanting to purge the Convention anew. Many were caught up in this strategic positioning, even Buonaparte, who wrote to Tilly admitting that he was 'a little affected by the catastrophe of the young Robespierre', whom he loved and believed to be pure, but asserted that, even if he were his own brother, he would have stabbed him with his own hand if he thought that he had aspired to tyranny.[3] After waiting forty-eight hours to verify the news, the representatives-on-mission, Albitte, Laporte and Saliceti, wrote to the Committee of Public Safety (6 August) denouncing the younger Robespierre, Ricord, and the 'liberticide' campaign in Italy that had been proposed by Buonaparte. There were strong reasons, they implied, for suspecting him of treason and fraud. What could he have been doing in a foreign country (they were referring to Genoa) in the first place?[4] In the atmosphere of paranoia created by the Terror, Buonaparte had become part of a defeatist plot to undermine the front.

Without waiting for the reaction of the Committee of Public Safety, the three deputies signed the order for Buonaparte's arrest and sent one of their compatriots, Arena, to carry it out. He reached Nice on the evening of 8 August. The next morning, a small troop of men consisting of a captain and eleven gendarmes made its way to Buonaparte's residence, where he was arrested. Buonaparte was in a difficult situation but was not yet lost. At that moment, a friend, the Comte Laurenti, came to his rescue and vouched for him so that he was simply placed under house arrest (at the Laurenti's).[5]

Tradition has it that Buonaparte was incarcerated in the Fort-Carré in Antibes, but there is no basis for this in the sources.[6]

One of the more puzzling aspects of this episode is Saliceti's behaviour towards Buonaparte. Not only were they compatriots, but they had been brothers in arms. The most likely explanation for Saliceti's behaviour is that he was simply trying to save himself by offering a sacrifice to the Committee of Public Safety. But it is also possible that Saliceti was becoming concerned about Buonaparte's ambition, and was perhaps jealous or resentful of his modest success. 'Buonaparte hardly deigns to look at me from the heights of his grandeur,' he complained in a letter written in Italian.[7] This is why Saliceti was probably not simply 'playing along' with his other two colleagues, as has sometimes been argued.[8] He knew full well what he was doing – he was trying to harm his rival. Convinced of his own innocence and perhaps believing in the virtue of revolutionary justice, Buonaparte wrote a statement addressed to Saliceti and Albitte where he emphasized his republican convictions.[9] He also thought it prudent to lay to one side his Jacobin credentials, and to distance himself from Robespierre.

Buonaparte was only one among dozens of officers arrested in the aftermath of the fall of Robespierre.[10] He was released, however, less than two weeks later.[11] In large part, he owed his freedom to the man who had him arrested in the first place, and who realized that it would be better for both of them if he went free. Saliceti was, even more than Buonaparte, Robespierre's man. The trial of one would have meant the trial of the other. After his release, relations with Saliceti took on a semblance of normality, but it is likely that Buonaparte never fully trusted him again, and may even have regarded him as his enemy.[12] On 24 August, Buonaparte was back at headquarters, only to find out that he had been relieved of his command. He had, in fact, only been released 'provisionally'. However, not only did he possess technical skills the army badly needed, but he was also extremely resourceful. It would only take him one month to get back on his feet.

In August 1794, the commander of the Army of Italy, General Pierre-Jadart Dumerbion, asked Buonaparte to draw up a plan to head off an expected Austrian counter-attack against the town of Savona. 'Present me with a plan such as only you know how to make, and I will do my best to carry it out.'[13] Buonaparte came up with a plan for attack on the towns of Cairo and Montenotte which may have been inspired by the memoirs of the Marquis de Maillebois, who had conducted a campaign over this terrain in 1745. Buonaparte was able once again to see the terrain first hand. He accompanied Dumerbion and the French army for a second time into Italy in September 1794, making note of certain geographical features, observing how his ideas could be put into practice. He witnessed, for example, his first pitched battle at Dego on 21 September, terrain that would be fought over again in 1796. It was there that he realized that the best plan of operation in Italy would be to separate the Piedmontese army from the Austrians. He was not the only one, though; a plan based on that same idea was submitted to the representatives-on-mission Louis Turreau de Linières and François-Joseph Ritter (who had replaced Saliceti and Albitte), who, in turn, submitted it for approval to the Committee of Public Safety. The Committee, no doubt inspired by Carnot, vetoed it. As we have seen, they were not interested in pursuing the campaign in Italy. Nevertheless, once back in Nice, Dumerbion praised Buonaparte for his part in the victories: 'I owe the skilful combinations that have assured our victory to the talent of General Buonaparte.'[14]

This was a good start to a career as a strategist, but nothing at this stage indicates Buonaparte could have become anything other than a 'good' general. After returning from Italy at the beginning of November, he busied himself preparing another plan to invade Piedmont, incorporating information that he had gathered while there, and which was the basis of the plan he was to effect with such success about eighteen months later. Although the plan received the support of the representatives-on-mission, Turreau and Ritter, the Committee of Public Safety, still influenced by the views of Carnot, remained unimpressed. The problem was that the Committee of Public Safety was conducting secret negotiations, some with Piedmont, while others were being conducted with Austria in Switzerland. Against this background, the French government was reluctant to pursue any serious military action in Italy. Buonaparte was, of course, unaware of this, but there was not much he could do about the Committee's decision to opt for a defensive war in any event. Since he had been in Italy, Dumerbion had been replaced by General Barthélemy Schérer, as a result of which Buonaparte lost what little influence he had in the Army of Italy. Schérer showed no interest in Buonaparte's plans and even thought they were mistaken. Where Buonaparte required lightness and speed, the ageing Schérer insisted on playing it safe.

Instead, the Committee of Public Safety focused on taking back Corsica. An expeditionary corps of about 10–12,000 men was assembled at Toulon for that purpose. Buonaparte asked Turreau to get him a posting there, and he duly arrived in Toulon around 15 December to organize the artillery for the expedition. On 5 December, the commissaries who had been assigned to the expedition had written to the Committee of Public Safety to say that everything was ready.[15] Despite this optimistic appraisal, preparations were still under way throughout the months of January and February 1795. The convoy finally set sail on either the 3 or 11 March, with Buonaparte on board the ship *Amitié*. But the British navy had been waiting for them for some time. A little off the island of Hyères, the two principal French vessels, the *Ça Ira* and the *Censeur*, engaged the enemy and came off the worse. That was enough for the rest of the fleet to turn tail and sail back to port. The plans to invade Corsica were scrapped, this time for good, and the troops destined for Corsica were assigned to the Army of Italy.

Buonaparte should have joined them, but Schérer considered him a political appointee. So he was told, by order of the Committee of Public Safety, to proceed immediately to join the Army of the West fighting insurgents in the Vendée. He was not, however, assigned to the artillery but was to take command of an infantry brigade. The number of artillery generals had exceeded the required maximum and Buonaparte was the youngest on the list. This may seem surprising, but he was still an unknown in Paris.[16]

Buonaparte was not informed of this decision until 7 May. He accepted the orders, although without any enthusiasm. He did not, despite what he later said on St Helena, refuse the position for fear of becoming involved in a civil war. He left Marseilles the next day, taking with him his brother, Luigi, and Captains Junot and Marmont. They took their time, travelling as though they were on holiday, stopping at towns along the way for two or three days before finally arriving in Paris on 25 May 1795. Mlle de Chastenay met Buonaparte and Marmont at Châtillon, where Buonaparte's party stopped for five days (they were staying with Marmont's family). At that time he was, according to her, 'thin and pale and his face was all that much more typical'. One assumes she was referring to his 'Corsican appearance'. In the society in which he found himself, republican generals like Buonaparte were not especially welcome, and those who met him considered him an imbecile.[17] The good woman did not know what to do with her guest, whose perfect and constant silence distressed her.

> His face made an impression on me . . . at Châtillon, we met at about two o'clock [for the main meal]. We were at table a long time, and when we got up, keen to speak with the general whose monosyllables had made a very different impression on me than on the rest of the company, I went over to him. I asked him a question about Corsica, and our conversation began. I believe it lasted more than four hours . . . On trying to recall since then something about the conversation, it seems that I soon discovered that the Republican general *had no principles and no republican convictions*. I was surprised, but his candour was complete in this respect.[18]

Buonaparte, Chastenay concluded, would have been an émigré if that path had offered any chance of success.

In this singular portrait, Buonaparte comes across as a political opportunist who is not motivated by either ideology or ideals. It is a new stage in his development. Up until his arrest as a Jacobin, one of the young Buonaparte's distinguishing character traits was his readiness to commit heart and soul to a particular cause. We can clearly see this in his espousal of Corsican independence, and then of the French Revolution, both of which he was eventually able to accommodate in his mind. The choice he was obliged to make between Corsica and France, between Paoli and the Revolution, was done reluctantly. But his political idealism remained more or less intact. That is why he was able to embrace Jacobinism, as we have seen with the publication of the *Souper de Beaucaire*, with as much vigour as he had embraced Corsica. This kind of idealism is, however, marked by its naïvety, any semblance of which was definitively purged from him with his arrest. It is understandable under the circumstances. Until this point in his life, every time he had committed to a political cause, it had been a deeply disappointing experience. From this time on, Buonaparte was perhaps not yet an opportunist, but certainly he was more of a political realist than ever before.

'My Tender Eugénie'

If Buonaparte's political experiences were slowly transforming him into an egocentric, at this stage of his life he was still a romantic. His first love, if that is not too strong a word, was Désirée Clary, a good-natured, plump sixteen-year-old with slightly bulging eyes whom he met in Marseilles at the beginning of 1794. He was introduced by his brother Giuseppe, who was courting Désirée's sister, the unattractive twenty-two-year-old Marie-Julie, whom Giuseppe married in August 1794. The meeting between Buonaparte and Désirée was not love at first sight. Indeed, it may even have been the prospect of a substantial dowry that persuaded Buonaparte to court her, the same reason his older brother was courting Julie.[19] And courting Désirée certainly did not prevent him later that year from vaguely considering marriage to a fifteen-year-old named Emilie, the daughter of the Comte de Laurenti.[20] Emilie's mother made it clear that she was too young for marriage and the matter was dropped; her parents prudently sent her to stay with cousins in the country. This brought Buonaparte back to Désirée, whom he insisted on calling by her middle name, Eugénie.

> 'The unfailing sweetness of your character,' he wrote to her while he was in Italy in September 1794, 'the happy candour that belongs only to you, inspires me, my good Eugénie, with friendship but, preoccupied by affairs, I did not think that this feeling would leave on my soul such a profound scar. Stranger to the tender passions, I was not on my guard against the pleasure of your company. Your charming person, your character, has little by little won the heart of your lover.'[21]

The tone of the letter is a little patronising. There is a passage where he recommends she buy a piano and get a good teacher, because 'Music is the soul of love, the sweetness of life, the consolation of suffering and the companion of innocence.' It is as though Buonaparte were hoping to fall in love. It is possible that he seduced Désirée and that he persuaded himself he loved her. He openly bragged only months before his death in 1821 that, 'Je lui ai pris le c ... et le p ... du c ...'[22] (This phrase could be decoded as, 'Je lui ai pris le con et le puit du cul.' That is, as well as having sex, he sodomised her.) It may have been little more than barrack-room braggadocio: in a letter to Désirée in June 1795 he alluded to 'that enchanting evening and those walks in which love united without satisfying us and made us drunk with hope'.[23]

Buonaparte's relations with Désirée may have had deeper roots. The two brothers were so close, especially at this stage of their lives, that Freud once speculated Napoleon may have been under the influence of a 'Joseph fantasy'.[24] By that he meant that Buonaparte, as a child, may have held a deep hostility towards his older brother, forced to compete with him for his mother's affection. As he grew older, though, his feelings were transformed into love. This is why, argued Freud, he was attracted to *Joseph*ine, and why he went to Egypt – 'to loom large in the brother's eyes'. Freud's thoughts on the subject may seem farfetched but they warrant consideration. The two brothers were close. It is no coincidence, for example, that Giuseppe wanted to leave the seminary at Autun in order to join the artillery, as though the older brother admired the younger brother so much that he had to imitate him. As for Buonaparte, who once described Giuseppe as endowed with a 'sweet, even-tempered and inalterable' character,[25] he wrote in the summer of 1795: 'No matter what events chance may place you in you know, my friend, that you cannot have a better friend, who is dear to you, and who sincerely desires your happiness.' And then he wrote something quite unexpected.

> Life is like a faint dream that [soon] disappears. If you leave [Giuseppe was about to go to Genoa] and you think it will be for some time, send me your portrait. We have lived so many years together, so closely united, that our hearts are merged, and you

know better than anyone how much mine is entirely yours. I feel in writing these lines an emotion of which I have had few examples in my life. I know that it will be a long time before we see each other and I can no longer continue my letter.[26]

In the same vein, on 6 September, Buonaparte wrote to his brother, 'If my hopes are seconded by the good fortune which never abandons me in my undertakings, I could make you happy and fulfil your desires.'[27] The attachment is deep, and to this extent, Désirée may have served no other purpose than to bring Buonaparte closer to his brother.

That he did not completely love her can be seen from his behaviour in Italy. There, sometime between 11 and 21 September, at the town of Loano, Buonaparte made the acquaintance of the representative-on-mission and zealous member of the Convention, Louis Turreau de Lignières, who had taken his wife on honeymoon to the south of France and northern Italy.[28] Buonaparte made an impression on him but, more importantly, he made an impression on his twenty-three-year-old wife, Louise Gauthier, whom he found 'very pretty and very kind'. Napoleon later recounted how he ordered an attack on an enemy advance post in order to impress her, and that it cost the lives of a number of men.[29] Since this particular phase of the campaign was over by 22 September, it is likely that Buonaparte accompanied the Turreaus back to Toulon, where they stayed several weeks. We are not sure what actually transpired between Louise and Buonaparte, but Napoleon confided in Emmanuel de Las Cases aboard the *Northumberland* on his way to St Helena that he was 'happy and proud of his little success'. The thought of Buonaparte seducing a woman on her honeymoon seems implausible, although he had also flirted with the wife of the representative-on-mission, Jean-François Ricord, earlier in the year. On those occasions, Buonaparte may have been using the wives to get to the husbands in order to advance his views and his career. His behaviour was so blatantly sycophantic that other officers apparently complained of it.

But he still maintained contact with Désirée. On his return from Italy, he wrote another, again slightly patronising, letter to her on 4 February 1795. He talked about some sort of theory of music he had written for her, and gave her a list of books she should read (few novels were included), so that by instructing herself she could 'learn to judge men and events'.[30] It is, in the words of Désirée's biographer, the letter of a 'thoughtful suitor rather than a passionate lover'.[31] Buonaparte was busy with preparations for an expedition to Corsica and seems to have had little time for her. She felt it and reproached him: 'the most sensitive of women loves the coldest of men.'[32] He scribbled off a letter on 12 February in which he maintained that: 'I have often longed for your feelings to match the strength of mine,' and then went on to give her some advice on how to sing scales.[33] By April, his letters were showing a little of the passion that later was to inspire his feelings for Josephine. 'I constantly have you on my mind,' he wrote on 11 April. 'Your portrait is engraved on my heart. I have never doubted your love, my tender Eugénie, why do you think that I could never love you?'[34]

When he learned that he had been taken off the list of artillery officers and assigned to the Vendée as an infantry officer, Buonaparte went to Paris to try to get the order overturned and to be given a command in the south of France. As his carriage drove off that day in May 1795, Désirée cried and then went straight to her room to scribble down a draft of what would be the first of many letters to him that summer. 'You have been gone for half an hour. The hour of our walk is nearing, but my friend will not come to get me. Oh, how I regret having let you go.' The feelings this time seem to have been mutual. The next day, Buonaparte arrived at Avignon, 'greatly pained at the idea of being so far from you for so long'.[35] What remains of his correspondence from Paris (for a time in June he wrote every couple of days) demonstrates that he had, indeed, become fond of her.[36]

Circumstances, however, were soon to prevent their relationship developing further. While he was in Paris, the Clary family moved to Genoa. Buonaparte apparently received a long letter from Désirée explaining the move and that the family was opposed to a union between them, although no trace of this letter exists. The news elicited from Buonaparte by far the longest letter he had ever written to her:

You are no longer in France, my deserving friend; were we not far enough apart? You have resolved to put the sea between us. I do not reproach you; I know that your position was delicate, and your last letter deeply moved me with the touching portrait of your suffering. Tender Eugénie, you are young. Your feelings will at first weaken, will declare themselves, and a little while after, you will find yourself changed. Such is the empire of time. Such is the fatal effect, infallible, of absence. I know that you will remain interested in your friend, but it will be nothing more than interest, than esteem.[37]

The rest of the missive is taken up with more advice, this time on what to do when she falls in love again. Curiously, the man he describes as the one she should choose above all others remarkably resembles how Buonaparte wanted to live his life. 'With a fiery imagination, a cool head, a strange heart and melancholic tendencies, one can shine among men like a meteor and disappear like one.'

Paris: The Decisive Months

The day after arriving in Paris, Buonaparte went to see François Aubry, who had been imprisoned during the Terror but who had managed to escape the executions carried out against so many others. He was now the Committee of Public Safety's main military expert (he had replaced Carnot in March 1795). Buonaparte hoped to be reinstated in the artillery of the Army of Italy, but that was hardly likely to happen with someone like Aubry, who professed an irreconcilable hatred towards Jacobins, and who wanted to purge the army of 'terrorists' and those whose rapid promotion during the Terror appeared suspect.[38] Buonaparte, it should be remembered, had been promoted at the height of the Terror. We do not know what transpired between the two men, but on 13 June, Aubry signed an order not only confirming Buonaparte's posting to the Vendée but also the 'demotion' to an infantry brigade. It was supposedly during this interview that Aubry made a remark about Buonaparte being so young, only to get the riposte, 'Citizen Representative, one grows old quickly on the field of battle.'[39]

For an officer in the artillery, a transfer to the infantry was considered to be such a slight that it would normally provoke a resignation.[40] The order by Aubry can thus be interpreted as deliberately provocative, as a way of getting rid of an officer he considered undesirable. In some respects, Buonaparte was lucky. About 40 per cent of generals in active service during the Terror were removed from their posts by Aubry in a purge of the officer corps during what is known as the Thermidorean reaction.[41] However, Buonaparte had the good sense not to resign. Instead, on 15 June, furnished with a medical certificate, he went to the Ministry of War and managed to get sick leave for two months (until 31 August). He was going to use that time to try to get a posting that suited him better. 'I am sick,' he wrote to his brother. 'When my health is re-established, I shall see what I will do.'[42]

He was buying time, and kept up the fiction as long as he stayed in Paris with Marmont, who was there without authorization, and Junot, who was supposedly acting as his aide-de-camp, all three lodging in a dingy hotel in the rue des Fossés Montmartre, whiling away the time at either the Palais Royal or various shows or, in Buonaparte's case, reading at the Bibliothèque Nationale.[43] He nevertheless sent his effects and his horses to the Vendée,[44] undoubtedly resigned to the fact that he would eventually have to leave Paris. It was during this period that he finalized his plans for an invasion of Italy.[45] On 30 July, he wrote to his brother saying 'The peace with Spain [signed with France in July 1795] makes an offensive war in Piedmont certain. They are discussing the plan I proposed, which will certainly be adopted.'[46]

For the present, neither Buonaparte nor his friends had much money (Buonaparte was on half pay) nor, at this stage, it would seem, many prospects for the future. He would frequently go for walks with either Junot or Horace Sébastiani, 'indignant about his obscurity, tormented by his genius and the triple need to learn, to act and to command.'[47] His 'genius' was no doubt seen in retrospect, but the sentiments expressed all those years later are consistent with what we know of Buonaparte. The walks would often lead towards the Observatory, which would apparently take his mind off things for a while. But the next day, 'a sad and threatening necessity would plunge him again into a situation more and more unbearable.' He would sometimes decide to take matters into his own hands and attempt to approach another influential political personality. At other times, though, he would stop short, literally in one instance before the door of the deputy and former terrorist, Fréron, as corrupt an individual as the Revolution threw up, unable to go through with his solicitation. This was a period in which everything for Buonaparte 'was disgrace; everything was suffering'.[48]

The relationship with Désirée was not to survive the separation, although this was not entirely Buonaparte's fault. She had stopped writing at the beginning of July 1795. He wrote to his brother complaining, 'I think that you are deliberately not talking to me of Désirée. I do not know if she is still alive.'[49] Their eventual rupture was to inspire another literary effort, another uncompleted sketch, this time a semi-autobiographical romance entitled *Clisson and Eugénie*.[50] It is the story of a twenty-six-year-old officer, Clisson, who falls in love and marries. But while he is away at war, his wife Eugénie betrays him with a young officer whom her husband, now a general, has sent to her as a messenger. When he finds out, the protagonist decides to find consolation by seeking out a glorious death on the battlefield. There is little doubt who Clisson or the sixteen-year-old Eugénie were meant to represent. The similarities between the fiction and what later happened in Italy between Buonaparte and Josephine are so close as to lead some historians to speculate that it might have been written at a later date.

As at other difficult times in his life, Buonaparte yet again turned to writing and, once more, he flirted with the idea of suicide. '[I] cling so little to life,' he wrote to Giuseppe, 'and look on it with so much anxiety, I constantly feel as if I were on the eve of a battle . . . If this continues, my friend, I will end up by not stepping aside when a carriage passes by.'[51] It reveals melancholy, tinged with self-pity, but it is highly unlikely that he ever seriously contemplated putting an end to it all. Mme Bourrienne, who had occasion to observe him often enough in Paris during this time, and who supposedly jotted down notes about events that most struck her, confirms that Buonaparte was suffering from a mild depression. She had this to say about an evening at the Théâtre Français, where a play, which was meant to be a tragedy, called *Le Sourd ou l'Auberge*

Pleine (The Deaf Man or the Full Inn) actually had the audience rolling with laughter. Buonaparte was the only person to 'keep an icy silence'. 'There was always something original in Bonaparte's manner of being, for he often disappeared when with us without saying anything, and when we thought that he was elsewhere other than at the theatre, we would see him in the second [boxes], in the third, or alone, looking as if he was sulking.'[52]

This melancholy would come back to haunt him throughout his life, especially when he was under duress or overworked. There were periods when he seems to have overcome it; there were others, like this time in Paris when his future was unclear, when it would reappear, dampening the spirit and deadening the soul. During the Italian campaign, for example, there were days when Bonaparte was completely despondent and when he thought of abandoning the army. Indeed, Bonaparte's moods could swing violently from elation, especially after a particularly hard-fought victory, to outright dejection before the start of a battle. Just before Arcola, for example, he wrote that his spirit was 'lacerated'. These mood swings can be explained by the sheer strain of command – he and his men marched hard, and fought almost non-stop for months – but there was an underlying pessimism that dominated Buonaparte's character.

His melancholy was reflected in an outward appearance that did not inspire trust. In her memoirs, the Comtesse de Ségur writes that he was contemptuously referred to as the 'little Italian', while one of the directors, the hunchback Louis-Marie de La Révellière-Lépeaux and his wife called him, perhaps not without some affection, their 'little general'.[53] The Duchesse d'Abrantès was probably correct when she wrote:

> At that period of his life, Napoleon was ugly . . . His features, which were almost all angular and sharp, have become rounder [since then], because they have been cloaked in flesh, of which there was an almost total absence. His hair, so singular for us today . . . was very simple then . . . but his complexion was so yellow at that time, and he looked after himself so little, that his badly combed, badly powdered hair, gave him an unpleasant appearance. His little hands have undergone the same metamorphosis; then they were thin, long

and black. [He had] an uncertain gait, with a bad round hat sunk deep over his eyes, letting his two badly powdered 'dog ears' [a hairstyle] escape . . . without gloves because, said he, it was a pointless expense, wearing badly made and badly polished boots.[54]

On top of that he spoke French badly, with a heavy Corsican accent, and was suffering from scabies contracted at Toulon.[55] In short, at this period of his life he came across as what the French called *minable* (pathetic) .

Increased career prospects were to drag him out of this insignificance. During the course of his stay in Paris events in Italy took a turn for the worse. Austria launched an unexpected offensive and the Army of Italy was forced to retreat to Loano. All the advantages that had been gained by weeks of campaigning were lost. Indeed, General François Kellermann, the victor at the cannonade of Valmy, who now commanded the Army of Italy, predicted that he might have trouble holding on to Nice if reinforcements were not sent immediately.[56] Alarmed by this news, Doulcet de Pontécoulant, another former Girondin, a member of the Committee of Public Safety (where he had replaced Aubry and now acted as a kind of minister of war), gathered together some of the deputies who had been representatives-on-mission with the Army of Italy to discuss the situation. During the course of these discussions, Boissy d'Anglas told him that he had met a young artillery general who had been with the Army of Italy but who was in Paris without a job.

That, at least, is one version of events. Another is that, armed with a letter of introduction, he obtained an interview with Barras, who remembered Buonaparte from Toulon as active, decisive, a bit of an intriguer certainly, but perhaps someone who could be useful to him one day.[57] Buonaparte argued that, rather than go to the Vendée, he should be posted to Nice. Besides, he had information on Italy that could be useful; he had even thought up some plans that the army might like to take a look at. Barras probably recommended that he go and see Pontécoulant. He did, and the minister met a young man with a haggard and ghastly complexion, and a frail and sickly appearance. But Pontécoulant was nevertheless impressed by Buonaparte's knowledge of the Italian terrain and his suggestions for conquering Italy, which 'gushed out of him like a volcano sends up the lava it has held back'.[58] When he asked Buonaparte to present a report on the subject – Pontécoulant was thinking that he would return a few days later – Buonaparte simply asked for pen and paper and rapidly wrote out on the spot, in writing that was barely legible, the plan for the Italian campaign.[59] It was a blueprint for what he would undertake as commander of the Army of Italy. Pontécoulant immediately sent him off to the Bureau Topographique.[60]

The Bureau had been set up by Carnot in 1792 to act as a kind of general staff to co-ordinate the war effort. Buonaparte was attached to the section dealing with operations in Italy. In this capacity, he became, in today's terms, an advisor to the government for military operations, one among many and very junior at that. A desk job, however, was obviously not entirely to his liking. Buonaparte contemplated leaving the French army and going into the service of either Russia or Turkey, a common enough practice for officers in the eighteenth century. The thought, nevertheless, did not prevent him from working hard in the short time he was employed in the Bureau. A stream of reports, instructions and suggestions flowed from his pen. 'I am overwhelmed with work,' he wrote to Giuseppe on 25 August, 'from one o'clock in the afternoon till five o'clock at the Committee and from eleven in the night till three o'clock in the morning.'[61] He expressed his views so forcefully that the Committee of Public Safety soon came around to adopting plans that led to an offensive conducted by General Barthélemy Schérer, reinstated as commander of the Army of Italy, in northern Italy between August and November. This, Buonaparte thought, simply put him in a stronger position to carry out his idea of going to Turkey. Pontécoulant supposedly tried to dissuade him, but to no avail.[62] On 20 August, the same day he was officially appointed to the Bureau, Buonaparte wrote to Giuseppe, 'If I ask, I would obtain permission to go to Turkey as general of the artillery, sent by the government to organize the artillery of the Great Seigneur, with a good wage and flattering titles. I would name you consul . . . The commission and the decree of the Committee of Public Safety appointing me in charge of the direction of the armies and the campaign plans have been so flattering to me that I fear that they will not let me go to Turkey; we shall see.'[63]

On 30 August he actually drafted a request to go. It was denied, something that he learned of on or before 5 September.[64] A member of the Committee of Public Safety, Jean Debry, interviewed Buonaparte, reviewed his request to go to Turkey on 13 September, and wrote in the margins of Buonaparte's letter, 'I believe that . . . the Committee of Public Safety must refuse to send away from the Republic, especially at this time, such a distinguished officer.'[65] On 15 September the Committee, presided over by Cambacérès, who was later to become one of Napoleon's most trusted and loyal servants, briefly deliberated Buonaparte's case on another matter, that is, his refusal to go to the Vendée. By this stage, Pontécoulant had been replaced by a man named Letourneur de la Manche, who was not sympathetic to Buonaparte's cause. The meeting concluded with the Committee issuing a decree which stated that, because of his refusal to join his post in the Vendée, Buonaparte was to be crossed off the list of officers employed by the Republic.[66]

Although Buonaparte had been usefully employed in the Bureau, his stubborn refusal to obey orders had led to this state of affairs. Still, angry at what he considered to be unfair treatment, Buonaparte turned up at Cambacérès' doorstep early one morning to plead his case. His arguments, or more likely the fervour with which he argued them, obviously impressed Cambacérès, for a short time later the order was rescinded.[67] In the meantime, Buonaparte renewed his attempts to get assigned to the Turkish army. It may simply have been a contingency plan, but it was like Buonaparte to have more than one option available to him. Eventually, the Committee of Public Safety gave way and issued a decree allowing him to undertake service in Constantinople. He was even allowed to designate the officers who could accompany him: he chose Nicolas-Marie Songis and Marmont, both artillery officers, and Junot and Jean-Baptiste Muiron, both of whom Buonaparte had met at Toulon.[68] The only reason, it seems, that he did not go in the end was because he asked that he and his officers should be paid three years' salary in advance, and also for an indemnity for the preparations of the expedition, models of the weapons needed, and a frigate to transport them. The Directory demurred, and so Buonaparte stayed. Eight days after being struck off the officers' lists, Buonaparte was given a chance to enter the national political arena.

8

The Political Appointee

General Vendémiaire

After six years of political unrest and two years of Jacobin Terror, the general election that was held in the autumn of 1795 witnessed a swing to the right; everyone associated with the Terror had been discredited in the eyes of the public. 'The government of the Convention,' wrote Marmont, 'having ceased being maintained by torture, had fallen into contempt and abjectness; all honest people ardently desired the [government's] fall and overthrow.'[1] This did not prevent former members of the Convention obstinately maintaining and perpetuating themselves in power. The men who had taken over the reins of power after the coup of Thermidor were an association of people with common interests, desperate men afraid for their lives, enemies of Robespierre for the most part, but who were just as cold-blooded and just as un-scrupulous.

About a year after Maximilien Robespierre's execution, these men introduced a new constitution (in August 1795) with a bicameral system: a lower house called the Council of Five Hundred, one third of whom were to be renewed every year; and an upper house called the Council of Elders, chosen from a list presented by the Five Hundred. There was also to be an executive council, called the Directory, made up of five men, one of whom would retire each year (chosen by lot). Rather than dissolve the Convention and call for elections, though, the deputies, knowing that they were unpopular, passed a decree stipulating that two-thirds of the members of the first new assembly to meet should be drawn from existing members of the Convention.[2] The 'law of two-thirds', as it became known, produced a 'terrible sensation' in public opinion, and was perhaps *the* decree that most alienated the Convention from 'honest people'.[3] Shortly after its introduction, on 24 September, groups of young men noisily demonstrated in the streets of Paris to cries of 'Down with the two-thirds'. At the Palais Royal, partisans and opponents of the decree came to blows: shots were fired at grenadiers doing their rounds, patrols were insulted, seditious shouts of 'Long live the king' and 'Down with the Convention' were heard.[4]

Despite the alarming situation, the Convention remained unprepared. 'What was most real and worse in our situation,' wrote Paul Barras, the former representative-on-mission at Toulon, 'was to be in the most complete disorder on every account, not to know what we were doing, and hardly to know what we wanted.'[5] On the morning of 4 October, the section Le Peletier, which had helped defend the Tuileries on 10 August, and was now the centre of the royalist agitation, took hold of the popular movement. Of the forty-eight sections in Paris, thirty-two mobilized. Around midday, they were in open revolt against the government, although, generally speaking, only the sections in the centre of Paris were bent on overthrowing the Convention. These were more prosperous than most of the sections, so the insurrection was bourgeois (and royalist) in nature, undoubtedly aggravated by economic concerns.[6]

A little before sunset, the rebels marched on the Tuileries, where the Convention was sitting. The commander of the Army of the Interior, General Menou, who is generally accused of lacking decisiveness during this crisis, went to meet them. Menou did not want to fire on citizens reclaiming free elections; he was a former royalist who sympathized with the rebels, and felt reluctant to let the band of volunteers he commanded loose on the city. Instead of giving the order to open fire, Menou negotiated with the rebels, persuading them to halt their march. He was probably acting with the implicit approval of those members of the Convention who also wanted to see free elections. In any event, the rebels were happy enough to bivouac overnight where they had stopped. They thus occupied the Palais Royal, the place Vendôme, the rue de la Loi, and the rue Saint-Honoré, not far from the Tuileries. They were also posted in the Church of Saint-Roch, which became the 'principal citadel of the insurgents'.[7]

Menou was consequently relieved of his command and Barras took over the defence of the Convention. Barras, a tall, dark, debauched, distinguished looking man, who had a 'tireless capacity for intrigue',[8] may have exaggerated the danger the government faced in order to enhance the victory that followed, but it was clear that the Convention was faced with a difficult situation. The forces lined up on the side of the Convention were not numerous – 5-6,000 men who slept on the ground in the courtyards and gardens of the Tuileries Palace. They had neither artillery nor munitions, while supplies were dispersed throughout Paris. Barras was officially invested with the command of these forces at four in the morning but, even before the hour of midnight had struck, he knew that his nomination was certain and had already acted decisively by recruiting people, choosing collaborators and organizing the defence of the government. Barras was a military professional, having served in the Indies before the Revolution. Officers who only a few weeks before had been discharged were now recalled. Only some of them answered the call – including Brune, Carteaux and Buonaparte – almost all of whom were without commands. They seized the opportunity to find a place in the army once again (all of them afterwards received commissions).[9] During the evening of 3 October, while Buonaparte was at the Théâtre Feydeau, he heard news of Menou's dismissal and immediately went to the Committee of Public Safety to find out what measures were being taken. It is there that Barras, asking for someone to take charge of the artillery (under his direction), had Buonaparte pointed out to him.[10]

Some contemporaries suggested that Buonaparte hesitated between the monarchists in revolt and the corrupt republicans in power, and that he was supposedly quite prepared to consider joining the monarchists, if the revolt started well; he only changed his mind when Barras gave him permission to requisition the artillery.[11] There is nothing to substantiate these rumours. On the other hand, one can discount almost entirely Napoleon's version of events recounted many years later on St Helena, where he portrays himself as hesitating, concerned that he might later be made a scapegoat, before coming up with the idea of demanding that Barras be made general-in-chief.[12] This is a complete misrepresentation of the facts. It is even unlikely that Buonaparte was made second-in-command.[13]

What we know is that around two or half past two in the morning, orders were given, probably by Buonaparte, to an officer by the name of Joachim Murat, to fetch cannon from the camp at Sablons, about ten kilometres away.[14] The cannon did not arrive in Paris until about six in the morning, at about the same time as the defenders of the Tuileries were still getting organized. Seven hundred muskets were distributed among the deputies, determined this time to fight it out. Some of them would have witnessed the mob storm the Assembly on previous occasions, often with dire consequences. Surrounded by superior forces, they waited. During this time, Barras looked after troop movements while Buonaparte was preoccupied with the placement of the cannon so as to prevent the insurgents from gaining access to the Tuileries.[15]

Around four in the afternoon, cannon fire was heard around the Church of Saint-Roch, where rebels were fighting with the troops who had remained loyal to the government. At one point in this fighting, according to tradition, Buonaparte gave the order to fire grapeshot from two eight-pounders into the mob in front of the church causing, so it is said, hundreds of deaths. By the end of the day's fighting there were as many as four hundred dead lying in the church itself, with another thousand or so bodies strewn around the streets outside.[16]

Did Buonaparte give the order to fire on the crowd?[17] It is highly unlikely. The only historian to have studied this episode at any length believes that Buonaparte was not involved in the shooting in front of the church. He also suggests that the cannonade did not and could not have taken place, given the topography of the streets, still much as they were two hundred years ago, and the difficulty (if not impossibility), of placing two

Artist unknown, *Journée du 13 vendémiaire an 4* (*Journée* of 5 September 1975), between 1795 and 1799. (*Bibliothèque nationale, Paris*)

eight-pounders in the street leading up to the church.[18] Certainly, the legend that grew up around Napoleon made much of this episode, exploited to an extent by contemporary prints and engravings of the scene. By the end of the Empire it was commonly accepted that Buonaparte did indeed fire on the crowds on the steps of the church.[19]

Whatever Buonaparte's role, the 'combat' was only one element in the events that took place that day. Wherever the rebels rushed headlong into the barricades erected to prevent their passage, they were unable to get past and soon became discouraged, a sentiment that was aggravated by the heavy rain that had fallen most of the day. Gradually they withdrew and went home. By six in the evening the firing had stopped, and by nine everyone had left. At two o'clock the next morning, Buonaparte wrote to Giuseppe:

> At last, everything is over; my first impulse is to think of giving you news of me. The royalists, formed by sections, were becoming daily more proud. The Convention ordered the disarming of the Le Peletier section, they beat off the troops. Menou, in command, it was said, was a traitor; he was immediately dismissed. The Convention named Barras commander of the armed forces: the

Committees named me second in command. We placed our troops; the enemy came to attack us at the Tuileries. We killed a lot of their people; they killed thirty men and wounded sixty. We have disarmed the sections and everything is calm.[20]

The letter ended with the singular phrase, 'As usual, I am not wounded.' Was he simply reassuring his family or was it the beginnings of a narcissism that would develop disproportionately as his power increased?

The repression that followed was mild, although Buonaparte's role in it remains obscure.[21] Barras was responsible for this. As victor, he did not press home his advantage. The force of the insurrection allowed him to measure the state of mind of the people. He did not want to be held at the mercy of extremists and to cut himself off from the moderate elements. Five days later, Barras went to the Convention in order to give an account of the insurrection, possibly using Buonaparte's report as the basis of his observations. In doing so, he presented several officers who were roundly applauded by the Convention, but not Buonaparte.[22]

Fréron – who had been taken with Carlotta-Maria (Pauline) and was even thinking of marrying her – stood up and declared that the Assembly should not forget General Buonaparte, who had been named during the night of 12 Vendémiaire* to replace Menou and who 'only had the morning in which to prepare himself' and to take the dispositions he took to protect the Republic.[23] Buonaparte might otherwise have been forgotten altogether. (Merlin de Douai, for example, who wrote a report on 14 Vendémiaire, does not mention Buonaparte at all.[24]) Not to be outdone, Barras stood up and declared that it was Buonaparte who had taken the necessary

* In October 1793, a new revolutionary calendar was introduced to replace the Christian calendar. The new calendar was dated from 22 September 1792, when the Republic was proclaimed. Thus the period from 22 September 1792 to 21 September 1793 became Year I of the Republic. The year was divided into twelve months of thirty days, with five supplementary days (called *sans-culottides*). Each month was divided into three periods of ten days, every tenth day (*decadi*) being a day of rest. Another decree gave each month a name appropriate to its season. Thus Vendémiaire (the month of vintage) ran from 22 September to 21 October, Floréal (the month of flowers) from 20 April to 19 May, Brumaire (the month of mist) from 22 October to 20 November, and so on. The new calendar ignored Sundays and Church festivals.

dispositions to defend the precinct near the Church of Saint-Roch and to place the men in their positions with a great deal of skill.[25] He then recommended that Buonaparte be named second-in-command of the Army of the Interior.

It was only fitting. Buonaparte represented the army, to which the Convention owed its continued existence. Until that time, it had been a revolutionary tradition to keep the army out of political struggles inside Paris. After Vendémiaire this was to change. Between 9 and 13 October, six battalions were brought into Paris. More troops were brought in by 25 October. The organization of this force was given to Buonaparte. In other words, Paris was occupied militarily, and the soldiers conducted themselves as if they were in a foreign city, assembling in the evening in streets near the Palais Royal, stopping passing women and treating them all like 'common prostitutes', taking their jewellery (on one occasion by simply tearing it off a woman's ears), breaking into private houses and stealing, drinking in cafés without paying, and generally threatening that if people 'did not toe the line, Paris would be put to fire and sword'.[26] Although Buonaparte was nominally in command, as with the Easter Sunday fiasco in Corsica, he does not appear to have had much control over the troops, at least not at first. But the population generally suffered this kind of behaviour wherever troops found themselves, and it was an indication of the increasing gulf between the army and the people of France.

As a reward for his role in suppressing the coup, Barras received a place in the newly formed Directory. Since he could not be a Director and head of the Army of the Interior at the same time, he handed in his resignation. He chose his second-in-command to replace him, probably because he thought Buonaparte was someone he could control. On 16 October, Buonaparte was promoted general of division. Ten days later, he was named commander-in-chief of the Army of the Interior. It was probably the most influential military position in the country, as the Army of the Interior was by far the largest in France. Overnight Buonaparte had become a figure to be reckoned with. And for what? For having fired, perhaps, a couple of cannon shot at a mob in front of a church? It is little wonder that he was known to the public as General Vendémiaire.

'Seizing the Moon with His Teeth'

There was no longer any question of Buonaparte going about in badly polished boots. Almost as soon as he was made second in command, Barras boasted that he gave Buonaparte the means by which he could buy the necessary materials to have new clothes made. One administrator recounted cheerfully, 'the Little Corsican has generously used the stores of the Republic.'[27]

If this were the case,[28] Buonaparte also spared a thought for his family. He sent his mother a significant sum of money – fifty to sixty thousand francs in coin and paper money (the *assignat*) so that she would want for nothing;* he wrote letter after letter of recommendation for his brother Giuseppe and, in December 1795, confided the incredible sum of 400,000 francs in him, making his family extremely well off (although we do not know where he got it from);[29] the ten-year-old Gerolamo was placed in an expensive college; and he attempted to find a place for Luciano as commissary for war in the Army of the North. Luciano was a difficult case. He had barely turned twenty-one, but he had an enormous political appetite unhindered by conscience or desire for hard work. Less than six months later, tired of his posting, he simply left for Paris without authorization. Luigi was completely different. Buonaparte got him nominated as lieutenant in his old regiment and, when he was promoted commander of the Army of the Interior, had him named as one of his own aides-de-camp. Luigi followed his brother everywhere: he was his table-companion, his secretary, his confidant, and enjoyed the fatherliness that his relationship seemed to bring out in Buonaparte.[30] Buonaparte's principal preoccupation during this period remained to serve his family, refusing nothing that was asked of him, and obtaining places for relatives like Ramolino or Arrighi, or his uncle, the Abbé Fesch, who was taken on first as secretary and then made commissary of war. In short, he really cared for his family, even though the sentiment was not always reciprocated.

Buonaparte now went about in a carriage and took up residence in a hotel looking out over the Place Vendôme which had belonged

---

* The livre was replaced by the franc in 1795.

to the Marquis de Créqui. It was there that he established his headquarters. He was, initially at least, viewed with suspicion by his staff, who had never seen a political animal as strange as this one. He also had to overcome the perception that he had come so far because Barras thought him a fool who was easy to manipulate. On this occasion, as on others, Buonaparte adapted, changing his outward behaviour to suit the circumstances. According to Marmont, who had been in Germany and was recalled by Buonaparte as one of his aides-de-camp, the man he met on his return to Paris was very different from the one he had left. 'He already had an extraordinary aplomb,' he wrote, 'an air of grandeur that was completely new to me, and the feeling of his importance that must have been growing continually.'[31]

Buonaparte set to work with his now customary zeal. The Army of the Interior was mainly occupied with the maintenance of law and order throughout France, counter-insurgency, and the enforcement of the draft. Buonaparte devised a series of regulations for the conduct of his new command. He insisted on being able to inform the Directory at any time of the situation in the capital. He also had direct access to the government's ministers.[32] One of his first measures was to reform the police.[33] He purged a number of army corps of royalists (those who had been named by Aubry, for example), and introduced other measures against royalists in Paris between the end of October and November. The Right was not the only faction to suffer. The Jacobin club in Paris was closed down, admittedly on the order of Barras, but it was Buonaparte who carried out the order (26 February 1796). There is no indication that Buonaparte baulked at persecuting those he had formerly considered his ideological brothers-in-arms, an indication that he had turned his back on the Jacobins in much the same manner as he had turned his back on Corsica and Paoli.

A less driven man would have been content with this important command, but his mind was on Italy, where Schérer's offensive had come to a halt. Undoubtedly, up until then Buonaparte's ambition was driven, in part, by material necessity. This had also been the case for Buonaparte's father, and one can see this pattern repeated once the family arrives in France after 1793. That is, everything the sons did, the political and social contacts they made and the positions they aspired to, was driven by the need to establish the family in its new homeland, and, in some respects, mirror the father's attempts to secure a prominent position in Corsica. But Buonaparte's ambition, perhaps driven by a need to gain the respect of others, and his willingness to risk everything for a military command that may very well have been beyond his talents, runs deeper. If his ambition was not appeased by the position of commander of the Army of the Interior – he was a political appointee, and everyone knew it – it was because he had yet to prove himself in the field. This is why he was so keen to obtain command of the army fighting in Italy, the region he was most familiar with.

The means by which he persuaded the Directory to give him command of an army is straightforward enough. Shortly after Vendémiaire, but before becoming commander of the Army of the Interior, Buonaparte had sent off a memorandum about matters along the Ligurian coast, and criticized Schérer for his incompetence. 'They [Schérer and his staff] have committed a grave mistake', began Buonaparte's 'Note on the direction that should be given to the Army of Italy', 'in not forcing the entrenched position at Ceva while the defeated Austrians were reeling back towards Acqui . . . The capture of Ceva and the concentration of our Army around that fortress are of such importance that they can induce the Court of Turin to make peace, and considerably reduce the enormous expenses that the Army of Italy costs the public treasury.'[34] He was suggesting to a cash-strapped Directory that a successful campaign would not be a burden on the treasury. In a second note dated 19 January 1796, Buonaparte insisted on the urgency of the moment. 'If the Army of Italy spends the month of February without doing anything, just as it has spent the month of January, the Italian campaign will be entirely lost. It must be understood that great success in Italy can only be gained during the winter. If one assumes that the Army of Italy gets underway at the earliest possible moment, it can march on Ceva, and storm the entrenched camp there before the Austrians, who are at Acqui, can join up with the Piedmontese.'[35] The Directory thought, however, that Schérer should carry out Buonaparte's plans. It was his refusal to do so that made the Directory think twice about Schérer's value as a general.

The reaction from those on the ground in Italy to the stream of plans and suggestions emanating from Paris was predictable, the more so since they knew who the plans were coming from – a general with Jacobin leanings who was also a political appointee. Indeed, one of the representatives-on-mission attached to Schérer, François-Joseph Ritter, became so frustrated with the orders from Paris that he wrote to one of the directors, Louis François Honoré Letourneur, complaining of the interference. 'I have said to you before that eternal project-mongers surround the government. I do not wish to name these individuals gnawed by ambition and greedy for posts above their abilities. You have judged them at the time and on the spot. Why then do you not oppose their chimerical and gigantic plans? Will you suffer the Army of Italy, commendable by its patience and its victories, to go to its destruction because some madmen show you on a map of a country, of which no accurate maps exists, that they can seize the moon with their teeth?'[36] Schérer attempted to circumvent the interference from Paris by proposing less ambitious projects of his own, and by asking for massive reinforcements. If they were not forthcoming, he wrote time and again, he asked to be relieved of his command. 'I beseech you, I implore you,' he wrote to the Directory, 'to send here a general of more resource and skill than I have, for I admit that I am incapable in the present conditions of sustaining the burden of command . . . I now request you as a special favour to send me a successor. My health is impaired by the fatigues of the body and the pains of the spirit and my moral and physical means are far below the task that you require of me.'[37]

After Buonaparte's ally, and now one of Barras' creatures, Saliceti, arrived in Nice to have talks with Schérer, he reported back to the minister of war, Lazare Carnot, that the situation in which the army found itself was 'distressing. Everything is lacking and especially transport. No preparations have been made to enter on campaign. Ritter and the general in chief do not appear prepared, in the actual state of affairs, to act. They say that they cannot march because they need mules and supplies, either in fodder for the transport and the cavalry, or medical supplies.'[38] Saliceti went on to say that it would certainly be better to have these things, but that, in their absence, 'would it not be more useful and more correct to procure them from the enemy, to attack in providing for the needs of the moment?' The enthusiasm of both Buonaparte and Saliceti for the projected campaign in Italy was in marked contrast to Schérer and Ritter, who had proven themselves incapable of obtaining the necessary provisions to launch a new offensive. So the Directory, tired of Schérer's complaining, and perhaps worn down by Buonaparte's continual badgering, finally accepted Schérer's resignation. On the same day (2 March), Buonaparte was appointed to fill the vacancy. Rumour of his appointment was reported as early as 27 February.[39] Certainly, Buonaparte must have known about his appointment well in advance; a few days previously he had written to the minister of war giving orders concerning the disposition of the Army of Italy.[40]

It was Carnot who insisted on making Buonaparte commander-in-chief of the Army of Italy.[41] He knew that Buonaparte's experience was extremely limited, but the two or three military operations in which he had participated – the suppression of the revolt at Toulon, the short campaign in Italy in the autumn of 1794, and the suppression of the royalist insurrection in Paris – had proved, at least, that he was a capable officer. Besides, his republican convictions were unquestionable. In some respects, his obscurity worked to his advantage; Barras was the first to assure everyone that Buonaparte's interests were limited to military matters and that he did not have a head for politics. In the final analysis, however, the Directors as a whole had to make the decision. Carnot, one of the most able of the Directors, had already noticed the plans drawn up by Buonaparte and agreed with Barras. Moreover, Carnot had fallen under the persuasive charms of Buonaparte, whom he liked to call in private 'his little captain'.[42] La Révellière-Lépeaux almost always sided with Barras. The two other Directors were at first reluctant, because they had hoped to place their own men into positions of importance: Letourneur, perhaps the least important of the directors, was a partisan of General Bernadotte; and Jean-François Reubell proposed General Championnet, who had been with the Army of the Sambre-et-Meuse, as a replacement for Schérer. Barras, however, dominated the proceedings and the Directory by his character and his 'moral' authority. The decision to appoint Buonaparte was, therefore, a unanimous one, but in name only. It is also evident from this that, in spite of Schérer's relatively good military reputation, he lacked any kind of political support within the Directory.[43]

The news reached the public immediately and was greeted with stupefaction, at least among the political elite, for whom the appointment bordered on the scandalous.[44] To confide a command of that importance in a young man of twenty-six who had only played a minor role to date, who had not won his promotion on the field of battle, and who was, therefore, without authority and without prestige in the eyes of the army, was considered madness. In reality, Buonaparte was not even experienced at manoeuvring a regiment, let alone an entire army. Many were indignant at what appeared characteristic of the courts of the absolute monarchs – a promotion based on patronage rather than merit. In a now well-known protest written a few days after the publication of the decree nominating Buonaparte, the minister of foreign affairs, Dupont de Nemours, wrote to Reubell, who had been opposed to Buonaparte's appointment:

> They say that you have given the Army of Italy, our last hope, to two Corsicans, Buonaparte and Saliceti, at least one of which is the creature and friend of Paoli. I can hardly believe that you have made this mistake . . . Don't you know what Corsicans are like? For the last two thousand years, no one has ever been able to count on them. They are *volatile* by nature. They're all out to make their fortunes! . . . Those people must always be held in subordinate [positions], even when they have talent and appear like they are honest people.[45]

Buonaparte's promotion to the command of the Army of Italy was not entirely a political appointment. Carnot initially wanted the Army of Italy to attack the Milanese, with a secondary drive against Acqui, largely in order to avoid giving any offence to the rulers of Piedmont. However, Buonaparte would not tolerate any political interference; he had to have complete control or he would simply not go. He was also adamant that the key to success in Italy lay in defeating Piedmont. He, therefore, bullied the Directory into changing his instructions so that the Army of

Italy was directed to take Ceva first, and then to push towards the Milanese.[46] Buonaparte had won his first political skirmish, but many more were to follow.

'A Proud Cajoler'

It was during these momentous weeks in Paris that he met the Vicomtesse de Beauharnais.

Josephine had been born Marie-Josephe-Rose de Tascher de la Pagerie on the island of Martinique. She signed her name Marie-Rose, and was known affectionately to her family as Yeyette. It was only at the insistence of Buonaparte that she came to use the name Josephine. Her first marriage, to Alexandre de Beauharnais, had been arranged. She was sixteen and he was eighteen and, two years later, she gave birth to first a son, Eugène, who was later to become viceroy of Italy, and then a daughter, Hortense, who was later to marry Buonaparte's brother, Louis. Alexandre, however, soon tired of his young wife. Not only was he a philanderer, he was not much of a gentleman either in a time when that mattered. He ended up treating her abominably, trying to blacken her reputation by constructing a sordid past that she had never had. A settlement was eventually arranged that gave her a pension and her daughter, and access to her son over the summer. Despite the separation, connection with the name Beauharnais was enough to implicate her during the height of the Terror. Not that Alexandre was anti-revolutionary. Like so many nobles he embraced the Revolution in its early years and even profited by it; he was elected deputy to the First Estate of the Estates-General in 1789, and he eventually rose to become president of the National Assembly in June 1791 at one of the most critical periods in the history of the Revolution – when the king and his family attempted to flee Paris. Alexandre was also a member of the Jacobin club, where he made a bit of a reputation as an orator. He even served for a time, in 1791, as its president, but that was really the climax of his political career. Although he was re-elected president of the National Assembly, a self-denying law prevented deputies from standing again for the new Legislative Assembly. As he was a soldier by profession, he decided to return to active life, but the man who had made an impression on the political landscape of revolutionary Paris, albeit a small one, proved to be less than inspiring as a soldier. Given command of the Army of the Rhine in May 1793, he failed in his attempt to relieve Mainz (it fell to the Prussians at the end of July), and resigned in August of the same year. Even so, he gave evidence of an ambition that was hardly to be suspected in the days of the *ancien régime*. It was perhaps because of his failings as a commander, or more likely simply because he was an aristocrat, that he was denounced and arrested as a 'suspect' in March 1794. Josephine was incarcerated soon after, probably for no other reason than that she too was an aristocrat and married to a 'suspect'. They were both incarcerated in the vermin-infested Carmelite prison, rue Vaugirard, the scene of some of the worst atrocities committed during the September massacres of 1792.

Josephine did not hold up terribly well in this environment; she wept a great deal and was so low-spirited that it made her companions uncomfortable.[47] Despite efforts to save Alexandre, and despite a solid dossier attesting to his revolutionary credentials, he appeared before the Revolutionary Tribunal on 23 July 1794, five days before the death of Robespierre, and was guillotined the next day along with forty-eight other people in what is now the Place de la Nation. Josephine survived. Legend has it that she escaped from the guillotine when an obscure clerk, by the name of Delperch de la Bussière, employed by the Committee of Public Safety, made her file disappear by eating the papers.[48] It is a wonderful story, captured of by Abel Gance in a scene in his silent film, *Napoleon*, but it is probably fictional even though de la Bussière certainly existed. Josephine later gave him a thousand francs 'in grateful remembrance', which indicates that there was some sort of connection between the two.

A more likely explanation for Josephine's survival is that the Terror abruptly came to an end with the death of Robespierre on 28 July 1794, only a few days after the execution of Beauharnais, and that the doors of the prisons were thrown open. Once she had gained her liberty, an aristocratic lady who found herself penniless and husbandless, she sought the protection of powerful men. Josephine soon earned a reputation, along with Mme Tallien and Mme Talma, of being a libertine. She used her charms to accumulate a number of lovers which included, among others, the Duc de Lorge, the Comte de Crenay, the Chevalier de Coigny, General Lazare Hoche, the Marquis de Caulaincourt (whose son we shall come across later) and, finally, Barras, who described her ungraciously – and hypocritically given his notorious lack of moral scruples – as the 'lustful Creole' who only loved 'out of interest'.[49] The extent to which she had become a prominent member of what some may have considered to be Paris' decadent society can be seen in the fact that she was made the protagonist in an unpublished pamphlet, *Zoloé et ses deux acolytes* (Zoloé and her Two Acolytes), that may have been written by the Marquis de Sade. In it one can find a description of the protagonist. 'Along with all that is seductive and captivating she enjoys an ardour for pleasure a hundred times greater than Laureda's, a usurer's avidity for money, which she squanders with the alacrity of a gambler, and a dizzying love of luxury grand enough to swallow up the revenue of ten provinces.'[50]

Legend has it that the first meeting between Bonaparte and Josephine came a few days after the government ordered all unauthorized weapons in the Paris sections Le Peletier and the Théâtre Français to be surrendered to the authorities. When a commissary visited the Beauharnais household to enforce the rule, Josephine's son, Eugène, protested at having to surrender the sword of his father, once a general in the armies of the Republic. To keep it, he was told to seek permission from the commanding general in Paris. In this way Buonaparte received a visit from a solemn fourteen-year-old asking, as a matter of honour, to retain his father's sword. Apparently moved by the request, Buonaparte agreed. He brought the authorization himself the next day to the Beauharnais household, where he is said to have met Josephine for the first time.

This, at least, is Eugène's own account, repeated often enough by others, but it is probably a fabrication.[51] Josephine's house was not even in the sections that were being disarmed.[52] In fact, we do not know how or when Buonaparte and Josephine met. The financier, Gabriel Ouvrard, suggests that it was in the salon of Mme Tallien, but it is also possible that it was at the house of Barras, which Buonaparte visited frequently.[53] Despite, or more possibly because of, the fact that Josephine was older (thirty-three compared to Buonaparte's twenty-six years), Buonaparte was impressed. He was drawn to her because of her sophistication and her experience – 'She was a real woman,' as Napoleon later put it, and 'she had the prettiest little backside possible.'[54] He went from a submissive Désirée, whom he had accused of indifference and on whom he had projected many of his own feelings, to a very self-assured woman of the world.

Within two weeks of their first meeting, Buonaparte had been promoted to commander-in-chief of the Army of the Interior and it was probably about this time that he became a more attractive prospect and Josephine started to pay him more attention. With all his new duties, however, the liaison might have lapsed before it had really even started. It was at this point that she kept his interest alive by writing to him on 28 October: 'You no longer come to see a friend who is fond of you. You have completely deserted her. You are wrong, for she is affectionately attached to you. Come tomorrow to lunch with me. I need to see you, and to talk with you about your affairs.'[55] Probably on the same day, Buonaparte replied: 'I cannot imagine what has been the cause of your letter, and I beg you to allow me the pleasure of believing that no one desires your friendship as much as I do, or is as ready to do what it takes to prove it.'[56]

This was the beginning of what was to become an ardent, if rather lopsided, love affair. Sometime in December, Buonaparte spent the night, his first, with her. As soon as he returned home in the early hours of the morning, he hurriedly wrote off the following note: 'I awake full of you. Your portrait and the memory of the intoxicating evening of yesterday leave my senses no rest. Sweet and incomparable Josephine, what strange power you have over my heart!'[57] It is testimony to the depth of his passion. The affair was his first serious involvement, and he experienced it with the 'full energy of his nature', undoubtedly flattered that Josephine paid him any attention at all.[58]

Paris after the fall of Robespierre had seen a return of the Salon and the role of women in political life.[59] Of the three women who dominated Parisian society during this period – Thérésa Tallien, Juliette Récamier and Josephine – 'Josephine may not have been the most beautiful,' wrote her friend,

Antoine Arnault, 'but she was without contradiction the most attractive: the regularity of her moods, the simplicity of her character, the kindness that animated her look . . . but also her accent: [there was] a certain natural indolence to Creoles which came through in her attitudes and in the way she moved.'[60] 'She was still charming during this period,' wrote the sometimes venomous Duchesse d'Abrantès. 'Her teeth were frightfully bad, but when her mouth was shut she had the appearance, especially at a few paces distant, of a young and pretty woman.'[61] Others have noted that little detail, which seemed to spoil her overall appearance for contemporaries. A friend of Josephine's, Antoine Hamelin, remarked that when she laughed she made sure to cover her mouth with a handkerchief. Luciano was probably right when he described her as 'not at all what one could call beautiful', but there was something about her that seemed to appeal to almost every man who met her.[62] Barras thinks that Buonaparte only approached people he thought might have some influence, such as Thérésa Tallien, for whom he had earlier declared his 'insurmountable passion'. Thérésa was considered to be one of the most beautiful women in Paris – 'No human being had been made out so beautiful by the hands of the Creator', according to the Marquise de la Tour du Pin – so it is not surprising that, according to Barras at least, she rejected Buonaparte with the scornful remark that 'she believed she could do better than him'. It was only after the rebuff that that he turned his attentions to Josephine, perhaps even under the mistaken impression that she was well off.[63]

After six months of courting, Buonaparte asked for Josephine's hand in marriage. What, one wonders, did two so very different people see in each other? The fact that they were both from the geographical and social margins of French society may have brought them closer together, but this did not prevent Josephine from hesitating before agreeing to marry General Vendémiaire, as she called him; she supposedly had to choose between Buonaparte, Hoche and Caulaincourt, all of whom were courting her.[64] Arguably, she accepted because she was no longer considered young, and thought that Buonaparte could offer her material security; he was on the ascendant. For women in the eighteenth century, marriage and dependency on a man were often seen as the path to happiness.[65] The idea that one would marry for love was not all that common in the nobility and does not, in any event, seem to have influenced Josephine's decision.[66] There is even a hint that Josephine suspected Buonaparte of using her to advance his career, or perhaps she had heard talk that Buonaparte thought she was rich and well-connected. 'So you think that I do not love you for you alone,' he wrote to her in a reproachful tone some time before their marriage. 'Ah, Madame, I would have had to have greatly changed!'[67] Buonaparte had, in the meantime, written to Désirée with an ultimatum: if she did not obtain the consent of her mother and her brother to marry him, it would be preferable to 'break off all relations'.[68] He knew full well that the mother (the father had died in 1794) would never agree to have another Buonaparte in the family.

It was not the first time Buonaparte had proposed to a woman. If the Duchesse d'Abrantès is to be believed, he had asked her recently widowed mother, Mme Permon, fourteen years his senior, to marry him.[69] She turned him down. He had also made overtures to a certain Mme de la Boucharderie, about whom we know very little, other than that she was also much older. We have already seen, though, that he was engaged to Désirée, just a girl, and how this did not prevent him from considering marriage with the fifteen-year-old daughter of the Comte de Laurenti, Emilie. Even before that, when Buonaparte was in Auxonne, he had courted Manesca Pillet, the richest heiress in town, and asked for her hand in marriage. Was he more interested in a large dowry than love? The fact that he was asking women of all ages to marry him means that the age difference between Josephine and Buonaparte is of no great significance. What Buonaparte's behaviour does show, however, is that he was lonely, emotionally immature – six proposals, including Josephine, in as many years – that he became infatuated rather quickly, that he perhaps did not take the proposals, or the women in question, as much to heart as he ought to have (since their rejections did not deter him from trying again), and that he was not sensible enough to think of the consequences of his actions, nor of what the object of his desire may have thought of him. Moreover, the choice of Josephine, a frivolous spendthrift who had had a number of lovers, was bound to displease Buonaparte's mother, Letizia.[70] It says a great deal about the son's relationship with the mother.

On 9 March 1796, Buonaparte and Josephine were married at the town hall of the second arrondissement (the building can be found at 3 rue d'Antin). He turned up two hours late for the wedding ceremony on the pretext that he had been absorbed in his work. Given his avowed feelings for Josephine, this is hardly credible. Even though he was preoccupied with preparations for his forth-coming campaign in Italy, his tardiness could be seen as a form of aggression, a sign of the egotism that dominated his relations with other people, even those he supposedly loved. It is commonly stated that Charles Leclercq conducted the ceremony: his name is on the certificate but, in fact, he got tired of waiting and left.[71] The ceremony was eventually held in the light of one flickering candle, and carried out by one Antoine Collin-Lacombe, a minor official with a wooden leg, at about ten in the evening. Jean Tallien, a former member of the Committee of Public Safety, and Barras were witnesses. Buonaparte's wedding gift to her was a gold and enamel medallion with the inscription 'To destiny'. On the marriage certificate, Josephine made herself a few years younger, while Buonaparte made himself a few years older.

Buonaparte kept the marriage a secret from his family, initially at least. In fact, he made sure that none of them was in Paris when it took place – Luciano was with the Army of the North, and Luigi was sent to Châtillon on the pretext of taking horses to the Army of Italy. This was not the first time that a Buonaparte had married without consulting the family. In 1794, the wilful Luciano married Christine Boyer, an illiterate innkeeper's daughter two years older than he, causing a good deal of consternation in the family, but not as much as Buonaparte's decision. He did not inform his mother until he arrived in Marseilles on 20 March on his way to the Italian front. Désirée Clary was also in Marseilles, but they did not meet. She found out what had happened, however, and sent him a letter in which she spoke of her hurt:

> You have made me unhappy for the rest of my life, and I yet have the
> weakness to forgive you. So you are married . . . I shall never

accustom myself to this thought, it is destroying me. I cannot bear it. I will let you see that I am more faithful than you to our pledges, and even though you have broken the ties that once bound us, I shall never promise myself to another, I shall never marry.[72]

Time heals all. Two years later, after a brief engagement to a French general by the name of Duphot, who was killed in Rome, two days before their wedding – once again she was knocked senseless with grief – she married another young, ambitious general by the name of Bernadotte, who later became Marshal of France and eventually King of Sweden.

While he was in Marseilles, Buonaparte spent two days trying to reconcile his mother to the marriage. The negotiation which followed was difficult, the resistance on the part of the mother strong. Buonaparte urged her to write a letter to Josephine, which she did, nine days after Buonaparte left, and which may have been dictated by her son. Josephine represented the kind of woman who would have been completely unacceptable in Corsican society, not because she had already been married (although that was bad enough), but because it was known she had taken a number of lovers. Giuseppe was upset because his plans for Buonaparte's marriage with his sister-in-law, Désirée, came to nothing, a marriage that would have united their fortunes and their interests. For Luciano and Luigi, however, both of whom knew Josephine in Paris, their surprise was even greater; to them she was no more than an 'old woman', guilty of stealing their brother from the clan.[73] Their dislike was to turn into a vendetta in which every means used to discredit her was legitimate as long as the goal – to chase her from the family – was achieved. For her part, Josephine had no idea what kind of family she was marrying into.

THE CONQUERING HERO, 1796–1798

9

Innovation

First Impressions

Nine days after his appointment as commander-in-chief, and thirty-six hours after marrying Josephine, Buonaparte was in a carriage speeding south for the Italian border. 'You are the constant object of my thoughts,' he wrote to Josephine only a few days into his journey, 'my mind is exhausted imagining what you are doing. If I see you sad, my heart is torn and my pain increases. If you are gay and playing with your friends, I reproach you for having soon forgotten the painful separation of three days ago.'[1] He wrote from his headquarters in Nice: 'Not one day has gone by without my loving you, without holding you in my arms,' signing the more French sounding 'Bonaparte'. 'Not one cup of tea have I taken without cursing the glory and the ambition that keeps me away from the soul of my life . . . If I leave you with the rapidity of the torrent of the Rhône, it is to see you all the more quickly. If I get up in the middle of the night to continue work, it is because it could advance by a few days the arrival of my sweet friend.'[2] If Bonaparte performed so brilliantly during this, his first campaign, it was largely because he was attempting to prove himself to Josephine. He admitted as much himself shortly after signing an armistice with Piedmont-Sardinia: 'It will be a happy day when you cross the Alps: it will be the greatest reward for my efforts and the victories I have won.'[3] Love sharpened and focused Bonaparte's physical and intellectual abilities; it channelled his energies so that he did everything in his power to guarantee victory.

However, no one could have foreseen what was to come: nothing in Bonaparte's life so far prepares us for his achievements in Italy. He had never commanded a division in battle before, let alone an army. Even *he* probably had no idea what he was capable of. Neither his personal choices, his erratic political career, his writings, nor certainly his military career had been in any way particularly outstanding, or even original. True, he had drawn up plans in the Bureau Topographique that had impressed his superiors, and he had studied maps of Italy for the last three years, undoubtedly fantasizing about what might have been available to him in different circumstances. He had also visited Italy twice and had inspected the terrain in the region where he was to fight his first battles. Indeed, he had read accounts of previous campaigns and everything else on Italy he could lay his hands on (in fact, most of his military ideas came from books, and not battlefield experience).[4] But a good tactician does not necessarily make for a great general.

Historians have examined Bonaparte's military education for clues to the 'brilliance' behind the campaign. They have dissected his every move, analyzing his defeat of an army with means that had frustrated more experienced generals before him. There is no doubt that, even though the diplomatic outcomes of the campaign were questionable, the military outcomes were entirely successful: the campaign was conducted with extraordinary energy and panache. However, historians have perhaps too easily accepted the version of the military campaign presented by Bonaparte himself. The Italian campaign was also a political campaign, a propaganda campaign (although the word was never used by contemporaries), designed to make it appear as though everything that happened did so according to a plan laid out by Bonaparte. It is this political campaign that shaped both the legend with which we are now familiar – the dynamic young general who triumphed against the odds – and the individual who became known to history as Napoleon. We see now that the whole time Bonaparte was fighting, he was also consciously cultivating an image from reports and dispatches he wrote himself from the field and sent to Paris. In these reports he enhanced his victories by exaggerating both the odds and the quality of the troops against which he fought. At the same time, he omitted any embarrassing setbacks that he or his generals had suffered by feeding the Directory inaccurate reports, and avoiding mention of any divisions in command during the more stressful periods of the campaign.[5] Moreover, the audience he cultivated was not in Italy, it was in France. Everything Bonaparte did in Italy, and, for that matter, years later in Egypt, thousands of kilometres away from Paris, was done in the hope of influencing public opinion in France.[6]

Rumours of Bonaparte's appointment reached the Army of Italy within a week. The reaction was predictable. Schérer's deputy chief of staff, Adjutant General Martin de Vignolle, wrote to Masséna: 'I think, if this news turns out to be true, that the government has committed a great stupidity. I think that Bonaparte has military talents,' Vignolle went on, 'but not enough, nor the experience to be commander-in-chief of the army.'[7] Louis Suchet, who was later to become a marshal under Napoleon, was of the same opinion. 'This Corsican has no other reputation than that of a good gun commander. As a general he is only known by the Parisians. This intriguer is supported by nothing.'[8] If the politicians and the public in Paris did not think much of his appointment, one could hardly expect the men he was to command to think any differently. First impressions were not good. When a sergeant by the name of Vigo-Roussillon saw Bonaparte for the first time, he could scarcely believe he was the new commander-in-chief. 'His appearance, his dress, his behaviour did not appeal to us [*ne nous séduisirent pas*]. Here is how he seemed to me then: small, skinny, very pale, with big black eyes in sunken cheeks, long hair falling from his temples to his shoulders forming, as they were called, "spaniel's ears". He was dressed in a blue coat, and wore over it a hazel coloured overcoat.'[9] General Landrieux, who admittedly never got on with Bonaparte in Italy, referred to him as that 'scarecrow of Toulon', and reported rumours that he had been given the command of the Army of Italy by Barras as a dowry for Josephine.[10] Others were similarly overcome by feelings of disappointment. Captain Jean-Baptiste Giraud, who did not lay eyes on Bonaparte until 27 April – well into the campaign – was unimpressed and referred to him as puny compared to generals such as Augereau, Masséna and Murat.[11] The troops were accustomed to being commanded by 'handsome men', he wrote, and, as their new general was not much to look at, some thought that he could not possibly possess any military abilities.[12]

Nor were Bonaparte's generals, all of whom had risen from the ranks, looking forward to engaging with the political upstart from Paris. On the day he formally took command of the army, on 27 March, Bonaparte summoned his commanders – André Masséna (one of the most talented commanders in the army), Jean-Mathieu Sérurier (who had lost most of his teeth from a musket shot), Amédée-Emmanuel de Laharpe (who was accidentally killed by his own men a few months later), and Pierre-François Augereau and Louis-Alexandre Berthier (both of whom would have long and successful careers by Bonaparte's side) – to a meeting at his headquarters at Nice. They all agreed, many years later, that he immediately imposed himself through his presence and his knowledge.[13] André Masséna, a sombre, reserved man who had served with Bonaparte at Toulon, recalled that he entered the room with a portrait of Josephine in his hand. A moment later, though, 'he put on his general's hat and seemed to have grown two feet. He questioned us on the position of our divisions, on their equipment, on the spirit and effective force of each corps, traced the course we were to follow, announced that the next day he would hold an inspection, and on the following day attack the enemy.' He apparently spoke to them with such dignity, precision and knowledge that they left convinced that at last they had a 'real captain'.[14] Pierre-François Augereau, a battle-hardened veteran whose language was as coarse as his manners, is supposed to have come away saying 'that the little bugger of a general scared him, and that he could not understand the ascendancy with which he felt overwhelmed from the outset'.[15] Auguste de Marmont, a brilliant young officer who had already known Bonaparte for a number of years, found in him 'an authority which he imposed on everybody'. Even though Bonaparte was awkward in his gait and posture, 'there was the master in his attitude, in his look, in his manner of speaking, and each of us, feeling it, was disposed to obey'.[16] Even the most cautious appraisal of such retrospective accounts cannot ignore the fact that so many agreed that Bonaparte made an immediate impression, though some, such as General Laharpe, still found time to complain about being commanded by a Corsican.[17]

An Army of Brigands

Bonaparte took over an army of about 63,000 men, of which only some 37,600 men were operational.[18] The rest were either on garrison duty or sick. The army was nevertheless experienced, composed of old soldiers of the line from the royal army, and volunteers from the Midi, the Cevennes, Languedoc, Dauphiné and Provence who had joined in 1792. They had been hardened to the difficulties of campaigning but were now in a bad state. The supply situation was indeed deplorable; morale was low; the troops were badly clothed and poorly fed, with no wine or tobacco, and they had not been paid in months.[19] A similar situation existed in the other revolutionary armies, but when General Berthier arrived at the end of 1795, he claimed that he had 'never seen such a ramshackle army'.[20] Even cleanliness became an effort under these conditions and some brigades simply stopped washing altogether.[21] The Venetian ambassador to Turin wrote in March that 'the continuous reports from the Riviera regarding the sad condition of the enemy army, its small number, and its lack of stores and provisions each day calm the fears originally felt by this court.'[22]

That situation had been considerably altered through the re-organization and re-equipment of the Army before Bonaparte's arrival, largely through the efforts of the commissary, Saliceti. Indeed, it could be argued that without Saliceti's efforts to refurbish the army, Bonaparte would not have been able to take the offensive as soon as he arrived.[23] Schérer had been determined not to go on campaign without all the necessary supplies and equipment, but Bonaparte knew that as long as he had alcohol for six days he would find whatever else he needed on the road.[24] A loan of seven million livres, extorted from the banks in Genoa, had been used to buy food, six hundred mules and four or five months' worth of wheat.[25] As a result, Masséna was able to pay his men and put shoes on their feet for the first time in months.[26] It was just as well; discontented troops were beginning to mutiny everywhere to shouts of 'Money or no soldiers'. Food and clothes seem to have appeased most of them, although two days before Bonaparte's arrival in Nice a battalion mutinied on the grounds they had no pay or shoes.[27] Bonaparte had inherited not so much an army as a gang of thugs who were forced to feed off the locals. Discipline was lacking and, as one of the commanders, Sérurier, complained, the officers were often as drunk as the soldiers.[28] The resentment these men left behind was so deeply felt among the people of the Midi that soldiers who returned on leave after hard-won victories in Italy were treated as 'Bonaparte's brigands', attacked and sometimes killed.[29]

On 31 March, a couple of days before the Army was to leave France and march into Italy, Bonaparte gave an improvised speech on the Place de la République in Nice. He told them that, although they had nothing, the territory they were about to enter was rich and could provide them with everything. Much later, this declaration was reworked into the now well-known Italian proclamation, which went, 'Soldiers! You are hungry and naked. The government owes you much; it can give you nothing. Your patience, the courage you have shown among these rocks are admirable; but they bring you no glory, no brilliant feats reflect upon you. I want to lead you into the most fertile plains on earth. Rich provinces, great towns will be in your power; there you will find honour, glory, and riches.'[30]

Anonymous, *Cristofano Saliceti, Commissario della Repubblica Francese presso l'Armata d'Italia* (Christophe Saliceti, commissary of the French Republic for the Army of Italy), date unknown. Château de Versailles. (*Courtesy of Photo RMN – © Droits réservés*)

The proclamation is apocryphal, dictated by Napoleon on board the *Bellerephon* while on his way to St Helena, but we know from eyewitness accounts that he said something along these lines, although there are contradictory reports on just how this was received by the men.[31] Pierre de Pelleport declared that it made little impact, while François Roguet and Nicholas-Philibert Desvernois declared that, on the contrary, it made quite an impression. Historians have always interpreted the proclamation as an open invitation to loot, and it can easily be read in this way,[32] even if this was probably not Bonaparte's original intention. In essence, he was letting his troops know that the beggarly state in which they had lived would soon end: the plains of northern Italy, some of the most fertile in Europe, lay ahead of them and they would now be able to live off the land. This is, undoubtedly, what the troops wanted to hear. There was little point in Bonaparte appealing to his men's sense of patriotism. Instead, he appealed to their desire for material comfort in the hope of regaining some control over them.[33]

The French left in their wake nothing but despair. After taking the town of Mondovi (21 April), where there was a well-stocked arsenal, Sérurier's men indulged in pillage and destruction that lasted a whole day. A few days later, an officer by the name of Franceschi complained that, 'In every village, in every country house, in every hamlet, everything is pillaged and devastated . . . Bed linen, shirts, old clothes, shoes, everything, is taken from the unfortunate inhabitant of a cottage . . . If he does not hand over money he is beaten senseless . . . Everywhere inhabitants flee . . . children cry and ask after bread.'[34] Officers as well as men trafficked in whatever they could lay their hands on. Saliceti even had his seal stolen so that forgeries could be issued in his name.[35] One officer remarked that the 'consummation' of guns went beyond anything that could be imagined, that is, men sold their guns to the local populations despite being in occupied territory. The selling of horses, equipment and clothes was minor in comparison. 'The soldier that we put shoes on yesterday is today barefoot. He sells his shoes in order to be given new shoes to sell them again.'[36] They were able to earn enough money in this way to buy other necessities.

One volunteer, Captain Jérôme Laugier, referred to the men's looting, in one instance at least, as an *orgie soldatesque* (barrack room orgy), and described groups of soldiers going from house to house in one town by the light of candles they had stolen from a grocer's, taking everything that they could lay their hands on.[37] General Vaubois complained to Berthier during his invasion of the Tyrol: 'The disorder was dreadful. In spite of the trouble we went to, the first night a general pillage took place; we beat, we shot, but we were not able to put a stop to the disorder.'[38] And it was not uncommon for soldiers to murder women after abducting and raping them.[39]

Artist unknown, *Unter den Königen war der Neufrank höflich und erbar jez ist er ein vertheidiger des Raubes un der Unzucht* (Under the Queen the new Frank was polite and compassionate now he is a defender of plunder and sexual assault), circa 1796. A popular print showing French soldiers abducting the wife and daughter of a peasant to take them to their bivouac. The caricatural nature of the print belies the enormous suffering peasants endured at the hands of troops of all armies. This type of behaviour was so common that the entry on 'brigands' in the *Encyclopédie* drew a direct connection between soldiers and brigandage.[40] (*Bibliothèque nationale, Paris*)

Bonaparte disapproved of such behaviour. His correspondence during this period is punctuated with indignant remarks about the depredations committed by his soldiers and exhortations to his generals about making examples.[41] Soldiers were indeed shot for a variety of petty offences, such as pilfering from a church or stealing a knife from a local inhabitant. By May hardly a day went by without some looters being shot. However, despite the severity of the punishment, pillaging continued.[42] 'You were deprived of everything at the beginning of the campaign,' Bonaparte pleaded with his men, 'you are today abundantly supplied . . . we would blush at commanding an army without discipline, unbridled, which only knows the law of force . . . I will know how to make the laws of humanity and honour respect to the little group of men without courage and without hearts who tread them underfoot. I will not tolerate brigands to soil our laurels . . . looters will be shot mercilessly, several have been already.'[43]

The executions had little effect. When Bonaparte gave orders to Masséna 'that the volunteers stop the pillage to which they have given themselves up and that they do not leave their posts',[44] Masséna's reply was to the point: 'If you don't want us to pillage, well then, we have to be fed, we have to be clothed and we have to be paid!'[45] That was hardly likely to happen, or at least not on a regular basis, and that was the problem. Pillage took place partly because the men were desperate for food and clothing and partly because they saw it as the natural right of conquerors. After the Treaty of Cherasco with the Piedmontese (28 April 1796), General Landrieux complained that, 'There was so little discipline in the marches that I saw entire brigades scattered, while only their officers followed the road. I spent the night outside [the village of] Bene to rally the looters. There were even those who fired on my regiment. Some were sabred . . . It is hardly possible to believe that in a country so abundant the distribution [of rations] was sometimes lacking in the evening!'[46] A sum of money called a *rachat de pillage* (pillage redemption) was given to the men in the hope that they would no longer need to pillage. Just before taking the town of Verona in the summer of 1796, for example, the men were each given twenty-four livres as long as they promised not to resort to looting. The operation cost 1.8 million francs, and it is not clear that it succeeded.[47]

Defeating Piedmont

Such was the band of marauders with which Bonaparte marched
into Italy, although it should be said in their defence that they were
no worse than any other army of the day, if perhaps a little more
filthy and unkempt than the norm.

The ultimate goal of the French strategy was to drive Austria out
of the war. In this, Italy was meant to be a secondary theatre of
operations. In 1795, Carnot devised a means of doing this – a two-
pronged attack against Austrian forces in Germany, accompanied
by a third prong across the Alps into Italy.[48] The objective was to
oblige the Austrians to split their forces. The campaign, however,
proved to be a disaster. In Germany, the troops were ill-equipped
and the generals in charge, Jean-Baptiste Jourdan and Jean-Charles
Pichegru, inept and incapable of co-ordinating their efforts. The
Austrians were able to defeat the two French armies and push them
back across the Rhine. The French fared a little better in Italy, with
some initial successes, but the offensive petered out through lack of
men and equipment. The overall strategy was not entirely abandoned, however, and was implemented again in a modified form in
1796. This time around, the main thrust against Austria was to come
from the commander of the Army of the Rhin-et-Moselle, General
Jean-Victor Moreau, who was ordered to push into south-west
Germany and eventually to meet up with Bonaparte, who was to
make his way across northern Italy and join Moreau in the Tyrol.
The Italian theatre of war, however, was regarded as secondary; the
main front was to be Germany. And yet, within a matter of months,
Bonaparte turned the Italian front into a campaign upon which the
whole war seemed to hinge.

He first turned on the Piedmontese army following a plan given to
him by the Directory but which he had written.[49] It was essentially
the same as that adopted by the French marshal, the Marquis de
Maillebois, who was at the head of the Franco-Spanish forces in Italy
during the War of the Austrian Succession in 1745.[50] Bonaparte was
to push the Piedmontese back towards Turin, and the Austrians back
beyond Milan and into their own territory. Battles were fought and
won at Montenotte (12 April, his first), and Dego (13–16 April),
preventing the Austrian and Piedmontese armies from linking up.

Indeed, Bonaparte made the Piedmontese retreat so quickly towards Turin that he broke what little will they had to resist. It was not that the Piedmontese could not have continued fighting; it was simply that they were tired of the war and no longer had the political desire or the will to go on.[51] The court of Vienna, aware of Piedmont's lack of motivation, had secretly warned the Austrian commander in the field, Baron von Beaulieu: 'Never lose sight of the fact that it is possible, not only that the court of Turin will unexpectedly make a separate peace, but that it will even join the enemy either through weakness or through treacherous politics.'[52]

Artist unknown, *Bataille de Montenote le 23 germinal an IV* (Battle of Montenotte, 11 April 1796), circa 1796. The caption accompanying the image read, 'The complete rout of the enemy with losses of 4,000 men, of which 2,500 were made prisoner, and the capture of several flags and cannon.' In fact, no more than 2,500 casualties were suffered on the Austrian side. The exaggeration of enemy losses was a technique Bonaparte would use to great effect throughout this and subsequent campaigns. (*Bibliothèque nationale, Paris*)

The Austro-Piedmontese alliance was, therefore, politically weak, and was strained by jealousy, mistrust, ill-will and fear of betrayal. Peace feelers had been put out by the King of Piedmont-Sardinia, Victor Amadeus, months before Bonaparte even entered the campaign. Caution, therefore, is needed about apportioning the responsibility for the defection of Piedmont from the Austrian alliance solely to Bonaparte. Certainly, he had achieved more over the first two weeks of the campaign than any other general in similar circumstances had done in months, but by that stage the Piedmontese monarchy was ripe for peace. On 23 April, the commander of the Piedmontese forces, General Michael Colli, brought Bonaparte the offer of an armistice. Bonaparte's response was to push forward to occupy the towns of Cherasco and Alba, thus making any link between the Piedmontese and Austrian forces impossible. On 26 April, the Piedmontese delegation arrived at Cherasco, about 130 kilometres south of Turin, to negotiate a separate peace, which Bonaparte accepted in accord with his instructions from the Directory.[53]

Before that, Bonaparte had written a (slightly) exaggerated account to the Directory of what had happened up until then: 'You have no idea of the army's military and administrative situation,' he complained. 'When I arrived, the army had been worked on by spiteful souls, without bread, without discipline, without obedience. I made examples; I put everything into raising the service, and victory did the rest. However, lack of carts, bad horses, and greedy administrators has left us absolutely destitute. My life here is inconceivable; I arrive tired, I have to work all night to carry out the administration, and go everywhere in order to re-establish order.'[54]

The accounts of the battles and the conditions in which they were fought, the missives that were regularly sent to the government and the people of Paris so that they were constantly kept abreast, were all techniques of self-promotion. Bonaparte, in other words, was particularly adept at flagging his own achievements. His brother Joseph, who was living in Genoa at the beginning of the campaign, one of his aides-de camp, Junot, and Murat were sent on to Paris with the flags taken from the enemy at Montenotte and Mondovi. It was a gesture reminiscent of ancient Roman generals sending the flags of defeated armies to the Senate. Bonaparte, the army and his victories must be in the limelight as long as possible. There was a pattern to this. Bonaparte would write a dispatch to the Directory, always published in the official newspapers, often accompanied by a dispatch from Saliceti (at least in the first months of the campaign) or Bonaparte's chief of staff, Berthier; then Bonaparte would send to Paris, with captured flags and other trophies, a general, who would often give a public address (this happened with Marmont, Lemarais, Bessières, Masséna and Sérurier); then another officer might arrive in Paris a few days, a few weeks or even months later with more flags from the same battle.[55] Other generals, like Moreau, Jourdan or Kléber, also published their letters to the Directory in newspapers – self-promotion thrived in the French as in other armies and navies of the period – but their accounts lacked the flair and excitement that Bonaparte was able to convey.[56] Like so many modern-day administrators, they were not writing to be read – indeed, it is more than likely that they had not recognized the importance of the press – whereas Bonaparte was writing for the public, instinctively aware of the importance of the newspaper as a medium. Moreover, many of the so-called letters to the Directory were also printed as posters destined for the walls of various French towns.[57] Bonaparte thus became closely associated with victory from the earliest phases of the campaign, and was constantly in the public eye.

The Piedmontese negotiators, General Sallier de La Tour, an old, mediocre soldier, and Colonel Joseph-Henri Costa de Beauregard, a gentleman from Savoy, arrived at Bonaparte's headquarters in Cherasco on 27 April at about half past ten on a rainy evening. When Bonaparte finally appeared his 'demeanour was grave and cold . . . His smooth chestnut hair was tied in a queue. It was not powdered and hung very low over his forehead and down the sides of his face; his eyes were red and tired. He had that wan and even complexion that the physiologists attribute to the melancholy temperament, and, according to them, is an indication of the greatest faculties of the soul. In conclusion, as we have already said, he totally lacked affability and grace.'[58] At one o'clock in the morning, after less than two hours of talks, Bonaparte took out his watch, looked at it and said, 'Gentlemen, I warn you that a general attack has been ordered for two o'clock . . . It may happen', he added, 'that I will lose battles, but I shall never lose time through idle talk or sloth.'[59] He then left Berthier to continue negotiating while he paced nervously up and down the room. By two o'clock, the 'amnesty', as Bonaparte called it in his Corsican French (he meant to say armistice), was signed.[60] Bonaparte was to win many battles, but seldom, if ever, was it followed by a diplomatic settlement that was satisfactory to both parties. It was one of the failings of the later Empire, that is, an inherent inability to negotiate a settled peace.

That night, Bonaparte and the negotiators did not sleep. After a frugal meal, he relaxed and started discussing the campaign, the mistakes he had made, and what he thought of the Austrian approach to war. By the end of the night, Bonaparte was leaning on the balcony of an open window watching the day break, and talking with Costa de Beauregard about the campaign to come, the outcome of which he seemed sure of. 'The impression that one had near this young man,' concluded Beauregard, 'was of a painful admiration; the intellect was dazzled by the superiority of his talents, but the heart remained oppressed.'[61] Later during the day Bonaparte wrote to Josephine revealing how ill at ease he was in the world of high and low politics: '. . . I have to prattle [*jaser*] with little gentlemen who visit as early as ten in the morning, and then listen to the twaddle and the stupidity of a hundred whippersnappers until one in the morning.'[62]

The campaign had lasted only ten days. In exchange for a suspension of hostilities, the French were granted a few fortresses, and the right of passage through Piedmontese territory, that is, the Piedmontese abandoned control of the Alpine passes. The question of a full treaty was postponed until later. Cherasco is sometimes qualified as the first act of insubordination by Bonaparte against the Directory,[63] but one should keep in mind that Saliceti was present, and that Bonaparte conferred with him before concluding the armistice.[64] Even so, Bonaparte was a little worried that the armistice might even be disavowed by the Directory.[65] In the event, it was not, although when news of the armistice reached Paris in the first days of May it does not seem to have made much of an impact. Of course, people longed for peace, but the topics of conversation were more likely to centre on the *assignats* or the newest hairstyle worn by Mesdames Bonaparte and Tallien.[66] The war was still being fought, and a definitive end to it had not yet been achieved. Bonaparte next took the battle into the enemy's own territory, into the Austrian Duchy of Milan.

'The Moral Force of Victory'

'I march tomorrow against Beaulieu,' Bonaparte wrote to the Directors. 'I will oblige him to cross the Po, I will pass it immediately after him, I will take all of Lombardy [the Duchy of Milan], and, in less than a month, I hope to be in the mountains of the Tyrol, to find the Army of the Rhine and with it carry the war into Bavaria.'[67] Instead of now taking the obvious route across the river Po at Valenza, Bonaparte sent his army east along the southern bank as far as Piacenza, into the heart of Austrian territory.[68] It was there that he was going to cross before the seventy-year-old Beaulieu had time to realize what was happening and to rally his forces to prevent the French from crossing. 'Yesterday morning,' Bonaparte wrote to the Directory, 'an artillery duel took place with the enemy posted on the far bank of the Po. This river is very large and very difficult to cross. My intention is to cross it as close as possible to Milan, so as to have no further obstacles before arriving at that capital. In this way, I will turn the three lines of defence that Beaulieu has prepared along the Agogno, the Terdoppio and the Ticino. Today I march towards Piacenza. Pavia finds itself turned and if the enemy persists in defending that town, I will find myself between him and his depots.'[69] It was a sensible if not a bold thing to do; if Bonaparte had not crossed the Po at Piacenza, he would have had to fight across the three northern tributaries (the Agogna, the Terdoppio and the Ticino) that Beaulieu had put between his army and the French.

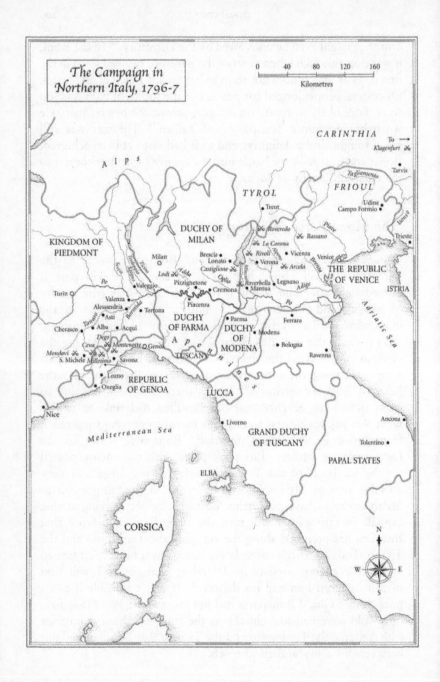

The Campaign in
Northern Italy, 1796-7

0   40   80   120   160
Kilometres

ALPS

CARINTHIA

To →
Klagenfurt

TYROL

FRIOUL

Tarvis

Tagliamento

Trent

Udine
Campo Formio

DUCHY OF
MILAN

Roveredo

Bassano

Piave

Trieste

La Corona

Milan

Brescia

Rivoli

Vicenza

KINGDOM OF
PIEDMONT

Adda

Lonato
Castiglione

Chiese

Verona

Arcola

Venice

Lodi

Mincio

THE REPUBLIC
OF VENICE

Pizzighetone

Riverbella

Legnano

Po

Valeggio

Cremona

Mantua

Adige

Turin

Valenza

Alessandria

Asti

Piacenza

ISTRIA

Tanaro

Bormida

Tortona

DUCHY
OF PARMA

Parma

Ferrara

Cherasco

Alba

Acqui

Modena

Adriatic Sea

Deto

Ceva

Montenotte

Genoa

DUCHY
OF
MODENA

Mondovi

S. Michele

Millesimo

Savona

Apennines

Bologna

TUSCANY

Ravenna

Loano

Onéglia

REPUBLIC
OF GENOA

LUCCA

Nice

Livorno

Ancona

Mediterranean Sea

GRAND DUCHY
OF TUSCANY

Tolentino

PAPAL STATES

ELBA

CORSICA

N
W   E
S

With impressive speed, therefore, Bonaparte moved on Piacenza, arriving on 7 May, in the Duchy of Parma. The Austrians apparently had not considered the possibility of a flanking movement. Now Beaulieu had to retreat rapidly north-east to cross the river Adda at Lodi, a small town of about 12,000 inhabitants, thirty-two kilometres south-east of Milan. It was here, on 10 May 1796, that one of the great myths of the Napoleonic era, which helped establish the idea of Bonaparte as an irresistible, invincible force, was created.

Early on the morning of 10 May, the French advance guard forced their way into Lodi, driving a weak Austrian covering force back through the town and across the river on the far side.[70] The river is not deep or terribly wide, but the current is strong. There the French had to abandon their pursuit. Facing them was a narrow wooden bridge about 200 metres long. (The bridge one sees at Lodi today was rebuilt further downstream.) To cover his retreat, Beaulieu left behind a force of less than 10,000 men. Three battalions of these troops, along with a dozen or so cannon, were drawn up on the other side of the bridge. When Bonaparte arrived, he placed two light guns aimed down the bridge to prevent the Austrians from destroying it. On their side, the Austrians raised a barricade under fire of French sharpshooters, who had found positions from windows and on the roofs of buildings at the edge of town. At some point, Bonaparte ascended the bell-tower of the Church of San Francesco, still there today, from which he could observe the enemy positions. The artillery duel carried on for several hours, increasing in intensity with the arrival of additional guns throughout the morning; Bonaparte eventually deployed twenty-four to thirty guns along the bank, firing on the Austrians' fourteen. He also sent cavalry to the north and south in search of a suitable crossing point. At about six in the evening, by which time reinforcements had arrived and the grenadiers had recovered from the morning's fighting, Bonaparte tried to arouse their enthusiasm with a short patriotic speech and then sent them charging across the bridge. The Austrians only had time to fire one round of grapeshot, but it decimated the French; the grenadiers were first stopped near the centre of the bridge, then fell back. It was at this point that a number of senior officers – Masséna, Lannes, Dallemagne, Cervoni, Berthier, but especially Dupas, whose nickname was *le général Z'en avant* – rushed on to the bridge to rally the flagging troops, taking them forward once more in a new assault. This time the charge proved irresistible, especially when the attackers discovered that the water at the Austrian end of the bridge was shallow and that they could station themselves beside the bridge to provide covering fire for the main party. Swarming over the Austrian guns, the grenadiers soon established a secure position. In the meantime, the cavalry had found a ford to the north of the town and now came upon the Austrian flank from the rear.

Artist unknown, *Passage du pont de Lody en Italie par l'armée republico-française commandé par le général en chef Napoléon Bonaparte* (Passage of the bridge at Lodi by the French-republican army commanded by the general-in-chief Napoleon Bonaparte), circa 1796. Note that Bonaparte, on a white horse, is at the head of the advancing column. (*Bibliothèque nationale, Paris*)

The whole affair had been little more than a skirmish, judging by the casualty list: the Austrians lost 335 killed and wounded, the French about 350. Saved by nightfall, the Austrians were able to withdraw in good order eastwards to join their main army at Cremona. Some military historians have, moreover, criticized the episode as unnecessary.[71] If Bonaparte had waited another day there would have been no need to storm the bridge. He had, in fact, been acting under the false assumption that he was facing the main Austrian army, and not just the rearguard. The action was also a failure, it could be argued, in that the Austrian forces were able to get away. It was not, by any means, a decisive engagement, but the consequences were important.

Beaulieu was forced to withdraw to the Austrian fortress of Mantua, thereby leaving Milan and the rest of Lombardy open to a French invasion, while some of the lesser Italian states (Parma and Modena) hurried to conclude peace with the French. And Lodi was also a tremendous blow to Austrian prestige: a professional army of 10,000 men had failed to hold a bridge against French conscripts. The Prussian military theorist, Karl von Clausewitz, later called it 'the moral force of victory', and added that 'there was no feat of arms which excited such amazement in Europe', inspiring enthusiasm in all those who were friends of France.[72] This was the purpose of the propaganda effort that was now spent on diffusing not only news of the battle, but images of it too. The resounding moral and psychological impact the representations of the crossing had on the public imagination in the construction of Napoleon Bonaparte, both in France and in the rest of Europe, was enormous. This is remarkable since Bonaparte was not personally involved in the crossing and in the memoirs of the day he is not even mentioned.[73] He had remained safely behind, as any general should, looking on as his men braved Austrian fire. And yet, within the space of a month, this 'feat' was as well known in Germany and England as it was in France, and was to become one of the cornerstones of the Napoleonic legend.

Bonaparte did this, first, by exaggerating both the odds facing the French and the role he played in the crossing. 'Beaulieu himself fled with his terrified army,' Bonaparte wrote to the French consul in Genoa. 'I pursued him beyond Cremona.'[74] This was patently false, but then for him the truth never got in the way of a good story. It is true that Bonaparte paid tribute to the heroism of his subordinates – in the official report at least – but in the popular accounts his role is pre-eminent. In a dispatch to Paris, the skirmish became a battle against the whole Austrian army under Beaulieu, while thirty pieces of artillery defended the crossing of the bridge. 'Although we have had some very heated actions since the beginning of the campaign . . . none has approached the terrible crossing of the bridge of Lodi,' and he went on to call it 'the most brilliant [victory] of the entire war.'[75]

I had all of my artillery placed in battery positions; the cannonade was very lively for several hours; as soon as the army arrived, it was formed into tight columns, the second battalion of *carabiniers* at the head and, followed by all the grenadier battalions, charged crying out '*Long live the Republic!*' They were on the bridge, which is about two hundred metres in length; the enemy's fire was terrible; the head of the column even appeared to hesitate: a moment's hesitation and all was lost. Generals Berthier, Masséna, Cervoni, Dallemagne, the *chef de brigade* Lannes and the *chef de bataillon* Dupas who all felt it, rushed to the front [of the column] and decided the outcome still in the balance.[76]

An even more romanticized account was written by Saliceti, now firmly behind his former protégé, and later distributed throughout Europe.

Once the column of republican heroes had been formed, he [Bonaparte] went along the ranks; his presence ignited the soldiers and he was welcomed with cries a thousand times repeated *Long live the Republic!* He had the charge sounded and the troops, with the speed of lightning, threw themselves at the bridge. The fire which the cannon and muskets spewed out stopped the column for a moment, and almost sent it reeling, but General Berthier, chief of staff, threw himself at its head . . . valiantly seconded by General Masséna and by the brigades generals Cervoni and Dallemagne.[77]

According to his own later accounts, Lodi gave Bonaparte a surge of self-confidence. Many years later on St Helena, reflecting on his life and career, Napoleon revealed as much to three of the four chroniclers who accompanied him into exile. To Baron Gourgaud, 'I saw the world flee before me as if I were being carried in the air.'[78] To the Comte de Montholon, 'It was only on the evening of Lodi that I believed myself to be a superior man, and that the ambition came to me of executing the great things which so far had been occupying my thoughts only as a fantastic dream.'[79] To Las Cases, 'Vendémiaire and even Montenotte did not lead me to believe I was a superior being. It was only after Lodi that the idea came to me that I could well become, after all, a decisive actor on the political scene. It was then that the first sparks of high ambition were born.'[80]

The turning point, however, seems to have come a few days after Lodi: on 13 May in the village of Pizzighettone, Bonaparte received a letter from the Directory instructing him to take the Milanese, and then to divide his army into two.[81] He was to leave a holding force under General Kellermann in Lombardy; the larger part of the army was to head south into central Italy, threatening Rome and Naples, which were at war with the French Republic. It was misguided: the situation had changed dramatically while the letter was drafted in Paris and the orders were no longer appropriate. Bonaparte refused to comply; it was the first time he had rebelled against authorities he had assiduously obeyed until then. When Bonaparte received the letter, he was standing near a fire in the corner of a room, even though the weather was already warm.[82] The opinion that he formed of his superiority, Bonaparte reflected many years later, was related to *that* moment. He felt that he was worth much more, that he was stronger than the government that had given him those instructions, that he was destined to 'save' France from an incompetent and inept government, and to finish the Revolution. 'From that moment, I glimpsed the goal and I marched towards it.' The goal, one has to assume, was either eternal glory or, more prosaically, ultimate power.

This looks like one of those defining moments sought after by biographers that helps illuminate the transformation of Bonaparte's character on the road to power but, since it comes from Napoleon's reminiscences on the island of St Helena, it needs to be treated with circumspection. Bonaparte is clearly describing *the* moment when it dawned on him that he was not an ordinary man, that fortune had great things in store for him. But even if these later reports regarding the 'revelation' at Pizzighettone are part of the myth-making exercise Napoleon spent his last years revelling in, one thing is clear: these first few weeks in May were decisive for Bonaparte's career, for the development of his character, and for the fate of France and the Directory.[83] Bonaparte was now consciously aware of his talent, and especially of the potential it held out for him, which no doubt fed his ambition. As his increasing belief in his own destiny grew, he became less likely to heed the directives from Paris, which could take weeks and months to reach him, when decisions had to be made quickly on the ground.

Written descriptions of the battle of Lodi were useful, and might well be read out in the cafés and *guingettes*** of Paris, but for a largely illiterate society visual images, through cheap engravings produced in large numbers, were a more direct manner of shaping public opinion.[84] This is what Bonaparte set about doing.

Shortly after the battle, Bonaparte received a series of engravings from the French ambassador at Genoa, a man by the name of Guillaume Faipoult. The contents of the engravings are unknown, but two days before Bonaparte's triumphal entry into Milan (15 May), he replied: 'I am much obliged for the engravings you sent me, which will delight the army. I would ask you to send, on my behalf, twenty-five louis [a considerable sum] to the young man who made them; encourage him to engrave the astonishing crossing of the bridge at Lodi.'[85] The young man in question was quite possibly Antoine-Jean Gros, then a member of Faipoult's entourage. A pictorial record of Bonaparte's deeds could be easily broadcast, not only to the people in France, but also to the conquered peoples of Italy. It should be noted, however, that the focus in these first engravings is on the troops that cross the bridge in the face of enemy fire, and not on Bonaparte.

---

* A small café, often in the open and usually outside the walls of Paris, in which music and dancing took place.

Thomas Charles Naudet, *Passage du pont de Lody en Italie par l'armée française* (Passage of the bridge at Lodi by the French army), between 1796 and 1802, engraving by Le Beau. (*Bibliothèque nationale, Paris*)

That the populist propaganda surrounding Lodi made some impression is evident in the following letter from the directors in Paris. Having initially ordered Bonaparte to split his army in two, dividing the command with Kellermann, the Directory was now forced to countermand its original orders. 'Immortal glory to the conqueror of Lodi,' they wrote back on 18 May. 'Honour to the general-in-chief who planned the bold attack on the bridge of that town, scouring the ranks of the French warriors, exposing himself to the most murderous fire of the enemy, and organizing everything to vanquish [the Austrians]!'[86]

The Directory could do little other than bend to Bonaparte's wishes. Not only had his exploits begun to inspire the people of Paris, he was also the general who had contributed the most money to the state's coffers. When the loot Bonaparte had taken from Italy arrived in Paris, the Directory was forced to shower even more praise on the victor of Lodi, and to celebrate the feats of the Army of Italy on the Champs de Mars (29 May 1796). This was an attempt to persuade Paris that the Directory was in control of the army but, with Bonaparte at its head, this was becoming increasingly doubtful.

10

Conquest and Pillage

The Entry into Milan

Lodi guaranteed Bonaparte the domination of Lombardy. A few days later, on 14 May 1796, Masséna was at Milan, a sizeable city of about 120,000 people. 'One enters Milan', wrote a French tourist a number of years later, 'almost without suspecting it. The town is situated on a plain covered with trees: one does not see it until the moment when one passes through the gates.'[1] The next day, a Sunday, Bonaparte arrived in a coach, escorted by 500 cavalry and 1,000 foot soldiers, and entered the town in a ceremony that recalled the triumphal entries of the Romans. He stopped not far from the ancient gateway, the Porta Romana, got out and mounted a small, sorry-looking white horse, Bijou, on which Bonaparte had conducted most of the campaign to date.[2] He rode alone. Masséna, Joubert, Kilmaine and Saliceti followed him. To remind the people of Milan who was now in control, a small group of Austrian prisoners preceded the procession. They advanced towards the gateway where the city dignitaries had come out to hand Bonaparte the keys to the city.

The Porta Romana was so narrow that the cavalry could only get through two at a time. Beyond that was a field where a triumphal arch of leaves and flowers had been erected for the occasion. The new National Guard of the city of Milan, dressed in green uniforms with tricolour cockades in their hats, formed a guard of honour along the route to the cathedral, keeping back the crowds who had come to see Bonaparte. Most of the spectators, as was to be the case throughout Bonaparte's conquest of Italy, were not of the people, but were bourgeoisie either sympathetic to the French cause or simply curious to see the man they had already heard so much about and the motley collection of soldiers he commanded. The contrast between the bourgeoisie of Milan and the scarecrow army made for a strange sight. The clothes the soldiers had worn out during the campaign had been replaced along the way with anything they could get hold of; they had no proper uniforms. In place of cartridge pouches, for example, many wore belts of goatskin; their heads were covered by bonnets of fox, sheepskin, rabbit and even cat. Only their weapons were in a decent state.[3] What impressed contemporaries most though was that 'these men, dying of hunger, generally small, weak, worn out by fatigue and privation, without clothes or shoes – men that one would take for the dregs of a wretched population – should have conquered the Austrian army.'[4]

This was Bonaparte's first triumphal entry in Italy. Its scale and importance were greatly exaggerated in reports back to Paris so that the French entered amid 'cries of joy' from an 'immense crowd'.[5] There is, in fact, some doubt as to when the crowds turned out to greet the French, on 14 May when Masséna entered the town, the next day when Bonaparte entered it, or perhaps on both occasions. General Marmont wrote to his father that their triumphal entry was made on 14 May.[6] On St Helena, Napoleon tried to gloss over any ambiguity by arguing that no troops had entered Milan before 15 May, but this was patently not the case.[7] It is likely, therefore, that the crowds which turned out on 15 May were less numerous and perhaps less exuberant than on the previous day. It is also likely that, over time, the two dates were fused into one scene in the minds of those representing the event.[8] Moreover, it is impossible to say whether the entry that took place in 1796 has not also been confused, at least in its pictorial representations, with the second entry that took place four years later after the battle of Marengo in 1800.[9] Nevertheless, Bonaparte's entry into Milan was made a key element of the Italian campaign. There were other French entries made during this period represented in engravings that could just as well have served as an image for propagandists. But it was this first entry into Milan that so inspired artists that it became one of the major events of what the Italians refer to as the *triennio rivoluzionario*, the three years of French occupation. The legend sanctioned retrospectively what local artists and emissaries of the Army of Italy instinctively knew to be an important and decisive moment.

A dozen or so engravings celebrating this event appeared between 1799 and as late as 1860. The best-known engraving was executed by Carl Vernet, a French painter of battle scenes, although it did not appear until 1804 in the series *Tableaux historiques de la campagne d'Italie* (Historical Scenes of the Italian Campaign).[10] Even though Vernet had accompanied the army to Italy, he had been absent at the time of the entry into Milan. Instead, he took another engraving of the Porta Romana (by Vallardi) and simply stuck Bonaparte in the middle of it.[11] He planted one of the symbols of the French Revolution, a gigantic Tree of Liberty, in the background (one can see it on the far right of the engraving) with a Phrygian bonnet on the top for good measure, and added a mythical welcoming message across the top of the arch – *Alla valorosa armata francese* (To the courageous French army). It was meant to emphasize the union between the French 'liberators' and the people of Milan. If one looks closely at the engraving, one can see distinct signs of this. To the right of the picture there is a group of Italian 'patriots', while an individual hands out tricolour cockades to the crowd; at least another dozen or so individuals are portrayed in gestures indicating their enthusiasm for the arrival of the French, one offering an olive branch to a cavalryman, a hussar embracing some women, and soldiers in a fraternal embrace, sharing a bottle of wine.[12]

It is probably this image that Stendhal, a collector of engravings, had in mind when he wrote the opening passages for *The Charterhouse of Parma*: 'On 15 May, 1796, General Bonaparte entered Milan at the head of that young army which had lately crossed the Lodi bridge and taught the world that after so many centuries Caesar and Alexander had a successor.'[13] Indeed, the descriptions of the entry were all modelled on ancient Roman triumphal entries with which educated contemporaries would have been thoroughly

Carl Vernet, *Entrée des français dans Milan* (Entry of the French into Milan),
between 1799 and 1807. (*Bibliothèque nationale, Paris*)

familiar. In fact, the entry was elaborately prepared by representatives of the Army of Italy (like Saliceti), and the French diplomats
present in Milan (who did everything in their power to influence
public opinion positively), and Italian 'Jacobins' (who called themselves 'patriots'). One of the latter was Carlo Salvador, an obscure
journalist who had been a political refugee in Paris, where he
befriended the radical, Marat. These Italian 'Jacobins' were anxious
to demonstrate the revolutionary zeal of the Milanese people.
Salvador, who had accompanied the French army into Italy, sent
a letter to his friends in Milan telling them that 'the time had come
to make the numerous patriots and the French partisans decide, that
the time had come to show themselves and to keep their cockades at
the ready.'[14] A few days before the arrival of the French, on 11 June,
Salvador entered Milan through the Porta Romana, where Italian
patriots awaited the coming of the French 'as the Israelites awaited
the Messiah', and 'fifty thousand cockades' reportedly made their
appearance.[15] Improbable as this may have been, there is no doubt
that Salvador attempted to galvanize patriot opinion by opening a

popular society, by distributing revolutionary pamphlets printed
before he entered the town, and by planting a Tree of Liberty
before the royal palace.

'I Thought Only of You'

The Austrian Archduke Ferdinand, ruler of the Duchy of Milan,
was forced to flee the city in the wake of the retreat of the
Austrian troops. A wag hung a sign outside his residential palace
that read, 'House for rent. See commissary Saliceti.'[16] When
Bonaparte first entered the town, however, he took lodgings in
the Archbishopric, followed by a bath and a nap, and later in the
day received delegations from the municipality. That evening, a
sumptuous banquet with two hundred guests was given in his
honour at the Palazzo Reale, where an orchestra played revolutionary songs like 'La Marseillaise', the 'Carmagnole', and the
'Ça Ira'. His heart was not in the celebrations, though. It was at
moments like these when Bonaparte's mind turned to Josephine.
Shortly after arriving, he left the ball and went to bed, where he
tormented himself with thoughts of his wife. He wrote to her
claiming that five or six hundred pretty and elegant women were
at his disposal, but that 'I thought only of you, it made everything unbearable'.[17]

When Joseph was sent on to Paris with the flags taken from the
enemy at Montenotte and Mondovi, he also carried a letter for his
sister-in-law: 'He will see you,' wrote the lovesick Bonaparte
speaking of his brother, 'he will breathe in your temple; you will
perhaps even accord him the unique and inestimable favour of a kiss
on the cheek, while I, I will be alone, and far, far away. But you will
come, won't you? You're going to be here, next to me, in my heart,
in my arms, on your mouth. Take wings, come, come! . . . A kiss to
the heart, *and then lower, much lower!*'[18] The Directory made sure
that his new bride could not follow him; they thought it best, at this
early stage of the campaign at least, that Bonaparte should not have
any distractions. Throughout the next twelve months, Josephine
was to spend less than two with her husband; usually it was just a
few days at a time and always in the public eye.

Bonaparte suffered deeply at the separation and wrote to her constantly. In the midst of the enormous logistical difficulties that came with taking over a battered army, at the outset of what was to be one of the most intense and most active campaigns of the revolutionary wars, Bonaparte's mind was occupied with Josephine, the thought of whom gnawed at him so that he was not only constantly exhausted from the hardships of the campaign, but also tormented by their separation. During the few moments of respite he allowed himself, he feverishly imagined what she might be doing in Paris, doubting whether she truly loved him (with good reason as it turned out). 'To die without being loved by you, to die without that certitude, is the torment of hell, the acute and striking image of absolute annihilation. It seems like I am suffocating.'[19] A few days later he wrote: 'The fear of not being loved by *Josephine*, the idea of her being inconstant, of her . . . But I am making trouble for myself. There are so many real difficulties! Do I need to invent them!!! You cannot have inspired a love without limit without sharing it . . .'[20]

Josephine was certainly not passionate about Bonaparte, although she may have felt some affection for him, or perhaps she was simply flattered by the devotion that she inspired in him. 'He is odd [*Il est drôle*], Bonaparte!' she once remarked, smiling, in her Creole accent. 'She was proud to know that he loved her almost as much as glory.'[21] She wrote to him every four days or so, so that her letters filled Bonaparte's 'days with pleasure', though he sometimes complained that they were too cold.[22] Unfortunately, we do not know what Josephine may have said to him; Bonaparte later destroyed the letters. In the meantime, while he was away busy with the day-to-day problems associated with conducting a campaign, Josephine was enjoying all that Paris had to offer – the theatre, appearing at all the balls and salons, receiving and visiting friends – which was a good deal more than she was accustomed to, since her husband had become the victorious general of Italy and was the topic of social conversation. It was around this time, May 1796, that Josephine met a young, dashing hussar nine years her junior, Lieutenant Hippolyte Charles, who had the reputation of being a bit of a wit, and who apparently made Jospehine laugh until she cried.[23] Although there is no certainty that they became anything more than close friends, given Josephine's passionate, sensual character, and that Charles had her letters to him burnt when on his deathbed, it is quite possible that they became lovers.

The Price of Liberty

A few days after entering Milan, in a proclamation to the people of Lombardy, Bonaparte declared that the French Republic, which had 'sworn hatred to the tyrants had also vowed fraternity to the people'. But there was an ominous warning in the proclamation: 'If the French victors wanted to consider the people of Lombardy as their brothers, they owed a just due . . . Their independence . . . is the result of the success of the French: it has to be seconded by the means [at their disposal].'[24]

Bonaparte was true to his word and fixed the price Lombardy would have to pay for its freedom from Austria – twenty million francs; he also requisitioned clothing and shoes and five to six thousand horses. Bonaparte paid for them in the worthless paper currency of the Directory, the *assignat*. The French commissaries, led by Saliceti, exacted two million francs from the citizens of Milan, while the looting carried out by the soldiers soon exhausted any goodwill the populace might have felt for the French. Within the space of two weeks, the French had managed to extract more than thirty-five million francs in cash alone.[25] Indeed, wherever Bonaparte went in Italy he imposed enormous levies of cash, usually presented as the price to pay for the liberation from Austrian troops: two million francs from the Duchy of Parma; ten million from the Duke of Modena; twenty million from Milan (five times the annual tax burden of the old regime); and two million from Genoa. He would soon also demand important collections of paintings. Moreover, individual generals, like Masséna, were renowned for their private exactions.

It was not simply a question of looting for looting's sake though. As we have seen, the Army of Italy was still in a deplorable condition. Bonaparte found himself caught between the suppliers of the army, for the most part unscrupulous men who short-changed and stole, but who had also lent large sums of money before the start of the campaign (Bonaparte still owed the Flachat company, for example, five million francs), and the directors who were pressing him to send the riches of Italy back to France. Carnot sent letters to Bonaparte urging him to 'not spare the Milanese particularly; immediately raise contributions in money during the first terror that the approach of our armies will inspire.'[26] Lombardy, in other words, was to be treated as conquered enemy territory. There is no notion of revolutionising Italy here. Short of cash, and despite all the rhetoric about liberating the peoples of Europe, the Directory and its generals had no illusions about what their ultimate mission in Italy was: to pillage and to send as much of their booty as possible back to France.[27]

The official contributions, as well as the large sums that were exacted from the Dukes of Modena and Parma, allowed Bonaparte to pay the army in cash, something that some soldiers had not seen in years. 'When I saw sixty francs,' reminisced one officer, 'I thought myself rich.'[28] 'It was the first time since 1793 that we received cash,' stated Captain Roguet.[29] 'The officers did not know what to do with the money they had been given,' wrote Vigo-Roussillon. 'As they did not have coats, canteens, or any form of transport, they bought jewellery. The watchmakers and jewellers saw their shops emptied in twenty-four hours, and everyone strutted around with two watches decorated with chains and ornaments that fell halfway down their thighs, just as the fashion was in Paris at that time. We transformed ourselves into *Incroyables*!'*[30]

Payment in hard cash was a significant step in binding the soldiers of the Army of Italy to Bonaparte.[31] Moreover, he did so on his own initiative, which caused some alarm among both the Directors and the commissaries attached to the army. Saliceti, who had been closely consulted by Bonaparte on all important measures until then, was not even told of this decision. 'The commander-in-chief', he complained to the Directory, 'took this resolution himself; he did not inform me, and I did not know about it until the army had already been informed.'[32] The fear was that it would set a precedent that would create discontent both among the men behind

---

* *Incroyables, Jeunesses dorés*, the *Merveilleux* and *Muscadins* were all terms used to describe young men and women with royalist leanings who, after the fall of Robespierre, flaunted their politics through extravagant dress.

the lines, who were not in a position to profit from the consequences of the army's pillaging, and perhaps also among the other armies of the Republic, which were paid in *assignats* whose value continued to fall. It is from this moment on that fundamental disagreements between Bonaparte and Saliceti began. It is another example of military power imposing its will over civilian power. It was a contagious model: the encroachments of the army over the administrative branches of the government multiplied at every level of the hierarchy. 'Everywhere officers, instead of addressing ordnance, carry out requisitions themselves. It is a system that has prevailed. In vain have we protested against the disruption of all order in the service and of all bookkeeping, abuses are recurring every moment.'[33]

Bonaparte's decision to pay his troops in cash was, therefore, quite an audacious act, more so than the later acts of disobedience surrounding the treaties with Austria or the creation of sister republics in spite of Paris. The Directory, for its part, seems to have conceded this power to Bonaparte. Its principal concern was not to lose what little control it had over him and it counted on doing so by maintaining its man, Saliceti, in the field. Increasingly, though, the troops felt loyalty towards the person capable of supplying their material needs, rather than towards the Republic that had failed them on so many occasions.[34] Contemporaries were aware that the longer the war dragged on, the longer the troops stayed away from France, the greater the danger that they would attach themselves to their generals. They had the example of the Roman Empire before them.

Lombardy in Revolt

French depredations were also bound to cause discontent among the faithful of Italy, for whom the invader was often perceived as a sacrilegious, murdering thief. They were right – anti-clericalism was strong in the French army – and apparently incurred the disapproval of the Virgin Mary, whose statues mysteriously changed colour, shed tears and even moved, signs that were almost inevitably interpreted as protests against the French occupation. In

Milan, for example, people reported that a statue of St Ambrose placed in a niche on the corner of Spadari and della Rosa streets, near the Ambrosian library, had raised its arm, holding a riding crop, when French troops had marched past. People flocked to the spot from all over Milan in the hope of seeing the miracle repeated. When nothing happened, the French were accused of opposing the miracle and were set upon and insulted in the streets. In order to put a stop to this, the authorities condemned the statue in a court of law for disturbing the peace. That night (22 May), a picket of dragoons dragged the statue from its place with a cord placed around its neck.[35]

All of this was part of the war of ideas being fought with political symbols between revolutionary and counter-revolutionary forces throughout Italy. The miracles the faithful claimed to have witnessed were given political meaning and were doubtless a reaction to the revolutionary symbols promoted by the French – Trees of Liberty, tricolour cockades and Phrygian bonnets – which then became obvious targets for anti-French sentiment. In Milan, for example, the very day after the French had dragged away the statue of St Ambrose, a large crowd of protestors gathered at the Cathedral Square, where they tore down the Tree of Liberty, a symbol of the Revolution. The crowd dispersed when a battalion of French soldiers turned up, but the signs were ominous. Religion often acted as the catalyst, but there were a number of reasons why Italians rose up against the French, not the least of which were the material exactions.[36] Within a short space of time, revolts broke out in Piedmont, followed by Lombardy, starting in Milan, and then continued the following month into the towns of Emilia-Romagna.[37] Bonaparte, who was at Lodi when he heard of the revolt, immediately returned to Milan, arriving in the afternoon of 25 May. There he ordered the French commander of the town, General Despinois (nicknamed 'General twenty-four hours' because the demand for supplies made on the civilian population often had to be carried out within that time), to execute a councillor and a priest who were considered to be the ringleaders.[38]

The revolts obliged Bonaparte to postpone a planned offensive against the Austrians and left him vulnerable to a counter-attack. He was forced to return to Milan the same day he left to start the offensive

(23 May): he gathered the municipal authorities, along with a number of clergy and nobles to tell them they had not done enough to prevent the unrest. Bonaparte then asked the archbishop, Monsignor Visconti, to publish a pastoral letter calling for calm and asking the clergy to encourage submission to the French. In the meantime, General Lannes, another future marshal of the Empire, had been sent ahead with a mobile column to pacify Pavia. Halfway between Milan and Pavia at the village of Binasco, where the aristocracy and the clergy were very powerful and very hostile to the French and the Revolution, he found the road littered with the corpses of soldiers. The sight of the French dead and the intense heat of the day was explosive. Lannes' soldiers shot indiscriminately and then, on the direct orders of Bonaparte, put the village to the torch until little of it remained, shooting all the men in the process, although the women and children were taken out of the village first. According to one historian, a pharmacist by the name of Carlo Rognoni managed to avoid the massacre and make his way to Bonaparte, where he threw himself on his knees and begged him to spare the village. Bonaparte is supposed to have replied coldly that his first and only concern was for the safety of the army and that a severe example had to be set. If true, and it is quite likely, then Bonaparte's later avowal that the sight of so much blood was horrible and that he was deeply affected by it seems hypocritical, unless he was only referring to French blood.[39] He had come a long way from the days at the Tuileries and the siege of Toulon when the sight of the dead and dying shocked him.

From Milan, Bonaparte issued a proclamation to the people of Lombardy threatening them with the fate of Binasco if they did not lay down their arms.[40] The archbishop of Milan, who had been sent to Pavia (about thirty-five kilometres south) with this proclamation, failed to arrange a surrender. The French had arrived there about two weeks before, imposing the usual heavy levies and requisitions. One of the first clashes that occurred, however, was not, as one might expect, between occupiers and occupied, but between supporters of the old regime and a group of political radicals.[41] Local Jacobins destroyed an ancient bronze equestrian statue of a Roman emperor called the 'Regisole'. It was a popular town icon that was inoffensive to most people, but the Italian Jacobins deemed it unacceptable to leave the statue of a tyrant in the town square next to their newly planted Tree of Liberty. Augereau, who commanded that section of the front, agreed to let them pull down the statue even though, according to one local diarist, he disapproved of the act. Nothing happened immediately after this attack on Pavia's symbol of local identity, but there were mounting signs of unrest. Armed peasants had started gathering in villages around the town.

It was only after the departure of the bulk of the French forces on 21 May that the people of Pavia felt bold enough to take the initiative. The trigger was the rumour – false as it turned out – of the defeat of Bonaparte before Mantua and the imminent return of the Austrians. The uncanny arrival of two escaped Austrian prisoners, acclaimed as 'angels who had descended from heaven', was considered proof by the crowds that the Austrians were indeed about to return. Twenty-eight churches in the town rang their bells simultaneously, and armed bands of peasants from the surrounding countryside swarmed into the city. To cries of 'Down with the cockades!', 'Long live the [Austrian] Emperor!' and 'Long live the House of Austria!', the Pavians cut down the Tree of Liberty, revenged themselves on collaborators, and killed a few isolated French soldiers. The peasants who had answered the tocsin were even angrier than the townsfolk because of French depredations. The commander of the French garrison – between 100 and 400 men (the accounts vary) – besieged in the citadel for two days, decided that, since they had no food, no artillery and no ammunition, it would be best to surrender. The French troops filed out of the citadel, each soldier accompanied by an 'honest' citizen, into a nearby seminary where a large meal awaited them.

The fact that not one French prisoner was harmed did not prevent the town from being sacked when it was stormed on 26 May, with dozens killed in the process. What little resistance there was soon faded away; the peasant 'rebels', anywhere between five and forty thousand according to the sources, emptied the streets in the 'blink of an eye' as the French arrived in force, leaving the townsfolk to their own fate. Those killed (between seventy and eighty) were the unlucky ones who could not get away fast enough and who were, for the most part, sabred by dragoons riding through the streets. Bonaparte then handed over the city to his soldiers for anywhere between three and twenty-four hours (also depending on the source). 'The town was delivered up to pillage, and while complete, the troops did not combine, as often happens in such cases, murder and other atrocities.'[42] Another contemporary account confirmed that no murders were committed and no women were raped. Some soldiers even protected women from the 'lubricity of their comrades'. According to Landrieux, soldiers who had got into disputes, or who had perhaps tried to prevent their comrades from committing atrocities, were killed by their own men, which suggests that outrages were indeed committed.[43] It was only at midday on 26 May that the call to arms was sounded, putting an end to the scenes that were taking place inside the town. One general went around with a patrol pulling the men into line, but Saliceti was still riding around at five in the evening threatening those who did not obey their officers with the death penalty.[44]

Carl Vernet, *Révolte de Pavie* (The Revolt of Pavia), between 1799 and 1807. (*Bibliothèque nationale, Paris*)

Rumours of the sacking of Pavia were probably much worse than what actually took place. Three times 'the order to burn the town expired on my lips', Bonaparte wrote to the Directory, but he decided not to because the French garrison had been well treated by the rebels.[45] Nor is there any evidence to support the reports that Bonaparte had the municipality, and even the hapless French officer who surrendered the citadel to the insurgents, shot.[46] On the other hand, insurgents found with weapons were summarily executed after being court-martialled by military tribunals at work in both Milan and Pavia, while a number of priests suspected of instigating the revolt were shot. Saliceti beggared the municipality of Pavia (a contribution of one million livres, to be paid within ten days, was imposed on the richest inhabitants implicated in the revolt), and had a large number of nobles and suspects arrested. Indeed, hundreds of hostages were deported to France to guarantee the future good behaviour of those left behind.[47] The day before the sacking of Pavia, on 25 May, Bonaparte issued another proclamation lamenting that nobles, priests and Austrian agents had been deluding the people.[48] The French army, he promised, would behave with generosity to all those who were peaceful, but would inflict terrible retribution on those who were not. Communities that did lay down their arms at once would not be burned to the ground, but any inhabitants found bearing weapons would be shot out of hand. Any priests or nobles found in those villages in revolt would be taken hostage and deported to France.

The massacre of the inhabitants of Pavia, far from tarnishing the image of Bonaparte as liberator, became a strand of the heroic legend, at least for contemporaries. The rebels were not victims of French repression, but traitors to liberty, allies, therefore, of the Austrian enemy. This particular episode, in which Bonaparte took pains to minimize the executions, would have given contemporaries the impression that they were seeing a more complete picture of the campaign and the difficulties the French troops faced with a recalcitrant populace.[49] From the start, the great majority of Italians had received the French invader with a mixture of fear and hostility. After their experiences in 1796, those feelings were intensified. Bonaparte blamed Catholic priests for inspiring the revolts and, in some respects, they were caused by Italian Jacobin excesses towards the Church. But the revolts risked developing into another Vendée. Fear of a war of attrition behind his lines was probably one of the reasons why the revolts were so ferociously put down. It was a warning to anyone who might be contemplating revolt. Months after the initial uprisings, when trouble flared again, Bonaparte wrote to General Rusca: 'Assemble all the magistrates, the heads of various monasteries and all the parish priests. Tell them from me, that as long as ministers of religion are motivated by true principles ... I will respect them, their property and their customs ... but when the sanctity of their ministry becomes, in the hands of evildoers, an instrument of civil war and discord, I will treat them without any consideration, and I will destroy their monasteries and punish personally every parish priest who behaves badly.'[50]

These examples could serve no purpose while French exactions continued. In the weeks that followed, there was a rash of insurrections after the sacking of Binasco and Pavia that demonstrate just how much anger, hatred and desperation can overcome any fear of reprisal. The British consul in Venice, Francis Drake, explained that the 'excesses and irregularities which they [the French] have committed in the provinces of Bergamo, Brescia, and Verona 'have completely disgusted the inhabitants of those provinces – in short, the French have none but enemies, upon their whole line of operation from Verona to Nice.'[51] Detachments of French soldiers were attacked and troops were besieged at Arquarta, where the road linking Genoa to Milan crosses the Apennines. The disturbances were brought to an end when most of the houses in the area were burnt down.[52] At the end of June 1796 a revolt broke out in Lugo, a small town south of the Po in the papal province of Reggio Emilia, when a religious symbol (the town's patron saint, St Hilary) was confiscated. Bonaparte ordered the town sacked and sixty insurgents shot.[53] Attempts by Cardinal Chiaramonti, bishop of Imola (the future Pope Pius VII) to prevent the uprising failed miserably, although, without his intervention, the reprisals could have been much worse.

Over the months that followed, the French would find it increasingly difficult to control the areas they had occupied, and had to contend with armed bands, known as *barbetti* in Piedmont, anywhere between 4,000 and 7,000 strong, who plundered French convoys, massacred the soldiers and terrorized pro-French Italians. Most of them, it was thought, were soldiers in the army of the King of Piedmont-Sardinia who had been stood down once peace was signed with France, but it is also likely that French deserters could be found among their ranks.[54] The court of Turin was in no position to combat them, and may even have been continuing the war through them.[55] The French were never able to eradicate them entirely. These bands, similar in many respects to the guerrilla movements that were later to spring up in Calabria and Spain, were numerous and particularly well organized. Bonaparte would always attempt to come across as respectful of 'all peoples', but he would never hesitate to use mobile columns against resisters, threatening that he would be 'terrible like fire from the heavens'.[56]

Liberating Italian Art

Bonaparte suspended his offensive against the Austrians, at least for the moment. He received instructions from the Directory, probably inspired by Carnot, to complete the conquest of Lombardy, but at the same time he was to take advantage of his successes, leave a holding force in the north under Kellermann, and turn against the enemies of France in central and southern Italy – the Duke of Parma, the pope and the King of Naples.[57] The sole purpose of this brief (less than one month) foray into the south seems to have been to loot and pillage, although admittedly it was at the same time dealing a blow to the enemies of the Republic by gaining control of the western Italian ports threatened by British occupation.

The expedition began on 15 June. Four days later, Bonaparte passed through Modena and arrived in Bologna, part of the Papal States, at midnight. There was little or no resistance; Bologna had once been an independent state and was not particularly sympathetic to the pope, who had suppressed its power and privileges over the years. Whatever joy the Bolognese may have felt at being liberated from Rome was, however, quickly dispelled when Bonaparte levied a contribution of two million francs in silver, while he took another two million 'in kind' from the town.[58] Bonaparte also imprisoned the cardinal legate and then packed him off to Rome to let the pope know his demands. The Holy See sent back the Chevalier d'Azara, the Spanish ambassador to Rome – who is said to have exerted more influence over the pope than anyone in his entourage – to mediate on his behalf (Rome did not recognize the French Republic).[59] Within a few days, an armistice was signed, pending negotiations that were to be carried out in Paris. But, in the meantime, the pope had to hand over the port of Ancona, one hundred paintings, vases and statues, five hundred manuscripts, provide twenty-one million francs in coin and goods, and allow the passage of French troops through the Papal States whenever it was requested.[60]

There was nothing new in Bonaparte's policy.[61] Requisitioning was a common practice during the *ancien régime*, while the demands in monetary contributions and the seizing of artworks dated back to 1794 with the French incursions into Belgium, the Rhineland and Holland. Armies had always lived off the land and had always levied contributions, but the practice was systematized as never before during the Terror.[62] In December 1793, the finance specialist for the Committee of Public Safety, Pierre Joseph Cambon, stood up in the Convention to argue that, even though France had brought 'liberty and equality' to its neighbours, it had not received the support that was their due. Those people should, therefore, be made to pay for their liberation.[63] The proposal was enthusiastically adopted, and, over the coming months and years, the argument was fine tuned. Official plunder was also put on the agenda under the guise of ideology – art could only thrive and prosper in a 'free' country and revolutionary France was, above all, the land of 'liberty'. The revolutionary government was spurred on by, among other people, artists who considered revolutionary France the legitimate successor of ancient Greece and which could, therefore, claim the heritage of mankind's patrimony.[64] In short, France had become, in the minds of some of its revolutionaries, the motherland not only of liberty but also of the arts.

We do not know whether Bonaparte subscribed to the revolutionary rhetoric of repatriating art, but even before the Directory's orders had arrived, he had organized the systematic pillaging of Italy's treasures. His motives appear to be more politically self-serving. By transferring Italy's art to the National Museum in Paris, he hoped to be remembered as a kind of modern-day Caesar.[65] What is certain, however, is that the art seizures were desired simultaneously by the government in Paris and by Bonaparte on the ground.[66] Bonaparte, therefore, adopted two different strategies, depending on the circumstances. In those countries that had been conquered by his armies – Lombardy, Romagna, the Holy See, and the region around Verona in neutral Venetian territory – Saliceti and the agents attached to the commission acted with the same freedom as their counterparts in Germany, requisitioning art as they saw fit. On the other hand, in those countries that asked to negotiate a peace settlement, Bonaparte demanded a certain number of art works as part of that settlement. He thus 'legally' extorted art treasures in the treaties signed on behalf of the French government and various Italian rulers. In this manner, Bonaparte was able to seize sixteen paintings from the Duke of Parma (the people of Parma particularly resented the loss of Correggio's *Madonna del S. Gerolamo*, considered a symbol of the city), twenty paintings from the Duke of Modena at Parma, while Perugia delivered Raphael's *Madonna of Foligno*, chosen personally by the general-in-chief, and twenty paintings from Milan (including works by Michelangelo, Raphael, Titian, Rubens, Giorgione and Leonardo da Vinci).[67] The pièce de résistance was a manuscript by Virgil that had belonged to Petrarch and contained his marginalia.

The manner in which these works of art were seized was thus fundamentally different from what had occurred in Belgium and Germany at the beginning of the French revolutionary wars, first, by the sheer size of the collections seized and, second, by the cultural and moral stakes at play. Belgium had been a question of simple plunder, but Bonaparte now systematized the acquisition of artworks by stipulating how many were to be handed over in official treaties. Moreover, on 6 May he wrote to the Directory asking for a detachment of artists capable of choosing what had to be taken.[68] The Directory had, in fact, already decided to do so. The Government Commission for the Search of Scientific and

Artistic Objects in Countries Conquered by the Armies of the French Republic was formed on 16 May and comprised the mathematician, Gaspard Monge; the distinguished chemist, Claude-Louis Berthollet; two naturalists, André Thouin and Jacques Julien de Labillardère; the sculptor, Jean-Guillaume Moitte; and the painter, Jean-Simon Barthélemy.[69] Two new members were later added to help Barthélemy: the artists Jean-Baptiste Wicar and Antoine-Jean Gros, who were already in Italy, while the Italian painter, Andrea Appiani, collaborated in Verona and Venice. In the meantime, awaiting their arrival, Bonaparte designated Pierre-Jacques Tinet, an artist attached to the Tuscan legation and who had been a member of the Commission for the Search of Artistic Objects in Belgium.[70] He had already selected works from Parma and Modena.

One is struck by how rapidly the commission worked. It left Paris in two large carriages a week after it had been formed, driving through France, crossing Mount Cenis in the rain and snow on mules, and arriving in Milan on 5 or 7 June. The members of the commission outdid each other trying to seize *chefs-d'oeuvre* from the defeated Italian cities. In Rome, the commission of experts drew up a list of 100 objets d'art, 500 manuscripts (Bonaparte had demanded 2,000) and eighty-three statues, including two of the most renowned classical works – the *Apollo Belvedere* and the *Laocoön*. Although the transfer was delayed by both popular resistance and Pope Pius VI's refusal to honour the armistice he had signed with France, they were eventually taken anyway. In February 1797, Bonaparte told the Directory, 'The commission of experts has reaped a good harvest in Ravenna, Rimini, Pescara, Ancona, Loreto and Perugia which will be sent to Paris. That, together with what we have from Rome, will mean that we have everything that is a work of art in Italy, save for a small number of objects in Turin and Naples.'[71] The boast was not quite true – Florence and Brescia remained untouched, as did many private collections – but the French were certainly thorough. By the end of the campaign, just under two hundred paintings and one hundred sculptures were confiscated.[72]

The news that the southern front was being run at a profit was welcome relief to a government having difficulty justifying its existence, let alone managing the difficult situation France still found itself in. Far from 'making war finance itself, the Directory proceeded to make war for the purposes of finance'.[73] And Bonaparte made sure he let the government in Paris know where the money was coming from. In May 1796, he reported that he had sent to Tortona at least two million francs' worth of jewels and silver, paid as part of the levy, and awaited the Directory's instructions for their disposal. At the beginning of June, the directors were told that he was sending another two million francs in gold bullion back to Paris and that they should make immediate arrangements for a safe escort from Lyons. Bonaparte also added that he was sending back 100 horses, the finest in Lombardy, 'to replace those poor creatures that at present pull your carriages.'[74] It was almost as if Bonaparte were taunting the directors. He also sent about one million francs in cash directly to the Army of the Rhine.[75] In July, he informed the directors that an eighty-wagon convoy of hemp and silk was heading for Paris.[76] Hardly a week went by in the summer and autumn of 1796 without some article in the Parisian press about the latest Italian art acquisitions, sometimes written by Bonaparte, but usually by one of the members of the commission. The publicity surrounding the artistic conquests in Italy was an obvious means of keeping his name in the papers as well as adding to his prestige as a general truly interested in the arts and sciences.

'My Life is a Perpetual Nightmare'

Despite the impressive victories that marked the opening phases of the Italian campaign, and the tremendous hoard Bonaparte was sending back to France, he was constantly gnawed by personal anxieties. He often spoke of his wife to Marmont with a certain 'open-heartedness' and 'impetuosity' that he would not allow himself in later years. 'In a trip I made with him during this period, whose object was to inspect the fortified towns of Piedmont that had been put in our hands, one morning, at Tortona, the glass on the portrait of his wife, which he always carried with him, broke. He went terribly pale and had the most painful sensation. "Marmont," he said to me, "my wife is either

sick or unfaithful".'[77] A number of attempts to get her to come
to Italy had failed. Bonaparte wrote first through Junot (sent to
Paris with twenty-two enemy flags), then through Murat asking
her to accompany them when they returned to Italy.[78] The
correspondence was briefly interrupted in May with the resumption of the campaign. Josephine had, in any event, excused her
absence by saying she was pregnant. 'So it is true that you are
pregnant. Murat [we do not know whether he was complicit in
the deception or not] wrote me, but he says that it has made you
sick and that it would not be prudent for you to undertake such
a long journey. So I will again be deprived of the happiness of
holding you in my arms! So I will again be several months away
from all that I love! Is it possible that I won't have the pleasure
of seeing you with your little stomach!'[79] He was so gratified by
the news that he wrote, 'Rather than know you to be melancholy, I think that I would find a lover for you myself.'

We do not know whether it dawned on Bonaparte that the
pregnancy was an excuse not to join him, but in any event the
elation was not to last.[80] Around the end of the month he resumed
his lament and even wrote to Carnot to complain that his wife had
not come and had taken a lover.[81] Bonaparte's letters during these
months swing between expressions of intense devotion – 'Never
has a woman been loved with more devotion, more warmth, and
more tenderness' – expressions of anguish – 'If I were to lose your
love, your heart, your adorable self, I would have lost all that makes
life happy and dear to me' – and frenzied reproach – 'You are a
monster whom I cannot explain' – sometimes in the same letter.
Bonaparte's moods alternated between fanciful expectations that
she was on her way – 'it would make me so happy that I could
become mad' – and despair that she had still not left Paris – 'My soul
had opened itself to joy; it is now filled with pain'.[82] In those
instances, he would insist that she stay in Paris, no longer write to
him and respect his 'exile': 'A thousand daggers are tearing my heart
apart; do not drive them in any further.'[83]

Glory was evidently not enough for Bonaparte at this stage of
his life. What he desperately needed was for Josephine to
reciprocate the love he felt. He tried to get it in much the
same way that he had hoped to obtain the love of his mother, by

performing great feats that would make her pay attention, and that would flatter *her* pride. Bonaparte felt nothing without her; he hardly knew how he had lived without knowing her. No glory, no *raison d'être*, no appetite, no sleep without 'you, you, and the rest of world no more exists for me than if it had been destroyed.' Honour and victory were important only in so far as they pleased Josephine, 'without which I would have left everything to be at your feet.' She had become a kind of sacred object for Bonaparte. 'Remember the dream I had in which I took off your shoes and your rags and let you completely enter my heart? Why did not nature arrange things that way?'[84] It eloquently expressed his feelings; he was saving her from poverty and was allowing her to enter his innermost being. That she did not reciprocate in the way he hoped for drove him to despair.

Louis Léopold Boilly, *Portrait de profil de Madame de Beauharnais* (Portrait in profile of Mme de Beauharnais), 1793. (*Courtesy of Photo RMN –* © *Gérard Blot*)

While Bonaparte moved into a new phase of the campaign against Austria, when Genoa, Tuscany, Rome and Naples all fell to his troops, when he entered Modena and Bologna in triumph, he found time to write letter after tormented letter to Josephine. He considered for a moment going to Paris to see her, although it is impossible to say how serious he was.[85] More certain is the torment he was left to confront alone. 'My life is a perpetual nightmare,' he wrote to her in the middle of June, the same day that he began his raid into central Italy. 'A terrible premonition prevents me from breathing. I no longer live; I have lost more than life, more than happiness, more than repose; I am almost without hope.'[86] His thoughts were becoming increasingly morbid. In the same letter he wrote that he would be happy to hold her for two hours against his breast and then to die together. To his brother, Joseph, he wrote:

> My friend, I am in despair. My wife, all that I love in this world, is ill. I can no longer think straight. You are the only man on earth for whom I have a true and constant affection. After her, after my Josephine, you are the only one who arouses in me a feeling of concern. Reassure me! Tell me the truth! You know I have never been a lover, that Josephine is the first woman I have adored. Her illness causes me to despair. Everyone abandons me. I am alone, a prey to my fears and to my misfortune. You likewise do not write. If she is well, let her make the trip; I ardently desire her to come. I need to see her, to press her to my heart. I love her madly, and I cannot continue, far from her. If she no longer loved me, I would have nothing left to do on earth.[87]

And yet Josephine still did not come. It was not entirely her fault. For over two months the Directory had denied her permission to leave the capital, although she certainly made good use of her supposed ailments to stay at home. Carnot admitted that the directors had been reluctant to let her go. 'We feared that your solicitude for her', he wrote on 21 May, 'might distract you from the tasks to which your glory and the safety of the *patrie* call you, and for a long time we resisted her desire.'[88] Passports were not issued until 24 June when Josephine was finally given permission to join her husband. Leaving Paris with her were Nicholas Clary

(Joseph's brother-in-law); General Junot; the Duc de Serbelloni, the Lombard delegate at Paris; Antoine Hamelin, a Paris acquaintance Josephine wanted to introduce to Bonaparte in the expectation of finding him a job; four servants; her little pug, Fortuné (which never left her side, slept on her bed, and on their wedding night had bitten Bonaparte on the leg hard enough to leave a scar); and Josephine's lover of two months, Hippolyte Charles. One of the servants, a maid by the name of Louise Compoint, was later sacked for granting 'favours' to Junot. He seems to have borne a grudge against Josephine as a result (it was he who later told Bonaparte about Josephine's infidelity during the Egyptian campaign). The six carriages needed for the party were given a cavalry escort. She left Paris with a heavy heart. A friend, Antoine Arnault, dined with her before she left. 'Poor woman!' he wrote, 'she dissolved into tears, she was sobbing as if she were going to the scaffold.'[89]

Josephine eventually arrived in Milan, avoiding Marseilles and her mother-in-law, on the evening of 10 July. Hamelin complained that the journey down would have been gay if it were not for Charles, who sulked every time Josephine did not give him her entire attention. Otherwise, Junot made them laugh with his 'soldierly wit'.[90] Bonaparte, however, was not there to greet her. He was near Verona, but he had left instructions that a courier was to leave at once to bring him news of her arrival. Three days later, they were reunited in Milan amid the splendours of the Serbelloni Palace. 'He loved his wife passionately,' wrote Hamelin. 'From time to time he would leave his study in order to play with her as if she were a child, would tease her, make her cry out, and overwhelm her with such caresses that I would go to the window and observe the weather outside.' Marmont also confirms that Bonaparte was ecstatic when Josephine finally arrived in Milan, 'for then he only lived for her and it was the same for a long time, never was love more pure, more true, more exclusive and possessed the heart of a man, who was so superior!'[91] But Hamelin went on to say that, as far as Josephine was concerned, 'she had never been in love for the simple reason that she had always been in love with someone else. I knew what to expect of Mr Charles, and I felt uncomfortable seeing this young general [Bonaparte] already covered in a glory that he reflected onto his wife, become the unfortunate rival of a little shrimp of a man whose only advantage was his good figure and the elegance of a wigmaker's boy.'[92]

Two days after their brief reunion, Bonaparte was off to fight what was to be the stage of the campaign that would put him in control of the entire Italian Peninsula. For all that, Bonaparte felt Josephine's absence acutely; over the following six days he wrote her five letters. The first, on 17 July at two o'clock in the afternoon, went:

Since I left you I have felt sad. My happiness is to be next to you. What nights, my dear friend, I spent in your arms! I go over in my mind the all that we did, the kisses, the tears, your lovable jealousy, and the incomparable charms of Josephine constantly re-ignite the bright and burning flame in my heart and in my senses. When will I be free of all worry, of all my affairs, to spend every moment next to you, to do nothing but to love you and to think of nothing other than the happiness of telling you, of proving it to you? . . . A few days ago, I thought I loved you but since I have seen you, I feel that I love you a thousand times more. Since I have known you I love you more everyday . . . Ah!, please, let me see some of your defects. Be less beautiful, less gracious, less tender, less good, and especially, never be jealous, never cry, your tears carry away all reason, and burn my blood. Believe me when I say that I am not capable of having a thought that does not belong to you nor an idea that is not subject to you.[93]

On 18 July, at two o'clock in the afternoon, having spent the night fighting before Mantua, where the Austrian army had retreated after being chased from the region of Milan, Bonaparte hurriedly wrote to Josephine: 'I spent the whole evening in Virgil's village [Mantua was the birthplace of Virgil], next to the lake, under the silver light of the moon. Not one hour without thinking of my Josephine. I saw you asleep, one of your hands was around my neck, the other on your breast. I held you close to my heart and I felt yours palpitate.'[94] This tenderness did not prevent the usual outbursts of possessiveness. He would open Josephine's mail (after having apparently asked her permission to do so), not out of jealousy, he argued, but so that there would be no remorse and no fear.[95] A couple of days later, suspicion pierces through his letters again: 'You must know Milan well by now. Perhaps you have found that lover you came here looking for. Only, you would have found him without my offering him to you. That idea worries me . . . But, no, we should have a better idea of our worth. While we are on the subject, I have been assured that you have known for a long time and *very well* that gentleman whom you recommend to me for a business venture. If that were the case, you would be a monster.'[96] He was referring to Hippolyte Charles, whose presence could hardly have gone unnoticed in Milan. In the very next sentence, however, Bonaparte was once again reassuring Josephine of his love and of his desire to breathe her breath while he lay next to her, to contemplate her 'graces', and to overwhelm her with caresses. He ended the letter, 'A thousand kisses, everywhere, everywhere.'

Clearly, Josephine's presence in Italy did not placate his jealous nature, perhaps because she was just as lax in writing to him as she had been in Paris: his letters were still full of reproaches to her on that count.[97] On such occasions he could be quite spiteful: 'You are mean and ugly,' he wrote to her in September, 'as ugly as you are inconsiderate . . . should a husband lose his rights because he is far from you, overwhelmed with work, tiredness, and sorrow? Without his Josephine, without the assurance of her love, what is left on earth, what would he do?'[98] The relief obtained from the arrival of a few letters was temporary; he would soon start admonishing her again.

It is possible that Josephine was also jealous, accusing Bonaparte of having opened his heart to another, a certain Mme Tarera, about whom we know nothing. Bonaparte took Josephine's reproach seriously enough to write reassuringly that his heart was hers by right of conquest and that the conquest was solid and eternal.[99] Josephine's little outburst could be seen as coquettishness, but she did ask Berthier to send her reports from headquarters assuring her of Bonaparte's devotion. Twelve letters from October 1796 to February 1797 exist.[100] Either Bonaparte's attentions were starting to affect her, or she was worried that he would find out about her affair with Hippolyte Charles. About that time, Josephine wrote to her aunt in Paris that Bonaparte was 'the best husband in the world. I never lack anything, for he always anticipates my wishes. All day long he adores me, as if I were a goddess. He could not possibly be a better husband. M. Serbelloni [who took the letter to Paris] will tell you how I am loved. He often writes to my children for he loves them very much.'[101] There is nothing in them about her own feelings.

Castiglione

At the end of July, the Austrians began the first of what were to be four attempts in the space of six months to relieve Mantua and re-establish control over northern Italy. Mantua, with an imposing fortress and a garrison of 12,000 men, was important to the Austrian line of defence in northern Italy. The problem Bonaparte faced was to maintain control over the territories he had conquered, to continue the siege of Mantua, and to fend off the Austrian army's attempts to relieve the siege with the limited forces available. That he succeeded in doing so was because Bonaparte exploited his central position to the full, moved his troops faster and concentrated them at critical points.

Austrian command of the relief army was given to General Wurmser, who had been sent to take over from Beaulieu in June. Beaulieu had lost the confidence of the army; most of his officers openly complained that they had hoped Beaulieu would be replaced by 'a younger man more capable of *bodily* exertion'.[102] In this they were to be disappointed. Wurmser was seventy-two compared to Beaulieu's sprightly seventy. He was full of energy, admittedly, but there was not much else going for him. 'He is undecided,' wrote the British attaché, Colonel Graham, attached to the Austrian army.[103] On the first of these counter-offensives, Wurmser divided his army into three columns. Two slowly advanced either side of Lake Garda, while the third column moved down the Brenta valley, further to the south-east. If the two columns advancing either side of Lake Garda had reunited at the southern end of lake, they would have presented Bonaparte with a formidable force. But they were kept apart, largely through the tremendous energy displayed by

Bonaparte, riding from front to front, in order to defeat the two forces separately. The parts played in this by Augereau, who halted Wurmser's advance guard at Castiglione (3 August 1796), and Masséna, who faced his Austrian counterpart, General Peter Vitus von Quasdanovitch, that same day at Lonato, were considerable. It gave Bonaparte time to defeat Quasdanovitch and then turn back with the bulk of his army to defeat Wurmser at Castiglione (5 August 1796).[104] Wurmser was obliged to retreat to the Tyrol, from where he had started his offensive, while the siege of Mantua, briefly postponed when troops were transferred to bolster the army confronting the Austrian offensive, was resumed. Wurmser made another thrust into Italy in September (the second counter-offensive), but this time he was so badly mauled (at the battles of Roveredo and Bassano) that he ended up within the walls of Mantua with half his army, while the other half had to slip back to the Tyrol with their tails between their legs.

Even before that, though, Bonaparte was considering marching on Vienna. This was a new development. Only a short time before, he had been content to follow the Directory's instructions to join with the French forces in Bavaria. Now he was suggesting that he could 'march on Vienna by the road to Trieste' and, to make it palatable to the Directory, 'we shall then have time to take the immense resources that this place contains.'[105] To this end Bonaparte pushed himself and his men implacably; he is supposed to have ridden five of his own horses to death over a period of three days.[106] Marmont complained to his father on one occasion that he had spent twenty-four hours in the saddle and, after three hours of rest, rode again for another fifteen.[107] Captain Dommartin wrote to his mother that he had spent sixty hours on horseback and only dismounted to change horses.[108] Even if this is an exaggeration, it gives an indication of the degree to which Bonaparte pushed his men. Forced marches were common and conditions for the men at the best of times were hard. The record was held by Augereau's division, which marched an incredible eighty kilometres in thirty-six hours at the height of the crisis leading to the battle of Castiglione, and ninety-six kilometres in two days before storming the mountain pass of Primolano.[109] This was *blitzkrieg* before its time – armies would normally march between sixteen and twenty kilometres a day – and was made possible by the extraordinary endurance and stamina of the French troops. It was a feat that would rarely be repeated during the Napoleonic wars, even if these incredible forced marches in Italy, followed by fighting and more fighting, became integral to Napoleon's approach to war. The memory of it led him later to regularly expect it of his men.[110] And, unlike other theatres of the revolutionary wars, where it was the allies who took the fight to the French,[111] in Italy it was Bonaparte, at least in the opening and closing stages of the campaign, who took the fight to the allies.

'It was extremely hot,' Captain Laugier later recalled during one day's march in the Venetian countryside on the road to Lonato. 'No food except a few ears of barely formed maize we tore off. At nine in the evening I still had not eaten, and I did not have any reserves from the previous day's bread ration. I then learned that thirst was more difficult to support than hunger and that great thirst occurs when one does not eat. I drank from all the streams without quenching my thirst and felt that water gave me little assistance.'[112] The next day only four ounces of bread were distributed. When Bonaparte rode by and saw his men sucking on 'ears of Turkish wheat', complaining there was no food, his only response was, 'I know, and you won't find any until you have taken Salo. There are no other resources than the enemy's magazines.'[113] Masséna complained to Bonaparte on 1 September that the 'soldiers suffer cruelly; at least two-thirds of my division want coats, vests, breeches, shirts etc., and are absolutely barefoot.'[114] By September, there were almost as many men in the hospitals as there were in the field (about 29,000 to 32,000).[115] 'The division does not only suffer from the privation of subsistence,' Masséna continued, 'but on the eve of an expedition into the mountains of the Tyrol, two-thirds of the troops were without clothes and literally barefoot.'[116]

11

Artists and Soldiers, Politics and Love

Rebirth – Arcola

In November 1796, Bonaparte was in a precarious position. He faced another concerted push from the Austrians (the third counter-offensive) to try to regain northern Italy and relieve the siege of Mantua. Bonaparte's intelligence estimated the combined Austrian forces to be about 50,000 strong against his 30,000. It left the young commander in a despondent mood:

> The weakness and exhaustion of the bravest men makes me fear the worst. We are perhaps on the eve of losing Italy. None of the expected help has arrived . . . I do my duty, and so does the army. My spirit is lacerated, but my conscience is clear . . . The wounded are the elite of the army. All our senior officers and our elite generals are out of action. All those who arrive are inept and do not have the confidence of the soldiers. The army of Italy, reduced to a handful of men, is exhausted . . . We are abandoned in the depths of Italy . . . Those brave men who remain see death as inevitable in the midst of such continual risks and with such slender forces. Perhaps the hour of the brave Augereau, the intrepid Masséna, of Berthier or mine is ready to sound. Then what would happen to these courageous people? This idea makes me wary: I no longer dare to face death.[1]

Interestingly, the refrain in this letter to the Directory was taken up by his men. One can find the very same phrases, for example, in a letter Dommartin wrote to his mother that same day.[2] Like everything Bonaparte wrote for public consumption, this kind of declaration has to be read circumspectly. It was a way of telling the world, 'Look how much I have accomplished with so little.' Admittedly, he was tired and exhausted, as were many of the men under his command. They had been fighting for months, many comrades had been lost, and it was starting to take its toll on morale. And yet, Bonaparte made an emotional appeal to his men for another concerted effort, in order to meet the two-pronged attack from the Austrians, one of which was commanded by General Josef Alvinczy. It resulted in the victory of Arcola.

The similarities between the battles of Arcola and Lodi were not lost on Bonaparte,[3] but although Lodi was a much longer bridge, and its outcome was immediately and obviously successful, it was Arcola that resulted in an intensive propaganda campaign to highlight Bonaparte's role. There are a number of possible explanations for this. It was the first time in the campaign that Bonaparte had been exposed to real danger, so it lent itself to an heroic construction.[4] It is also possible that, by the time of Arcola, Bonaparte had realized the glory that could be gained from an heroic crossing in the face of enemy guns. That is, the action could be better exploited a second time around. By Arcola, almost nine months had gone by since the opening of the campaign and much had been learned. This is apparent in the evolution of the images surrounding the battle. Certainly, the popular representations of the crossing of the bridge of Lodi, a subject that was suggested by Bonaparte himself, were not, on the whole, as visually sophisticated as those of Arcola, at least not as far as promoting Bonaparte is concerned. Portrayals of Lodi are more egalitarian: Bonaparte is not usually the central figure or he is not immediately recognizable. Arcola, on the other hand, was the object of a more concerted effort of self-promotion. Finally, it is just possible that Arcola represented a psychological turning point for Bonaparte. Two days after the battle, he wrote the following lines: 'At last my adorable Josephine, I am reborn: death is no longer before my eyes, and glory and honour are again in my heart. The enemy has been beaten at Arcola ... Mantua will be ours in eight days and, in your arms, I will soon be able to give you a thousand proofs of the ardent love of your husband. As soon as I can, I will return to Milan; I am a little tired.'⁵

In the first engravings of Arcola to appear, Bonaparte is accompanied by Augereau. Both are portrayed on horseback, side by side, crossing a bridge that was never crossed, each carrying a flag with the inscription 'The French People', followed by a dozen or so grenadiers in formation. We can see two cannon to the right crashing fire on the advancing French. In other engravings, Augereau appears by himself in the posture later attributed to Bonaparte. Over time, these representations gave way to images of Bonaparte crossing the bridge alone, at first on horseback, and then on foot, as Bonaparte displaced Augereau in the popular imagination. It was from this moment on that Bonaparte as an individual breaks away from the Army of Italy, which had, until then, always been portrayed collectively. It is the start of the myth of Bonaparte as invincible

Alexandre Chaponnier, *Passage du Pont d'Arcole* (Crossing of the Bridge at Arcola), circa 1798. (*Bibliothèque nationale, Paris*)

Paul André Basset, *Buonaparte, général en chef de l'armée d'Italie plantant un drapeau sur le pont d'Arcole* (Buonaparte, general-in-chief of the Army of Italy, planting a flag on the bridge at Arcola), between 1796 and 1799. (*Bibliothèque nationale, Paris*)

hero, even if those words were not used until the first half of 1797. The emphasis, moreover, especially in the pamphlet literature that was to follow, was on Bonaparte's youth, which to contemporaries made his achievements all the more remarkable.[6]

Bonaparte was not the only general attempting to rewrite the history of the crossing. Both Augereau and Berthier tried to promote their own version of events at Arcola without success.[7] Both had their portraits on the bridge painted, the former by

Charles Thévenin and the latter by Antoine-Jean Gros, which were shown at the Salon of 1798 along with portraits of at least six other generals. Gros' drawing of Berthier is similar, if not a mirror image, to the stance in which he portrayed Bonaparte two years later, with Berthier also clearly looking back at the men who are meant to follow him onto the bridge, his open hand gesturing towards it as though he were offering it to them.

These images were never meant to be accurate portrayals of a historical event. They were meant to glorify the individual and the heroic feats of the army. They symbolize the potential valour each revolutionary had within him. It is clear that, as far as the war of representations was concerned, Bonaparte had to contend with competing images and competing narratives of battle. He did not, indeed could not, at this early stage, completely dominate the

Pierre-Michel Alix, based on a drawing by Antoine-Jean Gros, *Portrait de Louis Alexandre Berthier* (Portrait of Louis Alexandre Berthier), circa 1798. (*Courtesy of Photo RMN – © Gérard Blot*)

Charles Thévenin, *Le Général Augereau conduisant la charge à l'attaque du Pont d'Arcole le 15 novembre 1796* (General Augereau leading the charge to attack the bridge at Arcola on 15 November 1796), 1798. (*Courtesy of Photo RMN – © Droits réservés*)

iconography. Other generals, including Jean Charles Pichegru (who had commanded the armies of the Nord, and the Ardennes), Louis Lazare Hoche (Moselle, Ouest, Sambre-et-Meuse), Jean Victor Moreau (Rhin-et-Moselle) and Pierre Beurnonville (Nord, Sambre-et-Meuse and Batavia) also recognized the importance of propaganda and were using engravings and prints to promote themselves. But their propaganda efforts, as well as their military victories, paled in comparison to Bonaparte's, or at least paled in comparison to Bonaparte's exploitation of them, which eventually enabled him to impose himself on the public imagination.

Exploiting Victory

On many levels the campaign of Italy was a war of representations.[8] Both Lodi and Arcola are clear examples of the disparity between the reality of battle and the manner in which it was portrayed in Bonaparte's accounts. He would not hesitate, for example, to misrepresent the results of battle by exaggerating his own or his troops' feats and minimizing losses.[9] The order of the day, issued after the battle of Montenotte, was thus full of inaccuracies: the enemy was not completely routed, Beaulieu was not there with 13,000 men, and the enemy had not lost 3,000 killed or wounded.[10] At Lodi, the 10,000 Austrian infantry became 14,000, the 1,500 cavalry became 4,000, and the 300-odd killed and wounded became 3,000.[11] A great deal was made of each victory, no matter how small. A long list of figures could be read in the proclamation of 10 March 1797, in which Bonaparte boasted of having won fourteen battles, seventy skirmishes, taken over 100,000 prisoners, 500 cannon, and sent thirty million francs and 300 pieces of art back to Paris.[12] The proclamation of 6 May summarized the campaign up until then in the most flattering light. In two weeks they had won, 'six victories, taken twenty-one flags, fifty-five cannon; several forts, conquered the richest part of Piedmont; taken fifteen thousand prisoners and killed or wounded more than ten thousand men.' The proclamation concluded with a tribute to the troops. 'You have won battles without cannon, crossed rivers without bridges, undertaken forced marches without boots, bivouacked without liquor and often without bread. The Republican phalanx, the soldiers of liberty were alone capable of suffering what you have suffered.'[13]

Bonaparte, quite literally, was constructing a narrative of their adventures in Italy, adventures he and the troops shared in common. His victories were amplified, the troops' morale was given a boost, and a bond between the commander-in-chief and his men was created in the process. He was not only enhancing the heroism of his men, as a reflection of his own image as hero, he was also demonstrating accomplishments as commander-in-chief. This was not only how he obtained the approval of the directors and the French people, but also how he maintained his freedom of action in Italy. As long as he kept up the pace, as long as the victories and the loot kept coming, the Directory would have to give him free rein to run the campaign.

The reverse side of the coin is that, as we saw with Arcola, Bonaparte did not hesitate to hide losses and defeats from the government and the people of Paris. Thus, no mention was made of the loss of over 180 field guns during the first siege of Mantua (a setback, admittedly, but not disastrous). Nor was any mention made of the defeat of Masséna's divisions on 12 September when about 2,000 men were lost.[14] When Bonaparte did mention any reversals it was always done in a way that highlighted the heroism of those taking part in the action, or the occasion was used to remind readers of previous victories. In a letter to the Directory (3 August 1796), subsequently published in the *Moniteur*, he briefly mentioned having 'suffered reverses' – a reference to the Austrians' taking Salo and Corona – but then immediately went on to say that 'already victory has started to come back to us under our flags.'[15] The setback at Cerea (11 September), in which Murat was badly mauled by Austrian cavalry, prompting Bonaparte to intervene personally (to no avail), was reported by Bonaparte to the Directory to look like a simple tactical manoeuvre to strengthen his hand.[16] In another article in the *Moniteur* that described a failed attempt to take Mantua, he wrote: 'Despite the canister shot from the fortress, the grenadiers advanced in order along the causeway; they even stormed a column [of troops] to take Mantua and when someone pointed out the enemy batteries on the ramparts they said: "At Lodi, there were many more." But the circumstances were not the same; I had them withdraw.' The article ended with, 'It was an extremely interesting day for us, and the advance guard performed well.'[17] What better way of hiding setbacks from both the government and the public than by focusing on the heroic nature of battle? Thus, in the visual representations that followed Arcola, Bonaparte and Augereau were portrayed not at a distance from the bridge, but actually on it, on horse or on foot, rushing forward as if they were succeeding in taking it.

This 'political exploitation of victory' was not as straightforward or obvious as it might appear to the modern reader.[18] To begin with, the newspaper as medium was relatively new, or at least access to it was. The explosion of newspapers that occurred on the eve of the French Revolution opened possibilities to those who wanted to influence and, indeed, create public opinion. Hundreds of broadsheets appeared during this period, many, it is true, not lasting more than one issue, but many more enjoying a run of a couple of years. Access to the press, then, quickly became an important means of communicating a political message or, more rarely, of promoting one's image. Thus, the *Moniteur* announced victory after victory (Montenotte, Millesimo, Dego, Ceva, and the armistice with Piedmont) in the first couple of weeks of the campaign.[19] This is one of the more remarkable aspects of Bonaparte's early career. Almost intuitively, it would seem, he was aware of the power of this medium, and took full advantage of what it had to offer. We have no idea where this awareness came from. Did he simply look around him, make a mental note of what was being done in the newspapers of the time and then, when he was in a position to do so, exploit the medium for his own personal advantage? Was he inspired by a particular revolutionary or military figure who had done something similar? Although we cannot assess the true impact of this correspondence, we can assume, from the artistic outpouring that soon followed, that Bonaparte's exploits inspired others.

Equally important was the style in which the accounts were written.[20] Bonaparte made sure that he always appeared in control of events, and he or his men were almost always at the centre of the heroic action being described. But suspense was one of the keys to his writing style. Other generals also used the press to promote their victories, but, by and large, their accounts were dry, revealing little to excite the imagination of the reader. Not only are Bonaparte's letters more numerous, but they are also invariably written with a flair and dynamism not found elsewhere. One can imagine the readers in the cafés and clubs of Paris impatiently awaiting the next issue to find out the latest news.

Bonaparte seldom referred to himself in these letters and would often suppress his feats in favour of the heroic actions of his generals, a gesture that did not go unnoticed. The *Décade philosophique*, for example, picked up on Bonaparte's evident humility. Bonaparte, favourably compared to Alexander, did not order these conquests for himself, but in the name of the *patrie*, in the name of twenty-five million men bound by a common interest, and 'that is such a great and moving idea!'[21] It was left to others, like Saliceti, who at the beginning of the campaign often signed off on reports that were also printed in the papers, to praise the role of the general-in-chief. In a letter sent to the Directory after the victories of Millesimo (13 April) and Dego (14–15 April), for example, Saliceti wrote, 'the commander-in-chief has acquired during this victory through the wisdom of his actions, his ability to direct them, by his ability to proceed during the action to points where his presence could be necessary, the reputation of a general worthy, in every respect, of the national confidence.' He was soon comparing Bonaparte with the 'most famous generals of Europe'.[22]

At the same time, poets and songwriters, if they were not directly employed to compose odes to the conqueror of Italy, spontaneously joined the myth-making process, as though they instinctively recognized a subject of heroic proportions.[23] Little by little, other newspapers, and other artists, took up the refrain portraying Bonaparte breaking the chains of slavery and liberating the people of Italy. A concert of praise was eventually to be heard not only in France but also in Holland, Germany, Italy, and even in England, where Bonaparte's exploits were the subject of newspaper articles.

Bonaparte's exploits also generated a demand for visual representations. Between 1796 and 1798, about thirty-seven different portrait engravings of Bonaparte were made in Italy.[24] As we have seen, some of these engravings were commissioned by Bonaparte, although we know little about the actual process involved and how he went about this.[25] The vast majority of engravings, however, appear to be spontaneous manifestations of the legend, a product designed to meet the popular demand for some kind of representation of the victor of Italy. What is notable about these portraits is that, since most of the artists, and the general public, for that matter, had no idea what Bonaparte actually looked like, they simply invented a likeness.[26] In fact, so little was known about Bonaparte during this period that many people did not even know how to say his name; in at least part of the Army of Italy the men pronounced Bonaparte, 'Bonnappete'.[27] But then a likeness, or even a reasonably accurate representation of Bonaparte, was not a prerequisite. The name was distinctive enough and served as a marker. The important thing was that people identified with what he represented, not with who or what he really was. In this respect, it was not until engravings by Andrea Appiani appeared around 1798, when Bonaparte was already away in Egypt, that a standardized Bonaparte portrait began to emerge.

Love and Self-Pity

'I am so felled with exhaustion, citizen directors, that it is impossible for me to tell you of all the military moves that preceded the battle of Arcola.'[29] It was no doubt the reason why Bonaparte spent almost a week, between 19 and 25 November, at Verona. There he had time to think again about his wife. 'I would be so happy to assist at your loveable toilet, small shoulder, a small white breast, supple, very firm; on top of that, a little expression [*une petite mine*] with a Creole headscarf. You know that I do not forget those little visits; you know, the little black forest. I give it a thousand kisses and am impatient for the moment when I will be there . . . To live in Josephine, is to live in Elysium. Kisses on the mouth, on the eyes, on the shoulder, on the breast, everywhere, everywhere.'[30]

The Many Faces of Bonaparte

Bonaparte sat for five artists in Italy: Appiani in Milan, Louis Lafitte in Florence, Bacler d'Albe and Gros back in Milan, and Francesco Cossia in Verona.[28] Since there was no existing iconography, and since few knew what Bonaparte actually looked like, other artists had to imagine the hero, imagine a resemblance. This was occurring as late as 1799, when Bonaparte was away in Egypt. The images that follow are largely French, but around ninety-two engravings were produced and distributed in France, Italy, parts of Germany, Austria, England, Spain and Switzerland between 1796 and 1799. This selection of portraits reflects, therefore, with varying degrees of intensity, the impression Bonaparte had made on the public imagination, from the relatively naïve (Le Clerc, Fairburn), to the heroic (Appiani, Schiavonetti), to the more or less realistic (Alessi, Momal), to more dynamic representations of Bonaparte as victorious general (Vernet, Hennequin).

Pierre Thomas Le Clerc, *Buonaparte général en chef de l'armée de la République française en Italie, nt. corsicain* (Buonaparte, general-in-chief of the French army in Italy, Corsican nationality), between 1796 and 1799. (*Bibliothèque nationale, Paris*)

John Fairburn, *General Buonaparte, engraved from the original portrait drawn from the life by citizen l'auteur at Paris, 1797.* (*Bibliothèque nationale, Paris*)

Andrea Appiani, *Le Général Buonaparte* (General Buonaparte), 1798.
(*Bibliothèque nationale, Paris*)

Drawn by Luigi Schiavonetti from a painting by Francesco Cossia,
Buonaparte, 1797. This is the earliest known British engraving of Bonaparte,
published by John Shlunt of Piccadilly, 10 July 1797. (*Bibliothèque nationale,
Paris*)

G. Alessi, *Buonaparte*, 1796. One of the first engravings, by a Milanese artist, was reproduced with varying degrees of quality in at least twenty other versions. The caption reads 'Ajaccio saw him born. The universe is filled with his glory.' (*Bibliothèque nationale, Paris*)

Jacques François Momal, *Buonaparte, général en chef de l'armée d'Italie* (Buonaparte, general-in-chief of the Army of Italy), circa 1799. (*Bibliothèque nationale, Paris*)

Carl Vernet, *Buonaparte*, circa 1797. The bridge of Arcola is in the distance. (*Bibliothèque nationale, Paris*)

Drawn by Philippe Hennequin from a painting by Appiani, *Buonaparte: nommé général en chef de l'armée d'Italie* (Buonaparte, named general-in-chief of the Army of Italy), circa 1798. Appiani, a Lombard painter, was a fervent admirer of Bonaparte, whom he probably met in Milan. (*Bibliothèque nationale, Paris*)

At the same he realised, if not yet consciously, that Josephine was being unfaithful. Two days later he wrote:

> I no longer love you, on the contrary I detest you! You are ugly, very clumsy, very stupid and a drudge. You no longer write to me at all, you do not love your husband; you know how much pleasure your letters give him and you do not write. Six lines haphazardly thrown down! What do you do all day, Madame? What important business takes from you the time to write to your good lover [*bien bon amant*]? What attachment has stifled and cast to one side the love, the tender and constant love that you promised him? Who could be this wonderful new lover who consumes your time, tyrannises your days and prevents you from looking after your husband? Beware, Josephine, one fine night the doors will burst open and I shall be before your bed! You know, Othello's small dagger![31]

The letter was partly in jest (it ends in 'I soon hope to hold you in my arms and to cover you with a million kisses as hot as the Equator, and as we approach the great circle of the sphere . . . a little kiss well planted on the little scamp'), but reflects the outbursts of passion that Bonaparte was prone to, and the torment he was suffering because of Josephine's absence.

When Bonaparte did eventually get back to Milan on 27 November, Josephine was not there. She had gone off to Genoa with her lover, Hippolyte Charles, bored with Milan,[32] despite being fêted by all the princes of Italy. She realized how much Bonaparte loved her, and seems to have been happy enough at the thought,[33] but not enough to prevent her from finding comfort in the arms of her lover. 'I ran to your apartment,' Bonaparte scrawled off to her, bitterly disappointed. 'I left everything to see you, to hold you in my arms . . . You were not there; you run around towns with parties, when I approach you draw away from me, you no longer care for your dear Achilles. A caprice made you fall in love with him; inconstancy now renders you indifferent . . . The unhappiness I feel is incalculable; I have no right to expect it. I will be here till the 29th. Do not trouble yourself, amuse yourself, you are made for happiness, the whole world will only be too happy to please you, and your husband alone is very, very unhappy!!!'[34]

The next day, however, his disappointment gave way to self-pitying. He was prepared to tolerate everything as long as she loved him: 'I do not want to disturb in the least the outings that are offered you, I am not worth it . . . To love only you, to make you happy, to do nothing that would annoy you, that is my destiny and my aim in life . . . When I sacrifice to you all my desires, all my thoughts, every moment of my life, I obey the ascendancy that your charms, your character and your whole person have taken over my unfortunate heart. I am wrong if nature, less favourable, has not given me the attraction needed to captivate you, but what I deserve from Josephine is respect, esteem, and compassion. I love her passionately and her alone.' At the end of the letter, he wrote 'I have reopened the letter to give you a kiss and a . . . [sic] Ah! Josephine . . . Josephine!'[35] 'Come,' Berthier wrote anxiously to her. 'He is afflicted and gravely upset.'[36] Josephine returned sometime at the beginning of December, and Bonaparte was so happy that reconciliation soon followed.

The public image Bonaparte projected – the victorious, confident young general who swept aside all in his path – could not have been more different from the insecure behaviour that characterized his love life. With Josephine, he appeared almost entirely dependent on her for his happiness and was content with the few scraps of affection she threw his way. There is something almost pathetic about *this* Bonaparte's sexual obsession with the woman he loved, and the little he received in return. Indeed, he was probably so passionate about this woman *because* he received so little in return. With his men, however, Bonaparte was a different person – cool, resolute, exacting and vigorous. He was, after all, playing a part. André-François Miot, an envoy sent from Paris, remarked when he first met Bonaparte in June that he saw 'none of those marks of familiarity between him and his companions that I had observed in other cases, and which was consistent with republican equality. He had already assumed his own place, and kept others at a distance.'[37]

This distinction between Bonaparte's personal and public personae was to change, however, and Josephine's absence in November may have been a turning point.[38] After the resumption of the campaign at the beginning of 1797, Bonaparte's letters to her practically ceased. There are only seven for the months of January and February 1797 (compared to the thirty-odd letters in the previous nine months), and then nothing. Admittedly, Josephine was by his side more often (at Bologna, for example, in February, and at the Doge's summer residence at Passeriano in September and October), and she was used on one occasion on a political mission (she accompanied a delegation to Venice in September, where she also caught up with Hippolyte Charles), but there were also long periods of absence during which no letters were forthcoming. It is not that Bonaparte had had a change of heart; he still loved her, as we will shortly see from his behaviour when they were together again in the summer of 1797; but that the pain and suffering she caused him may have obliged him to rethink his relations with her. He may have finally come to the realization that Josephine was not capable of returning the affection he lavished on her. Besides, the tables had turned somewhat since Paris. When Bonaparte married her shortly before heading off to Italy in March 1796, he was an unknown. She, on the other hand, was an experienced woman of the world who had entry into the highest political and social circles in France. Nine months later – time enough for the passion to wane somewhat – he had proved himself to be one of the most capable generals in the revolutionary armies, was administering conquered peoples and provinces, and was experiencing a growing popularity. It is not surprising that he did not feel as dependent on her.

Breaking Free

Problems were looming elsewhere as well. By this stage, profound tensions had developed between Bonaparte and the commissaries accompanying the Army of Italy; it may be that Saliceti and Garrau increasingly resented Bonaparte's growing power. The conflict was going to come to a head by early 1797.[39]

By the end of 1796, the French had managed to extract between forty and forty-five million livres from the occupation of Italy, about fifteen of which were actually sent to Paris. The commissaries of the Army of Italy were thus among the principal agents of the government and prolonged the Directory's precarious life by furnishing it with the necessary financial means.[40] On the ground in Italy, however, Bonaparte was keen to marginalize the commissaries. As he confided in Miot in June: 'The commissaries of the Directory . . . count for nothing in my policy. *I do what I want*; let them get on with the administration of public revenues, they are welcome to it, at least for the moment, but the rest does not concern them. I do not expect they will remain in office for long, and may the Directory send me no more.'[41] Bonaparte knew the Directory was about to send two more commissaries to Italy in an attempt to limit his powers, which he found intolerable. When Garrau later made the mistake of giving an order to General Vaubois, the commander in charge of the occupation of Livorno, Bonaparte replied in a tone that would have cost the position of any other general: 'When you were a representative of the people, you had unlimited power; everyone believed it a duty to obey you. Today you are commissaries of the government invested with great power, but practical instructions regulate your functions; keep to them.'[42]

In October, Bonaparte took another radical step when he made a decision that was outside his competency. He wrote to the commander of Lombardy, General Baraguey d'Hilliers. 'The overseers of the government continue to steal, to interfere with the police and everything that does not concern it; fix these enormous abuses. As first agent of the Republic in Lombardy, it is up to you to destroy all the abuses, and to re-establish things as they should be.'[43] In effect, Bonaparte simply gave the authority Saliceti and Garrau had exercised over Lombardy to one of his generals. No mention of the commissaries was made; it was as though they did not exist. The decision was taken without consulting the Directory, indeed, without even warning the commissaries. In fact, it was Baraguey d'Hilliers who informed the Directory that Bonaparte had arrogated the 'civil and administrative authority' to himself.[44] When Garrau got the letter from Baraguey d'Hilliers informing him that he had been relieved of his duties, he whipped off a reply to Bonaparte (4 November) to warn him that he was playing a dangerous game. Nevertheless, because Garrau wanted to avoid a head-on collision with Bonaparte, he did not oppose the decision outright.[45] Bonaparte had carried out a kind of coup d'état against the French civil authorities in Italy. The Directory had either to recall Bonaparte or recall the commissaries, but it could not let the conflict drag on indefinitely. Before making a decision, however, they decided to learn as much about the situation as they could. In November 1796, the thirty-year-old General Henri Clarke, a personal friend of Lazare Carnot, was officially charged with negotiating a peace treaty with Vienna, but, on his way, he was to go through Italy with a second, secret mission: to find out about the situation in Italy, that is, whether it was ripe for independence, as well as investigate Bonaparte's 'morality and talents'.[46] It was a belated and half-hearted attempt on the part of the Directory to regain control of affairs in Italy, hoping that Clarke would be able to influence Bonaparte to do its bidding.

When Clarke arrived in Milan at the end of November, he found Bonaparte 'haggard, thin, the skin sticking to his bones, the eyes shining with a constant fever'.[47] Despite his physical appearance, however, Bonaparte inspired confidence. 'There is no one here who does not regard him as a genius', wrote Clarke to the Directory, 'and he really is . . . He has great influence over the individuals who compose the republican army . . . His judgement is sure. His decisions are followed through with energy and vigour. His composure under the liveliest of actions is as remarkable as the extreme rapidity with which he can change his plans when unforeseen circumstances demand it.'[48] For his part, Bonaparte treated Clarke with a great deal of suspicion – hardly surprising since the Directory had not seen fit to warn Bonaparte that it was sending an envoy – and even accused him of being a spy for the Directory.[49] The fact that he was a pen-pusher who had never seen active service did not help matters.

Clarke, nevertheless, did his job, sending long dispatches to the government in Paris about the situation in Italy. He realized that the people of Lombardy were coming to hate the French because of the French army's exactions, but he also praised the conduct of Bonaparte. He wrote, for example, 'General Bonaparte has behaved in this country with wisdom, steadfastness, and a lot of skill. He has reassured and welcomed priests who could have been our most dangerous enemies. He has taken rides in carriages in one part of Lombardy with the archbishop of Milan and had the good sense to allow him, while by his side, to bless a superstitious people kneeling to receive this ridiculous favour.'[50] Even before Clarke's reports on the commissaries were sent to Paris, the Directory decided it was time to recall them to France (7 December), partly because it was facing a revolt – all the generals-in-chief in all the Republican armies were crying out for the suppression of the commissaries – but mostly because it was obliged to look to the two armies which remained fundamentally republican, the Army of the Sambre-et-Meuse and the Army of Italy.[51]

The abolition of the commissaries was going to have important consequences for the development of Bonaparte's political power, but it needs to be kept in context. It was part of the struggle between civilian and military authorities that had been waged with varying degrees of intensity ever since the beginning of the war, and which was to continue even after Bonaparte came to power.[52] For the first time since the sixteenth century, a French army in the field did not have a civilian representative at the commander-in-chief's side.[53] The countries occupied by French troops were, in effect, delivered up to the arbitrary power of those in command. The generals were now absolute masters of the situation in their respective occupied territories, and were able to proceed with requisitions without restrictions being placed on them. If the situation was bad while the civil authorities accompanied the armies, it became much worse in their absence.[54]

Rivoli

In the wake of the battles of Lodi and Arcola, Bonaparte persuaded the Directory to send reinforcements by holding out before them the prospect of even more loot. 'The more men you send, the easier it will be to not only feed them, but in addition we will be able to raise more contributions for the benefit of the Republic.'[55] Bonaparte had received several new brigades to bring his field strength to 34,500 men, as well as the 10,000 men involved in laying siege to Mantua, and as many more again maintaining the lines of communication.[56] Supplies, though, remained a constant problem. Shortly after the battle of Arcola, Bonaparte sent off an angry letter to the commissary, Garrau: 'The army is without shoes, without pay, without clothes, the hospitals lack everything, our wounded are lying on the floors, and in the most horrible state of destitution . . . The evil [*mal*] is so great that a remedy is necessary. I beg you reply to me during the day whether you can provide for the needs of the army.'[57] Joubert wrote to Bonaparte to complain: 'We are dying of hunger, my ovens are ready, but we have no flour. It is one o'clock in the afternoon, and no bread . . . I do not even dare go out. They shout at me: bread . . . the most dismal silence reigns over the camps, and I have seen soldiers look for food in the bushes.'[58] The lament was taken up in a letter to General Lebley: 'the penury of the troops has not ceased. In November, by a bitter cold in the Alps, snow covered the ground. Many soldiers have neither shoes nor coats [*roupes*]. The companies that are at Corona are obliged to remain indoors because they are barefoot. Only a few men can be found to go reconnoitring. If there are any manoeuvres to carry out [in the snow], our shoes become absolutely ruined. I have half-brigades that have not left the mountains that are absolutely naked.'[59]

In these conditions, the French had to meet another (the fourth and final) Austrian counter-offensive designed to relieve Mantua, which began in January 1797. It was a three-pronged attack – one was directed against Legnano, a second against Verona and the third and main attack against the village of Rivoli, about thirty-two kilometres north-west of Verona. There a three-day battle was fought, beginning on 14 January. Bonaparte himself did not arrive until around two in the morning after the first day's battle, which was carried out by Joubert, and he immediately went to inspect the enemy's positions. Bonaparte later recalled that 'the moonlight was superb. [I] climbed the different heights and observed the lines of the enemy fires. They filled the country between the Adige [river] and Lake Garda, and the atmosphere was ablaze with them. One could easily distinguish five camps, each composed of a column.'[60] He thus saw at one glance the disposition of the Austrian forces and issued orders for the battle for the next day. One only has to stand outside Rivoli today and look out over the valley floor below to understand how comprehensive Bonaparte's view was. The exterior of the church in the main street of Rivoli is pretty much as it was in 1797. Bonaparte is thought to have used the tower as a lookout.

During the course of the second day, the Austrians appeared to be on the verge of victory. Instead, it ended in their total defeat, the loss of almost half the army (most of them as prisoners) and the retreat of the rest back to the north. Local oral tradition has it that peasants from the region, who were pro-Austrian, and who had gathered on one of the heights to watch the course of the battle, as was customary in the eighteenth and nineteenth centuries, cheered when they saw an Austrian force under the command of General Lusignan arrive at the rear of the French; they thought the Austrians were about to carry the day. This is said to have alerted Bonaparte and he was able to take the necessary steps to counter-attack. It is an interesting anecdote, but there is little in it. Bonaparte knew well in advance that the Austrians were attempting to outflank him and reacted accordingly, dealing with the bulk of the Austrian forces before turning on the unfortunate Lusignan's column.

Carl Vernet, *Bataille de Rivoli les 25 et 26 nivôse an 5* (The battle of Rivoli, the 13 and 14 January 1797), between 1799 and 1807. Rivoli much as it can be seen today, minus the highways that have been cut around the mountains. (*Bibliothèque nationale, Paris*)

Rivoli, it has been argued, was the first of the three great Napoleonic victories (the other two are Austerlitz and Jena), the first of the three great blows that destroyed the *ancien régime* in Italy and Germany.[61] The battle not only inflicted an overwhelming defeat on the Austrian army under Alvinczy – the Austrians suffered an astounding 43 per cent loss in dead, wounded and prisoners[62] – it also had important consequences for Bonaparte's reputation. When news of the battle reached Paris on 27 January 1797, it could not have arrived at a more propitious moment for the government. The Prussian ambassador reported that one of the phrases most heard during that day was: 'We needed an event like this, because we were starting to get discouraged – Vive Bonaparte!'[63] The battle marked the end of the Austrian attempt to recapture Italy. On 2 February 1797, Mantua fell at last, after a siege that had lasted, on and off, for eight months. The Austrian garrison had held out under appalling conditions. Thousands had died of sickness and malnutrition. As far back as October 1796, months before the city's fall, fifty to sixty people were dying each day; about 5,000 Austrian troops had died in the previous two months.[64] Only half of the 30,000-strong Austrian garrison was fit enough to actually march out of the town, leaving behind many thousands who were expected to die in the days that followed.

In Paris, the Austrian surrender at Mantua was considered an even greater victory than Rivoli: it seemed to leave control of the whole Italian Peninsula in the hands of the French, and peace appeared to be within sight. Bonaparte's popularity was material for the police reports. The Army of Italy now appeared to be the 'bulwark' of the Republic on the exterior, as well as its 'guarantee from within'. It was even said that those persecuted during the uprising of Vendémiaire were now prepared to pardon Bonaparte.[65] Indeed, it is safe to conclude that, from February and March 1797, Bonaparte became a noted and respectable figure in Parisian public opinion.[66] The fall of Mantua, however, was to pose a problem for the Directory. Until now, Italian patriots in Paris clamouring for an independent Italy had always been fobbed off with a 'wait until Mantua falls' attitude. Now that it had, it was going to be more difficult to resist their demands.[67] What is more important, and something, perhaps, that the directors suspected, is that Bonaparte now felt himself to be the veritable master of Italy. It is from this time on that we see him increasingly direct the diplomatic negotiations that were carried on with various Italian states according to his own political views. This is certainly what was about to happen in the Papal States.

12

The Apprenticeship of Power

Invading the Papal States

After the battle of Rivoli, Bonaparte again marched south, this time to take on the pope. The Directory implored Bonaparte to do everything in his power to destroy the Papal government by replacing the temporal power of the Church. Although not as rabidly anti-clerical as its Jacobin predecessors, the Directory nevertheless considered the Catholic Church to be an 'enemy of freedom' and an irreconcilable foe of the Republic. 'The Directory wishes you to understand that it is not giving you an order, but is merely formulating a request. It is too far from the scene of events to be able to judge the real state of things. It leaves that to the zeal and prudence which have always directed you in your career . . . No matter what steps you decide on in this case, and whatever the result may be, the Executive Directory will always consider that you have acted with the best intentions and the sincere desire to serve your country to the best advantage . . .'[1]

This is an extraordinary document. First, it demonstrates the extent of the changed relationship between Bonaparte and the Directory. The Directory no longer ordered Bonaparte; rather it politely asked him whether it was convenient. Second, the Directory was now giving Bonaparte a free hand to suppress the Papal States if he saw fit.[2] Bonaparte seized the opportunity to do so. He headed south on 30 January 1797, invading the region of Romagna with a division of troops, partly formed by Italian legions, enough to intimidate Pius VI but not enough to march on Rome.[3] The small Papal army made up of Swiss mercenaries offered little resistance.

There was only one battle, at Faenza, about fifty kilometres south-east of Bologna, followed by the flight of the pontifical troops. Pope Pius VI, an inveterate enemy of the Revolution, was obliged to sue for peace on 12 February. This resulted in the Treaty of Tolentino (19 February), which formally ceded Avignon and the Comtat Venaissin (both integrated into France since 1791), Bologna, Ferrara and the Romagna, a huge indemnity of more than thirty million francs, and a further great haul of art treasures – over one hundred paintings and sculptures, and five hundred manuscripts.[4] (Bonaparte had hoped to get much more, but was compelled to settle for less.) He justified his decision to conclude peace, once again without the involvement of Paris, by dangling the financial windfall in front of the Directory: 'thirty millions are worth ten times Rome'. After taking Bologna, Ferrara and the Romagna away from the pope, Bonaparte believed that Rome could not survive: 'this ancient machine', he wrote to his government, 'will collapse [se détraquera] all by itself.'[5]

The interest of this aspect of the Italian campaign resides entirely in Bonaparte's religious politics. The Treaty of Tolentino is often considered a sort of forerunner of the Concordat with the Catholic Church that would be implemented a couple of years after Bonaparte came to power. Until that happened, France was torn apart by what could, euphemistically, be called the religious question.

The revolutionary government in Paris had attempted to reform the Church's temporal organization in the same way that it attempted to reform the state. To do so, the National Assembly came up with a Civil Constitution of the Clergy in July 1790. Church lands were nationalized, contemplative orders were closed, priests became paid functionaries of the state, and diocesan and parish boundaries were redrawn to conform to new departmental boundaries. None of this occurred, however, without opposition from some priests. The National Assembly attempted to resolve this problem in November 1790 by requiring all priests to swear an oath of loyalty to the Civil Constitution of the Clergy.[6] It was a mistake of cataclysmic proportions. Only about half of parish priests (called jurors) took the oath, and only four or five bishops (the rest are referred to as non-juring or refractory priests). The oath, in effect, created a vast chasm between those who favoured the Revolution and those who remained loyal to the Church by obliging people to take sides.

In March 1791, many months later, Pope Pius VI issued a papal bull condemning the Civil Constitution. As a result, many priests who had initially taken the oath retracted. At the same time, the pope condemned the Declaration of the Rights of Man and of the Citizen. The Declaration was carefully debated and voted by the National Assembly in August 1789, at the very beginning of the Revolution, and remains one of the fundamental documents emerging from it, a guiding light of human rights. The Declaration guaranteed (among other things) freedom of speech, freedom of association and freedom of religion. It was this last principle that Rome objected to, and it did so on the grounds that Catholicism was the one and true apostolic faith. It could not, therefore, be put on an equal footing with Protestantism and Judaism. From the moment the pope, in effect, came out against the Revolution, a compromise between the Revolution and the Church was impossible. It was the question of religion, perhaps more than any other issue, that convinced Louis XVI that he could no longer co-operate with the National Assembly, and that flight was necessary.[7]

At first the revolutionary state persecuted all those priests who failed to take the oath, and eventually even those priests who did so. From 1793 onwards, that is, during the Terror, a policy of de-christianization was carried out, during which time the state attempted to eliminate altogether the Catholic Church as an institution in France. Non-juring priests were persecuted and sent to their deaths in their thousands, while the Church was forced underground. There were also a couple of desultory and vain attempts to replace Catholicism with new 'cults'. First was the Cult of Reason, whose highlight was a ceremony in the cathedral of Notre Dame (re-baptized the Temple of Reason), in which an opera singer dressed in white, wearing a Phrygian bonnet and holding a pike, incarnated Liberty. A year later followed the Cult of the Supreme Being, the climax of which was a ceremony organized by the artist, David, on the Champ de Mars (June 1794) that attracted around 500,000 people – virtually all of Paris – and in which Robespierre played at being the new 'pope'. It was one of the most carefully staged festivals of the Revolution.[8]

The intensity of de-christianization certainly diminished after the fall of Robespierre in 1794 – the Directory even allowed churches to be re-opened – but anti-religious sentiments were still very strong among (former) Jacobins within both the government and the army. This anti-clerical trend was probably best represented in the Directory by La Révellière-Lépeaux, who had founded (another) new religion dubbed Theophilanthropy, but also by Reubell and Barras, who were bent on destroying the Papal government. At one stage Reubell suggested creating two or more popes.[9] On the other hand, there were directors like Carnot who wanted to come to an agreement with the pope, and who wanted to guarantee religious liberty, while the foreign minister, Delacroix, had entered into negotiations with the papacy at the beginning of 1796 to lend weight to the religious pacification in France.[10]

The Directory's lack of consistency, both in France and in Italy, helps explain Bonaparte's ambivalent attitude towards the Church. Although he was raised a Catholic, and would have had to attend mass on a regular basis at Brienne and the *Ecole militaire*, Bonaparte was never an ardent believer and stopped attending mass sometime after graduating.[11] In the early stages of the Italian campaign, Bonaparte showed himself to be conciliatory towards the Church. On his entry into Milan, for example, he declared to the archbishop, Filippo Visconti, who had come out to meet him: 'Each person will be able to recognize his God, and practise the cult inspired by his conscience, without fear of seeing it not respected.'[12] These words, which may not have exactly reassured Catholics, nonetheless served as the basis of the relations between the French and the institutions they put in place in Italy, and the Church. Bonaparte seems to have understood how powerful religion in Italy was and modified his behaviour accordingly. But some of Bonaparte's setbacks in 1796 had encouraged the pope to lean towards Vienna and Turin. After Rivoli and the fall of Mantua, Bonaparte was free to do as he liked in Italy. Many thought that he would break the temporal power of the pope, and the letters from Bonaparte during this period support this. He was indignant at 'the obstinate bad faith of the court of Rome', and wanted to convince 'all Italy of the stupid drivel of his old cardinals'.[13] If he attacked the Papal States, however, it was not out of hatred for religion, nor out of a desire to destroy the papacy, but rather for strategic reasons: to financially exploit the territories of central Italy; and to eliminate any threat to his right flank before a resumption of the campaign against Austria.[14]

It was while he was in the Papal States that, on 9 February 1797, Bonaparte experienced another revelation, this time more intellectual than 'spiritual'. It took place in the port town of Ancona, on the Adriatic Sea, some nine months after Lodi. Ancona, with its population of Greeks, Albanians, Bosnians and Turks, was strategically important for relations with Constantinople. This was one of the reasons it was occupied in the first place. Bonaparte was a child of the Mediterranean, and it was here that the possibility of conquests further afield opened up to him. At the end of his five-day stay he wrote to the Directory: 'One can reach Macedonia from [here] in twenty-four hours and Constantinople in ten days . . . We have to maintain the port of Ancona when peace is concluded so that it always remains French. It will give us great influence over the Ottoman Porte, and will make us masters of the Adriatic Sea.'[15] Six months later Bonaparte reiterated those initial sentiments: 'Corfu and the Ionian islands are more valuable to us than the whole of Italy . . . The empire of the Turks is crumbling day by day: the possession of these islands will enable us to support it, as far as that is possible, or to take our share of it.'[16] Bonaparte's horizons were starting to extend beyond Europe towards much larger and much more ambitious political objectives.

'Turn Their Thoughts towards the Idea of Liberty'

After Ancona, Bonaparte slowly made his way back north. He was in no hurry to return to Milan, partly because the patriots of Lombardy were awaiting his arrival in the hope that he would allow them to hold primary assemblies to elect deputies to a congress of representatives, something he was doing his best to delay.[17] It is commonly accepted that, before his entry into Milan, Bonaparte was opposed to the creation of an Italian Republic in the north of Italy. In fact, the attitude of both Bonaparte and the Directory was ambiguous at best. Certainly, Bonaparte wanted to be perceived by Italian patriots to be sympathetic to their cause. Shortly before marching into Italy, he issued a proclamation directed at them: 'Your misfortune, your attachment to the great cause make you interesting to humanity and ensure for you the esteem of the French people . . . The government of the Republic will always know how to recognize the peoples who, by their generous efforts, will help to throw off the yoke of tyranny . . . Piedmontese patriots, the eyes of Europe are fixed on Italy, the army will know how to secure victory and the happiness of the peoples [of Italy]!'[18] It was an opportunistic appeal to Italian revolutionaries to help the French.

Bonaparte thus flirted with Italian revolutionaries. When he marched into Piedmont, the army was followed by a group of about 150 revolutionary Italians who had planned a general insurrection and the installation of a provisional revolutionary government. The Directory had certainly considered the possibility of provoking a republican insurrection in Piedmont, but this was only in the event that Paris was unable to come to an agreement with the court of Turin over an offensive-defensive alliance, something that both the Directory and Bonaparte were prepared to consider.[19] Various Italian patriots had been active in Paris soliciting the Directory 'to give back to Italy with its liberty its former splendour', although they were hardly given a warm welcome.[20] The group was organized by Filippo Buonarroti, a descendant of Michelangelo and a future accomplice of the French radical, Gracchus Babeuf, but was nevertheless under the close supervision of Buonarotti's friend, Saliceti. Buonarroti had obtained permission from the Minister of Foreign Affairs to assemble around Genoa all those Italian patriots who had had to flee to France to escape persecution. They clearly indicated the manner in which they hoped to act in several reports that were addressed to the Minister of Foreign Affairs.[21]

In the summer and autumn of 1796, however, neither Bonaparte nor especially the Directory was inclined to listen to radical Italians intent on a united Italy.[22] For one thing, Bonaparte's opinion of Italians was not particularly flattering. He found them 'effeminate, superstitious, hypocritical and cowardly'.[23] Given that Corsicans were closer in language and customs to Italians than to the French, this is ironic but it accords with the general French perception that their southern neighbours were politically immature and morally defective. The French consul to Genoa, Fourcade, wrote, 'There can be no question of republicanizing Italy. The people are not at all inclined to accept liberty, neither are they worthy of this boon.' And he went on, 'Italians in general are linked to the human species only by the forms which characterize them, and by the vices which dishonour them.'[24] Fear may have been behind this kind of rhetoric – fear of ignorant and fanatical counter-revolutionary masses – but there may have been a degree of cultural superiority involved here too: the peoples of Europe had demonstrated time and again since the beginning of the revolutionary wars that they were not mature enough to appreciate the benefits of liberty.[25] Much of this vituperation was the result of the Italian reaction to French occupation – resistance, murder, revolts – almost as though the French were hurt that the Italians did not continue to welcome them with open arms, in spite of the depredations committed by the troops, army suppliers and commissaries alike.[26] The consequence was a profound contempt for those over whom the French ruled.

It translated into a lack of confidence in the ability of Italians to determine their own political future. Carnot is reported to have said that, 'All ideas of independence would collapse before an Austrian regiment.'[27] The original aim of the campaign was to oust the Austrians from Italy and to render Lombardy subservient to France by either creating an independent Lombard state or attaching it to Piedmont. Bonaparte kept to this line of thinking and thus opposed the projects of the Piedmontese patriots, especially since Buonarroti was compromised in a plot to overthrow the government in Paris in May 1796. This was partly the problem. For the directors, as well as many in the French political elite, Italian patriots were condemned by association with Jacobinism, in their eyes the same thing as anarchism.[28] Revolution broke out in Piedmont and a republic was actually proclaimed by an Italian patriot, Giovanni Antonio Ranza, in the town of Alba, about 130 kilometres from Turin.[29] He had been militating for an independent Piedmontese republic since 1793. It was meant to be the first step towards a republic for the whole of Italy. The rebels then presented an address to Bonaparte calling on him to free all of Italy from tyranny. However, Bonaparte ignored their pleas and even wrote back to the Directory telling them that 'you should not count on a revolution in Piedmont', and that the Piedmontese people were not yet politically ripe.[30]

Within the space of a few weeks, however, Bonaparte had a change of heart about Italian patriots, at first those in Lombardy, and later those in central Italy.[31] They must have made an impression on him. On 16 May, Bonaparte encouraged the patriots in Lombardy with a vague declaration that hinted at independence. 'People of Italy, the French army has come to break your chains; the French people is the friend of all peoples; come confidently before us; your property, your religion and your customs will be respected! We are waging war as generous enemies and we only begrudge the tyrants who subjugate you.'[32] This type of language was used in the early years of the Revolution when the French declared they had come to liberate the oppressed peoples of the world. The rhetoric had been abandoned as unrealistic in the latter part of 1793,[33] but Bonaparte made use of it partly because he was new to politics and was unsure how to deal with the peoples over whom he ruled, and partly because he himself believed in it. (It was only much later when he saw how the Italians reacted to French domination – that is, by rebelling whenever they could – that he abandoned the 'liberator' rhetoric for a much more pragmatic approach to government.) A week later, he wrote to the Directory enquiring what he should do if the people of Lombardy asked him to organize a republic. 'This country is much more patriotic than Piedmont,' he wrote. 'It is closer to liberty.'[34] There was, indeed, some proof that the Milanese educated elite were inclined towards a republic: a (short-lived) political club was formed in Milan with over 800 members, most of them lawyers or merchants. Bonaparte even allowed 'moderate' Italian patriots to take control of a number of towns, to print newspapers, and to form a 'Lombard Legion' (in the image of the French National Guard), to which he gave the green, white and red tricolour that later became the Italian national flag.[35]

The response from Paris to Bonaparte's question was less than encouraging. The Directory at first fobbed Bonaparte off with vague answers about wanting to know more about the 'disposition of its inhabitants' so they could judge whether they would be 'susceptible to independence'. 'In the meantime,' they instructed him, 'turn their thoughts towards the idea of liberty.'[36] This attitude did not help solve Bonaparte's problem of what to do with the Italian states under French control. In his official correspondence and in his proclamations, Bonaparte gave the impression that he intended to promote a free people, but it was only after he had repulsed the Austrian attempt to regain control of northern Italy in January 1797 that he began to carry out his own policies on the ground, in direct contrast to the instructions he had followed from Paris.[37] It is evident that, far from his base of operations in France, Bonaparte's supply lines would remain precarious as long as Italian governments sympathetic neither to the Revolution nor to the French remained in power. This was demonstrated when Bonaparte, after leaving Milan to go on the offensive against the Austrians in May, was obliged to turn back to take care of the uprisings that had broken out. Over the coming months when unrest had to be put down in Piedmont, Bonaparte became convinced that a combination of the pope and *ancien régime* rulers were behind the revolts.[38] Although this was not altogether the case, the establishment of friendly and compliant governments would secure his rear and his supply lines.

At some stage during the autumn of 1796, Bonaparte must have decided that it was more practical to create small sister republics – rather than create some sort of unified peninsula, an idea that he briefly toyed with – and that, for the moment at least, this was easier to do south of the river Po than in Lombardy. On 16 October 1796, 110 deputies elected by provisional governments in Modena, Reggio, Bologna and Ferrara met in Modena. After two days of deliberation, the assembly declared the foundation of a 'Cispadane Confederation', a kind of military association that was to raise an Italian Legion of 25,000 men. Bonaparte was present, although laid up most of the day with a fever and a bad headache.[39] (What this says about Bonaparte's state of health is difficult to say. Was he simply exhausted from the campaigning, or did he subconsciously realize the enormity of his act of defiance against the Directory?)

Enthusiastic about the results, he declared, 'I thought the Lombards were the most patriotic people in Italy, but I am beginning to believe that Bologna, Ferrara, Reggio, Modena surpass them in energy.'[40] Bonaparte attempted to allay any fears the Directory may have had by insisting that 'the revolution here does not have the same character as it had at home', and that fanaticism would not do any harm.[41]

Faced with a fait accompli, the Directory reiterated its reserves about starting a 'revolutionary conflagration' in Italy and intimated that it might, nevertheless, be forced to hand over parts of Italy to Austria.[42] The Confederation laid the political foundations of a sister republic, which was officially proclaimed two months later, at another congress held at Reggio (27 December). The Cispadane Republic, as it was called, started with high hopes; Bonaparte wrote them a flattering letter saying that one day he hoped to see Italy figure among the powers of the world.[43] Even though it had an army, and adopted a constitution and a flag, its existence proved to be short-lived.

'Has the Rhine Been Crossed?'

Once Bonaparte had reorganized and consolidated his conquests, he could turn his attention to delivering the final blow to Austria. At the beginning of 1797, another concerted, three-pronged attack by the armies of the Rhine (under Moreau), the Sambre-et-Meuse (under Hoche) and Italy (under Bonaparte) was to deal that blow, although this time the main thrust would come from Italy. The Directory had finally realized that Italy, and not Germany, was the main theatre of war, and promised to reinforce the army until it reached a strength of about 80,000 men.[44] Success, in principle, was dependent on both Moreau and Hoche in Germany, but neither of them seemed in any hurry to move. Writing from the foot of the Alps at Gorizia, which he occupied on 22 March, Bonaparte insisted that 'if the Rhine is not crossed very soon it will be impossible for us to maintain our positions. I wait with impatience the return of my courier to know whether the Rhine has been crossed. It is possible that within eight days I will be at Klagenfurt, fourteen relays from Vienna, with the greater part of my army. If Moreau can march in order to occupy the enemy and to prevent it from turning, by Innsbruck, on my flank, the campaign could be successful and carry us very far. If, on the contrary, the Army of the Rhine are late in taking the offensive, I will find myself, alone against all, obliged to retreat to Italy.'[45]

On the day of Bonaparte's letter, Masséna took the pass of Tarvis: the gateway to Austria was in the hands of the French. Still, Bonaparte demanded a simultaneous and concerted push from the Army of the Rhine. Bonaparte's letters during this period attest to his concern on this point: 'Here we are in Germany,' he wrote on 25 March. 'It is essential then that the armies of the Rhine should also enter; when you read this letter I do not have the slightest doubt that the greater part of the forces that the Emperor has on the Rhine will already have turned against us.'[46] On the same day, he wrote to Carnot: 'Has the Rhine been crossed? It is clear that in four or five days, when my movements will have been unmasked and the enemy will have felt the danger to which it is exposed, the Rhine will practically be abandoned in order to fall on me. If in that case Moreau does not march quickly on the enemy . . . I will be beaten and will be obliged to regain Italy . . . if fortune does not act like a cruel stepmother, and the Rhine is crossed quickly, this campaign offers great hopes for us.'[47]

Bonaparte's constant complaints to the Directory served a purpose, namely, to minimize whatever gains might eventually be achieved by rival generals in Germany, thereby making it appear as though he were fighting at a tremendous disadvantage. In some respects, of course, this was true. Neither Hoche nor, especially, Moreau had got very far since the opening of the campaign in February, supposedly owing to lack of funds. The Directory even ordered Bonaparte to send money seized from the pope to the Army of the Rhine.[48] Consequently, after inflicting a defeat on the Archduke Charles at Neumark (29 March), Bonaparte decided, quite suddenly, to write a personal letter to his Austrian counterpart proposing an armistice to allow peace negotiations, ostensibly on humanitarian grounds. 'The general-in-chief and his brave soldiers are waging war but desire peace. Has the war not lasted six years? Have we not killed enough people and done enough harm to a sorrowful humanity? It is crying out on all sides. Europe, which had taken up arms against the French Republic, has laid them down. Your nation remains alone, and yet blood is going to flow more than ever.'[49] Bonaparte, the conqueror, was now portraying himself to the world as a man of peace.[50]

There was a reason for this. It was obvious that, with commanders of the calibre of Hoche and Moreau in Germany, it was only a question of time before the French armies would be victorious against the Austrians, and that the path to Vienna would be laid open. It was vital, therefore, if Bonaparte wanted to maintain his reputation, and to earn all the credit for bringing peace to the continent, to bring the war to an end as quickly as possible. The means to do so were diplomatic and military – approach the Austrians with an offer of peace while threatening them with a decisive military defeat. Of course Bonaparte, once again, undertook this diplomatic initiative without the approval of the Directory, but he nevertheless explained his reasons in a letter to his political masters the next day.[51] If the answer from the court of Vienna was negative, Bonaparte planned to publish both letters in a manifesto that would be made available to the Austrian public. The letters would give the impression that Bonaparte had striven for peace but that his efforts had been rejected. (He was to use the same tactic with Britain as First Consul in 1800.) If Vienna said yes, then peace preliminaries could be started. The archduke sent the proposal straight back to Vienna, where the Austrian chancellor, Baron Franz Maria von Thugut, faced with an extremely hostile public who blamed him for the prolongation of the war, was finally ready to talk peace. To demonstrate that he was speaking from a position of strength, Bonaparte had his troops push on to the town of Leoben, where, on 6 April, he was only about 120 kilometres from Vienna.

Refugees had been pouring into Vienna, fleeing the French advance, since March. Their numbers were so great that the Austrian Emperor ordered the police to divert the human flood around Vienna and into Hungary and Bohemia so as not to add to the already chaotic conditions within the imperial capital.[52] By the beginning of April, those who could began to leave the city in droves, including the women and children of the royal family. At one stage, enormous placards were circulated throughout the palace carrying the order to prepare baggage as quickly as possible and to get ready to leave; it created a moment of panic at the court.[53] Those who remained behind, however, demanded an end to the war. The English ambassador reported back that 'the clamours for peace have become louder and more importunate than at any other period of the war.' The Prussian ambassador reported that the discontent of all classes had reached its peak and was directed at the person of Baron Thugut.[54]

On 6 April, two Austrian generals, Heinrich Josef Bellegarde and Maximilien Merveldt, arrived at Bonaparte's headquarters at Judenburg in Styria to ask for an armistice, which Bonaparte granted for just six days to allow plenipotentiaries to be sent from Vienna. His position was, in fact, much more vulnerable than it looked – both the Tyrol and Venice were unreliable and threatened to cut off communications: 'If, contrary to my expectations, the negotiations do not succeed, I will be at a loss as to what course of action to take. I will nevertheless try to draw the enemy into some kind of clash, defeat him and oblige the Emperor to abandon Vienna. But I will be obliged to return to Italy after this, if the armies of the Rhine remain inactive, as at present.'[55]

But, as Bonaparte expected, it was unlikely not to succeed: he was probably aware, from information that his spies were feeding him,[56] that the Austrian court was in no position to continue the struggle, and that the population of Vienna was terrified of the approaching French. (The military situation could nevertheless change dramatically overnight, as events in Verona were about to demonstrate.) General Merveldt, who had gone off to Vienna to carry the news of the armistice, came back a few hours before its expiration, accompanied this time by the ambassador of Naples to Vienna, Marzio Mastrilli, Marquis del Gallo, a personal friend of the empress. The reason that an Italian was involved had nothing to do with the campaign itself; the imperial chancellor, Baron Thugut, did not trust an Austrian to negotiate the settlement. Besides, it would be convenient to blame disadvantageous terms on a foreigner.[57] On the afternoon of 18 April 1797, the preliminary peace treaty of Leoben was signed, bringing the war virtually to an end on the continent. That left only Britain in the fray.

According to the terms of the treaty, each side agreed not to interfere in the other's domestic affairs. In other words, the French would not seek to foment sedition in the Habsburg territories, and the Habsburgs would not attempt to restore the Bourbons to the French throne. Since Francis II had made peace with France in his capacity as ruler of the Habsburg monarchy, a congress was to be held later to negotiate peace between France and the Holy Roman Empire. For the present, Francis II ceded Belgium to France in return for just compensation to be arranged in the definitive peace. In reply, the French armies were to evacuate all Austrian territory. This was straightforward enough and fell within the logic of the eighteenth-century great-power politics – if a country lost a war it was expected to give up territory, while weaker states were often partitioned in the search for an 'equitable' exchange of territory. So, too, were the secret articles, which contained some sensational material, and which bring us back to the introduction of sister republics.

The Liberator of Italy

Nothing in Italy, at this time of shifting fronts and territorial boundaries, was permanent. In May 1797, Bonaparte got news of election results in the Cispadane Republic. 'The choice has been very bad. Priests have influenced all the elections.'[58] Bonaparte, therefore, simply decided to do away with the sister state altogether, and to incorporate its territory into a newly pro-claimed Cisalpine Republic (Gaspard Monge thought up the name) centred on Milan. It was announced to the people of Lombardy at the end of June 1797; their freedom a gift from the people of France. It was up to the people of Italy to show they were worthy of it.[59] About a week later (9 July), in Milan, with more than 400,000 people present, the Cisalpine Republic was inaugurated with great pomp in a ceremony remarkably similar to the Feast of the Federation held in Paris on 14 July 1790.[60] Only a year before the city had been in revolt against the French, but now those same people were celebrating (although, despite what Bonaparte may have said, with less enthusiasm than the French would have liked), the foundation of their political liberty.[61] Is it any wonder that many (but not all) Italian patriots recognized in Bonaparte the liberator of Italy?

There are any number of examples of this in the engravings from the period. One of the most important is that by Philippe-Auguste Hennequin, destined for an Italian public and probably executed sometime after April 1797. One can see Virgil's tomb in the background, a reminder of Italy's former greatness.[62] Bonaparte is in the centre, embracing an opulent 'Italy' (dressed with a Minervan helmet) to whom a muscular athlete, Hercules, probably representing the French people, presents a statuette of liberty, or perhaps equality. Bonaparte's body is turned more towards the figure of Hercules, a radical image of the people in the French Revolution, than towards Minerva/Italy; at this stage he was perceived, and wanted to be perceived, as being close to the people.[63] The chains Hercules is holding signify that he has broken away from both Austrian political power and the power of the Church. That is why the three figures are standing on a two-headed eagle, the symbol of the Habsburg dynasty, but one can also see in the very foreground the broken cross of the pope. Bonaparte later played on these themes in his declarations to the Italian people.

The constitution Bonaparte gave the Cisalpine Republic, after consulting with a group of Italian patriots, was an imperfect copy of the French constitution of 1795, which had already been used for the Cispadane – that is, an executive (made up of directors) would dominate a bicameral legislative; both the executive and the legislative had, in principle, popular sovereignty as their base.[64] In reality, and in order to be sure that only his men were in place in the different elective functions, Bonaparte chose the members of the executive and the two assemblies himself. The Italian notables were wary of a power structure that, in their eyes, had produced the Terror, but Bonaparte, while he may have despised the people as much as the notables, was bent on changing Italy while preserving local customs. All of this put the Directory in Paris in a difficult position. They were torn between their own revolutionary ideals and the practical necessity of keeping Italy as a pawn in the forthcoming negotiations with Austria. The Directory was aware that the majority of Italians did not hold the same views as the handful of radicals pressing for independence

Philippe-Auguste Hennequin, *La Liberté de l'Italie, dédiée aux hommes libres* (The Liberty of Italy, dedicated to free men), 1797–8. (*Bibliothèque nationale, Paris*)

and a constitution, but it was perhaps better to place the friends of revolutionary France in positions of power than to let hostile governments continue in office.

The Italian sister states were created not out of a desire to revolutionize Italy, but out of the need to create a stable base for the French army in regions where state structures were decomposing.[65] What Bonaparte wanted most of all, and this is a lesson he was to apply later to his Empire, was a modernized state structure capable of organizing men and money to pursue the war. Those who did not co-operate would find that the wrath of the French people would be like that of 'an exterminating angel'.[66] In short, Bonaparte's motives for creating sister republics were military, not ideological, and to this extent it was better to have a number of small states he could control than a united Italy that might prove to be intractable.[67] A system of domination that relied only on the military and the financial structures that had been put in place was doomed to failure. Others had realized this. Faipoult wrote from Rome in 1797: 'We do not want to hold Italy in perpetual tutelage by formidable armies, we have to conquer minds . . . We should not on the one hand lavish the sentimental title of sister or daughter to the new republics and on the other act as if the French, superior in liberty, were to receive from them preferential tributes, or onerous and arbitrary enjoyments.'[68] The French did not have enough troops to spread throughout north and central Italy, nor could they continually rely upon mobile columns to patrol these territories. Bonaparte was thus obliged to exploit the current of opinion, or at least that which coincided with the politics of revolutionary France, and thereby satisfy some of the Italian patriots' political aspirations. If he did not invent the notion of sister republics, he was at least instrumental in bringing about their existence, in spite of resistance from the Directory, so that he transformed northern Italy into one vast experiment for his political ambitions. This may not have been a conscious decision, but once the process had started Bonaparte had little choice but to carry it to its logical conclusion.

Bonaparte was not the first, and certainly not the last, Republican general to follow an independent political path by establishing satellite states in conquered territories. Much earlier, General Charles Dumouriez had done the same thing in Austrian Belgium and Holland by working towards the creation of the Belgian Republic in the hope of becoming its Protector.[69] When the Convention declared in favour of the system of 'natural frontiers' in December 1792 (the 'natural limits' of France were marked by the Atlantic Ocean, the Rhine, the Alps and the Pyrenees), Dumouriez refused to co-operate and went to Paris at the beginning of January 1793 in the hope of getting the Convention to change its policy.[70] When this failed, and he had the agents of the French government arrested in March 1793, his troops turned against him. Hoche attempted a similar policy in Germany in 1797 by advising the Directory to create a Cisrhenan Republic centred on Mainz.[71] His death in September of that year put an end to this project. More typical was the attitude of General Championnet, commander of the army in Rome, who, at the end of 1798, was ordered to push into Naples. Despite formal instructions from the Directory, he established the Neapolitan (later the short-lived Parthenopean) Republic.

The trend is clear. The impulse to create sister republics – one of the most inspired inventions of revolutionary politics and the precursor of the post-1945 puppet states of Eastern Europe[72] – was coming from the generals on the ground, and they were driven by one motive: to feed the war. It was not part of the Directory's policy. On the contrary, from very early on in the war, the revolutionary government had kept an eye on its generals to prevent them from implementing their own ideas. Hence the need to attach commissaries to the army, who were partly there to oblige the generals to obey directives from Paris, but also to prevent them from getting out of hand. Once the Directory abolished the civilian commissaries within the Army of Italy under Bonaparte and the Army of the Sambre-et-Meuse under Hoche in January 1797, it was more difficult for Paris to control generals in the field. (On the other hand, a commissary continued to watch over Moreau, rightly suspected of royalist sympathies, at the head of the Army of the Rhin-et-Moselle.) In some respects, Bonaparte had paved the way for generals like Championnet or Joubert, who vainly tried to become the head of first the Batavian Republic, and then the

Cisalpine Republic in 1798. The political power and money enjoyed by Bonaparte in northern Italy obviously made his peers
envious, but then the French government was gradually losing
control over the military, which, ever since the fall of Robespierre
and the Committee of Public Safety, increasingly went its own way.

At Leoben, Bonaparte was attempting to preserve his Italian conquests – which, to an extent, he considered his personal territory –
as well as trying to find a territorial solution to northern Italy that
guaranteed some sort of stability.[73] The existence in northern Italy
of a nascent Cispadane Republic (under French tutelage), a decrepit
Republic of Venice, and Lombardy (whose existence would be
threatened by Austria if it were not for the French) was obviously
not a formula for success. This is why Bonaparte came up with the
idea of creating a large Italian state – the Cisalpine Republic – while
Venice was to be partitioned between Austria and France. Bonaparte informed the Directory that the towns of the Venetian *terra
ferma*, along with Bologna, Romagna and Ferrara, had petitioned in
favour of incorporation into the Cisalpine at the beginning of
July.[74] It was a way of letting them know in advance what he
was about to do, without their permission. In effect, Bonaparte
incorporated the once Austrian territory of Lombardy and the
Cispadane into the Cisalpine Republic on 27 July. In return,
Austria received the mainland territories of the Venetian Republic,
especially Istria and Dalmatia, but not the city of Venice. The
French occupied the Ionian islands – Corfu, Cephalonia and Zante.
Bonaparte, as we have seen, was already thinking about French
expansion into the Mediterranean. Effectively, Bonaparte and the
Austrian emperor had divided a state that was nominally neutral
and which did not belong to either of them, in much the same way
that Poland had been partitioned earlier in the century (I will return
to what that meant for Venice in the next section). It was, in the
words of one historian, the 'execution of a crime against a free and
neutral people.'[75]

When details of the Treaty of Leoben filtered through to both
Vienna and Paris, it caused dismay. Thugut was unhappy because
the Austrians lost over four million souls (from Belgium and
Lombardy) in exchange for two and a half million new Venetian

subjects, a relative diminution in strength compared to its traditional rivals, France and Prussia.[76] In terms of eighteenth-century great-power rivalry, the status quo had not been maintained and the preliminaries were, therefore, disadvantageous. One can understand why the court of Vienna was not happy, but the directors in Paris were not happy either, presumably because their primary objective – the left bank of the Rhine – was not even mentioned in the treaty. In other words, they considered the conditions too lenient, an understandable position given the series of crushing defeats sustained by the Austrian army. Bonaparte, however, had foreseen the government's reaction and had pre-empted any negative response by deliberately leaking news of the agreement – General Leclerc, the courier carrying the treaty to Paris, his soon to be brother-in-law was ordered to spread the news along the way – knowing that French public opinion would be firmly behind such a peace.[77]

There was certainly an explosion of joy, not only in Paris but in the rest of the country. For example, in the town of Montauban, about eighty kilometres north of Toulouse, celebrations in Bonaparte's honour are said to have lasted three days.[78] Therefore, the government, which was unpopular among some sections of the French populace, would have found it very difficult not to ratify the treaty. The prime consideration in the government's decision, however (the directors voted 4–1 in favour of ratification), was not Bonaparte's popularity, nor the outburst of joy in favour of peace, but his assurance that this was only a preliminary agreement and that France could get the left bank as well when it came to the definitive treaty.[79] In fact, within only weeks of signing the preliminaries with Austria, Bonaparte informed the Austrians that he had changed his mind. When the Austrian envoy, the Marquis del Gallo, arrived in Italy at the end of May to exchange the formal ratifications of the terms of Leoben, he was tersely informed that France now wanted the left bank of the Rhine as well. A congress would be organized in the town of Rastatt to work out the details. In diplomatic terms, this was outrageous, but its was typical of Bonaparte; he knew the Austrians were in no position to renew the war.

The most important thing to note of Leoben, however, is what it reveals about Bonaparte's relations with the Directory.[80] In a letter explaining his actions, there is a thinly veiled threat – 'My civilian career will, like my military career, be one and simple.'[81] This could loosely be translated as, 'if you don't accept the treaty I'll resign from the army and take up politics'. By this stage Bonaparte had total control over the direction of policy in Italy; the Directory was a feeble adjunct, no longer consulted, and whose views were no longer taken into consideration.

The Veronese Easter

The question of Venice was the most delicate part of the preliminaries of Leoben.[82] Despite the fact that the French had partially occupied and fought numerous battles on Venetian territory since June 1796, Venice was still nominally neutral territory. Bonaparte, therefore, had to find some means to conquer La Serenissima in order to fulfil his obligations to Austria. This was not a moral problem for Bonaparte, who hated what he described, in an angry tirade to the Directory, as 'the most absurd and tyrannical of all governments; beside there is no doubt it wanted to profit by the moment we were in the heart of Germany to murder us. Our Republic has no more bitter enemies.'[83] Moreover, the people of Venice were described as an 'inept, cowardly people, by no means made for liberty' and as 'a soft people, effeminate and cowardly, without land nor water and we want nothing to do with them'.[84] A week or so before the signing of Leoben, Bonaparte threatened the doge, Lodovico Manin, on 9 April 1797, in a letter delivered by General Junot in person: 'Do you think that at a time when I am in the heart of Germany, that I am powerless to [make you] respect the foremost people of the universe? ... The blood of my brothers in arms shall be avenged.'[85] After it was read out, Junot flung the letter on a table in front of him, turned around, and stormed out of the Collegio, where he had been received, to a boat waiting to take him back to the French Legation.

Much of this was simply cold political calculation, the result of a number of 'incidents' that had taken place on Venetian territory, at Bergamo, Brescia and Cremona, almost certainly with the complicity of French officers on the ground, fomenting trouble against the government in Venice.[86] During this time, while Bonaparte was busy in the Austrian Alps, the French suffered a backlash in other parts of the Veneto: about fifty French troops were killed on the road from Milan to Bergamo; the French consul's residence on the Venetian-ruled island of Zante was sacked; and a detachment of French troops on Lake Garda was attacked by a mob of peasants from the region of Salo. The worst 'incident', however, occurred in Verona the day after Easter Sunday, as pen was being put to paper at Leoben.[87] On 17 April, in what came to be called the *Pasque Veronesi*, or Veronese Easter, a quarrel between French troops and local inhabitants resulted in the deaths of four soldiers. The reprisal was immediate and brutal – cannon were discharged into crowds of people in the town, the reaction to which was an immediate and general insurrection both in Verona and the neighbouring countryside. The bishop of Verona had apparently incited his flock to rebel by preaching that it was 'meritorious and agreeable to God to kill the French'.[88] God may not have seen things in quite the same light but the sermon nevertheless inspired many Veronesi to go on a rampage, hunting down and killing French troops, including a number of soldiers lying wounded in the hospitals of Verona, as well as locals who had collaborated. It is impossible to know how many were actually killed, but it was probably closer to a few dozen than the few hundred usually cited by historians. The bulk of the garrison managed to hold out in the fortress, well stocked with provisions, until reinforcements entered the city and suppressed the insurrection. There was no looting, but eight of the rebel ringleaders were arrested, tried, and immediately put to death by firing squads, while another fifty or so were placed in irons and sent to French Guyana, the equivalent of a slow death sentence. Furthermore, the town had to pay for its insolence by supplying forty thousand pairs of boots, as well as clothing in similar quantities, vast sums of money, and the usual hoards of paintings, sculptures and works of art that were shipped off to Paris.

The Veronese Easter occurred shortly before an attack on a French vessel in Venice, on 19 April, when the fortress of S. Andrea

J. Duplessi Bertaux, *L'assassinat des Français a Vérone, en Italie. Le 28 germinal an 5ème de la République française* (The assassination of the French at Verona, in Italy, on 17 April 1797), circa 1797. The image captures an incident that took place in front of one of the city's three strongholds, the Castel Vecchio. (*Bibliothèque nationale, Paris*)

bombarded a privateer named, ironically, the *Libérateur de l'Italie*. The French captain and four of his crew were killed in the process. The massacre of the French troops at Verona, which may also have been incited by *agents provocateurs*, and the attack on the French vessel in Venice were all the excuse Bonaparte needed to overthrow the Venetian government and install a puppet regime. 'After such a horrible betrayal,' he wrote to the Directory, 'I do not see any way other than to wipe the Venetian name from the face of the map. The blood of all Venetian nobles is needed to appease the spirits of the French whose throats they have cut.'[89] And again, 'If French blood is to be respected in Europe, if you do not want them to mock us, blood must flow, the noble Venetian admiral who presided over this assassination has to be publicly condemned.'[90] The patricians of Venice may have tried to buy their way out of the predicament by bribing Barras with 600,000 francs; he is supposed to have promptly pocketed the money and let Bonaparte do as he liked.[91] Demoralized, the Great Council, including the doge, resigned and a new pro-French provisional municipality was established in its place (12 May 1797).

A few days later, on 15 May, French troops arrived at the gates of the capital – the first time foreign troops had entered the city in its thousand-year existence – under the command of General Louis Baraguey d'Hilliers. Earlier Bonaparte had promised Venetian envoys, sent to negotiate with him while he was in Austria, that he would act like an Attila.[92] In a way he did, by wiping the Venetian Republic from the face of the map, and by looting as many of the Republic's art treasures as he could.

The Court at Mombello

In a letter Bonaparte wrote to Barras shortly after Leoben, he complained, 'I am sick . . . I need rest; I ask for my resignation, back it if you are my friend.'[93] It is true that Bonaparte was exhausted, but then there was also a tendency to exaggerate, and the passages in his correspondence referring to the burdens of greatness and the emptiness of victory are central to his thinking throughout his public life. A young French playwright and poet, the Marquis Carrion de Nisas, who saw Bonaparte at Mombello after Leoben, described him in the following manner: 'On his faded and pale cheeks, in that demoralizing fatigue, I in vain sought the physiognomy of the conquering hero I had imagined. The brow, furrowed by worry, is that of the victor! That head which has shaded so many laurels bows under the weight of worries, and his soul seems to describe itself by a look in which I read sadness, deep reflection and the most sombre serious-ness.'[94]

Hyperbole aside, Bonaparte needed to rest – there was not much else to do while the terms for a definitive peace were worked out – and so he spent the next ten weeks or so (17 May to the beginning of July 1797) at the magnificent château of Mombello, a short distance from Milan and not far from Lake Como. The military campaign was over, and Bonaparte now planned to give much more

Antoine-Jean Gros, *Portrait en buste de profil de Bonaparte, général en chef de l'armée d'Italie* (Portrait of Bonaparte in profile, general-in-chief of the Army of Italy), circa 1796. Bonaparte in Italy, looking perhaps a little worse for wear. (*Courtesy of Photo RMN – © Michèle Bellot*)

attention to the political campaign to both promote himself and to attack various elements on the French political stage. One of the first things he did was shape his life according to the conventions of the world to which he aspired. That is, Bonaparte formed a small court around his person.

He had made war successfully, corresponded with the Republic's agents throughout Italy and in Paris, negotiated treaties with a number of states, been involved with the finances of the army, and, importantly, had more or less ignored directives from Paris without suffering any political repercussions. In short, he had become used to running things his own way. Now he needed to fashion his public appearances in such a way as to increase the aura of power. Thus the aides-de-camp did not dine daily with the commander, as was the rule in most other armies; it became an exception and a privilege to be invited to dine at his table. Nor did he dine in private, but in public, like a sovereign. Italians who came to catch a glimpse of the conqueror of Italy were allowed into the galleries to watch while he ate, a display reminiscent of Louis XIV's performances. Bonaparte received homage as if he had been born to it. The salon at the château of Mombello was extended into the garden by a vast tent. Everyone who was intelligent, ambitious or simply enthusiastic about Italy could be found there consorting with bureaucrats, administrators and French generals.[95] Pontécoulant has left a description of the atmosphere that reigned at Mombello:

> His [Bonaparte's] attitude was not that of pride or self-importance, one could distinguish the assurance of a man who is conscious of his superiority and who feels up to the position he occupies. No other, moreover, treated public opinion with such consideration as Bonaparte at that time, all the while appearing to despise it or wanting to suppress it. Anybody who was presented to him and who was preceded by a reputation was sure to be welcomed with affected politeness and flattering consideration. That person became the object of special attention on his part, and of a kind of ... discrimination ... His lively mind, his singularly expressive face, his look ... his physiognomy ... everything was used to subdue the less benevolent, and master of himself, surrounded by the prestige of his glory enhanced by the simplicity of his costume and his habits, he subjugated with an incredible facility all those whom he wanted to seduce.[96]

There are two observations about Bonaparte's behaviour that are worth pointing out. First, the apparent contradiction in playing the monarch to a closed circle outside France, while publicly espousing the republican cause, was far from characteristic of generals in the French Republican armies. During the *ancien régime*, it was expected of senior officers, that is, from colonels upwards, to operate a common table for unit and/or staff officers while on campaign. It was, in fact, one of the many financial burdens associated with

holding senior military office. This tradition was also often maintained as a display of wealth and magnificence; sumptuary edicts
were introduced to try and restrict this luxuriousness and extra-
vagance. That is, the table was an element in the competitive
struggle between high-ranking officers. This practice ceased with
the republicanization of the French army, so it is curious to see that
Bonaparte resurrected the tradition.[97] Bonaparte, it must be emphasized, was the only republican general to maintain a table in this
manner. Moreover, he gave a personal twist to the tradition by
shifting to a 'court' style of dining, completely out of keeping with
standard military practice. We do not know where the inspiration
for this type of behaviour came from – was he influenced by
Josephine's knowledge of pre-revolutionary etiquette? – but if it
outraged die-hard republicans, none put their concerns in writing.

Bonaparte did, however, confide in André-François Miot de
Melito in June 1797: 'Do you believe that I triumph in Italy for
the Carnots, Barras, etc. . . . I wish to undermine the Republican
party, but only for my own profit and not that of the former
dynasty . . . As for me, my dear Miot, I have tasted authority and I
will not give it up.'[98] Miot's account was written from notes taken
at the time. Even though he was fundamentally hostile to Napoleon, it is safe to assume that they are reasonably accurate. This sort
of statement, coupled with Bonaparte's court-like behaviour, reveals, therefore, not only his ambition for the post-campaign
period, but also a much deeper desire to be treated almost as
though he were a monarch. The passage in Miot's memoirs describing the small court at Mombello is sometimes used by biographers to demonstrate that Bonaparte had now become a
'conqueror in his own right',[99] but Bonaparte's behaviour in Italy
(and later in Germany and Egypt) reveals another aspect of his
character.

The second notewothy observation about Bonaparte's behaviour
is that the formalized etiquette with which he surrounded himself
seems to have served the same purpose as it did at any eighteenth-
century court. It placed a distance between the prince, or in this case
the general, and those in his entourage, so that they were obliged to
look up to him. It also created an aura of uniqueness; it was in Italy
that poets first alluded to Bonaparte as the 'saviour' during the early

stages of the campaign. One anonymous acclamation, for example, exclaims, 'I praise this hero, child of Italy. Who, having become French, has saved his *patrie*.'[100] An engraving by Bonvalet, which dates from 1797, was based upon a popular song, *Ha rendez grâce à la nature* (Ah, give thanks to nature), which already presented Bonaparte as the saviour. Pro-Bonaparte newspapers were constantly referring to him as the 'preserver of liberty', while writers

Bonvalet, *Buonaparte: général en chef de l'Armée d'Italie* (Buonaparte: General-in-Chief of the Army of Italy), circa 1797. (*Bibliothèque nationale, Paris*)

lauded 'the young artillery officer of twenty-eight years' as the Caesar that France needed and had found.[101]

Bonaparte gathered the family around him at Mombello. His wife, of course, who had stayed on in Italy (although we know few details about their relationship during this period), but also his mother, his three sisters, Joseph, Louis (who had accompanied his brother to Italy as an aide-de-camp) and his stepson, Eugène de Beauharnais. It was on this occasion that the Bonaparte and Beauharnais families were to come face to face for the first time, at least for a couple of weeks. The Bonapartes seem to have been reserved, circumspect, no doubt sensing that it was too soon to move against Josephine, but they were gathering ammunition to use at a later date. On 14 June, there was a double wedding of sorts. The sixteen-year-old Pauline, considered to be at the height of her beauty, was pushed by her brother into marriage with a serious young man of twenty-four, General Victoire-Emmanuel Leclerc, in the hope that it would tame her romantic ardour. She had had an inappropriate liaison, probably innocent, with the deputy Fréron, and was desperately in love despite the difference in their age – he was forty and had, moreover, fathered two illegitimate children by an actress he kept in Paris. The family, or rather Letizia and Bonaparte, soon put a stop to it. Leclerc was a friend Bonaparte had met at the siege of Toulon, indeed a friend of the family, and had known Pauline for some years. Even though he was blond, Leclerc apparently resembled Bonaparte somewhat and became so devoted to him that he supposedly imitated his mannerisms. The second wedding was that of the twenty-year-old Elisa, the name that Maria-Anna took sometime between 1794 and 1796 while she was living in Marseilles. She had married six weeks previously in a civil ceremony a fellow Corsican, Felix Bacciochi, a thirty-five-year-old an officer of no particular merit, who was also a friend of Pozzo di Borgo and a Paolist. The two families had been rivals in Ajaccio, although their union does not seem to have presented a problem.

The prima donna of the La Scala opera house in Milan, Giuseppina Grassini, was invited to attend Mombello, while Josephine played the hostess over a round of elegant soirées, dances, games, excursions to the lakes of Maggiore and Como, and hunts in the nearby forests. She appears to have been more attentive to Bonaparte during this period, frequently caressing him in public, perhaps because the family was there, only too ready to judge her for her lack of devotion. Miot has left us with a description of one of these excursions to Lake Maggiore. He found himself, along with Berthier, in a carriage with Bonaparte and Josephine. 'During the trip he was gay, animated, told us several anecdotes from his youth, and told us that he had just turned twenty-eight. He showed particular care to his wife, often taking conjugal liberties with her, which left us not a little embarrassed, Berthier and me. But his free manners were marked with such a lively sentiment of affection and tenderness for that woman as likeable as she was good, that we could easily forgive them.'[102] Whatever suspicions may have plagued Bonaparte's mind about Josephine's fidelity seem to have been dispelled, at least for the moment.

There is no doubt that Italy was a decisive experience in the formation of his character and that he would return to France much more politically savvy and certainly more politically astute than when he had left. He had, to put it mildly, come a long way since the Battle of Montenotte, when he had set out to provide a diversion to the main thrust of the French forces into Germany. Since then, he had fought in eleven major battles; he had ruled over millions of people; he had created, and dissolved, states; he had negotiated treaty after treaty; he had dealt with sovereigns of every kind, something that no doubt enormously enhanced his own self-esteem; and he had navigated potentially dangerous waters between the Catholic Church and the Revolution in Italy. In short, he had wielded enormous real power, both military and political, and had amassed enormous wealth along the way. It is not so much that all this power had gone to his head – although admittedly, after experiencing power, he certainly did not want to relinquish it – but that it gave him a direction, an identity and a purpose in life that he had striven for as a young man but had only glimpsed in Corsica and in the early days of the Revolution.

Personally, too, the period in Italy was a formative experience. His love for Josephine had been tested, more as a result of her lack of ardour than anything else, and although he still felt passionately about her, his emotional dependence seems to have waned. On another level, as a soldier, he had known death, and had lost thousands of men and dozens of officers who had been close to him, or at least were personally known to him. Most importantly of all, though, Bonaparte came away from Italy with a belief in his own destiny, feeling that history had reserved a place for him, and that there were even greater accomplishments ahead. His ambition was limited only by his imagination, which was why he had cast his gaze east, towards the Orient. The change that had taken place in Bonaparte is perhaps best expressed by his relations with those around him. Bonaparte's secretary, Bourrienne, asserted that it was at Mombello that Bonaparte no longer permitted those close to him to use the informal 'tu'.[103] But then power of the magnitude that Bonaparte wielded in Italy almost automatically places a barrier around those exercising it. He may have waxed lyrical to the Directory about how much he needed to steep his soul among the masses once again, but Bonaparte, in fact, did nothing of the kind.[104] On the contrary, as we have seen at Mombello, he went out of his way to foster the trappings of power, and consequently to distance himself from others. Certainly he was now less spontaneous and cooler towards those around him, and he was a good deal more cynical in his dealings with other men than he had been in his youth. Some of these traits had been acquired in Corsica, but they were developed and refined in Italy. His ability to 'play' Italian patriots, for example, is testimony to that. Just as importantly, his political ideas had also started to evolve, and his views towards the Directory, the councils, and indeed the people of Paris were now quite contemptuous. He had become confident, arrogant even, in the face of so many victories. He would gradually come to the realization that he could exist, as a political entity, independently of the government in Paris.

13

Bonaparte the 'Italique'

Defending 'Liberty and its Friends'

If the year 1797 had been an apprenticeship in ruling conquered peoples and territories, it also saw Bonaparte refining the techniques of self-promotion he had embarked on in the early stages of the campaign. This legend-building reveals a great deal not only about the development of Bonaparte's personality, but also about how he wanted others to perceive him. In some respects, Bonaparte was giving the French people an image of what they desired, and they, in turn, projected on to him the kind of character they wanted – namely, a youthful, selfless, virtuous, victorious Republican general. It was a type of collective transference. During the early stages of the campaign, Bonaparte's motives for projecting this image were quite simple: he needed to build a reputation and enhance his own prestige by glorifying his military feats. We have seen in previous chapters how this was done, but it was echoed by authors in newspapers, pamphlets and even books throughout France and Europe. Between the spring of 1796 and the end of 1797, seventy-two pamphlets appeared, sometimes reaching 3,000 run-offs, all on the subject of Bonaparte or his victories in Italy.[1] Many examples from these pamphlets could be given,[2] but the unsolicited praise from these journalists tells us that Bonaparte inspired them as an heroic subject.

The praise, however, was by no means unanimous. In fact, by 1797 Bonaparte was coming under increasing attack from the royalist press in Paris. Like the pro-government press, the royalists noted the similarities between Bonaparte and Caesar, but they did so in a negative way: 'Is the Rubicon already crossed?' asked the *Messager du Soir* after a proclamation from Bonaparte in July 1797, calling on his troops to defend the Republic against its internal enemies. 'Will we avoid a military Republic by going to prostrate ourselves at the feet of the dictator?'[3] This particular newspaper had been warning against Bonaparte's dictatorial ambitions since the end of March 1796.[4] Those dubbed Clichyans, that is royalists who increasingly made up the members of the two Councils, attempted to minimize the efforts of the young general, lobbying in favour of a return to peace in foreign policy, through newspapers like *La Quotidienne*, *Le Miroir*, *Le Mémorial* and *Le Thé*.[5] *La Quotidienne* ridiculed the flowery discourses and the untruthful proclamations, downplaying his victories and highlighting his defeats, his victims and the excesses committed. Buonaparte, as they insisted on calling him, was portrayed as a Jacobin fanatic, an angel of death, pursuing his own 'philosophical crusade'.[6] For them, it was a question of unmasking the exaggerated accounts emanating from Italy, and, until it was banned in September 1797, it never ceased to point out the contradictions and to amplify the rumours propagated by the Austrians and Italians, to denounce the cynicism and the greed of those generals who pillaged the Italian states, and to accentuate the suffering and the abnegation of the simple soldier. Although Bonaparte was not the only general to be targeted in this manner, he seems to have been singled out by the royalist press.

The animosity of the Clichyans is understandable given that Bonaparte was perceived, above all else, as the general of Vendémiaire who helped put down a royalist uprising in Paris, as the destroyer of *ancien régime* Italy, the despoiler of Rome, the founder of the Cisalpine Republic, and the protégé of Barras. The Clichyan (and moderate) newspapers were also more numerous than those on the left, and their watchword in the build-up to the elections in March 1797 was 'Peace without annexations'.[7] Bonaparte was clearly annoyed with the royalist press, something that is apparent in his correspondence during this period. He vented his anger in a letter to the Directory, threatening to resign if they did not rein them in (this is the way he would always react whenever his actions came under scrutiny).[8] In July 1796, for example, when the Directory felt it necessary to deny the rumours that had been circulating about Bonaparte working only for himself and not for the nation, he replied in a fit of pique to Carnot that, 'If there is a single honest man of good faith in France who suspects my political intentions and doubts my conduct, I shall renounce instantly the happiness of serving my country.'[9] Bonaparte wanted the Clichyan press banned, and went so far as to threaten them indirectly with violence.[10] At Bonaparte's suggestion, the different corps of the army sent petitions to Paris against the Clichyans to mark the celebration of 14 July. At the same time as he demanded his immediate recall, he urged the Directory to carry out a coup against them, offering his support and declaring that it was the only way to 'save the republic and to conclude peace within twenty-four hours.' A proclamation from that period calls on the troops to make ready to defend the Republic against its internal enemies.[11]

This is not the only way in which Bonaparte reacted to such criticisms. After he had suffered a number of attacks in the two Councils because of his handling of affairs with Venice (23 June), Bonaparte decided to publish his own newspapers.[12] He may have got the idea of using the press for his own ends from patriotic newspapers like the *Journal républicain de Marseilles*, distributed among the troops during the siege of Toulon by Dugommier, or perhaps from his time in Paris, where he would have seen firsthand the influence of the press on public opinion. In any event, he was certainly not the first general to create his own newspaper. Dugommier had also founded *L'Avant-Garde de l'Armée des Pyrénées orientales* (March–October 1794). Indeed, the Revolution saw the appearance of a number of newspapers, often subsidised, written by and for the army. But Bonaparte's newspapers differ from these other papers, and from the generals behind them, by their references to destiny, and the creation, deliberate or not, of the aura of myth, which came to dominate his later life.

Two newspapers were founded by Bonaparte, his agents, or members of his family (we do not know how these papers were financed, but it was probably with money looted from the Italian people).[13] The *Courrier de l'armée d'Italie ou le Patriote français à Milan, par une société de républicains* (The Courier of the Army of Italy or the French Patriot in Milan, by a Society of Republicans), was created on 20 July 1797. It was something Bonaparte had thought about doing after Lodi in May 1796, but in Paris the Council of Elders initially rejected the proposal, perhaps fearing the self-serving use to which he could put it.[14] When he asked for permission again around June 1797, having thrown the Austrians out of Italy, they could hardly refuse him.[15] Directed as much at the Army of Italy as the people of France, it appeared every second day (from 20 July 1797 to 2 December 1798, 248 issues appeared over a period of eighteen months), was available in Milan and Paris, and was distributed free of charge. Because many of the articles were taken up by other newspapers, like the republican *Ami des Lois*, the *Révélateur* and the *Journal des Hommes libres*, it reached a wider audience.

A second, less substantial and more moderate newspaper, *La France vue de l'armée d'Italie* (France viewed from the Army of Italy), was created only two weeks after the *Courrier*. *La France* was distributed in Milan, Lyons and Paris, but only once or twice every ten days. Although relatively short-lived, it tells us a great deal about Bonaparte's political ambitions and expectations. Only eighteen issues appeared in all – the first issue is dated 29 July and the last issue 6 November 1797 – and, despite the fact that some of the articles were reprinted in pro-Bonapartist newspapers like the *Clef du Cabinet*, and Bonaparte boasted of it having 'the greatest effect in Paris', it is impossible to tell to what extent the newspaper might have been read, and therefore to what extent Bonaparte's name was being diffused. We simply cannot know the extent to which this propaganda had an impact on its target audience, whether the soldiers read the newspapers around the camp fires at night, or whether their views of the government in Paris or of Bonaparte were influenced as a result. But the content is nonetheless worth looking at for what it tells us about Bonaparte.

At the top of the first few editions of the *Courrier* was a quote from the *philosophe*, Raynal: 'The Republic lost the little that remained of action and life; the cadaver had to be reanimated. That resurrection was not impossible because people were generally disposed to trying any remedy; the difficulty was in finding some that worked.' The implication was clear; the Republic was suffering. Was Bonaparte the remedy? By looking 'objectively' at the political goings-on in Paris, driven as they were by passion, factions and hatred, the paper presented itself as moderate, above factions and capable of unifying the French under one banner. Everything suggested that the man capable of doing just that was Bonaparte.

Responsibility for the *Courrier* was initially granted to Marc-Antoine Jullien, a young (six years Bonaparte's junior) former editor of *L'Orateur plébéien*, who had been a collaborator and follower of Robespierre and who had also contributed to the Jacobin *Journal des Hommes Libres* (sometimes referred to as the 'Journal des Tigres' by contemporaries). Jullien had written a letter to Bonaparte in June 1796, expressing the naïve desire to be received into the Army of Italy so that it would become for him 'the school of virtue, the temple of friendship, the sanctuary of glory'. He went on to salute Bonaparte not only as the 'victorious leader of the heroes of the Army of Italy,' but also as 'the liberator of oppressed nations whose laurels are stained only with the blood of the enemies of humanity.'[16] We do not know whether this letter actually reached Bonaparte, or even if it was sent. Nevertheless, dissatisfied with the Republic and wishing to escape recrimination for his revolutionary past (he was proscribed for his association with the Babouvists), Jullien went to Italy to join the Lombard Legion, where he distinguished himself by preventing the capture of half a million gold ducats by an Austrian privateer between Venice and Trieste.[17] Irrespective of how Jullien came to his attention, by April 1797 he was employed by Bonaparte as editor of the *Courrier*. The collaboration, however, lasted only three months; the political conceptions of the two men, especially over Italy, were fundamentally different.

The objective of the *Courrier* was not to report news; it was meant to analyse the political situation in France, to rectify false reports and rumours about Italy in the Parisian press, to 'defend liberty and its friends against tyranny or terror', and, especially, to defend Bonaparte, and to act as a conduit for calculated indiscretions regarding Bonaparte's intentions.[18] But the *Courrier* also exacerbated the differences between the people of Paris and the army: in the issue of September 1797, it announces, 'Anarchy reigns, the government is weak and powerless . . . One should no longer conceal these fatal truths.'[19] The patriotism of the troops in Italy was contrasted with the corruption of the government and the enemies of the Republic: 'On 14 July, we honour the memory of our illustrious comrades who have died in our midst, and we have before our eyes the price of their blood, of our long and arduous labours, *our victories* [. . .]. If ever Liberty wavers, look at those glorious standards, then follow the impulse of your honour, and woe betide the factious, woe betide our external enemies! They have already been killed or dispersed. The Republican constitution, to which you have sworn, has once again been saved.'[20] The message was clear: the army was fighting and dying for the Republic, earning them the right to sweep aside all those they considered unworthy. Much of the newspaper was concerned with denouncing those who posed a threat to the Republic, in particular those 'Clichyans and their arsenal of conspiracies and secret schemes against the *patrie* . . . the silence of the law or rather the indifference of the tribunals, murderous accomplices who encourage and inflate their cohorts.'

La France was first edited by Michel-Louis Regnaud de Saint-Jean d'Angély, a former deputy of the Estates-General. He had been in favour of a compromise between aristocrats and patriots and, in 1795, supported a restoration of the monarchy.[21] As with Jullien, Bonaparte and Regnaud soon fell out, so that Regnaud edited only the first six issues of *La France*. Regnaud had the reputation for being irascible, but the reason for the separation was probably an article that appeared in the sixth issue that advised acting with moderation and trust in Paris where the royalists dominated the Council of Five Hundred. It appeared before the coup of Fructidor (about which more below) and was thus a disavowal of sorts of the events in which Bonaparte was to be directly implicated.[22] Thereafter, the paper was given to an obscure personality with no journalistic experience, Chicoilet de Corbigny, and it rapidly declined. The choice of Regnaud as editor-in-chief is nevertheless interesting in that it prefigures the politically conciliatory approach Bonaparte would demonstrate when he came to power.

Bonaparte's radical politics – he was still tainted with Jacobinism at this stage – were up to a point counter-balanced by *La France*, much more moderate in its outlook and in some respects a rejection of the Jacobin image he still projected. This tells us that Bonaparte now refused to be categorized politically, that he wanted to present himself as someone who was above factions, although it is impossible to tell whether the editors were expressing the general lassitude with factional fighting in France,[23] or whether they were interpreting Bonaparte's views. The papers were, by format and content, aimed at different groups of readers. Both addressed a middle-class readership, but the *Courrier* was aimed at the new revolutionary elite and expressed Bonaparte's views on Italy, while *La France* was aimed at the more politically traditional elements in French and Italian society.[24] *La France* was, above all, destined for those in favour of centrist politics, who wanted to safeguard the benefits of the Revolution and maintain law and order, but who might have been wary of the Jacobin tendencies evident in the Army of Italy.

The focus of both newspapers, however, was Bonaparte – the simplicity of the general, his refusal of all dictatorships, his disdain for luxury, the purity of his morals.[25] Here, too, a contrast was meant to be drawn between Bonaparte and the politicians of the Directory, some of whom, like Barras, were notoriously debauched. Bonaparte, on the other hand, was indulged by Providence, a hero without reproach, a just man for the oppressed, inflexible against oppressors, a zealous republican, a friend of law and order, and a barrier against anarchy, the man who could bring about peace. In the second issue of the *Courrier*, in an article subtitled 'On rumours of war and peace', Jullien intimated that the problem was in France, not in Italy.[26] *La France* was even clearer – it asserted that peace was in the hands of Bonaparte: 'within fifteen days we will know whether we have peace or war. The general-in-chief is going to carry one or the other in the folds of his scarf.'[27] Both newspapers endeavoured to impress their readers with the notion that the royalists were an obstacle to peace, and that the Army of Italy was the vanguard of the Republic. The rhetoric found an echo among the left back home; petitions were sent to Bonaparte from all over France expressing solidarity with the general and his army.[28] In other respects, it was to force the hand of the Directory to act, and to prepare the coup against the royalists that took place on 18 Fructidor.

Entering the Political Fray: The Coup of Fructidor

Bonaparte's behaviour in Italy, where he had created a political system in the north so that he could better control his conquests, was becoming the rule rather than the exception among the generals of the French republican armies. That is, they were progressively interfering more and more in the politics of those territories they occupied, treating them as their personal fiefs. It was only a matter of time before a general with enough audacity turned his gaze towards the domestic situation in Paris, which, for republicans and neo-Jacobins at least, was becoming worrying.[29] The partial elections of March–April 1797 proved to be a resounding success for the royalists (although they took place amid the general indifference that had characterized every election since 1791). Of the 234 deputies who had to be replaced, 182 were royalist and included a former minister to Louis XVI. As a result, the three directors with distinctly republican leanings – Barras, Reubell and La Révellière-Lépeaux – disconcerted by this backlash, simply decided to annul the elections, expel the two other directors (Barthélemy and Carnot, who had argued that, since the royalists had won the elections, they should govern, even if it meant a restoration of the monarchy), and call upon the army to help them purge the chambers. Hoche, Kléber and Bernadotte, who had allied themselves with the chambers, hesitated.[30] Bonaparte, who had allied himself with the executive, that is, Barras, did not. He sent Augereau and his hussars, famous for their republican sentiments, to Paris to see through this legislative coup.[31] That, at least, is how historians have traditionally portrayed Augereau's departure for Paris, but one memorialist, the Comte de Lavalette, tells us that Barras summoned Augereau. If true, this would have suited Bonaparte, who considered his subordinate to be a troublemaker.[32] Relations between the two men had been strained; Augereau had political ambitions of his own, and relations between the two men had been strained.[33]

At three o'clock in the morning on 4 September 1797 (18 Fructidor by the revolutionary calendar), a cannon was fired to announce to the people of Paris that another revolutionary *journée* had begun. In sharp contrast with those which had preceded it, it was carried out from above, by politicians and generals, and not from below. In any event, the cannon shot was the signal to the troops and the police to take up the positions assigned to them by Augereau. Posters on the walls in the streets of Paris announced that a royalist plot was in the making.[34] Despite clashes between troops and royalist bands in the weeks leading up to the coup, the day itself was bloodless. Carnot, warned of his imminent arrest, managed to escape; Barthélemy, struck dumb with fear, let himself be taken; General Pichegru was also arrested, and the fact that he had conquered Holland for the Republic made no difference. Fifty-three deputies were arrested along with forty-two royalist journalists.

Bonaparte could rejoice in having undone a supposed plot against the Republic and that the Army of Italy had played an important role in the collapse of the royalists, but he realised that the coup was only a temporary solution and that the Directory was, in many ways, compromising the existence of the Republic. It also showed the extent to which republicans were increasingly turning to the army for the survival of the regime.[35] It was only a matter of time before a general figured out the implications.[36] The army's intervention at home showed that the regime was now increasingly dependent on force for its survival. If we include Vendémiaire, this was the second time the army helped the Directory through a political crisis. This is certainly how many in the army saw themselves, as defenders of the Republic. In the Army of Italy, at least, this was partly owing to the message Bonaparte had been propagating over the previous year or so. By the summer of 1797, many republicans in the army were disillusioned with the government in Paris, and its perceived corruption and inefficiency. One general by the name of Dupuy wrote, on 17 July 1797, 'The time has come where prudence is reprehensible. The Directory cannot object. The knives are suspended over its own head, and there is no salvation either for it or the Constitution other than a holy insurrection.'[37] Under these conditions, it is not surprising that generals like Hoche and Bonaparte emphasized their republican opinions. Bonaparte gave the example on 14 July 1797: 'Soldiers, I know that you are deeply affected by the misfortune that threatens the *patrie*, but the *patrie* is not in any real danger . . . Mountains separate us from France; if you have to, you will cross them with the speed of an eagle, to maintain the Constitution, defend liberty, and to protect the government and republicans.'[38] The letter, published in the *Moniteur*, caused something of a stir in Paris; Bonaparte was essentially threatening to march on Paris to clean out the royalists.[39]

The coup of Fructidor was thus part of the political struggle going on in Paris between royalists and republicans,[40] but that struggle also had important, far-reaching foreign political implications. The army silenced the royalists who, as partisans of peace without annexations and without the creation of sister republics, were now in a minority. Moreover, the two 'moderate' directors who were most in favour of peace (Carnot and Barthélemy) were expelled from the Directory. With them went their plans to return France to her old frontiers as the necessary price of a lasting peace.[41] The elimination of Carnot, especially, was a decisive blow against the partisans of 'smaller limits'. He was replaced by Philippe Merlin de Douai, (nicknamed 'Merlin Suspect' because of his role in introducing the 'law of suspects' during the Terror), who wanted to increase the number of sister republics and who was an important ally for La Révellière-Lépeaux. Merlin was a complicated figure who would prove perfectly capable of using extra-legal means to defend the Republic. As for the other directors, they were supporters of retaining all French conquests and, if possible, of expanding them even further. With Reubell, La Révellière-Lépeaux and Barras, the policy of natural frontiers that was first suggested in 1792 had finally won the day, as had the concept of sister republics and annexations. The two tendencies were mutually supportive and gave Bonaparte much greater scope to act according to his will. The coup of Fructidor, then, brought an even more assertive tone to French foreign policy. Over the next eighteen months, France was to expand by creating a number of sister republics (the Ligurian, also created by Bonaparte in 1797, the Roman, Helvetic and Parthenopean).

The coup was also a turning point that revealed Bonaparte's higher political ambitions, a kind of dress rehearsal for the coup of 18 Brumaire that brought him to power two years later. Bonaparte was perhaps preparing for the post-Italian period, and in this he was much more politically astute than his rivals. Unlike Hoche, who courted the Jacobin majority in the Councils, Bonaparte was thick with the executive directors, those most likely to instigate a change of government. Unlike Hoche, who sent troops from the front to the environs of Paris in July 1797 and was thereby condemned for violating the Constitution (which forbade troops from coming within sixty kilometres of Paris without the authorization of the Councils), Bonaparte managed to send Augereau and his troops on the pretext that they were on leave from the campaign in Italy, thus supporting the Directory without making any waves. Moreover, as a result of the coup of Fructidor, the Directory, more than ever, was now dependent on Bonaparte, even if it attempted to distance itself from him. When one of Augereau's aides-de-camp arrived in Passariano towards the end of September with instructions that bypassed Bonaparte, he rushed off a letter asking to be dismissed: 'No power on earth would be capable of making me stay in service after that horrible mark of ingratitude from the government.'[42] Not only had his health been considerably altered, he argued, but also his soul needed to gain renewed strength from the people. Histrionics aside, the Directory could not accept his resignation; every other leading general was either suspect or discredited.[43] Bonaparte was aware of this, and went ahead to negotiate peace terms with Austria without consulting the Directory.

'Drunk with Happiness'

Six months passed between the preliminaries of Leoben and the Treaty of Campo Formio that brought the war between France and Austria formally to a conclusion. Initially, the negotiations were long and arduous because many of the preliminary articles were obscure and difficult to interpret, but also because all three parties – Bonaparte, the Directory and Austria – had an interest in prolonging the talks: Bonaparte in order to establish his authority in northern Italy more firmly; the Directory because it wanted to wait and see how the domestic developments in France would turn out; while Austria hoped that a royalist majority would take power in France so that it could renege on the concessions it had made at Leoben.

The coup of Fructidor changed all that. The Austrians could no longer procrastinate in the hope that a restoration would take place in France, something that Thugut had counted on for some months. The new government decided that peace was necessary as quickly as possible to compensate for the alarm the coup had caused among some sections of the public.[44] Bonaparte, fearing that the Directory might transfer negotiations with Austria to Paris so that peace would be concluded without him, or that perhaps they would even be given to Augereau, who had just been named commander-in-chief of the Army of Germany, hurried to finish the negotiations at Campo Formido, a village between Passariano and Udine on Venetian territory. (Camp Formido is commonly known as Campo Formio. A French secretary left out the 'd' by mistake and the name has stuck ever since.) Under threat of a resumption of hostilities, Austria finally signed a peace agreement on the night of 17–18 October, one that was very different from what had been agreed at Leoben. In return for the loss of Belgium, Lombardy and parts of Germany, the Austrians were to receive the archbishopric of Salzburg, Bavaria east of the Inn, and keep Venice. This last clause was deeply resented not only by Italian patriots who dreamed of a free and united Italy, but also by the rest of Europe, which saw in the annexation of Venice proof that republican France had become 'just another rapacious exponent of great-power politics'.[45] Indeed, Bonaparte had to threaten to resign again in order to have this clause accepted by the Directory.[46] The French got Belgium, indirect control over what was once Lombardy (now the Cisalpine Republic, formally recognized by Austria), the Ionian islands, and the promise of Austrian assistance to gain most of the left bank of the Rhine when peace was negotiated with the Holy Roman Empire. In a long letter to the foreign minister, Talleyrand, Bonaparte explained his reasons for making so many concessions to Austria. He insisted on the necessity of concentrating all efforts against Britain, at the risk of losing the French colonies.[47] Not only did Campo Formio partition northern Italy, it also paved the way for the partition of Germany. That was some time in the future. For the moment, Bonaparte's peace brought the French two concrete advantages: an evident hegemony in Italy; and the role of arbiter in the reconstruction of Germany.[48]

The war had done an enormous amount for the personal prestige of Bonaparte, but its outcome was, in fact, indecisive. The governments of both France and Austria were decidedly unhappy about the terms of the treaty. For the Austrians, the treaty was no more than a truce. As soon as they had signed it, they were sounding out the British about the possible revival of an anti-French coalition.[49] The directors baulked at what they considered its mildness, and would have preferred to reject it.[50] There had been acute disappointment in Paris at Bonaparte's failure to secure Austrian consent to cede the left bank of the Rhine in its entirety. Reubell and Merlin de Douai, hostile to Bonaparte's Italian policy and especially to the transfer of Venice to Austria, at first refused to ratify the treaty. There were, as far as we can tell, heated debates over what to do, and certainly there was division in the two legislative councils.[51] The reaction among the dominant political faction, the Jacobins, was not much better. They had learned to hate Bonaparte, considered the treaty to be an 'abominable treason', and protested that the articles had to be redressed at a future congress (to be held at Rastatt in Germany).[52] The fact that the government in France eventually did concede to Bonaparte's treaty was, in some respects, a further sign of their increasing dependence on the army, which now seemed to be dictating the direction of foreign policy.

This had implications that few at the time realized. For one, the policy of natural frontiers, although it had not existed in practice for some time, was now officially overturned and replaced with that of expansion through sister republics. It made the international situation inherently unstable.[53] The foreign minister, Talleyrand, was perhaps aware of this when he later criticized the direction affairs were taking by arguing, 'can one not say that the Treaty of Campo Formio and every other treaty we have signed are nothing but military capitulations by the enemy of little permanent worth?'[54] The deputy, Emmanuel Joseph Sieyès, who was later to play an important role in Bonaparte's accession to power, also declared that Campo Formio was not a peace treaty, but rather a call to war.[55]

Even Bonaparte was supposedly not particularly happy with the treaty, which he knew to be 'entirely impolitic, extremely unfavourable for the present and even more so for the future', although it is highly unlikely he had the international situation in mind when he said this.[56] Indeed, the treaty highlighted two shortcomings in Bonaparte: his apparent ignorance of the state of affairs in Germany; and his inability to think in long-term objectives. One can perhaps understand Bonaparte's inability to be 'diplomatic', to compromise, to have the necessary patience for a successful outcome in any negotiation. He was, after all, a soldier, but more than that it was simply contrary to his nature. To Bonaparte, the object of the negotiation process was to impose one's will on the defeated in the immediate and short term. The consequences for the future of France and its place in the European states system, or indeed for the future of Europe itself, were never entertained.

A good example of this is the statements Bonaparte made to the young Austrian plenipotentiary, Count Johann Ludwig Cobenzl, one of Austria's most competent diplomats, during the negotiations at Campo Formio. According to Cobenzl, Bonaparte not only believed himself to be the equal of any king but, indeed, to be above them. He also regarded the Mediterranean as belonging to France. Even more worrying to the future peace of Europe, however, was Bonaparte's boast that if he had 100,000 peasants in Russia, he would turn them into soldiers and declare war on the sovereigns of Europe, taking over the Russian throne.[57] This could easily be dismissed as bluster, the façade of a revolutionary republican trying to intimidate an Austrian royalist into concluding peace quickly, but the fact that he made these statements to the key Austrian diplomat is, I think, an indication of Bonaparte's state of mind. It was always how he handled negotiations, and it was always this – an unthinking rush to impose his will – that, once he was in power, got him into ever deeper waters.

If the Directory was unhappy about the Treaty of Campo Formio, the same cannot be said about the people of France. When news of the treaty reached Paris, the people were 'drunk with happiness', according to the expression used by the police. Some of the Paris cafés changed their names to Café de la Paix, while in the theatres that evening the crowds burst into applause every time the

Artist unknown, *Prinz Carl und General Bonaparte als Friedenstifter* (Prince Charles and General Bonaparte as Peacemakers), circa 1797. Note the French and Austrian soldiers in the background embracing and holding hands. There were numerous prints celebrating the signature of the preliminaries at Leoben, all designed to underline the nature of Bonaparte as pacifier and his ability as an adept diplomat. (*Bibliothèque nationale, Paris*)

word 'peace' was mentioned, or when actors ad-libbed and introduced it into their roles.[58]

Bonaparte had managed to do what no other general or politician had been able to do – bring the war on the Continent to an end. Military victory and peace are generally two sides of the same coin, but the people of Paris seem to have been more genuinely impressed by the fact that Bonaparte had brought the war to an end than by his military prowess. An indication of this is that plays – the theatre was the principal form of entertainment at the time and was often used to comment on current affairs – that had earlier highlighted Bonaparte's military exploits, like *La Bataille de Roverebella, ou Buonaparte en Italie*

(10 February 1797), *La Reddition de Mantoue* (23 February 1797), or *La Prise de Mantoue* (27 February 1797), were not particularly well received in Paris.[59] This might have had something to do with the fact that they were mediocre love stories in which Bonaparte sometimes did not appear. But even what might be called the first theatrical manifestations of the Bonaparte legend, such as *Le Pont de Lodi* (December 1796), were much less successful than the plays that had peace as their subject. About seven plays appeared in the months of April and May 1798 dramatizing the preliminaries with Austria. In October and November, a dozen or so plays and impromptu operas appeared with either peace or Bonaparte as their subject. One of them, entitled the *Hymne sur la Paix*, contained the following rhyme:

> Glory to the conqueror of Italy!
> Glory to the hero of the universe!
> A hundred different peoples belong
> To the same motherland.
> You whom history has immortalized,
> Surrender to this young Frenchman:
> You fought for victory,
> He fought for peace.[60]

None of the military victories, therefore, made as much of an impact on the French imagination as the announcement of peace at Leoben and Campo Formio.[61] It can be assumed that Bonaparte was aware of this. He seems to have played up to the desire for peace in France: on a number of occasions he presented himself as someone who preferred to negotiate an honourable peace rather than wage an all-out war. From the moment Leoben and Campo Formio were signed, the prestige surrounding Bonaparte was considerably enhanced. 'At last, we are going to enjoy the benefits of peace,' wrote one contributor in the *Journal des Campagnes*. 'Thanks to you, invincible armies that destroyed the efforts of all of Europe in league against our liberty.'[62] A poem on the signature of the peace preliminaries celebrated Bonaparte for bringing the war to an end:

> To Bonaparte,
> Young hero, conqueror of Italy,
> Pursue, amaze, fell the pride of kings:
> May your successes consolidate our laws:
> Astound your enemies and those of the *patrie*.
> You will not stifle the passion of envy:
> Well then, earn it by new exploits.[63]

The poetry is mediocre, but the sentiments are clear. Another pointed out that, 'Hannibal did not do what Bonaparte has done in Italy; Scipio did not surpass him and a grateful Rome honoured him with the name of the African.'[64] Bonaparte was now referred to in some circles in Paris as *l'Italique* (the 'Italic'). This compared him directly with ancient Roman generals, like Scipio, dubbed the 'African' for his conquests in that country, and Drusus, dubbed 'Germanicus' for his victories against the Germans.

'A Pure and Great Giant of Glory'

Peace, therefore, magnified Bonaparte's prestige. But there was, nevertheless, the question of what to do about Campo Formio, and about Bonaparte. One way for the Directory to gain time was to name Bonaparte commander-in-chief of the Army of England, which had just been formed – the Directory had to reward Bonaparte for concluding peace even if it was not particularly keen on doing so – and also to send him off to Rastatt to take part in the negotiations regarding the application of the clauses of the treaty in Germany. It was an effective means of keeping Bonaparte away from Paris for as long as possible, without their motives being questioned.[65] It may even have been a trap set by the Directory: every other general who had been involved in a landing directed at either England or Ireland had failed.[66] Tension between Bonaparte and the Directory, then, was apparent if muted. He suspected that most of the directors feared rather than admired him, and that they had named him commander-in-chief of the Army of England to keep him away from the theatre of his conquests, to separate him from the army that was so devoted to him.[67] In fact, the bulk of the troops earmarked for the Army of England were to come from the Army of Italy.

Peace may have considerably enhanced his reputation, but peace and inaction were Bonaparte's enemies. Another campaign and further victories were essential if he were not to become just another general in the crowd. And so Bonaparte accepted both the new command and the diplomatic posting. He was now directly invited to take part in politics at the highest levels, although he does not seem to have been in any great hurry to leave his miniature court at Mombello for Rastatt, where he planned to arrive around the end of November.[68] There was still work to do. Officers had to be designated for the Army of England, maps had to be assembled and plans drawn up, naval material from Venice had to be evacuated, and cannon made in the same calibre as the English so that the French could use their shot once they arrived. The Directory also began to put its administrative machinery into gear so that, for example, the different points where the navy was to be concentrated, from the Adriatic to the North Sea, were decided on 11 December 1797. The organizational effort put into the expedition against England, later transformed into the Egyptian expedition, is a telling sign that the Directory, far from being a weak and inefficient government, was, after six years of almost continual war, still able to muster imposing military strength.

Bonaparte's arrival at Rastatt on the evening of 25 November caused a sensation.[69] His *berline* was drawn by eight horses, the number usually reserved for kings, and accompanied by an escort of thirty hussars. On 29 November, the Directory invested Bonaparte with the powers necessary to evacuate and take possession of all territories pertaining to the articles of the Treaty of Campo Formio. Consequently, on 9 December 1797, Bonaparte started writing instructions in the name of the Directory to the plenipotentiaries at Rastatt as well as orders to General Jacques-Maurice Hatry, who was blockading Mainz.[70] From a military point of view he was acting almost like a generalissimo. Indeed, this is what Talleyrand, in a letter to Barras dated 29 November, suggested – that Bonaparte should be placed in command of both the armies of Italy and Germany. Together with the command of the Army of

England, this would have given him almost total control over the whole French army.

This was not to happen, though, and Bonaparte did not stay in Rastatt long. The Directory had a change of heart, and ordered him back to Paris. Barras probably needed Bonaparte to intimidate the opposition in Paris, especially within the Directory, where the self-appointed master of France seems to have entered into a struggle with Merlin de Douai.[71] Bonaparte left Rastatt on 3 December only a week after having arrived. He understood what was expected of him and possibly imagined playing a greater political role in Paris than Barras intended.

In contrast to his grandiose entry into Rastatt, Bonaparte arrived in Paris unannounced, after an absence of almost eighteen months, on 5 December at five o'clock in the evening, in civilian dress and in a simple *voiture de poste* (mail coach). Josephine was not there (there are no letters from this period, which in itself speaks a good deal about the state of their relationship). Although no longer with her lover, she had taken her time travelling back from Italy, a voyage that lasted for two and a half months. This is perhaps one reason why, for the next month, until her return at the beginning of January, he avoided the public eye and went out as little as possible. When Bonaparte did go out in public, he appeared not as the glorious conqueror of Italy in military uniform, but modestly, as a simple citizen.[72] Despite this, whenever Bonaparte appeared, crowds gathered to shower him with applause.[73] According to the Duchesse d'Abrantès, all Paris was at Bonaparte's feet: 'All classes united to welcome him on his return to his country. The lower orders cried, Long live General Bonaparte! Long live the victor of Italy! The peacemaker of Campo Formio! The bourgeoisie said, May God preserve him for our greater glory and deliver us from the *Maximum** of the directors. The upper classes rushed with enthusiasm to acclaim a young man who in one year had gone from the battle of Montenotte to the Treaty of Leoben, from victory to victory! He may have made mistakes, even big ones, since that time, but in those days he was a pure and great giant of glory.'[74] But it

* The General Maximum set at a fixed price all wages and all essential food items. Introduced by the Convention, it was eventually hated by Parisians.

was the image of the humble hero, who did not seek out public acclaim, and who wore civilian dress, that was most remarked upon by contemporary observers. When he attended the theatre, for example, he 'hid from the applause that always follows him when he is recognized.'[75] At least one anecdote reported by the press, in this instance while Bonaparte was on the coast inspecting the ports, played to this theme:

> General Bonaparte was at Dunkirk and wanted to attend a comedy, and as his plans were discovered, a considerable crowd turned out to wait for him. Faithful to his principles of modesty, he was dressed in bourgeois attire, and went and mixed with the spectators in the pit. One of his [Bonaparte's] neighbours asked him if the person he saw in a box was Bonaparte; he replied, I do not think so. Another citizen asked him the same question pointing out another person . . . Not at all, replied a third person standing next to the general, I know Bonaparte and he is much taller.[76]

The message Bonaparte wished to was clear: as victorious hero he was at heart modest and unassuming. It seems out of keeping with the image he fostered in Italy. In fact, it was a studied, remarkably sensitive calculation designed to enhance his reputation, and to avoid the Parisian political quagmire. Here too, just as at Mombello, Bonaparte was performing a role he knew would be acceptable to the political elite. To have been hailed as a military hero would have made many in the two councils feel uneasy and would have conjured up images of Caesar returning to Rome after the campaigns in Gaul. The interesting thing is that Bonaparte was perhaps the first figure in modern history to foster the illusion of avoiding public acclaim, when his real goal was to attract it. It was a ploy that worked.

The day after his arrival in Paris, Bonaparte met with the directors in the apartments of Barras, where he was warmly received by his host and La Révellière-Lépeaux, cordially by Reubell, and coldly by the two others.[77]

However, it is his public audience with the Directory at the Luxembourg Palace, held a few days later on a 'sad and cold'

December morning, which is worth reflecting on.[78] Bonaparte left Josephine's house in the rue Chantereine at about ten o'clock in the morning in a simple carriage, accompanied by Barras. The avenues leading up to the palace were so full of people who had turned out to see him that they were impassable. The courtyard of the palace itself was transformed into an immense 'room' almost entirely covered by a tent, decorated with the trophies of war. At half past twelve, Talleyrand led the general, flanked by Berthier, Joubert and Championnet carrying the flags they had captured in Italy, 'all taller than he [Bonaparte] but almost stooped by the respect they showed him',[79] to the position where he was to be officially received – an altar to the *patrie* in the courtyard of the palace. Bonaparte advanced towards them among frenetic acclamations of 'Vive Bonaparte' and 'Vive le Directoire', and deafening applause. The five directors were sitting in front of the altar of the *patrie* – above which were three statues representing Peace, Liberty and Equality – surrounded by their ministers and the diplomatic corps.[80] Twelve hundred musicians and the choir of the Conservatory sang the 'Hymn of Liberty'.

When the crowds quietened, Talleyrand spoke, praising the 'conqueror of Italy', a term that was often used in the pamphlet literature, as the author of peace with the Holy Roman Empire, and as future conqueror of England. 'And when I think [Talleyrand concluded] of all that he did to be forgiven that glory, of the manner for simplicity which characterizes him, of his love for the abstract sciences ... when no one could be unaware of his profound contempt for ostentation, for luxury, for display, the contemptible ambitions of the common mortal, ah!, far from doubting what one might call his ambition, I feel that we might have to appeal to him one day to tear him away from his studious retreat. All of France will be free; he may never be. That is his destiny.'[81]

It is a remarkable declaration. Either by design, or simply because he, too, had been seduced by Bonaparte's performance as humble citizen, Talleyrand helped propagate the image of an apolitical conqueror. Moreover, Talleyrand was brazen enough to compare the corrupt directors with Bonaparte, and at the same time plant the idea that he might be called upon to save and govern France.

Bonaparte could hardly have hoped for more. In turn, he gave a short speech, 'with a sort of affected nonchalance, as if he wanted people to understand that he had little liking for the regime he was called to serve',[82] concluding, 'When the happiness of the French people is based on better organic laws, all of Europe will become free.'[83] Even if little of the speech was heard – the crowd was too large and too noisy – the rhetoric was clear. It was a threat to the existing regime.

Abraham Girardet, *Fête donnée à Bonaparte, au Palais national du Directoire après le traité de Campo Formio* (Festival given to Bonaparte at the National Palace of the Directory after the Treaty of Campo Formio), 1802. (*Bibliothèque nationale, Paris*)

The key moment seems to have been the official presentation of the treaty of peace to the Directory. Bonaparte charged Berthier with this propaganda exercise in which he appears as the avenger of Vercingetorix: 'We needed two thousand years to produce a successor. He has all your virtues; in a more enlightened century you would have had his talents and fortunate Gaul would not have known slavery.'[84]

Not everyone in the crowd, and especially the directors, were impressed by the theatricality surrounding the ceremony.[85] Bourrienne noted that the atmosphere was 'icy cold', while the members of the Directory and Bonaparte's clique sized each other up, perhaps trying to assess the other's worth.[86]

This ceremony was followed by other public marks of confidence in the weeks that followed: a banquet was given by the two legislative councils to Bonaparte on 24 December. It was a means of rendering homage to the Army of Italy while at the same time asserting the pre-eminence of civilian power, especially that issued from the coup of Fructidor, over military power. On 3 January 1798, the day after Josephine's return to Paris, Talleyrand gave a reception at the Hôtel Galiffet, ostensibly in her honour, to which over 500 people were invited and where people danced a new dance – *The Buonaparte*. The invitations specified that no English merchandise be worn. At midnight, Chénier's music was performed in honour of Bonaparte. The ball was preceded by fireworks in which a 'Vive la République' appeared in coloured letters. Bonaparte, uncomfortable in social situations, arrived at about half past ten in the evening and had left by one o'clock in the morning.

Bonaparte had almost certainly quarrelled with his wife about Hippolyte Charles. The same day Josephine arrived in Paris, she sacked her maid, Louise Compoint, for sleeping with Junot. Compoint then exacted revenge on her mistress by telling Bonaparte everything.[87] Did he believe her? Did he confront Josephine only for her to calmly deny the accusation? We do not know, but witness reports of how morose they were at the ball suggest that a scene had taken place, and that she had probably managed to lie her way out of the predicament.[88] Josephine continued to maintain a liaison with Charles and her affections for him would appear much warmer than those she felt for her husband. A couple of months later, in

March, when Joseph had a talk with Bonaparte about Josephine's involvement in some shady business dealings, she complained in a letter to Charles: 'Yes, my Hippolyte, I hate them all [she was referring to the Bonaparte family]. You alone have my tenderness, my love.' And she went on to say, 'I will do everything I can to see you during the day. If I cannot, I will pass by Bodin's [one of the businessmen she was embroiled with] this evening, and tomorrow morning I will send Blondon [Bonaparte's servant] to give you a time when we can meet at the Mousseaux gardens [the present-day Parc Monceau]. Goodbye, my Hippolyte, a thousand burning kisses, as passionate as my heart and just as loving.'[89]

Bonaparte never persisted with his accusations, perhaps fearing the worst, perhaps fearing the consequences, both personal and political, of a scandal involving a young hussar and his wife. It was something he could not afford as he was about to enter into politics. Moreover, Josephine still had close contacts with highly placed politicians like Barras. He is supposed to have once said to his family around the dinner table on Corsica, 'Women especially are the only real and efficient protective machines.'[90] So Bonaparte focused on politics, despite the troubles at home, and calculated how best to enter the arena. Talleyrand may also have helped him, at least some of the way. Bonaparte had his first official meeting with the Directory's foreign minister the day after he arrived in the capital (5 December), although they had quite possibly met briefly on the same evening of his arrival at Talleyrand's residence, where they supposedly remained behind closed doors for several hours.[91] The conversation was not reported, but Talleyrand recalled his first impressions many years later: 'At first glance, Bonaparte seemed to me to have a charming figure. Twenty battles won is most becoming in a young hero with fine eyes, a pale and almost consumptive look.'

Was Bonaparte already thinking of assuming power and sounding out Talleyrand about the possibility? Perhaps. He certainly believed the government had become dependent on him for its survival.[92] He had command of a sufficient amount of force at this stage, and perhaps enough popularity, to sweep away the Directory if he were so inclined. It is doubtful, though, that he wanted to; his political acumen, undoubtedly developed during his stay in Italy, would have led him to the conclusion that the time was not ripe.

Instead, Bonaparte approached Barras, through the intermediary of Jean Tallien, to find out whether he could get himself elected to the Directory, but for that a constitutional change was necessary – a director had to be over forty – and that was unlikely to happen. There was talk of a coup, although it was not Bonaparte's idea at the outset. When he arrived in Paris, he was almost immediately approached by generals like Moreau and Kléber, who suggested to him the idea of a coup that would put an end to the Directory. The prestige of these generals was considerable and they were both, to a greater or lesser extent, disaffected with the Directory: Moreau, because of his attitude during the coup of Fructidor, was temporarily released from duty; Kléber, a sincere republican, reproached the Directory for having left the army in total poverty during the German campaign of 1796, and blamed it for that campaign's failure.[93] When Bonaparte approached Barras he was fobbed off, and had to let the idea go. He had taken an enormous risk in revealing a political ambition that might not have been previously suspected. This is perhaps one of the reasons, if one contemporary is to be believed, why, during the four months he was in Paris between the end of the Italian campaign and his departure for Egypt, Bonaparte was never seen without spurs, and why he always had a horse saddled and ready in his stables.[94] The malcontents were, however, persistent and came from every side of the political spectrum. General Desaix, a noble and a product of the military schools of the *ancien régime*, also approached Bonaparte about the possibility of a coup, but one that was to be under his direction. At about the same time, Bonaparte received advances from royalists – Josephine was being used as an intermediary in this context – who wanted to use him to bring about a restoration.[95]

It is clear from this that certain sections of both the political and especially the military elite were so disaffected with the Directory that they had resolved to get rid of it. One contemporary, at least, was convinced that Bonaparte seriously considered the possibility of a coup, that he examined its chances of success, but then abandoned the idea.[96] He now knew, however, that high-ranking military from the Army of Germany were prepared to involve and perhaps support him – he could naturally count on his own officers – and that anti-Jacobin sentiments in certain sections of the army, coupled with a feeling of overall powerlessness at the inability of the Directory to govern efficiently, could eventually serve his ends. He would have to wait until the Directory's authority had dwindled more, but as long as he was capable of conserving the confidence that his victories in Italy had gained him, the possibility of taking part in a coup would always be there.

THE CIVILIZING HERO, 1798–1799

14

A Grandiose Exile

The Decision

The Treaty of Campo Formio left France fighting only one enemy –
Britain. There had been a half-hearted attempt to negotiate a peace
settlement with Britain at Lille, where negotiations started in mid-
June. In late September 1797, however, they were broken off,
essentially because leaders on both sides of the Channel lacked
the political will to pursue them to a decisive outcome.[1] The British
resisted what they feared would be a humiliating surrender, while
three of the directors were simply opposed to peace. The failure
underlined what was to be the major stumbling block to a general
settlement in Europe for years to come: the difficulty in finding an
equitable basis for reconciliation between the two powers – one
land, one maritime – when both were determined to keep their
respective conquests.

The negotiations had been made difficult by a number of factors,
not the least of which was the impact of the coup of Fructidor (4
September 1797) on the Directory's attitude towards Britain. The
new Directory was much more belligerent, and believed itself to be
'the master of Europe'.[2] Within a few days of assuming power it
recalled its negotiators, who were suspected of being too moderate,
and replaced them with men who were enemies of the faction that
wanted to keep France within its old territorial limits. By 19
September, the negotiations had broken down, and the French
put the blame on the British. They were not entirely wrong: the
internal divisions within the British government were too great at
this stage. While the prime minister, William Pitt, may have been

prepared to compromise, the foreign secretary, Lord Grenville, was inflexible on the Belgian question, as was George III. For the French, then, Britain was the supreme obstacle on the path towards a general peace. Bonaparte recognized this early on when he suggested to Talleyrand, 'destroy England [and] Europe is at our feet.'[3]

The problem of defeating Britain was compounded by the deplorable state of the French navy. At the outset of the Revolution, it was the second largest in the world, and included seventy-three ships of the line and sixty-three frigates (with four more of each under construction). Even the French state's financial crisis did not slow the ship-building programme. By 1793, the French had eighty-eight ships of the line and seventy-three frigates, compared with the British fleet's 115 ships of the line and sixty frigates.[4] Moreover, recently built vessels, such as the *Dauphin-Royal* (re-baptized the *Sans-Culotte* and later the *Orient*), the largest naval vessel of its time, and the *Franklin*, launched in 1790, were considered superior to the equivalent British ships. If the French vessels outclassed their English equivalents, the Revolution had an insidious impact on the navy, interfering with its organization, stimulating insubordination among the rank and file, and persecuting aristocratic officers.[5] Consequently, a considerable number of naval officers emigrated at the outset of the Revolution, so that by 1792 only two out of nine vice-admirals, eighteen out of forty-two captains, and 170 out of 356 lieutenants remained.[6] To this must be added the lack of money available to maintain the navy, as well as the perennial problem of finding enough sailors to man them (a problem compounded by the civil war in the west of France, a region where sailors were traditionally recruited), and the fact that the French were often unable to train their crews because the British fleets blockaded their ports.[7] On one occasion in July 1795, when a French squadron managed to sail from Brest, two-thirds of the 12,000 sailors in the fleet had never put to sea before.

The lack of qualified manpower goes some way towards explaining the poor performance of the French navy in its encounters with the British. Courage among French crews was not lacking, but they were very conscious of their inadequacies compared with the technical superiority of the more numerous and better-trained

British sailors. In battle, this manifested itself in a lack of determination and, often, a refusal to undertake audacious moves. Between January 1793 and December 1797, in various skirmishes between the French and the British, the French lost 204 ships, of which thirty-five were ships of the line and sixty-one were frigates, with 108 other vessels. The British losses for the same period seventy-seven ships, of which fourteen were ships of the line, twenty frigates, and forty-three others.[8] With the construction of new vessels, the superiority of the British navy was overwhelming. French naval inferiority, however, was not an insurmountable obstacle to an invasion of Britain. It was simply a question of controlling the Channel for a specific, limited period of time so that troops could be transported from the mainland to the English coast. The important thing was to keep Britain unsure about where the landing would take place.

It was under Bonaparte's leadership as commander of the Army of England that, in November 1797, France began assembling an invasion force with the aim of defeating her last remaining enemy. The idea of invading England was not new. Recently, for example, there had been a combined Franco-Spanish attempt in 1779, during the American War of Independence, aborted because of epidemics that decimated the ships' crews. From 1793 onwards, the Committee of Public Safety, and later the Directory, seriously considered an invasion of both England and Ireland. With that in mind, General Hoche was put in charge of an invasion attempt against Ireland in December 1796, and even though the expedition was a fiasco – the fleet was dispersed by bad weather – it seemed to prove that, in principle, it was possible. A couple of small books on the history of these invasion attempts appeared in 1798 in order to demonstrate that, in principle; 'it has always been easy to cast troops onto the shores of England'.[9]

Bonaparte, however, had serious doubts about the feasibility of an expedition to England. In the first days of February 1798, when he finally decided to inspect the ports in the Pas de Calais and Belgium in person (General Caffarelli was sent to inspect those in the department of the Nord, General Kléber those in Normandy and General Desaix those in Brittany), he may have already decided to find an excuse not to pursue the enterprise. In any event, when he returned to Paris from his inspection tour on 20 February, and without even waiting for the other generals' reports, he submitted a memorandum to the Directory underlining the impracticality of an invasion, highlighting the problems such an enterprise would entail: the difficulty of avoiding the Royal Navy long enough to make the crossing; the impracticality of using small boats to transport thousands of men; and the fact that the French navy was not adequately prepared and did not have full compliments of crews.[10] As a result, he recommended that either the focus be shifted to the conquest of Hamburg and the Electorate of Hanover, or that an expedition be sent to the Levant (the eastern Mediterranean) to threaten Britain's commerce with India.

The possibility of occupying the Electorate of Hanover, nominally the territory of the English king, George III, as well as Hamburg, would have intensified the economic war the Directory had led against Britain since the French victories of 1797, when it declared that British goods aboard neutral ships were liable to confiscation. At the beginning of 1798, the Directory intensified the economic war when it authorized the capture of any vessel with British goods on board, and closed French ports to any ship that had touched at a British port. The occupation of Hanover, however, would take the economic war a step further – it would be the start of an indefinite expansionist programme on the Continent in order to plug the breaches of the blockade. The Directory thought this would embroil it in a conflict with the northern European powers and wisely decided against it, but it is worth noting that Bonaparte would do exactly that after he had come to power a few years later. Another option was to channel French expansionist ambitions overseas, thereby threatening Britain's commercial relations with its colonies.

This is why, in this particular instance, India was raised as an eventual objective. Since the Americans had won their independence from Britain, India had become the central pillar of its imperial structure. If the French managed to repeat their success there too, it was thought, the whole imperial edifice would come crashing down. France might even recoup some of its colonial losses in India. Egypt was thus presented as a vital key in the link to India and a viable alternative to continued war on the Continent.[11]

A colonial expedition would offer the advantage of undermining Britain, while preserving stability on the Continent by preventing further expansion beyond France's natural limits.

There were practical reasons for taking Egypt, too. During February and March 1798, when the plan for an expedition to Egypt was drawn up, there were no British warships in the Mediterranean – they had withdrawn at the end of 1796, leaving the French in effective control – making a successful invasion more likely. Egypt as potential colony had, moreover, been discussed in political circles for a number of months, largely as a result of two papers Talleyrand presented to the National Institute. The first (delivered on 4 April 1797) was on commercial relations between Britain and the United States,[12] in which he warned that dreams of a mighty alliance between France and its sister republic in the New World were doomed to failure; the British were in an unassailable position with respect to its commercial potential because of traditional connections with the American continent. In fact, Talleyrand was laying the groundwork for the argument he delivered in his second paper three months later (3 July 1797). The future, he contended, lay in colonial expansion – that is, in colonizing new lands with French citizens.[13] The need to replace French colonies lost to the British in the Americas, the convenience of finding colonies closer to home, and the need not to be outdone by a rival nation were all arguments put forward by Talleyrand in this second paper to justify a colonial enterprise. However, he argued that new colonies were not to be sought in the New World, which was already controlled by the British, but should be sought in Africa; he mentioned Egypt as a possibility.

It is difficult to know where Talleyrand's sudden interest in colonial affairs came from. It is possible that he was the voice of some kind of colonial lobby, businessmen who had lost everything at Saint-Domingue (Haiti) when the slave revolt broke out there in 1791. Saint-Domingue had been the jewel in the French colonial crown and by far the richest colony in the world.[14] In any event, although Talleyrand may have been proposing a new direction in revolutionary foreign policy, Egypt has to be placed within the context of the colonial question in France. The idea of invading Egypt had been contemplated by Louis XV's foreign minister, the

Duc de Choiseul, who advised the king to open negotiations for the cession of Egypt to France by the Ottoman Empire, but nothing came of it. The loss of French territory in North America in 1763, and of the French islands in the Caribbean to the British as a result of the revolutionary wars, made it imperative to reconstruct the country's colonial empire. That is why France, during this period, was sending out missions to the Pacific, as far as Australia. As for Egypt, the debate in late eighteenth-century French politics centred around the question of whether France should intervene to shore up the crumbling Ottoman Empire by attempting to renew and modernize it from within, or whether it should reach an agreement with Russia and Austria to partition the spoils. Increasingly, towards the end of the eighteenth century, the view that there might be more to gain from the role of predator than that of protector of the Ottoman Empire gained ground in Paris. Attention began to centre on the weak spot of the empire, Egypt. In the course of the 1780s, French diplomatic missions were sent all over the eastern Mediterranean to explore the possibility of an invasion. It resulted in a series of memoranda on the subject, some of which went so far as to suggest the possibility of opening communications with India through the Red Sea.

The idea inspired Talleyrand. A week or so after becoming foreign minister (16 July 1797), perhaps encouraged by the reception of his 'colonial policy', he decided to collect the assorted plans for an invasion of Egypt that had been submitted to the French Ministry for Foreign Affairs over the previous thirty years. On 23 July 1797, Talleyrand submitted three reports to the Directory marking the conjuncture of two ideas: the conquest of Egypt, and intervention in India. The first of these enterprises was a sure means of achieving the second. There does not seem to have been any prior understanding between him and Bonaparte on a projected Egyptian expedition, although sometime later they exchanged ideas on the subject. On 16 August, for example, Bonaparte wrote suggesting that French support for the Porte was pointless: 'we will see it fall in our time.'[15] (Some contemporaries believed that the Ottoman Empire was on the verge of dissolution: the Sultan had been unable to subdue rebellious pashas in the Balkans or the Mameluke beys in Egypt.) Again on 13 September 1797, Bonaparte wrote to Talleyrand to suggest, 'Why don't we seize the island of Malta? . . . If we are obliged to cede the Cape of Good Hope to the English when peace is concluded, then we should seize Egypt . . . I would like it if, citizen minister, you were able to make some enquiries and let me know how the Porte would react to our expedition to Egypt.'[16] Talleyrand's reply was immediate and in the same vein: 'Your ideas on that matter are great, and its usefulness must be felt . . . if conquest was made, it would have to be, as far as the Porte is concerned, to thwart Russian and English intrigues, which are so often renewed in that unfortunate country. Such a great service to the Turks would easily engage them to leave us completely in control with all the commercial advantages we need. Egypt, as a colony, will soon replace the produce from the West Indies.'[17]

The primary motivation seems to have been economic. For the moment things were left at that, but a few months later Talleyrand used the discussion surrounding the replacement of the French ambassador to the Porte, Aubert-Dubayet, who had died after a short illness, as a pretext to bring Egypt back on to the agenda. Two reports, unsolicited, were consequently addressed to the Directory on the question of the Orient, urging it to shelve the invasion project currently being prepared against Britain in favour of an invasion of Egypt. The first report was submitted on 27 January 1798, only a week or so before Bonaparte left on his inspection tour of the French ports (there may very well have been collusion between Talleyrand and Bonaparte over this, even though there is nothing in the written evidence to suggest it). The Ottoman Empire, argued Talleyrand, was on the verge of collapse, and its European provinces would be the prey of the imperial houses of Russia and Austria. 'Egypt, which nature has placed so close to us, and which presents immense advantages from the point of view of commerce', would be a substitute for the colonies in the Caribbean. 'Egypt', he went on to say, 'is nothing for Turkey, where the Porte does not have the shadow of authority.'[18]

The conquest of Egypt was thereby officially open for discussion. A second report was submitted two weeks later on 14 February 1798, largely plagiarized from a submission by the French consul in Egypt, Charles Magallon, and held out as Talleyrand's own vision of a country that would welcome the French as liberators.[19] Magallon, sick of the large sums of money the Mamelukes had been extorting from French merchants and their general interference with commerce, had been urging his government to intervene for some years. In his report, Talleyrand raised the possibility of an Ottoman government too weak to intervene and which could be easily won over by an able negotiator, of a Europe afraid of war with France, but more interestingly, of opening a route to Suez and striking a blow at Britain in India. Egypt, in short, would be easy pickings and would prepare the expansion of French influence westward across the northern coast of Africa, and eastward to the remotest regions of Asia. 'We will penetrate every part of the immense continent of Africa,' Talleyrand imagined rather fancifully, 'and discover there the rivers of the interior, the mountains and the mines of iron and gold in which that country abounds.'[20]

This might help us understand the foreign policy choices open to the directors around this time, but it does not explain Bonaparte's role in an overseas colonial adventure. It was largely because Bonaparte, with the support of Talleyrand, exerted pressure on the directors in favour of the idea that the decision to launch an expedition was finally made, despite vigorous objections from Reubell and La Révellière-Lépeaux, who both favoured an invasion of Britain.[21] Bonaparte's role in the inception of the expedition was, therefore, fundamental. He was, more than any other individual, including Talleyrand, the motivating force. One French historian has argued that Bonaparte was the agent of European imperialism,[22] and it would be fair to say that French colonial ambitions best found their expression in the person of Bonaparte.

It has been argued that Bonaparte's fascination with the Orient may have dated from his days at Valence or Auxonne, when he read and took notes on a number of works – including the Abbé de Marigny's *Histoire des Arabes* (1750) and Baron François de Tott's *Mémoires sur les Turcs et les Tartares* (1785). We also know that, in Corsica in 1792, he met Constantin François de Chasseboeuf, who wrote under the pseudonym of Volney and who was the author of a travelogue on Egypt. If the fascination was there from an early age, the idea for an expedition to Egypt took time to develop. It was considered a possibility from the time of the Italian campaign.[23] In April 1797, Bonaparte received a visit from a French diplomat, Raymond Verninac, returning to Paris from Constantinople, where he had been minister plenipotentiary. On his way home he had been arrested by the Neapolitan authorities and spent several months in prison. When released, rather than go straight to Paris, he decided to visit Bonaparte near Leoben; whether this was his own initiative or he was summoned by Bonaparte is uncertain. Verninac was well informed on the situation in the Orient. While in Constantinople, he had sent a commissary, Charles-François Dubois-Thainville, to investigate conditions in Egypt. Dubois-Thainville addressed a report to Verninac from Smyrna in September 1796 in which he came to much the same conclusions as those expressed by Bonaparte and Talleyrand a year later – the Ottoman Empire was in a state of dissolution and chaos, and Egypt could be had for the trouble of taking it.[24]

In September 1797, during his stay in the Italian town of Passariano, Bonaparte received a visit from General Desaix, who had come to Italy expressly to visit the victorious general he had heard so much about in Germany. Desaix jotted down some brief but interesting notes on his interview with Bonaparte that simply ran, 'Ideas on Egypt, its resources. Project about it. Development. Peace with Austria, England. Departure from Venice of 10,000 men and 8,000 Polish troops for Egypt; to take it, advantage, details. With five divisions, two thousand cannon [he probably meant 200]. Collection of all the means, of men well informed. Travels, Savary, Volney, etc.'[25] Bourrienne confirms that at Passariano, with his task in Italy almost at an end, Bonaparte had indeed turned his gaze towards the Orient; he talked to his generals and close associates almost every day about Egypt.[26] This is supported by Bonaparte's letter to the Directory in which he declared that he had occupied the Ionian islands (General Gentili landed on Corfu in July 1797) and in which he stated that, 'The time is not far when we will think that in order truly to destroy England, we have to take Egypt.'[27] It was from about this time that Monge started collecting maps and memoranda on Egypt for Bonaparte's use.[28]

Four months later, Bonaparte had returned from Rastatt, and the decision had been made not to risk a descent on England. What was left for him to do? Given his impatient nature, his precarious political position in Paris, the tensions that existed between himself and the Directory, and the habit he had acquired of running his own show, he no doubt concluded that it would be preferable to continue in the role he had written for himself in Italy. If he could not seize power in France, then he could do so elsewhere at the head of his own army.[29] It was probably this consideration above all else that made the Orient so attractive.

During sessions held on 1 and 2 March 1798, the Directory decided to postpone the invasion of England and to examine the principle of an invasion of Egypt. Given that Talleyrand had prepared the way, it did not take much to convince the Directory that Egypt was a viable alternative. When, on 5 March, Bonaparte submitted a detailed report on what he considered to be the manpower neces-sary for a successful mission, the directors quickly acceded.[30] On 16 March, a decree written by Merlin de Douai ordered the minister of the interior, Letourneur, to place the necessary troops and *matérial* at Bonaparte's disposal. Finally, on 12 April, the directors ordered the formation of a new Army of the Orient, naming Bonaparte commander-in-chief; in fact, the Directory had given Bonaparte carte blanche as early as 5 March. Some contemporaries believed that the Directory wanted to remove Bonaparte and that this was the purpose of the expedition, but there is no foundation to the story.[31] It is more likely that Bonaparte wanted to be rid of the Directory.[32] However, the rumour that the Directory wanted to get rid of Bonaparte had the advantage of making him out to be the victim of the Directory's machinations. Many people, it seems, both in the government and in the public sphere, hoped that something untoward would happen to Bonaparte – at least a third of the capital, according to one secret report, despised him[33] – but sending him off on an expedition, and risking some of the most experienced troops in the process, would have been an extravagantly expensive means of getting rid of him. Indeed, the fact that they gave him the command of the Army of the Orient showed their confidence in his military abilities. A number of newspaper articles in the days and weeks after his appointment supported this view. The *Ami des Lois*, for example, featured an article by the editor and deputy, François-Martin Poultier d'Elmotte, entitled 'Bonaparte and Saint Louis', which was an emotional appeal to conquer Egypt. 'Oh, you who have just set Italy and the left bank of the Rhine free, Egypt is calling you! . . . Bonaparte, in leading our victorious phalanx to the banks of the Nile . . . you will change by that campaign alone the face of the earth . . . Oh Bonaparte! Attach your already immortal name to this great revolution of the universe.'[34]

The Directory's instructions to Bonaparte, dated 12 April 1798, reveal its foreign policy goals. A new route to India needed to be found, and since the English occupied the Cape of Good Hope, Egypt was considered essential. By taking control of the isthmus of Suez, the French would gain possession of the Red Sea and, from there, access to India.[35] French frigates were to sail from the Île de France (Mauritius) and the Île Bourbon (Réunion) to Suez and remain under Bonaparte's orders, presumably with an eventual invasion of India in mind. The English may have been worried (the stock exchange plummeted when news of a French landing in Egypt reached London), but they need not have been.

The Philosopher General

Egypt was not only a military but also an intellectual expedition. There had been scientific expeditions in the eighteenth century before – the circumnavigation of the world by Louis-Antoine de Bougainville in 1766–9 and Jean-François de La Pérouse in 1785–8; the exploration of the Indian and Pacific Oceans by Antoine Bruny d'Entrecasteaux in 1791–3; and Nicolas Baudin's expedition to map Australia in 1800–2. One cannot ignore the fact that there were also geopolitical considerations, namely, the desire to defeat Britain other than by a direct invasion of England. But Bonaparte's expedition to Egypt was the first of its kind, in that military conquest and science were closely associated from the earliest phases of the expedition onwards.[36] Antoine Thibaudeau, who voted for the death of Louis XVI, recalled that Bonaparte recruited officers and soldiers, scientists and men of letters, workers and artists from all over France:

He gathered instruments, tools, books, machines, models. It looked as though he, taking into consideration all these measures, like Columbus, was going to explore a world and bring to it civilization. Everything was assembled at Toulon; it seemed as if Paris was migrating to the Mediterranean ... Bonaparte took the attitude of a high priest who was the only one to know the key to a profound mystery. He exercised great power over everything that concerned the expedition. Republican or royalist, aristocrat or Jacobin, it did not matter as long as they could serve his needs.[37]

A brilliant engineer, General Caffarelli, assisted him in his choice of men, but it was Bonaparte who made the final decision, giving priority to the members of the Institute and to students of the recently created *grandes écoles*. Bonaparte's experience in Italy, where he had organized a commission to catalogue the artistic 'requisitions', was of some help to him in selecting scientists, artists and engineers. In a France that had been torn apart by civil war for more than six years Bonaparte had, perhaps unwittingly, hit upon a formula for national union centred on his person. The political backgrounds of his scientists (or soldiers) did not matter, it seemed, as long as they were prepared to work for the common good. We will see that Bonaparte used these same principles when he came to power.

Most scientists who were approached accepted the offer. Some, like the painter David, politely refused to become involved in an adventure about which few details were known. Others, like the young graduate of the (*Ecole Polytechnique*, Chabrol de Volvic, used his social status and relations to get on the list.[38] A rare few, like Dominique-Vivant Denon, author of a forgotten libertine fable, *Point de Lendemain* (1777), and who was later to play an important role as director of the Louvre, used their contacts with Josephine to join the expedition. In the end, 167 scientists were recruited, a small number of which were among the most prominent members of the French academic community; the majority were young with little or no experience and were probably attracted by the general air of mystery and excitement that surrounded the mission. One should not assume, however, that all those drawn to the expedition had lofty motives. Among the hundreds of other civilians accompanying the expedition was a collection of what Denon referred to as 'amphibians' – ruthless adventurers, corrupt suppliers and a ragbag of dreamers who 'had left Paris to look for new pleasures in Cairo'.[39] They were, for the most part, to be sadly disappointed.

The unprecedented number of scientists in Bonaparte's company can only be understood in the context of the Republic's preoccupation with collecting data in order to assess the economic and agricultural potential of a country.[40] It was a methodology the French had first applied in France itself and would later apply throughout the Empire. But there is another, arguably more important, element to consider – the scientific aspect of the expedition was an integral part of the image Bonaparte wanted to project. He had started, in the early stages of the campaign in Italy, using the Parisian press to present himself as a kind of Cato or Cincinnatus – a general philosopher capable of abandoning the art of warfare for the world of letters and sciences.[41] This tendency continued on his return to Paris when, for example, he published a letter in the *Moniteur* extolling the conquest of ignorance as something that was more valuable than military conquest.[42]

Bonaparte recognized that, if he were ever to achieve power and be accepted by the French elite, it was important to be seen as something more than just a conqueror. As we have seen, when Bonaparte returned to Paris after the Italian campaign he made a point of being seen in civilian dress. He also went out of his way to woo the capital's intellectual elite by associating with writers, scientists and artists. At his house in the rue de la Victoire,* he held literary or musical evenings in order to attract influential artists and writers – Antoine Arnault, Jacques-Henri, Bernardin de Saint-Pierre, Jean-Louis Ducis, Gabriel Legouvé, Louis Lemercier and Volney. The reward came when Bonaparte was elected to the National Institute in December 1797, replacing the disgraced Lazare Carnot. Bonaparte succeeded in being elected because he managed to cultivate the right contacts, even while he was on

---

* The rue Chantereine had been re-baptized in his honour at the end of December 1797 by the Department of the Seine. It still holds the name rue de la Victoire, although the house, which would have been around no. 60, is long gone.

Francesco Cossia, *Buonaparte*, September 1798. Bonaparte as enlightened warrior, surrounded by various symbols, such as a sword (the warrior) and lightning striking the symbols of the Catholic religion (a mitre and the cross), as well as books (enlightenment), a lyre, a palette (painting and the arts), and an owl (knowledge or wisdom). Bonaparte, then, as friend of the arts, whose army was in the service of Reason and anti-clericalism. (*Bibliothèque nationale, Paris*)

campaign in Italy.[43] At Mombello, Bonaparte had formed a bond with Monge and Berthollet, who would both follow him to Egypt. Bonaparte's election was not entirely without foundation: he had always been interested in the sciences, having a predilection for mathematics and the exact sciences. After his election, he wore the uniform of a member of the Institute whenever he made a public appearance. All his correspondence bore the heading, 'Bonaparte, member of the National Institute, General-in-Chief', thus expressing his obvious preference for the civilian rather than the military title. To be an amateur of the arts and sciences was not only to rally the country's elite around his person, it was also to act as a patriot avid to work towards the reconstruction of revolutionary France.

This made it possible for Bonaparte to cloak the invasion in the guise of a 'civilizing mission'.[44] The Ottoman Empire was widely seen as a perfect representation of what despotism stood for outside revolutionary France. Indeed, the Orient's 'despotism' had been a favourite theme among eighteenth-century French political thinkers.[45] In the debate that took place in revolutionary France, Egyptians were widely seen as incapable of liberating themselves from the Ottoman yoke. Since Turkish rule was seen as inherently evil, it was logical to assume that a profound modification of Egyptian institutions would enhance the lives of Egyptians. The argument was elaborated in an article in the *Décade philosophique*, a newspaper founded by Bonaparte in Egypt,[46] but it was also present, for example, in Volney's play *Les Ruines*, first performed in Paris in 1791, in which the author prophesied the fall of the Ottoman Empire and the rise of the diverse nations that made it up.[47] Much later, when the results of the scientific mission were published in the massive *Description d'Egypte*, French scientists justified the expedition by arguing that Egypt, which had 'transmitted its knowledge to so many nations' was now 'plunged into barbarism', groaning under the weight of the most arbitrary government in the world. Bonaparte was thus a conqueror who had come to abolish the tyranny of the Mamelukes, and to 'make the inhabitants' lives more pleasant and to procure for them all the advantages of a perfected civilization'.[48] The contradiction inherent in the rhetoric of 'liberating' the country from the Mamelukes while at the same time subjecting it to French 'domination' seems to have escaped contemporaries.[49]

Moments of Doubt

The departure had to be hastened. Too many people were curious about the massive fleet that was being assembled at

Toulon and its eventual destination – Naples, Portugal or the Levant? The British had withdrawn from the Mediterranean at the end of 1796, but they could order their ships back at any time. Any delays, therefore, threatened the safety of the French fleet. Artists and engineers were given orders to leave for Lyons on 18 April. Bonaparte was meant to leave Paris on 23 April – he wrote to the admiral in command of the fleet, Vice-Admiral Brueys, informing him of his intention to[50] – and even the newspapers of 25 April announced that Bonaparte had left the city during the night of 22–23, having dined with Barras and attended a performance of *Macbeth* at the Théâtre Feydeau. In fact, Bonaparte was still in Paris. News of an incident at the French embassy in Vienna made him decide to stay. On the evening of 13 April, someone in the French embassy had hoisted a large tricolour flag with the words 'Liberty, Equality, Fraternity' emblazoned across it. Within a short time, an excited and volatile crowd had gathered before the embassy; the police asked the ambassador, General Bernadotte, to take it down. He refused, declaring that it was the responsibility of the police to maintain order. At one point, Bernadotte appeared at the doorway of the embassy brandishing his sword and yelling at the crowd to disperse. It was hardly the most appropriate gesture in the circumstances, but Bernadotte was not known for his finesse. The mob laid siege to the embassy and eventually got inside and ransacked the place. In protest, Bernadotte left Vienna, which in diplomatic terms was the equivalent of a declaration of war.

When the incident became known to the Parisian public it caused as much surprise as irritation.[51] The morning after the news reached Paris (23 April), the directors held a meeting to discuss what to do. According to Barras, Bonaparte and Talleyrand invited themselves along. The meeting lasted from about ten o'clock in the morning until five o'clock in the evening, at the end of which the directors decided to send Bonaparte to Rastatt to demand public satisfaction from the Holy Roman Emperor. Bonaparte dispatched letters to halt preparations for the expedition to Egypt and to have the troops put at his disposal.[52] Furthermore, without consulting either Talleyrand or the Directory, Bonaparte sent a letter to the Austrian plenipotentiary at Rastatt, Count Johann Ludwig Cobenzl, in which he threatened Austria with a merciless struggle if it refused to come to an agreement with France.[53]

Renewed war with Austria seemed imminent; Bonaparte consequently hesitated about leaving Europe.[54] It would have been another opportunity to prove himself on the field of battle and, through victory, to move one step closer to political power. If, on the other hand, war did not break out and he left for Rastatt where, he assumed, he could impose a definitive settlement on Austria and the Empire, he would then return to Paris as the great peacemaker, even the arbiter of France's destiny.[55] This is certainly the impression that Bonaparte gave Miot de Mélito in a conversation with him on the subject,[56] and this is also what the Directory may have realized, especially when they got wind of the letter Bonaparte had sent to Cobenzl. They decided, on 27 April, not to send Bonaparte to Rastatt after all; the Directory, in the meantime, had understood that the Austrians were not using the incident to precipitate a break with France. Barras went to Bonaparte's house in the rue de la Victoire to announce the news.[57] 'The interview', Miot wrote, 'lasted hardly a quarter of an hour. Barras came out first and left the salon, having hardly exchanged two words with Mme Bonaparte. The general appeared after him, said nothing, and went back into his study, abruptly closing the door after him.'[58] Judging by Bonaparte's reaction, he did not particularly want to hear what Barras had told him. Was he having second thoughts about the whole expedition? It seems probable. According to one witness, Bonaparte was more frequently and more insistently solicited during this period to take part in a coup than ever before.[59] The idea obviously tempted, not to say troubled, him; but he was still aware that the time was not yet right.

Whatever doubts may have crossed Bonaparte's mind, the conversation with Barras undoubtedly helped him see more clearly. The next day he wrote to Admiral Brueys and Generals Kléber and Caffarelli informing them that he would send a courier on 30 April with the order to embark and to leave with the fleet for Genoa, where he would join them. A couple of days later, when he encountered the Directory at a session of the Institute, their attitude was openly hostile. Bonaparte had outstayed his welcome in Paris, even if people like Antoine Arnault were still trying to persuade him to remain.[60] He hastened the preparations for departure. At three o'clock in the morning of 4 May, Bonaparte, accompanied by Josephine, left for the south of France.

15

Confronting Egypt

Toulon

Bonaparte arrived in Toulon, a confusion of soldiers, sailors, generals, admirals and officers, who had invaded the town and its cafés, on 9 May. His reputation had grown significantly since Italy, and his arrival electrified the troops, who were now reassured they would be led to victory, wherever that might be. Bonaparte, one officer suggested, was like one of the conquistadors who inspired soldiers to risk their lives in the search for gold in the New World.[1] The analogy can be linked to Talleyrand's rhetoric about 'the mountains and the mines of iron and gold in which that country abounds'. When Bonaparte decided to inspect the arsenal at Toulon, he was quickly surrounded by a crowd of admirers pressing in on him from all sides, crying out 'Vive Bonaparte!' His escort had trouble containing the crowd and he had to find refuge in one of the armouries.[2]

As was his custom by now, Bonaparte issued a proclamation to the army that contained some resounding phrases, such as, 'You have made war in the mountains, on the plains and have besieged cities; you have yet to make war on the seas',[3] and which compared the Army of Egypt with the Roman legions that fought at Carthage. Bonaparte astutely made use of classical history and compared the Republic of France (Rome) to Britain (Carthage). In fact, it is possible that the passage quoted above was inspired by a play that appeared in Paris in January 1798, entitled *Scipion l'Africain*, which drew a parallel between Scipio and Bonaparte that was recognized and appreciated by the public. One line in particular met with bravos from the audience: 'And it is at twenty-eight/That he has almost eclipsed our greatest conquerors!'[4] The proclamation also referred to the French bringing liberty to mankind (a claim reminiscent of the *philosophe* Volney).[5] As in Italy, and as we shall see with the Empire, the reality of political and economic domination was accompanied by the rhetoric of a civilizing mission. The Enlightenment, and indeed science, given the number of scholars that were persuaded to accompany the expedition, was thus harnessed in the service of conquest and exploitation.[6] Bonaparte's claim was that he came not so much to conquer Egypt as to bring it civilization.

These references would probably have gone straight over the heads of the vast majority of troops waiting to embark in and around Toulon. Bonaparte had another message for them. We know from the memoirs that he addressed the troops (one has to assume that he did so on a number of occasions), and that he spoke briefly of the sufferings they had endured in the Alps, the lack of supplies, and their poverty. But he also reminded them of the spoils they had procured through the conquest of Italy and held out the same prospects of loot and pillage, as well as six acres (*arpents*) of land in France on their return from the expedition.[7] It was an astute move and had the desired effect. A distinct change in attitude now came over troops who had been dubious about the whole affair. 'He promises the equivalent of six acres of land to each solider on his return to his homeland as a result of the expedition. He talks about interest, honour . . . People are dying to leave, imploring the winds,' wrote Jullien, who had re-entered Bonaparte's service at the insistence of Caffarelli, 'worry and suspicion have disappeared. Everyone is running to the ships.'[8] It was an empty promise; the reward was never mentioned again.

Bonaparte still had to decide whether he was going to take Josephine with him or not. According to one witness, General Alexandre Dumas, the father of the author of the same name, he arrived at headquarters early one morning only to find the two of them in bed and Josephine in tears because, Bonaparte told him, he could not make up his mind whether to take her.[9] In the end, Bonaparte thought it best for Josephine to wait in France until news came through that the expedition had successfully eluded the British fleet. If she did not receive orders to leave Toulon within two weeks, she was to go and wait at a resort in Plombières in the Vosges mountains – a spa town famous for its waters, said to increase fertility.[10] From her letters, it is likely she had every intention of joining him. She admitted to Barras that she was so distressed at being separated from him that she could not overcome her unhappiness, and that she liked him a good deal 'in spite of his little shortcomings'.[11] Her feelings had obviously deepened since Italy, although why this was so remains unclear. Certainly, it would have been politically imprudent to act as anything other than the faithful wife. But it is also likely that she had simply fallen into step with Bonaparte, had become used to being his companion, and even that his love for her had stirred her own feelings. We know that Bonaparte wrote to her from Egypt – 'He says that he cannot live without me'[12] – and that he even told her to embark at Naples, where he sent a frigate, the *Pomone*, to bring her to him.

One of the reasons Josephine was unable to join him was because of a fall she suffered while at Plombières in June.[13] She had been on the first floor of a building with some friends when one of them called to her from a wooden balcony to come and see a little dog that was walking past in the street. When they all rushed to the balcony, it collapsed beneath them, throwing everyone some five metres or so to the ground below. Although no one was seriously injured, a colonel who happened to be standing below the balcony had his leg broken and Josephine suffered from some 'pelvic injuries'. In fact, she seems to have suffered some kind of internal injuries; she complained of horrible pains to the lower stomach.[14] The local doctor, a man by the name of Johannes Florentius Martinet, consulted with his colleagues and devised a regimen of baths, douches, bleedings and leechings.[15] She convalesced for two months, during which time she said she did 'nothing but cry'. After all this, she still had every intention of following Bonaparte to Egypt.[16] It was only when she returned to Paris in September 1798,[17] and news of Nelson's victory before the Nile greeted her, that she prudently decided to remain where she was.

The Crossing

The speed with which Bonaparte completed preparations for Egypt impaired the efficiency of the expedition. While most of the equipment had been gathered, there were important omissions, possibly in order to keep the army's destination secret: no flasks or canteens to carry water were issued, for example.[18] Despite this, at five o'clock on the evening of 18 May 1798, Bonaparte ordered the beat-to-quarters and had six cannon shots fired. It was the signal to all those who had shore leave to board their ships.

The next morning the fleet set sail in calm weather and good winds. It must have been an impressive sight. When the diverse fleets eventually rendezvoused, it was made up of thirteen ships of the line (with a firing capacity of 1,026 cannon), as well as six frigates, and thirty-six other warships of various sorts, and more than 280 ships used to transport the troops. When the combined fleet was in sailing order, it covered an area of more than ten square kilometres. The Directory had managed to assemble the largest concentration of ships since the Battle of Lepanto between a Christian alliance and Ottoman forces in 1571.

Bonaparte completely eluded Horatio Nelson, who was about 120 kilometres south of Toulon. The British had re-entered the Mediterranean early in May, greatly increasing the risk of the French operation. But, by then, the whole enterprise had gained a momentum of its own and could not be reversed.[19] Besides, Bonaparte did not have any accurate knowledge of the British fleet's whereabouts: if he had he might have aborted the enterprise. The curious gathered along the coastline to watch the ships pass out, while music on board floated across the harbour to the spectators.[20] There was excitement and trepidation among those on board, many of whom would never have experienced the sea before and were travelling abroad for the first time. 'In spite of the military equipment, we set sail as though it were a pleasure cruise,' wrote Antoine Thibaudeau. Dominique Denon spoke of nothing but *bayadères* (dancers), 'of the pure skies and the perfumes that one breathed in the Promised Land.'[21]

Speculation was rife about the destination of the expedition not only among the officers and the scientists, but also in the Paris press in the days and weeks leading up to the departure.[22] England, Ireland, Sicily, Malta, Sardinia and Naples were all proposed, but Egypt seems to have been high on the list. Denon implies in the opening lines of his *Voyage dans la Basse et la Haute-Egypte* that he knew the destination, but his account was written after the event.[23] We nevertheless know, for example, that officers passing through Avignon in April 1798 bought so many copies of Volney's *Voyage en Egypte* that there was only one copy in the town when an army supplier by the name of Grandjean passed through on his way to Toulon.[24] If the destination was a secret, it may have been an open one among certain scientists and officers.

The crossing of the Mediterranean would mean weeks in extremely uncomfortable conditions. Not only were the ships crammed full of supplies, munitions and cannon, but also thousands of troops, scientists, civilians and administrators vied with thousands of sailors for living space, with little or no opportunity to wash or clean clothes. On board, too, were a few hundred women who had been brought along as washerwomen and canteen attendants for the campaign. The army had forbidden men to bring their wives or mistresses, though this did not prevent some generals from doing so, or others from sneaking their wives on board dressed in uniform. These women usually disclosed themselves once the army was ashore, although their presence would lead to a clash of cultures in Egypt. Below decks, little conflicts about precedence and position broke out between officers of the navy and the army, and the scientists. To pass the time, men either gambled or sat around telling stories of their exploits late into the night, the boredom being broken now and then when someone fell overboard.[25] In the evenings, plays were put on by some sailors and soldiers. It was almost invariably the same fantasy: the deliverance of a slave girl from a harem and her old Turkish master by a French soldier, who would then, of course, marry her.[26]

There is ample evidence that many were seasick, at least for the first few days of the crossing.[27] The smell of filthy men and women would no doubt have mingled with the stench of the bilge and the thousands of live cattle, sheep and horses. Bonaparte was probably seasick too,[28] but at least his quarters on the *Orient* gave him a bedroom, a dining room and a salon to himself. There he whiled away his time in discussion with the scientists and officers on subjects ranging from mathematics and chemistry to religion. A strict etiquette was observed throughout the crossing, based on the usages adopted at court, in much the same manner as at Mombello. This would not have failed to offend the republicans in the expedition. A tailor by the name of François Bernoyer, for example, who came on board the *Orient* one evening for dinner, observed: 'I do not know if, in adopting this system, Bonaparte believes he is giving himself more splendour or more consideration, but the fact is he is mistaken, for nothing honours a man more than love of the *patrie* and love of liberty.'[29]

The fleet's first task was to rendezvous with the convoys from other Mediterranean ports. The fleet from Toulon met the fleet sailing from Genoa two days after leaving port on 21 May, off the coast of Monaco. They then sailed along the island of Corsica to meet up with the convoy out of Ajaccio. From 29 May on, they followed the Sardinian coast in search of the convoy out of Civita Vecchia under the command of General Desaix. When they failed to meet them and ran across, instead, a corsair who told them of the presence of Nelson's fleet in the Mediterranean, the French commanders began to worry. However, neutral ships that were intercepted along the way reassured them about the strength of the British fleet – fourteen ships of the line – so Bonaparte decided not to wait for Desaix and to head straight for Malta. The decision was right in the circumstances: Desaix, as it turned out, was already heading for Malta, the expedition's first objective, and a union of all the convoys took place off that island on 9 June.

Malta

The conquest of Malta was another project that Bonaparte had been contemplating since Italy. In fact, he had conceived of the idea after the conquest of the Ionian islands in July 1797. In the summer of that year, Bonaparte wrote several letters to the Directory and to Talleyrand about the necessity of taking Malta, an essential base for operations in the eastern Mediterranean.[30] Both Talleyrand and the Directory were in agreement on this point in order to anticipate the action of Austria, Britain or Russia in the Mediterranean. In other words, Malta was a geopolitical consideration perfectly in keeping with French interests in the Mediterranean; it was a question of capturing it before someone else did.

The Order of St John of Malta, nominally in control of the island, had declined dramatically since its peak in the sixteenth century. Its military power had been reduced to about 1,500 troops, most of whom were of French descent. But the fortifications surrounding the island were still impressive enough to constitute a real obstacle. Bonaparte, therefore, tried to avoid a siege by asking for authorization to enter the port, La Valetta, in order to take on supplies and fresh water. The knights, justifiably suspicious, gave the authorization to admit only four vessels at a time. It was an unrealistic demand for a fleet of that size and it was all the pretext Bonaparte needed to invade the island. His proclamation declared that he was 'ready to take by force what should have been accorded him'.[31]

The invasion took place on four different beachheads on 10 June 1798. By 11 June, the grand master of the Order, the ineffectual German-born Baron Ferdinand von Hompesch, asked for a ceasefire so that negotiations could be started. The rapid surrender of the fort of La Valetta must rest, not with von Hompesch, but with certain pro-French knights who acted against him. It was, however, the uprising of the civilian population that largely led to that result. The hatred felt by the populace for the knights was greater than their repugnance for the French. The vice, luxury and greed of the Order were known to every islander, as was the reputation of France as a liberator from oppression (even if the reputation was undeserved). There is no doubt that, at this time, the islanders preferred the rule of the French, even if they were later to regret it.

A convention was signed the next day: the Order had to agree to cede to France its sovereign rights over the island and its dependencies. The grand master was to receive a comfortable pension and the knights much more modest pensions to be collected in their country of origin. A small number of knights decided to join the French expedition, and were to play an important role in the administration of Egypt. Every other knight aged under sixty was expelled from the island.

Artist unknown, *Vue de la Prise de l'isle de Malthe* (View of the taking of the island of Malta), circa 1798. (*Bibliothèque nationale, Paris*)

Bonaparte swiftly set about imposing the French administrative system on the islanders.[32] He called together a commission of nine local notables, and one French commissary, to reorganize the civil, judicial and administrative machinery: in effect, he gave the people of Malta the principle of equality before the law. But the commission's main purpose seems to have been to supervise the collection of taxes and to take the necessary measures concerning supplies. The tricolour cockade was introduced, but only those who had shown themselves loyal to the French Republic were allowed to wear it. Following the ancient Roman practice, the male children of the notables were to be sent off to France to receive an education. Municipalities and a National Guard, with French officers, were created. The island was divided into *cantons* and *arrondissements*. Religious liberty was assured; both Greek

Orthodox and Jews received permission to practise their religions freely. Everything was centred on the French military government under the command of General Vaubois, who was to stay on the island with 3,000 men. Malta represented the first application of Napoleonic ideas in terms of government.[33] Just as importantly, Bonaparte used the conquest of the island for what might be called his Islamic policy. He advised the French consuls at Alger, Tunis and Tripoli to announce the conquest to their respective Turkish provincial governors, called 'beys', and inform them that he had liberated 2,000 Muslim slaves found on the galleys of the Order of Malta; he asked that they reciprocate the gesture by liberating any Christians who might be found on their galleys.[34]

If the French attempted to bring an enlightened administrative machinery to Malta, their attempts were compromised by the army, which looted churches, monasteries, convents and the Public Treasury of precious objects in order to obtain some much-needed ready cash when it got to Egypt.[35] The sanctioned plunder of the churches and monasteries severely strained relations between the Maltese and the French. Even worse, however, was the suppression of all monasteries. Despite the terms of the capitulation, Bonaparte ordered all secular monasteries to be closed, except for one for each order, and their buildings and lands to be sold. The experience of France and Italy should have taught the revolutionaries to act with caution in dealing with Roman Catholic communities. The two ideologies were totally incompatible: the revolutionaries felt they were bound to suppress, or at least minimize the impact of what they considered to be superstition. Still, Bonaparte's conduct in Malta was hardly less provocative than the behaviour of any other republican general. On this, as on other points, dissension on the method of government arose between Regnaud de Saint-Jean d'Angély, who had been appointed by Bonaparte as commissary in the administration of the civil government, and Vaubois, commander-in-chief of the military forces. In Vaubois' opinion, the dissatisfaction of the Maltese with the French government of the islands was to be attributed to Regnaud's excessive zeal in carrying out Bonaparte's orders. Thus, Regnaud's attempt to introduce civil rather than religious marriages shocked people, but it was the sale of the Carmelite possessions that alienated the Catholic Maltese and that brought about a revolt against French rule on 2 September 1798, well after Bonaparte had gone and less than three months after the French had occupied the island. The French were driven into La Valetta by a peasant army and were still being besieged there, with the help of the British navy, in 1800.

Bonaparte did not wait to see the implementation of his reforms, or the popular reaction they would provoke. On 18 June, eight days after he took possession of Malta, the fleet raised anchor and set sail (minus the garrison that he left in place and a few scientists who decided that they did not want to continue).[36] It was only after having left Malta that news about the destination of the expedition began to leak out. Bonaparte was obliged to inform the captain of each vessel where they were headed, in the event that they were separated from the fleet during the crossing. If a few had already guessed, it seems to have come as a great surprise to others. Kléber, although he may have exaggerated, mentioned that there were not forty people in all who were in the know about the expedition's objective. A lot of speculation had certainly taken place and any number of destinations had been suggested – Crimea, even Sicily and Portugal, though the last two were behind them. When Egypt was eventually revealed, the men questioned each other, 'Did you know? And you?'[37] According to one of the first contemporary descriptions left by a member of the expedition, the rest of the voyage passed with relative ease, despite some concern about the vulnerability of the fleet to an attack by the British.[38]

Nelson's failure to intercept the French fleet might have been considered a calamity by the British but, as events would prove, it was not. Owing to Nelson's shortage of frigates, he could neither find the French fleet nor keep the commander-in-chief of the Mediterranean fleet, the Earl of St Vincent, informed of his own movements. As a result, Nelson's reinforcements were unable to find him before 1 June, but with only one brig to reconnoitre the whole eastern Mediterranean – his frigates had been dispersed in a storm – it was going to take time to seek a decisive victory.

Having criss-crossed the western Mediterranean without finding the French, Nelson was convinced that the constant westerly winds must mean that, if Bonaparte had sailed east beyond Sicily, he would be going to Alexandria. He did not reach this conclusion until after 15 June.[39] His guesswork was confirmed off Sicily when Nelson learned of Bonaparte's attack on Malta. Nelson hurried after him in pursuit, fearful that Bonaparte intended to invade India. The history of both the French interests in Egypt, and their co-operation with Mysore against the British, pointed to a combined attack as the probable goal of a French army at sea in the eastern Mediterranean and to Egypt as its probable destination. 'If they have concerted a plan with Tippoo Sahib to have vessels at Suez,' wrote Nelson to St Vincent, 'three weeks at this season is a common passage to the Malabar Coast . . . was I to wait patiently till I had certain accounts from Egypt . . . before I could hear of them they would have been in India.'[40]

In his haste, Nelson overtook Bonaparte – the two fleets crossed, unaware of the other's presence, during the night of 22–23 June – and reached Alexandria on 28 June, three days before the French. Since the French were not there when he arrived, Nelson then wrongly assumed that Egypt was not their destination. He swept north again as far as the coast of Anatolia to find out whether they were on their way to Syria or the Straits of Bosphorus. Two days after Nelson left Egypt, the French fleet arrived. Nelson has been criticized for not waiting for Bonaparte off Egypt,[41] but there was no reason he should have. If the French fleet was not off Egypt, Syria and Anatolia were the other likely landing sites. The British brig *Mutine* left Alexandria only two hours before the arrival of Bonaparte's leading frigate, *La Junon*.[42]

'Like Fish on the Plains of Saint-Denis'

At daybreak on 1 July 1798, the 'inhabitants of Alexandria, seeing that the surface of the water was covered with vessels, were seized by fear and terror'.[43]

Earlier that morning, as land and then Alexandria came into sight, more than forty thousand men would have strained from the crowded decks to get a view of the monotonous shoreline where, every now and then, a minaret or a tower could be distinguished. Around midday, a frigate broke away from the mass of sails to explore the port – which was closed to merchant shipping because the windows of a number of harems opened onto it[44] – but reported back that it was too shallow to navigate. In the meantime, the wind had come up and the sea had become so rough that even experienced sailors were sick. The ships, thrown about on their anchors by the swell, were at risk of ramming each other. It was considered best to move the fleet further east, to the bay of Aboukir, and to postpone the landing until the next day.

Then the French consul at Alexandria, Magallon, came on board the flagship *Orient* with the worrying news that Nelson had been off the coast only forty-eight hours before. Anxious that the British fleet might reappear, Bonaparte ordered the army to disembark immediately.

> Nothing is like the difficulty of disembarkation in those moments. One has to see the longboats next to the ships tormented by the swell rise above the porthole or disappear into the abyss as soldiers laden with their arms and hanging onto ropes had to wait several minutes for the moment to throw themselves into the arms of the sailors. Even though the order to disembark was signalled to the entire fleet at nine in the morning, it was almost five in the evening before thirty or so boats had gathered and moored around a Maltese galley where the general-in-chief was, and which he had chosen in preference to get closer to land.[45]

The troops waiting in the boats thus spent the day under a blazing sun, drenched by the waves, horribly tossed about, and violently colliding with each other.[46]

General Menou, a man with a violent temper who was said to have clubbed to death an army supplier in Turin,[47] disembarked first with his division at about nine o'clock in the evening near a mosque known as the Marabout Tower, a four-hour-march from

Alexandria. Bonaparte disembarked about one o'clock in the morning. Surrounded by his general staff, who formed a kind of watch around him, he lay on the beach and slept for two hours while the rest of the troops were brought ashore.[48] At three o'clock in the morning, Bonaparte ordered the troops to assemble; only about 5,000 men had so far managed to land, but Bonaparte was in a hurry to get them safely within the walls of Alexandria before Nelson reappeared. It had been impossible to get any horses or artillery on shore, while at daybreak the sea swelled up even more violently so that it was impossible to count on reinforcements.[49] In silence, the small army trudged the eleven or twelve kilometres through the sand to Alexandria. Bonaparte marched ahead of them on foot with his head wrapped in a handkerchief. According to one witness, he constantly slapped General Berthier on the back, saying, 'Well, Berthier, here we are at last.'[50]

For more than an hour, the army marched ankle-deep in sand along the coast. 'I greatly suffered from the crossing,' Bonaparte wrote to his brother, Joseph, after it was all over. 'This climate overwhelms me, it will change us all.'[51] It should have been a forewarning of what to expect. Around dawn, a few Bedouins, as well as a detachment of cavalry from Alexandria, harassed the column for the length of the crossing; many men considered themselves lucky to have reached Alexandria alive.[52] The Bedouins managed to kill a number of stragglers and to capture and rob some prisoners, among whom were several women. 'Others that were captured and taken were splendidly buggered by the children of Ismail and then sent back; two dragoons of the 20th regiment were submitted to this rude ordeal.'[53] A few days later, a group of about thirty-seven French prisoners was exchanged for the bargain price of a sheep or a goat for each soldier.[54] It was rumoured that the Bedouins preferred to rape the male prisoners and simply beat the female prisoners.[55] Fear of sodomy, which can be found throughout eighteenth-century French literature,[56] served to reinforce European notions of Oriental depravity and no doubt increased the disdain of the troops for the inhabitants of the country.[57]

By sunrise, Bonaparte came to the Pillar of Pompey. Built of red granite and standing twenty-five metres high, it was erected at the end of the third century to commemorate the Emperor Diocletian's siege of the city. Bonaparte climbed up its base in order to get a better view of the area. From there he could see the crenellated walls of Alexandria and a few minarets. By the end of the eighteenth century, the town was no more than a skeleton of its former ancient self. In the third century, during the Roman Empire, the population had reached over 500,000. When Bonaparte landed in Egypt, it was a small town of about 6,000 people, having been ravaged some thirty-odd years previously by catastrophic epidemics. The desert sands had enveloped what little was left of the palaces and monuments that testified to its glorious past, while the ramparts, which were crumbling in parts, could not hold out long against a persistent enemy. When the column arrived within reach of the city, the three divisions took up positions around the wall, in front of the modern town. The order to attack was given. The commander of Alexandria was waiting for them but, within a short time, the French, impetuous

Artist unknown, *Vue de la prise d'Alexandrie par l'armée française aux ordres de Bonaparte le 4 prairial an 6* (View of the taking of Alexandria by the French army under the orders of Bonaparte, 23 May 1798), circa 1798. Note the Pillar of Pompey in the foreground, under which were buried about fifty French troops. (*Bibliothèque nationale, Paris*)

and thirsty, had managed to breach and scale the wall. If Bonaparte's claim to the Directory that 'every house was a citadel' is an exaggeration,[58] we know that resistance was strong:[59] 'The Turks know how to die,' wrote one French officer, 'but they do not surrender. They do not ask for mercy from the victors, and they do not accord any to the vanquished.'[60]

Resistance of any sort inevitably led to reprisals. No eighteenth-century military commander – and Bonaparte was no exception – was capable of totally controlling the men under his command. The fact that the French were lacking even the most basic supplies – they ate dried figs while waiting for provisions to arrive[61] – did not help matters. Some battalions were sent ashore without rations; all lacked water. The march on Alexandria was, therefore, painful and led one second lieutenant, Nicholas-Philibert Desvernois, to remark that they were 'like fish on the plains of Saint-Denis'.[62] Besides, there was an understanding that pillage and rape were the rewards for the hardships soldiers were forced to endure during a siege. The greater the hardships, the greater the loss of life incurred by the besiegers, the worse the massacre of the civilian population. Eyewitnesses like Bourrienne and Thurman later made a point of saying there were no reprisals against the civilian population of Alexandria, a cause for suspicion in itself. General Boyer, on the other hand, a member of the general staff, reported that once the town was taken, soldiers gleefully massacred over a period of about four hours those who had taken refuge in the mosques.[63] This is confirmed by Pierre Millet, a private in Kléber's division, who relates how, having come under sniper attack from a nearby mosque, a general ordered them to force the gate and to spare no one inside: men, women and children, old and young, were bayoneted and only about a third of those inside survived.[64]

As for those French troops killed during the storming of the city, a ditch was dug at the bottom of the Pillar of Pompey, where about fifty were buried. Their names were carved at the top of the column, while the regimental bands played funeral marches: 'Far from discouraging us,' wrote an officer by the name of Pierre Pelleport, 'the ceremony increased our ardour. We cried out "Long live the Republic! Long live Bonaparte!"'[65]

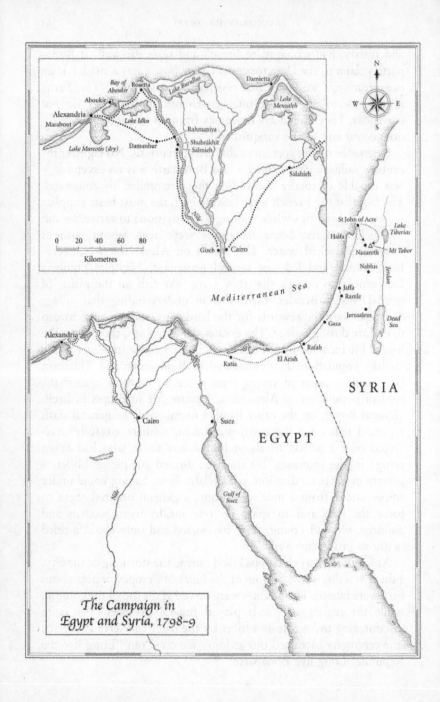

The Campaign in
Egypt and Syria, 1798–9

Sand, Melancholy and Suicide

While the fight for Alexandria was still taking place, Bonaparte distributed a proclamation to the Egyptian people. With the help of Venture de Paradis, an old Orientalist who knew Egyptian affairs well, having lived there for many years, it was translated into Arabic. The French version, deliberately altered, contained the 'peace at home, war against the châteaux' rhetoric so prevalent during the first years of the Revolutionary wars. At the same time, there was an attempt to Islamicize, or at least Egyptianize, the proclamation by using phrases from previous proclamations by Ali Bey, ruler of Egypt between 1763 and 1773, and Ghazi Hasan Pasha, an Ottoman commander who invaded Egypt in the 1780s. In both versions, however, Bonaparte portrayed himself as someone who had come to suppress the iniquities of the ruling class in Egypt, the Mamelukes, to restore the authority of the Ottoman regime, and to give Egyptians self-rule.* Moreover, the proclamation was imbued with the principles of the Revolution; Bonaparte had come to give them what they, naturally, ardently desired – liberty: 'all men are equal before God; wisdom, talent and virtue are the only things that distinguish them.'[66]

Even if Bonaparte's proclamation may have persuaded the people of Egypt that he was acting in accordance with Constantinople's wishes by liberating them from the Mamelukes, nobody was fooled by the Islamic additions to the French propaganda.[67] The bizarre mixture of French revolutionary vocabulary and Islamic political terms made little or no sense to the Egyptian elite. The divide between the two cultures, one evangelically revolutionary, the other Islamic, was too great for there ever to be an understanding. Most of the population waited to see what would happen. For the moment, they were more afraid of the Mamelukes than the French.

---

* Two Mameluke beys, Murad Bey and Ibrahim Bey, ruled Egypt at this time. Ibrahim assumed the title Sheik el-Beled, or leader of the nation. Murad was known as Emir el-Hadj and was overseer of pilgrimages to Mecca and commander of the army. Though he was more than fifty, Murad was a man of extraordinary energy, unlike Ibrahim who was considered avaricious and cowardly. There were frequent quarrels between the two and it is doubtful whether they would have coexisted much longer without the arrival of the French.

Since Alexandria could not furnish the French troops with adequate food and supplies (they had had to dig into the navy's rations), Bonaparte pressed on towards Cairo. Before doing so, Bonaparte left Kléber, convalescing from a head wound received during the storming of Alexandria, with a garrison of 6,000 men – more than the total population of the city. The best route for Bonaparte to take would have been along the Damietta branch of the Nile, but that would have meant re-embarking men and equipment and a sea crossing of thirty-six hours, a high-risk manoeuvre given the possible appearance of Nelson. Instead, Bonaparte chose to follow the canal, dry most of the year, which linked Alexandria to the Nile. Meanwhile, General Charles-François Dugua, who had met Bonaparte at the siege of Toulon and had campaigned with him in Italy, was sent along the coast with a division of troops to Rosetta, and from there was to proceed along a branch of the Nile until he met up with Bonaparte – a march that, although harsh, was to prove easy compared to what Bonaparte's troops were about to experience. Bonaparte had naïvely hoped to find enough drinking water for his men along the way. Instead, his men had to cross an arid region with few water holes. Only a few troops had had the time to find flasks or jugs to carry water before leaving Alexandria and they had still not been issued with canteens. To make matters worse, the troops were hardly equipped for desert conditions; their uniforms were made for the European climate, so they suffered terribly.

The seventy-two hour march that followed was a living hell. By the time the main body got to Damanhur, about forty-eight kilometres from Alexandria, it was to find that the advance party had drunk most of the water in the wells. Many of the troops, thinking they would be able to live off the land in much the same way as they had done in Italy, had thrown away their reserves of dry biscuits at the beginning of the march.[68] Their desolation in Alexandria quickly became a complete aversion for the country. The troops started to grumble, hardly surprising but not a good sign so early in the expedition. According to one witness, in the space of the five or six days it would take to cross the desert, five to six hundred men died, either of thirst or killed by Bedouins harassing the columns.[69]

'Never', lamented General Charles-Antoine Morand to a friend back home, 'could I describe to you the horrible country that we have come to conquer. Never will I be able to express what we have suffered from the first moment of our descent to this day.'[70] In these extreme conditions, suicide was not uncommon. Captain Joseph-Marie Moiret points to a number of instances in his memoirs, as does Adjutant-General Boyer in a letter to his father: 'Each day we march offers a similar spectacle.'[71] 'A gloomy silence dominated the ranks,' wrote one officer, 'mixed with complaints and sighs. Now and then, succumbing to the heat and to necessity, a soldier would stop as though asphyxiated, and fall dead in the middle of the road. Others, seized with a fever of the brain [un transport au cerveau], convulsively rolled around in the sand, or in a delirium, blew their brains out.'[72]

The general malaise seeped down to the middle and lower ranks: Napoleon later recalled that the 'army was hit by a wave of melancholy that nothing could overcome; its spleen was attacked'.[73] After a forced march through the desert without water and without bread, exposed to blinding sand storms, attacks by Bedouins and the loss of comrades to thirst,[74] morale was desperate. On reaching the Nile after three days of marching across the burning desert, several soldiers, rather than finding physical and psychological relief in the water and food they found there, simply decided to put an end to their suffering by drowning themselves.[75]

Bonaparte's depleted forces rendezvoused with General Dugua, whose column came up along the Nile without any difficulty. But the French were isolated, virtually cut off from their camp bases at Alexandria, Aboukir and Rosetta. A defeat at this stage would have put the whole expedition in jeopardy. Bonaparte decided to concentrate his forces at Rahmaniya, seventy-odd kilometres from Alexandria on the Nile, which permitted his men to rest. On 12 July, scouts told him the news he wanted to hear: the Mameluke army was not far off. Bonaparte brought up his troops and, on 13 July, the fighting started near a village called Shubrâkhît.

The Mameluke cavalry under Murad Bey was far superior to anything the French could put into the field: while charging, riders could fire off six shots from a carbine, a blunderbuss, and two pairs of pistols. During the attack, the Mameluke's *valet d'armes* could reload the weapons, thus enabling him to make multiple assaults on the enemy. The problem, therefore, was not entirely in the equipment or in the courage and skill of the riders. It was that the Mamelukes were totally unprepared for the sort of fighting they were about to encounter. Volney's travelogue gave a description of the Mameluke strategy:

> The strongest camp or the most audacious pursues the other; if they are equal in courage, they wait for each other or arrange a meeting, and there, without any regard for the advantage of position, the two troops approach each other in platoons, the hardiest march at the head; they accost each other, they defy each other, they attack. Each [Mameluke] chooses his man: they shoot if they can, and then pass on to the sabre, and it is there that they deploy the art of the horseman and the versatility of their horses. If one falls, the other is lost ... Often the battle is decided by the death of two or three people.[76]

The Mamelukes were exceptionally mobile and were specialists in guerrilla warfare. If they had decided to withdraw into Upper Egypt, they would have been practically invulnerable but, either because they were not aware of European warfare methods or out of a sense of duty to defend their communities, they decided to fight the French on open ground.

Bonaparte had one major advantage the Mamelukes were unaware of, and that was the 'square'. The square, formed by the infantry when threatened by cavalry, had been perfected by the Austrians and the Russians during the wars against the Ottoman Empire in the eighteenth century in order to deal with the Ottoman cavalry, similar in many respects to the Mamelukes. The French army introduced the manoeuvre in 1776. Although they had not used it in combat before, it was to become a fairly standard manoeuvre during the Napoleonic wars. Artillery pieces were put at the angles of the square. The cavalry looked for a weak point; if the infantry were well trained and disciplined, the square could usually hold off any attack. If they panicked and broke ranks, which sometimes happened, then it became a question of who could pick off the most fleeing soldiers.

The battle that took place at Shubrâkhît on 13 July was an anti-climax. The Mamelukes charged and circled the squares in the hope of finding weak points, lost a few men to gunfire, and then rode off. A more substantial battle was fought during this time on the Nile between five small vessels from the French flotilla and seven larger Mameluke craft. The fighting was bitter and prolonged and lasted the entire morning. It was only when Bonaparte ordered some field artillery to support the flotilla that the French gained the upper hand as a lucky shot blew up the Mameluke flagship.[77]

The rest of the march towards Cairo passed with soldiers venting their frustrations by massacring entire villages and pillaging anything they could find along the way. According to one witness, Sergeant François, an entire village of about nine hundred men, but not the women and children, was massacred to teach the indigenous population a lesson.[78] The irony of French peasants killing Egyptian peasants in the name of liberty was no doubt lost on them.[79] The orders of the day reminded the troops that they were here to fight the Mamelukes and not the Egyptians, and held officers responsible for the conduct of their troops. Pillaging took place at first because of a lack of food, but continued indefinitely. Nor did the troops hesitate to do so within sight of their generals and even Bonaparte, a sure sign that what little discipline was left had broken down altogether. As a result, the Egyptian population began to flee before the arrival of the French.

A major engagement did not take place until 21 July 1798, when the army approached Cairo. The battle that followed was later baptized the 'Battle of the Pyramids', which were just visible about twenty-four kilometres away. Bonaparte ordered the army to form into squares and waited for the Mamelukes to attack. He rallied his troops with the words, 'Soldiers, do your duty, think that from the top of these monuments a hundred generations are looking down at you.'[80] The largely uneducated rank and file probably had no idea what the monuments were; the historical significance of the battle would have been reserved for educated officers. The Mamelukes charged the French squares but their attacks were broken once again by the concerted firepower of gun and cannon. During this time the divisions commanded by Generals Bon and Menou took the trenches dug by Murad Bey on the other side of the river and attacked the Mamelukes from behind. They fled into the Nile, where many drowned. The whole action lasted about two hours, after which Murad withdrew with his Mamelukes to Upper Egypt.

Bonaparte wrote to the Directory to proclaim his victory and boasted that he had destroyed the main Mameluke army. In reality, the Mameluke losses were minimal; the 2,000-odd men who were killed that day were, for the most part, the infantry and valets who accompanied the Mamelukes.[81] In other words, the bulk of the Mameluke forces remained intact. Moreover, the Mameluke retreat was perfectly in accord with their tactics. If the number of deaths within their ranks reached certain proportions, they simply beat a retreat to fight another day, even if that meant losing a major city like Cairo. It was a clash of military cultures that, for the Mamelukes at least, would prove disastrous.

Detail, Louis François Lejeune, *La Bataille des Pyramides* (The Battle of the Pyramids), 1806. Detail of the disorderly Mamelukes charging the well-maintained, orderly squares. (*Courtesy of Photo RMN –* © *Gérard Blot*)

The French, in the meantime, looted the Mameluke dead and their baggage trains. Almost immediately, a kind of bazaar was established by the troops who bartered, bought and sold whatever they could lay their hands on: horses, weapons, clothes, camels – like a fish market on Holy Friday, remarked one observer. Some offered cashmere shawls for fifteen francs, others offered a camel or an Arabian horse for thirty francs, and others auctioned off carpets, caftans, saddles or stirrups to the highest bidder. In the midst of this extraordinary tumult, other men ate and drank, others yet again danced around in turbans still dripping blood, or draped themselves proudly in long cloaks lined with sable or vests embroidered with gold.[82] The next day, soldiers made hooks out of their bayonets and, tying them to ropes, tried to fish bodies out of the Nile in order to loot them. 'The catch was good,' wrote Marmont, 'there were soldiers who deposited as much as thirty thousand francs in the regimental coffers.'[83]

The bulk of the army marched on that afternoon to Gizeh, arriving at about nine o'clock in the evening. Throughout the night, within sight of some of the oldest monuments on earth, the troops, their spirits renewed, danced and sang in celebration of their victory. The people of Cairo, in the meantime, 'spent the night in the greatest fright'.[84]

A large number of people left . . . those who found no mount on which to ride or on which to load their household possessions, left on foot, carrying their baggage on their heads. Those who had the means and could find a donkey or some other beast, bought it at several times its value. Some went on foot themselves while their wives or daughters rode! Most of the women left unveiled, carrying their children in the darkness of night, and continued in this fashion all through Sunday and the next morning. They took with them all the money, baggage, and household furnishings they could carry, but once they had left the gates of Cairo behind, and were in the open countryside the Bedouin and fellahin confronted them, plundering most of them, robbing them of their possessions, their camels, and their money, in such great quantities as to be innumerable and incalculable: so much that without a doubt the property which left Cairo on that night was greater than that which remained in it . . .

Sometimes they [the Bedouins] killed anyone they could, or whoever did not easily surrender his clothing and possessions. They
stripped the women of their clothing and violated them, including
ladies and noblewomen. Some of the people returned home very
soon after, and those were the ones that delayed and heard what
befell the first group. Others took a chance and went on, relying on
their great numbers, supporters and guards, either surviving or
perishing.[85]

16

Conciliation and Terror: Governing Egypt

Tearing Away the Veil

After arriving in Gizeh, Bonaparte spent the night in the house of Murad Bey. When he awoke the next morning, he saw before him the enormous ramparts of the walls of Cairo. Cairo was by far the largest urban agglomeration in Egypt, with approximately 260,000 inhabitants – as large as Vienna or Moscow at the time – about 60,000 of whom might be described as 'urban proletariat', considered dangerous by the orthodox religious authorities because they were quick to revolt.[1] The notables of the city, therefore, took matters into their own hands and sent a delegation to Bonaparte at his headquarters at Gizeh, informing him that they were disposed to negotiate a capitulation.

Bonaparte made his triumphal entry into Cairo that same day, 24 July, and took as his residence the newly built palace of Muhammad Bey al-Alfi overlooking the square of Azbakiyya with its magnificent gardens and its pools connecting with the Nile. It was from these luxurious quarters on that same day that Bonaparte wrote to the Directory telling of his victorious march on Cairo.[2] His letter emphasized that, despite the terrible poverty of the population, the country held great potential, and underlined the necessity of rational development.

As with Alexandria, many French soldiers felt a deep sense of disappointment on entering Cairo. They had been expecting a European-style city; instead they found 'narrow, unpaved and dirty streets, dark houses falling to pieces, public buildings that look[ed] like dungeons, shops that look[ed] like stables'. Their appreciation of the inhabitants was not much better. They found:

people dressed in rags, pressed together in the streets or squatting, smoking their pipes ... hideous, disgusting, hiding their fleshless faces under stinking rags and displaying their pendulous breasts through their gowns; yellow, skinny children covered with suppurations, devoured by flies; an unbearable stench, due to the dirt in the houses, the dust in the air, and the smell of food being fried in bad oil in the unventilated bazaars.[3]

An artillery officer by the name of Jean-Pierre Doguereau agreed: 'The male and female inhabitants among the people are extremely ugly; the children are hideous; one can hardly make out their eyes which are always covered with flies.'[4]

It was the rhetoric of the colonizer, the descriptions a common leitmotif in European attitudes towards non-Europeans: the place was dirty, that is, if it could not be adequately ruled and managed by its own people, if its inhabitants were lazy, then it deserved to be conquered. However, not all the generals and scientists lodged in the bey's palaces were disappointed in Cairo. 'Magnificent lodgings,' Etienne Geoffroy Saint-Hilaire wrote home, 'immense gardens marvellously designed; abundant water flowing all around with a soft murmur; a multitude of different kinds of trees under which one can find a voluptuous shade.'[5] As for the rank and file, they quickly became accustomed to their surroundings so that General Morand could report that, 'the situation of the army is excellent. The anguish is disappearing, it [the army] is becoming used to its new circumstances. Awakened by the rich loot of the battle of the Pyramids, they have recovered their high spirits.'[6]

If the French considered the world in which they found themselves to be strange, the Egyptian perception of the French also suffered from cultural incomprehension. Al-Jabartī was shocked by the invaders' attitude towards sex. 'They have intercourse with any woman who pleases them and vice versa. Sometimes one of their women goes into a barber's shop, and invites him to shave her pubic hair. If he wishes he can take his fee in kind. It is their custom to shave both their moustaches and beard. Some of them leave the hair of their cheeks only.'[7] In an interesting example of what might be termed Occidentalism, the Egyptians generally considered the French to be filthy, lecherous drunks.[8]

On his second day in the Egyptian capital, Bonaparte was given a rude awakening. It seems that during a conversation with Jullien, Junot and Berthier, he was told of Josephine's affair with Hippolyte Charles (Junot, it should be remembered, had slept with Josephine's maid and had no doubt learned a few things). Bonaparte had long held suspicions of Josephine's infidelity, and this is not the first time that others had tried to tell him about her. To have his fears substantiated by people in his entourage added insult to injury. Hurt and despondent, he scribbled off a few lines to his brother, Joseph, telling him of his increasing need for solitude:

> I have a lot of domestic problems, for the veil is completely torn away. You are the only person left to me in this world; your friendship is very dear to me; if I were to lose this, or if you were to betray me, nothing could keep me from becoming a misanthrope. It is a sad state of affairs when all one's affections are concentrated upon a single person. You will know what I mean. See to it that I shall have a country place upon my arrival, either near Paris or in Burgundy. I count on passing the winter there and seeing no one. I am sick of human nature. I need solitude and isolation. Greatness wearies me, my feelings are dried up. Glory is empty at twenty-nine; I have exhausted everything: there is nothing left except to become truly egoist. I count on keeping my house; I will never give it to anyone. I have nothing more to live by.[9]

Bonaparte now knew for certain what he had previously been unable to admit to himself. Eugène, Josephine's son, who had accompanied Bonaparte as aide-de-camp, wrote to his mother: 'Bonaparte has been extremely sad for five days, as a result of an interview with Jullien, Junot and Berthier. This conversation has affected him more than I would have believed.'[10] It is fair to say that, from this point on, a change came over Bonaparte. He may not have lacked barefaced ambition before this revelation, but much of that ambition had been directed towards impressing, if not pleasing his wife. To an extent, therefore, he had been motivated by romantic ideals rather than ruthless political goals. That was about to change.

Adapting

Bonaparte did not, indeed could not, let others about him see that he was discouraged. Order had to be established in Cairo, where looting by its citizens continued even after the French arrived. (Indeed, the French were taking an active part in this, albeit unwittingly, by opening buildings to inspect and thus allowing Egyptians to enter once they had left.) Bonaparte was also keen to implement his 'Islamic policy' – the fruit of his discussions and reflections with Orientalists such as Venture de Paradis and Volney. Volney, who had published an account of his travels to Egypt in 1788, wrote that, if the French wanted to establish themselves there, they would have to conduct three wars: the first against the British; the second against the Porte; the third, the most difficult of all, would be against Islam. This war, Volney cautioned, would occasion so many losses that it was perhaps an insurmountable obstacle.[11]

Bonaparte had thought about Volney's analysis. With the help of his Orientalist advisors, he attempted to reconcile French revolutionary discourse with the political rhetoric of Islamic Egypt. But first he had to defuse the deep hostility of the Egyptian people towards the French invaders. One way was to present himself not as an innovator or a reformer, but as someone desiring to preserve and continue traditions. The key to power in Egypt, he believed, resided in the religious *ulama*, low-ranking government officials, and the *sheikhs* of Al-Azhar, the insitution Bonaparte called the 'Sorbonne of the Orient'. The French needed to get the *ulama* on their side so that they would not call for a jihad. The *ulama* and the *sheikhs* had enormous influence over public opinion and needed, therefore, to be closely associated with French power.

As soon as he arrived in Egypt, Bonaparte set about implementing this policy, with Alexandria as the testing ground. In particular, he attempted to establish political contact with the resident notables. On 4 July, Bonaparte, after reaching an accord with the principal *ulama*, constituted a veritable charter of relations between the French and the Egyptians. According to the terms of the agreement, the *ulama* kept the administration of justice and promised not to foment trouble against the French. The French, on the other hand, agreed not to mistreat the population, to respect property rights, and not to force the inhabitants to change religion or to introduce new religious practices.[12]

Unfortunately, the French ignored the subtleties of Egyptian politics, the differences existing between the religious element represented by the *ulama*, and the civil administration represented by the regime of Murad Bey. In obtaining the accord of the *ulama*, the French believed that they had achieved the agreement of the civil regime when they had done nothing of the sort. Nevertheless, Bonaparte's policies appeared to be on the right track. He was, in fact, applying the principles of association and indirect administration the French had applied in other conquered territories. The French reserved for themselves direct control over government, associating and subordinating local councillors and agents and exercising the executive through them. In this manner, the French intervened as little as possible in the affairs of the native populations, and tried not to disturb local customs. For example, when the order was given to disarm the local population of Alexandria, exception was made for the *imams, muftis* and *sheikhs*. The privilege was a judicious homage to their influence, which Bonaparte hoped to use for his own ends. A similar logic lay behind Bonaparte's order on 3 July that everybody in Egypt was to wear a tricolour cockade.[13] The *imams, muftis* and *sheikhs*, however, were ordered to wear the tricolour sash, as a sign of rank and the confidence the French had invested in them. In fact, it became an overt sign of collaboration.

A good deal of publicity was given to this measure in Alexandria, although the local elites had no intention, initially at least, of so closely and publicly associating themselves with the new occupiers. To do so would be to turn their backs on the Porte. Bonaparte apparently shocked the chairman of the new *diwan* (an assembly of notables) of Cairo, the first genuinely Egyptian council since the arrival of the Ottoman Turks in 1517.[14] Sheikh Abdullah el-Charkawi, the most popular of the Egyptian leaders, and the one closest to the people, was presented with a tricolour sash by Bonaparte, who expected him to wear it. El-Charkawi at first declined, worried about what impression it would make on the people, but the following day another member of the *diwan*, Sheikh al-Sadat, allowed Bonaparte to pin a cockade on him. When the rest of the *sheikhs* arrived, al-Sadat apparently told them:

'Don't oppose him in pinning on the rose [that is, the tricolour cockade], and when you leave remove it'. So they said nothing. [Bonaparte] got up and pinned a rose on everyone while they expressed contentment and he was happy with that. They were unable to refuse, especially when they saw the rose in the garment of the Sheikh. When the party was finished and they left his presence they removed it from their garments. Later, they used to put it on when they entered his reception room and when they left they removed it.[15]

At one point, Bonaparte thought about appearing in 'Turkish' garb himself, in an effort to encourage them to wear the French sash, but he was dissuaded from doing so.[16]

As early as 27 July, the administrative organizational system introduced into Alexandria and then Cairo was extended to all the occupied territories: a *diwan* was introduced into each province; an *agha* of Janissaries (a kind of chief of police) was put in charge of the police; and an intendant, supervised by a French official, was charged with raising taxes and with the revenues of the Mamelukes. In order to obtain hard cash quickly, a heavy tax was imposed on the merchants of the principal towns under French control. Hospitals were established and all available horses were requisitioned for the cavalry.

The French had arrived with the aim of transforming Egypt into a 'civilized', that is, a westernized society, by imposing the administrative methods of the *Grande Nation* and employing Enlightenment methods to study and measure the country.[17] This latter point is no better illustrated than by the publication of the expedition's scientific findings, the *Description de l'Egypte*, one of the most influential works of colonial scholarship ever produced.

Artist unknown, *Buonaparte donne l'écharpe tricolore à un bey d'Egypte*
(Bonaparte gives a tricolour scarf to a bey of Egypt), between 1798 and 1800.
Note the bey's submissive (head bowed, hands crossed over his chest), almost
grateful attitude, while Bonaparte's stance is that of a benevolent ruler. (*Paris,
Musée des Traditions Populaires*)

Twenty-two volumes appeared between 1809 and 1828, enabling
the French to 'engulf' Egypt with the instruments of western
knowledge and power.[18] But, in the process, Egypt succeeded,
up to a point, in 'Orientalising' the French.[19] Many of the French
adopted local habits, or at least adapted to local conditions by
assuming the exterior signs of daily life, such as smoking the
hookah, drinking Turkish coffee, and adopting traditional dress
and bathing customs. The ambiguity present in the imagery (above
and below) illustrates the difficulties the French experienced in
imposing their own culture, and the extent to which they absorbed,
however superficially, Egyptian culture in the process.

Artist unknown, *Bonaparte dans un costume Oriental, en compte avec le Pacha du Caire* (Bonaparte in Oriental costume, an exchange with the Pasha of Cairo), circa 1798. In actual fact, Bonaparte was dissuaded from wearing local costume by Tallien. (*Courtesy of RMN – © Daniel Arnaudet*)

The French also used local feast days to indoctrinate a largely illiterate population with French civic values, and to ingratiate themselves with the local population.[20] For example, on 18 August, a local ceremony was held to celebrate the flooding of the Nile. The ceremony was centred on the Nilometre, a column that measured the level of the river, and hence the fertility of the Nile valley for the coming year (it can still be seen today, although no longer in use). Bonaparte, who by this time had earned the nickname 'Sultan Kebir' or 'great sultan', appeared with his general staff, members of the *diwan*, the Mollah, who was keeper of the Nilometre, the *agha* of the Janissaries, and other local notables. If Egyptian feast days were kept, revolutionary festivals were also celebrated; the

Festival of the Republic, held on the 21 September (1 Vendémiaire), was organized in such a way as to reflect the marriage of East and West, of the Republic and its new subjects.[21] These crude attempts at creating a kind of Franco-Egyptian rapport were accompanied by a show of force in the guise of a military parade that was meant to intimidate the local population.

Inevitably, however, irreconcilable cultural differences created frictions between the colonizer and the colonized. The fact that the French wore green, for example, was seen as an affront; it was the colour traditionally reserved for the descendants of Mohammed.[22] Even measures the French considered 'enlightened', such as the cleaning of streets, the order to illuminate houses at night, and the closing of the insalubrious cemetery in the middle of Cairo, were viewed as provocations. So, too, was the conversion of the mosque of El Cheraïbi into a tavern, and the protected status given to the Copts – Christian Egyptians considered to be inferior by Muslim Egyptians. Psychologically and culturally, the people of Egypt were not prepared to accept the innovations introduced by the French. So, when the French transgressed Islamic religious rules, violent reaction was inevitable.

Disaffection

Bonaparte's attempts to conciliate the Egyptians could not work. Not only were the Egyptians unwilling, but most of the French occupiers were not convinced this was the right approach. 'There is not a soldier, not an officer, not a general,' wrote the diplomat Jean-Baptiste Poussielgue to the Directory, 'who does not most earnestly long to return to France; persuaded, as they all are, that they are sacrificing here, without any advantage to their country, their health and their lives.'[23] Not only was the landscape considered hostile, but there was a stark contrast between naïve French perceptions of the 'noble savage' – in vogue through the writings of Rousseau – and the behaviour of the Bedouins towards the invader.* Bonaparte described the Egyptians as 'horrible savages'

---

* The French did not generally make a distinction between the Mamelukes, the Bedouins and the local Egyptian populations.

and then lamented in a letter to his brother Joseph, 'O Jean-Jacques [Rousseau]! Why was it not your fate to see these men, whom you call "men of nature"? He would tremble with shame and surprise at having once admired them.'[24] Similar sentiments were echoed in a letter written by a French officer who commented that it was 'impossible for a Frenchman to wander alone within musket range of an inhabited area without risking being assassinated or becoming victim of the dreadful passion [sodomy] very much in vogue in this country above all with the Mamelukes and Bedouin Arabs. I know of several people who, in the town of Alexandria itself, were abducted at nightfall, and who suffered this frightening idiocy.'[25] For the majority of troops, the disappointment of the harsh living in Egypt, the material difficulties, and the increasing sense of isolation due to the English blockade meant that they felt threatened and insecure. In the face of soaring numbers of officers requesting permission to return home, attempts were made to thwart the disaffection: army doctors who granted medical certificates without any real cause were publicly reprimanded by an order of the day dated 19 Frimaire VII (9 December 1798), and those troops who made unjustified demands were denounced in front of their comrades. It was clear, however, that Bonaparte's troops were homesick.

This disaffection touched those close to Bonaparte. The chief army commissary, Simon de Sucy, a friend of Bonaparte's before the Revolution, managed to obtain the authorization that was coveted by so many. Unaware that war had broken out between the Kingdom of the Two Sicilies and France, his ship called in at Sicily. Those passengers who went ashore, including Sucy, were massacred on 20 January 1799.[26] Others, too, would have been safer staying in Egypt. A mineralogist, Déodat Dolomieu, appalled by Bonaparte's authoritarianism, wrote a report presented to the Institute of Egypt entitled *Tempus edax rerum* (Time destroys all things). It was dedicated to the ruins of Alexandria, but was rightly seen as an attack on Bonaparte. Dolomieu was quickly granted permission to return to France. He left much later than Sucy, but the British navy intercepted his boat off the coast of Italy, where he was arrested; his health deteriorated so badly in prison conditions that he died shortly after being released.

The majority, however, rank and file and officers alike, were condemned to remain. Disapproval increased to the point where their behaviour was close to revolt. 'The disgust in the army is general,' wrote one officer. 'The administration is disorganized. There exists among us an egoism and an ill-humour that make it impossible for us to live together.'[27] The morale of some officers became so bad that, in December 1798, there were rumours of a mutiny. Such insubordination was quickly dealt with as Bonaparte threatened summary executions if they continued to spread discontent.[28]

Distractions

It became a question of how Bonaparte could best blunt the sense of isolation. One way was to create institutional structures in Egypt reminiscent of those in France. Thus, the Institute of Egypt, a copy of the Institute of France, was opened in August 1798. Newspapers were set up: the *Courrier de l'Egypte* for the army, and the *Décade Egyptienne* for the scientific community. Concerts of military music were given daily at midday near the French military hospital in the hope of cheering the sick and wounded. Plays produced by amateur groups were encouraged in the hope not only of diverting the soldiers, but also of providing a means of 'civilizing' the Egyptians. And a European-style café with a garden (dubbed 'the Tivoli'), with a salon reserved for games and another for receptions, was opened. There were also bars and restaurants where beer was served.

Boredom, however, remained a problem. There was little to distract the men apart from playing cards, running about on donkeys and visiting a few tourist sites.[29] The heat deterred most from going about, and when they left the city it had to be with an escort. The pyramids were a favourite excursion because of their proximity – about two hours from Cairo. Many climbed to the top; some, undaunted by the grandeur of the monuments, carved their names in the rocks (graffiti can still be seen today in the interior of the burial chamber of the Pyramid of Cheops); others rolled off blocks of stone to see how far they would fall, or started taking pot shots; some even tried to ride their horses to the top.[30] (It is a myth, however, that the French used the sphinx for target practice with their cannon and knocked off its nose. The nose had been missing since at least the thirteenth century.)

This behaviour was characteristic – these were, after all, troops on leave – although others were more respectful. Charles Norry and some of his colleagues climbed to the top of the Pyramid of Cheops one morning in about thirty-five minutes.[32] 'Sitting on top of the summit, overwhelmed with fatigue, we examined, on the one side the immensity of the desert where the horizon has no limit, and on the other the Nile, passing through a vast and pleasant countryside. Beyond it is the harsh [mountain] chain of Mokattam which makes its way towards the Red Sea.'[33]

Artist unknown, *Bonaparte en haut d'une pyramide d'Egypte* (Bonaparte on top of an Egyptian Pyramid), circa 1799. In fact, he never climbed the pyramids, nor did he even visit the interior chambers. He did not want to crawl around on all fours. This did not prevent an article appearing in the *Moniteur*, and even a pamphlet appearing in Paris, describing the event and even a conversation supposedly held between Bonaparte and a number of *muftis* in the interior of the pyramid.[31] (*Bibliothèque nationale, Paris*)

The biggest preoccupation among the occupying forces was, however, the lack of available women. As we saw earlier, only a few wives and a few hundred women had been brought along as washerwomen and canteen attendants. These French women went about without veils, rode horses and mules, and wore cashmere shawls over their shoulders, shocking the local inhabitants, even those who were Christian. Bonaparte had asked the Directory to send the wives of the administrators to Egypt, along with a hundred or so single women, but the order was not acted on.[34] Officers with means were often able to find a concubine. A few married local women after a ceremony the *sheikhs* declared to be legal as long as the bridegroom pronounced the profession of faith, 'There is no God but God and Mohammed is his prophet'. This was not as exceptional as has been assumed and it seems that a great number entered into marriage this way. The most famous case is that of General Menou, who married the twenty-two-year-old daughter of a *sharif* (a descendant of Mohammed), by the name of Zobaïdah al-Bawab, who gave Menou a son. General Marmont later tried to explain Menou's behaviour by arguing that he was interested in her not so much for sex – 'she was no longer young, she was no longer pretty' – as for her social position, and it is true that some married in the hope of acquiring influence and wealth, but Menou seems to have been smitten.[35] A rare few, like General Berthier, were obsessed with the women they had left behind, in his case Mme Visconti, whom he had met in Milan. When a merchant by the name of Hamelin arrived in Egypt in January 1799, and went to pay his respects to Berthier in Cairo, he found him 'lying on a divan, in front of a portrait hanging from a wall' of Visconti.[36] Indeed, Berthier was torn between his desire to be reunited with his Italian mistress and his loyalty to Bonaparte: when given the opportunity to return home he hesitated for a long time before deciding to stay.

Some of the high-ranking officers – Admiral Perrée, for example – 'requisitioned' Armenian and Georgian women left by the beys 'for the welfare of the nation'.[37] 'Some were regarded as being beautiful, but of a corpulence that contrasted too much with the elegant and svelte waists of our French women.'[38] They were often quickly discarded when the officers 'realized they had come upon old stock! . . . Since then, they have passed through so many hands that

André Dutertre, *Almés ou danseuses publiques* (Almehs or public dancers).
Note the latticework, a symbol of virginity in western art. Obviously, because
the latticework is not intact, these women are not virgins. (*Reproduced from
the* Description de l'Egypte, *Bibliothèque nationale, Paris*)

today they are reduced to being the companions of our troops.'[39]
Others, including Bonaparte's son-in-law, Eugène, managed to buy
young female slaves – white women were generally preferred,
though Eugène was taken with two black girls.[40] However, the
vast majority of the more than 30,000 men had to make do with
local prostitutes, in ample supply and cheap. François Bernoyer
describes how he called a 'Sultan Ganache' (a pimp, in other words)
to bring him several women to choose from. He had trouble

making up his mind until 'one of them suddenly burst out laughing, as if to mock my timidity and the little daring I had shown in making my choice, and revealed herself completely naked. Her clever and decisive appearance, her big ravishing eyes, and especially her fourteen years of age transfixed me and I proclaimed her my sultaness.'[41]

Bonaparte also decided to take a woman. It seems that he made this decision after the realization that he had been cuckolded by Josephine. Sex as revenge, sex as a means of allaying the hurt, sex out of a need for the comfort of another? No doubt there were elements of all of these in Bonaparte's behaviour. He first took the sixteen-year-old daughter of Sheikh El-Bekri, a girl by the name of Zenab, but he apparently found her rounded figure and her perfume too much. (After the French left Egypt, Zenab was killed for having slept with an infidel and for being a collaborator.) Bonaparte's eyes then fell on Pauline Fourès, a dressmaker from Carcassonne, who had married a young lieutenant in the chasseurs. (When her husband was ordered to Egypt, she had donned an officer's uniform and stowed away on board his ship.) Blessed with a beautiful figure and complexion,[42] she soon became a noted figure in the Egyptian Tivoli. In December 1798, in a scene reminiscent of David and Bethsheba, Bonaparte made his first move by sending her husband back to Paris with an 'urgent commission'. The soldier had no choice but to leave, while his wife remained in Cairo.[43] She was soon installed in a villa adjoining the palace where Bonaparte had his headquarters.[44] It was not long before Bonaparte was parading her in public, apparently caring little about what others thought. On one occasion, according to an officer who was present at a dinner with several other French women, Bonaparte, deliberately or not, spilt water over Madame Fourès' dress and took her into his tent on the pretext of setting things right. They spent a long time alone together in the tent while the guests waited patiently at table.[45] Unfortunately for Bonaparte, Lieutenant Fourès' ship was captured only one day out of port. The British, through their spies, were well aware of Bonaparte's affection for Pauline and, rather than keep Fourès a prisoner, it seems they decided to send him back to Cairo where, after confronting Bonaparte in the role of the outraged husband, he demanded and obtained a divorce from his wife.

Bonaparte seems to have taken the affair with Pauline, who was nicknamed 'Cleopatra' by the troops and 'Bellilotte' by the officers (after her maiden name, Bellisle), seriously enough. He wrote to her from Syria (though the letters have never been found), and later instructed her to return to Paris. This she did, but arrived to find that Josephine and Bonaparte were reconciled. She, nevertheless, received a liberal allowance from Napoleon during the Empire and lived to the age of ninety.

Artist unknown, *Portrait de Madame Marguerite-Pauline Bellisle-Fourès (1778–1869)*. (*Courtesy of Photo RMN – © Droits réservés*)

The Plague

The situation of the French in Egypt changed dramatically from mid-December 1798 onwards with the appearance of the plague in Alexandria. It had been in Alexandria since the beginning of the year, probably brought there from Constantinople, but it took a few months to spread to the French population.[46] Marmont immediately gave orders to quarantine the city but, by 11 January 1799, in spite of the precautions taken, the French had already lost ninety-five men.[47]

The plague was present during the whole of the French expedition. The means of combating it, however, were ineffective since the aetiology of the disease was not yet known. Various remedies were suggested. Bonaparte ordered Marmont to strip a brigade of light infantry 'naked and to have them bathe in the sea, so that they scrub themselves from head to foot, that they wash their clothes well, and that they be careful to keep themselves clean'.[48] It was sound advice but unlikely to help. Although many contemporaries were under the impression that the plague was not contagious, quarantine was nevertheless systematically practised.[49] Special judiciary commissions were established to judge infractions against the sanitary rules. The death penalty could be demanded against those who did not respect the quarantine. In this manner, the French authorities succeeded in slowing down the spread of the disease but not in stopping it. In Cairo, three military hospitals were established: one in the citadel, and two others at the entry of the European quarters near the Nile. Bonaparte was particularly concerned that the sick were adequately cared for; any functionaries that were caught embezzling or neglecting their duties were severely punished. Thus, in January 1799, the surgeon of the hospital at Alexandria, a man by the name of Boyer, was found guilty of refusing to treat wounded soldiers who had come into contact with plague victims. Bonaparte declared: 'He will be dressed in women's clothes and led on a donkey through the streets of Alexandria with a sign on his back reading "Unworthy of being a French citizen; he is afraid of dying".'[50] Boyer was then shipped off back to France, but this was hardly likely to deter others from refusing to tend the sick and wounded.

Repression

While attempts were made to co-operate with local authorities and to respect some local customs, Bonaparte quickly let it be known that all opposition or criminal acts would be severely dealt with. He had initially been conciliatory with the people of Cairo, in order to counter the reputation of terror that had preceded their arrival, but continued unrest and revolts occurring throughout the first months of the French occupation led him to decide that it was important to take a harsh stance. In Cairo, measures were put in place in order to

quickly suppress any revolts. An early-warning system was introduced that allowed the French to take position anywhere in the city
as rapidly as possible. The guns of the citadel were positioned
pointing out over the city, and an order was given to destroy all the
gates in the narrow streets of Cairo that closed off the districts from
one another, thus permitting free communication between the
streets.[51] These measures, however, offended the Egyptians' because they interfered with their traditional living space. Finally, the
population had to surrender all firearms. Those who refused were
either subjected to corporal punishment – 100 lashes – or, if they
were caught with gunpowder or cannon, decapitation. Bonaparte
gave orders to General Menou that he had to be ruthless and have
five or six people decapitated every day in the streets of Cairo. For
the Egyptians, he wrote, to obey is to fear.[52]

The French thus maintained their rule through a mixture of
terror and the collaboration of local elites – a policy that had been
practised in Europe by the *ancien régime*, and which Napoleon
would use with varying degrees of success in the Empire. In this,
Bonaparte was able to call on the experience of his two leading
generals – Menou and Kléber – both of whom had served in the
Army of the Vendée, the army that Bonaparte had refused to join in
1795.

The annihilation of the village of Salmieh, located on the Nile, a
little distance from Lake Manzaleh, set the tone for French repression in the face of native resistance. On 7 August 1798, the division
of General Reynier entered the village and discovered several
Frenchmen who had had their heads cut off, or half cut off, and
their arms, legs and hands severed from their bodies. One chasseur
had been 'split from the left shoulder to the middle of his back'.
Earlier, General Leclerc had been sent with a group of about eighty
officers and men from the engineers to build ovens. According to
one account, after being captured they were sodomized and then
had various parts of their bodies cut off, including noses, ears and
genitals. Another officer recorded that: 'Those who escaped death
after these operations were forced to heat the ovens they had built
and were put inside by these cannibals. On our arrival, I saw those
unfortunate victims roasted in the ovens.'[53] The killings were

horrific, but the reprisals were ferocious. 'The village was sacked by the soldiers, and, when night fell, the neighbouring hamlets learned by the light of the conflagration that French vengeance had been terrible and complete.'[54]

Repression was not the only tactic used by the French. Local rule was often as much a matter of individual style as official policy. For example, in Rosetta, General Menou faced similar problems to those confronted by Kléber at Alexandria: the threat from the British navy; insecurity created by the Bedouins; attacks against couriers; and a raft of financial difficulties. For a while, Menou reacted differently.[55] An enthusiastic supporter of the conquest of Egypt, he believed it could be transformed into a French colony to replace those lost to the British in the West Indies. Egypt, he thought, had the potential to produce coffee, sugar, cotton, indigo and cochineal. France could thereby come to dominate commerce in Africa and India. Consequently, Menou initially encouraged the promotion of an exemplary attitude towards local populations. His troops received instructions to spare the inhabitants as much as possible, and to pay for whatever they bought; those soldiers caught committing acts of violence against civilians were dealt with mercilessly. Captain Laugier reported the case of a carter who was caught stealing money from a Turk, and was then executed on the spot.[56] A young interpreter, Amédée Jaubert, reported a similar incident: a soldier caught stealing a knife from an Arab was shot for his crime.[57]

When 'anodyne' reprisals against the local populations, such as taking hostages and imposing expiatory taxes in the face of continuing hostilities, did not work, Menou resorted to brutal repression. At the end of July 1798, after the killing of a French soldier, Menou decided to set an example by ordering two hundred villagers to be led to the place of the attack: the villagers were massacred and their village burnt. The example did not and could not serve its purpose. On 15 September, when Menou toured the interior of his province with Marmont and Denon to reassert the presence of the French and ensure communication lines with Cairo, they were caught in an ambush in one of the villages. It too was burnt to the ground in reprisal.[58]

Similar incidents occurred throughout Lower Egypt as the occupation was extended. Whenever it did, Bonaparte's deputies

spontaneously ordered reprisals and punishments for acts committed against the French. On receiving their reports, Bonaparte
either approved their behaviour or went a step further, for example,
ordering Dugua on one occasion to: 'Burn the village. Make a
terrible example of it and do not allow those Arabs [he was referring
to Bedouins] to come and inhabit the village again unless they
deliver ten hostages of leading chiefs to you, which you will then
send to me so that I can keep them in the citadel in Cairo.'[59]

By October, repression would begin to have an impact; the
'pacification' of the Delta had more or less been accomplished
and there were signs that the Egyptian population would eventually
be subdued. However, there would be important hurdles to overcome: the Ottomans would shortly enter the war, and the threat of
the British navy under Nelson was still very real. The devastating
defeat of the French fleet by Nelson off Aboukir would give
Bonaparte considerable cause to rethink seriously his plans for
the Orient.

17

Prisoner of his Conquest

The Battle of the Nile

When Nelson arrived at Alexandria on 28 June 1798, he found an empty harbour and no news of the French. He therefore headed for Syracuse in Sicily to take on supplies. It was not until a month later, while he was sailing towards Crete, that Nelson learned the French were in Egypt, and he set sail for Alexandria a second time. 'The utmost joy', wrote Captain Berry aboard Nelson's ship, the *Vanguard*, 'seemed to animate every breast on board the Squadron, at sight of the Enemy; and the pleasure which the Admiral himself felt, was perhaps more heightened than that of any other man.'[1]

The French first saw the approach of Nelson's fleet on the afternoon of 1 August. Their commander, Brueys, decided not to raise anchor and fight them in the open sea: men were detached from the ships for shore duties. Brueys, moreover, believed his fleet was in a good position to meet the English ships. It was lined up for about a kilometre with a shoal on the coastal side for protection, so that each English vessel would have to sail down the line and take thirteen French broadsides. Besides, it was already five o'clock in the evening and nightfall was not far off.

This failed to take account of Nelson's brilliantly improvised plan.[2] Nelson was in his fortieth year. He had already lost his right eye, and his right arm, in previous battles but was possessed of an immense ambition exacerbated by an inflated sense of self, a thorough and almost pathological hatred of everything French, and the somewhat disconcerting notion that he had a special relationship with God. But he was also determined, aggressive and talented. Rather than run the gauntlet of the French ships, Nelson focused on the front of the line first and had his own vessels anchor both on the outside and the inside of the French line so that very shortly eight English vessels were firing at five French vessels. The battle was engaged at half past six, just as the sun was going down, and was fought well into the night. Early on, Nelson was struck in the forehead by shrapnel and was taken below, where he spent the remainder of the action. The unfortunate Brueys, who would bear the blame for the defeat, had his leg blown off at the beginning of the fighting and died on the bridge at about half past seven. Rear Admiral Villeneuve, who commanded the end of the French line and who was later to be defeated at Trafalgar, chose not to weigh anchor and neither sailed against the British nor fled.

Artist unknown, *Vorstellung der merkwurtigen Seeschlacht, so zwischen der Französischen Kriegs Flotte, in der Bay von Rosetta u. den Englischen Admiral Nelsons d.2 u.3 Aug 1798 vorgefallen* (Illustration of the curious sea battle in the Bay of Rosetta between the French navy and the English Admiral Nelson that occurred on 2 and 3 August 1798), 1798. (*Bibliothèque nationale, Paris*)

At about nine o'clock in the evening, a fire broke out on board the *Orient*. 'The light thrown by the fire of the *Orient* upon the surrounding objects, enabled us to perceive with more certainty the situation of the two Fleets, the colours of both being clearly distinguishable.'[3] At about ten o'clock, Vice-Admiral Ganteaume, seeing that it was impossible to drown the gunpowder, ordered the evacuation of the ship. Fifteen minutes later, the biggest ship of the line Europe had ever seen blew up, throwing debris, both human and material, a great distance in the air. The shock of the explosion, heard for miles around, was followed by a hushed quiet that lasted anywhere between three and fifteen minutes – 'when the wreck of the masts, yards, &c. which had been carried to a vast height, fell down into the water, and on board the surrounding Ships'[4] – before combat started up again.

Six hundred thousand livres in gold and diamonds – treasure which had been pillaged from Malta and which was meant to bribe the beys, pay the army, and to coin a new currency in Egypt – also went down with the *Orient*. The battle petered out during the night, but at daybreak the next day, Nelson ordered his ships to attack the remaining five French ships of the line and two frigates. Although the French had put up a stiff resistance the previous evening, they had no fight left in them. Three headed for shore, where they ran aground, while the two remaining ships of the line, including that commanded by Villeneuve, and the two frigates, raised anchor and headed back to Europe, abandoning to their fate those who were unable to manoeuvre.

The French had suffered horrendous losses. One thousand seven hundred French sailors were either killed or drowned, and another 1,500 were wounded. British losses numbered 218 killed and 677 wounded. Two French ships of the line and two frigates had been sunk or burnt, while nine ships had fallen into the hands of the British. Over 3,200 men had been captured but, after a few days, all except 200 officers and specialists were handed back by the British because of a lack of supplies, on condition that they would not take any further part in the campaign. Though none of the British vessels were sunk or burnt, many suffered serious damage – the main reason they did not pursue Villeneuve.

The reasons for the French fleet's defeat lay in its position, the only possible site once Bonaparte decided that it should stay close to the Egyptian coast in the event that he wanted to return to France. The situation was complicated by the fact that Bonaparte had ordered Brueys to unload virtually all the supplies for the use of the army, making it impossible for the fleet to go to sea at short notice. Brueys had made repeated and desperate pleas for supplies to maintain the fleet at Aboukir, and to use at least one-third of his crews to look for provisions on shore. The insufficient number and the mediocrity of the French sailors (about half of the crews were under eighteen) were also significant factors, and so it is unlikely that, even if the French fleet had anchored closer to the shore, they could have survived the accuracy of the British bombardments. However, if Brueys had sent out a squadron to keep watch off the coast, he would have been warned of the approach of the British ships much earlier in the day, earning an arguably critical several hours' warning of the approach of Nelson.

A few days after the battle, Vivant Denon was with an expeditionary force when they came across a surreal scene on a moonlit beach at midnight. Four or five kilometres of shoreline were covered with the debris of the battle. Locals were burning the flotsam – masts, mountings, small boats – in order to extract the metal; they quickly fled as the French approached. But there was also the human flotsam that had been washed up, 'in poses as sublime as they were terrible'. 'Only a few months ago,' reflected Denon, 'all these beings, young, full of life, courage and hope, had been, by a noble effort, torn from the tears that I had seen flow, from the embrace of their mothers, their sisters, their lovers, and from the feeble hugs of their children.'[5] 'Our situation here is dismal,' wrote Captain Thurman shortly after the battle. 'Not only can we not chase from our spirits the memory of that fatal night, but the theatre of the disaster is right under our eyes . . . Every evening, the shore, on the other side of the harbour, is lined with fires along a distance of seven leagues [about thirty-four kilometres]: it is the Bedouins who are burning our wreckage in order to extract iron.'[6]

Menou called the defeat a 'calamity', while Jean Tallien, a member of the economic section of the Scientific Commission, wrote to Barras, admitting that 'consternation has overwhelmed us all'.[7] Tallien also brought the news to Bonaparte, who, in turn, tried to conceal the defeat from the Egyptian population, and his own men, as long as possible. News of the naval disaster did not reach Cairo for two weeks. The officer who had left Kléber's camp on 2 August took eleven days to cross hostile territory flooded by the Nile. He reached Bonaparte on 14 August, the day before Bonaparte's twenty-ninth birthday. Nevertheless, the rumour of the destruction of the French fleet by the British ran through Cairo. Bonaparte prohibited any commentary on or discussion of the defeat among the Egyptian population and imposed heavy fines on anyone caught talking about it. He also wrote to the Directory, putting all the blame on the conveniently dead Brueys' shoulders. The admiral, Bonaparte lied, had disobeyed his orders by remaining at Aboukir instead of taking shelter in the old port or plotting course for the island of Corfu.[8] Bonaparte even doctored the correspondence between himself and the admiral by sending fabricated extracts to the Directory.[9] (When Bonaparte became first consul in 1799, he had the most compromising items of correspondence removed from the military archives and others modified.)

The Battle of the Nile, it has been argued, marked the crucial turning point in the 'Second Hundred Years' War' between France and Britain: it condemned Bonaparte's Oriental empire to destruction even before it had been established; it marked the end of France as a naval power; and some have seen Trafalgar as its inevitable consequence.[10] This is an exaggeration. The battle was a brilliant tactical victory for Nelson, but it remained just that, tactical and not strategic. Had Bonaparte been planning to invade India in a joint campaign with Tippoo Sahib, the defeat of the French fleet would not have prevented him from doing so. He could have crossed at Suez. Moreover, the destruction of the French fleet was not a victory over the French army, even if Nelson made it difficult for the French to supply the army by blockading Egyptian ports. It encapsulates, in some respects, the problem of a land power facing a sea power.[11] But the British badly needed a political victory and pretended not to notice that the French army was still free to manoeuvre as it saw fit. To the British War Office, at least, which saw the presence of the French in Egypt as a danger to India, the Battle of the Nile was not a victory: it only provided the opportunity for one.[12] Certainly, the loss of the French fleet by no means made Bonaparte's situation as hopeless as Nelson thought, and Bonaparte still had transport ships at Alexandria.

Nevertheless, the naval defeat was an immediate and a personal blow towards Bonaparte's prestige. The disaster suggested that 'destiny' was hostile towards his project in the Orient. He did his best to make light of the disaster in his letters to the Directory: 'As great as this setback is, it cannot be attributed to the inconstancy of Fortune. She has not yet abandoned us. Far from it, she has helped us in this operation more than ever [he is referring to the fact that the British were absent long enough for the French to carry through the invasion].'[13] This was, of course, utter nonsense. Fortune prevented a return to Europe, an option that Bonaparte certainly did not want to forgo. In fact, it seems likely that the Egyptian expedition was never meant to be more than a hit-and-run campaign lasting only a few months. The defeat at Aboukir changed all of this and forced Bonaparte into an indefinite occupation.[14] Now, trapped in his conquest, Bonaparte had no option but to carry on. The defeat also meant that the Directory was in no position to send reinforcements to Egypt. The Army of the Orient was, therefore, totally isolated from Paris at a time when war was about to break out again on the Continent. The Directory was not even able to send precise orders to Bonaparte, and consequently gave him a free hand. 'It is up to you to decide, in accord with the elite of brave and distinguished men in your entourage. But, in whatever direction you turn your efforts, we expect vast schemes and illustrious results from Bonaparte's genie of fortune.'[15]

The dispatch, dated 4 November 1798, did not reach Bonaparte until 25 March 1799, by which time he and his troops were in Syria. One early chronicler has him poring over maps, measuring the distance that separated him from India.[16] It may be in this context that he sent a letter to Tippoo Sahib. Bonaparte had, in fact, three options open to him at this stage: to stay in Egypt and wait for the Turks to attack; to continue to India in the hope of provoking an insurrection against the British; or to march on Constantinople, thereby hastening the collapse of the Ottoman Empire.

The Revolt of Cairo

Although the sultan, Selim III, had posted Turkish ambassadors in all the major European states with instructions to send back detailed reports of their strength, policies and interests in common with Turkey, the dispatches he received in the spring of 1798 from his ambassador in Paris, Esseid Ali, were at best confused. Admittedly, Talleyrand had been playing a double game with the Ottoman envoy, hiding the fact that the expedition being prepared was indeed destined for Egypt by evasive replies to the Turkish ambassador's questions.[17] Moreover, Talleyrand had, in vain, attempted to localize the conflict to Egypt by sending a dispatch on 11 May to Pierre Ruffin, the French ambassador at Constantinople, informing him of what was about to take place. He argued that the expedition was directed at the Mamelukes and not at the Porte, so that it should be no cause for a rupture between Paris and Constantinople.[18]

Two weeks after the Turks learned of the invasion of Egypt, they reluctantly decided upon war against France. Not only had France been their traditional ally for over three centuries, war also meant accepting the help of the Porte's most hated rival, Russia. (The alliance between Russia and the Ottoman Empire to oust Bonaparte from Egypt was so improbable in terms of eighteenth-century diplomacy – they had been bitter enemies for decades – that it would be akin to Russia and the United States joining to fight China at the height of the Cold War.) As a result, some of the most influential men at the court of Constantinople, such as the Francophile reformists, the Grand Vizier and Sheikh ul-Islam, remained opposed to war until the end. Any hesitation in terms of great-power diplomacy, however, was outweighed by the growing popular clamour for war. On 2 September, Selim III, fearing that further resistance might cost him his throne, and compelled to choose between France and Russia, interned French diplomats at Constantinople in the castle of the Seven Towers, the equivalent of a declaration of war.[19]

The Porte published its declaration of war on 9 September. Bonaparte stubbornly refused to believe what was happening. As late as 30 October, after every *imam* in every mosque in

Egypt had read out the sultan's *firmin* (an official order emanating from the sultan) against the French, Bonaparte still seemed to doubt its authenticity. On two occasions, in October and again in November, he sent emissaries to an Anglo-Turkish fleet anchored off Alexandria to establish the reliability of the claim. As late as 11 December – three months after the French ambassador at Constantinople, Ruffin, had been taken to the Seven Towers – Bonaparte was still addressing letters to Talleyrand, as ambassador to Constantinople,* and to the Grand Vizier, thinking that it was still possible to communicate with the Porte.[20]

Bonaparte's arrogant refusal to believe in the Turks' declaration of war, which would fan the flames of revolt when it became general knowledge in Cairo, meant that he was insensitive to the signs of increasing tension between the French colonizers and the Egyptian population. And yet, by October 1798, it was clear the anxiety of the population of Cairo was growing. The measures taken by the French authorities against the plague – surveillance, isolation and quarantine – violated fundamental elements of Islamic life. Quarantine, for example, cut links between the sick and their relatives and was very unpopular; it could mean dying alone amid strangers rather than among family and friends.[21] The obligation to air all fabrics (clothes, carpets) for several days and to disinfect them by fumigation, followed by visits to houses to verify the application of the law, was also resented, but so too was the destruction of several blocks of houses in front of the mosque of al-Azhar, the regulation of burials destined to reduce the risk of epidemic, and the rumour that Egyptian women would soon be ordered not to wear the veil.[22] Their indignation was all the greater because the Christians and Jews, who willingly collaborated with the French, enacted a kind of social revenge on Muslims, humiliating them whenever they could. One of the most demeaning experiences for Muslims was the transgression of the Islamic law that forbade non-Muslims from riding horses, carrying swords and holding posts of authority.[23]

---

* The two men had come to an arrangement before Bonaparte's departure: Talleyrand would leave for Constantinople to persuade the sultan to accept the French incursion on Ottoman territory. It was naïve of Talleyrand to think that he could do so and, in any event, he never left France.

The greatest resentment, however, at least according to contemporary sources, was directed at a proposed real-estate tax.[24]

This may very well have been what sparked off the revolt in the city, but it came at a time when the hatred felt by the people of Cairo towards the French was given a religious justification. Selim III's proclamation calling on all Muslims to wage a jihad against the French was read publicly in the mosques by the *imams* during the Friday sermons. The French could not understand what the *imams* were saying and, as a result, the revolt came as a complete surprise to them. On the morning of 21 October 1798, the revolt started out as a classic riot, a protest against French exactions. During the riot, the commandant of Cairo and a number of his men were killed. It was the death of Dupuy, whose corpse was mistakenly identified as that of Bonaparte, that turned the riot into a general insurrection. All over the town, Christian and European houses were sacked (although the Egyptian neighbours of the French mostly did their best to protect them, often at the risk of their own lives). Bonaparte was away when the insurrection started – he was visiting Old Cairo a few kilometres away – and did not get back to the city until the middle of the day. He did not move to crush the insurrection at once, but went about restoring contact between the various French posts in the town and establishing artillery positions.

The next morning, the *sheikhs* from the *diwan* appeared before Bonaparte. He was angry but at length calmed down and asked them to organize a conciliatory mission to the rebels. However, the rebels interpreted this gesture as evidence of French weakness and refused to meet with the *sheikhs*. Around midday that day, Bonaparte gave the order to bombard the town and to exterminate everybody in the Grand Mosque.[25] The areas held by the rebels were hard hit, particularly the district of al-Azhar. The bombardment caused enormous destruction and was followed up by French soldiers, who overcame the barricades that had been erected. When they reached the Grand Mosque of al-Azhar, it was deliberately desecrated and sacked:

> [They] rode into the mosque on horses . . . And the French trod in the mosque of al-Azhar with their shoes, carrying swords and muskets. Then they scattered in its courtyard and its main praying

area and tied their horses to the *qibla* [the niche in mosques that indicates the direction of Mecca]. They ravaged the students' quarters and pools, smashing the lamps and chandeliers and breaking up the bookcases of the students . . . and scribes. They plundered whatever they found in the mosque, such as furnishings, vessels, bowls, deposits, and hidden things from closets and cupboards. They treated the books and Koranic volumes as trash, throwing them on the ground, stamping on them with their feet and shoes. Furthermore, they soiled the mosque, blowing their spit in it, pissing and defecating in it. They guzzled wine and smashed the bottles in the central court and other parts. And whoever they happened to meet in the mosque they stripped. They chanced upon someone in one of the [students' residences] and slaughtered him.[26]

At this stage, the rebels tried to negotiate, but Bonaparte refused to receive them. At about eight o'clock in the evening, the leaders of the movement surrendered in order to spare the rest of the population. Shots were heard until late at night but, by morning, the French were again in control of the city. About three hundred French had been killed and about ten times that number among the civilian population.

A general amnesty was proclaimed on 21 December, except for the leaders of the revolt and looters. The *agha* of the Janissaries and his lieutenant, a Greek adventurer by the name of Barthélemy Sera, continued to pursue the looters, and increased the number of arbitrary arrests without hesitating to torture their victims in order to obtain denunciations. They were also after weapons. Bonaparte himself asked the *sheikhs* and the *diwan* to give him the names of those guilty of having led the revolt. The *sheikhs* prevaricated, but they soon realized that the French had already identified the leaders and arrested them. The *sheikhs* nevertheless demanded that the *ulama* arrested be treated according to their high rank. Bonaparte complied by sentencing them to house arrest.

Bonaparte wanted to limit the repression, despite clamours from the army that an exemplary punishment be meted out. Surprisingly, the most vociferous in this outcry for revenge were the scientists and artists like Vivant Denon, who wrote to Menou on 30 October

1798: 'Perhaps all those whose eyes saw French soldiers give way should have been put to death without exception.'[27] This was very different language from that expressed in his *Voyages*, where he points out that if the lower classes were 'fanatical and cruel', the middle classes were 'perfectly human and generous, in spite of their customs, religion, and language, which made us so foreign to each other'.[28] Denon conceded that Muslims who had housed Frenchmen went out of their way to save them from the mob, among them an old lady who offered protection in her harem to Denon himself and to a number of scientists.

Bonaparte's clemency was, of course, a political tactic. (Indeed, clemency was to become a recurrent theme of paintings during the Empire.) While he allowed the *sheikhs* to kiss his hand in gratitude, he ordered Berthier to arrest and condemn six of the ringleaders. But instead of proceeding with a public execution, Bonaparte had them quietly decapitated in the citadel on 4 November 1798. As for those caught with arms, they were decapitated and their bodies thrown into the river Nile.[29] The victims:

> . . . were assembled in the grand courtyard. The executioner called them one after the other. They were made to pass through a small door communicating with another courtyard. There, the captive was received by two men who took him under the arms, as though to lead him before his judges. The executioner approached him with a handful of sand, which he immediately threw into his eyes. The condemned man, by a natural reflex, brought his two hands to his eyes and lowered his head: it was immediately cut off with a sword of damask steel that the executioner held hidden under his robes.[30]

The whole process took about five hours, from seven o'clock in the morning until noon. In this manner, at least eighty members of the rebellious junta were executed. One source – Bernoyer – asserts that more than two thousand were arrested and executed under the supervision of General Armagnac, although the figure of three hundred is probably closer to the truth.[31]

Bonaparte initiated measures to safeguard the French. The notables of each district were to be guarantors of public order, made to swear an oath to warn the French at the first sign of trouble.

Discipline was tightened among the French soldiers; they were to have their arms at hand at all times and to go to rallying points within the city if trouble broke out. Three companies of Greek sailors were created from the sailors of Murad Bey's fleet who had remained loyal to the French. They were given the task of maintaining the security of communications on the river. But, above all, Bonaparte concentrated the French living quarters outside city limits, on the island of Roudah at Gizeh. In doing so, Bonaparte had understood, consciously or not, the importance of separating occupier and occupied, a concept that would be applied throughout the French colonies in the nineteenth century.[32]

Beyond Cairo, the revolt inspired the Bedouins, who came dangerously close to the city walls. 'The greed and the audacity of the Bedouins is so great,' wrote one officer, 'that one cannot leave the walls of Cairo without risk of becoming their prey.'[33] Barthélemy the Greek was ordered to clear the region of the nomads and he did so in a manner that was both brutal and effective. Barthélemy, whose nickname was *Fart Rumân* (*Grain de Grenade* or pomegranate seed), was hated by the locals, not least because he was a Greek Christian who had been raised to a position of authority. Each day he rode out with his Mameluke escort, and would bring back Bedouin heads mounted on pikes.[34] On some days, a dozen or so heads were collected and placed in a sack. On one occasion, Barthélemy was tactless enough to empty the sack on to the desk of the military governor of the city, General Dupuy, to the horror of the assembled company. If Barthélemy could not find any Bedouins, it was said he would simply make do with peasants instead. The example no doubt served its purpose – further to terrify the local population into submission – but the choice of Barthélemy, a non-Muslim, to fill this post was impolitic.

The terror tactics ran parallel with attempts to conciliate the people of Cairo. On 21 December, shortly before his departure for Syria, Bonaparte announced a full pardon and the re-establishment of the *diwan* (although it was greatly reduced in power). His proclamation revealed a messianic tone not seen before in his writings, but which became one of the characteristics of the remaining campaign.[35] He spoke of his destiny in the Orient and of how it was directing all his operations:

> Is there a man so blind as not to see that destiny itself guides all my operations? Is there anyone so faithless as to doubt that everything in this vast universe is bound to the empire of destiny?
>
> Let the people know that, from the creation of the world, it is written that after destroying the enemies of Islam and beating the cross, I was to come from the confines of the Occident to accomplish my appointed tasks. Show the people that in more than twenty passages of the holy Koran, what has happened has been foretold and what shall happen has been explained . . .
>
> If I choose, I could call each of you to account for the most hidden feelings of his heart, for I know everything, even what you have told no one. But the day shall come when all men shall see beyond all doubt that I am guided by orders from above and that all human efforts avail naught against me. Blessed are they who, in all good faith, are the first to choose my side.[36]

This extraordinary document, in which Bonaparte claimed he could read the minds of those over whom he ruled, was a mistaken attempt to control Egyptians through religion. Was he playing at the Mahdi (the Prophet) in order to convince the Egyptians, whom he believed to be a superstitious people, that he had some connection with Allah, or did he really believe that Fate was written in the stars? There is probably a mixture of personal and political motivation behind his decision to present himself in prophetic guise. There was the example of Alexander the Great, who obliged the priestesses at the temple of Amon to hail him as the son of Jupiter, in full knowledge of the attitude of local people. Bonaparte no doubt acted under the misapprehension that he understood the people he now ruled as well as their belief systems.

The Decision to Invade Syria

On Christmas Eve 1798, Bonaparte set out with an armed escort and several scientists for Suez. Ostensibly, he was going to visit the

André Dutertre, *Bonaparte, général en chef de l'Armée d'Egypte* (Bonaparte, General-in-Chief of the Army of Egypt) 1798. (*Courtesy of photo RMN –* © *Gérard Blot*)

'Fountains of Moses', natural springs near the coast, a few kilometres south of Suez. In reality, Bonaparte met with a number of merchants from Hedjaz, Yemen and Muscat, in the hope of not only establishing contact with their rulers, but also to gather intelligence in preparation for the invasion of Syria.

When Bonaparte returned to Cairo in the first week of January 1799, he had already resolved to take the offensive against the enemy gathering on the frontier with Syria. It is not entirely clear whether the campaign in Syria was a continuation of the expedition to Egypt, or whether Bonaparte had more grandiose plans in mind. Napoleon always contended that his objective was either India and the creation of an empire in the Orient, or a return to France via Constantinople. Both these objectives were reiterated later during the Empire and on St Helena, where he also made allusions to Alexander the Great.[37] In exile he would argue: 'Look what might have happened if only I had won. I could have gone on to construct an empire in the east.' Although these views, like everything else he said on St Helena, need to be seen in the light of Napoleon's own myth-building, it is worth noting that he placed so much importance on the Egyptian and Syrian expeditions that he would spend the first years of his exile dictating his version of the campaign to General Bertrand. Since Syria would become the scene of Bonaparte's first defeat, it is understandable that he would dwell retrospectively on the potential of the expedition, portraying the campaign as an event whose success would have had implications for the world. Indeed, some contemporary memoirs argue that India was the objective; there would be rumours in the camp outside St John of Acre in Syria that Bonaparte was going to continue north, once he had taken the town, and crown himself 'King of Persia'.[38] Bonaparte may have been aware that he did not possess the strategic capabilities necessary to carry out such a scheme, but he may have hoped to recruit warlike minorities, such as the Druses, the Maronites and the Matuwellis in Syria, swelling the depleted ranks of his army for an Alexander-like conquest of the Orient.

These were options that Bonaparte undoubtedly considered, but we cannot be entirely sure of his intentions. Bonaparte often improvised and let circumstances take him in other directions – but a number of factors help point the way. Bonaparte never wanted to commit himself to a lengthy campaign away from France.[39] His original intention had been to return to France in the month of October 1798,[40] but this was frustrated by the loss of the French fleet in the Battle of the Nile. It is safe to assume that a prompt return there was still uppermost in his mind at the end of 1798 and the beginning of 1799.[41] Other options were considered, as can be seen from the letters he drafted to 'the brave and victorious Sultan, Tippoo Sahib', to the King of Ceylon, the sovereign of Tanjore and a number of other Oriental potentates whose names were left blank.[42] (These were never sent because of the difficulties of communicating with India by sea.) In a letter to Tippoo Sahib written in January 1799, Bonaparte announced that he would soon reach India at the head of an 'invincible army' in order to deliver him from the English. Such declarations can be regarded as wishful thinking. So, too, were the orders sent to French ships of war at the Ile de France and the Ile Bourbon to set sail for Suez in order to place themselves under Bonaparte's orders.[43] This was after his return from Syria!

A clearer indication of Bonaparte's intentions can be gleaned from his thoughts on the expedition to Syria in his correspondence. As early as September 1798, spies were being sent to reconnoitre in Syria, while supplies were stored in Salahieh, on the edge of the Sinai desert.[44] On 10 February, for example, the day he left Cairo to join the expeditionary force that had gathered at Katia near the Syrian border, Bonaparte wrote to the Directory declaring that his reasons for the pre-emptive attack were to assure the conquest of Egypt by striking at the forces gathering in Syria, and to eliminate Syria as a supply base for the British.[45] Bonaparte's main reason for an invasion of Syria, though, seems to have been to remove Ibrahim Bey, and to ward off an attack by land from the governor of Acre, Djezzar Pasha, thus averting any direct threat to Egypt. Whether he needed to go as far as Acre to do this is debatable, but given the logic of eighteenth-century warfare, it seems perfectly understandable that the elimination of Djezzar as a potential threat meant that he had to be destroyed. Bonaparte hoped that the whole matter would be finished within two months and that he would be back in Egypt in time to repel an expected attack by sea.

Throughout the months of November and December, French spies were reporting that Ibrahim Bey and Djezzar were planning an offensive. A number of Mameluke couriers managed to get through the French lines to join Murad Bey in Upper Egypt, but one letter intercepted by the French revealed that the Grand Vizier himself, Youssef Pasha, had announced the preparation of a combined Anglo-Turkish action against Egypt under the command of the governor of Damas, Abdallah Pasha. In response, Bonaparte sent Djezzar an ultimatum – he had already sent French officers on two separate occasions to try to reach an agreement – on 19 November: 'I do not want war if you are not my enemy, but it is time for you to explain yourself. If you continue to give asylum, at the borders of Egypt, to Ibrahim Bey, I shall regard this as an act of war and shall march on Acre.'[46]

By January, the Allied action against Egypt had begun. On 19 January, Marmont, who was acting as governor of Alexandria, arrived in Cairo to tell Bonaparte that an English squadron, reinforced by one Turkish and one Russian vessel, had begun bombarding the town. The decision to undertake the expedition to Syria had already been made by this stage, but Bonaparte nevertheless convoked a meeting of his generals. Three-quarters of them disapproved of the plan, although it seems only one general, Joseph Lagrange, had the courage to say so to Bonaparte's face.[47] It would have been far more sensible, they argued, to await the arrival of an invading army after a long, difficult and exhausting march across the desert. But even at this relatively early stage of his career, Bonaparte's entourage was afraid to contradict him openly. So, despite the opposition of some of his generals – the opinion of others was never an overriding consideration in matters that Fate alone could decide – Bonaparte decided to go ahead with his initial plan and to meet the enemy head on.

On 10 February, Bonaparte left Cairo to join his small army of about 13,000 men commanded by Kléber, Bon, Lannes, Reynier and Murat. This figure does not include Egyptian and Arab personnel, or the French civilian commissaries, a number of women, and a large contingent from the Scientific Commission. Bonaparte was the last to leave Cairo. He had been waiting for news of what was happening in Europe. Reports of the deterioration of France's position and the start of the war of the Second Coalition were worrying. Even before he set out for Syria, therefore, Bonaparte's thoughts had turned to Europe.

18

The Limits of Imagination

'All Human Effort against Me is Useless'

January 1799 was spent in preparation for the expedition, although, once again, to Bonaparte's discredit, they were carried out carelessly. True, supplies were stored along the route; recalcitrant Bedouin tribes were attacked; and numerous hostages were taken to ensure that Egypt remained quiet while the bulk of the army was away. Camels and sheep were seized from the Bedouins, and a dromedary regiment was created to carry dispatches and scouting parties. A portable Arab printing station was even assembled, while provincial commanders were reassigned, and more and more troops were taken from various regions to reinforce the expedition. But there were many organizational deficiencies. Bonaparte had little or no idea of the situation and obstacles he would encounter. Indeed, he was under the illusion that the army would be able to supply itself en route, as the Army of Italy had done. As a result, 'not only did he [Bonaparte] only bring enough supplies for a march which was supposed to last ten days when it lasted as much again, but he did not leave any orders for supply columns to be sent'.[1] Given the army's ordeal between Alexandria and Rahmaniya at the beginning of the invasion, it was incredibly negligent, especially as reports from spies were conflicting and contradictory.

The lack of preparations and logistics began to make themselves felt immediately. The march to Katia was difficult enough – 'After twenty-one hours of crossing shifting sands in blazing heat, we reached Katia sometime after two [in the morning]. It had been a dreadful day – officers and soldiers collapsed from thirst, hunger, fatigue, and heatstroke'[2] – but the march between Katia and El Arish, only eighty or so kilometres from the Egyptian border, was even worse.

After six to eight hours of marching, what was supposed to have been a two-hour halt was ordered. 'Each officer, non-commissioned officer and soldier, spout in hand, went to drink from the goatskins the camels were carrying. The water was hot, disagreeable and dirty like the water from a cobbler's tub,' wrote Sergeant François.[3] This did not prevent several soldiers from dying of thirst while, once again, several men, no longer able to take the hardship, blew their brains out. The men were so worn out that they stayed there for the rest of the day. They started out again at two o'clock in the morning to avoid the heat of the day, only to repeat the same scenario. That day, as the army hugged the coast, thirst drove several men into the sea, where they rashly drank saltwater then, unable to bear 'the fire that it had lighted in their bodies', shot themselves. Later that day, two brothers also committed suicide. When the division finally stopped at a well near Messoudieh, not far from El Arish, the stampede killed over thirty men. The wells quickly ran dry, but the men discovered that if they dug holes in the ground around the well they could find a little water in that way.[4] General Reynier, commanding the advance guard, had great trouble in getting his men, who lay exhausted on the ground, back on their feet. When he did, finally, more than a hundred men were left on the sand, dead from exhaustion. The rest of the army was in much the same state.

> Soldiers weighed down by their baggage, their weapons, water and supplies dragged themselves with difficulty across the burning sands . . . If they rested, it was on terrain they could hardly touch with their hands, and without finding the shade of a bush that could protect them from the ardour of the sun. To quench their thirst, they had nothing but brackish water over which they often argued and which even the horses refused to drink.[5]

On 8 February, Reynier, thinking that the route to Gaza was free, stumbled out of the desert on to the fort at the fishing village of El Arish. The existence of the fortress came as a complete surprise.

Much of the preparation for the expedition was based on the out-of-date accounts of travellers and reports lacking detailed information. Not only did the fortress have thick walls, not only was it defended by about one thousand Mamelukes, Arabs, Magrebins, Albanians and Turks, but the French troops that arrived in front of the town were in a terrible condition. Over the previous days, they had been eating sea sorrel, dug up from the sand, which caused dysentery.[6] Only a week or so into the campaign, the men were obliged to eat their horses, donkeys and camels.[7]

The capitulation of the fortress was indispensable to the expedition, not only for Egypt and Bonaparte, but because it guarded the access to Syria. The very next morning Reynier attacked. The outer defences of the town were easily stormed, with terrible consequences for the inhabitants who tried to resist. It was only when a breach was made after two days of continuous bombardment that Bonaparte offered very favourable conditions to the defenders: the garrison would be allowed to withdraw with the honours of war, on condition that they did not serve in Syria for the duration of the campaign, and, especially, that they left their supplies to the French.[8] Under the rules of warfare then prevailing, a garrison that refused to surrender once a breach had been made could be expected to be put to the sword.

On the evening of 20 February, the fort capitulated after a ten-day siege. The French occupied it immediately and, just as quickly, violated the accord they had signed with the Ottoman defenders. Bonaparte had had no intention of keeping his word. Contrary to the terms of the armistice, the men who surrendered were disarmed, and about 900 were more or less persuaded to join the French forces rather than perish in the desert on their way home (they all deserted at the first opportunity[9]). The Mamelukes were sent back to Egypt under escort. The rest went on to Syria where, given that the agreement with the French had been broken, they joined the Ottoman forces.

As for the town itself, the supplies had been sent there by Djezzar in preparation for his invasion of Egypt, but one of the surgeons accompanying the army, ordered to take the necessary measures to 'disinfect and sanitize' a number of rooms, soon realized that plague was present in the garrison. 'The courtyards of the fortress were filled with the bodies of men and animals, especially animals that were already in a state of putrefaction. The rooms of the soldiers were scattered with rags and all sorts of insalubrious and putrid objects.'[10] It was an ominous sign of things to come.

The next day, the army continued its march. On the road between El Arish and Gaza stand the columns of Rafah that symbolized the ancient divide between Africa and Asia.[11] A wire divided the village, separating the Asian from the African quarter. The first village they entered in Palestine was St Louis, some seventy-odd kilometres from El Arish, named after the French king who had led the thirteenth-century crusade there. The morale of the troops rose when they saw large numbers of olive trees, which reminded them of Provence. 'This place is surrounded by gardens in the European style, full of all sorts of fruit and vegetables.'[12] Memories of Provence, however, did not stop them from setting fire to thousands of trees, whether for warmth, to dry off (it had rained constantly since their entry into Gaza), or simply for fun.[13] It was during this period that Bonaparte issued a declaration to the people of Gaza, El Ramle and Jaffa in which he asserted that 'all human effort against me is useless, for I succeed in all that I undertake. Those who declare themselves my enemies die. The example that has just occurred at Jaffa and at Gaza will show you that if I am terrible towards my enemies, I am good towards my friends, and especially clement and merciful towards the poor.'[14]

On 24 February, the army finally reached Gaza, whose inhabitants did not repeat the mistake made by those of El Arish. Bernoyer described the scene:

> Some distance from the town a group of Turks without arms approached us: this was a delegation sent out to offer us all we could ask for. Bonaparte appreciated this prudent step and gave them presents. He told them that he had come only as their friend; that his intentions were only to punish the oppressors of the people but to grant the inhabitants complete independence.[15]

Is this hypocritical? Perhaps. The French revolutionaries as conquerors had a tendency to cloak pillage in the guise of 'liberty', but many (naïvely) did believe that they were bringing their message to the peoples of the world, that its significance was universal, and that it would inspire the inhabitants to whom it was given.

The fortress held out overnight and surrendered the next morning after light skirmishing. To their relief, the French found considerable stocks of supplies and ammunition.[16] It would appear that luck was once again on Bonaparte's side. If the garrison had decided to resist the French, it would have caused them problems on all sorts of levels, but especially regarding supplies. However, if Gaza fell without a shot fired it was because one of Bonaparte's Palestinian agents was an intimate friend of the governor of the town and had no trouble convincing him, with the help of an appropriate bribe, to save the inhabitants.[17] They were spared, but the town was thoroughly looted while the French spent three days recuperating from their long march.

The Ottoman forces at this point separated into different sections. The Ottoman troops fell back on Jaffa; the Mamelukes and the local contingents withdrew to Jerusalem and Nablus. Djezzar preferred to use the forts at his disposal to delay the French until reinforcements arrived from Turkey. The French would be obliged to stay close to the coast while guerrilla warfare on French supply and communication lines could be carried out from the interior. As long as the bulk of his forces remained more or less intact, Djezzar knew that there would be no significant desertion to the French. While resting at Gaza, Bonaparte considered moving to 'liberate' Jerusalem. He even sent proclamations to Jerusalem, Nazareth and Lebanon with the vague notion of recruiting the Christians who lived there. But in the course of a secret meeting at Gaza between Bonaparte and the governor of Jerusalem, who had travelled to meet Bonaparte with a Christian delegation, they counselled him not to enter the city until he had defeated the forces of Djezzar.[18]

The Massacre at Jaffa

On 28 February, the army continued its march. The desert between Gaza and Jaffa is an immense plain 'covered with hills of moving sand, which the cavalry only succeeded in crossing with much difficulty'.[19] Even the camels, accustomed to desert sands, had trouble crossing these dunes.[20] The army took ten hours to march about fourteen kilometres, and were obliged to triple the number of animals used to haul the artillery. To make matters worse, they were constantly harassed along the way by Bedouins, especially during the night, so that the army was obliged to bivouac in squares, with the horses, camels and baggage in the middle.[20] Moreover, the going was made much more difficult by the torrential rains that began the moment the French entered Syrian territory. 'The freshness of the wet ground and the humidity of the nights rendered sleep danger-ous; insects further troubled the repose of our warriors; often they had to spend part of the night warming themselves and did not fall asleep until the undeniable need for slumber had closed their eyes.'[22]

By 1 March, though, the army had left the 'ungrateful soil' of the desert, and taken Ramle.[23] Once again, the French were lucky enough to find considerable supplies, and once again that did not prevent the soldiers from looting and pillaging as they made their way up the coast. On 3 March 1799, Kléber arrived before Jaffa and took up position north of the town to isolate it from Acre and Nablus. The siege started the same day. At one stage, two French emissaries were sent to negotiate the surrender of the town. The reply was the appearance of their heads on pikes behind the wall. This time the town fell in less than three hours on 7 March and suffered much worse than the traditional pillaging. Jaffa was given up to rape and murder for two, possibly four, whole days (wit-nesses disagree on this point). The troops stopped only when they were exhausted from indiscriminately killing anyone that fell in their way, regardless of sex or age.[24] Bonaparte not only turned a blind eye, but in fact he was partly responsible. Before the last assault, he announced that the whole garrison would be executed. The troops understood that no quarter was to be given. Etienne-Louis Malus, a doctor who attended the plague victims at Jaffa, vividly recalled his impressions:

> The soldiers cut the throats of men and women, the old and the young, Christians and Turks, anyone who had a human face fell victim to their fury. The noise of the massacre, broken doors, ruined

houses, the sounds of shots and of the cleaning of swords, the shrieks of women, father and son one on top of the other (on the same pile of bodies), a daughter being raped on the cadaver of her mother, the smoke from the burnt clothes of the dead, the smell of blood, the groans of the wounded, the shouts of the victors who were quarrelling about the loot taken from a dying victim, angry soldiers who redoubled their blows the more their victim cried out in order to sink at last, satiated by blood and gold, without further feeling, on top of a heap of dead.[25]

One witness described some officers trying in vain to intervene, sabring their own men in the attempt to stop the massacre, but the 'ecstasy of blood, the frenzy of rape, [and] the fever of loot had annihilated all feelings of compassion and honour' among the troops.[26]

A commissary by the name of Jacques-François Miot, the Comte Miot de Melito's brother, attempted to explain the behaviour of the troops in his account of the event: 'The soldier, excited by the noise and the powder, gives vent to all the ferocity which the assault authorized: he wounds, he kills, nothing could stop him, and through it all his love of glory, increasing his ardour, causes him to forget a wound that he only notices at the end of the fighting.' Then followed the litany of obscenities that is now associated with the sacking of Jaffa (which were only added to the 1814 edition of his account).[27] What is not as well known, however, is that a large number of young girls and women were kidnapped, taken to the French camp and raped. Quickly, though, fights broke out among the troops over them. Bonaparte, hearing of this, ordered that all the women were to be led into the hospital courtyard by midday, on pain of a severe punishment. The order was punctually carried out; it was believed that they would be sent back into the ruins of the town where they would find refuge. However, a company of chasseurs was assembled to execute them.[28]

And the killing did not stop there. Of the 5,000 men who had defended the town, 2,000 were killed during the assault. The remaining 3,000 found refuge in a harem with a large courtyard. A battalion from Lannes's division had come across them but had been unable to get inside. The French troops were already talking about burning them alive when Eugène de Beauharnais and one of Bonaparte's aides-de-camp, Captain Croisier, intervened to prevent them.[29] Not thinking that Bonaparte had really meant he would execute the garrison, they started negotiations that led to their surrender on the condition that their lives would be saved. They were then marched off as prisoners of war to headquarters.

According to an account by Bourrienne, Bonaparte was sitting on a cannon before the breach in the ramparts talking to Lannes when he saw the long line of captives marching towards him. He apparently went white with rage and shouted, 'What do you want me to do with all of these prisoners? What the devil have you done?' Beauharnais and Croisier explained that they had wanted to avoid renewed bloodshed, but Bonaparte tersely replied: 'Yes, no doubt, if it were a question of old men, women and children! But not armed soldiers. You should have let them die and not bring me these wretches. What do you want me to do with them?'[30] According to the same account, Bonaparte started walking up and down, extremely agitated. He then made a dreadful choice – to execute the prisoners in spite of the promise that had been made by his aides-de-camp. He did not plan to take the responsibility alone, however. Assembling his general staff, he asked them to ratify his decision. They met three times in his presence and three times they were unable to bring themselves to do it. In the end, Bonaparte assembled all the division generals and, after a long and bitter debate, he finally bullied them into his way of thinking. Those who saw the generals leaving the room where the council was held tell us that they were pale and their features drawn. At the last minute, it seems that Berthier interceded – he felt responsible for their fate since he had helped negotiate their surrender – trying to persuade Bonaparte that the action was inhuman. 'Since you react in that way,' Bonaparte furiously threw back at him, pointing at a Capuchin convent that was in the vicinity, 'don't ever get involved in politics. Enter the [monastery] and if you want my advice, don't ever come out!'[31]

Bourrienne, however, is the only person who mentions a council. It is much more likely that Bonaparte alone made the decision, within twenty-four hours of their surrender. Kléber and Reynier were at Ramle. Berthier, Dommartin and Bon seem to have been the only generals present, and Berthier, at least, mentions nothing of this in his account of the campaign.[32] Bonaparte took out the Egyptians, about 500, who were sent back to their country. The rest, a mixture of Magrebins, Albanians, Damascans, Anatolians and Sudanese, were condemned to death by firing squad on the pretext that found among them were soldiers from El Arish who had not respected the agreement (there were, indeed, 300 or 400 soldiers from El Arish). There were other, more practical arguments that could be used to explain if not justify Bonaparte's decision. The army was short of supplies and was in no position to feed all those prisoners; there were simply not enough soldiers to escort them back to Egypt in the presence of a hostile population; if they were freed, there was a real danger that they would fight another day; Bonaparte was also determined to make a terrible impression on Djezzar. The young paymaster, André Peyrusse, sent his mother an account of what happened:

> The next morning all the Moroccans were taken to the seashore and two battalions began to shoot them down. Their only hope of saving their lives was to throw themselves into the sea; they did not hesitate, and all tried to escape by swimming. They were shot at leisure, and in an instant, the sea was red with blood and covered with corpses. A few were lucky enough to reach some rocks. Soldiers were ordered to follow them in boats and finish them off . . . Once this execution was over, we fondly hoped that it would not be repeated and that the other prisoners would be spared . . . Our hopes were soon disappointed, when, the next day, 1,200 Turkish artillerymen, who for two days had been kept without food in front of General Bonaparte's tent, were taken to be executed. The soldiers had been carefully instructed not to waste ammunition, and they were cruel enough to run them through with their bayonets. Among the victims, we found many children who, in the act of death, had clung to their fathers. This example will teach our enemies that they cannot count on French good faith, and sooner or later, the blood of these 3,000 victims will be upon us.[33]

Over a three-day period, from 8 to 10 March, the remaining prisoners were marched to a beach about a kilometre and a half south of the city and massacred.[34] Soon after the killing started, the order was given to spare powder and to bayonet to death those who remained. In a macabre choreography in which victims and perpetrators were required to participate, squares of French soldiers were formed, in the middle of which prisoners were placed; the troops then advanced and killed everyone in the square.[35] The French troops, used to the horrors of war, and responsible for many individual acts of atrocity, obeyed, 'but with a sort of loathing and dread'.[36] In the days that followed, the stench of the rotting corpses soon poisoned the air surrounding the French camp.[37]

Pillage, rape and murder, it has to be said, were the rule rather than the exception throughout the seventeenth and eighteenth centuries on the fall of a besieged town. Whether we are reminded of Frederick the Great in Moravia in 1741, or of the Seven Years' War, which saw atrocities committed by all sides, or the British massacres committed at Seringapatam, India, after it was stormed and captured in May 1799, or again the British sacking of the city of Badajoz in Spain in 1812, the wars of the eighteenth and the early nineteenth centuries were characterized by the indiscipline of the troops and the terrible exactions they carried out on the civilian populations. In 1788, for example, Prince Potemkin besieged the Turkish town of Otchakof. Potemkin, it should be noted, was regarded as a sophisticated, knowledgeable courtier but, after the final assault, the whole town was sacked and pillaged for three days running. More than 6,000 inhabitants were massacred. According to legend, two days after the town had been stormed, Russian soldiers would throw babies up into the air, catching them on their bayonets and crying out, 'At least they won't do any harm to Christians.'[38]
  There was nothing, sadly, out of the ordinary, then, in the massacre at Jaffa, except that it was calculated and took place after the storming of the town. The massacre was committed from a position of weakness, that is, out of a desire to impose authority and to terrorize the opposing camp.[39] Bonaparte must have hoped that news of the massacre would weaken any future resistance. To that extent it was a political act, but it also testifies to a complete disregard for human life bordering on the pathological, to an authoritarian, repressive style of rule that did not originate in

the 'Orient' but which already existed, to an extent, in Corsica and which was certainly present in Italy. For Bonaparte, people were pawns in his political and military calculations, to be dispensed with if they could not be useful. Those who might argue that Egypt allowed Bonaparte to throw off the mantle of European 'civilization' and adopt 'oriental' ways when dealing with political and/or military opponents have missed the point. The Revolution itself engendered a violent rhetoric,[40] so that, from the very beginning of the expedition, the French repressed their opponents as they were accustomed to doing in Europe. One should not forget the horrors Bonaparte and the French visited upon the people of Italy, nor where many of the French generals and troops had gained experience – in the Vendée, where, too, they had practised a policy of repression of astounding violence. In Egypt, the French perpetrators – hardened veterans, a long way from home, who had been brutalized over the years by their experiences – had even fewer qualms about killing people with whom they could not identify. As for Bonaparte, it is impossible to say whether his lack of humanity was an inherent, latent trait that had now come to the fore – had the realization that Josephine was unfaithful made him even more callous and unfeeling towards those around him? – or whether he had simply become immune to suffering. There was now a ruthlessness about him that was taking on alarming dimensions.

Fear and Contagion

The plague caught up with the French at Jaffa. The first cases appeared the day after the sacking, and were eventually to take the lives of 700 to 800 men. To avoid panic, the sick were isolated and any knowledge of the plague was publicly denied: for a time, Bonaparte refused to call it the plague and instead referred to it as a 'fever'. He forced the doctors accompanying the army to assert that it was not contagious, and in a way this was correct. The bubonic plague, which is what this was, is transmitted through flea bites rather than through exposure to people, although this was not known at the time. As a result, most of the medical attendants contracted the disease and died, while soldiers, ignorant of what they were dealing with, did not hesitate to steal the effects of those who died from the plague, thus inadvertently infecting themselves in the process.[41]

The morale of the army plummeted: the plague would have led men to look upon their comrades with great suspicion, watching for the first signs of sickness. The soldiers, if not actually sick, were weakened by long marches in the burning sands, by lack of food, and by setting up camp in places soaked by diluvian rains.[41] 'For ten days,' wrote Malus, who was in charge of the administration of the health service,

> I assiduously went [to the hospital] and I spent the morning in the stench of that cesspool, every corner of which was filled with the sick ... Half the garrison had already been struck down; about thirty soldiers a day died in that place ... one man in twelve escaped ... Moreover, the plague was in every house in town where inhabitants were still to be found ... The monastery of the Capuchins which had put itself under quarantine, was not able to avoid the contagion, and most of the priests died.[43]

Malus himself came down with the plague but survived.[44] Fear of contracting the plague remained uppermost in people's minds and dictated how they behaved and interacted with others. Some did their best to isolate themselves from the rest of the army. Several generals and high-ranking officers, for example, locked themselves in houses at Jaffa and only communicated with the outside world through spy holes or hatches. Some generals erected a palisade at twenty-five paces from their lodgings and would not even receive a piece of paper from the outside world unless it had been soaked in vinegar (widely believed to act as a disinfectant). Needless to say, even these measures did not prevent some of them succumbing to the plague.[45] The dead kept mounting up, but since no one wanted to touch them, the divisions belonging to Lannes and Bon were used to force both the inhabitants and prisoners to take away the corpses encumbering the streets and the houses.[46]

In order to avoid panic and impress the troops, Bonaparte, by now supremely confident in his own personal destiny, and perhaps wanting to demonstrate extraordinary powers, paid a visit to the sick at the hospital set up in a seventeenth-century Armenian monastery at Jaffa. The chief medical officer, Nicolas René Desgenettes, has left us with a description of what took place on 11 March 1799, when Bonaparte arrived, probably accompanied by most, if not all, of his staff.

> The general walked through the hospital and its annexe, spoke to almost all the soldiers who were conscious enough to hear him, and for one and a half hours, with the greatest calm, busied himself with the details of the administration. Finding himself in a very cramped and overcrowded room, he helped to lift, or rather carry, the hideous corpse of a soldier whose torn uniform was soiled by the spontaneous bursting of an enormous abscessed bubo.[47]

Bonaparte's grand gesture – witnessed by as many people as possible under the circumstances – had a rational motive. It was believed that fear helped the advance of the disease, so Bonaparte, thinking that the 'surest protection, the most efficacious remedy, was a display of moral courage',[48] made a theatrical gesture designed to convince others of the irrationality of their fears. 'It is one of the peculiarities of the plague', Bonaparte wrote much later, 'that it is most dangerous to those who fear it; those who allowed themselves to be mastered by their own fear are almost all dead.'[49] The gesture reassured the army. Jean-François Detroye, later killed at the siege of St John of Acre, commented in his diary: 'This action, profoundly political, has produced an excellent effect. People have been comforted.'[50]

The Siege of St John of Acre

On 14 March, the army continued on its way, arriving outside Haifa three days later (the French were given the keys to the town to avoid looting), where it discovered two British ships of war – the *Tigre* and the *Theseus* – that had arrived only a couple of days before. Their presence was a disaster for the French.[51] The British had intercepted the little fleet charged with transporting the French siege artillery, too heavy to carry overland, thus depriving Bonaparte of valuable equipment. Moreover, the Ottomans were now capable of supplying the town by sea, while the British ships bombarded the French. Present also were two specialists, Sir Sidney Smith and Colonel Picard de Phélippeaux, who were to play a major role in hindering Bonaparte's conquest of Syria. Djezzar's first reaction had been to flee, and he had those things he most valued – thirty women from his new harem and his personal treasure – put on a ship in the harbour of Acre for that purpose. It was only when Sir Sidney Smith sent Captain Miller from the *Theseus* to reassure Djezzar and to persuade him to regain his palace that he decided to stay. The presence of Djezzar within the town meant that the civilian population had either to die fighting or win. Once he decided to stay, however, Djezzar's role in the defence of the city was to be decisive.[52] To defend the town, Djezzar armed the civilian population, and had the Christians massacred in case they acted as a fifth column. (Although he was seventy years old, Djezzar continued to rule all Syria south of the river Aleppo with an iron fist and with immense cruelty, hence his nickname – 'the butcher'.) Their bodies were stuffed into boxes used for coffee and rice and thrown out to sea, where they were washed ashore. The French who found them were shocked at the contents, one of which included a French officer sent by Bonaparte six months earlier to negotiate with Djezzar, strangled to death on his orders.[53]

Acre should not have been an insurmountable obstacle to Bonaparte. He had brought with him 12,000 disciplined and experienced troops, while the defenders could count on only about 4,000 troops – Turks, Kurds, Bosnians, Albanians, Syrians and Anatolians. Nor were the walls of Acre particularly impressive by eighteenth-century standards (the walls one sees today were actually a second line of defence built by Djezzar after the French had raised the siege). If Bonaparte had arrived at Acre eleven days earlier – the time spent at El Arish – he would have taken it without any great difficulty. It was to be the difference between success and failure. Now, with the arrival of the British to reinforce the local garrison, Bonaparte was drawn into a protracted siege at a time when French morale was flagging. The troops had just marched hundreds of kilometres in scorching heat and pouring rain; they had seen and committed unspeakable horrors; they were hungry, tired, ill, and lacked the appropriate clothing and adequate equipment.

The first weeks of the siege nevertheless went by without any notable incidents, although there seems to have been disagreement about the best way to conduct it. If Bonaparte, instead of launching futile attacks against the walls of Acre, had waited for the siege guns, which started to arrive in Jaffa on 30 April and which were installed by 7 May, he might very well have taken the town. As things stood, however, he wasted both men and resources on hopelessly improvised attempts. In addition, he had the attacks from the British and Djezzar's allies to contend with. While Bonaparte was besieging Acre, Djezzar appealed to the warlike mountaineers of Nablus and to the Pashas of Aleppo and Damascus. At the beginning of April, some 7,000 warriors from the Nablus region reportedly gathered at Galilee, and the army of the Pasha of Damascus was said to be on the march to take the French in the rear. The most urgent task for Bonaparte was to meet the army on the banks of the river Jordan. He dispatched Murat with about 200 cavalry and 500 infantry in the direction of Damascus. At the same time, Junot with about 150 cavalry and 300 infantry was sent in the direction of Nazareth, where he was well received by the Christian population of the town. But, on 8 April, he found himself face to face with about 3,000 Turks, the advance guard of the coalition assembled by the Pasha of Damascus, a composite force of around 40,000 men.

News of a growing concentration of troops started to trickle in to Acre, so Bonaparte decided to take the initiative. On 9 April, he sent Kléber with some 2,500 men to reinforce Junot. On 16 April, however, Kléber and his men ran into a combined force of 35,000 men near Mount Tabor. Kléber boldly, and perhaps foolishly, attacked the army before daybreak in the hope that surprise would work in his favour. Instead, he found himself desperately trying to fend off the attacks of 25,000 cavalry behind squares for most of the day. At about four in the afternoon, after almost having run out of ammunition, Bonaparte appeared. He had marched forty kilometres overnight with a division of men from Acre. His sudden arrival and a few well-placed cannon shot were enough to make the Arab army flee.

On his return from Nazareth on the evening of 18 April, Bonaparte learned that Admiral Perrée's naval convoy had arrived at Jaffa carrying the heavy siege guns. But rather than await their arrival at the Acre encampment – it would have taken until the end of the month to drag them into place – he ordered another wave of assaults. The tailor, François Bernoyer, recalled:

> We went to the attack eight times against that town, without any result. In the night of 6 June, Bonaparte ordered the ninth attack: he wanted to take advantage of the fact that the Turk does not work after the setting of the sun ... that night attack was more successful than the others. The first guard was taken by surprise and in part killed: we spiked a few cannon and destroyed a few earthworks. That was all we were able to do ... The frequent assaults caused our army to diminish appreciably in number. All the obstacles that prolonged the siege started to create grumblings among the troops and officers. The glory of the army and especially that of Bonaparte were compromised: that is why every means were used.[54]

Bonaparte seemed impatient to end the siege because, it is safe to surmise, he had already decided to return to France. A man by the name of Boutros Bokty, a Syrian merchant who was born in Egypt and educated in France, arrived at the encampment of Acre in the evening of 18–19 April. He was accompanied by Winand Mourveau, sent by the Directory to Egypt. Bokty was a private messenger sent by the Bonaparte brothers, Joseph and Lucien, and is said to have transmitted a letter from Joseph urging Bonaparte to return to France. It is probably this letter that led to his decision to do so.[55] Without waiting for the heavy artillery, Bonaparte launched a new assault on Acre. It failed. French engineers worked twenty-one days on a mine that was exploded at nine o'clock in the morning of 24 April and which was meant to cause one of the main towers to come crashing down.

Its only effect was to blow up a corner of the tower ... The grenadiers boldly charged the breach, although it was clear that it was impossible to penetrate it. The enemy, installed at the top of the tower and hidden behind the battlements, flattened our troops with rocks, shells and hand grenades. However, since nothing could turn them back, the Turks resorted to two or three powder kegs, which they dropped on them. All our men were suffocated although a few managed to run away half-burned.[56]

The attempt had nearly exhausted their munitions supplies. The next day another assault was launched, and although one hundred or so grenadiers succeeded in penetrating the lower gallery of the tower, it, too, failed. The siege artillery started arriving on 30 April. Some successes were recorded in the days that followed but, on 7 May, a fleet of about thirty sails appeared in the distance. At first, the French believed that reinforcements had arrived from France, but their hope evaporated when Turkish and English flags became visible. The convoy was carrying 10–12,000 reinforcements from Rhodes under the command of Hassan Bey. A last desperate assault was launched that same day before the troops had time to disembark and reinforce the garrison. This time the French succeeded in penetrating the town, only to find that a trap had been laid for them.

The fire from the buildings, from the barricades across the street, from Djezzar's palace, took those who descended from the breach into the town both from the front and the back, and those who were already in the town started to retreat, as they were unable to hold the town. They abandoned two cannon and two mortars, which they had got hold of inside the ramparts. The whole column inside the town was affected by the retrograde movement. General Lannes went forward in order to arrest it and get the column to move forward again. The foot scouts, who had been held in reserve, now scaled the breach. The effect of the first rush wore off; General Lannes was dangerously wounded, General Rambaud was killed there ... Retreat became necessary, and the order was given.[57]

Part of the problem was that Bonaparte persisted in attacking the same part of the fortress, so that it was easy for the defenders to plan for an eventual incursion. By the evening of 8 May, the relief troops started to disembark and prevented any reinforcements from reaching the beleaguered French troops inside the town. According to Bernoyer, the remaining troops, who had managed to hold out in a mosque, were killed to the last man. Kléber arrived the next day, and there was a scene in which he publicly rebuked Bonaparte for conducting the siege so poorly.[58] Nevertheless, another assault was ordered for 10 May with the fresh troops from his division. This, too, was a failure. Almost incomprehensibly, Bonaparte launched another wave.[59]

19

The End of the Dream

Retreat and Revenge

The final assault proved too much for Bonaparte's men. Disgruntled, they blamed him, quite rightly, for their woes. Sidney Smith wrote to Nelson that the French grenadiers simply refused to mount the breach again 'over the putrid bodies of their unburied companions'.[1] This discontent manifested itself not only among the troops, but also among the officers. Murat is said to have referred to Bonaparte as the 'executioner' (*bourreau*) of his troops. 'One has to be very stubborn and very blind', he is reported as saying to his face, 'not to see that you will never reduce the town of St John of Acre. Since you did not succeed when your army was complete, it is not today that you will succeed.'[2] There was apparently no reaction; Bonaparte went back into his tent without responding.

St John of Acre was a new experience for Bonaparte. He had not, thus far, known defeat. It is probably why he persisted in the face of considerable difficulties, perhaps convinced that 'destiny' would eventually allow him to take the town. Over a two-month period, up to fourteen assaults (the sources vary) were launched, and all of them failed. For the first time in his military career, Bonaparte had suffered a serious setback, but this did not prevent him from sending back a letter to the *diwan* of Cairo announcing that he had razed Djezzar's palace and the walls of Acre, and that Djezzar himself had been seriously wounded.[3] Bonaparte also sent a letter to the Directory reporting on his victories in Syria and vaguely hinted at returning to Cairo: 'Besides, the season is too far gone. The goal I set myself has been fulfilled: Egypt calls.'[4] The explanation that he eventually gave for the retreat was that Acre was infested with the plague and that it was too dangerous to take the town.[5] Also, the proclamation Bonaparte issued to the army announcing the impending withdrawal read as if they were to return home victorious.[6] To that end, he gave the order to Berthier to select a sergeant major and two corporals to precede the army with the flags they had captured from the enemy. Each time they passed a village they were to enter with the flags displayed and to the sound of a marching band.

It was obvious that Bonaparte could not stay in Syria much longer. The arrival of the British fleet at Acre meant that the Turks were within easy striking distance of Egypt and he had to return to defend it. Before the retreat was effected, however, Bonaparte ordered the guns to fire at the city (between 12 and 15 May, and again on 20 May), partly to cover his retreat, but also to leave as much death and destruction behind him as he could. The subsequent withdrawal took place during the night of 20–21 May. The French left most of the artillery behind and used the horses and camels to transport the 1,000 to 1,200 sick and wounded. The most serious cases were to be transported from Acre or Tentura to Jaffa and then by ship to Damietta. About one o'clock in the morning of 21 May, the army reached Haifa, where it made a short halt to evacuate the sick and wounded. General Doguereau described the scene that confronted him:

> Near there, on Mount Carmel, there was still a hospital of plague victims in a monastery. The lack of means of transportation, as well as the need not to encumber the army with men who had come down with a sickness so terrible and so contagious, meant that the order was given to leave them. Those who were not so weak that they could not drag themselves along, came down from the mountain, standing with great difficulty, and walked following the army until exhaustion and sickness made them succumb. A few fortunate enough to have donkeys followed the army and recovered along the way. Plague victims, fallen on the ground, their rucksacks on their backs, could be found along the route appealing to every person who went by for the means to continue to follow

the army and to not be abandoned. We often saw that heartrending spectacle.[7]

After Haifa the army continued its march, following the route next to the sea. In the afternoon of 21 May, the army arrived at Tantura, where another seven to eight hundred sick and wounded were awaiting evacuation. The problem was that Admiral Perrée, who was meant to meet the army there with a flotilla of ships to help transport the sick to Egypt, decided to sail back to France without so much as attempting to consult either Bonaparte or the government in Paris. Bonaparte was now faced with the arduous task of transporting the sick by land. On 22 May, he ordered them to be divided into three categories: those who could walk, those who could ride, and those who would have to be transported by litter. The animals were only to be used for the transportation of the ill. All those able to walk were to march on foot, including Bonaparte, who gave up his horse to set an example, although it is highly unlikely that many other officers did so, or that he even walked very far. Rumours went around that the English had offered to take the sick and wounded on board their vessels and to transport them to Alexandria but that Bonaparte had refused, out of pride, even to contemplate negotiations with them.[8] The rumour seems to have been false, but it was enough that the troops believed it.

The reality of the retreat bore little resemblance to the largely impracticable orders issued by Bonaparte. Many of the wounded, and those too weak to keep up with the bulk of the army, were killed along the way by local inhabitants and by Bedouins who harassed the army. Fortunately for Bonaparte, Djezzar stayed within Acre and did not pursue the French. If he had, it is doubtful that the army would have been able to hold off an attack for long. The retreat probably caused more losses to the army than the two months' fighting that had taken place until then. This is, one might say, almost normal. The decision to withdraw from enemy territory was made because the army was no longer in any shape to continue. Physically enfeebled by the hardships they had undergone and the lack of decent food and shelter, the troops had to extend themselves even further by forced marches, with scenes reminiscent of what was later to become the long retreat from Moscow in 1812. As was to be expected, there were acts of depraved callousness. 'I saw amputated officers,' wrote Bourrienne, 'whose transport had been ordered and for which money had been distributed to reward the effort, thrown from underneath stretchers. I saw the amputated, the wounded, the plague-ridden or those only suspected of it abandoned.'[9]

'For it has to be said,' commented one soldier, 'fear and individual egoism sowed victims along the route from St John of Acre to Salahieh . . . The soldiers abandoned along the way a host of people who could have been saved . . . Amid the sandy steppes, would a man fall exhausted from fatigue, dying of thirst or of necessity? "Another plague victim" his neighbours would cry out avoiding him with a kind of horror, and the unfortunate soul would stay on the desert floor, where he was to expire after a long agony, when often a glass of water or a drop of alcohol would be enough to cure him of his momentary weakness. Sometimes this strange terror would change character from the inhuman to the stupid and the burlesque. A poor horse whose master had been struck down by the plague was met with more than two hundred gunshots, the soldiers imagining that the animal carried the germ of contagion within it and that it was prudent to kill it.'[10]

There were also acts of tremendous courage. During the siege a cannon ball from an English vessel killed three sergeant majors, took both legs off another, and one leg off a quartermaster sergeant. During the incident, Sergeant François recalled that the brains of one of his closest friends were splattered all over his face. Despite the deprivations and the difficulties suffered by everyone during the retreat, François and some friends nevertheless managed to carry one of their wounded comrades to Egypt on a stretcher.[11]

There was no such mercy shown towards the inhabitants of Palestine. The countryside between Jaffa and St John of Acre was devastated in a scorched-earth policy as the French retreated. Kléber, who was given command of the rearguard, was ordered to destroy everything in his wake.[12] Not only were the peasants' flocks taken away and killed for food and the crops ruined – standard practice for any marauding army – but every village the troops entered was burnt to the ground and the villagers massacred. Bonaparte and those who took part in the massacres later tried to justify their behaviour, arguing that the villagers had murdered some Frenchmen during the siege operations.[13] This was true, but the murders were certainly isolated incidents. Others argued that the massacres were carried out to make further acts of resistance impossible, and to prevent the enemy following the army.[14] It is more than likely, though, that the French were taking out their defeat on the inhabitants,[15] and on the Bedouins who often decapitated sick stragglers within view of the French. '[Bedouin] ferocity', wrote Pierre Millet, 'was such that everywhere we carried the most terrible incendiaries wherever we went. The villages and the countryside ready to harvest, and the wheat that had already been cut, everything was reduced to ashes.'[16]

The army stopped at Jaffa on 24 May to rest before continuing its march. A few hundred sick and wounded were then evacuated by sea, but several hundred more were left behind to try and make it back by foot. The problem of the sick and wounded who could not be moved – between thirty and sixty depending on the sources – was solved by Bonaparte who, according to Bourrienne, walked briskly through the hospital striking the yellow top of his boot with a riding crop.[17] There was no stopping to touch or help the sick this time. The decision was probably made impulsively but, once made, Bonaparte's mind was set. The sick too weak to be moved were to be given an overdose of opium to put them out of their suffering. It was a mercy killing. Desgenettes, the doctor in charge, protested and eventually refused. A pharmacist by the name of Royer agreed to carry out Bonaparte's orders out of a feeling of humanity for the victims (his part in the poisoning became so well known that he was stigmatized, forced to remain in Cairo after the departure of the French, and was later arrested and killed by the Turks). It seems, however, that the sick were not given a big enough dose – perhaps deliberately by Royer – and that they vomited the opium. When the British, and Sir Sidney Smith, arrived at Jaffa on 30 May and found seven men who had survived both the plague and the opium overdose, the veil of secrecy with which Bonaparte tried to shroud the incident was torn to shreds.[18] The news soon hit the press in

England, where it remained a popular anti-Bonaparte story for the duration of the Napoleonic Empire.

On 28 May, the defences surrounding Jaffa were destroyed by mines that had been prepared especially for that purpose before the army continued its march on to Gaza. Kléber's division formed the rearguard. By 30 May the army had reached Gaza, where it spent twenty-four hours recuperating. During that time, Bonaparte either evacuated or destroyed the provisions that had been stored in that town and, as with Jaffa, blew up the fortifications. Measures were then taken to ensure that the army had enough provisions and transport for the desert crossing that would lead them back to Egypt. The march, which began on the 31st, was relatively short. Much more difficult was the march that took place on 1 June when a long stretch between Khan-Younes and El Arish was crossed. 'The army was so exhausted, that it formed a long queue, many troops strayed in the desert and we had to fire several cannon shot near the wells where we halted to give direction to the lost.'[19] This particular phase of the return was considered one of the worst of the campaign. The road was littered in many places with the bodies of plague victims who, unable to keep up, were killed by Arabs.

On reaching El Arish, Bonaparte left a strong contingent of troops; it was to be the furthest outpost of the French in Egypt. The army was allowed to rest one day before continuing. Another two days were needed to cross the desert and to reach Katia before making a 'triumphal' entry into Cairo. On the journey between Katia and Cairo, which took about ten days, thirst and the heat once again proved to be the biggest problems. On 11 June, 'the heat was so excessive, that, given the lack of water and the weariness, we could hardly keep ourselves up. We saw several men faint: minutes became hours to those whose thirst made itself felt so keenly. We saw soldiers pierce a skin water-bag that was on a general's camel to quench their thirst.' Now and again, those who could no longer bear the suffering simply put an end to their torment by committing suicide, while those who managed to fight their way to drink a few drops of brackish water from the wells along the way caught dysentery. 'The water was so purgative that we felt its violent effects, for a few moments after having drunk it, we passed stools which weakened us so much that we could hardly keep on our legs.'[20]

Nevertheless, the majority of the troops managed to reach Cairo. The surviving troops had, of course, lost most of their equipment during the forced marches, and many were barefoot. Of the 13,000 men who had originally set out for Syria, only 8,000 were in reasonably good health and, refitted in brand new boots and uniforms, were selected to take part in the triumphal entry staged by Bonaparte with the active participation of the *diwan*, ordered to welcome them like heroes. The entry into Cairo was thus transformed into a military parade, as though a victorious army were returning home. They entered through the gate of Bab el-Nasr (the Gate of Victory) on 14 June as palm leaves were strewn on their path and a palm frond was put in every soldier's hat.[21] For the troops, the return to Cairo obviously elicited very different emotions from those they had felt when they first set eyes on it.

> We finally arrived in the great Cairo! What a sight! What joy! What rapture! What emotion! What effusions of the heart! What electrification! What palpitations! A host of the most pleasant ideas succeeded each other in our minds. We could have been in a new world judging by the agreeable sights that were offered to us. A huge crowd of people pressed along our path. Pashas, *sheikhs*, judges, Mamelukes, Janissaries and Frenchmen of all grades and all employments, to the sound of war-like music, went to a place called the Coubee. The general-in-chief, in dress uniform, preceded by his general staff, made the army march past him; the artillery salvoes were repeated and passed through the town in good order.[22]

The parade went on for five hours: as the troops passed through Bab el-Nasr, they would exit through another gate and eventually rejoin the march past. It was, moreover, a reaffirmation of the existence of Bonaparte, as it had been rumoured that he had been killed before Acre.

Thus ended the expedition to Syria. It had lasted four months and fourteen days. Although the triumphant entry into Cairo was meant to hide the defeat, no one was duped.[23] The expedition, in fact, greatly reduced Bonaparte's prestige among the people of Egypt, and marked the limit of Bonaparte's territorial conquests in the Middle East. The Muslim world undoubtedly and correctly interpreted Bonaparte's retreat from Syria as a French defeat. The capitulation of El Arish, the assault on Jaffa, the extension of the expedition to Nazareth – all of these events only assumed importance once back in France, when the myth-makers were able to get to work. Bonaparte presented the retreat not as having been forced by the French army's inability to overcome Acre, but determined by his will. The declarations he made, however, were not given much credence by the peoples of Egypt.[24]

Not only had the prestige of the Army of the Orient been affected, but the losses due to sickness and combat were irreparable. Over 2,200 had died, almost half of whom had succumbed to the plague, but another 2,300 were seriously ill or wounded, of whom about 100 were amputees and were therefore definitively out of action. In other words, more than a third of the army that had entered Syria were dead or disabled. The impact of the plague on these figures should not be overestimated: far fewer died from it than the victims of dysentery or what was called 'Egyptian ophthalmia' (conjunctivitis).[25] The army, which had been in Egypt a year, had been reduced through sickness and war to less than half its size. The rest had little hope of returning home. It was the elite who had died giving assault to Jaffa and St John of Acre, losses that could not be replaced as long as the British controlled the seas. Moreover, the army had suffered significant losses in *matériel*: artillery, horses, and supplies of all kinds that were either destroyed or left behind because of lack of transport. The navy, too, had seen its numbers diminish in the attempt to keep the army supplied.

A distinct characteristic of the campaign was that nothing had really been planned; the preparations for the expedition were hasty and ill-conceived. Despite the fact that Bonaparte had been thinking about invading Syria for some time, and that he had even written out some preliminary orders, it was only after his return from Suez that the preparations really started. One month later, the army was still lacking in the necessary supplies and transport and was often able to get out of critical situations only through a conjunction of favourable circumstances, such as the prompt capitulation of El Arish, the abandoned supplies found at Gaza, Ramle and Jaffa, and the general quality of the troops and their officers. Kléber noted in his pocket diary that Bonaparte never fixed on a plan and that everything went by fits and starts. 'Each day's business is transacted according to the needs of the day. He claims to believe in fate.'[26] Kléber's criticism is blunt and to the point. Although he admired Bonaparte's military genius and daring, Kléber believed that he was incapable of organizing and administering efficiently and that, since he insisted on doing everything himself, there were waste and deficiencies everywhere.

André Dutertre, *'Jean-Baptiste Kléber,'* circa 1798. Kléber succeeded Bonaparte as commander-in-chief when he left Egypt, but he was to die at the hands of an assassin, who was immediately captured and suffered a horrible death. After being tortured, the assassin was impaled. (*Courtesy of Photo RMN –* © *Gérard Blot*)

Bonaparte could not seriously think of occupying Syria for any length of time or of undertaking any new conquests. The almost immediate return to Egypt was necessary in order to protect the nascent colony against the possibility, ever present, of an Allied landing. Any victory in Egypt or Syria was a victory with no future. The day would inevitably come when, exhausted from war, cut off from communicating with the outside world, the French army would have to capitulate. The Directory, in any event, had decided to abandon any idea of reinforcing the Army of the Orient and to recall it to Europe. Instructions to Bonaparte to this effect were sent on 26 May 1799, underlining the fact, however, that the decision was his.[27] The instructions never reached him. Indeed, as he was completely cut off from Europe, none of the official messengers sent by the Directory succeeded in getting to Bonaparte. He had to make decisions based on the information to hand.

Aboukir: Defeat Atoned

Immediately after his return to Cairo, Bonaparte started to reorganize the army: hospitals and fortifications were inspected; mobile columns were formed in the provinces; companies of scouts were formed to carry out skirmishes; artillery was assigned to the infantry battalions; and the naval units were dissolved and amalgamated with the army.[28] Bonaparte even considered buying slaves from the Sudan in order to fill the gaps caused by the French losses. He also gave the order to fit out two frigates, the *Muiron* and the *Carrère*, in the port of Alexandria.

Apart from the reorganization of the army, the reaffirmation of the French presence meant, in real terms, an increase in repressive measures against the civilian population. All the Magrebins who had come to Egypt in response to the jihad against the French were condemned to death, as were Mamelukes who had re-entered Cairo without permission. Between 19 and 22 June, Bonaparte ordered thirty-two prisoners held in the citadel to be shot by firing squad, although General Dugua asked permission to replace the firing squads with decapitation in order to save munitions. He was also responsible for the deaths of a large number of prostitutes, possibly hundreds, who had spread venereal diseases among the soldiers; they were decapitated and their bodies sewn up in sacks and thrown in the Nile under the pretext of Islamic law that forbade intercourse with the infidel.[29]

Despite the repression, Bonaparte had every intention of returning to France with his 'prestige' intact. At a meeting of the Institute of Egypt on 4 July 1799, he ordered a study on the plague, probably in order to impute the failure of the Syrian campaign to the disease. He was particularly aggressive towards the medical personnel, which provoked the indignation of the chief medical officer, Desgenettes, and a vehement confrontation ensued. There had already been friction between Bonaparte and Desgenettes over the order to deny publicly the contagious nature of the plague and over the opium poisonings. Bonaparte now wanted the disease the 'charlatan' Desgenettes had refused to recognize officially confirmed. In other words, Bonaparte was indirectly blaming Desgenettes for the failure of the expedition to Syria.[30]

By July, Bonaparte's men blamed him for everything: the lack of organization, the lack of supplies, the casualness with which he had thrown his men into attack after attack against the walls of Acre, and even the plague. The troops had grumbled ever since arriving in Egypt, and, on one occasion at least, mutiny was in the air,[31] but now the commander-in-chief was booed, insulted, and even threatened by his men when he appeared among them in public.[32]

Bonaparte had one last battle to fight before he returned home. The Ottoman fleet consisting of five Turkish battleships, three frigates and fifty to sixty transports anchored off Alexandria on 11 July 1799, but did not start disembarking at Aboukir until 14 July. There were no more than 300 French soldiers to greet them behind mediocre entrenchments under the command of Major Godard. It nevertheless took the Ottoman army three days to overcome the small French garrison.

On his return from Syria, Bonaparte had declared that his campaign had destroyed or dispersed the troops that had been assembled for a Turkish offensive against him. The appearance of a Turkish fleet off Aboukir six weeks after Bonaparte had returned put the lie to the alleged success of his preventive campaign. The

Turks, it was evident, had not been defeated to the point where they could no longer mount an offensive against the French. It reinforced the impression the Egyptians had always maintained of their Turkish masters, that they had the power necessary to defeat the infidel. Faced with the arrival of a Turkish fleet off the coast and the danger of a Turkish invasion, a second threat appeared and, with it, the risk of another revolt by the local population.

As soon as Bonaparte received news of the Ottoman landing on 15 July, he gave orders for the mobile columns to march to Rahmaniya.[33] At the same time, he decided to concentrate the bulk of his forces dispersed throughout the country, including those stationed in Upper Egypt. The quicker victory was obtained the less the absence of the French in the interior of the country would be felt. A long campaign would have been detrimental to the French presence in Egypt because, even if the campaign was successful, it would have brought about the need to reconquer the country. In order to try to maintain his presence in Cairo, Bonaparte wrote another flamboyant proclamation in which he portrayed himself as the hero chosen by God to defend Islam against the (Trinitarian) Christians. Bonaparte was thus in the curious position of posing as the defender of Islam against the Muslim invaders. It was a kind of Islamic exegesis: 'In his wisdom,' Bonaparte declared, '[God] has decided that I will come in order to change the face of Egypt and to replace a devastating regime with a regime based on order and justice. He is thus giving a mark of his power, for what those who believe in three gods have never been able to do, we have done, we who believe in one [God] that governs nature and the universe.'[34]

The battle of Aboukir was a race against time in which the professionalism of the French army, in spite of the troops' disaffection with their commander, came to the fore. The concentration of Bonaparte's forces took place at Rahmaniya between 19 and 21 July. The next day the army took up position at Berket Ghitas, halfway between Alexandria and Rosetta, as Bonaparte did not know which town the Ottoman army intended marching on. The 24th was spent in approaching the enemy positions. Bonaparte had fewer than 10,000 men and a relatively strong cavalry of about 4,000; the Ottoman army was slightly numerically superior with an estimated 12–15,000 men.[35] But the Ottoman forces lacked audacity; instead of advancing on Rosetta, which would have cut off Alexandria and could very well have provoked a general uprising, they preferred to dig in and await the French attack.

The attack came at sunrise on 25 July. Bonaparte took an enormous risk: rather than wait for the enemy in squares, which until then had always proved impregnable, he decided to attack. With only 1,000 cavalry, Murat launched what is considered to be one of the most brilliant charges of his career. The attack was immediately exploited by the French infantry, so successfully that the battle served as a model in the Napoleonic wars to follow. Traditionally, the cavalry played a secondary role either before the battle, or afterwards in order to sweep down on an enemy already in flight. The cavalry charge was not commonly used in Europe. In Egypt, however, Murat was so impressed by the cavalry charges of the Mamelukes that he decided to emulate them. The result was that panic swept through the ranks of the Ottoman army and, in their hurry to flee, thousands drowned in the sea. Murat managed to capture Mustafa Pasha but there were still 3,000 Ottomans entrenched in the fort of Aboukir. After a siege that lasted until 2 August, they were forced, through exhaustion and thirst, to give themselves up.

Aboukir gave the French a few months' respite. The 'invasion' season in Egypt was relatively short. In winter, the seas were too rough to attempt a landing and, after August, the swelling of the Nile made travelling in the interior of the country virtually impossible. But the battle did little to resolve the dilemma in which Bonaparte now found himself.

The Flight from Egypt

Predictably, one of the first things that Bonaparte did after the battle was to send a messenger back to France to announce his 'brilliant' victory.[36] This time, the message got through as the ship arrived at Marseilles on 25 September. The effect that Bonaparte was looking for occurred: St John of Acre was forgotten, and the name of the conqueror again became synonymous with victory.

With this battle won, nothing further was keeping Bonaparte in Egypt. Sir Sidney Smith, who was now sailing off the coast of Egypt, considered the defence of the colonial empire in India to be more important than the revolutionary wars being fought out on European soil.[37] Accordingly, Smith believed that Bonaparte should be allowed to leave Egypt and, on 2 August, he sent his secretary, John Keith, to open up negotiations for an exchange of prisoners in Alexandria. General Menou, who commanded the French forces in the area, got negotiations under way. Menou's aide-de-camp, Merlin, wrote that, on 2 August, newspapers – the *Gazette de Francfort* and the *Courrier de Londres* – were given to the French to inform them of the situation in Europe. These newspapers were sent on to Alexandria by Merlin and then sent on to Bonaparte, who read them during the night of 2–3 August. The newspapers outlined the French defeats in Italy and Switzerland (which had taken place back in March 1799). Bonaparte locked himself away for four hours with Berthier to read the gazettes and talk over the situation. At the end of this time, the decision to return to France was definitively made,[38] though, as we have seen, Bonaparte had been contemplating this for some time. The news from France was the pretext he needed to abandon his men.

Bonaparte knew, through the exchange of prisoners, that the British were running short of supplies and water, and that they would shortly have to return to Cyprus to restock. He thus waited for the departure of the British ships blockading Alexandria (which took place on 12 August), before attempting his flight. As soon as he was informed of the British departure, he made a few last-minute preparations and, on the evening of 18 August, left Cairo on the excuse of a tour of inspection of Lower Egypt. It did not prevent rumours of his departure for Europe circulating almost as soon as he left. General Dugua, who was left in charge of Cairo, felt obliged to threaten anyone caught spreading the rumour with imprisonment.[39] Kléber, who was to succeed Bonaparte as general-in-chief, was summoned for an urgent interview, which was to take place at Rosetta on 24 August. But when Bonaparte arrived at the wells of Beydah, about fourteen kilometres from Alexandria, he and his entourage suddenly veered left and headed for the sea. It may be that he did not have the courage to confront Kléber, and who would in the circumstances? He was abandoning his army. Bonaparte had just enough time to inform Menou and to give him letters addressed to Kléber.

At Alexandria, on the night of the embarkation on 22 August, tensions played havoc with the nerves of those who were waiting to leave. Denon, who was with Lannes, Murat and Marmont, recalled: 'we understood each other without speaking; we could do nothing to while away the time. Time and again, we found ourselves back at the same window, observing the sea, questioning the movement of the smallest boat,' until finally, at one o'clock in the morning, Menou came to tell them that Bonaparte was waiting for them.[40] Junot and Desaix were to join him later. The embarkation took place in a less than dignified manner. 'Although we were on the shore for half an hour,' Antoine-François Merlin, recalled,

> the longboats had not yet arrived, and at the risk of waking the town, we were obliged to set off detonations to warn them of our arrival and to indicate the place where we were waiting for them. They finally replied to the signal without which they would not have found us for a long time and with the greatest difficulty, so black was the night. Once the longboats arrived, each of us, without distinction of rank or title, hurried to get on board that we got into the water up to our knees so great was our impatience, and so much did we fear being left behind. It was every man for himself to get on board the *Muiron* and we jostled each other with little care or consideration.[41]

At sunrise the next day, the little French fleet consisting of two frigates, the *Carrère* and the *Muiron*, and two sloops commanded by Vice-Admiral Ganteaume, took to the sea off the Egyptian coast.

The troops Bonaparte left behind learned of his desertion a few days later, and it aroused a good deal of anger.[42] Kléber was furious and had good reason to be: Bonaparte had left him with a country that was barely pacified; there would doubtless be further invasions to face, with an army that had been greatly reduced since its arrival.[43] General Dugua also justifiably felt himself to have been badly treated by Bonaparte – at sixty he had left his family, forsaken a new career as a deputy, and had come to Egypt on Bonaparte's request – and complained that they had been abandoned, 'without money, without powder, without shot, and a part of the troops without arms'.[44] Once the shock of Bonaparte's behaviour passed, however, they do not seem to have regretted his absence.[45] It was generally believed that, as long as Bonaparte remained in Egypt, there would be no negotiations with the English for their return, while the choice of Kléber as his successor was universally approved.[46]

Bonaparte's objectives in sailing to the Orient had been achieved. The romantic nature of the adventure, not necessarily the success or failure of his mission, was meant to lend prestige and glory to his name. In spite of the setbacks, there were any number of victories he could point to as proof of the 'success' of the mission. If Bonaparte decided to abandon his troops and slip back to France, it was because there was not much more that could be done other than sail on to India, which seems unlikely ever to have been his intention. Too much has been made of the fact that Bonaparte abandoned his troops in Egypt to their fate. He was certainly not the first revolutionary general to take leave of his command without permission. Jourdan, for example, deserted his army in the middle of the campaign in Germany and Switzerland 'for health reasons' in 1799. The flight from Egypt, then, was not only a desperate attempt to get out of an impasse; it was also a conscious decision to make a clean break and return to a new set of circumstances and a new set of opportunities. Moreover, the man who sailed back across the Mediterranean had changed considerably. His contempt for humanity, already present before he left France, had been strengthened by his experiences in Egypt and Syria. He now seemed to be possessed of a cynicism that would grow over the coming years as his own warped philosophy of life continued to develop. When Josephine saw him again, after sixteen months, she came away with the impression that Egypt had changed him; he had become, in his own words, 'truly egoist'.[47] The religious rhetoric characteristic of Bonaparte's proclamations in Egypt, meant for the consumption of the local population, may truly have played on his psyche, to the point where he believed that he had become the instrument of God, that is, of Fate or Destiny. We shall see the rhetoric unexpectedly reappear during his bid to take power in France. For the moment, Bonaparte had seen Rousseau's noble savage, and it had turned out to be a dog.[48]

SEIZING POWER, 1799

20

The Return of the Saviour

Like an 'Electric Shock'

On 6 October 1799, a messenger from the Directory entered the Council of Five Hundred. A secretary opened the message and read the contents out aloud. The Directory had just received a dispatch from General Bonaparte. As soon as the name Bonaparte was mentioned, cries of 'Vive la République' interrupted the reader. He continued – Bonaparte, returning to Egypt with his troops, had thrown back a Turkish army 18,000-strong at Aboukir. The name associated with the French naval disaster was thus transformed into a victory by a letter that was already two months old.[1] After the message was read a second time, the deputies spontaneously broke out into the revolutionary song 'Ça Ira'.[2] The Egyptian expedition, instead of plunging Bonaparte into obscurity, had made his reputation even greater than before.

Five days later, in the early afternoon, cannon fire from several places in Paris announced that Bonaparte had landed in France. A rumour announcing his arrival spread throughout the capital, greeted first with astonishment, then with a general explosion of joy.[3] The revolutionary songwriter Pierre-Jean de Béranger was with a group of people when news of Bonaparte's arrival came. 'Everyone got up spontaneously and gave a long cry of joy.'[4] By eight o'clock that evening, people were running through the gardens of the Palais Royal crying out 'General Bonaparte has landed at Fréjus!' The theatres had to interrupt their performances so that the audience could sing patriotic hymns. Antoine Thibaudeau, who was to rally to Bonaparte but who disapproved of the Empire, was at the Théâtre Français when news arrived of the landing: 'It was as though an electric shock had passed through the room. No one paid any attention to the show. People went from box to box, came out, entered, ran, unable to remain in one place . . . on every face, in every conversation, was written the hope of salvation and the presentiment of happiness.'[5] Military bands, on impulse, spilled out of their barracks on to the streets, filling the districts of Paris with martial music. The taverns stayed open and filled with workers drinking toasts to the 'return'. Rumour had it that Baudin des Ardennes, a leading Thermidorian and a member of the Institute was so overwhelmed with joy on hearing of Bonaparte's return that he died the next day of an apoplectic fit.[6].

The next day, when the news was confirmed, there were more spontaneous demonstrations. 'The expressions of universal joy', wrote one journalist in the *Gazette de France*, 'caused by the return

Artist unknown, *Débarquement du général Buonaparte a Fréjus, près Toulon* (Landing of General Buonaparte at Fréjus, near Toulon), circa 1799. (*Bibliothèque nationale, Paris*)

of this general are never ending.'[7] Indeed, it looked as though the whole country was in the grip of Bonaparte fever, kindled, in part, by the couriers that preceded Bonaparte's carriage, announcing his arrival from village to village.

Popular demonstrations were repeated all along the route of Bonaparte's journey, his triumphal procession on the way to Paris. 'At Avignon', wrote General Boulart,

> the crowd was enormous. At the sight of the great man, the air echoed with acclamations and shouts of 'Vive Bonaparte!' and this crowd, and that shout, accompanied him right up to the hotel where he put up. It was an electrifying scene . . . It was the first time I saw that extraordinary being. I contemplated him with a sort of voracity; I was in an ecstatic state. I didn't think he resembled the portraits I had seen of him. As early as that time, he was seen as being called to save France from the crisis into which the pitiful government of the Directory and the setbacks suffered by our armies had thrown it.[8]

At Aix, 'the entire city' turned out to greet the general as he passed through. Someone supposedly called out from the crowd: 'I don't need anything any more; Bonaparte is with us!'[9] Peasants from the Basses-Alpes escorted Bonaparte during the night by torchlight to protect him from brigands, who were rife in the region (this did not prevent his baggage being stolen near Aix). In his memoirs, Marbot, who was a simple hussar in 1798 but who would later become a general and baron of the Empire, recounts how he and his father encountered Bonaparte at Lyons.

> All the houses were lit and decked out with flags, guns were shot into the air, the crowds filled the streets to the point of preventing our carriage from advancing. People were dancing in the public squares, and the air echoed with the cry of 'Long live Bonaparte who has come to save the *patrie*!' The closer we got, the more the popular tide became compact and, on arriving at the door, we saw that it was covered by lanterns and guarded by a battalion of grenadiers. It was where General Bonaparte was staying.[10]

Marbot was, in fact, quite shocked to see the people 'run before Bonaparte as if he were already sovereign of France'. It summed up the problem facing Bonaparte – how to convince diehard republicans to accept him as the 'saviour'.

Bonaparte decided to stay in Lyons a while in order to receive the local authorities, as if he were already on an official tour of the country. We do not know whether Bonaparte was surprised by the popular reception he received, but he seemed to take everything in his stride. Within eighteen hours, a play was hastily written and improvised in his honour – *The Return of the Hero or Bonaparte at Lyons* – at the Théâtre des Célestins, where the actors read, or rather stammered out, their roles, holding their parts in their hands, intimidated by the presence of the man himself (13 October 1799). Invited to the theatre to see it performed, he affected humility, remaining at the back of his box while he pushed his aide-de-camp, Michel Duroc, to the front. Only when the crowd began chanting 'Bonaparte!' did he condescend to take his place in full view of the auditorium.[11]

'The Man Who Would Save France'

This unparalleled outburst of popular enthusiasm has to be placed in context.

Despite the treaty of Campo Formio (some historians argue because of it), peace had not settled over the Continent.[12] We have seen how both France and Austria considered the treaty to be little more than a truce. While the Austrians remained at home licking their wounds, the French continued their aggressive expansion into northern and south-eastern Europe. The Directory, in part dependent on the army for its survival, seems to have had little control over its generals in the field, and was often obliged to become the accomplice of conquest and annexation. The Dutch Republic was annexed and re-named the Batavian Republic in April 1798; Switzerland was incorporated into French territory and named the Helvetic Republic that same month; while, in the south of Italy, the Roman Republic was created out of parts of papal territory in February 1798, and the

Parthenopean Republic was formed in January 1799 out of the former Kingdom of Naples. Finally, in December 1798, the King of Piedmont, Charles Emmanuel IV (his father, Victor Amadeus III, died in October 1796), was forced to abdicate his territories on the Italian mainland (that is, Piedmont), and withdraw to the island of Sardinia.

All of this was enough to upset Austria and Britain, but the Russians, under Tsar Paul I, also looked upon these developments with concern. Paul I, who acceded to the throne at the end of 1796 after the death of his mother, Catherine the Great, was at first determined to pursue a policy of peace; he did not want to get involved in the war. He was a profoundly ideological and unpredictable man, however, and was not only offended when Bonaparte occupied the island of Malta – he was the protector of the Knights of St John – but was particularly sensitive to any interference in what he considered part of Russia's economic sphere – the eastern Mediterranean.[13] When a large fleet sailed from Toulon heading east, the Russians interpreted this as a direct threat against them.[14] Just as worrying were developments in Germany. When Bonaparte drove into Rastatt at the end of November 1797, and announced that France would be taking the left bank of the Rhine, it was obvious that the days of the Holy Roman Empire were numbered. And yet Russia, which had been a formal guarantor of the status quo in Germany for the last twenty-odd years, had not even been consulted. In short, Bonaparte's actions in the Middle East largely contributed to the creation of the Second Coalition, although few contemporaries would have made the connection.

The Tsar was therefore forced into a coalition against France, which would eventually include Britain (it had continued fighting alone since the end of the First Coalition), Austria (only too keen to get back at France after its previous defeats), the Ottoman Empire (since France had invaded Egypt), Naples (after being invaded in 1798) and Portugal (persuaded by British money to join). While Bonaparte was away 'civilizing' Egypt, revolutionary France was attacked by this new Second Coalition, or, it would be more accurate to say, France attacked the new coalition formed against it. Initial gains resulted from French offensives in Germany and Switzerland, but the French advantage did not last. In Germany, Archduke Charles defeated General Jourdan in two pitched battles (Ostrach and Stokach) in March. Jourdan resigned from his post and joined the opposition in the Council of Five Hundred while his army slowly disintegrated as it headed back across the Rhine. A similar scenario was played out in Switzerland, where initial French gains (under Moreau) were lost to a combined Austro-Russian army under the command of a flamboyant, coarse and aggressive (despite his seventy years) Russian general, Count Alexander Suvarov. In June 1799, a combined Anglo-Russian expeditionary force landed in Holland. In Italy, the Directory placed General Barthélemy Schérer back in control, where he outdid himself by losing Bonaparte's hard-fought gains in less than two months. Soon, the only foothold the French had in northern Italy was the city of Genoa. Moreover, the French position was made all the more tenuous by local populations who revolted in Tuscany, Lombardy and Piedmont, in what were known as the 'Viva Maria' riots (inspired by what local peasants thought was the apparition of the Virgin).[15] There were also revolts in the south of Italy: in Calabria, where a 'Christian Army' swept through the region; in Luxembourg and Belgium, where the 'Cudgel War' and the 'Peasants' War' (as they were respectively called) raged. In France, local revolts flared in the Massif Central, the Midi, the Pyrenees, Brittany and also the west of France, often as a reaction to conscription but also involving religious and ethnic issues.

The situation for the French government thus looked precarious to say the least. If the Republic survived, it had a good deal to do with the Allies' poor co-ordination and lack of co-operation, but it was also because the crisis at the front resulted in a neo-Jacobin revival at home. One consequence of this, and of the Directory's inability to resolve the country's military and economic problems, was another coup – the Coup of Prairial. In June 1799, three directors – La Révellière-Lépeaux, Merlin de Douai and Treilhard – were accused by Lucien Bonaparte of corruption, poor leadership and tyrannical actions, and were forced to resign under threat of prosecution. The Jacobins reinvigorated the war effort by introducing two new draconian laws spearheaded by the new minister of war, General Bernadotte. The first, the Law of Hostages, introduced in July, allowed for the internment of émigrés' relatives, supposedly as a deterrent to the assassination of local republicans, but essentially aimed at the sympathizers of the counter-revolution in the west of France. The second, introduced in August, was a forced loan from the rich to fill the coffers of the empty treasury, which succeeded in raising 100 million francs. These two measures, combined with the Jourdan Law – a massive call-up of men that resulted in more than 400,000 fresh troops – helped turn the situation around.

By the time news of the battle of Aboukir arrived in France at the beginning of October 1799, the French armies were gaining the upper hand. The Anglo-Russian force in Holland was defeated by Brune on 19 September; Masséna won a battle in Switzerland against the Russian forces under General Suvarov on 29 September. Moreover, the Directory eventually managed to contain the revolts inside France.[16] Only a week before Bonaparte landed in France, the Prussian ambassador in Paris was able to write home to Berlin to say, 'We have not seen a more perfect calm reign here for a long time', and he went on to say that the military victories had transformed the government into an imposing force.[17] Rightly or wrongly, however, the Directory was held responsible for France's internal and external military predicament. It is hardly surprising, therefore, that when news of Bonaparte's sudden arrival reached the army, as in Switzerland, for example, 'everyone saw in Bonaparte the man who would save France and end the Revolution'.[18] For the people of south and south-east France, who, outside Paris, seem to have been the most enthusiastic about Bonaparte's return, their response may have been prompted by the threat they felt at the recent invasion of northern Italy in 1798–9 by coalition armies. They saw in Bonaparte someone who could cross the Alps and contain the danger.[19] For the people of Paris, it may have been a kind of nostalgia for a time when Bonaparte's name and victory in Italy were indissolubly associated. He was mentioned in the cafés of Paris as early as April – five months before his return – as

someone who could straighten out the disastrous military situation and stand up to a general like Austria's Archduke Charles.[20]
One should not forget, either, that, during the Italian campaign,
Bonaparte had presented himself as a man of providence who
had given France peace: the memory of Campo Formio was still
present in people's minds.

In Italy poets had alluded to Bonaparte as the 'saviour' during
the early stages of the campaign. One anonymous acclamation,
for example, read: 'I praise this hero, child of Italy. Who, having
become French, has saved his *patrie*.'[21] Pro-Bonapartist newspapers constantly referred to him as the 'preserver of liberty',
while writers lauded him as the Caesar that France needed and
had found.[22] The saviour image was maintained during Bonaparte's absence in Egypt and Syria, thanks to both Louis and
Lucien, who published flattering articles about their brother in
Paris (Louis left Egypt in October 1798). Pamphlets had also
appeared calling for Bonaparte to be 'repatriated' from Egypt to
save the Republic from the 'clique' that had brought about the
loss of his conquests in Italy.[23] Only a few days before the
Coup of Prairial was carried out, a pamphlet appeared entitled,
'On Bonaparte, conversations between a soldier, a royalist and a
man of leisure', listing all the benefits that Bonaparte had already
brought France: glory to French arms, an end to factional
infighting, and peace to the nation. These, it argued, had all
been squandered by the politicians of the Directory, the implication being that only Bonaparte could restore them.[24] Similarly, Antoine Arnault wrote a number of inflammatory articles
highlighting Bonaparte and presenting him as the only man
capable of saving the Republic.[25] Pamphlets like these were
supplemented by a host of poems and songs that appeared
in the Parisian press after Bonaparte's return from Egypt.[26]
We do not know whether they were actually commissioned
by Bonaparte and his clique or whether they were spontaneously
written by pro-Bonaparte journalists. Almost certainly, though,
such literature prepared the ground for public acceptance
of the impending coup and singled Bonaparte out as the
obvious alternative.

Bonaparte was kept in the public eye in two other ways. The first was the procession of the Feast of Liberty. When news of the fall of Malta reached Paris, after Bonaparte had already landed in Egypt, the Directory decided to put on a festival that was one of the most original in a long line of odd republican ceremonies.[27] It was the triumphal entry into Paris, on a rainy day in July (in fact, on the 27th, the fourth anniversary of the fall of Robespierre), of the art objects looted by Bonaparte during the Italian campaign. A huge procession wound its way through the streets of Paris from the Jardin des Plantes to the Champ de Mars, where it was paraded in front of the directors, standing before an altar dedicated to the *patrie*. Throughout the ceremony, Bonaparte's name was not mentioned once, but his spirit hovered over the event. People could not possibly have failed to make the connection between Bonaparte, the victorious Army of Italy, and the art works paraded before them.[28]

Bonaparte was also kept in the public eye by the official reports he penned himself from Egypt and Syria, and which every now and then got through the British blockade (sometimes overland by way of Constantinople and Vienna). Even if months late, the news always reported victories of one kind or another. The French public knew, for example, that Bonaparte had taken Malta, that he had landed in Egypt, taken Alexandria, fought and won a battle before the pyramids, taken Cairo, and that he had set out into Syria.[29] The Directory even celebrated the army's entry into Alexandria more than two months after it actually occurred.[30] A number of engravings relating to the expedition circulated in France highlighting events such as the Battle of the Pyramids.[31] Journalists paid by the Bonaparte family also manipulated the news so that the Battle of the Nile was reported as an unfortunate event, an accident along the glorious path that was Bonaparte's, a minor victory for the British but not comparable to the taking of Malta in strategic importance. The Revolt of Cairo was also reported and played down. So, too, was the abandonment of the siege of St John of Acre, described as 'a tactical manoeuvre'; instead, Bonaparte had chosen to return to Egypt to prevent a landing of hostile Turkish forces. Besides, if the victory of Aboukir did not overshadow the suffering and misery caused by the plague, the blame for the defeats could be thrown squarely at the feet of the Directory.

A decided shift had taken place in the way Bonaparte's military victories were portrayed. In contrast to Italy, where there was often talk of the heroic feats of the army and of individuals within it, in Egypt there was almost no mention of the Army of the Orient. The Army of the Orient had become Bonaparte's army, the instrument of his ambition, an impression reinforced by the serialization of Berthier's *Relation de l'Expédition d'Egypte*, glorifying the commander of the Army of the Orient.[32] Even Bonaparte broke with the style he had developed in Italy, where he had tended to understate his own role in comparison with that of his men, and he now used the first person pronoun.[33] Thus, in his account of the taking of Alexandria, the public in France read that 'I marched all night', and 'I attacked Alexandria', or 'I was master of Rosetta'.[34] His army had been pushed into the background and, in its place, now there stood only one man, its commander-in-chief.

This trend can also be seen, to a lesser extent, in the imagery surrounding Egypt. Contrary to the Italian campaign, where more than 500 images were produced, very little visual representation of the Egyptian campaign was forthcoming, for the obvious reason of distance, and the rupture of communications with France after the Battle of the Nile.[35] But here, too, the few images that were produced during the campaign were all popular images that, curiously, since he was away on campaign, presented Bonaparte as a man of peace rather than as a warrior. There are several versions of the taking of Alexandria and of Cairo (the two illustrations here were printed in Augsburg), which emphasize the harmonious coming together of two civilizations as Bonaparte receives the keys from these two towns. In the case of Alexandria, fighting is still going on, but only in the background. In Cairo, there appears to be utter harmony against a backdrop of completely imaginary images of non-existent monuments. Given the lack of actual news, popular images such as these were portraying Bonaparte as bringing peace to peoples far away. The public had to wait until Bonaparte's return before visual representations of the expedition became more freely available.

Artist unknown, *Alexandria resa ai Franchi in Agosto, 1798* (Surrender of Alexandria to the French in August 1798), circa 1798. (*Bibliothèque nationale, Paris*)

When information was lacking, as was the case after the Battle of the Nile, journalists did what they always do in such a case: they speculated.[36] Newspapers published articles on what they thought was happening in Egypt, some conjecturing that Bonaparte was planning to attack the English in India (this was probably put around by the Bonaparte brothers in Paris),[37] while Volney wrote a series of articles for the *Moniteur universel* describing, predicting and developing 'the true situation, the probable tactics, the ideas, the administration and the fate of Bonaparte'.[38] At one stage, the *Journal des Hommes Libres* reported that Bonaparte, at the head of 200,000 troops, was only eighty-five leagues from Constantinople.[39]

In the face of such reports, any news of defeat and failure that might have slipped through could simply be discounted as the product of the enemy propaganda.[40] The general impression that Bonaparte was victorious was reinforced by the sudden arrival of news of the Battle of Aboukir in October 1799, shortly before Bonaparte's return to France. The first of Bonaparte's dispatches on the battle was made public on 6 October simultaneously in a

Artist unknown, *Cairo resa ai Republicani in Agosto 1798* (Surrender of
Cairo to the Republicans in August 1798), circa 1798. (*Bibliothèque
nationale, Paris*)

number of papers: the *Moniteur*, the *Journal des Hommes Libres*,
the *Clef du Cabinet* and the *Ami des Lois*. The next day, Bonaparte's proclamation to the Army of the Orient following the
retreat from Syria was published, but, in the popular imagination,
the victory at Aboukir somehow transformed the disastrous defeat
at St John of Acre.[41] These reports dominated the press in the week
preceding Bonaparte's arrival: he could not have planned it better
himself.[42]

The groundwork had been laid; when Bonaparte finally did arrive
in France his decision to abandon the army in Egypt could easily
be explained away. When he learned of the defeats of Jourdan
in Germany and Schérer in Italy he, in his own words,
'immediately left, that same hour, with the frigates *Muiron* and
Carrère, even though they were slow ships. I did not think of the

Artist unknown, *Reception du Général Buonaparte aux Indes par Tipoozaib, ami des Français* (Reception of General Bonaparte in India by Tippoo Sahib, friend of the French), circa 1799. (*Bibliothèque nationale, Paris*)

dangers; I had to be where my presence could be the most useful. Animated by these sentiments, I would have wrapped myself in my coat and sailed on a barque if there had not been any frigates.'[43] Noble, self-sacrificing, thinking not of himself but of the good of the *patrie*. The situation in Germany led one journalist in the *Décade philosophique* to write: 'the hero of Italy could lead our troops to new triumphs and to a new peace that Europe so much needs.'[44] Even newspapers that were not particularly pro-Bonaparte saw in his return the possibility of 'peace and happiness'.[45] Indeed, Bonaparte was called on not only to save France from the Coalition by defeating its enemies, but also to create a new paradise on earth. The workers of the Faubourg St Antoine, drinking in the cafés of the rue de Lappe and the rue de la Roquette, declared: 'We sing the triumph of our armies and the arrival of *our father, our saviour*, Buonaparte. We don't have any work, well then we will march en masse under the command of our good father Buonaparte.'[46]

Bonaparte, then, had returned to France to take up the work that had been compromised by the Directory, to set right the faults that had been committed in his absence, and to consolidate the successes that had been endangered. Bonaparte alone appeared capable of achieving victory and, therefore, of bringing about peace. The people, even according to one of his opponents, saw in him a general who was always victorious and who would bring about honour through victory,[47] and, in the eyes of the people, the means of bringing an end to the Revolution was to end the war.

France on the Eve of the Coup

At the turn of the nineteenth century, a French historian writing about Bonaparte's coup thought that France was never more ripe for a dictatorship than in 1799.[48] The implication was that France under the Directory was in crisis, and that a coup was necessary to save it. Historians have since questioned whether the Directory was as moribund as the conspirators who eventually overthrew the regime later made it out to be, or whether the Directory represented a force that would have survived had it been allowed to continue.[49]

The Directorial regime had lasted longer, over five years longer than any of its predecessors since 1789, and its achievements were remarkable. France had been expanded to include almost one hundred departments, which were more or less run by commissaries appointed by Paris (it was a system Napoleon would later copy when he introduced the prefects). Also, as we have seen, by the time Bonaparte set foot on French soil on returning from Egypt, the danger of an invasion had been averted and a royalist revolt in the south-west had been put down, demonstrating that the Directory was as capable of controlling the interior as it was of waging war on the frontiers.[50] Moreover, great strides had been made by the Directory in combating brigandage, even if the problem was still endemic in some regions.[51] By the autumn of 1799, some measure of economic and financial prosperity had returned to France. This was largely achieved when the government abolished the worthless paper money, the *mandats territoriaux* (which had replaced the equally worthless *assignats* in 1796), and then simply expunged the national debt, infuriating, it has to be said, many moneylenders in the process.

These achievements were not enough to assuage the belief among the people – and especially the French political elite – that France was in crisis and that the government was fundamentally corrupt.[52] 'Everyone cursed it,' wrote a former deputy to the Convention, Marc-Antoine Baudot, 'no one praised it.'[53] The state of France may have been relatively good, in spite of some serious problems. However, the *perceived* state of France was much worse.[54] Indeed, no better example of the disparity between the public's perception of a government and the successful implementation of its policies could be found.

Many factors led to that disparity, not the least of which was the Directory's own liberal attitude towards press censorship. At the beginning of the Revolution, press censorship had been virtually non-existent, with the result that hundreds of newspapers sprang up to voice a whole range of opinions from the extreme left to the extreme right. Once the Revolution entered its more radical phase, though, newspapers that did not meet with governmental approval were suppressed. The swing back to a more liberal regime after the fall of Robespierre saw a relaxation of censorship laws. The upshot was that greater freedom of the press led to greater criticism of the government. The opposition press, both on the left and the right, was unsparing in its attacks on the Director, which contributed to the general impression that the Directory was on the verge of collapse. In fact, the lawlessness in the months that preceded the Directory's fall was largely due to redoubled conscription, financial and material levies, and the transfer of troops from the interior to the frontiers, all to cope with the renewed war, and all of which provoked angry responses from those on whom the measures fell.

Just as importantly, there was a perceived moral decay of French society, and moral decadence was equated with political decadence. Contemporaries complained of the *daussières*, or the *bourdons*, the *barboteuses*, or the *Marie-toute-troussée*, all different synonyms for prostitutes. There were supposed to be 20–30,000 of them in the capital alone, invading the streets, palaces, gardens and quays of the river Seine.

Historians have made much of this, as though the supposed moral corruption that infected society was a reflection of the political corruption at the top. Outside France, contemporaries suggested that political upheaval could be traced back to French frivolity and lifestyles.[55] Illustrations of these decadent individuals

Jean-Louis Darcis after Carle Vernet, *Les Payables*, circa 1797. Note the sack of money being held by the gentleman. (*Bibliothèque nationale, Paris*)

– the *Jeunesses dorés*, the *Incroyables*, the *Merveilleux*, usually in prints by Carl Vernet or Louis Léopold Boilly – abound and are often used as proof that Directorial society was infused with self-centred, pleasure-seeking youth who cared little for events around them.[56] It is true that the new rich lost as much in one evening at a card game as a worker would earn in a year, but when was this ever not the case? It is also true that in contrast to this society of the rich and well-to-do, most of the population suffered from a deprivation of the most essential necessities, but when, too, was this ever not the case? In general, there was extreme poverty during most of the years of the Revolution, although economic hardships seem to have been a characteristic of the Directorial period. At the worst moments of the winter of 1795, for example, workers, or mothers who were no longer able to feed their children, were being pulled out of the river, having committed suicide. The food situation greatly improved in the following years owing to some good harvests, but during the last two years of the Directory (1798–9) there was a reduction in cereal prices that took place at the same time as an increase in the cost of living. In the last months of the Directory, these problems increased, especially in Paris, leading the brothers Goncourt to claim that Paris was hungry, thirsty, cold, and running out of patience.[57] One does not have to look much further to explain the unpopularity of the Directory among the peasantry. The solidarity that had been present at the beginning of the Revolution was long gone and replaced by a virulent individualism that only periods of famine and hardship can produce. In these circumstances, politicians were accused of setting a bad example.

On three occasions, the people of France expressed their discontent with the Thermidorians – those who had maintained themselves in power after the fall of Robespierre – by voting in either royalist or Jacobin majorities, or by simply staying away from the elections altogether. On the same three occasions the Directory had hit back, hard – in Vendémiaire IV (October 1795), in Fructidor V (September 1797), and Floréal VI (May 1798) – overthrowing the results of the elections in three parliamentary coups by removing deputies they objected to and replacing them with men of their own, thereby ignoring the wishes of the electorate. It was the type of action that was bound to engender, at the local level, a certain amount of disillusion in national politics. In Bonaparte's own words, the coups were as if 'three cannon balls had gone through the vessel [of state] and it has sunk.'[58] If there was a crisis in France in 1799, it was, above all, political. The government had become exclusive, recruiting within itself, detached from the nation. In short, it had become an oligarchy, and the fault was laid on the Constitution, which, many people believed, was responsible for the instability caused by the left and the inability of the government to keep them in check.

If the Constitution was at fault, changing it was no mean feat. Between the executive (a Directory made up of five members nominated by the assemblies) and the two legislative assemblies of which one, the Council of Five Hundred, had the power to propose and vote laws, while the other, the Council of Elders (appointed by the Five Hundred) had the power to approve or reject them, there was no means of resolving a conflict, except by force. In order to save the Republic that had been built upon the notables, it seemed vital to a great many people that the Constitution of the Year III (1795) be changed. The problem was that the Constitution was written in such a way that a majority in each assembly (remember one third were renewed every year) was required over a period of nine years in order for an amendment to be passed. Constitutional change, therefore, became virtually impossible.

Among the deputies were a number who aimed at bringing about a change of institutions that would lead to a stronger executive, but without recourse to violence. The nature of the executive had been a subject of contention for some years. Note the letter from Bonaparte to Talleyrand in which, as early as the Italian campaign, he called into question the executive, and, indeed, formulated the principles he would eventually enact two years later.[59] These revisionists were grouped around one man – Sieyès – an apostate abbé, a regicide, a vain man with little charm (although, apparently, he had a good voice and knew how to sing).[60] When he spoke – and because of his role in the early stages of the Revolution he was always listened to with respect – his face lit up, and his voice took on an authoritative, imperious tone. Talleyrand, who knew him well, wrote that Sieyès never discussed, he 'prescribed'. He left us this incisive portrait of the man:

He was always in a bad mood [*atrabilaire*]. It is possible that a natural indisposition, which prevents him from the commerce of women contributed to it. And yet, he did not disdain joking with them. Then he could be graceful, he could smile, employ a measured, malicious and relatively biting mockery, but never to the point of being pleasant. Proud and weak, he was necessarily envious and distrustful. Moreover, he had no friends, but a circle of the submissive and the faithful . . . He only speaks in catchphrases, but each one expresses a thought and indicates some reflection. In conversation he is serious, he is never stirring but he imposes.[61]

Artist unknown, *Emmanuel Joseph Sieyès*, 1797. Caricatured here as a furtive figure, he was also known to be irascible. One time, before the Revolution, when Sieyès was saying mass for the Duc d'Orléans and he realised that the prince had left in the middle of it, he is said to have stormed out of the church declaring that he did not say mass for the rabble.[62] (*Bibliothèque nationale, Paris*)

Sieyès was elected to the Directory in 1799 to replace Reubell, and became the oracle of the moderates. No sooner had Sieyès taken up his post, however, than the neo-Jacobin legislature hit back at the Directory (the Coup of Prairial) by purging it of three of the directors. They were nearly prosecuted by the Council of Five Hundred, but a vote on that narrowly missed being passed by three voices. Ironically, and bizarrely, in the circumstances, the most corrupt of all the directors, Barras, the *pourri* (rotten swine), as he was called, remained in power, while the choice of the three new directors seemed to guarantee future tensions and conflicts within the Directory.[63] Louis Gohier, who had once been minister of justice, and the more obscure General Jean Moulin were meant to be pro-Jacobin, while Roger Ducos soon allied with Sieyès in his hatred of the Jacobins. Sieyès went on the counter-attack and attempted to break the momentum of the neo-Jacobins, who were still in the majority in the Council of Five Hundred, by laying the groundwork for a revision of the Constitution. Given the impossibility of doing this legally, it meant that some sort of coup had to be prepared. So he went about recruiting allies in the Councils. Behind Sieyès and the revisionists, there was a whole group of well-to-do people who had profited from the Revolution by either creating or consolidating their businesses and who looked upon themselves as the only people capable of taking over and leading France.

The 'Sword'

By 1799, the idea of a new coup d'état had become acceptable; it had happened so often in the past that people had stopped thinking anything of it. The only element missing was a general who could help them with their plans, not so much to use against the Assemblies, but to protect the Assemblies from a popular outburst. This had, of course, occurred with coups in the past; Bonaparte had been associated with the Coup of Fructidor, for example. The conspirators were undoubtedly thinking along the same lines when they looked, during the autumn of 1799, for a 'sword' that could fill this role.

The choice was limited. Hoche – perhaps the only general to rival Bonaparte's reputation – died of tuberculosis in September 1797, when Bonaparte was still in Italy, while Jourdan, the victor of the battle of Fleurus in 1794, was one of the more prominent neo-Jacobins in the Council of Five Hundred. Only a short time before, Jourdan had introduced a motion that was deemed provocative because of its association with the Terror, declaring the *patrie en danger*. It was rejected after two days of impassioned debates. Besides, he had earned the nickname 'Jourdan the retreat' because of his poor military performance in Germany against the forces of the Second Coalition.[64] Bernadotte, minister of war, who also passed for a neo-Jacobin general, and who openly referred to Bonaparte as the *transfuge* (deserter), seems to have preferred to stay out of the conspiracy, choosing to observe developments from the sidelines.[65] Joubert would have been the most serious candidate: he had had experience in a coup in Holland in 1798,[66] but he had taken over the command of the Army of Italy in Bonaparte's absence in October 1798, where, showing a complete lack of political foresight, he got himself killed on 15 August 1799 at the Battle of Novi.

A suitable alternative to Joubert had to be found quickly. After considering Etienne Macdonald (who had fought in Italy in 1798), Augereau and Beurnonville, the conspirators decided to approach Moreau, one of the youngest generals in the army, former commander of the Army of the North as well as the Army of Rhin-et-Moselle and who, after briefly falling foul of the government, was given command of the Army of the Rhine. He was in that post when Sieyès approached him in October. Tradition has it that Moreau hesitated, and then renounced the idea when Bonaparte returned to France. 'There is your man,' he is supposed to have said to Sieyès on declining the offer. 'He will carry out your coup d'état better than I.'[67]

The traditional account is just a little too convenient; Bonaparte arrives in France at the moment when the conspirators happen to be looking for a general. As we have seen, the groundwork had been carefully laid by family and friends so that, well before Bonaparte set foot on French soil, the public, not to mention the political elite, already associated his name with a 'coup' against the Directory.[68] In

September 1799, for example, when the Directory organized a funeral celebration in honour of Joubert on the Champ de Mars, the deputy, Dominique Garat, a member of the Council of Elders, pronounced a eulogy that insistently repeated the name of Bonaparte at a time when everyone expected a 'great coup' to be directed against the government.[69] From October onwards, after the first victories of the republican armies against the Austro-Russian forces, Bonaparte's name took on increasing importance in the conversations of Parisians. The performance of the victorious generals in Italy, Switzerland and Germany automatically recalled Bonaparte's name in the public imagination. When news of the victory at Aboukir finally arrived in Paris on 6 October, the public responded accordingly: Bonaparte would save the Republic and bring about peace.

Negotiating a Role

Bonaparte arrived in the capital on the morning of 16 October and immediately went to his house in the rue de la Victoire, where he expected, or rather hoped, to find Josephine. The house was empty. Having learned of his sudden return, Josephine had thought it best to meet him on his way to Paris in order to stave off the inevitable scene, but, badly informed about his route, she had gone off to Châlons when Bonaparte had taken the route through Nemours. Joseph and Lucien had joined him en route – and no doubt gave Josephine a drubbing.[70] Letizia had moved in with Joseph, and Jérôme was still in an expensive and fashionable school in Paris, but the rest of the family was scattered: Louis, who had accompanied his two older brothers south on the way to meet Bonaparte, fell sick, perhaps with a bout of venereal disease contracted from a certain countess in Brescia while he had been campaigning with his brother in Italy,[71] and was left at Autun; Pauline was running around the countryside with her husband, General Leclerc; and Elisa was at Marseilles. Only Caroline was lodging in Paris with her sister-in-law, Hortense.[72]

When Bonaparte returned home to find an empty house, it supposedly had a 'terrible and profound' impact on him.[73] On her return from Châlons two days later, a scene in the best marital tradition was played out. Josephine, on her knees, cried and begged forgiveness in front of a closed door – she was, in the words of Barras, 'a true actor who knew how to play all roles'[74] – Bonaparte sulked, and may have even cried himself for a number of hours before, around four in the morning, he threw open the door and had it out with her. The heated argument must have done the trick; the story goes that Lucien, responding to an invitation to visit, arrived the next morning to find them in bed together (Josephine may have sent the invitation, without her husband's knowledge, in a little act of vengeance against the Bonaparte family).[75] Bonaparte may have considered divorce at one time or another;[76] it was a possibility as it had been introduced in 1792 but may very well have been considered socially unacceptable by the former nobility.[77] Besides, not only did Bonaparte probably still love Josephine, there were also practical considerations: he realized that a public divorce at this stage would damage his image. Moreover, he must have thought that her connections would be useful in the inevitable forthcoming push to power. 'Whatever might have been his wife's errors,' wrote Madame Junot,

> Bonaparte appeared entirely to forget them, and the reconciliation was complete . . . Of all the members of the family, Madame Leclerc [Pauline] was most vexed at the pardon that Napoleon had granted to his wife . . . Bonaparte's mother was also very unhappy, but she said nothing . . . As for Madame Bacciocchi [Elisa] she gave free vent to her ill-humour and disdain; the consequence was that her sister-in-law could never endure her . . . Caroline was so young that her opinion could have no weight in such an affair. As for Bonaparte's brothers, they were at open war with Josephine.[78]

This may have been because, while Bonaparte was in Egypt, Josephine had continued her liaison with Hippolyte Charles, although it is impossible to know how frequently they saw each other or even if their relationship remained physical. We do know, however, that Josephine attempted to break things off with Charles in February 1799, at about the time that Bonaparte was planning to march into Syria. The relationship had become strained over money

matters; both were involved in the Bodin Company, under inves-
tigation by the Ministry of War for fraudulent dealings with the
Army of Italy. Bodin himself was actually imprisoned and it looked
as though the company was going to become insolvent. Charles was
one of the co-directors. We do not know just how involved
Josephine was in all this, but the risk of financial embarrassment
and a public scandal no doubt encouraged her to distance herself
from everyone involved. She wrote to Charles in a tone that
smacked of disillusionment, asking him to see her for a few
moments, adding: 'You can be assured that after this meeting,
which will be our last, you will no longer be tormented by either
my letters or my presence.'[79] This was probably not the end,
though. There is some anecdotal evidence that the relationship
continued until either shortly before or shortly after Bonaparte
returned from Egypt in October 1799. To a friend, Josephine
complained of a letter containing such 'unreasonable' and 'unmer-
ited' reproaches that it was obvious the sender was trying to bring
about a rupture.[80] It can only be assumed that the person to whom
she is referring is Charles and that, this time, the impetus to break
came from him. If the letter was written after Bonaparte's return,
Charles may have realized how imprudent any further contact with
Josephine would have been. There is certainly no evidence of any
communication after October 1799.

The day after his arrival, Bonaparte appeared before the Directory,
which was called to session especially for the occasion. The directors – especially Moulin and Gohier – had considered punishing
Bonaparte for abandoning the army, but they thought better of
arresting a man who was so popular with the people.[81] During his
first public appearances, people were eager to note the changes that
had come over him since he left eighteen months ago: his skin was
obviously darker, his hair was cut short – he had had it cut in Egypt
because of the heat – but the cheeks were a little sunken and he still
generally had a wretched look about him.[82] Wearing an olive green
redingote, a round hat and a Turkish scimitar, Bonaparte arrived at
the Luxembourg Palace to read out a report on Egypt that lasted for
two and a half hours. At the end of it, with a hand on the pommel of
his sword, he swore that he would never draw it except in defence

of the Republic and its government.[83] This was grandstanding. Bonaparte probably had no intention of defending the government unless he was a part of it.

In order to enter the government, and this seems to have been his intention on returning to France, Bonaparte had to appear the most republican of republicans; no doubts could be cast on his sincerity and patriotism.[84] But he had to find significant support. This was one of the reasons Bonaparte, who was badly informed about the political realities in the capital, entered into talks with people from across the spectrum: the legal representatives of the government (Barras, Gohier and Moulin), who behind their backs Bonaparte called *pourris* (rotten); the 'popular party', represented by Jourdan; the Jacobins, among whom was his rival, Bernadotte; the royalists (through Barras); and, finally, the moderates led by people like Sieyès.[85] In this, Talleyrand seems to have been instrumental by acting as intermediary between Bonaparte and the representatives of the various factions in Paris. Talleyrand thus guided Bonaparte through the options that were presented to him. In the two weeks preceding the coup, Bonaparte received visits from the minister of police, Joseph Fouché; the former deputy and member of the Institute, Pierre-Louis Roederer, who was an outspoken critic of the Constitution and detested by royalists for having escorted Louis XVI to the Assembly on 10 August; his former editor in Italy, Regnaud de Saint-Jean d'Angély; Hugues Maret, a journalist with the *Moniteur universel*; Admiral Bruix (who, a few days before the coup, was ordered back to his posting at Brest by Sieyès; he decided to stay with Bonaparte[86]); Boulay de la Meurthe, one of the architects of the Coup of Fructidor; and Pierre-François Réal, a friend of Barras who was connected to the administration of Paris.[87] Officers of the National Guard, and leaders of the Paris districts, many of whom owed their posts to Bonaparte when he was commander of the Army of the Interior, also appeared on his doorstep. Other officers returned to Paris without permission to visit him. Bonaparte appeared as the leader recognized by certain sections of the military and the civilian elite alike.

Bonaparte not only received, but he also actively sounded out, potential players and rivals. On 22 October, less than a week after he arrived in Paris, the process began. He met briefly with Moreau, who avowed his hatred of the Directory and promised to remain neutral. The next day, Bonaparte had talks with two directors, Gohier and Moulin, about his eventual entry into the Directory.[88] They both opposed the idea because Bonaparte did not meet the minimum age requirement; the same objection was raised by Moulin. The legal path to power was thereby closed. Bonaparte had little option other than to find an alternative route. It must have been around this time that he made the decision to gain power by extra-legal means. The conversations he had had with people from all walks of life since his return from Egypt no doubt reinforced the notion that the Directory could not last much longer in its present state. If he could not be part of it, then he could help destroy it.

Later that day (23 October), possibly in the evening, he met with Sieyès and Roger Ducos. Bonaparte, it has to be said, had not gone out of his way to meet Sieyès. Indeed, at a dinner held the previous evening at the Luxembourg Palace he deliberately ignored him because he regarded Sieyès as being too compromised by his past and unacceptable to the Jacobins. Even so, Bonaparte obviously realized that he would have to deal with Sieyès on some level. On 24 or possibly 25 October, Sieyès and Ducos returned the visit. It was on this occasion that the possibility of overthrowing the government was openly discussed.[89] If a coup was to be successful, the conspirators had to be assured of at least three of the directors, as well as of the military commandant of Paris (Lefebvre) and the minister of war (Dubois-Crancé – Bernadotte was dismissed in September, accused of organizing an uprising against the government[90]).

On 28 October, Bonaparte was summoned to appear before the Directory. Ironically, the object of the meeting was to discuss Bonaparte's future. According to the directors, he had to resume service in the army, but they hardly had a chance to speak before Bonaparte went on the offensive.[91] Adopting an outraged tone, the 'conqueror of Egypt' spoke of the rumours that had been reported back to him: Barras had recently accused him of having amassed a fortune in Italy.[92] This offence alone, he said, justified his anger. It allowed him to change the subject and to prevent them from speaking about his nomination to an army posting. The directors, and especially Barras, were thus put into a position of having to defend themselves when they had planned on attacking Bonaparte. Gohier tried to defend Barras by remarking that, in effect, everything that a general confiscated was done in the name of the Republic. He concluded the debate by affirming that, in any event, the Directory was convinced of Bonaparte's probity. The meeting was brought to an end when Bonaparte, without formally refusing the command of an army, excused himself on the grounds that his health had been affected by his long stay in Egypt and that he was in need of rest.

Bonaparte had won time, but the desire of some of the directors to remove him from the capital was clear. If Bonaparte were to remain the 'sword' of the conspirators, it became urgent that a definitive, concrete plan be decided upon and that it be carried out soon. The conflict between Bonaparte and Sieyès was to recede into the background during the last stage of negotiations, carried out a little more than a week before the coup. The very day after the meeting with the directors, on 29 October, Bonaparte had an interview with Bernadotte at his brother's house at Mortefontaine, about forty kilometres north of Paris.[93] Joseph, convinced by his sister-in-law, Désirée Clary (married to Bernadotte), had been active in trying to bring about a rapprochement between Bonaparte and Bernadotte. He thus organized a dinner, which also included Lucien, Talleyrand, Roederer, Regnaud de Saint-Jean d'Angély and a few others. Mortefontaine was four hours by carriage from Paris over bad roads. Bonaparte, with Josephine, picked up Bernadotte and Désirée on the way. It was the first time Désirée and Bonaparte had seen each other since Marseilles.

Bonaparte and Bernadotte were to pass two days together in secret, long and sometimes bitter discussions. According to witnesses, relations between the two men were tempestuous and, in the end, Bonaparte was unable to persuade Bernadotte to join him. On the contrary, on his return to Paris, Bernadotte took part in a meeting of Jacobin deputies during which he probably told them of Bonaparte's intentions. Jourdan proposed bringing Bonaparte into the faction that controlled a large part of the Council of Five Hundred. Augereau, on the other hand, also part of the Jacobin faction, argued that Bonaparte had deserted the army in Egypt and deserved to be severely condemned or, at the very least, given a *coup de pied au cul* (kick up the backside).[94] Nothing, however, was decided; it demonstrates the lack of effective leadership among the left.

On 30 October, a decisive meeting with Barras took place during a dinner at the Luxembourg Palace. The two men had known each other now for about six years and used the informal 'tu' when speaking to each other. They were not exactly friends but they did have some things in common – Vendémiaire, which brought them both power, and Josephine – and Barras seems to have viewed Jérôme and Louis with a benevolent eye in their brother's absence.[95] Roederer tried to dissuade Bonaparte from attending, but Fouché apparently insisted on the meeting. He was probably helped in this respect by Josephine, working behind the scenes, who preferred Barras to Sieyès, perhaps because of a deal worked out with Fouché, but more likely because Sieyès was preferred by her brothers-in-law. If Barras was less odious to the Jacobins than Sieyès, he was unpopular with the people and had a bad reputation. During the dinner, the prospect of a coup was raised. Barras conceded that something had to be done to save the Republic, even if constitutional forms had to be abandoned. He proposed calling on another 'sword', General Hédouville, who had just arrived after a short stint on Saint Domingue, promising to give the command of the army to Bonaparte. Bonaparte considered Hédouville to be a man of excessive mediocrity, and it is highly unlikely that Barras ever considered the suggestion seriously. It was simply a way of sounding out Bonaparte. Bonaparte, slighted, left the dinner deciding not to use Barras at all. Barras realized the folly of his action. On the morning of 1 November, he came to Bonaparte's house to offer his services, convinced by Fouché and Réal that he had to repair the damage.[96] If a project was in the air, he said, he could be counted on. It was too late. Bonaparte had already decided he wanted nothing further to do with him.[97]

It was only after Bonaparte had definitively ruled out Barras that he turned to Sieyès, that is, he threw in his lot with the moderate left – those commonly referred to as the 'Ideologues'. The Ideologues, well represented at the Institute (where Bonaparte was also a member), were made up of lawyers, *philosophes*, writers, historians, geographers and scientists. They cut across the political spectrum. Some were downright counter-revolutionary, others were republicans, others royalists. Aside from Sieyès, other prominent adherents included Chateaubriand, Monge and Volney. What held them together were their ideas – explained and developed in their newspaper, the *Décade philosophique* – and especially the belief that reason should rule over all human activity.[98]

Bonaparte was brought into the conspiracy not because he was one of the few military men available with enough prestige to influence a large proportion of the army, but because he was seen to be in tune with these Ideologues. After all, he had made a point of being seen more often in public with the members of the Institute than with generals and politicians. He had, in fact, gone out of his way to associate himself with the Ideologues, in contrast to generals like Jourdan, Augereau and Bernadotte who appeared to represent a crude, vulgar militarism. Remember that Bonaparte, even before he left for Egypt, would appear in public dressed, not in military uniform, but in civilian clothes, and, where possible, he preferred to wear the uniform of the Institute, thus enhancing his reputation as 'the most civilian of all generals'. Moreover, after his return from Egypt he attended every single session of the Institute. This was to be an important aspect of his life in Paris in the weeks leading up to the coup, and is closely associated not only with the image that he wanted to present – that is, to reassure the bourgeoisie that he was a man in tune with the ideological currents of the time – but also with the aim of obtaining the approbation of a political elite steeped in the Enlightenment. Their approval was indispensable if the coup was to succeed and be something more than just another military coup.[99]

Not surprisingly, this was largely a performance. Bonaparte's behaviour, including the decision to wear civilian dress, not to receive any 'factional' leaders at home, and to be seen with members of the Institute, was done with one eye firmly focused on politics. Some contemporaries saw through this. 'His habits, his tastes, his manners, his speeches, his proclamations, the slightest word, even his character and the disdain he displayed for the military uniform

all revealed his ideas, his hope and his desire for usurpation,'
observed one witness, General Paul Thiébault (although, admittedly, he was writing from hindsight).[100] Most others, however,
seem to have been duped. The Ideologues slowly came round to
Bonaparte and considered him the person most likely to fulfil their
ambitions. An important element in their acceptance was that
Bonaparte appeared to be above the political faction fighting in
Paris. In the past, generals had had a tendency to intrigue with
politicians according to their own personal political leanings. Thus,
Joubert was definitely Sieyès' man; Hoche had plotted with Barras;
while Moreau had royalist sympathies. Bonaparte, on the other
hand, presented himself as a man alone. The Ideologues imagined
that he would help them create a government according to *their*
designs – that is, one that would be progressive and scientific.

It is clear that Bonaparte was as skilful at playing factional
politics as the best of them, but he was more adept at disguising
the fact. Of his two newspapers in Italy, one, the *Courrier de
l'armée*, had had Jacobin leanings while the other, *La France*,
was directed at the republican centre. In founding two newspapers that covered the centre and left, Bonaparte not only
attracted a wide republican audience but also avoided appearing
factionalist. By 1798, however, despite having once been a
Jacobin himself, and despite having flirted with them in spring
and summer of 1797, Bonaparte had turned away from the left.
One can only speculate upon his reasons – there is nothing in
his correspondence that leads to any positive assertions – but it
is more than likely that he had understood that the drift of
national politics had moved away from those associated with the
Terror. If he flirted with them again, briefly, in the days and
weeks leading up to the coup, it was because the Jacobins still
maintained some influence, at least in Paris. In the end, Bonaparte threw in his lot with the faction he considered most likely
to succeed – Sieyès and the Ideologues. These were the men
Bonaparte would first cultivate, then, once he had consolidated
his power, abandon. This is not to say that he had any more
respect for the Ideologues than he did for either the royalists or
the Jacobins, all of whom were castigated after the coup. The

choice was politically opportunistic, and in this he was no better
or worse than any number of political actors – such as Sieyès,
Talleyrand and Fouché – who had survived the vagaries of
revolutionary politics over the years by choosing sides carefully
at the opportune moment.

Important, too, was the role of Bonaparte's family in both the
lead up to the coup and on the day itself. One historian has even
referred to the conspiracy as a 'family affair'.[101] Joseph had been
elected to the Five Hundred as a Corsican deputy in 1797, but
he had almost immediately been sent as ambassador first to
Parma, and then Rome (accompanied by his sister-in-law,
Désirée, and her then fiancé, General Leonard Duphot). When
he returned to Paris at the beginning of 1798, he took up his seat
in the Five Hundred, but seems to have spent most of his time
reading, and fantasizing about becoming a writer. He nevertheless made some useful contacts for the time when his brother
would return. The twenty-four-year-old Lucien also played a
part in the preparations leading to the coup, although he may
not have had either his brother's or his family's interests at heart.
In fact, it is possible that he had had talks with Bernadotte, and
it is certain that he had had discussions with Sieyès, about
replacing the Constitution, despite the fact that, at the beginning
of his career as a deputy, he swore to die defending it.[102]
Bonaparte's unexpected arrival in France may not have entirely
fitted in with Lucien's own plans, and yet he played along, no
doubt fully aware of the opportunities the situation presented.
Elected as a deputy in 1798 – despite not being the constitutionally required minimum age – Lucien had been president of
the Five Hundred since before Bonaparte sailed from Toulon,
and was thus in a brilliant position to influence any political
intrigue directed against the house. The role he played on the
day of the coup was decisive. As for the rest of the family,
Bonaparte's brother-in-law, General Leclerc, married to Pauline,
was indispensable in making contacts with the heads of the
different military units in Paris, while Josephine was asked to
neutralize two of the directors, Barras, a former lover, and
Gohier, who aspired to become one.

The Plot

Events had moved with incredible rapidity. Less than one month after Bonaparte had returned from Egypt, he was one of the principal members of a plot to overthrow the government.

The eve of the coup was spent carrying out last-minute preparations. Notes were sent out, from lists drawn up by Berthier, inviting a number of officers to Bonaparte's house at the rue de la Victoire at six o'clock the following morning. Although the early hour was unusual for a visit, it was explained that Bonaparte would shortly afterwards be leaving on a voyage. Other messages were sent to the forty 'adjutants' of Paris – high-ranking officers in the National Guard – asking them to be at the Champs Elysées at seven o'clock in the morning for a review. The same order was sent to the colonels of the three cavalry regiments of the capital. Finally, all those who had accompanied Bonaparte to Egypt and had returned with him were ordered to appear at the crack of dawn at the rue de la Victoire. Each message specified that the summons was meant for the addressee only, to keep the whole affair as secret as possible. Horace Sébastiani, a young Corsican of twenty-eight with a brilliant and eventful career already behind him, was appointed commander of a regiment of dragoons. They were to be positioned on the Place de la Révolution (the present-day Concorde), not far from the Tuileries and the Bourbon Palace where the Elders and the Five Hundred respectively met. All of these measures, it should be noted, were taken without the knowledge of Sieyès. He would be confronted with them the next day and would be powerless to oppose the ascendancy of the military in what was meant to be a civilian coup.

That evening, Bonaparte was invited by Cambacérès to a dinner at the Ministry of Justice, which was said to be dull – people's minds were obviously elsewhere, anxious about the next day's events – although there are reports of Bonaparte in the days preceding the coup being gay and singing to himself, a sure sign that he was confident about the outcome.[103] At two o'clock the next morning, Bonaparte was still up sending orders to Moreau, Lefebvre and Macdonald to 'rise with the sun' and to come to his house on horseback; the officers would already be assembled. Josephine also sent a note – to the director Gohier, who had been courting her over a number of months – inviting him to breakfast at eight o'clock the next morning. The object was to keep Gohier at the Bonaparte household and, if possible, to keep him by Bonaparte's side and visible during the course of the morning. A member of the Directory in Bonaparte's company might influence troops hesitant about rallying to the conspirators.

Since the coup was well supported by ministers, deputies and other influential men, it had every likelihood of succeeding. The minister of police, Fouché, as we have seen, was aware of what was going on, although the details of the plot had been kept from him as he was not entirely trusted; Cambacérès (justice), Quinette (Interior) and Reinhard (foreign affairs) were all implicated. Strong personalities such as Talleyrand, Roederer, Benjamin Constant, Cabanis and Marie-Joseph Chénier were also involved, as were any number of bureaucrats, who had been persuaded to participate by Réal and Joseph, along with a sizeable minority of the deputies of the Five Hundred and the Elders, including the president, Lemercier (with Lucien, the presidents of both houses were involved). A number of high-ranking army officers – Sérurier, Bruix, Macdonald, Beurnonville, Murat, Lannes, Leclerc – were on the list kept by Berthier. Just as importantly, it was hoped that the garrison of Paris and its commander, General Lefebvre, would agree to be placed under Bonaparte's orders. This was a gamble: Lefebvre had not been let into the inner circle and, indeed, had declared that he was prepared to defend the regime against any plot hatched by Sieyès or Bonaparte.

There were other real dangers. The Jacobins were strong and dominated the Council of Five Hundred. The Jacobin clubs were still active and their newspapers attacked Sieyès daily, accusing him of preparing an 'oligarcho-royal system'.[104] All five directors had to resign so that a new constitution could be put in place, but only three of the directors had either been won over or neutralized; two of them – Gohier and Moulin – were not prepared to throw their lot in with the conspirators. The new minister of war, Dubois-Crancé, had registered his hostility towards the plot. In order to be successful, therefore, the coup had to be carried out quickly.

As soon as Bonaparte and Sieyès were in agreement, a plan was concocted to 'constitutionally immolate the Constitution'.[105] Three articles gave the Elders the right to change the place of residence of the legislative body, that is, to leave Paris for a calmer environment on the pretext that there was an insurrection looming in Paris. This would hardly have come as a surprise given the dozen or so popular *journées* that had occurred since the beginning of the Revolution. Once outside Paris, in an environment that could easily be surveyed, such as Saint-Cloud, it would be easier to extort from the two Assemblies a vote to overthrow the Constitution, and to replace it with a new provisional executive that would, naturally, include Sieyès and Bonaparte. The move outside of Paris would have the added advantage of depriving the Jacobins in the Five Hundred of their popular support base – that is, the people, who could be mobilized in the public galleries. The disadvantage was that the coup would have to be carried out in two movements, over two days, and would, therefore, leave time for potential opponents to rally. Nevertheless, the desire to get the Councils away from the populace dominated the planning. With hindsight, it is clear that the conspirators overestimated the influence of the Jacobins and underestimated the extent of popular apathy among the people.

Bonaparte approved the plan, reserving the right to modify it as he saw fit, and a date was fixed for 9 November (18 Brumaire).

21

The Coup as Farce

The First Act

In the early hours of the morning of 18 Brumaire (9 November), inside the Tuileries, the Inspectors of the Chambers – Mathieu-Augustin Cornet and Jean-François Baraillon – who had the right to summon the Councils and to dispose of the Directorial Guard, were busy writing invitations for an extraordinarily early session the next day.[1] Between five and six o'clock in the morning, non-commissioned officers of the Guard delivered the 150-odd invitations to the homes of the deputies. They deliberately did not convoke those members who were hostile to their plans. In buildings where more than one deputy resided, the 'good' deputy received the invitation, while the 'bad' deputy did not.[2]

Having dragged themselves out of their beds, donned their uniforms – designed by David, red togas with large plumed hats – the deputies hastened through the dark streets of Paris to the Tuileries. Everything would have looked normal around the palace.[3] There was not, as yet, one extra soldier to be seen in the surrounding streets. The first deputies started to arrive by six o'clock, filling the chamber of the Elders little by little. The session was opened between seven and eight o'clock in the morning, under the presidency of Lemercier. In the name of the Commission of Inspectors, Mathieu-Augustin Cornet read a vaguely phrased report in which he denounced a supposed plot that had been concocted by terrorists and the enemies of liberty.[4] Such formulations were by now common fare in the history of the Revolution. They had been fabricated so many times in the past to justify the illegal machinations of a radical minority of deputies that their significance must have been clear to all those who heard them. Cornudet (a deputy who had a reputation for being a moderate), Lebrun (renowned for his scruples, which were obviously not troubling him too much at this moment) and Fargues (an obscure Thermidorian) denounced in turn the Jacobin conspiracy and its attempts to re-establish the Terror according to a scenario that had been decided in advance.[5] Régnier, deputy for the Meurthe, then rose and got to the point – the Constitution provided for a procedure to safeguard the national representation by allowing it to meet not far from Paris. He proposed that the Council, therefore, be transferred and that Bonaparte be nominated the head of the 17th military division – Paris.

There was no debate. A decree made up of a number of articles was voted through: the transfer of the Councils to the Château of Saint-Cloud; the prohibition of all meetings between deputies until midday the next day (which should have made those not in the conspiracy very suspicious); the nomination of Bonaparte as head of the troops; and his summons before a commission in order to agree on the measures to be adopted. Sieyès initially ensured that the Directorial Guard be omitted from the list of troops over which Bonaparte was to have command, but Bonaparte rectified this omission with his own hand, thereby taking de facto control of the Guard.

Those inhabitants of the districts north of the Chaussée d'Antin awake between six and seven o'clock that morning would have seen an unusual sight – officers in full dress uniform walking through the streets, often singly, converging on one point, Bonaparte's house in the rue de la Victoire.[6] They had each been summoned by Bonaparte for a private audience, but even if they had not realized the real reason for being called so early in the morning – it was an open secret among the military in Paris – they would have soon understood the implications.[7] The Bonapartes' house was too small to contain them all. Most spilled out into the garden and the street, which was lined with dragoons, sabres drawn, put in place much earlier that morning by comander of the dragoons, Sébastiani. Only those who were to play an important part were allowed inside. Cavalry escorts and orderlies waited for orders. Other squadrons had been stationed in the streets up to the Chaussée d'Antin (then called rue de Mont-Blanc). Bonaparte, dressed in civilian clothes, greeted any high-ranking officers arriving in carriages and led them up the steps to the entrance. He then withdrew behind the closed doors of his study; they would open now and then to receive a distinguished arrival and then immediately shut again.

Finally, at about eight o'clock in the morning, the doors to the study were flung open and Bonaparte appeared in his general's uniform.[8] He held in his hand the decree from the Council of Elders, which had been delivered a little earlier by the Inspectors of the Chambers, Cornet and Baraillon. By his side stood General Lefebvre, commandant of the troops in Paris, who had been won over earlier that morning by a dramatic gesture from Bonaparte that brought tears to the man's eyes: he offered him the sword that he had worn in Egypt as a mark of affection. Bonaparte asked those present to help him save the Republic. He then mounted his horse (a superb black charger that had been lent to him by Admiral Bruix) and, a little ahead of the group of officers and troops following him, he led the way to the Tuileries. Along the way, sightseers began to follow them out of curiosity. Bonaparte, at the head of what was one of the most impressive collections of officers and generals the Republic could then muster (about sixty in all), advanced across the Place de la Révolution and down past a plaster statue of Liberty that had been erected in front of the Tuileries where the dragoons were formed in columns. In the garden of the Tuileries, the Consular Guard was lined up in front of the palace.

The palace and the gardens were now spilling over with people. The coming and going of so many soldiers, an unusual sight even in the capital city of a country that had been at war for years, had attracted a mass of onlookers who had come from the districts closest to the palace, that is, those inhabited by the bourgeoisie, by merchants and shopkeepers. Although news of the event had already reached the *faubourgs* and the outlying districts, they had not reacted. Despite the fact that this was clearly an attempt to overthrow the government, a festive atmosphere reigned. The idea seems to have delighted the crowd and it was significant that, unlike in previous revolutionary *journées*, they did not try to become involved. This was strictly a military affair.

Bonaparte entered the Tuileries at about ten o'clock. The deputies in the Council of Elders were standing in groups discussing the situation when Bonaparte was announced. They resumed their places; a solemn silence greeted his entrance.[9] He was followed by his general staff and a throng of uniforms. The president, Lemercier, welcomed them with a few words of greeting, a secretary read the decree that had been voted shortly before, then it was Bonaparte's turn to speak. It was the first time that he had had to address an assembly of such size and importance. He was first required to take an oath. The difficulty was getting around swearing an oath of loyalty to the Constitution. He managed to extract himself from this potentially disastrous situation by pronouncing a speech prepared in advance, and delivered with some hesitation, about the Republic dying, and about how he was going to defend it, helped by his 'companions in arms'.[10] Then, in an emotional conclusion, he asserted that he wanted a Republic based on the principles of liberty and equality: 'We will have it, I swear,' he is reported to have said, while the troops and the gathered assembly supposedly replied, as if on cue, 'We swear.'

Not all of the deputies, however, were convinced. Dominique Garat, for example, stood up and asked why there had been no mention of the Constitution, but Lemercier quickly shut him up, in the name of the Constitution, and said there would be no further discussion until they met the next day at Saint-Cloud.[11] The session was immediately closed. The deputies left the chamber shouting 'Vive la République'. They had, in fact, unwittingly just condemned it to death.

Between ten thirty and eleven o'clock, Bonaparte then went out into the gardens to speak to the troops and especially to the Directorial Guard, who would have little choice but to recognize him as their commander. As he was coming out of the palace, he noticed Bottot, Barras' secretary, sent to find out what was going on. In an inspired gesture, Bonaparte drew him to his side and addressed the crowd of soldiers and citizens that had gathered: 'The army has gathered around me, I have gathered around the legislative corps.' A loud round of applause followed. Bonaparte then turned towards the hapless Bottot and thundered at him:

What have you done with the France that I left in such a brilliant state? I left you peace, I found war! I left you victories, I find defeat! I left you millions from Italy, I find despoiling laws and misery everywhere! Our cannon have been sold, theft has been erected into a system! The state's resources have been exhausted! It has had recourse to vexatious measures, reproved by justice and good sense! Soldiers have been abandoned without means of defence! Where are the brave, the hundred thousand comrades I left covered in laurels? What have they become? This state of affairs cannot last. Within three years it will lead to despotism.[12]

Bonaparte had been looking for an opportunity to rail against the regime. By lambasting the poor Bottot he was accusing the regime collectively and Barras in particular. The remarks he made might have been unjust, even false, but it did not matter. References to the 'thieves' who had deprived the army and its soldiers of what they were entitled to, and an appeal to them to save liberty once again, were aimed at the troops gathered there. Inspired it may have been, but spontaneous it was not. The words he used were not even his own. He had found most of the expressions in a speech he had read a few days before and which had been addressed to the Jacobin club of Grenoble.[13] Bonaparte had simply appropriated it, as was his way, extracting what he considered useful.

This was a very different coup compared to the ugly scenes that had characterized the early years of the Revolution. It was orderly and well disciplined, accompanied by music, parades and fanfares. It resembled a military parade more than a traditional Parisian *journée*. And that was the problem, at least for sincere republicans – it was a military coup, the first of its kind in the modern era,[14] and was to inspire military coups throughout the nineteenth and twentieth centuries. Despite the republican, even revolutionary, rhetoric used by Bonaparte, the predominance of the military and Bonaparte's authoritarian behaviour on the day were leading to some unease among the civilian conspirators. They had already been completely eclipsed. Sieyès had been outmanoeuvred by a general who was meant to play a supporting role. Bonaparte had effectively taken charge of events from the very first. His 7,000 soldiers, led by officers who were personally devoted to him, gave him the key advantage over his rivals among the conspirators. Bonaparte's strategy during the first day had been allowed to develop unhindered by the civilians. Moreover, Sieyès had not even been informed of the military dispositions; in the proclamation posted that evening all over Paris justifying the coup, reprinted the next day in the *Moniteur*, Sieyès' name was nowhere to be found.[15] The leading role had been taken by the 'hero', the 'saviour' of the Republic. The posters insisted on the role that Bonaparte was now to play and underlined that his place was in Paris.

In the meantime, Talleyrand and Bruix were taking care of a small matter that was to dislocate the Directorial majority and put it in an impossible position. They arrived at the Luxembourg Palace where Barras, who had wanted to be part of the plot but now realized he had no choice but to abandon any hope of retaining power, signed the paper presented to him announcing his resignation. They also handed over a purse containing two million francs.[16] Barras was effectively paid off, and Bonaparte sent 100 dragoons to the Luxembourg to 'escort' Barras out of Paris and on to his estate at Grobois, in the Seine-et-Marne, where he would spend the rest of his days in retirement.[17] Solidarity between Barras and his colleagues, Gohier and Moulin, would have allowed the government a legitimacy that would almost certainly have resulted in its becoming a centre of resistance. Without Barras, Gohier and Moulin were lost. Gohier had been fooled into believing that it was not a question of destroying the government but of simply purging it by getting rid of Barras. The directors, therefore, were overthrown because they had spent most of their time duping, deceiving and betraying each other.

Despite the ease with which the first day of the coup had passed, the most dangerous moments still lay ahead. The plans and operations of the second day, the day that had necessarily to be unconstitutional, had been left entirely to chance. That day, Bonaparte would be obliged to admit that it was not simply a question of revising the Constitution and expelling a few directors, but of actually snapping the constitutional backbone. It was more than probable that the majority of the Five Hundred would oppose any such move, as well as the minority in the Council of Elders, who had been excluded from the first day's proceedings.

During the first day, Bonaparte had had conversations with his principal allies, but they had not had the opportunity to have a methodical discussion; there had been too many interruptions. Around seven o'clock that evening, a last conference took place among the principal conspirators in the hope of finally agreeing on a plan for the second day (Sieyès and Ducos were present, as were Lemercier, Regnier, Cornudet, Fargues, Lucien, Boulay de la Meurthe, Emile Gaudin, Chazal, Cabonis and a few others). Sieyès and Regnier (Bonaparte's future minister of justice) proposed a practical means of overcoming any potential opposition: they would simply arrest the forty or so Jacobin deputies, a solution in the purest revolutionary tradition. But Bonaparte and another conspirator, Boulay de la Meurthe, who would become one of Napoleon's loyal and capable administrators, categorically refused, not out of any scruples they may have had, but because it smacked of so many past coups. They did not want to abandon legal methods or act as though they feared 'being disavowed by the nation'.[18] Bonaparte wanted his coup to be different from all the rest; he could not afford to repeat past political errors. Besides, the Jacobins might yet be useful at some stage in the future.

One thing was agreed, that the Directory would be suppressed, and that a provisional consulate would be created. But there were far too many unanswered questions about the manner in which they were to proceed. How were they, at one and the same time, to use and to exclude the Assemblies? How were they to introduce the debate on the revision of the Constitution? Who was going to move the motion? What role were the Elders to play? The discussion went on late into the night without any definitive plan being reached. In the end, the outcome of the second day was left to chance, something that is perhaps a reflection of just how truly haphazard were the plans and how motley the alliance of conspirators. The civilian conspirators relied too heavily on the reputation of Bonaparte and his prestige as a military leader to suppress any opposition; Bonaparte relied too heavily on the civilian conspirators to carry the Councils along by expediency.

That night, Paris remained quiet. People went to the theatre as usual, in fact the theatres were full, even though it was raining hard.

The police reports indicate that, in some theatres, audiences sang the revolutionary song 'Le Chant du Départ'.[19] Most respectable people, it would seem, feared a return of the Jacobins and wanted Bonaparte to succeed, though some better-informed people had their doubts about where it would all lead.[20] At the Tuileries, the Palais-Bourbon, the Luxembourg Palace and on the banks of the river Seine, from the centre of Paris to Saint-Cloud, thousands of soldiers slept near their stacked muskets. Bonaparte had used them during the day as much to intimidate as to give a sense of security in case the *faubourgs* needed keeping in check, thereby reassuring the bourgeoisie.

Bonaparte returned to his house in the rue de la Victoire and is supposed to have said to Bourrienne, 'It didn't go too badly today; we will see about tomorrow.' Before he and Josephine went to sleep that night, he loaded two pistols and placed them by his bed.[21]

The Second Act

The seventeenth-century château of Saint-Cloud, where the Councils were to meet, had not been occupied since the fall of the monarchy in 1792. It was a familiar sight to anyone travelling to or from Paris, before it was burnt to the ground during the Prusso-German invasion of 1870. It was built in the shape of a horseshoe around a courtyard opening on to a terrace.

The rain that had been falling had cleared by morning but little time had been given to workers to prepare the château to receive the representatives of the people. In the right wing of the château, on the first floor, was the Gallery of Apollo; it was the largest room and was allocated to the Elders. As the château was too small for the Five Hundred, they were placed in a nearby annexe, the Orangerie, which was linked to the château by a narrow covered gallery. The apartments were to be occupied by Bonaparte, Sieyès, Ducos and their retinue. A few hundred metres from there, not far from the terrace, Sébastiani had placed his soldiers in reserve.

A great many other people, mostly curious sightseers, also

made the ten-kilometre journey to Saint-Cloud that day, attracted by the novelty of a coup unfolding in the countryside. The people, it seemed, were with the conspirators, or at least the crowds lining the route to the château who cheered Bonaparte's carriage as it passed were.[22] This did not prevent some of the conspirators from preparing for the worst, making sure they had a ready supply of cash on them, just in case.[23] Most of the newspapers had sent their reporters along as well. Itinerant traders set up stalls in the adjacent streets and hawkers sold newspapers. The moderate newspapers concentrated on the 'anarchist peril' and the coming abolition of the 'atrocious' laws and measures of 'pillage' – a reference to the forced loan – that had been adopted by the present government.[24] The Jacobin press denounced the directors Barras, Gohier and Moulin and hardly mentioned Bonaparte. Restaurants that had closed for the season opened for the occasion; fresh food had to be quickly bought, prepared and cooked, and tables laid in preparation to receive the deputies and sightseers.[25]

Gardina, *Vue du château de Saint-Cloud* (View of the Chateau of Saint Cloud), date unknown. (*Bibliothèque nationale, Paris*).

Bonaparte had spent a busy morning at his house in Paris sending out notes and orders organizing the troops under his command.[26] It would appear that the lack of resolution the previous evening, and the doubts that some of the civilian conspirators expressed to him that very morning, may have convinced him that the only way of winning the day was through force.[27] When Bonaparte arrived at the château – to cries of 'Vive Bonaparte' and, ironically, 'Vive la Constitution'[28] – he went directly to the two rooms that had been assigned to the Councils to see how far the work had progressed. They were still not ready; work had begun two hours late. Instead of hustling the deputies immediately into their respective chambers and into a prepared scenario, the conspirators let them mingle in the grounds, where they inevitably started to talk among themselves and to realize the extent to which they had been duped. The Jacobins of the Five Hundred were not the only ones who had doubts. A number of Elders, even those sympathetic to Sieyès, found that too much had been concealed from them the previous day and that the change of regime was taking an unexpected turn.

In the apartments that had been assigned to Bonaparte and his men, Bonaparte seemed nervous and impatient. General Thiébault was in the rooms adjacent to Bonaparte's. He recounted in his memoirs the following scene, which gives an insight into the stress under which Bonaparte was operating:

At last . . . a door opened and General Bonaparte appeared to say: 'Go and get Major X'. An aide-de-camp immediately left and a little later came back with the major. Warned, General Bonaparte reappeared, and addressed the officer with the greatest severity. By whose order did you move such and such a post? The officer named the person who gave him the order, observing that it was not the first order he had received from him. The response was very proper, which did not prevent General Bonaparte from continuing in the angriest of tones: 'There are no orders here but mine. Arrest that man and put him in prison'. Four lackeys (*séides*) threw themselves on the major and dragged him away.[29]

It was not until one o'clock that afternoon that Lucien, amid a general uproar, declared the session of the Five Hundred open.[30] It should have been evident from the start that he was not going to be able to control the deputies. It is doubtful that he even looked the part. He was, after all, relatively young, wore glasses because he was very short-sighted, spoke with a nasal twang and was unable to project his voice very far.

Lucien was immediately assailed by motions. The Jacobins, who occupied the first rows, sought physically to control access to the rostrum.[31] One of the deputies belonging to the conspirators, Emile Gaudin, who was later to be named minister of finance, immediately stood up and outlined the dangers the country was supposedly faced with. He demanded a commission be formed to examine the public danger and to propose measures to counter it. Until then, he

Jacques Sablet, *La salle du Conseil des Cinq-Cents à Saint-Cloud dans la soirée du 19 brumaire* (The room of the Council of Five Hundred at Saint Cloud in the evening of 19 Brumaire), circa 1800. The scene represents Lucien at the rostrum. The three future consuls are sitting in the centre of the piece. Jacques Sablet went to Saint-Cloud with his sketchbook to try to capture the events of the day. (*Courtesy of photo RMN* – © *Gérard Blot*)

continued, all deliberations should be suspended. It was an obvious ploy to stifle debate – a parliamentary commission would be much easier to control than an unruly assembly – but the Jacobins, past masters at manipulating assemblies, were not to be duped. Cries of 'No dictatorship!', 'Down with dictators!', 'Down with the Cae-sar!', 'Down with the Cromwell!' and 'We are free here; bayonets do not frighten us!' broke out from all sides.[32] Interruptions and insults drowned out the voice of Gaudin and the Jacobins forced him to step down from the rostrum.

The conspirators quickly found themselves paralysed by this uproar. Lucien tried, in vain, to calm things down but he was jeered and even threatened, while a crowd of deputies jostled with each other to try to get to the rostrum, shouting, 'The Constitu-tion or death'. For months the Jacobins themselves had been contemplating overthrowing the government and replacing it with a dictatorship. Now, their cries tinged with an appropriate amount of patriotic outrage, they had become its staunchest defenders. Pierre Delbrel, one of the Jacobin leaders, finally managed to speak and demanded that every deputy renew his oath of loyalty to the Constitution. The request was greeted with a thunderous round of applause. The neo-Jacobin deputy, Joseph-Marie Grandmaison, who had always played an active role in the Five Hundred, went even further. He proposed that emissaries be sent to the Elders, without delay, to get proof of the supposed plot and the danger to the Republic.

Fortunately for the conspirators, Grandmaison's dangerous pro-position was not acted upon. The Five Hundred then committed the most critical mistake of the day – they voted to renew their promise to defend the Constitution before any other debate could take place. No one dared renege, but, by agreeing to take the oath, form had to be respected: every single deputy would have to take the oath separately. The procedure would take hours to accomplish; the deputies thereby squandered a valuable opportunity to take control of events by wasting time in a long and futile theatrical gesture.

The Elders did not open their session until about two o'clock to the sounds of 'La Marseillaise'. Nothing had been omitted from the usual ceremony; even the orchestra of the Council made the journey from Paris. The president of the chamber had hardly opened the session when he, too, was besieged by shouts from all sides. A number of deputies not in the conspiracy demanded explanations of the so-called 'Jacobin plot'. The directors were called for: the Constitution required that the directors deliberate in the same building as the Elders. At about half past three a messenger arrived to announce that four of the directors had resigned and that the fifth had been placed under surveillance by order of General Bonaparte (all of which was untrue). The Directory no longer existed and the Elders were required to find a replacement. In the confusion that followed the session was suspended until a little before four o'clock.

Denouement

Not far from the Council of Elders, on the first floor, Bonaparte and the two directors, Sieyès and Ducos, were waiting. Bonaparte paced up and down, agitated. Sieyès, sitting near the fire, half-heartedly poked at it with a wooden stick.[33] Every five minutes or so, one of Bonaparte's aides-de-camp, Antoine Lavalette, would bring them news from the Council of Five Hundred. What he had to say was not encouraging. Messengers had been sent by the Jacobins to organize a movement in Paris and to raise the *faubourgs* in revolt. At Saint-Cloud, the people who customarily frequented the clubs in Paris started to appear in front of the château, attempting to slip past the guards and into the grounds. More seriously, Jourdan, Augereau and their followers had just arrived and suggested that Bonaparte abandon the coup.[34] In a room next to Bonaparte's, about thirty officers were packed in, anxious, waiting. Some, believing that the initiative had already been lost, started to discreetly steal away. Now and then, the door to the adjoining room would open and Bonaparte would appear, visibly nervous.

Shortly before four o'clock, Bonaparte, feeling that events were starting to slip out of control, decided to act. He walked across the apartments accompanied by his aides-de-camp and headed straight for the Council of Elders with the intention of rallying his flagging

support.[35] The authors of the coup had not counted on Bonaparte's
impatience. The session of the Elders had remained suspended up
until that time, but, when it was announced that Bonaparte was
about to appear, they quickly took their places. When Bonaparte
entered the Grand Salon, preceded by an usher, he placed himself in
the centre of the Assembly facing the president. Berthier and
Bourrienne were at his sides; his aides-de-camp and a few faithful
(including Joseph) followed him in, but he was certainly not as well
supported as on the preceding day. This may have been a deliberate
ploy to reassure the deputies that they had nothing to fear from the
military, or it perhaps may have been because, on coming among
the Elders without their permission, Bonaparte was crossing the
Rubicon. Moreover, it was no longer a question of pronouncing a
prepared speech, but of trying to convince the deputies of the
validity of his claims. This was an entirely new role for Bonaparte,
and one that he was unprepared for.

Bonaparte was suddenly seized with an attack of nerves. He
began to speak, but only muttered a few stock phrases ill-suited to
the circumstances, punctuating each idea with, 'That's all I have to
say.' The more he went on, the more embarrassing it became for all
concerned. His accusations against the Jacobin conspirators who
supposedly wanted to overthrow the Republic were especially
vague, but the worst thing he articulated, and which was indicative
of the febrile state of his mind, was a phrase he had already used
when he suppressed the revolt in Cairo – 'Remember that I march
accompanied by the God of War and the God of Fortune'.
Bourrienne concluded in his memoirs that: 'There was not the
least bit of sense in anything that he stammered with, it has to be
said, the most inconceivable incoherence. Bonaparte was no orator
. . . His place was amid a battery [of guns] rather than in the chair
of a president of the Assembly.' Seeing that Bonaparte was
having an adverse effect on the deputies, Bourrienne is supposed
to have pulled him gently by his coattails and whispered, 'Leave,
general, you no longer know what you are saying.'[36] He withdrew,
having given no proof of the Jacobin threat as the deputies had
demanded. His intervention had only discomposed the Elders, and
left a deplorable impression on them. Bonaparte had acted
as though he were haranguing a group of soldiers, incapable of

making the distinction between an assembly that deliberates and troops who obey.

From there Bonaparte went to the Council of Five Hundred, hoping to win the day either by carrying the deputies along with him or by putting the fear of God into them. If his intervention with the Elders was a fiasco, his intrusion into the Five Hundred was a disaster. The corridors leading to the room were so crowded that Bonaparte and his men had trouble clearing a path. When he finally reached the door, many of the deputies were so busy arguing with each other that his entry with a group of armed soldiers went unnoticed, even though he had committed an act that was strictly forbidden (the presence of armed men, other than its own guard, was prohibited in the Council of Five Hundred). Then, suddenly, Bonaparte and his men were noticed. There was a huge outcry: 'Down with the dictator!', 'Down with the tyrant!', 'Outlaw!', 'Down with Cromwell!' One deputy by the name of Guyot later bragged that he exhausted himself shouting 'Outlaw!'[37] Almost the whole assembly was standing in uproar against the man they had finally recognized as a Caesar. A number of them threw themselves on Bonaparte in an attempt to expel him from the room. A deputy by the name of Bigonnet later claimed that he grabbed Bonaparte by both arms and asked, 'What are you doing, what are you doing, you reckless man, leave, you are violating the sanctuary of law.'[38] Others ran from across the room, jumping over benches, surrounding Bonaparte, seizing him by the scruff of the neck, shaking him violently, and spitting insults at him. It was too much for Bonaparte: by all accounts he almost fainted.[39]

At the sight of their general in danger, the officers already stationed in the room dived into the mass of deputies. Murat, Lefebvre, Gardanne and the commissary Albon let fly with their fists. A few spectators in the public galleries took fright and thought it better to dash for the exits, thereby obstructing entry into the room. Spectators of both sexes, having jumped over the balustrade separating them from the deputies, became involved in the fray.[40] A brawl erupted between the conspirators and Jacobins. People were pushing and shoving, hitting out, and grabbing clothes. Some were trampled on. A woman shouted 'Vive Bonaparte!' and found an echo in the tumult. Deputies and soldiers scuffled with one another.

One deputy tripped on the carpet and fell flat on his face. Another, by the name of Destrem, a giant of a man, shouted right in Bonaparte's face, 'Is this the reason for your victories?' A grenadier by the name of Thomas Thomé cut his arm on the bayonet of one of his comrades as he rushed to Bonaparte's aid.[41] The soldiers were eventually able to tear Bonaparte away from the grasp of the outraged deputies. One officer took him by the shoulders, while four other soldiers protected him. They backed towards the door while Destrem laid into them with his fists. Bonaparte was finally dragged outside, held up by two grenadiers, as white as a sheet, his head to one side, almost unconscious. He had not been able to say one word the whole time.

During this time, cries of 'Outlaw!' had gone up. There was only one way to interpret this – they wanted his head. This could have left Bonaparte completely isolated as those terrified by the condemnation, the same that had been thrown at Robespierre before his downfall, began to distance themselves. According to their custom, the Jacobins called for a vote by show of hands. They now assailed the president, Lucien, demanding a vote to outlaw his own brother. In the face of the commotion, Lucien remained cool. He eventually managed to make himself heard above the noise. When the deputies had calmed down a little, he spoke – evenly, intelligently – trying to explain his brother's actions, that it was only normal he should enter the assembly to report on the situation. A deputy interrupted with: 'Today, Bonaparte has tarnished his glory, shame!' Another shouted: 'Bonaparte has acted like a king.' 'He has just forfeited the entire price of his services,' exclaimed another. 'Down with the dictator, down with tyrants!'[42]

With this, the assembly broke into an uproar once again; the Jacobin leaders demanded permission to speak. Lucien, however, was not short of expedients to prevent them from being heard. After speaking as president, Lucien had the right to step down from the chair, which he did, passing it to Chazal (pro-Bonaparte) to speak as a deputy. A Jacobin had beaten him to the rostrum, however, and Lucien was obliged to give way, but he stationed himself to the right of the speaker and refused to budge, despite the continual pushing and shoving among the deputies anxious to get next in line. In so doing, Lucien had forced a debate over whether his brother should be outlawed – the deputies would be compelled to discuss before they could vote – and had thus won some time.

Bonaparte went back to the room on the first floor. Sieyès and Ducos, a few generals and some of the faithful were with him. According to some eyewitnesses, Bonaparte just stood there for a moment, uttering incomprehensible phrases, hardly recognizing anyone present, even addressing Sieyès as 'general'.[43] He was visibly shaken by the ordeal he had just experienced. Everything depended on how he would now act. For the moment, however, Bonaparte and the others waited. Duquesnoy and Montrond, sent by Talleyrand, who throughout the day had kept himself informed of the mood of the two assemblies, had come to tell him that the Five Hundred had just declared him an outlaw (which was not true, but they were certainly on the verge of doing so). It was these words that finally convinced Bonaparte to act; he now had no choice but to resort to force. In this he was urged by his entourage, Murat and Leclerc and even Sieyès, who realized that the time had come for the army to intervene. Looking worn, Bonaparte drew his sword and, approaching an open window, cried out to the troops below, 'To arms, to arms'.[44]

Bonaparte entered the courtyard with his general staff to galvanize the troops, although what followed borders on the comedic. He mounted the same horse that he had trouble mastering the previous day; this time it may have even thrown him.[45] When he did eventually manage to control the beast and rode towards the grenadiers stationed in the courtyard and appealed to them with – 'Soldiers, can I count on you?' – there was no reply. These grenadiers acted as the guard to the Assembly, so it is not surprising that they hesitated. Bonaparte then rode on towards the outer courtyard where the regular troops, men loyal to him, were positioned. Those troops watched as he rode up and down the ranks on his intractable mount, shouting incoherently that they had tried to assassinate him, as if that were reason enough to overthrow the government. It was probably only because other high-ranking officers – Murat, Leclerc, Sérurier – took control and worked on the men, embellishing the assassination tale, that they eventually responded with the appropriate amount of indignation. Bonaparte could have used these men to disband the assembly, but an open clash with the Guards would have made for a bad impression. It was necessary to bring them around.

It was now almost five o'clock and getting dark; the interior of the palace was already dim. Outside, a mist had started to creep over the grounds.[46] The military men among the conspirators were aware that force would soon have to be used and yet no one seemed sure what had to be done. Lavalette later remarked that if a strong personality had confronted the Guards inside the palace, it would have been impossible to say how the day would have turned out.[47] But there, too, the neo-Jacobin generals – Jourdan and Augereau – were unable to summon the necessary courage either to rally the troops to the Councils or to use force against the conspirators.

In the Five Hundred, when Lucien finally managed to speak, he was unable to convince the Assembly to recall his brother.[48] Sporadic fighting was still taking place – Boulay de la Meurthe came to blows with another deputy at the foot of the rostrum – and Lucien's speech was lost in the general uproar. At one point, in a dramatic but pointless gesture, he took off his toga and threw it on the floor of the rostrum along with his hat, crying out: 'I have to renounce being heard and no longer having the means I declare deposed on the rostrum, as a sign of mourning, the marks of the popular magistrature.'[49] Lucien realized that he could no longer hope to control or influence the Assembly and that outside intervention was absolutely necessary. He recognized one of the inspectors, Frégeville, a Bonaparte sympathizer, and asked him to tell his brother: 'The session has to be interrupted within ten minutes, or I can no longer be held responsible for what happens.' Frégeville slipped outside of the Assembly to carry the message to Bonaparte, who now knew exactly how to act. Using the authority of his brother as president of the Five Hundred, Bonaparte ordered a captain of the Guard to take ten men, to enter the Assembly and to bring out Lucien.[50]

On entering the Orangerie, the captain shouted out in a loud voice: 'Vive la République.' The deputies thought that the army had come over to their side. The captain arrived at the foot of the rostrum, said a few words to the president, Chazal, and then invited

Lucien, still holding on to the rostrum for dear life, to follow him. Lucien, who did not seem to understand what he was asked to do, stood there dumbfounded, probably thinking that they had come to arrest him. The officer then stood behind Lucien and, lifting him under the arms off the ground, placed him at the foot of the rostrum amid the ten grenadiers who then dragged him outside. Tradition has it that once he was in the open Lucien recovered his senses; he harangued the Guard with his brother, declaring the vast majority of the Council under threat from a few dagger-wielding represen-tatives who were besieging the rostrum. He referred to them as 'audacious brigands', 'in the pay of England', and argued that it was they who were outlaws for having assailed the liberty of the Council.[51] He supposedly ended with another dramatic gesture. Drawing his sword and pointing it at his brother's breast, he swore that he would kill him with his own hand if he ever violated the 'Liberty of the French'.

With the president of the Five Hundred at his side, Bonaparte was given a semblance of legality, the lack of which had, until then, made the Guard hesitate: the Guard assumed that Lucien was speaking on behalf of the Five Hundred. At last, Bonaparte seems to have taken control, as he now gave the order to clear the rooms of deputies. It is difficult to unravel what follows in the confusion of soldiers, deputies and the public vying with each other within a limited space, and drummer boys adding to the general cacophony. Memories, let alone the accounts that were left, are unreliable, and can never tell the whole story, largely because different people saw different things at different times. It is possible, but unlikely, that Murat entered the room and roared, 'Citizens! You are dissolved', and that he turned to his men and shouted: 'Foutez-moi tout ce monde-là dehors' (Throw this lot out of here).[52] It is more likely that a certain chef de brigade, Dumoulin, was to have been the first to enter the Five Hundred – he later complained that his role that day was overlooked – and that, after Murat, Leclerc entered at the head of a column of grenadiers. It is likely that he announced: 'In the name of General Bonaparte, the legislature is dissolved. Good citizens must leave.'[53]

There are conflicting versions of what happened next. The official account later published during the Consulate has the troops advancing on the deputies with bayonets lowered.[54] In the uproar that ensued, benches were overturned as the deputies and public fell over each other in their hurry to get out, jumping out of windows in the process. But it suited the Brumairians, as they were to be known, to portray a weak, divided Five Hundred, and which acted in a cowardly fashion and without dignity by fleeing in fright. An alternative account relates a very different version of events:

> [My father, a member of the Five Hundred] often told me, [wrote General Auguste Petiet] concerning the invasion of the armed force in the Orangerie of Saint-Cloud things that were the opposite of the official accounts published by the Consuls. He maintained that the officer marching at the head of the troops shouted: '*All honest men leave or I will no longer be answerable for my actions!*' Everyone left the room without saying a word and it was not true that they jumped through the windows to escape more quickly.[55]

The truth probably lies somewhere in between: most deputies seem to have left in a dignified manner, and even had the time to take off their ceremonial clothes in adjoining changing rooms.[56] But a few deputies, seized by panic, appear to have decided on more expeditious methods, and some would have exited by the windows.[57]

The Final Scene

The victors spent the night at Saint-Cloud, but not without anxiety. It was still not known how Paris would react to the news of the violent dispersal of the Five Hundred. It would be prudent to present the event as an incident and not as the outcome of the day. The legality of what had occurred, however, would remain incomplete without support from both Councils. A lot of the deputies from the Orangerie were not far away, so Lucien, once again Lucien, had the idea of gathering a few of them together to form the semblance of an Assembly that would then proclaim itself to be the majority, and give the day's proceedings some kind of legal veneer. The regime that had been built on the death of Robespierre would not so much commit legal suicide, as suffer a kind of political euthanasia.

Ushers were sent to look for deputies. They were found in the taverns, *guingettes* and private homes surrounding Saint-Cloud. Carriages leaving for Paris were inspected and, if deputies were found, they were invited to come back to the château for an extraordinary session. The estimates vary as to how many members of the Five Hundred were actually present to play out the final scene – somewhere between thirty to one hundred[58] – but they were later dubbed the Council of Thirty by the Parisians. Article 75 of the Constitution stipulated that the Council of Five Hundred could not deliberate unless at least 200 of its members were not present. This is the reason the official accounts bloated the number to 350. In the Orangerie, by now almost dark, a few candles had been lit and placed on the bureau and on the rostrum, and the deliberations began.

Without going into the particulars,[59] at about eleven o'clock that night, Boulay de la Meurthe presented the report of a hastily formed 'commission' that had met to discuss a way forward. The report recommended that the Directory be dissolved and replaced by an 'executive commission' invested with full powers and composed of three consuls: Sieyès, Ducos and Bonaparte, in that order.[60] (Interestingly, the three consuls once belonged, respectively, to the clergy, the Third Estate and the nobility.) The consuls were given three objectives: to create order throughout the administration; to re-establish peace throughout the country; and to negotiate a solid and durable peace without.

After the report was voted, there was only one formality left. After each revolutionary change, an oath of loyalty was sworn either to the new regime or to the new Constitution.[61] It would have been nigh on sacrilegious not to follow what had already become a tradition. There was a problem, however. The Consulate was meant to be a provisional measure; the old Constitution may no longer have existed, but the new Constitution did not yet exist. To what, then, were they to swear an oath of loyalty? The difficulty was overcome when Lucien suggested that they swear an oath to the Republic, one and indivisible, and to such abstract principles as

liberty, equality and the representative system. The three consuls
were then invited to take the oath.

The assembly was slowly filling with people. Some had come
back from Paris, eager to show their willingness to rally to the new
regime. Some of the sightseers had hung around to watch the final
act of the play. Pauline was there, along with a few other women,
friends of the powerful. Some soldiers entered the room; servants
came and went. At two o'clock in the morning, the drums were
beaten and the consuls made their entrance, taking their place in
front of the president, Lucien, who addressed the weary spectators
before reading the oath. All three, with arms outstretched in the
Roman fashion, then replied: 'I swear.' The deputies automatically
cried out 'Vive la République', and then congratulated each other
on having saved the Republic. The same scene was played out
shortly afterwards in front of the Elders.

At about five o'clock that morning, Bonaparte left the Château of
Saint-Cloud and returned to his home in the rue de la Victoire in a
carriage, accompanied by Bourrienne, Sieyès, Gardanne and Lucien. On their way they passed a group of soldiers being marched
back to their barracks in Paris. They were singing the 'Ça Ira'.[62]
Bonaparte did not say a word the whole trip back, and there is no
indication of what he may have been thinking either about the day's
events, or about his assumption of power. When ever he spoke of
Brumaire again, it was always to reinforce the official version of
events. One thing is certain, though. If they had failed, Fouché
would certainly have had the conspirators arrested and executed.[63]
Bonaparte was thirty years of age – the same age as Paoli when he
was elected leader of the Corsican revolt – and he had just become
the most powerful man in France.

Epilogue

In Search of the Saviour

For a number of years the public had been indifferent to the political machinations of the Directory and the Councils. It was as though, according to one police report, they had been plunged into a 'lethargic sleep'.[1] In fact, if Paris remained calm, responses to the coup were a good deal more diverse in the provinces, where news of the overthrow of the Directory met a varied response, even within political factions, and where Jacobin clubs were still in operation. Many republicans simply did not know how to interpret the significance of the event. In Franche-Comté, for example, the neo-Jacobin reaction ranged from acceptance to open resistance.[2] In the Nord-Pas-de-Calais, Jacobins viewed Bonaparte as a tyrant; in the Doubs the authorities believed that the coup favoured the counter-revolution; Bonaparte's portrait was torn down from the municipality in the Jura and thrown into the fire; and in the Ardèche, the representative of the Directory denounced the man he called the new Cromwell.[3] In the vast majority of regions, however, news of the coup was greeted positively, if not with outright joy.

A similar range of responses could be seen in the army.[4] If the archives contain a number of flattering petitions to the consuls from armies in the field – the Army of the Rhine, for example, waxed lyrical about the coup – individual officers were less than enthusiastic. The new regime required an oath of loyalty; many refused to take it, even in the Army of Italy. Masséna, now in charge of a completely demoralized force, wrote to Bonaparte to say that certain divisions were against the coup.[5] A similar situation existed

in the Army of the North, where General Brune, considered too
republican, was ordered back to Paris despite a number of brilliant
victories.

In Paris, the republican press, although it might not have
agreed with Brumaire, tried to present it from a favourable angle
and stopped short of criticizing the coup, largely because of
characters like Sieyès and other veterans of the legislative assemblies associated with it. Their loyalty was not well founded.
Sieyès was to show himself incapable of producing a coherent
constitutional model, and thus did perhaps more than any other
person to pave the way for Bonaparte to take power.[6] The
moderate newspapers, like Roederer's *Journal de Paris* and *Le
Publiciste*, which were close to Talleyrand, necessarily lent un-
equivocal support to the new regime. Most of the seventy-three
newspapers in circulation in Paris at the time, however, were
royalist and openly criticized the events of 18–19 Brumaire over
a period of several weeks – the most radical among them were
l'Aristarque français, le Diplomate and *l'Ange Gabriel* – while a
number of anti-Bonaparte pamphlets appeared on the streets.[7]
None of this, of course, went unnoticed by the consuls.

This is, perhaps, why there was a concerted effort to justify the
coup, and why that effort focused on the person of Bonaparte
and the supposed attack on his life. The myth was probably the
result of a proclamation, written by Bonaparte himself the very
evening of the coup and pasted on the walls of Paris the next
day. It ran:

> I went to the Council of Five Hundred; alone, unarmed, head
> uncovered . . . Daggers . . . were immediately raised against their
> liberator [Bonaparte]; twenty assassins threw themselves on me
> and aimed at my chest. The grenadiers of the Legislative Corps,
> whom I had left at the entrance to the hall, ran to put themselves
> between me and the assassins. One of the brave grenadiers was
> struck and had his clothes torn by a dagger. They carried me
> out.[8]

This version of events would be perpetuated not only by the
procès-verbal of the Council of Five Hundred, but also in a

number of pamphlets and engravings in the weeks and months that followed, and it came to dominate the memoirs for the period.⁹ They transformed the farce of 19 Brumaire into a dramatic, theatrical adventure story.¹⁰

One of the most common engravings, which served as a prototype for others that followed, was by Charles-Melchior Descourtis.¹¹ Descourtis depicts Bonaparte in the room where the Five Hundred are gathered, surrounded by the grenadiers Thomas Thomé and Jean-Baptiste Pourée, who are protecting their commander from the deputies bent on striking him down (Barthélemy Arena is portrayed among the deputies). The scene is a fiction but it was a way for the conspirators to plant in the minds of contemporaries an association between the supposed attempted assassination of Bonaparte and the coup. Indeed, the attempted

C. Descourtis, *Séance du corps législatif a l'Orangerie de St. Cloud, apparition de Bonaparte et journée libératrice du 19 brumaire* (Session of the legislative body at the Orangerie, Saint-Cloud, appearance of Bonaparte and day of liberation, 10 November 1799), circa 1800. The image was accompanied by the proclamation that had been pasted on the walls of Paris the day after the coup. (*Bibliothèque nationale, Paris*)

assassination became a justification for the coup, thus distancing the true motives of the conspirators from the violence that is portrayed in the engraving.[12] The details in the engraving – the depiction of the Orangerie, the costumes of the deputies and the uniforms of the soldiers – lend the invention all the more credence. Important, too, is that the scene focuses on Bonaparte as the object of the attack, as victim, and, in the process, disregards every other player in the coup that day.[13] As with the bridge at Arcola three years earlier, the spotlight is turned on his image and person. Bonaparte again triumphs as an individual.

The theatres of Paris were quick to take up the refrain. Two days after the coup, on 12 November, a modest theatre called the Jeunes Artistes (Young Artists) performed a play called *Le Premier Rayon de Soleil* (The First Ray of Sunshine), in which a young general, (Bonaparte, of course) is believed to have been killed. His enemies want to tear down a mausoleum erected in his honour, but as they try to do so the general suddenly comes back to life, climbs up on to the mausoleum, and his terrified enemies prostrate themselves at his feet. Though it was wildly melodramatic, the public lapped it up. Brumaire as a theatrical subject was quickly taken up so that, within one week of the coup, just about every Parisian theatre of any note had written, rehearsed and performed pro-Bonaparte, anti-Jacobin plays based on the supposed events of the coup. On 13 November, the very popular Opéra-Comique performed *Les Mariniers de Saint-Cloud* (The Bargemen of Saint-Cloud). It was full of flattering remarks about Bonaparte and derogatory remarks about the deputies of the Five Hundred and the Elders, who were variously referred to as 'charlatans, intriguers, tyrants and brigands'. Although the public loudly applauded the play, Fouché, as minister of police, banned it for a while because, according to him, it 'bitterly recalled old memories that have to be effaced'.[14] This was also the case for *La Pêche aux Jacobins ou la Journée de Saint Cloud* (Fishing for Jacobins or the Day at Saint-Cloud), performed at the Troubadours Theatre. It was too violently anti-Jacobin for Fouché's liking. A note passed to the director of the establishment was enough to stop the performances. At the Théâtre du Vaudeville, *La Girouette de*

Saint Cloud (The Weathervane of Saint-Cloud) was being played. It contained the following lines.

> The flight to Egypt once
> Preserved the saviour of men,
> And yet a few malicious spirits
> Doubt it in the century in which we find ourselves,
> But one thing is certain in this day,
> Whatever one might think of the old miracle,
> It is from Egypt that there is a return
> That has brought a saviour to France.[15]

It was perhaps the first, but certainly not the last time, that a parallel would be drawn between Christ and Bonaparte as saviour. As late as January 1800, plays that had as their subject the 'Revolution of 18 Brumaire', as contemporaries referred to the coup, or which made some allusion to it, were still being well received by the public.[16]

As flattering as this was, Bonaparte soon put a stop to such theatrical representations. The police, moreover, began to forbid street singers from singing songs about Brumaire (we know, for example, that popular songs were sung in the cafés and the *guingettes* of Paris) and to confiscate caricatures of deputies.[17] In one of the most well-known caricatures of the times, the people are represented by a poor man who could breathe freely once again because a heavy load had been taken off his shoulders.

The new government obviously wanted people to forget about the coup as quickly as possible. The attitude is understandable. It had, after all, come to power through an illegal act, and, if it wanted to legitimize the new regime, it was best that the public was not constantly reminded of the fact.

That the coup succeeded at all, when it was so badly conceived and carried out, is indicative of the lack of support among the deputies for the regime they served. In the place of planning, Bonaparte had relied once again on Destiny, his 'star', to see him through. More than one supporter lost his nerve, and in the end the conspirators, or at least those in the army, reacted in the only way they knew how

Anonymous, *Ah! que je me sens soulage. Sept cent cinquante m'écrasent!* (Ah,
I feel relieved. Seven hundred and fifty were killing me!), circa 1799.
(Bibliothèque nationale, Paris)

– as soldiers, clearing obstacles out of their way with brute force.
Nevertheless, it was not because two drummer boys and a few
grenadiers cleared the Orangerie at Saint-Cloud on that day in
November that the Directory collapsed.[18] It collapsed, ultimately,
because of the Directory's own lack of respect for the republican
institutions that had been put in place after Thermidor, and a lack of
confidence in the people who represented those institutions.

One of the reasons for the monarchy's fall in 1792 had been a
general disaffection with the traditional forms of authority. People
had begun to believe that there were viable alternatives to the king,
and from there it was a small step to overthrowing the monarchy.
By 1799, the republican experiment was drawing to a close, even if
its institutions would survive a few more years. People were not

only dissatisfied with the alternatives that had been tried since the fall of the monarchy, but there was also a tendency to look back upon the *ancien régime* with nostalgia. Certainly one of the reasons no one lifted a hand to defend the Directory was because both the left and the right were reluctant to defend a government that was almost universally considered a failure.[19] Put another way, many moderate politicians simply could not abide the fact that others – royalists on the right, Jacobins on the left – challenged their authority.[20] This was why elections were overturned when they did not produce the desired outcome.

Nevertheless, all those who took part in the coup sincerely believed they were acting to save the Revolution, and that probably included Bonaparte himself. The conspirators were intent not so much on overthrowing the Republic as 'regenerating' it. There was, as yet, no question of one man assuming executive power and it would be unfair to conclude, as some have done, that these were men with only 'half-hearted republican convictions'.[21] The conspirators sincerely believed that they were replacing an arbitrary and incoherent regime riven with factionalism with what they hoped would be a more liberal and orderly one. Over the coming weeks and months, though, Bonaparte would go on to usurp the political process – something that no one could have foreseen – and place himself at the centre of the new constitutional provisions drawn up by the leaders of the coup.

Bonaparte was, in part, able to do this because he could draw on a groundwork of propaganda, myth-making and fact. He had gained huge popularity after leading the victorious campaigns against Austria in northern Italy. Propaganda, in turn, embellished these victories and glossed over any setbacks or defeats, giving the impression that Bonaparte was responsible for a series of uninterrupted successes. This was especially the case after the Battle of Rivoli and the fall of Mantua, when he gained his hero status. Another important message, reinforced in dozens of pamphlets in the weeks and months after the Brumaire coup, was the deplorable state of affairs in France before the arrival of Bonaparte. One pamphlet in particular, published anonymously, but written by Jullien, the former editor of Bonaparte's *Courrier de l'armée*, lamented that:

There was no national representation, no government, no constitution. Our conquests lost, our laurels tarnished, peace impossible except on dishonourable terms, our armies destroyed, the French name reviled by both enemies and allies, the republic fallen into the utmost debasement and misery, the aims of the revolution miscarried, the fruits of our labours, sacrifices and victories annihilated, the dregs of faction agitating and disputing with foreigners over the shreds of our country – that is what struck the observer.[22]

And that was just the start of a long list of similar complaints, written by Brumairians in a style of rhetoric stolen from Jacobin opposition pamphlets.[23] The fact that many of them were either false or grossly exaggerated was irrelevant. It had to be shown that Bonaparte had dragged France from the edge of the abyss, an image reinforced in numerous books, pamphlets and popular songs throughout the Consulate and the Empire.[24] The verse of one popular song repeated the harangue Bonaparte delivered to Barras' secretary, Bottot, on the first day of the coup.[25]

In periods of political crisis, 'saviours' often emerge, but they, and indeed sometimes the crisis in question, are largely inventions. This was the case in 1799, as it would be for other periods of French history: Napoleon III, and even Pétain and de Gaulle were portrayed as 'saviours'. If they succeeded, it was in large part because they fulfilled a profound need among the French.[26] Bonaparte filled a vacuum in the French political culture of his time: the need for a personality who would dominate the revolutionary landscape. Each time this had begun to happen in the past, the man in question either died – as with Mirabeau; was discredited as politically inept, as with Lafayette; or was sent to the guillotine, in the case of Danton and Robespierre. Besides, the Revolution's ideology worked against any one individual gaining a position of supreme political power. Barras, the longest surviving political leader in the revolutionary period, was able to stay in power so long because he was nominally one individual in a five-man executive. Bonaparte, however, seems to have filled a need for ordinary French men and women, as well as members of the political elite, to identify with and celebrate an individual who embodied republican virtues – honour, glory, and the possibility that an individual of relatively humble origins could achieve great things.[27]

This is undoubtedly why the 'saviour' image found such a positive echo in the French public. But it was a cultivated image that was, moreover, bred and reinforced over a long period of time until it was sanctified in memory. In 1807, Napoleon had the ship which brought him back to France from Egypt, the *Muiron*, displayed in the arsenal at Toulon with the inscription, 'In 1799, it brought the saviour back to France'.[28] As late as 1810, in an allegorical painting of Brumaire – Jean-Pierre Franque's *Allégorie sur l'état de La France avant le retour d'Egypte* – Bonaparte is woken from a dream by France, who, out of the shadows of the pyramids, calls on him to save her.[29] The figures behind the symbol

Jean-Pierre Franque, *Allégorie sur l'état de la France avant le retour d'Egypte* (Allegory on the State of France before the Return from Egypt), 1810. (*Courtesy of Photo RMN –* © *Droits réservés*)

of the *patrie* personify Crime and Blind Fury, while Plenty and the Altar of Law have been overturned. The message is clear: Bonaparte went to Egypt on a civilizing mission, and returned from there to bring 'pharaonic stability' to France. In other words, in spite of all the evidence, the Egyptian campaign invested Bonaparte with the political as well as the moral authority needed to put an end to the political woes being inflicted on France.

Later, Napoleon would make a vain attempt to use the saviour myth when he escaped from exile on Elba in 1814. On landing in the Golf-Juan, he is said to have proclaimed that he had come 'once again to save you [the French people] from anarchy.'[30] It was, in some ways, a hollow attempt to relive what he had been through fifteen years previously, this time, however, with the disastrous consequences that we know – defeat and again exile. On St Helena, Napoleon persisted with the myth, usually by reinforcing the image of a pre-Brumaire France brought back from the brink of the abyss by his arrival from Egypt.[31]

In Search of Bonaparte

Bonaparte's attentiveness to managing his image, and hiding his mistakes, will no doubt strike the reader as a particularly modern approach to politics. For all that, the French people did not unquestioningly accept the image that was given them. As we have seen, scepticism of and even hostility towards the image were expressed in the press when it was first being constructed. Nor, once the image-making process had begun, did Bonaparte always control its flow. Artists and journalists, inspired by the idea of the hero, contributed to its dissemination in newspaper articles, pamphlets and plays, by creating artistic works that mirrored the message coming from Italy. However, the representations Bonaparte did commission, the articles he wrote for newspapers, and his behaviour in certain contexts all reveal aspects of his character that were rarely openly expressed.[32]

This behaviour, and the images he projected on to the French public, can be interpreted both in personal and in political terms. In personal terms, Bonaparte created a distance between himself and those around him, as much in order to prevent familiarity as to create an aura of power.[33] One way of doing this was by adopting a strict etiquette, a technique he would continue to develop during the Consulate, thus keeping himself in 'deferential solitude'. This behaviour can also be interpreted as a desire to dominate, to rise above others. But that is only part of the answer. In fact, just as Bonaparte projected on to Paoli an idealized image of what he thought a freedom fighter cum father figure should be like, here, too, in some respects, he projected on to the French people an idealized portrait of how he wanted to be perceived.

In political terms, Bonaparte's propaganda in Italy was also part of a struggle with the Directory to break free from its hold and then to maintain his independence. Once he had done so, there were only limited options open to him: to gain power through the Directory, which, as we know, he was ineligible for at this time in his life; to fall into obscurity; or to become associated with a plot to take power by extra-legal means. This last option led to the coup of Brumaire. After that, the state was harnessed to promote his image.

Reflecting on Bonaparte as an individual on the verge of becoming the most powerful man in the most powerful country in Europe, it was obvious to many who came into contact with him that he was talented, intelligent and passionate. He was capable of inspiring others – authors, artists and soldiers – and all this at a time when the world did not lack inspiring men. There was, nevertheless, an all too human side to Bonaparte that sometimes stooped to the petty and the vindictive. His behaviour during the Easter Sunday murders in Ajaccio is a good example, as was his behaviour during certain moments of the Egyptian campaign. This callousness towards the lives of others, both his own men and certainly those who opposed him, is hardly exceptional in the character of a leading public personality, and is certainly no more marked in Bonaparte than in any other ruler, general or politician of the time. Power and empathy towards others are often inversely proportional – the more power, the greater the indifference. It is true that Bonaparte was not generally vindictive towards those close to him and who followed him loyally, even if they proved to be militarily or administratively incompetent. But when it was a question of sacrificing the lives of others in order to promote his own ambition, Bonaparte never hesitated.

Much of the energy that characterized Bonaparte as a young man was directed towards fulfilling an ideal outside of himself through politics, at first in Corsica at the local level, where he was faced with a harsh reality that did not at all coincide with his naïve preconceptions, and then in France. In both instances, his affiliation with Jacobinism proved disastrous. In Corsica, the Jacobins were associated with the anti-Paolist, pro-French clique that was temporarily expelled from the island in 1793. In France, the Jacobins were associated with the Terror that came to an end with the fall of Robespierre in July 1794, and which led to Bonaparte's short spell in prison. His refusal to fight in the Vendée further damaged his career. He was faced with two choices: to reluctantly carry out his orders, which he seems to have been on the verge of doing; or to dawdle in Paris in the hope that his connections would eventually get him a better posting. Relations had proved useful in the past. His links to Saliceti on Corsica led to his being appointed commander of the artillery at the siege of Toulon, where, among other people, he ran into Barras. Again in Paris, Barras, in charge of the defence of the Convention during the Vendémiaire troubles, no doubt remembered Bonaparte from Toulon as he cast around for officers to help suppress the uprising. The importance of connections, something that Carlo Buonaparte had perhaps instilled in his children, but which was certainly an integral part of the Corsican clan system, was fundamental on these two occasions. The right man, in the right place, at the right time?[34] The siege of Toulon and the Vendémiaire uprising, two important stages on the path to Bonaparte's public recognition, are often portrayed in this way, but one should also remember that, in the past, relations had also proved to be devastatingly detrimental to Bonaparte's career. This is perhaps why it is not so much a question of luck, coincidence, or concordance of circumstances – thinking that fuels the myth that Bonaparte was destined to become what he became – but more about an astute exploitation of the opportunities Bonaparte saw before him.

The military campaign in Italy illustrates this. There is little doubt that Bonaparte had a flair for battle, a natural, as yet largely untapped, talent that unexpectedly exploded on to the scene. Bonaparte's own youthful zeal, the intense surge of love he felt for Josephine, and the need to prove his capabilities both to himself and to others all combined to produce a warrior with a sense of mission. The 'hero' and the 'mission' were, as we have seen, notions that were deliberately fostered in the press of the day. This is where Bonaparte distinguished himself from other generals. He not only knew how to win battles, but he also knew how to exploit those victories politically. Consciously or otherwise, he created an image of himself, largely for public consumption, that he was obliged to live up to from that time on. And it is this image that has lived on, the image that finds such an echo through generations of history enthusiasts – the individual who takes control of his life, who rises above the masses, and who attains power through the realization of his dreams. It is the essence of the heroic myth.[35]

Bonaparte was himself deeply imbued with this naïve notion of the role of the individual in history. We know that, at Brienne, he had been exposed to a number of Latin authors – Homer, Virgil, Livy, Cicero and Cornelius among them – as well as Caesar's *Commentaries* and Plutarch's *Parallel Lives*. Did Plutarch offer him models of how great men were supposed to behave?[36] Possibly. Alexander and especially Caesar were examples Napoleon could reflect on throughout his life. He would also have been exposed to the great seventeenth-century French writers, Corneille and Racine, Fénélon and Bossuet. The *Histoire des chevaliers de Malte*, first published in 1726 and written by Abbé René Aubert de Vertot, was regarded as a classic text that had to be learned by heart at school.[37] He also read history, such as Jean-Charles Laveaux's *Vie de Frédéric II*, even if his reading was relatively superficial and provided few great insight into military strategy or tactics. It is perhaps from books like these that Buonaparte first gleaned the idea that it was possible for an individual as a soldier to make something of his life.

He could not, therefore, sit idly by after the successful military conclusion to the Italian campaign. By that time, he had not only had a taste of power and was determined to hang on to it, but he was also firmly convinced that he was destined to play a great role in history. Someone a little more foolhardy might have been tempted to gain power then and there; he was riding on a wave of popularity and he was being urged to participate in a coup by any number of people. But Bonaparte wisely concluded that the time was not ripe and that there was more to be gained by an exotic adventure in the Orient than in a potentially disastrous attempt to overthrow the government or invade England. In military terms, the Egyptian campaign was questionable to say the least. The objectives were vague, the means given to Bonaparte to carry them out proved insufficient, and, without the possibility of sustained reinforcements and supplies from France, the viability of the French presence so far from home was problematic to say the least. None of that mattered in the long run. Egypt was never about French colonial ambitions; it was about Bonaparte. It is unlikely that he planned to stay any longer than was necessary to enhance his already growing reputation. And that, despite serious setbacks, is exactly what he managed to do. By the time he returned home in October 1799, after literally abandoning his men, much of the groundwork had been laid. Little concerted propaganda was necessary; the idea of Bonaparte and the French in the Orient was enough to impress and inspire the popular imagination. He returned to France as though a saviour.

Bonaparte was astute enough, however, not to rush into anything without first feeling his way, without discussing his options. A coup against the Directory was going to take place with or without him; it was simply a question of negotiating a suitable role. The role that was assigned him and the role that he assumed were, however, two different things; he was, after all, brought on board somewhat reluctantly by occasional allies who turned to him as a last resort, and who had decided that he would play nothing more than a secondary, supporting role. Once again, Bonaparte showed what he could do when the opportunity presented itself: Toulon, Italy and Egypt are examples of what Bonaparte achieved where others had floundered. Brumaire, too, could have been disastrous. That it was not had little to do with Bonaparte's performance on the day – perhaps the worst of his career – and more with the actions taken by those in his entourage, especially his brother, Lucien.

Bonaparte, in other words, was not acting alone, nor was he the primary force behind the coup. Rather, he was acting in concert with, and was, initially at least, subordinate to many other politicians who had been working towards the coup months before he returned from Egypt. In some respects, power fell into Bonaparte's lap because those around him were too ineffectual to grab it themselves. The Brumairians knew they wanted to overturn the Constitution of 1795, but had given little thought to what they would do next. The end of democracy in France is inevitably associated with the rise of Bonaparte. However, it is worth underlining that democracy was being eroded well before Bonaparte came on the scene. The number of coups between 1795 and 1799 and the consequent political disaffection attest to this. In short, the social-political climate made Bonaparte possible, even if he contributed to that climate with military campaigns that destabilized not only the foreign political situation, but also the domestic political landscape.

Chances are the Directory was bound to fail, and that given the increasing militarization of French society, it was only a matter of time before a general came on the scene. But then, why not a general like Washington? This is where the role of the individual in history comes into play. Once Bonaparte became involved in the conspiracy he was able to hijack the whole process to his own advantage, to impose himself and his own agenda on the conspirators, and to use the circumstances to his own ends. This ability is what distinguished Bonaparte from many of his contemporaries. But none of that was obvious once the coup was over. Even if the words Bonaparte used to reproach the Directory on the first day of the coup in front of the Tuileries Palace – 'within three years it will lead to despotism' – were portentous, nobody riding back in that carriage from Saint-Cloud on that fateful day in November 1799 could have envisaged what kind of political institutions and structures would evolve over the next few months and years. Not even Bonaparte.

Notes

Prologue: The Bridge at Arcola

1 Marcel Reinhard, *Avec Bonaparte en Italie d'après les lettres inédites de son aide de camp Joseph Sulkowski* (Paris, 1946), p. 178.

2 Reinhard, *Sulkowski*, pp. 177–9.

3 Jean-Gabriel Peltier, *Examen de la campagne de Buonaparte en Italie par un témoin oculaire* Paris, 1814), pp. 73–4.

4 *Corr[espondance de Napoléon I publiée par ordre de l'empereur Napoléon III]*, 32 vols (Paris, 1858–1870), ii. n. 1197 (19 November 1796).

5 Edmond Chevrier, *Le Général Joubert, d'après sa correspondance* (Paris, 1884), p. 62 (22 November 1796).

6 Cited in Reinhard, *Sulkowski*, p. 171 (13 November 1796).

7 Cited in Reinhard, *Sulkowski*, p. 171 (13 November 1796).

8 *Moniteur universel*, 2 December 1796.

9 *Moniteur universel*, 2 December 1796.

10 Report by Jean Debry in the Council of Five Hundred. Cited in Michel Vovelle, 'Naissance et formation du mythe napoléonien en Italie durant le trienno. Les leçons de l'image', in Luigi Samarati (ed.), *Napoleone e la Lombardia nel Triennio Giacobino (1796–1799)* (Lodi, 1997), p. 32.

11 *Moniteur universel*, 2 January 1797; Vovelle, 'Naissance et formation du mythe napoléonien', p. 32.

12 *Moniteur universel*, 9 December 1796. 'Arcole, en tes vallons fameux par nos guerriers,/Les larmes du vainqueur ont mouillé ses lauriers.'

13 On Gros and his first painting of Bonaparte see, David O'Brien, *After the Revolution: Antoine-Jean Gros, Painting and Propaganda under Napoleon* (University Park, 2006), pp. 31–7.

14 J.-B. Delestre, *Gros et ses ouvrages* (Paris, 1845), pp. 30–1 (6 December 1796).

15 Delestre, *Gros et ses ouvrages*, pp. 33–4.

16 Antoine-Marie Chamans, Comte de Lavalette, *Mémoires et souvenirs du comte de Lavalette* (Paris, 1994), pp. 138–9.

17 Christopher Prendergast, *Napoleon and History Painting: Antoine-Jean Gros's La Bataille d'Eylau* (Oxford, 1997), p. 146.

18 John L. Connolly, 'Bonaparte on the Bridge', *Proceedings of the Consortium on Revolutionary Europe* (1985), p. 50.

19 Christian-Marc Bosséno, '"Je me vis dans l'histoire": Bonaparte, de Lodi à Arcole, généalogie d'une image de légende', *Annales historiques de la Révolution Française*, 313 (1998), 463–5, has retraced the figure of Bonaparte in Gros's painting to the classic representations of the goddess of History.

20 O'Brien, *After the Revolution*, p. 34.

21 See Edouard Pommier, 'L'invention du monument aux Grands Hommes (XVIIIe siècle)', in *Entretiens de la Garenne Lemot. Le culte des Grands Hommes au XVIIIe siècle. Actes du Colloque 3 au 5 octobre 1996* (Nantes, 1998), pp. 8–23; Jean-Claude Bonnet, *Naissance du Panthéon: essai sur le culte des grands hommes* (1998); Bonnet, 'Naissance du Panthéon', *Poétique*, 33 (1978), 46–55; Mona Ozouf, 'The Pantheon', in Pierre Nora (ed.), *Realms of Memory: Rethinking the French Past*, trans. Arthur Goldhammer, 3 vols (New York, 1996–8), iii. pp. 325–46; James A. Leith, 'Youth Heroes of the French Revolution', *Proceedings of the Consortium on Revolutionary Europe* (1986), 127; Leith, 'Nationalism and the fine arts in France, 1750–1789', *Studies on Voltaire in the Eighteenth Century*, 89 (1972), 926–7; and David A. Bell, *The Cult of the Nation in France. Inventing Nationalism, 1680–1800* (Cambridge, Mass., 2001), ch. 4.

22 For the following see Annie Jourdan, *Les Monuments de la Révolution, 1770–1804. Une histoire de représentation* (Paris, 1997), pp. 89–138.

23 Jourdan, *Les Monuments de la Révolution*, pp. 110, 125.

24 Ozouf, 'The Pantheon', p. 328.

25 *Courrier de l'Armée d'Italie*, 15 but also 23, 25 October, 2, 4, 22 November 1797.

26 Germaine de Staël, *Considérations sur la Révolution française* (Paris, 1983), p. 328.

1 The Pleasure of Recognition

1 Frédéric Masson and Guido Biagi, *Napoléon inconnu, papiers inédits (1769–1793)*, 2 vols (Paris, 1895), i. p. 145.

2 Dorothy Carrington, *Portrait de Charles Bonaparte* (Ajaccio, 2002), p. 58.

3 Frédéric Masson, *Napoléon et sa famille* (Paris, 1897), i. p. 41.

4 'Discours de Lyon', in Masson and Biagi, *Napoléon inconnu*, ii. p. 305.

5 Joseph Bonaparte, *Mémoires et correspondance politique et militaire du roi Joseph* (Paris, 1853–4), i. p. 37.

6 The absence of a religious ceremony was a fairly common practice in Corsica in the eighteenth and into the nineteenth century. It was, nevertheless, a valid union in the eyes of the families concerned. See Madeleine-Rose Marin-Muracciole, *L'honneur des femmes en Corse du XIIIe siècle à nos jours* (Paris, 1964), pp. 278–87. In fact, the couple do not seem to have kept house together until 1767, two children and three years after signing the dotal settlement.

7 We think that Letizia was born in 1749. For a discussion of her age see Dorothy Carrington, *Napoleon and His Parents: On the Threshold of History* (London, 1988), p. 17, n. 12. This minimum age for marriage in the eyes of the Church was fourteen for boys and twelve for girls, that is, the age of puberty.

8 Carrington, *Portrait*, pp. 15–20; Carrington, *Napoleon and His Parents*, pp. 24–5.

9 Carrington, *Napoleon and His Parents*, p. 27.

10 Carrington, *Portrait*, pp. 23–4; Carrington, *Napoleon and His Parents*, pp. 28–9.

11 Henri Gatien Bertrand, *Cahiers de Sainte-Hélène: 1818–1819* (Paris, 1959), p 136.

12 James Boswell, *An Account of Corsica; The Journal of a Tour to the Island; and Memoirs of Pascal Paoli* (Glasgow, 1768), pp. 351–2; and Boswell, *The Journal of a Tour to Corsica; and Memoirs of Pascal Paoli* (London, 1951), p. 68. See also Peter Martin, *James Boswell. A Life* (New Haven, 1999), pp. 204–7.

13 Pierre Carboni, 'Boswell et Paoli: Un Plutarque écossais et son Lycurgue corse', in *Entretiens de la Garenne Lemot. Le culte des Grands Hommes au XVIIIe siècle. Actes du Colloque 3 au 5 octobre 1996* (Nantes, 1998), pp. 109–18.

14 Boswell, *Journal*, p. 68.

15 The literature on Paoli in French, Italian and English is extensive. Relevant to this chapter are C. Ambrosi, 'Pascal Paoli et la Corse de 1789 à 1791', *Revue d'Histoire Moderne et Contemporaine*, 2 (1955), 161–184; D. Carrington, 'The Achievement of Pasquale Paoli (1755–1769) and its Con-

sequences', *Proceedings of the Consortium on Revolutionary Europe*, 16 (1986), 56–69; J. Defranceschi, 'De la légende à l'histoire', pp. 131–145; and Fernand Ettori, 'Paoli, Modèle du Jeune Napoléon', in *Problèmes d'Histoire de la Corse*, pp. 89–99. P. A. Thrasher, *Pasquale Paoli. An Enlightened Hero, 1725–1807* (1970), is an adequate account of his life.

16 D. Carrington, 'Pascal Paoli et sa "Constitution" (1755–1769)', *Annales historiques de la Révolution Française*, 218 (1974), 508–41.

17 'Exposé historique', in Carrington, *Portrait de Charles Bonaparte*, p. 95.

18 V. de Caraffa (ed.), 'Mémoires historiques sur la Corse par un officier du régiment de Picardie, 1774–1777', *Bulletin de la Société des sciences historiques et naturelles de la Corse* (1889), 33.

19 Gabriel Feydel, *Mœurs et coutumes des Corses* (Paris, 1798), pp. 17–18.

20 C. F. Dumouriez, *La vie et les mémoires du général Dumouriez* (Paris, 1822), i. pp. 132–7; Voltaire, 'Le Siècle de Louis XV', in *Œuvres historiques* (Paris, 1957), p. 1552.

21 Dumouriez, *La vie et les mémoires*, i. p. 98.

22 L. Letteron (ed.), 'Opérations militaires de la réduction de la Corse du 1er au 25 mai 1769, par M. de Guibert, major général de l'armée commandée par M. le comte de Vaux, lieutenant général des armées du roi', *Bulletin de la Société des sciences historiques et naturelles de la Corse* (1913), 38–9; Chevalier de Lenchère, 'Journal des campagnes de 1768 & 1769 en Corse par le chevalier de Lenchère', *Bulletin de la Société des sciences historiques et naturelles de la Corse* (July 1889), pp. 455–6; Dumouriez, *La vie et les mémoires*, i. p. 124.

23 Carrington, *Napoleon and His Parents*, p. 45; Robert G. Stewart, 'The Portraits of Henry Benbridge', *American Art Journal*, 2 (1970), 65.

24 Emmanuel de Las Cases, *Le Mémorial de Sainte-Hélène*, 2 vols (Paris, 1983), i. p. 82. Luciano, along with a number of other prominent Ajacciens, declared himself a loyal subject of His Very Christian Majesty, Louis XV only three weeks before the battle of Ponte Nuovo (Xavier Versini, *M. de Buonaparte ou le livre inachevé* (Paris, 1977), pp. 21–2).

25 Between the years 1772 and 1776, the Picardy Regiment, for example, lost 312 men in Corsica, although many of these would probably have died as a result of sickness. Caraffa, 'Mémoires historiques sur la Corse', 95–8.

26 Christine Roux, *Les 'Makis' de la résistance Corse, 1772–1778* (Paris, 1984).

27 Alphonse Chuquet, *La Jeunesse de Napoléon*, 3 vols (Paris, 1897–9), i. p. 22.

28　Carrington, *Portrait*, p. 52.

29　J. M. P. McErlean, *Napoleon and Pozzo di Borgo and After, 1764–1821: Not Quite a Vendetta* (Lewiston, 1996), pp. 16–17.

30　John McErlean, 'Scholarships for the Bonapartes: The Political Background', *Napoleonic Alliance Gazette*, 4 (2003), 21.

31　On the nature of Letizia's relationship with Marbeuf, see Carrington, *Portrait*, pp. 71, 125–6.

32　On the order and the school at Brienne, see Arthur-Emile Prévost, *Le Collège et les premiers maîtres de Napoléon. Les Minimes de Brienne* (Troyes, 1915).

33　The following is based on Masson and Biagi, *Napoléon inconnu*, i. pp. 53–86; Chuquet, *Jeunesse*, i. pp. 85–180; Carrington, *Napoleon and His Parents*, pp. 141–62.

34　Chuquet, *Jeunesse*, i. pp. 86–8.

35　Chuquet, *Jeunesse*, i. p. 190.

36　Chuquet, *Jeunesse*, i. p. 89.

37　Cited in Carrington, *Portrait*, p. 35.

38　Prévost, *Les Minimes de Brienne*, pp. 36–7.

39　Cited in Carrington, *Napoleon and His Parents*, p. 145.

40　Recently made nobles made up around 10 per cent of the officers graduating in the second half of the eighteenth century (David Bien, 'La réaction aristocratique avant 1789: l'exemple de l'armée', *Annales. Economies. Sociétés. Civilizations*, 29 (1974), 518–19).

41　Jay M. Smith, *The Culture of Merit: Nobility, Royal Service, and the Making of Absolute Monarchy in France, 1600–1789* (Ann Arbor, 1996), pp. 243–4.

42　Carrington, *Napoleon and His Parents*, pp. 142–3, 154–6.

43　These stories were often cited by earlier biographers, such as the pamphlet by J.-T. Bigrat, *Buonaparte dévoilé aux yeux de la France et l'Europe entière* (Paris, nd), pp. 3–4. The mattress story is in Bertrand, *Cahiers: 1816–1817*, p. 286. The garden story is related by C. H., *Some account of the early years of Buonaparte, at the Military School of Brienne* (London, 1797), p. 19. The author of this pamphlet has been identified by Vincent Cronin, *Napoleon* (London, 1971), p. 453, as, possibly, Cumming of Craigmillar, an English boy who was Napoloeone's contemporary at Brienne.

44　The anecdote, often repeated by historians, is told by Napoleon in Las Cases, *Mémorial*, i. pp. 91–2.

45　*La France vue de l'armée d'Italie. Journal de politique, d'administration et de littérature française et étrangère*, n. 15.

46 *Traits caractéristiques de la jeunesse de Bonaparte et réfutation des différentes anecdotes qui ont été publiées a ce sujet* (Leipzig, 1802), pp. 17–18.

47 See, for example, Philippe-Paul, Comte de Ségur, *Histoire et mémoires* (Paris, 1877), i. p. 72; and Antoine-Vincent Arnault, *Vie politique et militaire de Napoléon* (Paris, 1822), i. p. 2.

48 Louis-Antoine Fauvelet de Bourrienne, *Mémoires de M. de Bourrienne, ministre d'Etat sous Napoléon* (Paris, 1829), i. pp. 15–16. Jean Tulard (ed.), *Bibliographie critique des mémoires sur le Consulat et l'Empire* (Geneva, 1971), pp. 25–6, believes the memoirs were probably written by Charles de Villemarest, who had been attached to Talleyrand's office.

49 Carrington, *Napoleon and His Parents*, pp. 162–3.

50 Jean-Antoine Chaptal, *Mes souvenirs sur Napoléon* (Paris, 1893), p. 175.

51 Carrington, *Napoleon and His Parents*, pp. 161–2.

52 On the professionalization of the army officer corps see David Bien, 'The Army in the French Enlightenment: Reform, Reaction and Revolution', *Past & Present*, 85 (1979), 68–98. Bien asserts that the artillery was both one of the most highly professional of all sectors of the armed forces in the late eighteenth century and one sector in which noble dominance was least marked. See also S. F. Scott, 'The French Revolution and the Professionalization of the French Officer Corps', in M. Janowitz and J. van Doorn (eds), *On Military Ideology* (Rotterdam, 1971), pp. 8–18.

2 'You Will Be My Avenger'

1 François Vigo-Roussillon, *Journal de Campagne (1793–1837)* (Paris, 1981), p. 128.

2 Arthur Young, *Travels in France* (London, 1889), p. 103 (25 October 1787).

3 Louis-Sébastien Mercier, *Tableau de Paris*, in *Paris le jour, Paris la nuit* (Paris, 1990), pp. 189–90.

4 Rafe Blaufarb, *The French Army, 1750–1820. Careers, Talent, Merit* (Manchester, 2002), p. 21; Smith, *The Culture of Merit*, pp. 200–202.

5 For Buonaparte at the *Ecole militaire* see Masson and Biagi, *Napoléon inconnu*, i. pp. 87–127; Chuquet, *Jeunesse*, i. pp. 181–264; Carrington, *Napoleon and His Parents*, pp. 175–83, 191–4.

6 Las Cases, *Mémorial*, i. p. 678.

7 Robert Laulan, 'La chère à l'Ecole militaire au temps de Bonaparte', *Revue de l'Institut Napoléon*, 70 (1959), 18–23.

8 Robert Laulan, 'Pourquoi et comment on entrait à l'Ecole royale

militaire de Paris', *Revue d'Histoire Moderne et Contemporaine*, 4 (1957), 146–7.

9 Carrington, *Napoleon and His Parents*, p. 178; Chuquet, *Jeunesse*, i. pp. 260–1.

10 Laure, Duchesse d'Abrantès, *Mémoires de la duchesse d'Abrantès* (Paris, 1967), i. pp. 49–50.

11 Théodore Iung, *Lucien Bonaparte et ses Mémoires, 1775–1840*, 3 vols (Paris, 1882), i. pp. 21–22.

12 Joseph, *Mémoires*, i. p. 26.

13 See Ettori, 'Paoli, Modèle du Jeune Napoléon', pp. 93–5. On the subject of eighteenth-century interest in Corsica, see T. E. Hall, 'The Development of Enlightenment Interest in Eighteenth-Century Corsica', *Studies on Voltaire and the Eighteenth Century*, 44 (1968), 165–85.

14 Masson and Biagi, *Napoléon inconnu*, i. pp. 82–3.

15 See Francis Beretti, *Pascal Paoli et l'image de la Corse au dix-huitième siècle* (Oxford, 1988), pp. 190–210.

16 Ettori, 'Pascal Paoli, modèle du jeune Bonaparte', pp. 89–99.

17 Nira Kaplan, 'Virtuous Competition among Citizens: Emulation in Politics and Pedagogy during the French Revolution', *Eighteenth-Century Studies*, 36 (2003), 241.

18 'Sur la Corse', in Masson and Biagi, *Napoléon inconnu*, i. p. 141.

19 'Discours de Lyon', in Masson and Biagi, *Napoléon inconnu*, ii. p. 295.

20 'Première lettre sur la Corse', in Masson and Biagi, *Napolèon inconnu*, i. p. 396.

21 'Discours de Lyon', Masson and Biagi, *Napoléon inconnu*, ii. p. 299, and 'Lettre de M. de Buonaparte à M. Matteo Buttafuoco, député de la Corse à l'Assemblée Nationale', Masson and Biagi, *Napoléon inconnu*, ii. p. 181. Lycurgus was a ninth century BC Spartan lawgiver, traditionally considered the founder of the Spartan constitution. Solon was a sixth century BC Athenian statesman responsible for a number of important economic, legal and political reforms.

22 The story is accepted at face value by Chuquet, *Jeunesse*, i. p. 262, even though it was refuted by the author of an anonymous booklet who claimed to be a comrade of Buonaparte at both Brienne and Paris – *Traits caractéristiques de la jeunesse de Bonaparte*, pp. ix–x.

23 *Traits caractéristiques de la jeunesse de Bonaparte*, p. 30.

24 H. T. Parker, 'Napoleon's Youth and Rise to Power', in Philip Dwyer (ed.), *Napoleon and Europe* (London, 2001), p. 33.

25 This theme is also picked up in Andy Martin, *Napoleon the Novelist* (London, 2000), pp. 45–7.

26 Carrington, *Napoleon and His Parents*, p. 123.
27 See the entry 'Indentification' in J. Laplanche and J.-B. Pontalis (eds), *The Language of Psycho-Analysis* (New York, 1973), p. 207.
28 It was still being talked about years later. See Albert Soboul, 'Témoignage sur le général Bonaparte en l'an IV', *Annales historiques de la Révolution Française*, 27 (1955), 380–81.
29 Chuquet, *Jeunesse*, i. p. 262.
30 Cited in Bien, 'The Army in the French Enlightenment', p. 82.
31 Chuquet, *Jeunesse*, i. p. 263.
32 Harold T. Parker, 'The Formation of Napoleon's Personality: An Exploratory Essay', *French Historical Studies*, 7 (1971), 21.
33 Joseph, *Mémoires*, i. p. 29.
34 Chuquet, *Jeunesse*, i. pp. 211–12; Carrington, *Napoleon and His Parents*, pp. 186–9.
35 Masson and Biagi, *Napoléon inconnu*, i. p. 120, n. 2.
36 Masson and Biagi, *Napoléon inconnu*, i. p. 121.
37 Some contemporaries remarked on the indifference of the French towards death and compared it to the mourning practices of the ancient Greeks and 'primitive' peoples, both attached to their dead. See Margaret Fields Denton, 'Death in French Arcady: Nicolas Poussin's *The Arcadian Shepherds* and Burial Reform in France c. 1800', *Eighteenth-Century Studies*, 36 (2003), 202–3.
38 Carrington, *Napoleon and His Parents*, p. 192; Bertrand, *Cahiers, 1818–1819*, pp. 136–7.
39 Bertrand, *Cahiers, 1818–1819*, p. 136.
40 Las Cases, *Mémorial*, i. p. 566.
41 Carrington, *Napoleon and His Parents*, pp. 90–2, 192.
42 Carrington, *Portrait*, pp. 66–7, 72–3, 192.
43 The anecdote related by Bertrand, *Cahiers: 1818–1819*, p. 137, seems plausible.
44 Iung, *Lucien Bonaparte*, i. p. 49. Although this is more charactetistic of Bonaparte after 1800 than before.
45 For Buonaparte's first posting see Masson and Biagi, *Napoléon inconnu*, i. pp. 129–40; Chuquet, *Jeunesse*, i. pp. 265–89.
46 See Marcel Leijendecker, 'Un amour inconnu de Buonaparte', *Revue des études napoléoniennes*, 36 (1933), 52–5.
47 Las Cases, *Mémorial*, i. p. 101; F. G. Healey, *Rousseau et Napoléon* (Geneva, 1957), p. 4.
48 Healey, *Rousseau et Napoléon*, p. 5.
49 Joseph, *Mémoires*, i. p. 32.

50 Las Cases, *Mémorial*, ii. pp. 363–4.

51 Masson, *Napoléon dans sa jeunesse*, pp. 145–6; Healey, *Rousseau et Napoléon*, pp. 13–14, 22–45.

52 Jean Hanoteau (ed.), *Memoirs of General de Caulaincourt, Duke of Vicenza*, 3 vols (London, 1950), ii. p. 241.

53 Cited in Martin, *Napoleon the Novelist*, p. 14.

54 Bien, 'The Army in the French Enlightenment', p. 72.

55 One contemporary went so far as to remark that, without the prostitutes, the shops around the Palais Royal would have to close. François-Marie Mayeur de Saint-Paul, *Tableau du nouveau Palais-Royal* (Paris, 1788), ii. pp. 127–8.

56 Frédéric Masson and Guido Biagi, *Napoléon, manuscrits inédits, 1786–1791* (Paris, 1907), p. 21.

57 My thanks to Michael Sibalis for making this point.

58 Masson and Biagi, *Manuscrits inédits*, p. 173, n. 1.

59 Masson and Biagi, *Napoléon inconnu*, ii. pp. 528–9.

60 Ernest Hauterive, 'Lettres de jeunesse de Bonaparte', *Revue des Deux Mondes* (15 December 1931), 774 (28 March 1789).

61 For this period at Auxonne see Masson and Biagi, *Napoléon inconnu*, i. pp. 212–25; Chuquet, *Jeunesse*, i. pp. 304–60.

62 Hauterive, 'Lettres de jeunesse', 771 (28 March 1789).

63 Hauterive, 'Lettres de jeunesse', 775 (28 March 1789).

64 David Chandler, *The Campaigns of Napoleon* (London, 1966), pp. 139–40.

65 Smith, *The Culture of Merit*, pp. 214–15.

66 Hauterive, 'Lettres de jeunesse', 776 (15 April 1789).

67 Hauterive, 'Lettres de jeunesse', 780 (May 1789).

68 Hauterive, 'Lettres de jeunesse', 784 (22 July 1789).

69 Masson and Biagi, *Napoléon inconnu*, i. p. 214, n. 1.

70 Masson and Biagi, *Napoléon inconnu*, i. p. 360.

3 Corsica in Revolution

1 Félix de Romain, *Souvenirs d'un officier royaliste* (Paris, 1829), ii. pp. 13–14.

2 For Corsica in revolution see Masson and Biagi, *Napoléon inconnu*, ii. pp. 87–126; Chuquet, *Jeunesse*, ii. pp. 65–145; Emile Franceschini, 'La Corse aux premiers jours de la Révolution', *Revue de la Corse*, 62 (1930), 49–62; 63 (1930), 110–18; 64 (1930), 157–71; 65 (1930), 209–220; Antoine

Casanova and Ange Rovère, *Peuple corse, révolutions et nation française* (Paris, 1979); Casanova and Rovère, *La Révolution française en Corse* (Paris, 1989); Antoine Casanova, 'Caractères originaux et cheminements de la Révolution en Corse (1789–1797)', *Annales historiques de la Révolution Française*, 260 (1985), 140–172; Jean Defranceschi, *La Corse française (30 novembre 1789–15 juin 1794)* (Paris, 1980); Defranceschi, *La Corse et la Révolution française* (Ajaccio, 1991); McErlean, *Pozzo di Borgo*, pp. 29–68.

3 Jean Defranceschi, 'Le rôle de lieutenant Bonaparte aux débuts de la Révolution française en Corse', *Revue de l'Institut Napoléon*, 134 (1978), 6.

4 Romain, *Souvenirs*, ii. pp. 45–8.

5 Raoul Girardet, 'The Three Colours: Neither White nor Red', in Nora (ed.), *Realms of Memory*, iii. pp. 5–6. The tricolour may have had another origin, representing the three orders – white for the clergy, red for the nobility and blue for the Third Estate.

6 Chuquet, *Jeunesse*, ii. p. 69.

7 François Pomponi, 'Sentiments révolutionnaires et esprit de parti en Corse au temps de la Révolution', in *Problèmes d'Histoire de la Corse*, pp. 147–78; Louis Monestier, *Compte rendu des opérations des commissaires civils envoyés en Corse* (Paris, 1791), pp. 14–20; Constantin François de Chasseboeuf, Comte de Volney, *Précis de l'Etat de la Corse* (Nucariu, 1989), pp. 62–3; Stephen Wilson, *Feuding, Conflict and Banditry in Nineteenth-Century Corsica* (Cambridge, 1988). Although Wilson's book concerns the nineteenth century, it is safe to assume that the same ties applied in the later eighteenth–early nineteenth centuries.

8 J. Busquet, *Le droit de la vendetta et les 'paci' corses* (Paris, 1920), intro. and pp. 265–322; Wilson, *Feuding, Conflict and Banditry*, esp. ch. 2.

9 On the Bonapartist clan in Corsica, see Fernand Beaucour, 'Un fidèle de l'empereur en son époque: Jean-Mathieu-Alexandre Sari (1792–1862)', (thèse de 3e Cycle, l'université de Lille III, 1972), pp. 9–19, 42–77.

10 McErlean, *Pozzo di Borgo*, p. 40.

11 François Gilbert de Coston, *Biographie des premières années de Bonaparte*, 2 vols (Paris, 1840), ii. pp. 94–9; Masson and Biagi, *Napoléon inconnu*, ii. pp.92–6; Chuquet, *Jeunesse*, ii. p. 79.

12 Pozzo Di Borgo claimed to have had a hand in drawing up the letter (McErlean, *Pozzo di Borgo*, p. 41).

13 Defranceschi, 'Le rôle de lieutenant Bonaparte', p. 4.

14 For details of the rioting, see Masson and Biagi, *Napoléon inconnu*, ii. pp.

97–100; Chuquet, *Jeunesse*, ii. pp. 84–8; Franceschini, 'La Corse aux premiers jours', 64 (1930), 163–9.

15 Casanova, 'Caractères originaux', 169 and 170.

16 Masson and Biagi, *Napoléon inconnu*, ii. pp. 99–100; J. B. Marcaggi, *La Genèse de Napoléon, sa formation intellectuelle et morale jusqu'au siège de Toulon* (Paris, 1902), p. 192; Ambrosi, 'Pascal Paoli', p. 168.

17 Ambrosi, 'Pascal Paoli', p. 168.

18 These concerns are explained by R. Emmanuelli, 'Le gouvernement de Louis XVI offre à la république de Gênes la rétrocession de la Corse (1790)', *Annales historiques de la Révolution Française*, 46 (1974), 623–40.

19 Jacques Godechot, 'L'Empire napoléonien', *Recueils de la Société Jean Bodin*, 31 (1973), 437; and David A. Bell, 'Nation-Building and Cultural Particularism in Eighteenth-Century France: The Case of Alsace', *Eighteenth-Century Studies*, 21 (1988), 472–90.

20 Mirabeau and Saliceti's speeches in Mirabeau, *Collection complète des travaux de M Mirabeau aîné à l'Assemblée nationale* (Paris, 1791), ii. pp. 511–514.

21 Marcaggi, *Genèse de Napoléon*, p. 96.

22 This view is at odds with Steven Englund, *Napoleon: A Political Life* (New York, 2004), pp. 26–9, who argues that Napoleon was less 'pure' Corsican patriot and Francophobe than he was a 'citizen of the French Revolution'.

23 Masson and Biagi, *Napoléon inconnu*, i. p. 146.

24 Napoleon to Paoli, 12 June 1789, in Masson and Biagi, *Napoléon inconnu*, ii. p. 64, although there are doubts about the authenticity of this letter (Thierry Lentz (ed.), *Napoléon Bonaparte. Correspondance Générale* (Paris, 2004), i. p. 77, n. 7).

25 Masson and Biagi, *Napoléon inconnu*, ii. pp. 82–3. The Gothic style was very much in fashion at the end of the eighteenth century. See E. J. Clery, *The Rise of Supernatural Fiction, 1762–1800* (Cambridge, 1995).

26 'Nouvelle Corse', Masson and Biagi, *Napoléon inconnu*, ii. p. 79.

27 Masson and Biagi, *Napoléon inconnu*, i. pp. 415–19; and ii. pp. 17–19.

28 'Lettres sur la Corse à Monsieur l'abbé Raynal', Masson and Biagi, *Napoléon inconnu*, ii. p. 128 (written sometime between September 1789 and February 1791).

29 Chuquet, *Jeunesse*, ii. pp. 129–34.

30 Defranceschi, 'Le rôle de lieutenant Bonaparte', p. 14. The letter, though, has never been found.

31 Chuquet, *Jeunesse*, ii. pp. 122–3; Defranceschi, 'Le rôle de lieutenant Bonaparte', pp. 14–15.

32 Defranceschi, 'Le rôle de lieutenant Bonaparte', pp. 17–18.

33 Masson and Biagi, *Napoléon inconnu*, ii. pp. 107–15 (see p. 115 for quote).

34 Louis-Antoine Perelli, *Lettres de Pascal Paoli* (Bastia, 1895), iv. p. 33.

35 See Defranceschi, 'Robespierre et la Corse', in Jean-Pierre Jessenne et al (ed.), *Robespierre* (Villeneuve d'Ascq, 1994), p. 371.

36 Masson and Biagi, *Napoléon inconnu*, ii. pp. 105–6; Chuquet, *Jeunesse*, ii. pp. 110, 124.

37 Masson and Biagi, *Napoléon inconnu*, ii. p. 109; Chuquet, *Jeunesse*, ii. p. 110. Joseph gives a brief description of the journey in his *Mémoires*, i. p. 44.

38 Chuquet, *Jeunesse*, ii. p. 130.

39 McErlean, *Pozzo di Borgo*, p. 56.

40 Chuquet, *Jeunesse*, ii. p. 131.

41 *Correspondance Générale*, i. p. 89.

42 Chuquet, *Jeunesse*, ii. pp. 135, 310–11; McErlean, *Pozzo di Borgo*, pp. 60–61.

43 See Colin Lucas, 'The Theory and Practice of Denunciation in the French Revolution', *Journal of Modern History*, 68 (1996), 768–85.

44 Masson and Biagi, *Napoléon inconnu*, ii. pp. 123–4.

45 Chuquet, *Jeunesse*, ii. p. 136.

46 Masson and Biagi, *Napoléon inconnu*, ii. pp. 180–93; Chuquet, *Jeunesse*, ii. pp. 136–45.

47 Chuquet, *Jeunesse*, ii. p. 145.

48 Masson and Biagi, *Napoléon inconnu*, ii. p. 199.

49 McErlean, *Pozzo di Borgo*, pp. 67–8.

4 Ambition Awakened

1 Masson and Biagi, *Napoléon inconnu*, ii. pp. 195–6; Chuquet, *Jeunesse*, ii. p. 147.

2 'Impressions de voyage', in Masson and Biagi, *Napoléon inconnu*, ii. pp. 214–15.

3 On Buonaparte's second stay at Auxonne and Valence, see Masson and Biagi, *Napoléon inconnu*, ii. pp. 195–213; Chuquet, *Jeunesse*, ii. pp. 147–225.

4 For this and the following on Auxonne, see Chuquet, *Jeunesse*, ii. pp. 147–9.

5 Chuquet, *Jeunesse*, ii. pp. 167–8.

6 *Correspondance Générale*, i. p. 100.

7 Masson, *Napoléon et sa famille*, i. p. 47.

8 Eugène Ledoux, 'Bonaparte à Besançon', *Mémoires de l'Académie des sciences, belles-lettres et arts de Besançon*, (1900), 272–83.

9 Masson and Biagi, *Napoléon inconnu*, ii, p. 199.

10 *Correspondance Générale*, i. p. 101.

11 Chuquet, *Jeunesse*, ii. pp. 202.

12 See Timothy Tackett, *When the King took Flight* (Cambridge, Mass., 2003), esp. pp. 151–78 on the reaction in the provinces; and Tackett, 'Collective Panic in the Early French Revolution, 1789–1791: A Comparative Perspective', *French History*, 17 (2003), 161–6.

13 Chuquet, *Jeunesse*, ii. pp. 205–6.

14 On the importance of the oath in eighteenth-century society, see Lynn Hunt, *Politics, Culture and Class in the French Revolution* (Berkeley, Cal., 1984), pp. 20–1, 24. On the history of festivals, see Mona Ozouf, *Festivals and the French Revolution* (Cambridge, Mass., 1988).

15 My thanks to David Bell for pointing this out.

16 Chuquet, *Jeunesse*, ii. p. 188.

17 Chuquet, *Jeunesse*, ii. pp. 206–7.

18 Masson and Biagi, *Napoléon inconnu*, ii. pp. 208–9.

19 See his letter dated 8 February 1791 in Masson and Biagi, *Napoléon inconnu*, ii. pp. 195–6.

20 See Jean Tulard, 'Robespierre vu par Napoléon', in *Actes du colloque Robespierre* (Paris, 1967), pp. 36–8; Eugène Déprez, 'Les origines républicaines de Bonaparte', *Revue historique*, 97 (1908), 316–36. For his later espousal of Robespierre as an example of strong political leadership, see Antoine Casanova, *Napoléon et la pensée de son temps: une histoire intellectuelle singulière* (Paris, 2000), pp. 158–73.

21 Masson and Biagi, *Napoléon inconnu*, ii. p. 213.

22 This is stressed by Masson and Biagi, *Napoléon inconnu*, ii. pp. 334–6.

23 Masson and Biagi, *Napoléon inconnu*, ii. p. 335.

24 Frédéric Masson, *Napoléon dans sa jeunesse: 1769–1793* (Paris, 1907), p. 244.

25 Chuquet, *Jeunesse*, ii. p. 240–51.

26 Chuquet, *Jeunesse*, ii. p. 244.

27 On the election, see Masson and Biagi, *Napoléon inconnu*, ii. pp. 341–5; Chuquet, *Jeunesse*, ii. pp. 246–60; Marcel Mirtil, *Napoléon d'Ajaccio* (Paris, 1947), pp. 120–60; Sébastien Silvani, *Deux compagnons de Napoléon. Les frères Bonelli de Bocognano* (Paris, 1932), pp. 21–6; McErlean, *Napoleon and Pozzo*, pp. 92–4.

28 Masson and Biagi, *Napoléon inconnu*, ii. p. 343; Chuquet, *Jeunesse*, ii. p. 247.

29 Chuquet, *Jeunesse*, ii. pp. 247–8. It is generally agreed that he used the money left to the family from the death of Archdeacon Luciano the previous October, but Jean Defranceschi, *La jeunesse de Napoléon. Les dessous de l'histoire* (Paris, 2001), pp. 154–7, argues that Giuseppe abused his position in the administration to settle outstanding affairs in the family's favour. It was the money gained from this misappropriation that was used in the election.

30 For a later period, see Colin Lucas, 'The Rules of the Game in Local Politics under the Directory', *French Historical Studies*, 16 (1989), 352.

31 Chuquet, *Jeunesse*, ii. p. 248.

32 Lucas, 'The Rules of the Game', 352.

33 Anecdote in Tommaso Nasica, *Mémoires sur l'enfance et la jeunesse de Napoléon Ier jusqu'à l'age de vingt-trois ans* (Paris, 1865), pp. 145–7.

34 Chuquet, *Jeunesse*, ii. pp. 245–9, who treats this episode at length, relies on Nasica's *Mémoires sur l'enfance*. Defranceschi, *La jeunesse*, pp. 158–60, believes that the stories surrounding the election are a fiction.

35 Masson and Biagi, *Napoléon inconnu*, ii. pp. 344–5; Chuquet, *Jeunesse*, ii. p. 249.

36 The details of this incident can be found in Masson and Biagi, *Napoléon inconnu*, ii. pp. 349–84; Chuquet, *Jeunesse*, ii. pp. 261–95; Marcaggi, *Genèse de Napoléon*, pp. 293–317; François Chailley-Pompei, 'Les troubles de Pâques 1792, d'après le manifest de la municipalité d'Ajaccio', in *Problèmes d'Histoire de la Corse*, pp. 179–89; and Defranceschi, *La jeunesse*, pp. 160–9, who questions the whole episode and even argues that the reports historians have relied upon to explain the incident are either false or have been tampered with. Defranceschi's version of events, however, raises more questions than it answers.

37 'Mémoire justificatif du bataillon des volontaires sur l'émeute du mois d'avril', in Masson and Biagi, *Napoléon inconnu*, ii. pp. 357–84 (19 April 1792).

38 Chuquet, *Jeunesse*, ii. p. 290.

39 Chuquet, *Jeunesse*, ii. p. 294.

40 On Buonaparte's stay in Paris, see Masson and Biagi, *Napoléon inconnu*, ii. pp. 387–409; Chuquet, *Jeunesse*, iii. pp. 4–16; Marcaggi, *Genèse de Napoléon*, pp. 323–52.

41 T.C.W. Blanning, *The Origins of the French Revolutionary Wars* (London, 1986), chs. 3 and 4; and Blanning, *The French Revolutionary Wars,*

1787–1802 (London, 1996), pp. 37–69. See also Gunther E. Rothenberg, 'The Origins, Causes, and Extension of the Wars of the French Revolution and Napoleon', *Journal of Interdisciplinary History*, 18 (1988), 771–93; and for the political climate which led to war, see Gary Savage, 'Favier's Heirs: The French Revolution and the *Secret du Roi*', *Historical Journal*, 41 (1998), esp. 251–8.

42 Peter McPhee, *The French Revolution, 1789–1799* (Oxford, 2002), p. 92.

43 Rothenberg, 'The origins, causes, and extension of the wars', 772.

44 Indeed, in a letter written the previous year, he was convinced that France would not go to war (Masson and Biagi, *Napoléon inconnu*, ii. p. 209).

45 Bourrienne, *Mémoires*, i. pp. 32–3.

46 Napoleon to Joseph, 22 June 1792, Masson and Biagi, *Napoléon inconnu*, ii. p. 393.

47 Jennifer Harris, 'The Red Cap of Liberty: A Study of Dress Worn by French Revolutionary Partisans 1789–94', *Eighteenth-Century Studies*, 14 (1981), 283, 285–6, 292.

48 Chuquet, *Jeunesse*, ii. pp. 369–74.

49 Chuquet, *Jeunesse*, ii. pp. 366–9.

50 Chuquet, *Jeunesse*, iii. p. 17.

51 On the vicissitudes of appointments and dismissals in the army, see Jonathan Devlin, 'The Directory and the Politics of Military Command: The Army of the Interior in South-East France', *French History*, 4 (1990), 199–223.

52 Napoleon to Joseph, 7 August 1792, Masson and Biagi, *Napoléon inconnu*, ii. p. 404.

53 Napoleon to Joseph, 29 May 1792, Masson and Biagi, *Napoléon inconnu*, ii. p. 387.

54 See the account by Jean-Philippe-Gui Le Gentil Paroy, *Mémoires du comte de Paroy: souvenirs d'un défenseur de la famille royale pendant la Révolution (1789–1797)* (Paris, 1895), pp. 352–4, who narrowly escaped the mob.

55 Las Cases, *Mémorial*, ii. pp. 114–15.

56 Joseph, *Mémoires*, i. p. 47.

57 Paroy, *Mémoires du comte de Paroy*, p. 351.

58 Napoleon to the administrators of the district of Versailles, 1 September 1792, Masson and Biagi, *Napoléon inconnu*, ii. p. 407.

5 Disillusion

1 Masson and Biagi, *Napoléon inconnu*, ii. pp. 385–6; Defranceschi, *La jeunesse*, p. 176.

2 Chuquet, *Jeunesse*, ii. p. 292.

3 Masson and Biagi, *Napoléon inconnu*, ii. pp. 385–6.

4 McErlean, *Napoleon and Pozzo*, p. 51, n. 80.

5 A good account of the expedition is in Masson and Biagi, *Napoléon inconnu*, ii. pp. 416–47; Chuquet, *Jeunesse*, iii. pp. 25–58; Marcaggi, *Genèse de Napoléon*, pp. 359–84; and E. Peyrou, *L'Expédition de Sardaigne. Le Lieutenant-Colonel Bonaparte à la Maddalena (1792–1793)* (Paris, 1912); Guy Godlewski, 'Bonaparte et l'affaire de la Maddalena', *Revue de l'Institut Napoléon*, 90 (1964), pp. 1–12. The Abbé Letteron (ed.), *Pièces et documents divers pour servir a l'historie de la Corse pendant les années 1790–1791* (Bastia, 1891), i. pp. 1–293, contains a large number of documents concerning the expedition.

6 Chuquet, *Jeunesse*, iii. p. 27.

7 Peyrou, *L'Expédition de Sardaigne*, p. 17.

8 Iung, *Lucien Bonaparte*, i. p. 74.

9 *Mémories de Lucien Bonaparte, Prince Canino, écrits par lui-même* (Paris, 1836), p. 13.

10 Iung, *Lucien Bonaparte*, i. pp. 53, 54–5.

11 For the following, see Masson and Biagi, *Napoléon inconnu*, ii. p. 417; Chuquet, *Jeunesse*, iii. p. 33; Defranceschi, *La jeunesse*, pp. 29–30.

12 Peyrou, *L'Expédition de Sardaigne*, p. 123.

13 It proved a disaster. The men, or rather the boys, since the majority of them seem to have been around fifteen and sixteen and had never known war, panicked during the night and, crying treason, threw themselves into the sea, where it was reported that 700 of them drowned (Peyrou, *L'Expédition de Sardaigne*, p. 93).

14 Chuquet, *Jeunesse*, iii. p. 46.

15 Letteron, *Pièces et documents*, i. pp. 189–97.

16 Peyrou, *L'Expédition de Sardaigne*, p. 135.

17 Letteron, *Pièces et documents*, i. pp. 199–200; Defranceschi, *La Corse française*, pp. 122 and 125.

18 Masson and Biagi, *Napoléon inconnu*, ii. pp. 439–41.

19 Defranceschi, *La jeunesse*, p. 190, n. 86.

20 Chuquet, *Jeunesse*, iii. p. 53.

21 Godlewski, 'Bonaparte et l'affaire de la Maddalena', 10.

22 Defranceschi, *La jeunesse*, p. 192.

23 Coston, *Biographie de Bonaparte* i. p. 235; Chuquet, *Jeunesse*, iii. pp. 88–9.

24 According to Defranceschi, *La Jeunesse*, p. 192.

25 Chuquet, *Jeunesse*, iii. p. 82.

26 Chuquet, *Jeunesse*, iii. pp. 263–7.

27 Leonard Macaluso, 'The Political Lives of Antoine Christophe Saliceti', (PhD, University of Kentucky, 1972), pp. 70–5.

28 Chuquet, *Jeunesse*, iii. pp. 116–19; Marcaggi, *Genèse de Napoléon*, pp. 397–8, 428.

29 Iung, *Lucien Bonaparte*, i. pp. 61–73, here p. 65.

30 Masson and Biagi, *Napoléon inconnu*, ii. pp. 427–9.

31 This, however, is refuted by Jacques-Barthélemy Salgues, *Mémoires pour servir à l'histoire de la France* (Paris, 1814), i. p. 80.

32 Masson and Biagi, *Napoléon inconnu*, ii. pp. 427–30; Chuquet, *Jeunesse*, iii. pp. 121–7.

33 Chuquet, *Jeunesse*, iii. p. 126.

34 Masson, *Napoléon dans sa jeunesse*, p. 325.

35 Jean Defranceschi, 'De la légende à l'histoire: Paoli et les frères Bonaparte,' in *Problèmes d'Histoire de la Corse*, pp. 131–45; Antonello Pietromarchi, *Lucien Bonaparte. Prince romain* (Paris, 1980), pp. 19–21.

36 Escudier read the address to the Convention (*Archives Parlementaires de 1787 à 1860*, lxi. pp. 88–90 (2 April 1793). It was published in the *Moniteur* (4 April 1793).

37 Masson and Biagi, *Napoléon inconnu*, ii. p. 426.

38 McErlean, *Napoleon and Pozzo*, p. 127; Masson and Biagi, *Napoléon inconnu*, ii. pp. 430–1; Chuquet, *Jeunesse*, iii. pp. 131–2; Marcaggi, *Genèse de Napoléon*, pp. 409–10.

39 For the following, see Masson and Biagi, *Napoléon inconnu*, ii. pp. 431–6; Chuquet, *Jeunesse*, iii. pp. 133–6; Marcaggi, *Genèse de Napoléon*, pp. 411–18.

40 Chuquet, *Jeunesse*, iii. p. 137.

41 Chuquet, *Jeunesse*, iii. pp. 137–8.

42 The following is based on Chuquet, *Jeunesse*, iii. pp. 143–4.

43 Wilson, *Feuding, Conflict and Banditry*, p. 83. Saliceti's house was also burned down.

44 *Mémoires de Lucien Bonaparte*, pp. 31–2.

45 Chuquet, *Jeunesse*, iii. pp. 142–3.

46 'Position politique et militaire du Département de Corse au 1er juin 1793', Masson and Biagi, *Napoléon inconnu*, ii. p. 465.

47 Abrantès, *Mémoires*, i. p. 217.

48 *Réponse de M. Saliceti, . . . au libelle et aux délations de M. Buttafoco, . . . contre M. de Paoli et les patriotes corses* (Paris, 1790); Chuquet, *Jeunesse*, iii. pp. 77, 85–6.

49 Iung, *Lucien Bonaparte*, i. pp. 66–71.

50 Chuquet, *Jeunesse*, iii. p. 88.

51 Blanning, *French Revolutionary Wars*, p. 118; Alan Forrest, *The Soldiers of the French Revolution* (Durham, 1990), pp. 111–15.

52 *Le Souper de Beaucaire*, p. 11.

53 'Position politique et militaire du Département de Corse au 1er juin 1793', in Masson and Biagi, *Napoléon inconnu*, ii. p. 469.

54 This idea was first expressed, in somewhat different terms, by Frédéric Masson in Masson and Biagi, *Napoléon inconnu*, ii. p. 503: 'Just as France had made him a Corsican, so Corsica made him a Frenchman.'

55 Abrantès, *Mémoires*, i. p. 38.

6 The Jacobin

1 The best accounts in English on the federalist revolt of Toulon are Malcolm Crook, *Toulon in War and Revolution. From the ancien régime to the Restoration, 1750–1820* (Manchester, 1991), ch. 6, much of which can be found in Crook, 'Federalism and the French Revolution: The Revolt of Toulon in 1793', *History*, 65 (1980), 387–97; and William Cormack, *Revolution and Political Conflict in the French Navy, 1789–1794* (Cambridge, 1995), ch. 7. For the background to the revolt, see Hubert C. Johnson, *The Midi in Revolution. A Study of Regional Political Diversity, 1789–1793* (Princeton, NJ, 1986), pp. 222–49. For the broader context, although Toulon has been excluded, see Paul R. Hanson, *The Jacobin Republic Under Fire: The Federalist Revolt in the French Revolution* (University Park, Pa., 2003).

2 Cormack, *Revolution and Political Conflict*, pp. 162–72.

3 Over 1,000 Corsican refugees, mostly from well-off families, would find their way to Marseilles (Defranceschi, *La Corse française*, p. 247).

4 Masson, *Napoléon et sa famille*, i. p. 74.

5 Iung, *Lucien Bonaparte*, i. pp. 95–6.

6 Pietromarchi, *Lucien Bonaparte*, pp. 24–5.

7 Masson, *Napoléon et sa famille*, i. pp. 80–2.

8 Louis, Comte de Pontécoulant, *Souvenirs historiques et parlementaires du comte de Pontécoulant, ancien pair de France: extraits de ses papiers et de sa correspondance, 1764–1848*, 4 vols (Paris, 1861–63), i. pp. 325–6. If

his younger brother, Brutus-Luciano, is to be believed, Buonaparte already aspired to the position of commander of Paris as early as 1793 (Iung, *Lucien Bonaparte*, i. p. 134).

9 Such as J. M. Thompson, *Napoleon Bonaparte: His Rise and Fall* (Oxford, 1958), p. 29. They follow the lead set by an anonymous pamphlet during the Restoration, *Napoléon Buonaparte, lieutenant d'artillerie, documents inédits sur mes premiers faits d'armes en 1793* (Paris, 1821).

10 Bertrand, *Cahiers, 1818–1819*, p. 424. The remark about not wanting to get involved in a civil war was part of the image-making process that continued while he was in exile.

11 Chuquet, *Jeunesse*, iii. pp. 156–9.

12 *Correspondance Générale*, i. p. 128.

13 Maurice Contestin (ed.), *Le Souper de Beaucaire* (Paris, 1993), pp. xiii–xv.

14 Georges Roux, *Monsieur de Buonaparte* (Paris, 1964), p. 181.

15 Cited in Roux, *Monsieur de Buonaparte*, p. 182. Barras is still awaiting his biographer.

16 Crook, *Toulon*, pp. 139–40; Jennifer Mori, 'The British Government and the Bourbon Restoration: The Occupation of Toulon, 1793', *Historical Journal*, 40 (1997), 699–719.

17 Blanning, *Origins of the Revolutionary Wars*, pp. 138–57; Clive Emsley, *British Society and the French Wars 1793–1815* (London, 1979), pp. 19–28; Jeremy Black, *British Foreign Policy in an Age of Revolutions, 1783–1793* (Cambridge, 1994), pp. 404–71; John Ehrman, *The Younger Pitt* (London, 1983), ii. pp. 206–58; Paul W. Schroeder, *The Transformation of European Politics, 1763–1848* (Oxford, 1994), pp. 113–18. Most historians argue that Britain went to war against France for strategic reasons and that ideology had little to do with it. For another point of view, see Philip Schofield, 'British Politicians and French Arms: The Ideological War of 1793–1795', *History*, 77 (1992), 183–201; Mori, 'The British Government and the Bourbon Restoration', 699–719.

18 Alphonse Aulard, *Recueil des actes du Comité de Salut public*, 28 vols (Paris, 1889–1951), vii. pp. 79–80 (26 September 1793).

19 On the siege, see Chandler, *Campaigns*, pp. 20–29.

20 Aulard, *Recueil*, vii. pp. 316–21, 392–3 (8 and 12 October 1793).

21 See, for example, *Corr.* i. nos. 2 and 3.

22 *Corr.* n. 1 (25 October 1793). A much more detailed plan was sent to the Minister of War on 14 November (*Corr.* i. n. 4).

23 Thompson, *Napoleon Bonaparte*, pp. 36–7.

24 Macaluso, 'The political lives of Saliceti', p. 94.

25 Aulard, *Recueil*, vii. pp. 596–7 (23 October 1793).

26 *Correspondance Générale*, i. p. 138.

27 Claude-Victor Perrin, Duc de Bellune, *Mémoires de Claude-Victor Perrin, duc de Bellune* (Paris, 1847), i. p. 170; *Corr.* i. n. 8 (25 November 1793); Macaluso, 'The political lives of Saliceti', p. 97.

28 Aulard, *Recueil*, ix. pp. 56–7 (30 November 1793).

29 *Corr.* xxix, p. 14.

30 Zénon Pons, *Mémoires pour servir à l'histoire de la ville de Toulon, en 1793* (Paris, 1825), pp. 155–6.

31 N. A. M. Rodger, *The Command of the Ocean. A Naval History of Britain, 1649–1815* (London, 2004), p. 427.

32 Ian Germani, 'Representations of the Republic at War: Lille and Toulon, 1792–1793', *Canadian Journal of History*, 29 (1994), 89.

33 Edmond Poupé (ed.), *Lettres et correspondance de Barras et de Fréron en mission dans le Midi* (Draguignan, 1910), pp. 97–8 (25 December 1793). The assertion by Alan Schom, *Napoleon Bonaparte* (London, 1997), p. 22, that Bonaparte was responsible for the executions that took place is a misreading of the sources.

34 Auguste-Frédéric Marmont, *Mémoires du Maréchal Marmont, duc de Raguse, de 1792 à 1841* (Paris, 1857), i. p. 45.

35 Aulard, *Recueil*, ix. pp. 555–6 (20 December 1794).

36 Aulard, *Recueil*, ix. pp. 556–7 (3 January 1794).

37 Poupé, *Lettres et correspondance*, pp. 98–9, 101 (25 and 26 December 1793).

38 Poupé, *Lettres et correspondance*, p. 93 (25 December 1793).

39 Pons, *Mémoires*, pp. 169–71.

40 A-Jacques Parès, 'Relation inédite sur la fusillade du Champ de Mars, à Toulon', *Var historique et géographique*, 50 (1932), 427–8.

41 See Paul Cottin, *Toulon et les Anglais en 1793* (Paris, 1898), pp. 355–7; Crook, *Toulon*, p. 150.

42 See, for example, McLynn, *Napoleon*, p. 76; Englund, *Napoleon*, pp. 65, 72.

43 *Moniteur universel* (7 December 1793).

44 Charles James Fox, *Napoleon Bonaparte and the Siege of Toulon* (Washington, 1902), pp. 102–6.

45 General Amédée Doppet, *Mémoires politiques et militaires du général Doppet* (Paris, 1797), pp. 180–1.

46 Gunther E. Rothenberg, *The Art of Warfare in the Age of Napoleon* (Bloomington, 1978), p. 36. According to Chandler, *Campaigns*, p. 28,

between 1789 and 1794, various revolutionary governments had sacked 680 general officers, of which half had been executed.

47 Masson, *Napoléon et sa famille*, i. p. 80.

48 *Correspondance Générale*, i. pp. 149–69.

49 Corr. i. n. 13 (4 January 1794).

50 Jonathan D. Devlin, 'The Army, Politics and Public Order in Directorial Provence, 1795–1800', *Historical Journal*, 32 (1989), 96–7.

51 *Archives parlementaires de 1787 à 1860*, lxxxv. p. 470 (25 February 1794); Paul Gaffarel, 'Les Bonapartes à Marseilles', *La Révolution française*, 62 (1912), 269–74.

52 Aulard *Recueil*, xii. p. 421 (5 April 1794).

53 *Corr.* i. nos. 27 and 30 (21 May and 20 June 1794); Chandler, *Campaigns*, pp. 30–2.

54 Blanning, *French Revolutionary Wars*, p. 101.

55 On Piedmont before the French invasion, see Michael Broers, *Napoleonic Imperialism and the Savoyard Monarchy, 1773–1821. State Building in Piedmont* (Lewiston, 1997), pp. 24–164; and Broers, 'Revolution as Vendetta: Patriotism in Piedmont, 1794–1821', *Historical Journal*, 33 (1990), 575–8.

56 Jean-Lambert A. Colin, *L'Education militaire de Napoléon* (Paris, 1893), pp. 92–6.

57 Marmont, *Mémoires*, i. p. 50.

58 *Corr.* i. n. 30 (20 June 1794).

59 Colin, *L'Education militaire de Napoléon*, pp. 443–7, 'Note sur la position politique et militaire de nos armées de Piémont et d'Espagne', 19 July 1794.

7 Shifting Political Sands

1 Pasquale Villani, 'Agenti e diplomatici francesi in Italia (1789–1795). Un giacobino a Genova: Jean Tilly', *Società e storia*, 65 (1994), 529–58.

2 Marmont, *Mémoires*, i. p. 51.

3 Coston, *Biographie de Bonaparte*, ii. pp. 286–7 (7 August 1794). The letter is a bit of a conundrum. The tone makes it difficult to believe that Buonaparte had previously denounced Tilly. If he had, and was writing to him in his hour of need, then it is a little hypocritical to say the least. Either Buonaparte did not denounce Tilly, or this letter, which is not in the archives, is not by Buonaparte.

4 Aulard, *Recueil*, xv. pp. 717–20 (6 August 1794). Two letters were sent

on that day from a small town called Barcelonette, halfway between Nice and Grenoble. The second letter, cited above, denounces Buonaparte as being Augustin Robespierre's and Ricord's man. See also Thompson, *Napoleon Bonaparte*, pp. 44–6.

5 A. Augustin-Thierry, 'Un amour inconnu de Bonaparte', *Revue des Deux Mondes*, 110 (1940), 228–9.

6 Jean Tulard and Louis Garros, *Itinéraire de Napoléon au jour le jour, 1769–1821* (Paris, 1992), p. 61.

7 George Mauguin, 'Saliceti et l'arrestation de Bonaparte à Nice', *Revue des études napoléoniennes*, 39 (1934), 262.

8 Jacques Godechot, *Les Commissaires aux armées sous le Directoire. Contribution à l'étude des rapports entre les pouvoirs civils et militaires*, 2 vols (Paris, 1941), i. p. 241.

9 Coston, *Biographie de Bonaparte*, ii. pp. 289–91.

10 Schom, *Napoleon*, p. 25, gives the figure of seventy-four general officers but without citing his source.

11 Aulard, *Recueil*, xvi. pp. 328–9 (24 August 1794).

12 See Abrantès, *Mémoires*, i. pp. 173, 215, 218, 228.

13 Cited in Tulard and Garros, *Itinéraire de Napoléon*, p. 62.

14 Felix Markham, *Napoleon* (London, 1963), p. 13.

15 Aulard, *Recueil*, xviii. pp. 542–3 (5 December 1794).

16 Marmont, *Mémoires*, i. p. 60.

17 Victorine de Chastenay, *Mémoires: 1771–1815* (Paris, 1987), pp. 203–4.

18 Chastenay, *Mémoires*, pp. 205–6 [my underline].

19 Gabriel Girod de l'Ain, *Joseph Bonaparte. Le roi malgré lui* (Paris, 1970), pp. 51–2.

20 See Augustin-Thierry, 'Un amour inconnu', pp. 228–9.

21 Gabriel Girod de l'Ain, *Désirée Clary, d'après sa correspondance inédite avec Bonaparte, Bernadotte et sa famille* (Paris, 1959), p. 42.

22 Bertrand, *Cahiers: janvier-mai 1821*, p. 32.

23 Girod de l'Ain, *Désirée Clary*, p. 61.

24 Freud to Thomas Mann, November 1936, in Ernest L. Freud (ed.), *Letters of Sigmund Freud* (New York, 1960), pp. 432–4.

25 Bonaparte to Josephine, in Chantal de Tourtier-Bonazzi (ed.), *Napoléon. Lettres d'amour à Joséphine* (Paris, 1981), p. 63 (24 April 1796).

26 *Corr.* i. n. 42 (24 June 1795).

27 *Corr.* i. n. 65 (6 September 1795).

28 For the following, Félix Bouvier, *Un amour de Napoléon* (Paris, 1900), p. 29.

29 Las Cases, *Mémorial*, i. pp. 122 and 123.

30 Girod de l'Ain, *Désirée Clary*, p. 45.

31 Girod de l'Ain, *Désirée Clary*, p. 46.

32 Cited in Girod de l'Ain, *Désirée Clary*, p. 46.

33 Girod de l'Ain, *Désirée Clary*, pp. 46–7.

34 Girod de l'Ain, *Désirée Clary*, p. 50.

35 Girod de l'Ain, *Désirée Clary*, pp. 51–2.

36 Girod de l'Ain, *Désirée Clary*, pp. 61–2.

37 Girod de l'Ain, *Désirée Clary*, pp. 63–5. A number of lines from this letter can be found in Buonaparte's short story, *Clisson and Eugénie*.

38 Salgues, *Mémoire*, i. p. 133; Pierre-François Pinaud, *Cambacérès, 1753–1824* (Paris, 1996), p. 72.

39 Pontécoulant, *Souvenirs historiques*, i. p. 326.

40 Marmont, *Mémoires*, i. pp. 62–4.

41 Howard G. Brown, 'Politics, Professionalism, and the Fate of Army Generals after Thermidor', *French Historical Studies*, 19 (1995), 143–8.

42 *Corr.* i. n. 41 (22 June 1795).

43 According to Gustave Mouravit, *Napoléon Bibliophile* (Paris, 1905), pp. 28–9.

44 Joseph, *Mémoires*, i. p. 134 (19 July 1795).

45 *Corr.* i. n. 49 (July 1795). A revised version, *Corr.* i. n. 50 (July 1795), insisted on the need to separate Piedmont and Austrian forces.

46 *Corr.* i. n. 54 (30 July 1795).

47 Marmont, *Mémoires*, i. p. 62.

48 Ségur, *Histoire et Mémoires*, i. pp. 144–5.

49 *Corr.* i. n. 47 (25 July 1795).

50 The text can be found in Jean Tulard (ed.), *Napoléon Bonaparte. Oeuvres littéraires et écrits militaires* (Paris, 2001), ii. pp. 331–43. It was probably written from about the middle of August through to the middle of September 1795.

51 Joseph, *Mémoires*, i. p. 142 (12 August 1795). One is reminded of André Maurois' assertion that 'The need to express oneself in writing springs from a maladjustment to life, or from an inner conflict, which the adolescent (or the grown man) cannot resolve.' Cited in Catherine Drinker Bowen, 'The Biographer's Relationship with His Hero', in Stephen B. Oates (ed.), *Biography as High Adventure* (Amherst, 1986), p. 67.

52 Bourrienne, *Mémoires*, i. pp. 53–4.

53 François-Yves Besnard, *Souvenirs d'un nonagénaire* (Paris, 1880), ii. p. 112.

54 Abrantès, *Mémoires*, i. p. 173.

55 Las Cases, *Mémorial*, i. p. 115.
56 Chandler, *Campaigns*, p. 37.
57 Paul Barras, *Mémoires de Barras, membre du Directoire*, 4 vols (Paris, 1895–6), i. pp. 242–3, 245.
58 Pontécoulant, *Souvenirs historiques*, i. p. 327.
59 Pontécoulant, *Souvenirs historiques*, i. pp. 330–4; Colin, *L'Education militaire de Napoléon*, pp. 232–6.
60 *Corr.* i. n. 56 (20 August 1795); Pontécoulant, *Souvenirs historiques*, i. pp. 337, 338.
61 *Corr.* i. n. 58 (25 August 1795).
62 Pontécoulant, *Souvenirs historiques*, i. pp. 342–4.
63 *Corr.* i. n. 56 (20 August 1795).
64 Joseph, *Mémoires*, i. p. 146 (5 September 1795).
65 *Corr.* i. n. 61 (30 August 1795), 2.
66 Pontécoulant, *Souvenirs historiques*, i. pp. 345–6.
67 Pinaud, *Cambacérès*, pp. 72–3; Jean-Jacques Régis de Cambacérès, *Mémoires inédits. Eclaircissements publiés par Cambacérès sur les principaux événements de sa vie politique*, 2 vols (Paris, 1999), i. p. 345.
68 Pontécoulant, *Souvenirs historiques*, i. pp. 344 and 420–2.

8 The Political Appointee

1 Marmont, *Mémoires*, i. p. 82.
2 See D. M. G. Sutherland, *The French Revolution and Empire: The Quest for a Civic Order* (Oxford, 2003), pp. 259–60. Barry M. Shapiro, 'Self-Sacrifice, Self-Interest, or Self-Defense? The Constituent Assembly and the "Self-Denying Ordinance" of May 1791', *French Historical Studies*, 25 (2002), 625–56, argues that this was not done out of a sense of self-sacrifice, but because few deputies had any desire to be re-elected.
3 According to de Staël, *Considérations*, p. 319.
4 Henry Zivy, *Le treize vendémiaire an IV* (Paris, 1898), pp. 36–7.
5 Barras, *Mémoires*, i. p. 253.
6 Zivy, *Le treize vendémiaire*, p. 23. Counter-revolutionary *journées* have elicited little work. A good treatment in English of this particular episode can be found in George Rudé, *The Crowd in the French Revolution* (Oxford, 1959), pp. 160–77; H. Mitchell, 'Vendémiaire, a Revaluation', *Journal of Modern History*, 30 (1958), 191–202.
7 Pontécoulant, *Souvenirs historiques*, i. p. 369.

8 L. M. La Révellière-Lépeaux, *Mémoires* (Paris, 1895), i. pp. 337–8; Chastenay, *Mémoires*, p. 343.

9 Zivy, *Le treize vendémiaire*, p. 70.

10 Las Cases, *Mémorial*, i. pp. 818–19.

11 Pontécoulant, *Souvenirs historiques*, i. pp. 365–6. Barras, *Mémoires*, i. p. 250, goes so far as to accuse Buonaparte of negotiating with the section Le Peletier.

12 Las Cases, *Mémorial*, i. pp. 818–19.

13 Jean Tulard, *Napoléon ou le mythe du sauveur* (Paris, 1977), p. 76.

14 Baron Fain, *Manuscrit de l'an III, 1794–1795* (Paris, 1829), pp. 352–3.

15 Fain, *Manuscrit de l'an III*, p. 355.

16 See, for example, Schom, *Napoleon*, p. 27; McLynn, *Napoleon*, pp. 95–6; Englund, *Napoleon*, p. 79.

17 Ségur, *Histoire et mémoires*, i. pp. 167–8.

18 Zivy, *Le treize vendémiaire*, pp. 90–2.

19 See, for example, Salgues, *Mémoire*, i. pp. 161–8.

20 *Corr.* i. n. 72 (6 October 1795).

21 Pontécoulant, *Souvenirs historiques*, i. p. 365, n. 1.

22 *Rapport du général Buonaparte sur la journée du 13 vendémiaire, Corr.* i. n. 73 (7 October 1795). Description of uprising written by Paul Barras, *Rapport fait à la Convention Nationale au nom du Comité de Salut Public* (30 Vendémiaire an IV), at a time when he was particularly well disposed towards Buonaparte.

23 Masson, *Napoléon et sa famille*, i. p. 125.

24 Philippe-Antoine Merlin de Douai, *Rapport fait au nom des Comités de Salut Public ...* (Paris, 1796). Nor is he mentioned in any of the pamphlet literature of the day, much of it royalist, which leads one to assume that Buonaparte's role was by no means prominent. See Pierre-François Réal, *Essai sur les journées des treize et quatorze Vendémiaire* (Paris, an IV); *Précis historique de la Révolution du 13 vendémiaire et de celles qui l'ont causé* (Paris, 1796); *Précis historique et circonstancié des événemens qui ont précédés et suivis la journée du 13 vendémiaire* (Paris, 1796); Auguste Danican, *Notice sur le 13 vendémiaire, ou Les Parisiens vengés* (Paris, an XII).

25 P.-J.-B. Buchez and P.-C. Roux, *Histoire parlementaire de la Révolution française*, 40 vols (Paris, 1838), xxxvii. pp. 50–1.

26 A[rchives] N[ationales] AFII 140B, Rapport général de la Surveillance, 22 September 1795 (30 Vendémiaire IV); Aulard, *Paris pendant la réaction thermidorienne*, ii. pp. 348–9, 353.

27 Barras, *Mémoires*, i. pp. 284–5.

28 According to G.-J. Ouvrard, *Mémoires de G.-J. Ouvrard sur sa vie et ses diverses opérations financières*, 3 vols (Paris, 1826–27), i. pp. 21–2, Mme Tallien arranged for Buonaparte to obtain clothes before 13 Vendémiaire.

29 *Correspondance Générale*, i. p. 281.

30 Masson, *Napoléon et sa famille*, i. pp. 129–30.

31 Marmont, *Mémoires*, i. p. 86.

32 Barras, *Mémoires*, ii. p. 51.

33 Jean Tulard, 'Le recrutement de la Légion de police de Paris sous la Convention thermidorienne et le Directoire,' *Annales historiques de la Révolution Française*, 36 (1964), 46–50.

34 *Corr.* i. n. 75 (12 October 1795).

35 *Corr.* i. n. 83 (19 January 1796).

36 Gabriel Fabry, *Campagne de l'armée d'Italie, 1796–1797*, 4 vols (Paris, 1914), iii. p. 121 (3 February 1796); Godechot, *Les Commissaires*, i. pp. 179–80.

37 Fabry, *Campagne de l'armée d'Italie*, iii. pp. 124–5 (4 February 1796).

38 Fabry, *Campagne de l'armée d'Italie*, iii. p. 160 (22 February 1796). Saliceti was appointed commissioner of the Army of Italy, probably at Buonaparte's insistence, on 30 January.

39 Alphonse Aulard, *Paris pendant la réaction thermidorienne et sous le Directoire*, 5 vols (Paris, 1898–1902), iii. pp. 6–7; Ramsay Weston Phipps, *The Armies of the First French Republic*, 5 vols (Oxford, 1968), iii. p. 276–7.

40 Corr. i. nos. 87 and 88 (29 February 1796).

41 Phipps, *Armies of the Republic*, iv. p. 5; Huntley Dupre, *Lazare Carnot. Republican Patriot* (Oxford, Oh., 1940), p. 215; Barras, *Mémoires*, ii. p. 69; Vincent-Marie Viennot de Vaublanc, *Mémoires sur la Révolution de France*, 4 vols (Paris, 1833), ii. p. 395.

42 Jean and Nicole Dhombres, *Lazare Carnot* (Paris, 1997), p. 434.

43 Howard G. Brown, *War, Revolution, and the Bureaucratic State: Politics and Army Administration in France, 1791–1799* (Oxford, 1995), p. 203. Schérer became Inspector-General of Cavalry and eventually served as Minister of War between 1797 and the beginning of 1799.

44 See, for example, Thiébault, *Mémoires*, ii. pp. 4–5.

45 'Opinion de Du Pont (de Nemours) sur Bonaparte, en l'an IV'. *Révolution française*, 35 (1898), p. 376 (6 March).

46 Spenser Wilkinson, *The Rise of General Bonaparte* (Oxford, 1930), pp. 77–8.

47 Ernest John Knapton, *Empress Josephine* (Cambridge, Mass., 1982), p. 83.

48 Knapton, *Josephine*, p. 89.

49 Barras, *Mémoires*, ii. p. 56.
50 Cited in Maurice Lever, *Sade. A Biography* (New York, 1993), pp. 514–15.
51 Eugène de Beauharnais, *Mémoires et correspondance politique et militaire du prince Eugène*, 10 vols (Paris, 1858), i. pp. 31–2; Lavalette, *Mémoires*, p. 127.
52 Barras, *Mémoires*, i. p. 264.
53 Ouvrard, *Mémoires*, i. pp. 19–20; Bernard Chevallier, Maurice Catinat and Christophe Pincemaille (eds), *Impératrice Joséphine. Correspondance, 1782–1814* (Paris, 1996), pp. 122–3.
54 Bertrand, *Cahiers: janvier-mai 1821*, p. 98.
55 *Joséphine. Correspondance*, p. 31.
56 Bonazzi, *Lettres d'amour*, p. 45. There is some difference of opinion about the date of this letter. Tourtier-Bonazzi has the 20th October but others have opted for the 28th.
57 Bonazzi, *Lettres d'amour*, pp. 46–7.
58 Marmont, *Mémoires*, i. pp. 93–5.
59 For Salons under the Directory, see Steven Kale, *French Salons: High Society and Political Sociability from the Old Regime to the Revolution of 1848* (Baltimore, 2004), pp. 71–5.
60 Antoine-Vincent Arnault, *Souvenirs d'un sexagénaire* (Paris, 2003), pp. 392–3.
61 Abrantès, *Mémoires*, ii. p. 44.
62 Iung, *Lucien Bonaparte*, i. pp. 135–6.
63 Barras, *Mémoires*, ii. pp. 51, 57–9. Napoleon admitted as much to Bertrand, *Cahiers: janvier-mai 1821*, p. 99.
64 Ségur, *Histoire et mémoires*, i. p. 176; Claire-Elisabeth Rémusat, *Mémoires de madame de Rémusat, 1802–1808*, 3 vols (Paris, 1880), i. p. 141–2.
65 See, for example, Mme de Genlis' injunctions on marriage in Anne L. Schroder, 'Going Public against the Academy in 1784: Mme de Genlis Speaks out on Gender Bias', *Eighteenth-Century Studies*, 32 (1999), 376.
66 James F. Traer, *Marriage and the Family in Eighteenth-Century France* (Ithaca, NT, 1980), pp. 70–1.
67 Bonazzi, *Lettres d'amour*, p. 48.
68 Girod de l'Ain, *Désirée Clary*, p. 91.
69 Abrantès, *Mémoires*, i. pp. 293–4.
70 Carrington, *Napoleon and His Parents*, p. 92.
71 Knapton, *Josephine*, pp. 119–20.
72 Girod de l'Ain, *Désirée Clary*, pp. 96–7.
73 Masson, *Napoléon et sa famille*, i. pp. 134–5. An unflattering portrayal of Josephine by Lucien is in Iung, *Lucien Bonaparte*, i. pp. 135–6.

9 Innovation

1 Bonazzi, *Lettres d'amour*, pp. 49–50 (14 March 1796).

2 Bonazzi, *Lettres d'amour*, p. 51 (30 March 1796).

3 Bonazzi, *Lettres d'amour*, pp. 68–9 (29 April 1796).

4 Chandler, *Campaigns*, p. 137.

5 See, for example, André Masséna, *Mémoires d'André Masséna, duc de Rivoli, prince d'Essling, maréchal d'Empire*, 7 vols (Paris, 1966), ii, pp. 140–1, for an argument between Augereau and Bonaparte.

6 Christian Marc Bosséno, '"Les signes extérieurs." Diffusion, réception et image de la culture révolutionnaire française dans l'Italie du *Triennio* (1796–1799)', 2 vols, (PhD, Université Paris I Panthéon-Sorbonne, 1995), i. p. 34.

7 Fabry, *Campagne de l'armée d'Italie*, iii. p. 324 (13 March 1796).

8 Pierre de Pelleport, *Souvenirs militaires et intimes du général Vte de Pelleport* (Paris, 1857), i. p. 38.

9 Vigo-Roussillon, *Journal*, pp. 29–30.

10 Jean Landrieux, *Mémoires de l'adjutant-général Jean Landrieux* (Paris, 1893), i. p. 33. Lucien was spiteful enough to propagate the rumour (Iung, *Lucien Bonaparte*, i. p. 135).

11 Jean-Baptiste Giraud, *Le Carnet de campagne du commandant Giraud* (Paris, 1898), p. 19 (27 April 1796); and Hilarion Puget, Marquis de Barbentane, *Mémoires du lieutenant-général Puget-Barbantane* (Paris, 1827), p. 152, for an unflattering physical description.

12 Vigo-Roussillon, *Journal*, pp. 29–30.

13 Ségur, *Histoire et mémoires*, i. p. 193. Bonaparte may have been forewarned of their hostile attitude and modified or adapted his behaviour in consequence.

14 Chaptal, *Mes souvenirs*, pp. 204–5.

15 Ségur, *Histoire et mémoires*, i. p. 194; Parker, 'Formation of Napoleon's Personality', p. 20.

16 Marmont, *Mémoires*, i. pp. 296–7.

17 Bulletin from de la Rivière, P[ublic] R[ecords] O[ffice], FO 28 Genoa (12 April 1796).

18 Chandler, *Campaigns*, p. 54.

19 For the lack of supplies and the ensuing consequences, see Forrest, *Soldiers of the French Revolution*, pp. 125–42; Devlin, 'The Army, Politics and Public Order', 92–3, 100.

20 Cited in A. Dry, *Soldats ambassadeurs sous le Directoire*, 2 vols (Paris, 1906), ii. p. 25.

21 Giraud, *Carnet de campagne*, p. 16 (20 April 1796).

22 Cited in Piero del Negro, 'The Republic of Venice meets Napoleon', in *L'Europa scopre Napoleone 1793–1804* (Alessandria, 1999), i. p. 83.

23 Godechot, *Les Commissaires*, i. p. 254.

24 Report from de la Rivière, PRO, FO 28 Genoa (14 March 1796). Alcohol may have been given to the men before they went into battle, but the evidence for this is anecdotal. See Rory Muir, *Tactics and the Experience of Battle in the Age of Napoleon* (New Haven and London, 2000), pp. 199–200.

25 Drake to Grenville, PRO, FO 28 Genoa (29 March 1796); André Fugier, *Napoléon et l'Italie* (Paris, 1947), p. 24; although Macaluso, 'The political lives of Saliceti', pp. 129–33, lists much smaller sums.

26 Godechot, *Les Commissaires*, i. p. 251.

27 Ségur, *Histoire et mémoires*, i. p. 189.

28 Cited in Cécile Delhorbe, 'Retouche à la biographie d' Amédée Laharpe', *Revue historique vaudoise*, 72 (1964), 138.

29 Devlin, 'The army, politics and public order', 105.

30 *Corr.* i. n. 91 (27 March 1796).

31 Pelleport, *Souvenirs militaires*, i. p. 37; François Roguet, *Mémoires militaires du lieutenant général Cte Roguet* (Paris, 1862), i. p. 215; Nicholas-Philibert Desvernois, *Mémoires du général baron Desvernois* (Paris, 1898), pp. 39–40.

32 Chandler, *Campaigns*, p. 53; Schom, *Napoleon*, p. 42.

33 Bulletin from la Rivière, PRO, FO 28 Genoa (29 March 1796).

34 Franceschi to Bonaparte, 24 April 1796, cited in Reinhard, *Sulkowski*, p. 27.

35 Martin Boycott-Brown, *The Road to Rivoli. Napoleon's First Campaign* (London, 2001), p. 290.

36 Cited in Reinhard, *Sulkowski*, p. 152.

37 Jérôme-Roland Laugier, *Les Cahiers du capitaine Laugier. De la guerre et de l'anarchie* (Aix, 1893), p. 107.

38 Cited in Reinhard, *Sulkowski*, pp. 150–1.

39 *Examen de la campagne de Buonaparte*, pp. 82–3.

40 Alan Forrest, 'The Ubiquitous Brigand: The Politics and Language of Repression', in Charles Esdaile (ed.), *Popular Resistance in the French Wars. Patriots, Partisans and Land Pirates* (London, 2005), p. 28.

41 *Corr.* i. n. 214 (22 April 1796), n. 220 (24 April 1796), n. 233 (26 April 1796), n. 366 (9 May 1796). See also n. 308 (3 May), n. 376 (9 May 1796) and n. 615 (11 June 1796) which made the penalty for looting execution by firing squad in the presence of the troops.

42 Chevrier, *Joubert*, p. 36 (6 May 1796).

43 *Moniteur universel*, 17 May 1796.

44 *Corr.* i. n. 205 (22 April 1796).

45 Masséna, *Mémoires*, ii. p. 43.

46 Landrieux, *Mémoires*, i. p. 61.

47 Reinhard, *Sulkowski*, p. 240.

48 Steven T. Ross, *Quest for Victory. French Military Strategy, 1792–1799* (South Brunswick, 1973), pp. 91–8.

49 Instructions in Antonin Debidour, *Recueil des actes du Directoire exécutif* (Paris, 1910), i. pp. 717–22 (2 March 1796).

50 Colin, *L 'Education militaire de Napoléon*, pp. 338–9; Félix Bouvier, *Bonaparte en Italie, 1796* (Paris, 1899), p. 197.

51 Ferrero, *The Gamble*, p. 19, stresses this point.

52 Fabry, *Campagne de l'armée d'Italie*, iv. p. 140.

53 Debidour, *Recueil des actes du Directoire exécutif*, ii. pp. 227–31 (25 April 1796).

54 *Corr.* i. n. 220 (24 April 1796).

55 Wayne Hanley, *The Genesis of Napoleonic Propaganda, 1796–1799* (New York, 2005), pp. 59–63.

56 Marc Martin, *Les origines de la presse militaire en France de la fin de l'Ancien régime à la Révolution (1770–1799)* (Vincennes, 1975), p. 296.

57 See, for example, *Buonaparte, général en chef de l'armée d'Italie, au Directoire exécutif* (9 August and 10 September 1796), both of which also appeared in the *Moniteur*.

58 Charles Albert Costa de Beauregard, *Un homme d'autrefois* (Paris, 1877), pp. 333 and 341.

59 Costa de Beauregard, *Un homme d'autrefois*, p. 334.

60 Boycott-Brown, *The Road to Rivoli*, p. 280.

61 Costa de Beauregard, *Un homme d'autrefois*, p. 339.

62 Bonazzi, *Lettres d'amour*, p. 67 (29 April).

63 Albert Sorel, *L'Europe et la Révolution française*, 8 vols (Paris, 1893–1904), v. p. 68.

64 Raymond Guyot, *Le Directoire et la Paix de l'Europe* (Paris, 1911), p. 165.

65 See his letter to the Directory in *Corr.* i. n. 233 (26 April 1796).

66 Aulard, *Paris pendant la réaction thermidorienne*, iii. pp. 169–70 and 180.

67 *Corr.* i. n. 257 (28 April 1796).

68 Chandler, *Campaigns*, p. 78; Blanning, *French Revolutionary Wars*, p. 151.

69 *Corr.* i. n. 337 (6 May 1796).

70 On Lodi, see Chandler, *Campaigns*, pp. 77–85; Blanning, *French Revolutionary Wars*, pp. 145–7; Boycott-Brown, *The Road to Rivoli*, pp. 309–27.

71 Owen Connelly, *Blundering to Glory. Napoleon's Military Campaigns* (Wilmington, DE, 1987), p. 29.

72 Carl von Clausewitz, *La Campagne de 1796 en Italie* (Paris, 1999), pp. 80–81.

73 See, for example, Masséna, *Mémoires*, ii. pp. 63–4.

74 Cited in Bouvier, *Bonaparte en Italie*, p. 531.

75 *Corr.* n. 382 (11 May 1796).

76 *Moniteur universel*, 20 May 1796.

77 *Moniteur universel*, 20 May 1796. The article was also printed in Italian newspapers.

78 Gaspard Gourgaud, *Journal de Sainte-Hélène 1815–1818*, 2 vols (Paris, 1944), ii. p. 94.

79 Charles Montholon, *Récits de la captivité de l'empereur Napoléon à Sainte-Hélène*, 2 vols (Paris, 1847), ii. p. 424. The account in which Bonaparte was nicknamed the *petit caporal* (little corporal) during this battle by admiring troops (Las Cases, *Mémorial*, i. p. 132) is apocryphal. Napoleon was never known by that epithet before 1815.

80 Las Cases, *Mémorial*, i. p. 117.

81 Debidour, *Recueil des actes du Directoire exécutif*, ii. pp. 328–33 (7 May 1796). Also pp. 437–39 (21 May 1796).

82 Bertrand, *Cahiers de Sainte-Hélène; janvier-mai 1821*, p. 78.

83 Guyot, *Le Directoire*, p. 171.

84 In all, about fifteen different engravings of Lodi were produced. The French author, Stendhal, *Napoléon* (Paris, 1998), p. 380, wrote many years later that within a month of the event a rough woodcut print of the crossing could be found in inns in the smallest villages in the most remote parts of northern Germany.

85 Bonaparte to Faipoult, *Correspondance inédite, officielle et confidentielle de Napoléon Bonaparte* (Paris, 1809), i. p. 158 (13 May 1796). Although the literacy rates varied from region to region, generally speaking, less than half the male, and a little more than a quarter of the female, population could read. The percentages were higher in urban centres than in the country, and in Paris it has been estimated that almost 90 per cent of men and 80 per cent of women were literate, that is, they could sign their names (Hugh Gough, *The Newspaper Press in the French Revolution* (London, 1988), p. 195).

86 Debidour, *Recueil des actes du Directoire exécutif*, ii. pp. 415–19 (18 May 1796).

10 Conquest and Pillage

1 André Thouin, *Voyage dans la Belgique, la Hollande et l'Italie* (Paris, 1841), ii. pp. 42–3.
2 Boycott-Brown, *The Road to Rivoli*, p. 332.
3 Vigo-Roussillon, *Journal*, pp. 34–5.
4 Cited in Phipps, *Armies of the Republic*, iv, p. 46.
5 *Moniteur universel*, 7 June 1796; Roguet, *Mémoires*, i. pp. 242–3.
6 General Marmont, *Mémoires*, i. p. 322.
7 *Corr.* xxix. p. 122.
8 Bosséno, ' "Les signes extérieurs" ', pp. 58 and 68.
9 Vovelle, 'Naissance et formation du mythe', 28.
10 Bonaparte may have played some part in bringing about this series of engravings, modelled on a similar series for the French Revolution (Annie Jourdan, 'Images de Napoléon – un *imperator* en quête de légitimité', *Modern & Contemporary France*, 8 (2000), 435).
11 Christian-Marc Bosséno, 'La guerre des estampes. Circulation des images de thèmes iconographiques dans l'Italie des années 1789–1799', *Mélanges de l'Ecole française de Rome, Italie et Méditerranée*, 102 (1990), 371.
12 Bosséno, ' "Les signes extérieurs" ', pp. 48 and 50.
13 Stendhal, *The Charterhouse of Parma*, trans. Robert Andrew Parker (New York, 1999), p. 1.
14 Bosséno, 'La guerre des estampes', p. 371; Vovelle, 'Naissance et formation du mythe', 24, 26.
15 Archives des Affaires Etrangères, Correspondance politique, Milan, 55, ff. 47–51, Salvador to the minister for foreign affairs (28 May 1796).
16 Paul Gaffarel, *Bonaparte et les Républiques italiennes, 1796–1799* (Paris, 1895), p. 4.
17 Bonazzi, *Lettres d'amour*, p. 75.
18 Bonazzi, *Lettres d'amour*, pp. 64–5 (24 April).
19 Bonazzi, *Lettres d'amour*, p. 56 (3 April).
20 Bonazzi, *Lettres d'amour*, p. 61 (7 April).
21 Arnault, *Souvenirs*, p. 392.
22 Bonazzi, *Lettres d'amour*, pp. 54, 61, 64, 67, 74, 90.
23 Antoine-Romain Hamelin, 'Douze ans de ma vie, 1796–1808', *Revue de Paris*, 6 (1926), p. 10.
24 *Corr.* i. n. 453 (19 May 1796).
25 Albert Pingaud, *La domination française dans l'Italie du Nord (1796–1805). Bonaparte, président de la République italienne*, 2 vols (Paris,

1914), i. p. 137. This figure was based on reports sent by Saliceti to the Directory.

26 Debidour, *Recueil des actes du Directoire exécutif*, ii. p. 329 (7 May 1796); Carnot to Bonaparte, *Correspondance inédite, officielle et confidentielle*, i. p. 153 (7 May 1796); Bouvier, *Bonaparte en Italie*, p. 606.

27 Vovelle, 'Naissance et formation du mythe', 36, 38.

28 Laugier, *Les Cahiers*, p. 87.

29 Roguet, *Mémoires*, i. p. 244.

30 Vigo-Roussillon, *Journal*, p. 35.

31 Something that was picked up on by Pierre-Louis Roederer in an article in the *Journal de Paris* (25 July 1796).

32 Cited in Godechot, *Les Commissaires*, i. pp. 295–6.

33 Cited in Godechot, *Les Commissaires*, i. p. 297.

34 For the process whereby the army and the nation became separated, see John A. Lynn, 'Toward an Army of Honor: The Moral Evolution of the French Army, 1789–1815', *French Historical Studies*, 16 (1989), 159–61.

35 Félix Bouvier, 'La révolte de Pavie (23–26 mai 1796)', *Revue historique de la Révolution française*, 2 (1911), 534.

36 See Anna Maria Rao, 'Révolution et Contre-Révolution pendant le Triennio italien (1796–1799)', in Martin, Jean-Clément (ed.), *La Contre-Révolution en Europe* (Rennes, 2001), pp. 233–40.

37 Vittorio Scotti Douglas, 'The Italian Anti-Napoleonic Insurgencies', in *L'Europa Scopre Napoleone 1793–1804* (Alessandria, 1999), ii. pp. 583–4.

38 *Corr.* i. n. 494 (25 May 1796).

39 *Corr.* i. n. 536 (1 June 1796).

40 *Corr.* i. n. 493 (25 May 1796).

41 Blanning, *French Revolutionary Wars*, p. 166; Martin Boycott-Brown, 'Guerrilla Warfare *avant la lettre*: Northern Italy, 1792–97', in Esdaile (ed.), *Popular Resistance in the French Wars*, pp. 54–8.

42 Marmont, *Mémoires*, i. p. 180.

43 Landrieux, *Mémoires*, i. pp. 70–1; Bouvier, 'La révolte de Pavie', pp. 426–7.

44 Bouvier, 'La révolte de Pavie', p. 425.

45 *Corr.* i. n. 536 (1 June 1796).

46 *Moniteur universel*, 14 June 1796; *Corr.* i. n. 536 (1 June 1796). An account that was repeated in other memoirs, such as Ségur, *Histoire et Mémoires*, i. p. 229.

47 *Corr.* i. n. 496 (26 May 1796); Godechot, *Les Commissaires*, i. pp. 302, 304.

48 *Moniteur universel*, 14 June 1796.

49 Annie Duprat, 'La construction de la mémoire par les gravures: Carle Vernet et les *Tableaux historiques des campagnes d'Italie*', in Jean-Paul Barbe and Roland Bernecker (eds), *Les intellectuels européens et la campagne d'Italie, 1796–1798* (Münster, 1999), pp. 202–3.

50 *Corr.* ii. 1365 (7 January 1797).

51 Drake to Grenville, PRO FO 28 Genoa (11 June 1796).

52 Jacques Godechot, *The Counter-Revolution: Doctrine and Action, 1789–1804*, trans. Salvator Attanasio (London, 1972), p. 304.

53 See Godechot, *The Counter-Revolution*, pp. 305–9, for the circumstances surrounding this particular revolt.

54 AN AFIII 72, pl. 291, Clarke to the Directory, 6 December 1796 (16 frimaire an V); Jean Tulard, 'Quelques aspects du brigandage sous l'Empire', *Revue de l'Institut Napoléon*, 98 (1966), 33; Boycott-Brown, 'Guerrilla Warfare', pp. 46–51; Michel Iafelice, *Barbets! Les résistances à la domination française dans le pays niçois (1792–1814)* (Nice, 1998), pp. 51–64.

55 Broers, *Napoleonic Imperialism and the Savoyard Monarchy*, p. 189.

56 See, for example, his proclamation to the people of Tyrol (14 June 1796), in *Moniteur universel*, 26 June 1796.

57 Guyot, *Le Directoire*, pp. 168–9.

58 *Corr.* i. n. 685 (26 June 1796).

59 E.E.Y. Hales, *Revolution and Papacy: 1769–1846* (London, 1960), p. 99.

60 *Corr.* i. n. 676 (23 June 1796).

61 For the background to this, see Edouard Pommier, *L'art de la liberté. Doctrines et débats de la Révolution Française* (Paris, 1991); Pommier, 'Idéologie et musée à l'époque révolutionnaire', in Michel Vovelle (ed.), *Images de la Révolution française*, pp. 57–78. For Bonaparte's role in the Italian confiscations, on which the following is based, see Ferdinand Boyer, 'Les responsabilités de Napoléon dans le transfert à Paris des oeuvres d'art de l'étranger', *Revue d'Histoire Moderne et Contemporaine*, 11 (1964), 241–62; Boyer, 'Le général Bonaparte et la recherche des objet de Sciences et d'Art en Lombardie (1796)', *Revue de l'Institut Napoléon*, 122 (1972), 7–17; and Edouard Pommier, 'La saisie des oeuvres d'art', *Revue du Souvenir napoléonien*, 408 (1996), 30–43.

62 For this aspect of what Bénédicte Savoy calls the French policy of 'cultural appropriations', see *Patrimoine annexé. Les biens culturels saisis par La France en Allemagne autour de 1800*, 2 vols (Paris, 2003), i. pp. 13–54.

63 Rothenberg, 'The origins, causes, and extension of the wars', 786–7.

64 See Pommier, 'La saisie des oeuvres d'art', 31.

65 A few days before the creation of the Commission, indeed only a few weeks into the campaign, Bonaparte wrote to the French representative at Genoa, Faipoult, asking him for information about the forts of Parma, Piacenza and Modena, but especially about the paintings, statues and other 'curiosities' there (*Corr.* i. n. 280 (1 May 1796).

66 Pommier, *L'art de la liberté*, p. 399.

67 AN, AF III, 198, for lists of the confiscations carried out in 1796 in Piedmont, Lombardy and Parma.

68 *Corr.* i. n. 337 (6 May 1796).

69 *Correspondance des Directeurs de l'Académie de France à Rome, 1791–1797* (Paris, 1907), xvi. pp. 414–18.

70 Marie-Louise Blumer, 'La Commission pour la recherche des objets d'arts', *Révolution française*, 87 (1934), p. 75. Tinet's selection proved a great disappointment when the seven cases he sent to the Louvre were unpacked six months later (Andrew McClellan, *Inventing the Louvre. Art, Politics, and the Origins of the Modern Museum in Eighteenth-Century Paris* (Cambridge, 1994), p. 118; Savoy, *Patrimoine annexé*, i. p. 64).

71 *Corr.* ii. 1509 (19 February 1797).

72 See McClellan, *Inventing the Louvre*, pp. 118 and 119–20.

73 Blanning, *French Revolutionary Wars*, p. 160.

74 *Corr.* i. n. 539 (1 June 1796); Blanning, *French Revolutionary Wars*, p. 160.

75 *Corr.* iii. n. 2145 (3 September 1797).

76 *Corr.* i. n. 710 (2 July 1796).

77 Marmont, *Mémoires*, i. pp. 187–8.

78 Bonazzi, *Lettres d'amour*, pp. 64, 66 (24 and 29 April).

79 Bonazzi, *Lettres d'amour*, pp. 69–70 (13 May).

80 Indeed, it seems like an excuse that Josephine used on more than one occasion. See Bonaparte's reference to her 'little stomach' in a letter dated November 1796 (Bonazzi, *Lettres d'amour*, p. 120).

81 Brotonne, *Lettres inédites*, p. 6.

82 Bonazzi, *Lettres d'amour*, pp. 73 (18 May) and 76 (8 June).

83 Bonazzi, *Lettres d'amour*, p. 78 (8 June).

84 Bonazzi, *Lettres d'amour*, pp. 86–9 (15 June).

85 Bonazzi, *Lettres d'amour*, pp. 80–4 (14 June) and 86 (15 June).

86 Bonazzi, *Lettres d'amour*, p. 85 (15 June).

87 *Correspondance Générale*, i. p. 453.

88 Cited in Dupre, *Lazare Carnot*, p. 220.

89 Arnault, *Souvenirs*, p. 392.

90 Hamelin, 'Douze ans de ma vie', pp. 11–12.

91 Marmont, *Mémoires*, i. p. 188.

92 Hamelin, 'Douze ans de ma vie', p. 15.

93 Bonazzi, *Lettres d'amour*, pp. 93–4 (17 July).

94 Bonazzi, *Lettres d'amour*, p. 96 (18 July).

95 Bonazzi, *Lettres d'amour*, p. 97.

96 Bonazzi, *Lettres d'amour*, pp. 102–3 (21 July).

97 Bonazzi, *Lettres d'amour*, p. 113 (30 August).

98 Bonazzi, *Lettres d'amour*, p. 117 (17 September).

99 Bonazzi, *Lettres d'amour*, pp. 104–5 (22 July).

100 Knapton, *Josephine*, p. 140.

101 *Joséphine. Correspondance*, p. 47.

102 J. Holland Rose, 'The Despatches of Colonel Thomas Graham on the Italian Campaign of 1796–1797', *English Historical Review*, 53 (1899), p. 117.

103 Rose, 'The Despatches of Colonel Thomas Graham', p. 118.

104 It is a good example of what Chandler, *Campaigns*, pp. 191–201, considers a great Napoleonic battle, although in embryonic form.

105 *Corr*. i. n. 889, p. 548 (14 August 1796).

106 Chandler, *Campaigns*, p. 95.

107 Marmont, *Mémoires*, i. p. 314.

108 Alfred de Besancenet, *Le general Dommartin en Italie et en Egypte* (Paris, 1887), p. 260 (17 October 1796).

109 Chandler, *Campaigns*, p. 95.

110 Rothenberg, *The Art of Warfare*, p. 140.

111 Blanning, *French Revolutionary Wars*, p. 119.

112 Laugier, *Les Cahiers*, p. 97.

113 Laugier, *Les Cahiers*, p. 98.

114 Masséna, *Mémoires*, ii. pp. 167–9.

115 Reinhard, *Sulkowski*, p. 108.

116 Masséna, *Mémoires*, ii, pp. 169, 171.

11 Artists and Soldiers, Politics and Love

1 *Corr*. ii. n. 1182 (13 November 1796).

2 Besancenet, *Dommartin en Italie et en Egypte*, p. 263 (13 November 1796).

3 *Corr.* ii. n. 1196 (19 November 1796). For the following analysis of the images surrounding Lodi, see Vovelle, 'Naissance et formation du mythe', 28, 30, 32, 34; Bosséno, ' "Je me vis dans l'histoire" ', 449–65.

4 O'Brien, *After the Revolution*, p. 34.

5 Bonazzi, *Lettres d'amour*, pp. 121–2 (19 November 1796). The line about Mantua falling was optimistic; it was to hold out until February 1797.

6 See Jean-Yves Leclercq, 'Le mythe de Bonaparte sous le Directoire (1796–1799)', (Mémoire de Maîtrise, Université de Paris I, 1991), pp. 159–61.

7 O'Brien, *After the Revolution*, p. 35.

8 Bosséno, 'La guerre des estampes', 367–400.

9 Thompson, *Napoleon Bonaparte*, p. 64.

10 *Corr.* i. n. 139 (12 April 1796).

11 *Corr.* i. n. 381 (10 May 1796).

12 *Corr.* ii. n. 1552 (10 March 1797).

13 *Corr.* i. n. 234 (26 April 1796) and *Moniteur universel*, 17 May 1796.

14 *Moniteur universel*, 17 September 1796.

15 *Moniteur universel*, 13 August 1796.

16 *Corr.* i. n. 1000 (16 September 1796). See the account by Sulkowski in Reinhard, *Sulkowski*, p. 119.

17 *Moniteur universel*, 17 June 1796.

18 The expression is Tulard's, *Napoléon*, p. 83.

19 *Moniteur universel*, 25, 27, 28 and 29 April and 4, 5 and 10 May.

20 Hanley, *Genesis of Napoleonic Propaganda*, pp. 35–47.

21 *Décade philosophique*, 18 June 1796.

22 *Moniteur universel*, 19 May 1796. It was published in the official newspaper of the Directory, *Le Rédacteur*, 26 April, 18 May 1796.

23 One can consult the thirty-odd Bonaparte songs collected by Pierre Constant in *Les Hymnes et Chansons de la Révolution* (Paris, 1904), not to mention the songs dedicated to the Army of Italy.

24 Bosséno, ' "Les signes extérieurs" ', p. 92.

25 For how Bonaparte recruited some artists to his cause, see Hanley, *Genesis of Napoleonic Propaganda*, pp. 128–36.

26 Annie Jourdan, *Napoléon. Héros, Imperator, Mécène* (Paris, 1998), p. 152.

27 See André Dupont-Ferrier, 'Trois lettres inédites d'un caporal-fourrier aux Armées des Alpes et d'Italie (1795–1797)', *Annuaire-bulletin de la société de l'histoire de France*, 66 (1929), 140.

28 Xavier F. Salomon and Christopher Woodward, 'How England first saw Bonaparte', *Apollo*, 162 (2005), 54.

29 *Moniteur universel*, 1 December 1796.

30 Bonazzi, *Lettres d'amour*, p. 123 (21 November).

31 Bonazzi, *Lettres d'amour*, pp. 124–5 (23 November).

32 *Joséphine. Correspondance*, pp. 41–2, 47 (23 July and 6 September 1796).

33 *Joséphine. Correspondance*, pp. 42, 47.

34 Bonazzi, *Lettres d'amour*, pp. 127–8 (27 November).

35 Bonazzi, *Lettres d'amour*, pp. 129–30 (28 November).

36 Knapton, *Josephine*, p. 141.

37 Comte Miot de Mélito, *Mémoires du Comte de Miot de Mélito* (Paris, 1873), i. pp. 86–7.

38 Bruce, *Napoleon and Josephine*, p. 188.

39 Hamelin, 'Douze ans de ma vie, 1796–1808', p. 16. Godechot, *Les Commissaires*, i. chs. 2 and 3 is fundamental for this.

40 Godechot, *Les Commissaires*, i. pp. 566, 568.

41 Miot, *Mémoires*, i. p. 86. My italics.

42 *Corr.* i. n. 773 (20 July 1796).

43 *Corr.* ii. n. 1113 (25 October 1796).

44 Baraguey d'Hilliers to the commissaries of the Directory in Lombardy (26 October 1796), cited in Godechot, *Les Commissaires*, i. p. 529.

45 Godechot, *Les Commissaires*, i. pp. 530–1.

46 Directory to Clarke (16 November 1796), cited in Godechot, *Les Commissaires*, i. p. 550. On Clarke's mission, see Sydney Biro, *The German Policy of Revolutionary France* (Cambridge, Mass., 1957), pp. 704–29.

47 Cited in Tulard and Garros, *Itinéraire de Napoléon*, p. 89.

48 Clarke to the Directory, 7 December 1796, cited in L. Houdard, 'Les généraux Bonaparte et Clarke en Italie, 1797', *Revue des études napoléoniennes*, 34 (1932), 158.

49 Godechot, *Les Commissaires*, i. p. 551.

50 AN AFIII 72, pl. 291, Clarke to the Directory, 16 frimaire an V; Godechot, *Les Commissaires*, i. p. 551; Ludovic Sciout, *Le Directoire* (Paris, 1895), ii. p. 127.

51 Godechot, *Les Commissaires*, i. pp. 560 and 652–4; Debidour, *Recueil des actes du Directoire exécutif*, iv. p. 430 (7 December 1796).

52 Francis Pomponi, 'Pouvoir civil, pouvoir militaire et régime d'exception dans les "régions" périphériques au temps du Consulat', *Annales historiques de la Révolution Française*, 2 (2003), 147–69.

53 Godechot, *Les Commissaires*, i. p. 650.

54 See, for example, the report to the Directory cited in Jean-Paul Bertaud, *La Vie quotidienne des soldats de la Révolution, 1789–1799* (Paris, 1985), pp. 279–80.

55 *Corr.* ii. n. 1094 (17 October 1796).
56 Chandler, *Campaigns*, p. 114.
57 *Corr.* ii. n. 1201 (19 November 1796).
58 Chevrier, *Joubert*, p. 69.
59 Chevrier, *Joubert*, p. 70.
60 *Corr.* xxix. pp. 214–15.
61 Ferrero, *The Gamble*, pp. 151–2.
62 Rothenberg, *The Art of Warfare*, p. 41.
63 Report from Sandoz-Rollin, 27 January 1797, in Paul Bailleu (ed.), *Preußen und Frankreich von 1795 bis 1807. Diplomatische Correspondenzen*, 2 vols (Leipzig, 1881), i. p. 110.
64 L. Houdard, 'La situation sanitaire au siege de Mantoue, 1796–1797', *Revue des études napoléoniennes*, 31 (1930), p. 109.
65 For the police reports mentioning Bonaparte's popularity, see Aulard, *Paris pendant la réaction thermidorienne*, iii. pp. 762, 766 (21 and 23 February 1797); and iv. pp. 40, 42–43 (4 and 5 April 1797).
66 Leclercq, 'Le mythe de Bonaparte', p. 237.
67 Guyot, *Le Directoire*, pp. 332, 343.

12 The Apprenticeship of Power

1 Debidour, *Recueil des actes du Directoire exécutif*, iv. p. 787 (3 February 1797).
2 Debidour, *Recueil des actes du Directoire exécutif*, iv. pp. 628, 741, 787 (7 and 27 January and 3 February 1797).
3 Guyot, *Le Directoire*, p. 344.
4 Marta Turner, 'The Treaty of Tolentino and French Art Confiscations', *Risorgimento. European Review for Italian Modern History*, 2 (1981), 5–12.
5 *Corr.* ii. n. 1510 (19 February 1797).
6 See Timothy Tackett, *Religion, Revolution, and Regional Culture in Eighteenth-Century France. The Ecclesiastical Oath of 1791* (Princeton, NJ, 1986).
7 John Hardman, *Louis XVI* (New Haven, Conn., 1993), pp. 182–4.
8 Ozouf, *Festivals*, pp. 110–18.
9 Gerlof D. Homan, *Jean-François Reubell* (Hague, 1971), pp. 114, 130.
10 Guyot, *Le Directoire*, pp. 179–82.
11 A brief overview of Bonaparte's attitude towards religion can be found in Jacques-Olivier Boudon, *Napoléon et les Cultes* (Paris, 2002), pp. 39–46.

12 Cited in Jacques Godechot, *La Grande Nation. L'expansion révolution-naire de La France dans le monde de 1789 à 1799* (Paris, 1983), p. 407.

13 *Corr*, ii. n. 1402 (20 January 1797).

14 Hales, *Revolution and Papacy*, pp. 99, 102.

15 *Corr*. ii. n. 1497 (15 February 1797).

16 *Corr*. iii. n. 2103 (16 August 1797).

17 *Corr*. ii. n. 1544 (6 March 1797).

18 *Correspondance Générale*, i. p. 315 (31 March 1796).

19 Debidour, *Recueil des actes du Directoire exécutif*, ii. pp. 229-30 (25 April 1796). On the negotiations with Turin in 1796, see Broers, *Napoleonic Imperialism and the Savoyard Monarchy*, pp. 193-5.

20 AN, AFIII, 71, letter to the Directory signed by G. Selvaggi, N. Celantano, J. B. Serra and G. Sauli (13 prairial IV), but attached to it is a report from the ministry of general police (25 prairial IV) that qualifies these individuals as 'terrorists'.

21 Jacques Godechot, 'L'armée d'Italie (1796-1799)', *Cahiers de la Révolution Française*, 4 (1936), 15.

22 Guyot, *Le Directoire*, pp. 189-90; and Blanning, *French Revolutionary Wars*, pp. 172-3.

23 *Corr*. iii. n. 2292 (7 October 1796). See also T.C.W. Blanning, 'Liberation or Occupation? Theory and Practice in the French Revolutionaries' Treatment of Civilians outside France', in Mark Grimsley and Clifford J. Rogers (eds), *Civilians in the Path of War* (Lincoln, 2002), p. 115.

24 Cited in Michelle Vovelle, *Les Républiques-sœurs sous le regard de la Grande Nation, 1795-1803* (Paris, 2000), p. 35.

25 Blanning, 'Liberation or Occupation?', p. 115.

26 For further French reactions, see Emmanuelle Sayag-Boyer, 'La liberté en Italie, d'après les Archives de l'Armée d'Italie: Vérité et apparence d'un aspect de la campagne de Bonaparte (1796-1797)', *Revue du Souvenir napoléonien*, 408 (1996), 44-49.

27 Cited in Guyot, *Le Directoire*, p. 314.

28 Jacques Godechot, 'Les Français et l'unité italienne sous le Directoire', in *Regards sur l'époque révolutionnaire* (Paris, 1980), p. 308.

29 Elizabeth Eisenstein, *The First Professional Revolutionist: Filippo Michel Buonarroti (1761-1837)* (Cambridge, Mass., 1959), pp. 27-8.

30 *Corr*. i. n. 257 (28 April 1796).

31 Vovelle, *Les Républiques-soeurs*, p. 22.

32 *Corr*. i. n. 234 (26 April 1796); *Moniteur universel*, 17 May 1796, declaration dated 6 May.

33 T.C.W. Blanning, 'The Abortive Crusade', *History Today*, 39 (1989), pp. 35–6.

34 *Corr*. i. n. 437 (17 May 1796).

35 Godechot, *Grande Nation*, pp. 245–6; Blanning, *French Revolutionary Wars*, p. 173.

36 Debidour, *Recueil des actes du Directoire exécutif*, ii. p. 514 (31 May 1796).

37 *Corr*. i. n. 453 (19 May 1796); ii. nos. 1035 (26 September), 1059 (2 October 1796), 1101 (19 October 1796); xxix, *Campagnes d'Italie*, pp. 75–7, 282–4.

38 *Corr*. ii. n. 1060 (2 October 1796).

39 Bonazzi, *Lettres d'amour*, p. 119 (17 October 1796).

40 *Corr*. ii. n. 1099 (17 October 1796).

41 *Corr*. ii. n. 1095 (17 October 1796).

42 Debidour, *Recueil des actes du Directoire exécutif*, iv. pp. 153–4 (28 October 1796).

43 *Corr*. ii. n. 1349 (1 January 1797).

44 Chandler, *Campaigns*, p.122.

45 *Corr*. ii. n. 1618 (22 March 1797).

46 *Corr*. ii. n. 1632 (25 March 1797).

47 *Corr*. ii. n. 1637 (25 March 1797).

48 AN AF III, 440, Directory to Bonaparte, 31 March 1797.

49 *Corr*. ii. n. 1663 (31 March 1797).

50 Ferrero, *Gamble*, p. 173. Bonaparte later referred to this letter as a case of play-acting.

51 *Corr*. ii. n. 1666 (1 April 1797).

52 Karl Roider, *Baron Thugut and Austria's Response to the French Revolution* (Princeton, NJ, 1987), pp. 236–7.

53 Albert Sorel, *Bonaparte et Hoche en 1797* (Paris, 1896), p. 48.

54 Eden to Grenville, 1 April 1797, in Hermann Hüffer and Friedrich Luckwaldt, *Der Frieden von Campo-Formio* (Innsbruck, 1907), i. 2, pp. 153–5, and n. 3.

55 *Corr*. ii. n. 1703 (8 April 1797).

56 Biro, *The German Policy*, p. 737.

57 Roider, *Baron Thugut*, pp. 242–3; Schroeder, *Transformation*, p. 166.

58 *Corr*. iii. n. 1762 (1 May 1797).

59 *Corr*. iii. n. 1966 (29 June 1797). The Republic was inaugurated on 9 July. In France, there was a debate in the press about what to do with Italy and about the legitimacy of Bonaparte's actions there. See Anna Maria Rao, 'Les républicains démocrates italiens et le Directoire', in Philippe Bour-

din and Bernard Gainot (eds), *La République directoriale*, 2 vols (Moulins, 1998), ii. pp. 1070–6. See also Bernard Gainot, 'Révolution, Liberté = Europe des Nations? La sororité conflictuelle', in Jean-Paul Bertaud (ed.), et al., *Mélanges Michel Vovelle* (Paris, 1997), pp. 457–68; Jean-Louis Harouel, *Les Républiques soeurs* (Paris, 1997), pp. 35–48; Antonio de Francesco, 'Aux origines du mouvement démocratique italien: quelques perspectives de recherche d'après l'exemple de la période révolutionnaire 1796–1801', *Annales historiques de la Révolution Française*, 308 (1997), 333–48. One of the best works in Italian on the subject is by Carlo Zaghi, *L'Italia di Napoleone dalla Cisalpina al Regno* (Turin, 1986), esp. pp. 99–229.

60 *Corr.* iii. n. 1839 (27 May 1797).

61 It is possible that there were more acclamations for Bonaparte and his army than for the new Republic. See Pingaud, *La domination française*, i. p. 163; *Corr.* iii. n. 2003 (11 July 1797).

62 This is taken from Jérémie Benoît, *Philippe-Auguste Hennequin* (Paris, 1994), p. 148.

63 On the origins and evolution of Hercules as allegory, see Lynn Hunt, 'Hercules and the Radical Image in the French Revolution', *Representations*, 1 (1983), 95–117. I think it is safe to disregard the view propounded by Darcy Grimaldo-Grigsby, *Extremities: Painting in post-Revolutionary France* (New Haven, Conn., 2002), p. 78, that there is a homosexual element involved here.

64 Pingaud, *La domination française*, i. pp. 162–3. In a letter to Talleyrand, he outlined a constitution for Lombardy in which the executive was given a larger share of power than the legislative (*Corr.* iii. n. 2223 (19 September 1797)). Bonaparte's views on government in this letter are said to anticipate the constitution he implemented on coming to power (Luigi Mascilli Migliorini, *Napoléon* (Paris, 2004), p. 132).

65 Blanning, *French Revolutionary Wars*, p. 174; Ferrero, *Gamble*, p. 223.

66 *Corr.* ii. n. 1035 (26 September 1796).

67 Sciout, *Le Directoire*, ii. p. 123; Sorel, *L'Europe et la Révolution française*, v. p. 108.

68 Cited in Vovelle, *Les Républiques-soeurs*, p. 31.

69 Simon Schama, *Patriots and Liberators. Revolution in the Netherlands, 1730–1815* (London, 1992), pp. 151–2.

70 On the origins of the politics of 'natural limits', see Josef Smets, 'Le Rhin, frontière naturelle de la France: genèse d'une idée a l'époque révolutionnaire, 1789–1799', *Annales historiques de la Révolution Française*, 1998 (314), 675–83.

71 See Smets, 'Le Rhin, frontière naturelle de la France', 691–6.
72 Blanning, *French Revolutionary Wars*, pp. 169, 171.
73 See Pingaud, *La domination française*, i. pp. 159–61.
74 *Corr.* iii. n. 2003 (11 July 1797).
75 Godechot, *Grande Nation*, p. 195.
76 Roider, *Baron Thugut*, p. 246.
77 Godechot, *Grande Nation*, pp. 193–4; Guyot, *Le Directoire*, pp. 365–6.
78 *Ami des Lois* (29 April 1797).
79 *Corr.* iii. n. 1748 (22 April 1797); Schroeder, *Transformation*, p. 168.
80 Schroeder, *Transformation*, p. 169.
81 *Corr.* ii. n. 1745 (19 April 1797). Also *Corr.* ii. n. 1078 (8 October 1796).
82 Godechot, *Grande Nation*, p. 195.
83 *Corr.* ii. n. 1745 (19 April 1797).
84 *Corr.* iii. n. 1836 (27 May 1797).
85 Cited in Amable de Fournoux, *Napoléon et Venise 1796–1814* (Paris, 2002), p. 89.
86 Edmond Bonnal de Ganges, *Chute d'une République. Venise* (Paris, 1885), pp. 126–35. A good account of the uprisings and the last days of the Venetian Republic can be found in John Julius Norwich, *A History of Venice* (London, 1983), pp. 616–31; and Angus Heriot, *The French in Italy, 1796–1799* (London, 1957), pp. 118–31.
87 On this particular episode, see Fournoux, *Napoléon et Venise*, pp. 92–6; Francesco Vecchiato, 'La resistenza antigiacobina e le Pasque Veronesi', in Gian Paolo Marchi and Paola Marini (eds), *1797 Bonaparte a Verona* (Venice, 1997), pp. 180–200; Gian Paolo Romagnani, 'Dalle "Pasque veronese" ai moti agrari del Piemonte', in Anna Maria Rao (ed.), *Folle Controrivoluzionare. Le insorgenze populari nell'Italia giacobine e napoleonica* (Rome 1999), pp. 89–122.
88 *Corr.* iii. n. 1766 (3 May 1797).
89 Sorel, *Bonaparte et Hoche*, pp. 67–8.
90 Sorel, *Bonaparte et Hoche*, p. 66.
91 For this, see George B. McClellan, *Venice and Bonaparte* (Princeton, 1931), pp. 203–7, but who, nevertheless, insists that there is nothing to substantiate this claim.
92 Cited in Norwich, *A History of Venice*, p. 625.
93 Brotonne, *Lettres inédites*, p. 8 (26 September 1797).
94 Cited in Ernest J. Knapton, 'A Contemporary Impression of Napoleon Bonaparte in 1797', *French Historical Studies*, 1 (1960), 479.
95 Miot de Mélito, *Mémoires*, i. p. 150.
96 Pontécoulant, *Souvenirs historiques*, ii. p. 471–2.

97 My thanks to David Parrott, New College, Oxford, for these details.

98 Markham, *Napoleon*, p. 38; Schom, *Napoleon*, p. 65; McLynn, *Napoleon*, p. 153.

99 See, for example, Migliorini, *Napoléon*, p. 128; Schom, *Napoleon*, p. 63; Markham, *Napoleon*, p. 35.

100 *Bonaparte général d'armée* (Paris, an V).

101 *Ami des Lois*, 15 thermidor V (2 August 1797); François-Réné-Jean de Pommereul, *Campagne du général Buonaparte en Italie pendant les années IVe et Ve de la République française* (Paris, 1797), p. 3.

102 Miot de Mélito, *Mémoires*, i. pp. 173–4.

103 Schom, *Napoleon Bonaparte*, p. 64.

104 *Corr*. iii. n. 2255 (25 September 1797).

13 Bonaparte the 'Italique'

1 Jean-Paul Bertaud, 'L'expédition d'Egypte et la construction du mythe napoléonien', *Cahiers de la Méditerranée*, 57 (1998), 282.

2 See, for example, the poem published in pamphlet form entitled *Bonaparte général d'armée* (Paris, an V).

3 *Messager du Soir*, 23 July 1797. The proclamation it refers to is in *Corr*. iii. n. 2010 (14 July 1797). The proclamation caused a stir in certain circles in Paris, where a military coup was feared (Aulard, *Paris pendant la réaction thermidorienne*, iv. pp. 243–4 (25 July 1797)).

4 See, for example, *Messager du Soir*, 30 March 1796 (dated 26 March by mistake); Jeremy Popkin, *Right-Wing Press in France, 1792–1800* (Chapel Hill, 1980), p. 86.

5 *Le Thé*, 18, 29 April, 1, 4, 12 May 1797. Hawkers were able to play upon the title by yelling out in the streets, 'Qui veut du Thé? Prenez votre Thé. Il est fort le Thé. Voila du Thé' (Who wants some Tea, Take your Tea, The Tea is strong, Here is some Tea) (Louis Gabriel-Robinet, 'Napoléon journaliste', *Les Annales Conferencia* 115 (May, 1960), 6). The Clichyans were named after the place outside Paris at which they met.

6 See, for example, *La Quotidienne*, n. 304 (24 February 1797).

7 Godechot, *The Counter-Revolution*, p. 289.

8 *Corr*. iii. n. 1970 (30 June 1797); n. 2014 (15 July 1797).

9 *Corr*. i. n. 858 (9 August 1796).

10 *Moniteur universel*, 12 August 1797.

11 *Corr*. iii. n. 2010 (14 July 1797).

12 See Vovelle, *Les Républiques-soeurs*, pp. 156–7; Martin, *Les origines de la*

presse militaire en France, p. 353. A summary of the criticisms directed against Bonaparte in the Council of Five Hundred can be found in *Procès verbal des séances du Conseil des Cinq-Cents* (Paris, 1796), 105–9. A good analysis of Bonaparte's newspapers can be found in Hanley, *Genesis of Napoleonic Propaganda*, pp. 72–98.

13 Another newspaper, the incongruously named *Journal de Bonaparte et des hommes vertueux*, was in circulation for a short time (February and March 1797) in Paris. It was meant to inform the capital of the exploits, as well as extol the merits, austerity, frugality, simplicity and severity, of Bonaparte. For reasons that are not known, the paper ceased running after about forty issues – only eleven have survived – but it set the tone for the two other newspapers founded by Bonaparte in Italy.

14 Martin, *Les origines de la presse militaire en France*, pp. 340–1.

15 Jacques Godechot, 'L'expansion française et la création de la presse politique dans le bassin méditerranéen', *Cahiers de Tunisie*, 2 (1954), 153–4.

16 Daline, 'Marc-Antoine Jullien', 37 (1965), pp. 201–3.

17 Daline, 'Marc-Antoine Jullien', 38 (1965), p. 390; Isser Woloch, *Jacobin Legacy; The Democratic Movement under the Directory* (Princeton, NJ, 1970), pp. 164–5; R. R. Palmer, (ed.), *From Jacobin to Liberal: Marc-Antoine Jullien, 1775–1848* (Princeton, NJ, 1993), pp. 80–1.

18 *La France vue de l'armée d'Italie*, n. 1 (no dates). Martin, *Les origines de la presse militaire en France*, p. 310.

19 *Courrier de l'Armée d'Italie*, 12 September 1797.

20 *Courrier de l'Armée d'Italie*, 26 July 1797.

21 See Olivier Blanc, *L'éminence grise de Napoléon: Regnaud de Saint-Jean d'Angély* (Paris, 2002). Regnaud and Bonaparte did, however, maintain a long relationship, and Regnaud continued to write articles for the paper.

22 Martin, *Les origines de la presse militaire en France*, p. 312.

23 The political commentator, Benjamin Constant, expressed a similar wish in a pamphlet entitled *De la force du gouvernement actuel de La France et de la nécessité de s'y rallier* (Paris, 1796), in which he defended the notion of a centre-left government. The pamphlet is reprinted with a preface and notes by Philippe Raynaud (Paris, 1988), pp. 13 and 27–90.

24 Martin, *Les origines de la presse militaire en France*, pp. 311–12.

25 *La France vue de l'Armée d'Italie*, n. 1.

26 'Sur les bruits de paix et de geurre', *Courrier de l'Armée d'Italie*, 22 July 1797.

27 *La France vue de l'Armée d'Italie*, n. 5.

28 Woloch, *Jacobin Legacy*, p. 71.

29 On the increasing political power of the revolutionary generals, and Bonaparte in particular, see Jean-Paul Bertaud, *La Révolution armée. Les soldats citoyens et la Révolution française* (Paris, 1979), pp. 322–7.

30 Pontécoulant, *Souvenirs historiques*, ii. pp. 239–41, 256; François Furet and Denis Richet, *La Révolution française* (Paris, 1973), p. 403.

31 Pontécoulant, *Souvenirs historiques*, ii. pp. 241; Furet and Richet, *La Révolution française*, p. 354.

32 Lavalette, *Mémoires et souvenirs*, p. 164; Barras, *Mémoires*, ii. pp. 496–7, who states simply that Bonaparte gave Augereau leave.

33 Laurence Couturaud, *Augereau, l'enfant maudit de la gloire* (Paris, 1990), p. 65.

34 Jacques Godechot, *Le comte d'Antraigues, un espion dans l'Europe des émigrés* (Paris, 1986), p. 164. The Directory was using information intercepted by Bonaparte in Italy implicating General Pichegru in a plot to overthrow the Republic.

35 See, for example, V. Daline, 'Marc-Antoine Jullien après le 9 thermidor', *Annales historiques de la Révolution Française*, 37 (1965), 201.

36 Blanning, *French Revolutionary Wars*, p. 182.

37 Cited in Godechot, 'L'Armée d'Italie', p. 23.

38 *Moniteur universel*, 23 July 1797.

39 Aulard, *Paris pendant la réaction thermidorienne*, iv. pp. 243–4 (25 July 1797).

40 Or what Colin Lucas, 'The Rules of the Game', 346, prefers to call 'Jacobin republicans' and 'conservatives'.

41 On the debate between the partisans of 'natural frontiers' and those in favour of France's 'ancient limits' see Smets, 'Le Rhin, frontière naturelle de la France', 683–98; Godechot, *Grande Nation*, pp. 71–4; Blanning, *French Revolutionary Wars*, pp. 91–2.

42 *Corr*. iii. n. 2255 (25 September 1797).

43 Tulard, *Napoléon*, p. 86.

44 Miot de Mélito, *Mémoires*, i. pp. 179–80.

45 Blanning, *Origins of the Revolutionary Wars*, p. 175.

46 *Corr*. iii. n. 2255 (25 September 1797).

47 *Corr*. iii. n. 2307 (18 October 1797).

48 Blanning, *French Revolutionary Wars*, p. 179. Blanning believes there was a third, the possibility of transforming the Mediterranean into a French lake, but given the state of the French navy it was unlikely that they would ever pose a serious threat to the Royal Navy.

49 Blanning, *Origins of the Revolutionary Wars*, p. 176.
50 Sorel, *L'Europe et la Révolution française*, v. p. 253; Guyot, *Le Directoire*, pp. 543–6; Schroeder, *Transformation*, p. 171.
51 Bailleu, *Preußen und Frankreich*, i. p. 155 (28 October 1797).
52 Bailleu, *Preußen und Frankreich*, i. p. 162 (28 November 1797).
53 Howard Brown, 'The Search for Stability', in Brown and Miller (eds), *Taking Liberties*, p. 34.
54 George Pallain, *Correspondance diplomatique de Talleyrand. Le ministère Talleyrand sous le Directoire* (Paris, 1891), pp. 424–33.
55 Bailleu, *Preußen und Frankreich*, i. p. 157 (6 November 1797).
56 Miot de Mélito, *Mémoires*, i. pp. 216–17.
57 Cited in Emile Dard, *Napoléon et Talleyrand* (Paris, 1935), p. 62.
58 Aulard, *Paris pendant la réaction thermidorienne*, iv. pp. 414–15, 417 (26 and 27 October 1797).
59 L. Henry Lecomte, *Napoléon et l'Empire racontés par le théâtre, 1797–1899* (Paris, 1900), pp. 3–6. Some examples can be seen in Aulard, *Paris pendant la réaction thermidorienne*, iv. pp. 458, 466, 473.
60 Lecomte, *Napoléon et l'Empire*, pp. 14–15.
     Gloire au vainqueur de l'Italie!
     Gloire au héros de l'univers!
     Il fait d'une même patrie
     Dépendre cent peuples divers.
     Vous qu'immortalisa l'histoire,
     Cédez à ce jeune Français:
     Vous combattiez pour la victoire,
     Il a combattu pour la paix.
61 The police reports noted that public opinion ardently desired peace. See Aulard, *Paris pendant la réaction thermidorienne*, iii. pp. 320 (16 July 1796), 388 (12 August 1796), 425 (1 September 1796), 582 (19 November 1796), 599 (30 November 1796), 749 (14 February 1797), 766 (23 February 1797).
62 *Journal des Campagnes et des armées*, 3 May 1797.
63 *Journal des Campagnes et des armées*, 9 April, 3 May 1797.
     A Buonaparte
     Jeune héros, vainqueur de l'Italie,
     Poursuits, étonnes, abats l'orgueil des rois:
     Que tes succès affermissent nos lois:
     Confonds tes ennemis et ceux de la patrie.
     Tu n'étoufferas point la rage de l'envie:
     Eh bien, mérites-la par de nouveaux exploits.

64 Pommereul, *Campagne du général Buonaparte*, p. 274.

65 Albert Espitalier, *Vers Brumaire. Bonaparte à Paris, 5 décembre 1797–4 mai 1798* (Paris, 1914), pp. 17–19.

66 Jean Tulard, *Les Thermidoriens* (Paris, 2005), p. 171.

67 Miot de Mélito, *Mémoires*, i. pp. 180–1.

68 *Corr.* iii. n. 2354 (12 November 1797).

69 The best modern account of the Congress of Rastatt is to be found in Karl Härter, *Reichstag und Revolution 1789–1806* (Göttingen, 1992), pp. 539–66.

70 *Correspondance Générale*, i. p. 1314.

71 Espitalier, *Vers Brumaire*, pp. 29–35.

72 *Gazette Européenne*, 8 November, 22 December 1797.

73 *Gazette Européenne*, 8 December 1797.

74 Abrantès, *Mémoires*, ii. pp. 343–4.

75 *Le Rédacteur*, 1 January 1798; *Clef du Cabinet*, 24 February 1798.

76 *Clef du Cabinet*, 24, 27 February 1798.

77 Bailleu, *Preußen und Frankreich*, i. p. 162 (8 December 1797).

78 Chastenay, *Mémoires*, p. 239.

79 Staël, *Considérations*, p. 340.

80 Aulard, *Paris pendant la réaction thermidorienne*, iv. pp. 487–8, 489.

81 Dard, *Napoléon et Talleyrand*, p. 23.

82 Staël, *Considérations*, p. 340.

83 Dard, *Napoléon et Talleyrand*, p. 23.

84 *Moniteur universel*, 2 November 1797. There were accompanying poems and madrigals composed for the occasion. Marie-Joseph Chénier wrote 'Chant de retour', with music by Méhul. *Recueil complet des discours prononcés par le citoyen Barras . . . et accompagné de la description fidèle de cette fête, et des hymnes qui y ont été chantés* (Paris, n.d.).

85 Puget, Marquis de Barbentane, *Mémoires*, p. 204.

86 Bourrienne, *Mémoires*, ii. pp. 20–1.

87 Bertrand, *Cahiers: janvier–mai 1821*, p. 98.

88 Chastenay, *Mémoires*, p. 240. A good description of the banquet is to be found in Frédéric Masson, *Le Département des affaires étrangères pendant la Révolution, 1787–1804* (Paris, 1877), pp. 427–8.

89 Josephine to Hippolyte Charles, *Joséphine. Correspondance*, p. 60 (17 March 1798).

90 Iung, *Lucien Bonaparte*, i. p. 76.

91 Charles-Maurice de Talleyrand, *Mémoires du prince de Talleyrand*, 5 vols (Paris, 1891–92), i. p. 259.

92 Miot de Mélito, *Mémoires*, i. p. 171.
93 Henri Laurens, *L'expédition d'Egypte, 1798–1801* (Paris, 1997), p. 38.
94 Arnault, *Souvenirs*, p. 608.
95 Espitalier, *Vers Brumaire*, pp. 110–12.
96 Mathieu Dumas, *Souvenirs du lieutenant-général comte Mathieu Dumas, de 1770 à 1836* (Paris, 1839), iii. pp. 155–7.

14 A Grandiose Exile

1 Schroeder, *Transformation*, pp. 172–6.
2 Sorel, *L'Europe et la Révolution française*, v. pp. 225–6.
3 *Corr.* iii. n. 2307 (18 October 1797).
4 Blanning, *French Revolutionary Wars*, pp. 196–7, 201.
5 For an overview of this interpretation, see Cormack, *Revolution and Political Conflict*, ch. 1.
6 Blanning, *French Revolutionary Wars*, p. 199; J. M. Thompson, *The French Revolution* (London, 1955), p. 429.
7 Cormack, *Revolution and the French Navy*, pp. 24–6; Blanning, *French Revolutionary Wars*, pp. 210–15.
8 Clément de La Jonquière, *L'Expédition d'Egypte (1798–1801)*, 5 vols (Paris, 1899–1907), i. pp. 16 and 17.
9 P. F. Tardieu, *Notice historique des descentes qui ont été faites dans les Isles Britanniques* (Paris, 1798), p. 43; Charles Millon, *Histoire des descentes qui ont eu lieu en Angleterre, Ecosse, Irlande et isles adjacentes* (Paris, 1798).
10 *Corr.* iii. n. 2419 (23 February 1798).
11 On this point, see Geoffrey Symcox, 'The Geopolitics of the Egyptian Expedition, 1797–1798', in Irene Bierman (ed.), *Napoleon in Egypt* (Reading, 2003), pp. 21–2.
12 *Mémoires sur les relations commerciales des Etats-Unis avec l'Angleterre* (Paris, n.d.).
13 *Essai sur les avantages à retirer de colonies nouvelles dans les circonstances présentes* (Paris, n.d.).
14 Stuart Harten, 'Rediscovering Ancient Egypt: Bonaparte's Expedition and the Colonial Ideology of the French Revolution', in Bierman (ed.), *Napoleon in Egypt*, p. 33.
15 *Corr.* iii. n. 2106 (16 August 1797).
16 *Corr.* iii. n. 2195 (13 September 1797).
17 Pallain, *Talleyrand sous le Directoire*, p. 155.

18 Georges Lacour-Gayet, *Talleyrand, 1754–1838*, 4 vols (Paris, 1928–1934), i. pp. 306–7.

19 La Jonquière, *L'Expédition d'Egypte*, i. pp. 154–68.

20 Lacour-Gayet, *Talleyrand*, i. p. 308.

21 Reubell, 'Memoire justificatif', *Revue d'histoire diplomatique* lxii (1949), 80; La Révellière-Lépeaux, *Mémoires*, i. pp. 307–8.

22 Henry Laurens, *Les Origines Intellectuelles de l'Expédition d'Egypte. L'Orientalisme Islamisant en France (1698–1798)* (Istanbul, Paris, 1987), p. 106.

23 See Marmont, *Mémoires*, i. pp. 349–50.

24 J. Christopher Herold, *Bonaparte in Egypt* (London, 1962), p. 14.

25 Ronald Zins (ed.), *Journal de voyage du général Desaix, Suisse et Italie (1797)* (Paris, 2000), pp. 150, 175–6.

26 Bourrienne, *Mémoires*, i. p. 230.

27 *Corr.* iii. n. 2103 (16 August 1797).

28 Indeed, Miot suggests that Monge put the idea into his head. Miot de Mélito, *Mémoires*, i. p. 217. The choice of an invasion of the Orient or of England is also considered in *La France vue de l'Armée d'Italie*, n. 18.

29 Miot de Mélito, *Mémoires*, i. p. 217.

30 *Corr.* iv. n. 2426. His calculations were confirmed by a report from the Minister of the Navy delivered on 2 March (Thompson, *Napoleon Bonaparte*, p. 96).

31 François Bernoyer, *Avec Bonaparte en Egypte et en Syrie* (Paris, 1981), p. 45 (7 July 1798); Aulard, *Paris pendant la réaction thermidorienne*, v. pp. 179 (24 October 1798), 210 (16 November).

32 Martyn Lyons, *France under the Directory* (Cambridge, 1975), p. 203; A. B. Rodger, *The War of the Second Coalition, 1798 to 1801. A Strategic Commentary* (Oxford Press, 1964), pp. 21–2.

33 Espitalier, *Vers Brumaire*, p. 184.

34 *Ami des Lois*, 17 April 1798, cited in Maurice Herbette, *Une ambassade turque sous le directoire* (Paris, 1902), pp. 223–4.

35 *Corr.* iv. n. 2495 (12 April 1798).

36 On this aspect of the expedition, see Marie-Noëlle Bourguet, 'Science and Memory: The Stakes of the Expedition to Egypt (1799–1801)', in Howard G. Brown and Judith A. Miller (eds), *Taking Liberties: Problems of a New Order from the French Revolution to Napoleon* (Manchester, 2002), pp. 92–109; and Bourguet, 'Des savants à la conquête de l'Egypte? Science, voyage et politique au temps de l'expédition française', in Patrice Bret (ed.), *L'expédition d'Egypte, une enterprise des Lumières 1798–1801* (Paris, 1999), pp. 21–36. Other works on the expedition include Jean-Joël Brégin,

L'Egypte de Bonaparte (Paris, 1991); Patrice Bret, *L'Egypte au temps de l'Expédition de Bonaparte, 1798–1801* (Paris, 1998); Yves Lassius, *L'Egypte, une aventure savante* (Paris, 1998); and Robert Solé, *Les Savants de Bonaparte* (Paris, 1998).

37 Thibaudeau, *Mémoires sur la Convention et le Directoire*, ii. p. 346.

38 Gilbert Chabrol de Volvic, *Souvenirs d'Egypte* (Paris, 1998), pp. 17, 20–1.

39 Dominique-Vivant Denon, *Voyage dans la Basse et la Haute-Egypte* (Paris, 1990), pp. 79–80.

40 Stuart Woolf, 'Towards the history of the origins of statistics', in Jean-Claude Perrot and Stuart Woolf (eds), *State and Statistics in France, 1789–1815* (New York, 1984), pp. 81–94; and Woolf, 'French Civilization and Ethnicity in the Napoleonic Empire', *Past and Present*, 124 (1989), 96–120.

41 Dominique Garat, a member of the Council of Elders, described Bonaparte in this manner. See also Bonaparte's 'Lettre sur les moyens de faire fleurir les sciences et les arts en Italie', *Moniteur universel*, 10 July 1796. Cato the Elder (234–149 BC) was a Roman general who was also considered the foremost orator of his age. Lucius Quinctius Cincinnatus was a legendary hero often cited as an example of old-fashioned Roman simplicity and frugality.

42 *Corr*. iii. n. 2392 (26 December 1797).

43 Bonaparte's posturing as patron of the arts and sciences in Italy has been underlined by Jourdan, *Napoléon*, pp. 66–8.

44 Even if the term was never used by contemporaries, the idea of a secular civilizing mission dates from this period. See Alyssa Goldstein Sepinwall, *The abbé Grégoire and the French Revolution. The Making of Modern Universalism* (Berkeley, Cal., 2005), pp. 155, 232.

45 See Thomas Kaiser, 'The Evil Empire? The Debate on Turkish Despotism in Eighteenth-Century French Political Culture', *Journal of Modern History*, 72 (2000), 6–34.

46 *Décade philosophique*, no. 20, 20 germinal an VI, p. 81.

47 Constantin François de Chasseboeuf, Comte de Volney, *Les Ruines* (Paris, 1979).

48 Edmé-François Jomard, et al., *Description de l'Egypte ou Recueil des observations et des recherches qui ont été faites en Egypte pendant l'expédition de l'armée française*, 26 vols (Paris, 1821–1830), i. p. v, vi–vii, viii, ix; Edward W. Said, *Orientalism* (London, 1995), p. 85.

49 Juan R. I. Cole, 'Mad Sufis and Civic Courtesans: The French Republican Construction of Eighteenth-Century Egypt', in Bierman (ed.),

Napoleon in Egypt, p. 55. Shmuel Moreh, 'Napoleon and the French Impact on Egyptian Society in the Eyes of Al-Jabarti', in Bierman (ed.), *Napoleon in Egypt*, pp. 87–8, points out that the same rhetoric – that is, restoring Egypt to its former greatness – was used by the Arabs to justify their conquest of the region in the seventh century.

50 *Corr.* iv. n. 2540 (22 April 1798).

51 Roider, *Baron Thugut*, pp. 274–6; Bailleu, *Preußen und Frankreich*, i. pp. 186–8 (25 April 1798).

52 *Corr.* iv. nos. 2544, 2545, 2546 (23 April, 1798).

53 *Corr.* iv. n. 2547 (25 April 1798).

54 Barras, *Mémoires*, iii. pp. 214–15.

55 Espitalier, *Vers Brumaire*, p. 263.

56 Miot de Mélito, *Mémoires*, i. pp. 218–19.

57 Barras, *Mémoires*, iii. pp. 216–17; Espitalier, *Vers Brumaire*, pp. 275–7.

58 Miot de Mélito, *Mémoires*, i. p. 220.

59 Arnault, *Souvenirs*, p. 607.

60 Arnault, *Souvenirs*, p. 607.

15 Confronting Egypt

1 Dominique di Pietro, *Voyage historique en Egypte pendant les campagnes des généraux Bonaparte, Kléber et Menou* (Paris, 1818), pp. 38–9. Also Sulkowski, 'Lettre de Malte', in Adam Skalkowski (ed.), *Les Polonais en Egypte* (Paris, 1910), p. 2. The literature dealing explicitly with the expedition to Egypt is limited. Fundamental is the five volume collection of documents by La Jonquière, *L'Expédition d'Egypte*. A recent up-to-date account in French is to be had in Laurens, *L'expédition d'Egypte*. The only account in English, still very readable, is Herold, *Bonaparte in Egypt*. For the military aspects, see Chandler, *Campaigns*, pp. 205–49.

2 Bernoyer, *Avec Bonaparte*, p. 14 (18 May 1798).

3 *Corr.* iv. n. 2570 (10 May 1798).

4 Lecomte, *Napoléon et l'Empire*, p. 27. The simile is interesting in another respect; we know how much the Roman Republic feared the victor of the Carthaginians and for the safety of its institutions.

5 Laurens, *L'expédition d'Egypte*, p. 50.

6 Rana Kabbani, *Imperial Fictions. Europe's Myths of Orient* (London, 1986), p. 6.

7 Vigo-Roussillon, *Journal*, p. 56; Pelleport, *Souvenirs militaires*, i. p. 107;

Louis de Laus de Boissy, *Bonaparte au Caire, ou Mémoires sur l'expédition de ce général en Egypte* (Paris, 1799).

8   Cited in Daline, 'Marc-Antoine Jullien', 38 (1966), 394–5.

9   Alexandre Dumas, *Mes Mémoires*, 10 vols (Paris, 1863–1884), i. p. 138, although Dumas' memoirs are less than reliable.

10   Josephine to Barras, *Joséphine. Correspondance*, p. 63 (26 May 1798).

11   Josephine to Barras, *Joséphine. Correspondance*, p. 67 (18 June 1798).

12   Josephine to Barras, *Joséphine. Correspondance*, p. 70 (16 July 1798).

13   Knapton, *Empress Josephine*, p. 157; Bruce, *Napoleon and Josephine*, p. 239.

14   Josephine to Barras, *Joséphine. Correspondance*, p. 68 (2 July 1798).

15   He published the details of Josephine's treatment in his *Journal physico-médical des eaux de Plombières* (Remiremont, 1798).

16   Josephine to Mme Marmont, *Joséphine. Correspondance*, pp. 69 and 71 (6 and 27 July 1798).

17   Josephine to Barras, *Joséphine. Correspondance*, p. 75 (16 September 1798).

18   Vigo-Roussillon, *Journal*, p. 64.

19   Symcox, 'The geopolitics of the Egyptian expedition, 1797', pp. 24–5.

20   Charles Norry, *Relation de l'expédition en Egypte* (Paris, Year VII), p. 2; Bernoyer, *Avec Bonaparte*, p. 17 (9 June 1798).

21   Thibaudeau, *Mémoires sur la Convention et le Directoire*, ii. p. 346.

22   Charles-Antoine Morand, *Lettres sur l'expédition d'Egypte* (Paris, 1998), p. 5 (25 May 1798); Louis-George Thurman, *Capitaine Thurman. Bonaparte en Egypte* (Paris, 1902), pp. 2 and 3 (27 germinal an VI and 4 floreal vi 2); Laval Grandjean, *Journaux sur l'Expédition d'Egypte* (Paris, 2000), p. 36; Louis Bricard, *Journal du canonnier Bricard, 1792–1802* (Paris, 1891), p. 297; Aulard, *Paris pendant la réaction thermidorienne*, iv. pp. 591–2 (31 March 1798).

23   Denon, *Voyage*, p. 39.

24   Grandjean, *Journaux*, pp. 36–7; S[ervice]H[istorique de 1']A[rmée de]-T[erre], Mémoires et Reconnaissances, Extraits du journal des campagnes d'Egypte et de Syrie par André Peyrusse, M1 582, f. 5 (6 messidor an VI).

25   Edouard de Villiers du Terrage, *Journal et Souvenirs sur l'Expédition d'Egypte (1798–1801)* (Paris, 1899), p. 24; Bernoyer, *Avec Bonaparte*, pp. 18 and 20 (9 June 1798).

26   Villiers du Terrage, *Journal et Souvenirs*, p. 23.

27   Grandjean, *Journaux*, p. 43; Morand, *Lettres sur l'expédition d'Egypte*, p. 10 (9 June 1798); Villiers du Terrage, *Journal et Souvenirs*, p. 21; Bernoyer, *Avec Bonaparte*, p. 18 (9 June 1798).

28 At least according to Bourrienne, *Mémoires*, ii. pp. 70–1.
29 Bernoyer, *Avec Bonaparte*, p. 20 (9 June 1798).
30 *Corr.* iii. n. 2195 (13 September 1797).
31 *Corr.* iv. n. 2629 (10 June); n. 2641 (13 June 1798).
32 *Corr.* iv. n. 2643 (13 June) and nos. 2668, 2669, 2670, and 2671 (16 June), 2691, 2694, 2695, 2696, and 2697 (18 June 1798).
33 Laurens, *L'expédition d'Egypte*, pp. 54–5.
34 Lavalette, *Mémoires et souvenirs*, p. 184. All of these diplomatic overtures remained without a reply, with the exception of one from the Sheriff of Mecca, who depended for his revenues on the pilgrim caravans from Cairo.
35 See, for example, Bernoyer, *Avec Bonaparte*, p. 23 (18 June 1798).
36 Villiers du Terrage, *Journal et Souvenirs*, pp. 31–2.
37 Henry Laurens (ed.), *Kléber et Bonaparte, 1798–1800*, 3 vols (Paris, 1988), i. p. 534.
38 Pierre-Dominique Martin, *Histoire de l'expédition française en Egypte*, 2 vols (Paris, 1815), i. p. 148.
39 Nicholas Harris Nicolas (ed.), *The Dispatches and Letters of Vice Admiral Lord Viscount Nelson*, 7 vols. (London, 1845–1846), iii. p. 31 (15 June 1798).
40 Cited in Edward Ingram, *Commitment to Empire: Prophecies of the Great Game in Asia, 1797–1800* (Oxford, 1981), p. 59.
41 Rodger, *Second Coalition*, p. 53.
42 Chandler, *Campaigns*, p. 217.
43 Niqula ibn Yusuf al-Turk, *Histoire de l'expédition des Français en Egypte* (Paris, 1839), p. 19.
44 Anna Piussi, 'Images of Egypt during the French Expedition (1798–1801): Sketches of a Historical Colony' (PhD, St. Antony's College, Oxford, 1992), p. 118.
45 Sulkowski, 'Notes sur l'expédition d'Egypte', in Skalkowski (ed.), *Les Polonais en Egypte*, pp. 16–17.
46 Jean-Pierre Doguereau, *Journal de l'expédition d'Egypte* (Paris, 1997), p. 11; Thurman, *Bonaparte en Egypte*, pp. 17–18.
47 Marmont, *Mémoires*, i. p. 411.
48 Jean Gabrielle de Niello Sargy, *Mémoires sur l'expédition d'Egypte* (Paris, 1825), p. 44.
49 Sulkowski, 'Notes sur l'expédition d'Egypte', p. 18.
50 X.-B. Saintine (ed.), *Histoire de l'expédition française en Egypte*, 3 vols (Paris, 1830), i. p. 167; Jacques-François Miot, *Mémoires pour servir à l'histoire des expéditions en Egypte et en Syrie* (Paris, 1804), p. 33.

51 *Copies of Original Letters from the Army of General Bonaparte intercepted by the fleet under the command of Admiral Lord Nelson* (London, 1798), i. p. 4 (6 July 1798).
52 See, for example, Shechy to Miot, *Copies of Original Letters*, ii. p. 32 (26 July 1798).
53 Morand, *Lettres sur l'expédition d'Egypte*, p. 83 (3 July 1798).
54 Pelleport, *Souvenirs militaires*, i. p. 114; Charles François, *Journal du capitaine François* (Paris, 1903), i. p. 193 (3 July 1798).
55 *Corr.* xxix. p. 433. *Copies of Original Letters*, i. p. 26 (9 July 1797).
56 Volney, *Voyage en Syrie et en Egypte* (Paris, 1959), p. 108, for example, refers to the Mamelukes as 'addicted to that abominable wickedness which was at all times the vice of the Greeks and of the Tartars'. Jaubert, in *Copies of Original Letters*, i. p. 26 (9 July 1797), refers to it as 'Socrates is said to have treated Alcibiades.'
57 Rudi C. Bleys, *The Geography of Perversion: Male-to-Male Sexual Behaviour outside the West and the Ethnographic Imagination, 1750–1918* (New York, 1995), pp. 79–80; and Stephen O. Murray and Will Roscoe, *Islamic Homosexualities: Culture, History, and Literature* (New York, 1997), pp. 161, 165.
58 *Corr.* iv. n. 2765 (6 July 1798).
59 Chabrol de Volvic, *Souvenirs*, p. 27.
60 Morand, *Lettres sur l'expédition d'Egypte*, p. 41 (8 July 1798).
61 Chabrol de Volvic, *Souvenirs*, p. 27.
62 Desvernois, *Mémoires*, p. 99.
63 *Correspondance de l'armée française en Egypte* (Paris, an VII), p. 158; Pierre-François Boyer, *Historique de ma vie* (Paris, 2001), p. 34.
64 Pierre Millet, *Le chasseur Pierre Millet. Souvenirs de la campagne d'Egypte (1798–1801)* (Paris, 1903), p. 44.
65 Pelleport, *Souvenirs militaires*, i. p. 114; François, *Journal*, i. p. 192 (2 July 1798).
66 *Corr.* iv. n. 2723 (2 July 1798).
67 Laurens, *L'Expédition d'Egypte*, pp. 107–9.
68 Morand, *Lettres sur l'expédition d'Egypte*, p. 47 (8 July 1798).
69 Niello Sargy, *Mémoires*, pp. 57 and 58.
70 Morand, *Lettres sur l'expédition d'Egypte*, p. 46 (8 July 1798).
71 Joseph-Marie Moiret, *Memoirs of Napoleon's Egyptian Expedition, 1798–1801* (London, 2001), p. 51; *Correspondance de l'armée française*, p. 175; Boyer, *Historique*, p. 36.
72 Saintine (ed.), *Histoire de l'expédition française en Egypte*, i. p. 164.

73 Henri Gatien Bertrand, *Campagne d'Egypte et de Syrie, 1798–1799* (Paris, 1847), i. pp. 153–4.

74 Dominique Larrey, *Relation historique et chirurgical de l'expédition de l'armée d'Orient, en Egypt et en Syrie* (Paris, 1803), pp. 7 and 9.

75 *Copies of Original Letters*, i. pp. 143–4 (28 July 1797).

76 Volney, *Voyage en Syrie et en Egypte*, p. 106.

77 Chandler, *Campaigns*, p. 223.

78 François, *Journal*, i. p. 203 (19 July 1798).

79 Elliot Colla, ' "Non, non! Si, si!" ': Commemorating the French Occupation of Egypt (1798–1801)', *Modern Language Notes*, 118 (2003), 1058.

80 Morand, *Lettres sur l'expédition d'Egypte*, p. 64 (21 July 1798); Eugène, *Mémoires et correspondance*, i. p. 41.

81 Laurens, *L'Expédition d'Egypte*, pp. 126–7.

82 Miot, *Mémoires* (1804), p. 50.

83 Miot, *Mémoires* (1804), p. 51; Marmont, *Mémoires*, i. p. 384.

84 Niqula al-Turk, *Histoire de l'expédition des Français*, p. 33.

85 *Napoleon in Egypt. Al-Jabartī's Chronicle of the French Occupation, 1798* (Princeton, NJ, 1993), pp. 39–40.

16 Conciliation and Terror: Governing Egypt

1 Laurens, *L'expédition d'Egypte*, p. 129.

2 *Corr.* iv. n. 2834.

3 S[ervice] H[istorique de[']]A[rmée de] T[erre], Mémoires et Reconnaissances, Journal tenu à l'armée d'Orient par le chef de brigade Detroye, M1 526, ff. 52–53 (29 thermidor an VI); and Morand, *Lettres sur l'expédition d'Egypte*, pp. 71–2 (19 September 1798). The references to uncovered breasts among Egyptian women is interesting. Muslim women, of course, covered their breasts; there is, indeed, an injunction in the Koran that they should do so. However, the French may very well have been describing clothing worn by peasant women where the djellaba (the long black robe commonly worn) was open wide enough at the neck to reveal the breasts. There is an illustration in the *Description de l'Egypte* that effectively shows a 'woman of the people' with uncovered breasts. My thanks to Afaf Marsot for help on this point.

4 Doguereau, *Journal*, p. 25.

5 Etienne Geoffroy Saint-Hilaire, *Lettres écrites d'Egypte* (Paris, 1901), p. 69 (24 August 1798).

6 Morand, *Lettres sur l'expédition d'Egypte*, p. 65 (9 July 1798).

7 *Al-Jabartī's Chronicle*, pp. 28–9. To have a hairless face was the sign of a slave, and even though the French were masters, they could still be considered the slaves of others more powerful if they did not wear a beard (Geoffroy Saint-Hilaire, *Lettres écrites d'Egypte*, p. 74 (3 August 1798)).

8 For the attitude of Egyptians towards the French, see André Raymond, 'Les Egyptiens et les Lumières pendant l'expédition française', in Patrice Bret (ed.), *L'expédition d'Egypte, une entreprise des Lumières 1798–1801* (Paris, 1999), pp. 106–12; and of the French towards the Egyptians, Cole, 'Mad Sufis and Civic Courtesans', in Bierman (ed.), *Napoleon in Egypt*, pp. 47–62.

9 Bonaparte to Joseph, *Correspondance Générale*, ii. p. 200 (25 July 1798); La Jonquière, *L'Expédition d'Egypte*, ii. p. 208; Joseph, *Mémoires*, i. p. 189 (25 July 1798).

10 Frédéric Masson, *Madame Bonaparte, 1796–1804* (Paris, 1920), pp. 139–40. Neither Bonaparte's letter to Joseph nor Eugene's letter to his mother ever reached their destination. They were captured by the British and published on 24 November in the *Morning Chronicle*.

11 Laurens, *L'expédition d'Egypte*, p. 131.

12 Text in La Jonquière, *L'Expédition d'Egypte*, ii. pp. 65–6.

13 *Corr.* iv. nos. 2733 (3 July), and 3239 (4 September 1798); Laus de Boissy, *Bonaparte au Caire*, pp. 147–8.

14 On the workings of the *diwan*, see Sami A. Hanna, 'The Egyptian Mind and the Idea of Democracy', *International Journal of Middle East Studies*, 1 (1970), 241–2.

15 *Al-Jabartī's Chronicle*, pp. 59–60.

16 Laurens, *L'expédition d'Egypte*, p. 163; La Jonquière, *L'Expédition d'Egypte*, iii p. 16.

17 There is no place here for a discussion of whether the French occupation was necessary for Egyptian society to modernize itself. Contemporary historians reject this notion and point out that modernization was already taking place before Bonaparte's arrival. See Afaf Lufti al-Sayyid Marsot, 'L'Expédition d'Egypte et le débat sur la modernité', *Egypte/Monde Arabe*, 1 (1999), 47–54; and Colla, 'Commemorating the French Occupation of Egypt', 1043–69.

18 Said, *Orientalism*, p. 83–7. On the ideological implications of the *Description*, see Anne Godlewska, 'Map, Text and Image. The Mentality of Enlightened Conquerors: A New Look at the *Description de l'Egypte*', *Transactions of the Institute of British Geographers*, 20 (1995), 5–28.

19 Grigsby, *Extremities*, p. 122; and on the Egyptian 'feminization' of the French, see Colla, 'Commemorating the French Occupation of Egypt', 1063–4.

20 Piussi, 'Images of Egypt', pp. 122–7.

21 Laurens, *L'expédition d'Egypte*, pp. 171–2.

22 Villiers du Terrage, *Journal et Souvenirs*, p. 72.

23 *Copies of Original Letters*, iii. p. 114.

24 *Copies of Original Letters*, i. pp. 3–4 (6 July 1798).

25 *Copies of Original Letters*, i. p. 105 (27 July 1798). The account may be exaggerated, or a rumour, and it did not preclude some Frenchmen from seeking homosexual relationships. We know, for example, that Desaix had a young black boy and a Mameluke, 'as beautiful as an angel', in his 'seraglio' (Herold, *Bonaparte in Egypt*, p. 230).

26 Jacques de Coursac, *Un ami dauphinois de Napoléon Bonaparte, Simon de Sucy, ordonnateur en chef de l'armée d'Egypte* (Paris, 1932), pp. 217–24.

27 Shechy to Miot, *Copies of Original Letters*, ii. p. 35 (26 July 1798).

28 Ségur, *Histoire et Mémoires*, i. pp. 428–9.

29 Doguereau, *Journal*, p. 23 (written about August 1797).

30 Vigo-Roussillon, *Journal*, p. 89; Jean-Joël Brégin, *L'Egypte de Bonaparte* (Paris, 1991), pp. 204–12; and the article reproduced in annex by G. Legrain, 'Les graffiti de l'expédition'.

31 *Moniteur*, 27 November 1798; *Relation du voyage aérostatique du général Buonaparte* (Paris, an VII).

32 Villiers du Terrage, *Journal et Souvenirs*, p. 77.

33 Norry, *Relation de l'expédition en Egypte*, p. 43.

34 *Corr.* iv. n. 2874 (28 July 1798).

35 Marmont, *Mémoires*, ii. pp. 3–4. On this episode, see Rene Khoury, 'Le mariage musulman du général Abdallah Menou', *Egyptian Historical Review*, 25 (1978), 65–93. Some of these Egyptian women adopted the French style of dress and accompanied their husbands in public. We do not know what happened to Zobaïdah after the French left Egypt. Tradition has it that she accompanied Menou to France and lived in Marseilles after his death in 1810, only to return to Egypt in her old age.

36 Hamelin, 'Douze ans de ma vie, 1796–1808', p. 557.

37 Admiral Perrée to Ami Le Joille (10 thermidor an 6), in Saladin Boustany (ed.), *The Journals of Bonaparte in Egypt* (Cairo, 1977), x. p. 56; Niello Sargy, *Mémoires*, p. 72.

38 Niello Sargy, *Mémoires*, p. 194.

39 Bernoyer, *Avec Bonaparte*, p. 94 (13 November 1798).

40 Norry, *Relation de l'expédition en Egypte*, p. 46; Bernoyer, *Avec Bonaparte*, pp. 98–101 (13 November 1798).

41 Bernoyer, *Avec Bonaparte*, pp. 94–5 (13 November 1798).

42 Knapton, *Josephine*, p. 162.

43 *Corr.* v. n. 3774 (17 December 1798).

44 Niello Sargy, *Mémoires*, pp. 199–209.

45 Ségur, *Histoire et Mémoires*, i. p. 426.

46 Daniel Panzac, *La peste dans l'empire ottoman, 1700–1850* (Louvain, 1985), pp. 327–8.

47 Marmont, *Mémoires*, i. pp. 412–15.

48 *Corr.* v. n. 3909 (28 January 1799).

49 Girez to Ramcy, *Copies of Original Letters*, ii. p. 57 (28 July 1798).

50 *Corr.* v. n. 3818 (8 January 1799). Not the general of the same name quoted above.

51 See SHAT, Mémoires et Reconnaissances, Journal de Detroye, M1 526, ff. 38–9 (17 thermidor an VI).

52 *Corr.* iv. n. 2907 (31 July 1798).

53 François, *Journal*, i. p. 220 (7 August 1798).

54 Louis Reybaud (ed.), *Histoire scientifique et militaire de l'expédition française en Egypte* (Paris, 1830–6), iii. p. 261.

55 Laurens, *L'expédition d'Egypte*, pp. 144–6.

56 La Jonquière, *L'Expédition d'Egypte*, ii. p. 71, n. 2.

57 *Copies of Original Letters*, i. p. 15 (8 July 1798).

58 Marmont, *Mémoires*, i. pp. 393–5.

59 *Corr.* iv. n. 3252 (6 September 1798).

17 Prisoner of his Conquest

1 *Dispatches and Letters of Nelson*, iii. p. 49.

2 A good account of the battle can be found in Edgar Vincent, *Nelson: Love and Fame* (New Haven, 2003), pp. 259–64; and Blanning, *French Revolutionary Wars*, pp. 189–96.

3 'Battle of the Nile', in *Dispatches and Letters of Nelson*, iii. p. 51.

4 'Battle of the Nile', in *Dispatches and Letters of Nelson*, iii. p. 52.

5 Denon, *Voyage*, pp. 82–3.

6 Thurman, *Bonaparte en Egypte*, pp. 35–6 (17 thermidor VI).

7 *Copies of Original Letters*, i. pp. 185 and 197 (4 August 1797).

8 *Corr.* iv. n. 3045 (19 August 1798).

9 Laurens, *L'expédition d'Egypte*, p. 151. See also Charles-Yves Cousin, *Bonapartiana, ou Recueil des réponses ingénieuses ou sublime, actions héroïques et faits mémorables de Bonaparte* (Paris, 1801), i. pp. 30–1, in which Brueys bears the blame for the defeat but in which Bonaparte nobly states that he made up for any mistakes by a glorious death.

10 Blanning, *French Revolutionary Wars*, p. 196; Martine Acerra and Jean Meyer, *Marines et Révolution* (Rennes, 1988), pp. 98, 143, 215.

11 Brendan Simms, 'Britain and Napoleon', in Dwyer (ed.), *Napoleon and Europe*, pp. 189–90.

12 Ingram, *Commitment to Empire*, pp. 92–3.

13 *Corr.* iv. n. 3045 (19 August 1798).

14 Symcox, 'The Geopolitics of the Egyptian Expedition', p. 23.

15 La Jonquière, *L'Expédition d'Egypte*, iii. pp. 261–8.

16 Ségur, *Histoire et Mémoires*, i. p. 427.

17 Maurice Herbette, *Une Ambassade turque sous le Directoire* (Paris, 1902), pp. 225–6, 229–36.

18 For a summary of the diplomatic dealings around the expedition, see La Jonquière, *L'Expédition d'Egypte*, ii. pp. 587–609.

19 It is interesting to note that Talleyrand had assured Ruffin in a letter dated 3 August that he had nothing to fear from the Seven Towers (Herbette, *Une Ambassade turque*, p. 237).

20 *Corr.* v. nos. 3747 and 3748 (11 December 1798).

21 Panzac, *La peste dans l'empire ottoman*, pp. 332.

22 This last measure is mentioned in Niqula ibn Yusuf al-Turk, *Histoire de l'expédition des Français en Egypte*, p. 76; Panzac, *La peste dans l'empire ottoman*, pp. 328–9.

23 Moreh, 'Napoleon and the French impact on Egyptian society', pp. 83 and 84.

24 *Al-Jabartī's Chronicle*, pp. 83–96; SHAT, Mémoires et Reconnaissances, André Peyrusse, M1 582, f. 15 (8 brumaire an VI).

25 *Corr.* v. n. 3524 (22 October 1798).

26 *Al-Jabartī's Chronicle*, p. 93.

27 Herold, *Bonaparte in Egypt*, p. 199.

28 Denon, *Voyage*, pp. 117–18.

29 *Corr.* v. n. 3527 (23 October 1798).

30 Bernoyer, *Avec Bonaparte*, p. 91 (no date).

31 Niello Sargy, *Mémoires*, p. 187.

32 See F. Charles-Roux, *Bonaparte, gouverneur d'Egypte* (Paris, 1936), p. 251.

33 Morand, *Lettres sur l'expédition d'Egypte*, p. 74 (19 September 1798).

34 Laurens, *L'expédition d'Egypte*, p. 217; Reybaud (ed.), *Histoire scientifique et militaire*, iv. pp. 128–31.

35 Laurens, *L'expédition d'Egypte*, pp. 238–9.

36 *Corr.* v. n. 3785 (21 December 1798).

37 Las Cases, *Mémorial*, i. pp. 155, 168; *Memoirs of General de Caulaincourt*, ii. p. 234; Henry Laurens (ed.), *Campagnes d'Egypte et de Syrie* (Paris, 1998), pp. 8, 22, 210.

38 Ségur, *Histoire et Mémoires*, i. p. 427, 439–40; Claire Rémusat, *Mémoires*, i. pp. 274–5; Bernoyer, *Avec Bonaparte*, p. 152 (19 April 1799); Bourrienne, *Mémoires*, ii. pp. 242–5; Auguste Marmont, *Voyage du maréchal duc de Raguse en Hongrie, en Transylvanie . . . en Syrie, en Palestine et en Egypte* (Paris, 1837), iii. pp. 97–9.

39 Joseph, *Mémoires*, i. p. 189.

40 *Corr.* iv. n. 3259 (8 September 1798).

41 *Corr.* v. n. 3952 (10 February 1799), where he speaks of returning to France.

42 Some are in *Corr.* v. nos. 3899, 3900, 3901 (25 January 1799).

43 *Corr.* v. nos. 4236 and 4237 (30 June 1799).

44 *Corr.* iv. nos. 3215 (2 September) and 3360 (21 September 1798).

45 *Corr.* v. nos. 3952 (10 February) and 4035 (13 March 1799).

46 *Corr.* v. n. 3644 (19 November 1798).

47 Bernoyer, *Avec Bonaparte*, p. 134 (20 March 1799).

18 The Limits of Imagination

1 Vigo-Roussillon, *Journal*, pp. 81–2.

2 SHAT, Mémoires et Reconnaissances, André Peyrusse, M1 582, f. 24 (15 pluviose an VI).

3 François, *Journal*, i. pp. 255–6 (7 February 1799).

4 François, *Journal*, i. pp. 256–7 (8 February 1799).

5 Miot, *Mémoires* (1804), p. 118.

6 Vigo-Roussillon, *Journal*, p. 82.

7 Etienne-Louis Malus de Mitry, *L'Agenda de Malus. Souvenirs de l'expédition d'Egypte, 1798–1801* (Paris, 1892), p. 119; Niello Sargy, *Mémoires*, p. 245.

8 *Corr.* v. nos. 3979 and 3981 (18 February 1799).

9 Malus, *L'Agenda*, pp. 122–3.

10 Larrey, *Relation historique*, pp. 92 and 93.

11 Doguereau, *Journal*, p. 65.

12 Millet, *Souvenirs de la campagne d'Egypte*, pp. 79–80.

13 Malus, *L'Agenda*, pp. 128, 129; Miot, *Mémoires* (1804), p. 124; Bernoyer, *Avec Bonaparte*, pp. 141–2 (20 March 1799); Beauharnais, *Mémoires*, i. p. 53.

14 *Corr.* v. n. 4022 (9 March 1799).

15 Bernoyer, *Avec Bonaparte*, p. 142 (20 March 1799).

16 Bernoyer, *Avec Bonaparte*, p. 142 (20 March 1799).

17 According to Jacques Derogy and Henri Carmel, *Bonaparte en Terre Sainte*, p. 153.

18 Derogy Carmel, *Bonaparte en Terre Sainte*, p. 163. There is no truth to the claim that Bonaparte was thinking of establishing a Jewish state in Palestine. See Henry Laurens, 'Le projet d'Etat juif attribué à Bonaparte', *Revue d'Etudes Palestiniennes*, 33 (1989), 69–83.

19 Louis-Alexandre Berthier, *Mémoires du Maréchal Berthier . . . Campagnes d'Egypte*, 2 vols (Paris, 1827), i. p. 50.

20 François, *Journal*, i. p. 275 (28 February 1799).

21 Niello Sargy, *Mémoires*, p. 252.

22 Miot, *Mémoires* (1804), p. 223.

23 François, *Journal*, i. p. 275 (2 March 1799).

24 Millet, *Souvenirs de la campagne d'Egypte*, p. 82; François, *Journal*, i. p. 280 (7 March 1799).

25 Malus, *L'Agenda*, pp. 135–6.

26 Saintine (ed.), *Histoire de l'expédition française en Egypte*, ii. pp. 344–5.

27 Miot, *Mémoires* (1804), pp. 137–8.

28 Bernoyer, *Avec Bonaparte*, pp. 147–8 (19 April 1799).

29 Eugène glosses over this episode in his memoirs and even justifies his father-in-law's decision, Beauharnais, *Mémoires*, i. pp. 54–5.

30 Bourrienne, *Mémoires*, i. pp. 179–82.

31 Nicolas-René-Dufriche, Baron Desgenettes, *Souvenirs d'un médecin de l'expédition d'Egypte* (Paris, 1893), pp. 15–16.

32 Herold, *Bonaparte in Egypt*, p. 276.

33 La Jonquière, iv. p. 271. Also Miot, *Mémoires* (1814), pp. 145–8.

34 According to Detroye, the number massacred over the three days came to 2,441 (SHAT, Mémoires et Reconnaissances, Journal de Detroye, M1 527, f. 54 (20 ventose an VII)). Bonaparte boasted of 4,000 executions in a letter to the Directory (*Corr.* v. n. 4035 (13 March 1798)). For the location see Nathan Schur, *Napoleon in the Holy Land* (London, 1999), p. 67.

35 Vigo-Roussillon, *Journal*, p. 83.

36 Vigo-Roussillon, *Journal*, p. 84.

37 Bernoyer, *Avec Bonaparte*, p. 146 (19 April 1799).

38 Cited in Sorel, *L'Europe et la Révolution française*, i. pp. 85–6.

39 Jacques Semelin, 'In consideration of massacres', *Journal of Genocide Research*, 3 (2001), 381–2.

40 See Jean-Clément Martin, 'Les mots de la violence: les guerres révolutionnaires', in Stéphane Audoin-Rouzeau, Annette Becker, et al. (eds), *La violence de guerre 1914–45* (Paris, 2002), pp. 27–42.

41 Niello Sargy, *Mémoires*, p. 283.

42 Malus, *L'Agenda*, p. 128.

43 Malus, *L'Agenda*, pp. 140–3.

44 Malus, *L'Agenda*, pp. 143–6.

45 François, *Journal*, i. p. 281 (7 March 1799).

46 François, *Journal*, i. p. 283 (7 March 1799).

47 La Jonquière, iv. p. 284. Other published accounts have Bonaparte rapidly walking through the rooms where the sick lay, carefully avoiding any contact with them, and hitting his boot with a riding crop as he did so. But they seem to have confused two separate visits (Bourrienne, *Mémoires*, ii. p. 257).

48 Darcy Grimaldo-Grigsby, 'Rumor, Contagion, and Colonization in Gros's *Plague-Stricken of Jaffa* (1804)', *Representations*, 51 (1995), 8–9; Las Cases, *Mémorial*, i. p. 149.

49 *Corr.* xxx. p. 29.

50 SHAT, Mémoires et Reconnaissances, Journal de Detroye, M1 527, f. 57 (22 ventose an VII).

51 Laurens, *L'expédition d'Egypte*, pp. 269, 270–1.

52 There has been a tendency for British historians to lay all the credit for Bonaparte's defeat on Sidney Smith but this is contested by Amnon Cohen, *Palestine in the 18th Century* (Jerusalem, 1973), pp. 28–9.

53 Schur, *Napoleon in the Holy Land*, p. 89.

54 Bernoyer, *Avec Bonaparte*, p. 161 (1 July 1799).

55 See *Corr.* v. n. 4102 (19 April 1799) in which Bonaparte states that he expected to take Acre on 5 or 6 May, and that he would leave for Cairo immediately after.

56 La Jonquière, *L'Expédition d'Egypte*, iv. p. 453.

57 Louis-Alexandre Berthier, *Relations des campagnes du général Bonaparte en Egypte et en Syrie* (Paris, 1799), pp. 93–4.

58 Laurens, *Kléber en Egypte*, i. pp. 57–61; ii. pp. 475–8.

59 La Jonquière, *L'Expédition d'Egypte*, iv. pp. 496–7.

19 The End of the Dream

1 J. Barrow (ed.), *The Life and Correspondence of Sir Sidney Smith*, 2 vols (London, 1848), i. pp. 309–10 (30 May 1799).
2 Bernoyer, *Avec Bonaparte*, p. 163 (1 July 1799).
3 *Corr.* v. n. 4136 (16 May 1799).
4 *Corr.* v. n. 4124 (10 May 1799).
5 *Corr.* v. n. 4156 (27 May 1799).
6 *Corr.* v. n. 4138 (17 May 1799).
7 Doguereau, *Journal*, pp. 107–8.
8 Vigo-Roussillon, *Journal*, p. 87.
9 Bourrienne, *Mémoires*, ii. p. 250.
10 Reybaud (ed.), *Histoire scientifique et militaire*, vi. pp. 459–60.
11 François, *Journal*, i. p. 332 (20 May 1799).
12 See, for example, SHAT, Mémoires et Reconnaissances, André Peyrusse, M1 582, f. 61 (6 messidor an VII); Laurens, *L'expédition d'Egypte*, pp. 282–3.
13 See, for example, *Mémoires du maréchal Berthier*, i. pp. 99–100; François, *Journal*, i. pp. 334–5 (23 May 1799); Miot, *Mémoires* (1804), pp. 233–4.
14 Miot, *Mémoires* (1804), pp. 233–4.
15 Bourrienne, *Mémoires*, ii. p. 251.
16 Millet, *Souvenirs de la campagne d'Egypte*, p. 129.
17 Bourrienne, *Mémoires*, ii. p. 257. This scene is sometimes confused with the first visit to the sick at Jaffa. On the poisoning, see Marmont, *Mémoires*, ii. pp. 12–14; François, *Journal*, i. pp. 335–6 (26/27 May 1799); La Jonquière, *L'Expédition d'Egypte*, iv. pp. 575–83; Herold, *Bonaparte in Egypt*, pp. 307–8. There is no doubt that Bonaparte ordered the poisoning, although no one seems to have died as a result.
18 A French translation of Sidney Smith's letter to Nelson is in La Jonquière, *L'Expédition d'Egypte*, iv. pp. 588–92.
19 François, *Journal*, i. p. 338 (4 June 1798).
20 Sergent Bonnefons, 'Un soldat d'Italie et d'Egypte. Souvenirs (1792–1801)', in *Souvenirs et cahiers sur la campagne d'Egypte. Extraits du Carnet de la Sabretache* (Paris, 1997), pp. 56–7.
21 Reybaud, *Histoire scientifique et militaire*, vi. pp. 4–7.
22 Bonnefons, 'Un soldat d'Italie et d'Egypte', pp. 58–9.
23 Vigo-Roussillon, *Journal*, p. 89.
24 *Corr.* iv. nos. 4136 and 4137 (16 and 17 May 1799).

25 H. Mollaret and J. Brossollet, 'A propos des "Pestiférés de Jaffa" de A. J. Gros', *Jaarboek van het Koninklijk Museum voor schoone kunsten* (1968), p. 282.

26 Laurens, *Kléber en Egypte*, ii. p. 545.

27 La Jonquière, *L'Expédition d'Egypte*, v. pp. 166–8; Iung, *Lucien Bonaparte*, i. p. 270.

28 Laurens, *L'expédition d'Egypte*, pp. 302–3; La Jonquière, *L'Expédition d'Egypte*, v. pp. 191–226.

29 La Jonquière, *L'Expédition d'Egypte*, v. p. 231.

30 Herold, *Bonaparte in Egypt*, p. 317; *Victoires, conquêtes, désastres, revers et guerres civiles des français, de 1792 à 1815*, 29 vols (Paris, 1818), x. pp. 312–14.

31 Marmont to Bonaparte, 22 January 1799, in Marmont, *Mémoires*, i. pp. 442–3.

32 Bernoyer, *Avec Bonaparte*, p. 163 (1 July 1799).

33 *Corr.* v. nos. 4281–3 (15 July 1799).

34 *Corr.* v. n. 4296 (21 July 1799).

35 Herold, *Bonaparte in Egypt*, pp. 318–19.

36 *Corr.* v. n. 4323 (28 July 1799).

37 Laurens, *L'expédition d'Egypte*, pp. 313–15; Herold, *Bonaparte in Egypt*, pp. 321–2.

38 Marmont, *Mémoires*, ii. pp. 31–2.

39 Reybaud, *Histoire scientifique et militaire*, vi. pp. 289–90.

40 Denon, *Voyage*, p. 290.

41 Cited in La Jonquière, *L'Expédition d'Egypte*, v. p. 609.

42 Villiers du Terrage, *Journal et Souvenirs*, p. 223.

43 Herold, *Bonaparte in Egypt*, p. 341.

44 Dugua to Barras, September 1799, Laurens (ed.), *Kléber en Egypte*, iii. pp. 6–7; and Dugua to Barras, 13 October 1799, *Copies of Original Letters*, iii. p. 153.

45 N.-J. Colbert de Chabanis, *Traditions et souvenirs, ou Mémoires touchant le temps et la vie du général Auguste, Colbert (1793–1809)* (Paris, 1863–73), ii. p. 294.

46 Vigo-Roussillon, *Journal*, pp. 102–3.

47 Claire Rémusat, *Mémoires*, i. p. 142; *Correspondance Générale*, ii. p. 200 (25 July 1798).

48 Pierre-Louis Roederer, *Autour de Bonaparte. Journal du comte P.-L. Roederer* (Paris, 1909), p. 165.

20 The Return of the Saviour

1 *Moniteur universel*, 6 October 1799.

2 Albert Vandal, *L'avènement de Bonaparte* (Paris, 1903), i. p. 231. In addition to Vandal, the standard accounts of the coup of Brumaire, on which I have drawn for the following chapters, are: Albert Ollivier, *Le Dix-huit brumaire* (Paris, 1959); Jean-Paul Bertaud, *1799, Bonaparte prend le pouvoir. La République meurt-elle assassinée?* (Brussels, 1987); Thierry Lentz, *Le 18-Brumaire. Les coups d'Etat de Napoléon Bonaparte* (Paris, 1997); Jean Tulard, *Le 18 Brumaire: Comment terminer une révolution* (Paris, 1999); Malcolm Crook, *Napoleon Comes to Power: Democracy and Dictatorship in Revolutionary France, 1795–1804* (Cardiff, 1998). Also worth consulting are Jacques-Olivier Boudon (ed.), *Brumaire. La prise de pouvoir de Bonaparte* (Paris, 2001); and Isser Woloch, *Napoleon and his Collaborators: The Making of a Dictatorship* (New York, 2001), ch. 1.

3 Paul Thiébault, *Mémoires du général baron Thiébault* (Paris, 1895), iii. pp. 56–7.

4 Pierre-Jean de Béranger, *Ma biographie, ouvrage posthume de P.-J. Béranger* (Paris, 1857), i. p. 70.

5 Antoine-Claire Thibaudeau, *Mémoires de A.-C. Thibaudeau* (Paris, 1913), p. 1.

6 Vandal, *L'avènement*, i. pp. 233–4; *Le Publiciste*, 17 October 1799 (25 vendémiaire VIII).

7 *Gazette de France*, 29 vendémiaire VIII (21 October 1799); *Le Publiciste*, 17 October 1799 (25 vendémiaire VIII).

8 Jean-François Boulart, *Mémoires militaires du général Baron Boulart* (Paris, 1892), pp. 67–8. The account was written many years after the event but Boulart's memoirs are generally accurate.

9 *Ami des Lois*, 30 vend. VIII (22 October 1799).

10 Jean-Baptiste Marbot, *Mémoires du général baron de Marbot*, 3 vols (Paris, 1891), i. pp. 46, 49.

11 Lavalette, *Mémoires et souvenirs*, pp. 225–6; Maurice Albert, *Les Théâtres des boulevards: 1789–1848* (Paris, 1902), pp. 176–7. Other plays were to follow: *Le Retour à l'Espérance, ou l'Arrivée du général Bonaparte* (20 October 1799), *L'Heureux Retour* (22 October), *Le Héros de retour d'Egypte* (26 October), *Les Nouvellistes de Pantin, ou le Retour inattendu* (30 October), and *Le Premier rayon de soleil* (12 November) (Lecomte, *Napoléon et l'Empire*, pp. 45–7).

12 Blanning, *French Revolutionary Wars*, pp. 226–56; Blanning, *Origins of*

the Revolutionary Wars, pp. 173–204; Schroeder, *Transformation*, pp. 177–209.

13 The best biography on Paul is Roderick E. McGrew, *Paul I of Russia* (Oxford, 1992).

14 Blanning, *Origins of the Revolutionary Wars*, p. 191.

15 Godechot, *Grande Nation*, pp. 526–30.

16 See, for example, Howard G. Brown, 'Revolt and Repression in the Midi Toulousain (1799)', *French History*, 19 (2005), 234–61.

17 Bailleu, *Preußen und Frankreich*, i. p. 340 (3 October 1799).

18 Auguste Bigarré, *Mémoires du général Bigarré: 1775–1813* (Paris, 2002), p. 105.

19 Marmont, *Mémoires*, ii. p. 51.

20 Nicole Gotteri, 'L'esprit publique à Paris avant le coup d'Etat de Brumaire an VIII', in Boudon (ed.), *Brumaire*, p. 18.

21 *Bonaparte général d'armée* (Paris, an V).

22 *Ami des Lois*, 15 thermidor V (2 August 1797); Pommereul, *Campagne du général Buonaparte*, p. 3.

23 The view that Bonaparte had been 'deported' to Egypt by the Directory seems to have gained authority. The Directory was forced to respond by publishing a booklet of over 100 pages – *Bonaparte en Égypte, ou Dialogues entre Pitt et deux voyageurs anglais, Bruce et Yrwin* (Paris, 1799) – emphasizing that the expedition had been entirely conceived by Bonaparte (Leclercq, 'Le mythe de Bonaparte', pp. 245–6).

24 *Sur Bonaparte, conversations entre un soldat, un royaliste et un rentier* (np, nd).

25 Lentz, *Le 18-Brumaire*, p. 267.

26 See the poems in *Le Rédacteur*, 16 October (24 Vendémiaire), 22 October (30 Vendémiaire), 27 October 1799 (5 Brumaire VIII).

27 Patricia Mainardi, 'Assuring the Empire of the Future: The 1798 Fête de la Liberté', *Art Journal*, 48 (1989), 155–63; Martin Rosenberg, 'Raphael's Transfiguration and Napoleon's Cultural Politics', *Eighteenth Century Studies*, 19 (1985–6), 191.

28 Blumer, 'Commission', p. 249.

29 *Journal des Hommes Libres*, 16, 20, 28 thermidor VI (3, 7, 15 August 1799); *Moniteur universel*, 20 August, 16 and 29 September 1799; *Corr.* iv. n. 3045 (19 August 1799).

30 Thierry Lentz, *Le Grand Consulat, 1799–1804* (Paris, 1999), p. 40.

31 Tulard, *Napoléon*, pp. 160–1.

32 *Journal des Hommes Libres*, 12 October 1799; *Moniteur universel*, 11 October 1799; the *Clef du Cabinet*, 7 October 1799.

33 cf. Hanley, *Genesis of Napoleonic Propaganda*, pp. 37–9.

34 *Moniteur universel*, 24 October 1799.

35 Christian-Marc Bosséno, ' "*Du haut de ces monuments . . .*". L'Expédition d'Egypte dans la constitution de la légende napoléonienne', *Revista Napoleonica*, 1 (2001), 16–18, and for the following.

36 Hanley, *Genesis of Napoleonic Propaganda*, pp. 64–5, 67–8. An interesting view of the press in Bonaparte's absence can be found in Ian Germani, 'Where is General Bonaparte? Press reports of Napoleon's expedition to Egypt', *Western Society for French History*, 24 (1997), 61–70.

37 *Journal des Hommes Libres*, 20 thermidor VI (7 August 1798).

38 *Moniteur universel*, 19 and 21 November 1798.

39 *Journal des Hommes Libres*, 7 messidor VII (25 June 1799).

40 *Clef du Cabinet*, 4 and 13 thermidor (23 July and 1 August 1799).

41 *Moniteur universel*, 7 October 1799.

42 Hanley, *Genesis of Napoleonic Propaganda*, p. 69.

43 *Corr.* v. n. 4382 (10 October 1799). The theme was taken up by the press (*Le Publiciste*, 16 and 22 October 1799 (24 and 30 Vendémiaire VIII)).

44 *Décade philosophique*, 1 November 1799.

45 Aulard, *Paris pendant la réaction thermidorienne*, v. pp. 759, 760 (13 and 14 October 1799).

46 Gotteri, 'L'esprit publique à Paris', pp. 23–4.

47 'Le dix-huit Brumaire. Extrait des mémoires du maréchal Jourdan', *Carnet historique et littéraire*, 7 (1901), p. 164.

48 Vandal, *L'avènement*, i. p. 216.

49 A good discussion of the public relations problems facing the regime and why it fell is to be found in Jon Cowans, *To Speak for the People. Public Opinion and the Problem of Legitimacy in the French Revolution* (London, 2001), pp. 176–84. For an overview of the historiography and some of the problems facing the Directory – brigandage, religion, war, royalism, Jacobinism – see Howard G. Brown, *Ending the French Revolution. Violence, Justice, and Repression from the Terror to Napoleon* (Charlottesville, 2006), pp. 5–8, 23–46.

50 Steven T. Ross, 'The Military Strategy of the Directory: The Campaigns of 1799', *French Historical Studies*, 5 (1967), 170–87; Sutherland, *The French Revolution*, p. 296.

51 Howard G. Brown, 'Organic Society to Security State: The War on Brigandage in France, 1797–1802', *Journal of Modern History*, 69 (1997), 668, 681–3; Devlin, 'The Army, Politics and Public Order', 91, states that brigandage was on the rise in Provence at the end of the Directory.

52 Many of the memoirs from the period focus on the domestic disorder and the military defeats, but they are often written by Brumairians. See, for example, Cambacérès, *Mémoires inédits*, i. pp. 419–20, 423, 424, 435; Bertrand Barère de Vieuzac, *Mémoires de Bertrand de Barère* (Paris, 1843), iii. p. 86; Thibaudeau, *Mémoires*, p. 2; Iung, *Lucien Bonaparte*, i. pp. 191–3; Anne-Jean-Marie Savary, *Mémoires du duc de Rovigo, pour servir à l'histoire de l'empereur Napoléon* (Paris, 1829), i. pp. 23–4, 234–6. The portrayal of the Directory as corrupt and inefficient during the nineteenth and into the twentieth centuries was motivated by political agendas on both the left and the right (Susan Locke Siegfried, *The Art of Louis-Leopold Boilly: Modern Life in Napoleonic France* (New Haven, 1995), p. 57).

53 M.-A. Baudot, *Notes historiques sur la Convention nationale, le Directoire, l'Empire et l'exil des votants* (Geneva, 1974), p. 15.

54 For what Bernard Gainot calls a 'crisis in political representation', see his 'La légende noire du Directoire', in *Napoléon, de l'histoire à la légende* (Paris, 2000), pp. 18–25.

55 Contemporaries in Hamburg certainly made a connection between a nefarious French influence and a decline in local civic identity (Katherine Aaslestad, *Place and Politics: Local Identity, Civic Culture, and German Nationalism in North Germany during the Revolutionary Era* (Leiden, 2005), pp. 149–55), while British visitors to Paris drew a link between political change and perceived French character traits (Rebecca L. Spang, 'The Frivolous French: "Liberty of Pleasure" and the End of Luxury', in Brown and Miller (eds), *Taking Liberties*, p. 116).

56 Siegfried, *The Art of Louis-Leopold Boilly*, pp. 70–84. Spang, 'The Frivolous French', pp. 110–25, is one of the few historians to ask why 'rivolity' became a central motif of representations of the Directory. It continued well into the Restoration. See also Ronald Schechter, 'Gothic Thermidor: The *Bals des victimes*, the Fantastic, and the Production of Historical Knowledge in Post-Terror France', *Representations*, 61 (1998), 78–94.

57 There is an interesting passage describing the state of France at the end of the Directory in Edmond and Jules de Goncourt, *Histoire de la société française pendant le Directoire* (Paris, 1992, first published in 1855), pp. 309–12.

58 'Souvenirs du comte Le Couteulx de Canteleu', in *Mémoires sur les journées révolutionnaires et les coups d'Etat* (Paris, 1875), ii. p. 216.

59 *Corr.* iii. n. 2223 (19 September 1797).

60 José Cabanis, *Le Sacre de Napoléon* (Paris, 1970), p. 34. On Sieyès, see Jean-Denis Bredin, *Sieyès. La clé de la Révolution française* (Paris, 1988); and Paul Bastid, *Sieyès et sa pensée* (Paris, 1978).

61 Talleyrand, *Mémoires*, i. pp. 212–13.

62 At least according to an anecdote told by Napoleon on St Helena in Las Cases, *Mémorial*, ii. p. 438.

63 Thiébault, *Mémoires*, iii. p. 65; Woloch, *Napoleon and his Collaborators*, p. 10.

64 Gotteri, 'L'esprit publique à Paris', p. 17, n. 10.

65 Thiébault, *Mémoires*, iii. p. 64; Achorn, 'Bernadotte or Bonaparte?' *Journal of Modern History*, 1 (1929), 381, argues that even if the Jacobins supported Bernadotte there is no contemporary evidence linking the two.

66 Schama, *Patriots and Liberators*, pp. 348–53.

67 There is, in fact, no source for this anecdote, first related by Vandal, *L'avènement*, i. p. 233, other than what appears to be family oral tradition (whose family we are not told). It is often repeated: Furet and Richet, *La Révolution française*, p. 506; McLynn, *Napoleon*, p. 207; Schom, *Napoleon*, p. 197; Englund, *Napoleon*, p. 158.

68 On this point, Iung, *Lucien Bonaparte*, i. pp. 268–74.

69 Dominique Garat, *Éloge funèbre de Joubert, prononcé au Champ-de-Mars* (Paris, 1799); Gotteri, 'L'esprit publique à Paris', p. 21; Jean-Paul Bertaud, *Guerre et société en France de Louis XIV à Napoléon Ier* (Paris, 1998), p. 171.

70 Iung, *Lucien Bonaparte*, i. p. 275.

71 Iung, *Lucien Bonaparte*, i. p. 268.

72 Vandal, *L'avènement*, i. pp. 243, 245.

73 Abrantès, *Mémoires*, ii. p. 89.

74 Barras, *Mémoires*, ii. p. 61.

75 Claire Rémusat, *Mémoires*, i. pp. 147–9.

76 According to Barras, *Mémoires*, i. pp. 31–4.

77 Barras, *Mémoires*, i. pp. 31–4. On the other hand, Roderick Phillips, *Family Breakdown in Late Eighteenth-Century France: Divorces in Rouen, 1792–1803* (Oxford, 1980), pp. 160, 162, suggests that while hesitation was the only 'respectable attitude', divorce was generally widely accepted. Phillips, however, does not make a distinction between social classes.

78 Abrantès, *Mémoires*, ii. pp. 91–2.

79 Josephine to Hippolyte Charles, *Joséphine. Correspondance*, p. 81 (February 1799).

80 Josephine to Mme de Krény, *Joséphine. Correspondance*, p. 93 (end of 1799, possibly October according to Knapton, *Josephine*, p. 166).

81 Buchez and Roux, *Histoire parlementaire*, xxxviii. p. 154.

82 Vandal, *L'avènement*, i. p. 249.

83 Louis-Jérôme Gohier, *Mémoires de Louis-Jérôme Gohier, président du Directoire au 18 brumaire* (Paris, 1824), i. pp. 200–1.

84 Vandal, *L'avènement*, i. p. 255.

85 Joseph Fouché, *Mémoires de Joseph Fouché, duc d'Otrante* (Osnabrück, 1824), i. p. 109.

86 Buchez and Roux, *Histoire parlementaire*, xxxviii. p. 164; *Moniteur universel*, 7 November 1799.

87 Vandal, *L'avènement*, i. pp. 246–7; Lentz, *Le 18-Brumaire*, pp. 225–9.

88 Gohier, *Mémoires*, i. pp. 205–11.

89 Vandal, *L'avènement*, i. p. 259; Tulard and Garros, *Itinéraire de Napoléon*, p. 134.

90 In fact, Barras and Sieyès were wary of Bernadotte's popularity (Achorn, 'Bernadotte or Bonaparte?', 392–7).

91 Gohier, *Mémoires*, i. pp. 217–18; Lentz, *Le 18-Brumaire*, pp. 247–8.

92 It was true; of the 120 million francs that had been collected in Italy, about half was sent to Paris, and half was used to supply the army. It is inconceivable that Bonaparte would not have taken his share of the profit. Similarly, it is estimated that Moreau recovered about forty-four million francs in Germany, of which he kept eight million for himself. See Miot de Mélito, *Mémoires*, ii. p. 134. It would appear that Joseph was left in charge of the finances in his brother's absence and that the whole family invested in properties with money given to them by Bonaparte: Josephine had the house in the rue de la Victoire, and had bought Malmaison in her husband's absence; Joseph bought a sumptuous private hôtel in Paris, rue du Rocher, as well as the château at Mortefontaine; Letizia had renovated and extended the family home at Ajaccio; Pauline had been given a house in the same street as Josephine's. On Bonaparte's return, though, he does not seem to have had much cash at his disposal (Vandal, *L'avènement*, i. p. 283; Pierre-Louis Roederer, *Oeuvres du Comte P.-L. Roederer*, 8 vols (Paris, 1854), iii. p. 295).

93 Lentz, *Le 18-Brumaire*, p. 246.

94 Lentz, *Le 18-Brumaire*, p. 246.

95 Vandal, *L'avènement*, i. pp. 243–5, 257–8; Lentz, *Le 18-Brumaire*, p.211.

96 Fouché, *Mémoires*, i. pp. 116–17; Gohier, *Mémoires*, i. pp. 221–3.

97 Cambacérès, *Mémoires inédits*, i. pp. 432–3, questioned Bonaparte on

why he chose Sieyès over Barras, but was never able to get an answer from him.

98 See the entry by André Cabanis, 'Ideologues', in Jean Tulard (ed.), *Dictionnaire Napoléon* (Paris, 1989), pp. 902–4.

99 'Souvenirs du comte de Canteleu', pp. 216, 218 and 219.

100 Thiébault, *Mémoires*, iii. p. 60.

101 Bertaud, *Bonaparte prend le pouvoir*, p. 25. On the role of business and the financial backing received by the conspirators, see Lentz, *Le 18-Brumaire*, pp. 253–69; Lentz, *Le Grand Consulat*, pp. 93–6.

102 Iung, *Lucien Bonaparte*, i. pp. 240–1, 249, 268–74; Gilbert Martineau, *Lucien Bonaparte: Prince de Canino* (Paris, 1989), p. 50.

103 Cambacérès, *Mémoires inédits*, i. pp. 440–1; Vandal, *L'avènement*, i. pp. 298–9.

104 Aulard, *Paris pendant la réaction thermidorienne*, v. pp. 730–1, 765; Bastid, *Sieyès*, pp. 224–6; Bredin, *Sieyès*, pp. 437–8; Woloch, *Jacobin Legacy*, p. 396. They also attacked Bonaparte, but less so, perhaps because Lucien was friendly with a number of neo-Jacobins.

105 Vandal, *L'avènement*, i. p. 269.

21 The Coup as Farce

1 Mathieu-Augustin Cornet, *Notice historique sur le 18 brumaire, par le président de la Commission des inspecteurs du Conseil des Anciens* (Paris, 1819), p. 9.

2 Vandal, *L'avènement*, i. p. 301.

3 *Le Publiciste*, 10 November 1799 (19 Brumaire VIII).

4 *Moniteur universel*, 10 November 1799.

5 Lentz, *Le 18-Brumaire*, pp. 285–6.

6 Vandal, *L'avènement*, i. pp. 303–4.

7 Lavalette, *Mémoires*, p. 228.

8 Vandal, *L'avènement*, i. pp. 307–8.

9 Roederer, *Oeuvres*, iii. p. 297.

10 *Moniteur universel*, 10 November 1799.

11 Vandal, *L'avènement*, i. pp. 314–15; Lentz, *Le 18-Brumaire*, pp. 291–2.

12 Vandal, *L'avènement*, i. p. 316.

13 *Journal des Hommes Libres*, 10 November 1799 (14 Brumaire VIII); Vandal, *L'avènement*, i. p. 316.

14 Jean Tulard argues, on the other hand, that there was nothing to distinguish Brumaire from any other revolutionary *journée*, and that,

like previous coups, it was the victory of one government faction over another (Tulard, *Napoléon*, p. 29).

15 *Corr.* vi. n. 4389 (10 November 1799).

16 Lentz, *Le 18-Brumaire*, p. 299.

17 Vandal, *L'avènement*, i. p. 327.

18 Woloch, *Napoleon and his Collaborators*, p. 20.

19 Alphonse Aulard, 'Le lendemain du Dix-Huit Brumaire', in *Etudes et Leçons sur la Révolution Française* (Paris, 1902), p. 224; Vandal, *L'avènement*, i. p. 344.

20 Staël, *Considérations*, p. 358; Norman King and Etienne Hoffman, 'Les lettres de Benjamin Constant à Sieyès', *Annales Benjamin Constant*, 3 (1983), 89–92.

21 Bourrienne, *Mémoires*, iii. p. 81; Vandal, *L'avènement*, i. p. 344; Lentz, *Le 18-Brumaire*, p. 310.

22 Vandal, *L'avènement*, i. p. 349.

23 Roederer, *Oeuvres*, iii. p. 301.

24 Vandal, *L'avènement*, i. p. 346.

25 Pierre-Louis Roederer, *Mémoires sur la Révolution, le Consulat et l'Empire* (Paris, 1942), p. 109.

26 Vandal, *L'avènement*, i. p. (although nothing appears in the *Correspondance*).

27 This, at least, is the contention of Vandal, *L'avènement*, i. p. 348.

28 Vandal, *L'avènement*, i. p. 354.

29 Thiébault, *Mémoires*, iii. pp. 68–9.

30 *Moniteur universel*, 11 November 1799.

31 Combes-Dounous, *Notice sur le dix-huit brumaire* (Paris, 1814), 19–24; Jean-Adrien Bigonnet, *Coup d'état du dix-huit brumaire* (Paris, 1829), p. 23; Woloch, *Napoleon and his Collaborators*, p. 21.

32 Combes-Dounous, *Notice sur le dix-huit brumaire*, p. 35.

33 Lavalette, *Mémoires*, p. 230.

34 According to Joseph, *Mémoires*, i. p. 79.

35 Vandal, *L'avènement*, i. pp. 366–71.

36 Bourrienne, *Mémoires*, iii. pp. 85–6; Lavalette, *Mémoires*, p. 231. A more coherent version can be found in Vincent Lombard de Langres, *Le dix-huit brumaire, ou tableau des événements qui ont amené à cette journée* (Paris, 1799), pp. 199–203; and *Moniteur universel*, 12 November 1799.

37 Lavalette, *Mémoires*, p. 232; Cambacérès, *Mémoires inédits*, i. p. 439; Woloch, *Napoleon and his Collaborators*, p. 69.

38 Bigonnet, *Coup d'état du dix-huit brumaire*, p. 27.

39 Combes-Dounous, *Notice sur le dix-huit brumaire*, p. 24.

40 Combes-Dounous, *Notice sur le dix-huit brumaire*, pp. 35–7; Bigonnet, *Coup d'état du dix-huit brumaire*, pp 26–7; Vandal, *L'avènement*, i. pp. 374–5.

41 Auguste Petiet, *Mémoires du général Auguste Petiet, hussard de l'Empire* (Paris, 1996), p. 69.

42 *Moniteur universel*, 11 November 1799; Bigonnet, *Coup d'état du dix-huit brumaire*, p. 27; Vandal, *L'avènement*, i. pp. 375–6.

43 Thiébault, *Mémoires*, iii. p. 70; Roederer, *Oeuvres*, iii. p. 302; Vandal, *L'avènement*, i. pp. 377–8.

44 Roederer, *Oeuvres*, iii. p. 302.

45 Roederer, *Oeuvres*, iii. p. 302; Buchez and Roux, *Histoire parlementaire*, xxxviii. p. 217; Vandal, *L'avènement*, i. pp. 379–83.

46 Vandal, *L'avènement*, i. p. 382.

47 Lavalette, *Memoires et Souvenirs*. p. 232.

48 Vandal, *L'avènement*, i. pp. 383–4.

49 Vandal, *L'avènement*, i. p. 384.

50 Vandal, *L'avènement*, i. pp. 385, and for the following.

51 Vandal, *L'avènement*, i. pp. 386–7.

52 Vandal, *L'avènement*, i. p. 389, is the first person to assert this, repeated by other historians, but his source was a 'renseignement particulier' (note p. 590).

53 According to Combes-Dounous, *Notice sur le dix-huit brumaire*, pp. 39–40, which is among the more accurate accounts of that day.

54 *Procès-verbal de la séance du Conseil des Cinq-cents tenue à Saint-Cloud le 19 brumaire an VIII* (Saint-Cloud, n.d.). It was repeated in memoirs such as: Thiébault, *Mémoires*, iii. p. 70; Fouché, *Mémoires*, i. p. 144; Jean-Roche Coignet, *The Note-Books of Captain Coignet* (London, 1998), pp. 55–6.

55 Petiet, *Mémoires*, p. 68; Lentz, *Le 18-Brumaire*, p. 335. Aulard, 'Le lendemain', p. 221, is also convinced that the Five Hundred behaved in a dignified manner.

56 Vandal, *L'avènement*, i. note p. 590.

57 Combes-Dounous, *Notice sur le dix-huit brumaire*, p. 40.

58 Fifty, according to Thiébault, *Mémoires*, iii. p. 70 (who was not there); Vandal, *L'avènement*, i. p. 395.

59 Vandal, *L'avènement*, i. pp. 394–402; Lentz, *Le 18-Brumaire*, pp. 337–51.

60 The adoption of ancient Roman appellations for the government was an attempt, according to J.-C. Assali, 'Napoléon et l'Antiquité', *Revue du*

Souvenir napoléonien, 333 (1984), 16, to legitimize the new regime. We do not know, however, who came up with the idea.

61 For this scene, Vandal, *L'avènement*, i. pp. 399–400.

62 Aulard, *Paris pendant la réaction thermidorienne*, v. p. 789.

63 Lavalette, *Mémoires et Souvenirs*, p. 233.

Epilogue

1 Gotteri, 'L'esprit publique à Paris', p. 19.

2 Danièle Pingué, 'Les "néo-jacobins" franc-comtois et le 18 Brumaire', in Jean-Pierre Jessenne (ed.), *Du Directoire au Consulat*, 4 vols. iii. *Brumaire dans l'histoire du lien politique et de l'Etat-nation* (Villeneuve-d'Ascq, 2001), pp. 37–41.

3 For reactions to the coup, see Aulard, 'Le lendemain', pp. 232–43; the series of articles in Jean-Pierre Jessenne (ed.), *Du Directoire au Consulat*, 4 vols. iii. *Brumaire dans l'histoire du lien politique et de l'Etat-nation* (Villeneuve-d'Ascq, 2001); Elisabeth Berlioz (ed.), *La situation des départements et l'installation des premiers préfets en l'an VIII (23 septembre 1799–22 septembre 1800)* (Paris, 2000); Lentz, *Le Grand Consulat*, pp. 149–66.

4 See Lentz, *Grand Consulat*, pp. 158–62.

5 Vandal, *L'avènement de Bonaparte*, i. pp. 473–4.

6 Isser Woloch, 'Réflexions sur les réactions à brumaire dans les milieux républicains provinciaux', in Jean-Paul Bertaud, et al., *Mélanges Michel Vovelle* (Paris, 1997), pp. 310 and 316–7. On Sieyès and the constitution, see Bastid, *Sieyès*, pp. 231–77.

7 A summary of the contents of those newspapers containing material critical of the new regime can be found in AF IV 1329, Bureau central du canton de Paris, 4 February 1800 (15 pluviose VIII).

8 *Corr.* vi. n. 4391 (19 November 1799).

9 *Procès-verbal de la séance du Conseil des Cinq-cents; Moniteur universel*, 12 and 13 November 1799; Arnault, *Souvenirs*, pp. 768–9, simply repeats the Bonapartist version of events; as does Dumont, *Détail des événemens qui ont eu lieu hier dans la commune de Saint-Cloud* (Paris, 1799). Lucien Bonaparte, *Révolution de brumaire, ou relation des principaux événements des journées des 18 and 19 brumaire* (Paris, 1845), pp. 107–8, 124–5, adamantly stuck to his account of the event forty-five years later. Other accounts, such as Combes-Dounous, *Notice sur le dix-huit brumaire*, p. 36, and Bigonnet, *Coup d'état du dix-huit brumaire*, p.

98, deny seeing anyone attempting to assassinate Bonaparte. Alphonse Aulard, 'Bonaparte et les poignards des Cinq-Cents', *La Révolution Française*, 27 (1894), 113–27, was the first to debunk the legend.

10 The exception is Fouché, *Mémoires*, i. pp. 139–44, who has Bonaparte fleeing Saint-Cloud on a horse, chased after by Murat, who brought him to his senses.

11 The iconography surrounding Brumaire is relatively thin, a dozen engravings in all but, in comparison, there are only thirty engravings depicting the fall of the monarchy on 10 August. Of course, the number of woodcut prints made from these engravings could reach the hundreds. They were sold for only one sou and were, therefore, within everyone's reach (David M. Hopkin, 'Sons and Lovers: Popular Images of the Conscript, 1798–1870', *Modern & Contemporary France*, 9 (2001), 22). See Stéphane Roy, 'Le retentissement de Brumaire en image: rupture ou continuité?', in Jessenne (ed.), *Brumaire dans l'histoire*, pp. 581–93; Barthélémy Jobert, 'Les représentations contemporains du Dix-huit Brumaire dans les Arts', and Bruno Foucart, 'Les images du coup d'Etat et la formation de la Légende', in Boudon (ed.), *Brumaire*, pp. 115–30 and 131–50; and Gainot, 'La légende noire du Directoire', pp. 15–16.

12 Pierre Serna, 'Le Directoire . . . Un non lieu de mémoire à revisiter', in Bourdin and Gainot (eds), *La République directoriale*, i. p. 54.

13 Boudon, 'L'incarnation de l'état de Brumaire', p. 343.

14 Lecomte, *Napoléon et le'Empire*, pp. 48–9.

15 *La Girouette de Saint-Cloud: impromptu en un acte, en prose mêlé de Vaudeville*, Paris, Théâtre du Vaudeville, 14 November 1799, p. 17.

La fuite en Egypte jadis
Conserva le sauveur des hommes,
Pourtant quelques malins esprits
En doutent au siècle où nous sommes,
Mais un fait bien sur en ce jour,
Du vieux miracle quoi qu'on pense,
C'est que de l'Egypte un retour
Ramène un sauveur à la France.

16 AF IV 1329, Tableau de la situation de Paris, 3 January 1800 (13 nivose VIII).

17 AF IV 1329, Bureau central du canton de Paris, 18 January 1800 (28 nivose VIII). It is possible that much of this material was written by royalists and that their scorn was directed at republicans, reason enough for Bonaparte wanting to put a stop to it (Aulard, 'Le lendemain', pp. 226–8).

18 Sorel, *L'Europe et la Révolution française*, v. p. 487.

19 Jourdan, 'Le dix-huit Brumaire', *Carnet historique*, p. 161.

20 Lynn Hunt, David Lansky and Paul Hanson, 'The Failure of the Liberal Republic in France, 1795–1799: The Road to Brumaire', *Journal of Modern History*, 51 (1979), pp. 734–59.

21 Hunt, Lansky and Hanson, 'The Road to Brumaire', pp. 757–8.

22 *Entretien politique sur la situation actuelle de La France et sur les plans du nouveau gouvernement*. Translation in Palmer, *From Jacobin to Liberal*, pp. 94–100 (December 1799), here p. 95.

23 Gainot, 'La légende noire du Directoire', p. 16.

24 See, for example, Cousin, *Bonapartiana*, ii. pp. 52–8; Jean Saint-Sardos de Mantagu Mondenard, *Considérations sur l'organization sociale, appliquées à l'état-civil, politique et militaire de La France et de l'Angleterre*, 3 vols (Paris, 1802), i. 35–76; Jean Chas, *Coup d'œil d'un ami de sa patrie, sur les grandes actions de l'empereur Napoléon* (Paris, 1804), pp. 34–42; Barré, Radet and Desfontaines, *Chansons populaires, composées pour les fêtes du couronnement* (Paris, 1804); Joseph Dusaulchoy de Bergemont, *Histoire du couronnement* (Paris, 1805), pp. iii–vii; Louis Dubroca, *Les Quatre fondateurs des dynasties françaises, ou Histoire de l'établissement de la monarchie française, par Clovis. . . Pépin et Hugues Capet; et . . . Napoléon-le-Grand . . .* (Paris, 1806), pp. 285–7. On the manner in which Brumaire was rewritten in the history books of the period, see Pierre Serna, 'Refaire l'Histoire, écrire l'Histoire ou comment raconter le 18 Brumaire entre 1800 et 1802', *Cahiers d'histoire*, 77 (1999), 101–20; and Tulard, *Les Thermidoriens*, pp. 225–35.

25 Alphonse Aulard, *Paris sous le Consulat* (Paris, 1903), i. p. 8 (16 November 1799).

26 On Pétain and de Gaulle, both military as well as political leaders, see Robert Gildea, *The Past in French History* (New Haven, 1994), pp. 79–81. They touched what Gildea calls 'the fibre of the [French] nation'.

27 Woloch, *Napoleon and his Collaborators*, pp. 14–15.

28 Thompson, *Napoleon Bonaparte*, p. 157, n. 1. The vessel was dismantled in 1850.

29 Todd Porterfield, *The Allure of Empire. Art in the Service of French Imperialism, 1798–1836* (Princeton, NJ, 1998), p. 76.

30 Cited in Sudhir Hazareesingh, *The Legend of Napoleon* (London, 2004), p. 16.

31 Las Cases, *Mémorial*, ii. pp. 8–9. 'The fact is that without us the *patrie* was lost and we saved it.'

32 Jourdan, 'Images de Napoléon', 434.

33 Las Cases, *Mémorial*, i. pp. 128, 132.

34 Ellis, *Napoleon*, p. 21, uses this expression.

35 An idea that is developed by Luigi Mascili Migliorini, *Le mythe du héros. France et Italie après la chute de Napoléon*, trans. Laurent Vallance (Paris, 2002), pp. 33–7.

36 As England, *Napoleon*, p. 20, suggests.

37 Chuquet, *Jeunesse*, i. p. 105.

Select Bibliography

Aaslestad, Katherine. *Place and Politics: Local Identity, Civic Culture, and German Nationalism in North Germany during the Revolutionary Era.* Leiden: Brill, 2005.

Abrantès, Laure Junot, Duchesse de. *Mémoires complets et authentiques de Laure Junot, duchesse d'Abrantès: Souvenirs historiques sur Napoléon, la Révolution, le Directoire, le Consulat, l'Empire, la Restauration.* 13 vols. Paris: J. de Bonnot, 1967–8.

Acerra, Martine, and Meyer, Jean. *Marines et Révolution.* Rennes: Ouest-France, 1988.

Achorn, Erik, 'Bernadotte or Bonaparte?' *Journal of Modern History*, 1 (1929): 378–99.

Albert, Maurice. *Les Théâtres des boulevards: 1789–1848.* Paris: Société française d'imprimerie et de librairie, 1902.

Ambrosi, Christian, 'Pascal Paoli et la Corse de 1789 à 1791', *Revue d'histoire moderne et contemporaine*, 2 (1955): 161–184.

Arnault, Antoine-Vincent. *Souvenirs d'un sexagénaire.* Paris: Honoré Champion, 2003.

Assali, J.-C., 'Napoléon et l'Antiquité', *Revue du Souvenir napoléonien*, 333 (1984): 2–23.

Audoin-Rouzeau, Stéphane, Becker, Annette, et al. (eds). *La violence de guerre 1914–15: approches comparées des deux conflits mondiaux.* Paris: Éd. Complexe, 2002.

Augustin-Thierry, A., 'Un amour inconnu de Bonaparte', *Revue des Deux Mondes*, 110 (1940): 225–33.

Aulard, Alphonse, 'Bonaparte et les poignards des Cinq-Cents', *La Révolution Française*, 27 (1894): 113–27.

Aulard, Alphonse. *Recueil des actes du Comité de Salut public.* 28 vols. Paris: Imprimerie nationale, 1889–1951.

Aulard, Alphonse. *Paris pendant la réaction thermidorienne et sous le Directoire.* 5 vols. Paris: Cerf, 1898–1902.

Aulard, Alphonse. *Etudes et Leçons sur la Révolution Française*. Seconde Série. Paris: Alcan, 1902.

Aulard, Alphonse. *Paris sous le Consulat*. 4 vols. Paris: Cerf, 1903–9.

Barbaud, C. and Carbo, L., 'Le retour d'Egypte, escale à Ajaccio: une semaine ignorée de la vie de Bonaparte', *Revue des études napoléoniennes*, 19 (1922): 161–98.

Barbe, Jean-Paul, and Bernecker, Roland (eds). *Les intellectuels européens et la campagne d'Italie, 1796–1798*. Münster: Nodus Publikationen, 1999.

Barras, Paul. *Mémoires de Barras, membre du Directoire*. 4 vols. Paris: Hachette, 1895–6.

Barré [Pierre-Yvon], Radet [Jean-Baptiste] and Desfontaines [François-Georges]. *Chansons populaires, composées pour les fêtes du couronnement*. Paris: Collin, 1804.

Barrow, J. (ed.). *The Life and Correspondence of Sir Sidney Smith*. 2 vols. London: R. Bentley, 1848.

Baudot, Marc-Antoine. *Notes historiques sur la Convention nationale, le Directoire, l'Empire et l'exil des votants*. Paris: 1893.

Beaucour, Fernand, 'Un fidèle de l'empereur en son époque: Jean-Mathieu-Alexandre Sari (1792–1862)', thèse de 3e Cycle, l'université de Lille III, 1972.

Beauharnais, Eugène de. *Mémoires et correspondance politique et militaire du prince Eugène*. 10 vols. Paris: Lévy frères, 1858–60.

Beauregard, Charles Albert Costa de. *Un homme d'autrefois*. Paris: Plon, 1877.

Bell, David A., 'Nation-Building and Cultural Particularism in Eighteenth-Century France: The Case of Alsace', *Eighteenth-Century Studies*, 21 (1988): 472–90.

Bell, David A. *The Cult of the Nation in France. Inventing Nationalism, 1680–1800*. Cambridge, Mass.: Harvard University Press, 2001.

Benoît, Jérémie. *Philippe-Auguste Hennequin*. Paris: Arthéna, 1994.

Béranger, Pierre-Jean de. *Ma biographie, ouvrage posthume de P.-J. Béranger*. Paris: Perrotin, 1857.

Beretti, Francis. *Pascal Paoli et l'image de la Corse au dix-huitième siècle*. Oxford: Voltaire Foundation, 1988.

Berlioz, Elisabeth (ed.). *La situation des départements et l'installation des premiers préfets en l'an VIII (23 septembre 1799–22 septembre 1800)*. Paris: Documentation française, 2000.

Bernoyer, François. *Avec Bonaparte en Egypte et en Syrie, 1798–1800: 19 lettres inédites*. Paris: Editions Curandera, 1981.

Bertaud, Jean-Paul. *La Révolution armée. Les soldats citoyens et la Révolution française*. Paris: Laffont, 1979.

Bertaud, Jean-Paul. *1799, Bonaparte prend le pouvoir. La République meurt-elle assassinée?* Brussels: Editions Complexe, 1987.

Bertaud, Jean-Paul, et al. (ed.), *Mélanges Michel Vovelle*. Paris: Société des Etudes Robespierristes, 1997.

Bertaud, Jean-Paul, 'L'expédition d'Egypte et la construction du mythe napoléonien', *Cahiers de la Méditerranée*, 57 (1998): 281–8.

Bertaud, Jean-Paul. *Guerre et société en France: de Louis XIV à Napoléon ler*. Paris: A. Colin, 1998.

Berthier, Louis-Alexandre. *Mémoires du Maréchal Berthier . . . Campagnes d'Egypte*. 2 vols. Paris: Baudouin Frères, 1827.

Berthier, Louis-Alexandre. *Relations des campagnes du général Bonaparte en Egypte*. Paris: Didot, 1799.

Besancenet, Alfred de. *Le général Dommartin en Italie et en Egypte. Ordres de service. Correspondences. 1786–1799*. Paris: Téqui, 1887.

Besnard, François-Yves. *Souvenirs d'un nonagénaire*. 2 vols. Paris: Champion, 1880.

Bien, David D., 'La réaction aristocratique avant 1789: l'exemple de l'armée'. *Annales. Economies. Sociétés. Civilizations*, 29 (1974): 505–34.

Bien, David, 'The Army in the French Enlightenment: Reform, Reaction and Revolution', *Past & Present*, 85 (1979): 68–98.

Bierman, Irene A. (ed.), *Napoleon in Egypt*. Reading: Ithaca Press, 2003.

Bigarré, Auguste. *Mémoires du général Bigarré: 1775–1813*. Paris: Grenadier, 2002.

Bigonnet, Jean-Adrien. *Coup d'état du dix-huit brumaire*. Paris: Au Bureau du Censeur Européen, 1829.

Bigrat, J.–T. *Buonaparte dévoilé aux yeux de la France et l'Europe entière*. Paris: Impr. des nouveautés, nd.

Biro, Sydney Seymour. *The German Policy of Revolutionary France. A Study in French Diplomacy during the War of the First Coalition, 1792–1797*. 2 vols. Cambridge, Mass.: Harvard University Press, 1957.

Black, Jeremy. *British Foreign Policy in an Age of Revolutions, 1783–1793*. Cambridge: CUP, 1994.

Blanc, Olivier. *L'éminence grise de Napoléon: Regnaud de Saint-Jean d'Angély*. Paris: Pygmalion, 2002.

Blanning, T.C.W. *The Origins of the French Revolutionary Wars*. London: Longman, 1986.

Blanning, T.C.W., 'The Abortive Crusade', *History Today*, 39 (1989): 33–8.

Blanning, T.C.W., 'The French Revolution and Europe', in Lucas (ed.), *Rewriting the French Revolution*, pp. 183–206.

Blanning, T.C.W. *The French Revolutionary Wars, 1787–1802*. London: Arnold, 1996.

Blanning, T.C.W., 'Liberation or Occupation? Theory and Practice in the French Revolutionaries' Treatment of Civilians outside France', in Grimsley and Rogers (eds.), *Civilians in the Path of War*, pp. 111–35.

Blaufarb, Rafe. *The French army, 1750–1820. Careers, talent, merit.* Manchester: Manchester University Press, 2002.

Bleys, Rudi C. *The Geography of Perversion: Male-to-Male Sexual Behaviour outside the West and the Ethnographic Imagination, 1750–1918.* Washington Square, N.Y.: New York University Press, 1995.

Blumer, Marie-Louise, 'La Commission pour la recherche des objets d'arts', *Révolution française*, 87 (1934): 62–88, 124–50, 222–59.

Bonaparte en Égypte, ou Dialogues entre Pitt et deux voyageurs anglais, Bruce et Yrwin. Paris: Desenne, 1799.

Bonaparte, Joseph. *Mémoires et correspondance politique et militaire du roi Joseph.* 10 vols. Paris: Perrotin, 1853–4.

Bonaparte, Lucien. *Mémoires de Lucien Bonaparte, Prince Cannino, écrits par lui-même.* Paris: Charles Gosselin, 1836.

Bonaparte, Lucien. *Révolution de brumaire, ou relation des principaux événements des journées des 18 and 19 brumaire.* Paris: Charpentier, 1845.

Bonaparte, Napoléon. *Correspondance de Napoléon I publiée par ordre de l'empereur Napoléon III.* 32 vols. Paris: Plon, 1858–70.

Bonaparte, Napoléon. *Napoléon Bonaparte. Correspondance Générale*, edited by Thierry Lentz. 12 vols. Paris: Fayard, 2004–.

Bonnal de Ganges, Edmond. *Chute d'une République. Venise. D'après les Archives secrètes de la République* Paris: Firmin-Didot, 1885.

Bonnefons, Sergent, 'Un soldat d'Italie et d'Egypte. Souvenirs (1792–1801)', in *Souvenirs et cahiers sur la campagne d'Egypte. Extraits du Carnet de la Sabretache.* Paris: Teissèdre, 1997.

Bonnet, Jean-Claude, 'Naissance du Panthéon', *Poétique*, 33 (1978): 46–55.

Bonnet, Jean-Claude. *Naissance du Panthéon: essai sur le culte des grands hommes.* Paris: Fayard, 1998.

Bosséno, Christian-Marc, 'La guerre des estampes. Circulation des images de thèmes iconographiques dans l'Italie des années 1789–1799', *Mélanges de l'Ecole française de Rome, Italie et Méditerranée*, 102 (1990): 367–400.

Bosséno, Christian-Marc, ' "Les signes extérieurs." Diffusion, réception et image de la culture révolutionnaire française dans l'Italie du *Triennio* (1796–1799)', 2 vols. (PhD, University of Paris I Pantheon Sorbonne, 1995.)

Bosséno, Christian-Marc, ' "Je me vis dans l'histoire": Bonaparte, de Lodi à Arcole, généalogie d'une image de légende', *Annales historiques de la Révolution Française*, 313 (1998): 449–65.

Bosséno, Christian-Marc, ' "*Du haut de ces monuments . . .*". L'Expédition d'Egypte dans la constitution de la légende napoléonienne', *Revista Napoleonica*, 1 (2001): 11–27.

Boswell, James. *An Account of Corsica, the Journal of a Tour to that Island and Memoirs of Pascal Paoli.* Glasgow: E. and C. Dilly, 1768.

Boudon Jacques-Olivier (ed.). *Brumaire. La prise de pouvoir de Bonaparte*. Paris: Éd. SPM, 2001.

Boudon, Jacques-Olivier. *Napoléon et les Cultes*. Paris: Fayard, 2002.

Boulart, Jean-François, *Mémoires militaires du général Baron Boulart sur les guerres de la république et de l'empire*. Paris: Librairie illustrée, 1892.

Bourdin, Philippe, and Gainot, Bernard (eds). *La République directoriale*. 2 vols. Moulins: Société des Etudes Robespierristes, 1998.

Bourguet, Marie-Noëlle, 'Des savants à la conquête de l'Egypte? Science, voyage et politique au temps de l'expédition française', in Bret (ed.), *L'expédition d'Egypte*, pp. 21–36.

Bourguet, Marie-Noëlle, 'Science and Memory: The Stakes of the Expedition to Egypt (1799–1801)', in Brown and Miller (eds), *Taking Liberties*, pp. 92–109.

Bourrienne, Louis-Antoine Fauvelet de. *Mémoires de M. de Bourrienne, ministre d'Etat, sur Napoléon, le Directoire, le Consulat, l'Empire et la Restauration*. 10 vols. Paris: Ladvocat, 1829.

Boustany, Saladin (ed.). *The Journals of Bonaparte in Egypt: 1798–1801*. 10 vols. Cairo: al-Arab, 1971–7.

Bouvier, Félix. *Bonaparte en Italie, 1796*. Paris: Cerf, 1899.

Bouvier, Félix. *Un amour de Napoléon*. Paris: L. Gougy, 1900.

Bouvier, Félix, 'La révolte de Pavie (23–26 mai 1796)', *Revue historique de la Révolution française*, 2 and 3 (1911–12): 519–39, 72–89, 257–75, 424–46.

Bowen, Catherine Drinker, 'The Biographer's Relationship with His Hero', in Oates (ed.), *Biography as High Adventure*, pp. 65–9.

Boycott-Brown, Martin. *The Road to Rivoli. Napoleon's First Campaign*. London: Cassell, 2001.

Boycott-Brown, Martin, 'Guerrilla Warfare *avant la lettre*: Northern Italy, 1792–97', in Esdaile (ed.), *Popular Resistance in the French Wars*, pp. 45–66.

Boyer, Ferdinand, 'Les responsabilités de Napoléon dans le transfert à Paris des oeuvres d'art de l'étranger', *Revue d'histoire moderne et contemporaine*, 11 (1964): 241–62.

Boyer, Ferdinand, 'Le général Bonaparte et la recherche des objets de Sciences et d'Art en Lombardie (1796)', *Revue de l'Institut Napoléon*, 122 (1972): 7–17.

Boyer, Pierre-François. *Historique de ma vie*. Paris: Vouivre, 2001.

Bredin, Jean-Denis. *Sieyès. La clé de la Révolution française*. Paris: Fallois, 1988.

Brégin, Jean-Joël. *L'Egypte de Bonaparte*. Paris: Perrin, 1991.

Bret, Patrice. *L'Egypte au temps de l'Expédition de Bonaparte, 1798–1801*. Paris: Hachette, 1998.

Bret, Patrice (ed.). *L'expédition d'Egypte, une entreprise des Lumières 1798–1801*. Paris: Académie des Sciences, 1999.

Bricard, Louis. *Journal du canonnier Bricard, 1792–1802*. Paris: Delagrave, 1891.

Broers, Michael, 'Revolution as Vendetta: Patriotism in Piedmont, 1794–1821', *Historical Journal*, 33 (1990): 573–97.

Broers, Michael. *Napoleonic Imperialism and the Savoyard Monarchy, 1773–1821. State Building in Piedmont*. Lewiston: Edwin Mellen Press, 1997.

Brown, Howard G. *War, Revolution, and the Bureaucratic State: Politics and Army Administration in France, 1791–1799*. Oxford: Clarendon Press, 1995.

Brown, Howard G., 'Politics, Professionalism, and the Fate of the Army Generals after Thermidor', *French Historical Studies*, 19 (1995): 133–52.

Brown, Howard G., 'From Organic Society to Security State: The War on Brigandage in France, 1797–1802', *Journal of Modern History*, 69 (1997): 661–95.

Brown, Howard G., and Miller, Judith (eds). *Taking Liberties. Problems of a New Order from the French Revolution to Napoleon*. Manchester, 2002.

Brown, Howard G., 'The Search for Stability', in Brown and Miller (eds), *Taking Liberties*, pp. 20–50.

Brown, Howard G., 'Revolt and Repression in the Midi Toulousain (1799)', *French History*, 19 (2005): 234–61.

Brown, Howard G. *Ending the French Revolution. Violence, Justice, and Repression from the Terror to Napoleon*. Charlottesville: University of Virginia Press, 2006.

Bruce, Evangeline. *Napoleon and Josephine: An Improbable Marriage*. London: Weidenfeld & Nicolson, 1995.

Buchez, Philippe-Joseph-Benjamin, and Roux-Lavergne, Pierre-Célestin. *Histoire parlementaire de la Révolution française*. 40 vols. Paris: Paulin, 1834–8.

Busquet, Jacques. *Le droit de la vendetta et les 'paci' corses*. Paris: A. Pedone, 1920.

Cabanis, José. *Le Sacre de Napoléon*. Paris: Gallimard, 1970.

Cambacérès, Jean Jacques Régis de. *Mémoires inédits. Eclaircissements publiés par Cambacérès sur les principaux événements de sa vie politique*. 2 vols. Paris: Perrin, 1999.

Caraffa, V. de (ed.), 'Mémoires historiques sur la Corse par un officier du régiment de Picardie, 1774–1777', *Bulletin de la Société des sciences historiques et naturelles de la Corse* (1889): 1–266.

Carboni, Pierre, 'Boswell et Paoli: Un Plutarque écossais et son Lycurgue corse', in *Entretiens de la Garenne Lemot. Le culte des Grands Hommes au XVIIIe siècle. Actes du Colloque 3 au 5 octobre 1996* (Nantes, 1998), pp. 109–18.

Carrington, Dorothy, 'The Achievement of Pasquale Paoli (1755–1769) and its Consequences', *Proceedings of the Consortium on Revolutionary Europe*, 16 (1986), pp. 56–69.

Carrington, Dorothy. *Napoleon and His Parents: On the Threshold of History*. London: Dutton, 1988.

Carrington, Dorothy. *Portrait de Charles Bonaparte. D'après ses écrits de jeunesse et ses mémoires*. Ajaccio: Alain Piazolla, 2002.

Carrington, Dorothy, 'Pascal Paoli et sa "Constitution" (1755–1769)', *Annales historiques de la Révolution Française*, 218 (1974): 508–41.

Casanova, Antoine, and Rovère, Ange. *Peuple corse, révolutions et nation française*. Paris: Editions sociales, 1979.

Casanova, Antoine, 'Caractères originaux et cheminements de la Révolution en Corse (1789–1797)', *Annales historiques de la Révolution Française*, 260 (1985): 140–172.

Casanova, Antoine, and Rovère, Ange. *La Révolution française en Corse*. Paris: Privat, 1989.

Casanova, Antoine. *Napoléon et la pensée de son temps: une histoire intellectuelle singulière*. Paris: Boutique de l'Histoire, 2000.

C. H. [Cumming of Craigmillar]. *Some Account of the Early Years of Buonaparte, at the Military School of Brienne; and of his Conduct at the Commencement of the French Revolution*. London: Hookham and Carpenter, 1797.

Chabrol de Volvic, Gilbert. *Souvenirs d'Egypte*. Paris: Ville de Paris, 1998.

Chailley-Pompei, François, 'Les troubles de Pâques 1792, d'après le manifest de la municipalité d'Ajaccio', in *Problèmes d'Histoire de la Corse (de l'Ancien Régime à 1815). Actes de colloque d'Ajaccio*. Paris: Société des Etudes Robespierristes, Société d'Histoire Moderne, 1971, pp. 179–89.

Chandler, David. *The Campaigns of Napoleon*. London: Weidenfeld & Nicolson, 1966.

Chaptal, Jean-Antoine. *Mes souvenirs sur Napoléon*. Paris: Plon, 1893.

Charles-Roux, François. *Bonaparte, gouverneur d'Egypte*. Paris: Plon, 1935.

Chas, Jean. *Coup d'œil d'un ami de sa patrie, sur les grandes action de l'empereur Napoléon, depuis ses opérations militaires à Toulon jusqu'à son avènement au Trône*. Paris: Brochot, 1804.

Chastenay, Victorine de. *Mémoires: 1771–1815*. Paris: Perrin, 1987.

Chevallier, Bernard, and Pincemaille, Christophe. *L'impératrice Joséphine*. Paris: Payot, 1996.

Chevallier, Bernard, Catinat, Maurice, and Pincemaille, Christophe (eds). *Impératrice Joséphine. Correspondance, 1782–1814*. Paris: Payot, 1996.

Chevrier, Edmond. *Le Général Joubert, d'après sa correspondance*. Paris: Fischbacher, 1884.

Chuquet, Alphonse. *La Jeunesse de Napoléon*. 3 vols. Paris: Colin, 1897–9.

Clery, E. J. *The Rise of Supernatural Fiction, 1762–1800*. Cambridge, CUP, 1995.

Cohen, Amnon. *Palestine in the 18th Century. Patterns of Government and Administration*. Jerusalem: Magnes Press, 1973.

Coignet, Jean-Roche. *The Note-Books of Captain Coignet: Soldier of the Empire, 1776–1850*. London: Greenhill, 1998.

Cole, Juan R. I., 'Mad Sufis and Civic Courtesans: The French Republican Cconstruction of Eighteenth-Century Egypt', in Bierman (ed.), *Napoleon in Egypt*, pp. 47–62.

Colla, Elliot, ' "Non, non! Si, si!": Commemorating the French Occupation of Egypt (1798–1801),' *Modern Language Notes*, 118 (2003): 1043–69.

Combes-Dounous, Jean-Jacques. *Notice sur le dix-huit brumaire, par un témoin qui peut dire*. Paris: F. Schoell, 1814.

Connelly, Owen. *Blundering to Glory. Napoleon's Military Campaigns*. Wilmington, DE: Scholarly Resources, 1987.

Connolly, John L., 'Bonaparte on the Bridge', *Proceedings of the Consortuim on Revolutionary Europe*, 15 (1985): 45–65.

Connolly, John L., 'Napoleon as Hercules', *Proceedings of the Consortium on Revolutionary Europe*, 17 (1987): 647–66.

Constant, Benjamin. *De la force du gouvernement actuel de la France et de la nécessité de s'y rallier*. Preface and notes by Phillippe Raynaud. Paris: Flammarion, 1988.

Constant, Pierre. *Les Hymnes et Chansons de la Révolution*. Paris: Imprimerie nationale, 1904.

Copies of Original Letters from the Army of General Bonaparte intercepted by the fleet under the command of Admiral Lord Nelson. 3 vols. London: J. Wright, 1798.

Cormack, William. *Revolution and Political Conflict in the French Navy, 1789–1794*. Cambridge: CUP, 1995.

Cornet, Mathieu-Augustin. *Notice historique sur le 18 brumaire, par le président de la Commission des inspecteurs du Conseil des Anciens*. Paris: Lheureux, 1819.

Correspondance de l'armée française en Egypte, interceptée par l'escadre de Nelson, publiée à Londres. Paris: Garnery, an VII.

Coston, François Gilbert de. *Biographie des premières années de Bonaparte*, 2 vols. Paris: Marc Aurel, 1840.

Coursac, Jacques de. *Un ami dauphinois de Napoléon Bonaparte, Simon de Sucy, ordonnateur en chef de l'armée d'Egypte*. Paris: Firmin-Didot, 1932.

Cousin, Charles-Yves, dit Cousin d'Avalon. *Bonapartiana, ou Recueil des réponses ingénieuses ou sublimes, actions héroïques et faits mémorables de Bonaparte*. 2 vols. Paris: Fillot, 1801.

Couturaud, Laurence. *Augereau, l'enfant maudit de la gloire*. Paris: Kronos, 1990.

Cowans, Jon. *To Speak for the People. Public Opinion and the Problem of Legitimacy in the French Revolution*. London: Routledge, 2001.

Cronin, Vincent. *Napoleon*. London: HarperCollins, 1971.

Crook, Malcolm, 'Federalism and the French Revolution: the revolt of Toulon in 1793', *History*, 65 (1980): 387–97.

Crook, Malcolm. *Toulon in War and Revolution. From the ancien régime to the Restoration, 1750–1820*. Manchester: Manchester University Press, 1991.

Crook, Malcolm. *Napoleon Comes to Power: Democracy and Dictatorship in Revolutionary France, 1795–1804*. Cardiff: University of Cardiff Press, 1998.

Daline, V., 'Marc Antoine Jullien après le 9 thermidor', *Annales historiques de la Révolution Française*, 36, 37, 38 (1964, 1965, 1966): 159–73, 187–203, 390–412.

Danican, Auguste. *Notice sur le 13 vendémiaire, ou Les Parisiens vengés*. Paris: np, 1796.

Debidour, Antonin (ed.). *Recueil des actes du Directoire exécutif*. 4 vols. Paris: Imprimerie nationale, 1910–17.

Defranceschi, Jean, 'De la légende à l'histoire: Paoli et les frères Bonaparte', in *Problèmes d'Histoire de la Corse (de l'Ancien régime à 1815). Actes de colloque d'Ajaccio*. Paris: Société des Etudes Robespierristes, Société d'Histoire Moderne, 1971, pp. 131–145.

Defranceschi, Jean, 'Le rôle de Lieutenant Bonaparte aux débuts de la Révolution française en Corse', *Revue de l'Institut Napoléon*, 134 (1978): 3–20.

Defranceschi, Jean. *La Corse française (30 novembre 1789–15 juin 1794)*. Paris: Société des Etudes Robespierristes, 1980.

Defranceschi, Jean. *La Corse et la Révolution française*. Ajaccio: Cyrnos et Méditerranée, 1991.

Defranceschi, Jean, 'Robespierre et la Corse', in Jessenne et al. (ed.), *Robespierre*, pp. 369–80.

Defranceschi, Jean. *La jeunesse de Napoléon. Les dessous de l'Histoire*. Paris: Lettrage, 2001.

Delestre, Jean-Baptiste. *Gros et ses ouvrages, ou mémoires historiques sur la vie et les travaux de ce célèbre artiste*. Paris: Jules Labitte, 1845.

Denon, Dominique-Vivant. *Voyage dans la Basse et la Haute-Egypte*. Paris: Pygmalion, 1990.

Denton, Margaret Fields, 'Death in French Arcady: Nicolas Poussin's *The Arcadian Shepherds* and Burial Reform in France c. 1800', *Eighteenth-Century Studies*, 36 (2003): 195–216.

Déprez, Eugène, 'Les origines républicaines de Bonaparte', *Revue historique*, 97 (1908): 316–36.

Derogy, Jacques, and Carmel, Henri. *Bonaparte en Terre Sainte*. Paris: Fayard, 1992.

Desgenettes, Nicolas-René-Dufriche, Baron. *Souvenirs d'un médecin de l'expédition d'Egypte*. Paris: Lévy, 1893.

Desvernois, Nicholas-Philibert. *Mémoires du général baron Desvernois*. Paris: Plon, 1898.

Devlin, Jonathan D., 'The Army, Politics and Public Order in Directorial Provence, 1795–1800', *Historical Journal*, 32 (1989): 87–106.

Devlin, Jonathan D., 'The Directory and the Politics of Military Command: The Army of the Interior in South-East France', *French History*, 4 (1990): 199–223.

Dhombres, Jean and Nicole. *Lazare Carnot*. Paris: Fayard, 1997.

Doguereau, Jean-Pierre. *Journal de l'expédition d'Egypte*. Paris: La Vouivre, 1997.

Doppet, General François Amédée. *Mémoires politiques et militaires du général Doppet, contenant des notices intéressantes et impartiales sur la Révolution française*. Paris: Carouge, 1797.

Dry, A. *Soldats ambassadeurs sous le Directoire*. 2 vols. Paris: Plon, 1906.

Dubroca, Louis. *Les Quatre fondateurs des dynasties françaises, ou Histoire de l'établissement de la monarchie française, par Clovis . . . Pépin et Hugues Capet; et . . . Napoléon-le-Grand . . .* Paris: Dubroca, 1806.

Dumas, Alexandre. *Mes mémoires*. 10 vols. Paris: Lévy, 1863–84.

Dumas, Mathieu. *Souvenirs du lieutenant-général comte Mathieu Dumas, de 1770 à 1836*. 3 vols. Paris: Charles Gosselin, 1839.

Dumont [first name unknown]. *Détail des événemens qui ont eu lieu hier dans la commune de Saint-Cloud*. Paris: Gauthier, 1799.

Dumouriez, C. F. *La vie et les mémoires du général Dumouriez*. 4 vols. Paris: Baudouin, 1822–4.

Dupont-Ferrier, André, 'Trois lettres nouveaux de la bataille de Rivoli', *Annuaire-bulletin de la société de l'histoire de France*, 66 (1929): 133–42.

Duprat, Annie, 'La construction de la mémoire par les gravures: Carle Vernet et les *Tableaux historiques des campagnes d'Italie*', in Barbe and Bernecker (eds), *Les intellectuels européens et la campagne d'Italie*, pp. 199–207.

Dupre, Huntley. *Lazare Carnot. Republican Patriot*. Oxford, Oh.: Mississippi Valley Press, 1940.

Dusaulchoy de Bergemont, Joseph-François-Nicolas. *Histoire du couronnement ou relation des cérémonies religieuses, politiques et militaires, qui ont eu lieu pendant les jours mémorables consacrés à célébrer le Couronnement et le Sacre de Sa Majesté Impériale Napoléon Ier, Empereur des Français*, Paris: Dubray, 1805.

Dwyer, Philip G. (ed.). *Napoleon and Europe*. London: Longmans, 2001.

Ehrman, John. *The Younger Pitt. The Reluctant Transition*. London: Constable, 1983.

Eisenstein, Elizabeth. *The First Profesional Revolutionist: Filippo Michel Buonarroti (1761–1837)*. Cambridge, Mass.: Harvard University Press, 1959.

Ellis, Geoffrey. *Napoleon*. London: Longman, 1997.

Emmanuelli, René, 'Le gouvernement de Louis XVI offre à la république de Gênes la rétrocession de la Corse (1790)', *Annales historiques de la Révolution Française*, 46 (1974): 623–40.

Emsley, Clive. *British Society and the French Wars 1793–1815*. London: Macmillan, 1979.

Englund, Steven. *Napoleon: A Political Life*. New York: Scribner, 2004.

Entretiens de la Garenne Lemot. Le culte des Grands Hommes au XVIIIe siècle. Actes du Colloque 3 au 5 octobre 1996. Nantes: Institut Universitaire de France, 1998.

Esdaile, Charles J. (ed.). *Popular Resistance in the French Wars. Patriots, Partisans and Land Pirates*. London: Palgrave Macmillan, 2005.

Espitalier, Albert. *Vers Brumaire. Bonaparte à Paris, 5 décembre 1797–4 mai 1798*. Paris: Perrin, 1914.

Ettori, Fernand, 'Pascal Paoli, modèle du jeune Bonaparte', in *Problèmes d'Histoire de la Corse*, pp. 89–99.

Fabry, Gabriel. *Campagne de l'armée d'Italie, 1796–1797*. Paris, 1900–14.

Fain, Baron François, *Manuscrit de l'an III, 1794–1795*. Paris: Delaunay, 1829.

Feydel, Gabriel. *Mœurs et coutumes des Corses*. Paris: Garnery, 1798.

Forrest, Alan. *The Soldiers of the French Revolution*. Durham: Duke University Press, 1990.

Forrest, Alan, 'The Ubiquitous Brigand: The Politics and Language of Repression,' in Esdaile (ed.), *Popular Resistance in the French Wars*, pp. 25–43.

Foucart, Bruno, 'Les images du coup d'Etat et la formation de la Légende', in Boudon (ed.), *Brumaire*, pp. 131–50.

Fouché, Joseph. *Mémoires de Joseph Fouché, duc d'Otrante*. 2 vols. Osnabrück: Proff, 1824.

Fournoux, Amable de. *Napoléon et Venise 1796–1814*. Paris: Perrin, 2002.

Fox, Charles James. *Napoleon Bonaparte and the Siege of Toulon*. Washington: Law Reporter Company, 1902.

Franceschini, Emile, 'La Corse aux premiers jours de la Révolution', *Revue de la Corse*, 62 (1930): 49–62; 63 (1930): 110–18; 64 (1930): 157–71; 65 (1930): 209–20.

Francesco, Antonio de, 'Aux origines du mouvement démocratique italien: quelques perspectives de recherche d'après l'exemple de la période révolutionnaire 1796–1801', *Annales historiques de la Révolution Française*, 308 (1997): 333–48.

François, Charles. *Journal du capitaine François (dit le dromadaire d'Egypte)*. Paris: Carrington, 1903.

Freud, Ernest L. (ed.). *Letters of Sigmund Freud*, trans. Tania and James Stern. New York: Basic Books, 1960.

Fugier, André. *Napoléon et l'Italie*. Paris: Janin, 1947.

Furet, François, and Richet, Denis. *La Révolution française*. Paris: Fayard, 1973.

Gabriel-Robinet, Louis, 'Napoléon journaliste', *Les Annales Conferencia*, 115 (May, 1960): 5–21.

Gaffarel, Paul, 'Les Bonapartes à Marseilles', *La Révolution française*, 62 (1912): 255–76 and 289–314.

Gaffarel, Paul. *Bonaparte et les Républiques italiennes (1796–1799)*. Paris: Alcan, 1895.

Gainot, Bernard, 'La légende noire du Directoire', in *Napoléon, de l'histoire à la légende* (Paris, 2000), pp. 15–25.

Garat, Dominique. *Éloge funèbre de Joubert, prononcé au Champ-de-Mars*. Paris: Gratiot, 1799.

Geoffroy Saint-Hilaire, Etienne. *Lettres écrites d'Egypte*. Paris: Hachette, 1901.

Germani, Ian, 'Representations of the Republic at War: Lille and Toulon, 1792–1793', *Canadian Journal of History*, 29 (1994): 51–94.

Germani, Ian, 'Where is General Bonaparte? Press Reports of Napoleon's Expedition to Egypt', *Proceedings of the Western Society for French History*, 24 (1997): 61–70.

Gildea, Robert. *The Past in French History*. New Haven: Yale University Press, 1994.

Girardet, Raoul, 'The Three Colours: Neither White nor Red', in Nora (ed.), *Realms of Memory*, iii. pp. 3–26.

Girod de l'Ain, Gabriel. *Désirée Clary, d'après sa correspondance inédite avec Bonaparte, Bernadotte et sa famille*. Paris: Hachette, 1959.

La Girouette de Saint-Cloud: impromptu en un acte, en prose mêlé de Vaudeville. Paris, Théâtre du Vaudeville, 14 novembre 1799.

Godechot, Jacques, 'L'armée d'Italie (1796–1799)', *Cahiers de la Révolution française*, 4 (1936): 9–32.

Godechot, Jacques. *Les Commissaires aux armées sous le Directoire. Contribution à l'étude des rapports entre les pouvoirs civils et militaires*. 2 vols. Paris: Presses universitaires de France, 1941.

Godechot, Jacques, 'L'expansion française et la création de la presse politique dans le basin méditerranéen', *Cahiers de Tunisie*, 2 (1954): 146–71.

Godechot, Jacques, 'L'Empire napoléonien', *Recueils de la Société Jean Bodin*, 31 (1973): 433–55.

Godechot, Jacques, 'Les Français et l'unité italienne sous le Directoire', in *Regards sur l'époque révolutionnaire*. Paris: Privat, 1980, pp. 303–27.

Godechot, Jacques. *La Grande Nation. L'expansion révolutionnaire de La France dans le monde de 1789 à 1799*. Paris: Aubier Montaigne, 1983.

Godechot, Jacques. *Le comte d'Antraigues, un espion dans l'Europe des émigrés*. Paris: Fayard, 1986.

Godlewaska, Anne, 'Map, Text and Image. The Mentality of Enlightened Conquerors: A New Look at the *Description de l'Egypte*', *Transactions of the Institute of British Geographers*, 20 (1995): 5–28.

Godlewski, Guy, 'Bonaparte et l'affaire de la Maddalena', *Revue de l'Institut Napoléon*, 90 (1964): 1–12.

Gohier, Louis-Jérôme. *Mémoires de Louis-Jérôme Gohier, président du Directoire au 18 brumaire*. Paris: Bossange, 1824.

Goncourt, Edmond and Jules de. *Histoire de la société française pendant le Directoire*. Paris: le Promeneur, 1992.

Gotteri, Nicole. 'L'esprit publique à Paris avant le coup d'Etat de Brumaire an VIII', in Boudon (ed.), *Brumaire*, pp. 15–25.

Gough, Hugh. *The Newspaper Press in the French Revolution*. London: Routledge, 1988.

Gourgaud, Gaspard. *Journal de Sainte-Hélène 1815–1818*. 2 vols. Paris: Flammarion, 1944.

Grandjean, Lieutenant Laval. *Journaux sur l'Expédition d'Egypte*. Paris: Teissedre, 2000.

Grimaldo-Grigsby, Darcy, 'Rumor, Contagion, and Colonization in Gros's *Plague-Stricken of Jaffa* (1804)', *Representations*, 51 (1995), 1–46.

Grimaldo-Grigsby, Darcy. *Extremities: Painting in Post-Revolutionary France*. New Haven, Conn.: Yale University Press, 2002.

Grimsley, Mark, and Rogers, Clifford J. (eds.). *Civilians in the Path of War*. Lincoln: University of Nebraska, 2002.

Guyot, Raymond. *Le Directoire et la paix de l'Europe, des traités de Bâle à la deuxième Coalition (1795–1799)*. Paris: 1911.

Hales, E. E. Y. *Revolution and Papacy: 1769–1846*. London: Eyre and Spottiswoode, 1960.

Hall, Thad E., 'The Development of Enlightenment Interest in Eighteenth-Century Corsica', *Studies on Voltaire and the Eighteenth Century*, lxiv (1968): 165–85.

Hamelin, Antoine-Romain, 'Douze ans de ma vie, 1796–1808', *Revue de Paris*, 6 (1926): 5–24, 281–309, 544–66, 811–39.

Hanley, Wayne. *The Genesis of Napoleonic Propaganda, 1796–1799*. New York: Columbia University Press, 2005.

Hanna, Sami A., 'The Egyptian Mind and the Idea of Democracy', *International Journal of Middle East Studies*, 1 (1970): 238–47.

Hanoteau, Jean (ed.). *Memoirs of General de Caulaincourt, Duke of Vicenza.* 3 vols. London: Cassell, 1950.

Hanson, Paul R. *The Jacobin Republic Under Fire: The Federalist Revolt in the French Revolution.* University Park, Pa.: Pennsylvania State University Press, 2003.

Hardman, John. *Louis XVI.* New Haven, Conn.: Yale University Press, 1993.

Harouel, Jean-Louis. *Les Républiques sœurs.* Paris: PUF, 1997.

Harris, Jennifer, 'The Red Cap of Liberty: A Study of Dress worn by French Revolutionary Partisans 1789–94', *Eighteenth-Century Studies*, 14 (1981): 283–312.

Harten, Stuart, 'Rediscovering Ancient Egypt: Bonaparte's Expedition and the Colonial Ideology of the French Revolution', in Bierman (ed.), *Napoleon in Egypt*, pp. 33–46.

Härter, Karl. *Reichstag und Revolution 1789–1806. Die Auseinandersetzung des immerwährenden Reichstags zu Regensburg mit den Auswirkungen der Französischen Revolution auf das alte Reich.* Göttingen: Vandenhoeck & Ruprecht, 1992.

Hauterive, Ernest, 'Lettres de jeunesse de Bonaparte (1789–1792)', Revue des Deux Mondes (15 December 1931): 767–92.

Hazareesingh, Sudhir. *The Legend of Napoleon.* London: Granta, 2004.

Healey, F. G. *Rousseau et Napoléon.* Geneva: Droz, 1957.

Herbette, Maurice. *Une Ambassade turque sous le Directoire.* Paris: Perrin, 1902.

Heriot, Angus. *The French in Italy, 1796–1799.* London: Chatto & Windus, 1957.

Herold, J. Christopher. *Bonaparte in Egypt.* London: Hamish Hamilton, 1963.

Homan, Gerlof D. *Jean-François Reubell. French revolutionary, patriot and director (1747–1807).* The Hague: Martinus Nijhoff, 1971.

Hopkin, David M., 'Sons and Lovers: Popular Images of the Conscript, 1798–1870', *Modern & Contemporary France*, 9 (2001): 19–36.

Houdard, L, 'La situation sanitaire au siege de Mantoue, 1796–1797', *Revue des études napoléoniennes*, 31 (1930): 101–10.

Houdard, L, 'Les généraux Bonaparte et Clarke en Italie, 1797', *Revue des études napoléoniennes*, 34 (1932): 157–62.

Hüffer, Hermann and Luckwaldt, Friedrich. *Der Frieden von Campo-Formio. Quellen zur Geschichte der französischen Revolution.* 3 vols. Innsbruck: Verlag der Wagner'schen Universitäts Buchhandlung, 1907.

Hunt, Lynn, Lansky, David, and Hanson, Paul, 'The Failure of the Liberal Republic in France, 1795–1799: The Road to Brumaire', *Journal of Modern History*, 51 (1979): 734–59.

Hunt, Lynn, 'Hercules and the Radical Image in the French Revolution', *Representations*, 1 (1983): 95–117.

Hunt, Lynn. *Politics, Culture and Class in the French Revolution*. London: Methuen, 1984.

Iafelice, Michel. *Barbets! Les résistances à la domination française dans le pays niçois (1792–1814)*. Nice: Serre, 1998.

Ingram, Edward. *Commitment to Empire: Prophecies of the Great Game in Asia, 1797–1800*. Oxford: OUP, 1981.

Iung, Théodore (ed.). *Lucien Bonaparte et ses Mémoires, 1775–1840*. 3 vols. Paris: G. Charpentier, 1882–3.

Janowitz, M., and van Doorn, J. (eds). *On Military Ideology*. Rotterdam: Rotterdam University Press, 1971.

Jessenne, Jean-Pierre (ed.). *Du Directoire au Consulat*. 4 vols. iii. *Brumaire dans l'histoire du lien politique et de l'Etat-nation*. Villeneuve-d'Ascq: 2001.

Jessenne, Jean-Pierre (ed.), et al. *Robespierre. De la Nation artésienne à la République et aux Nations*. Villeneuve d'Ascq: Centre d'Histoire de la Région du Nord et de l'Europe du Nord-Ouest, 1994.

Jobert, Barthélémy, 'Les représentations, contemporains du Dix-huit Brumaire dans les Arts', and Bruno Foucart, 'Les images du coup d'Etat et la formation de la Légende', in Boudon (ed.), *Brumaire*, pp. 115–30.

Johnson, Hubert C. *The Midi in Revolution. A Study of Regional Political Diversity, 1789–1793*. Princeton, NJ: Princeton University Press, 1986.

Jomard, Edmé-François, et al. *Description de l'Egypte ou Recueil des observations et des recherches qui ont été faites en Egypte pendant l'expédition de l'armée française*. 26 vols. Paris: Panckoucke, 1821–30.

Jonquière, Clément de la. *L'Expédition d'Egypte (1798–1801)*. 5 vols. Paris: Charles-Lavauzelle, 1899–1907.

Jourdan, Annie. *Les Monuments de la Révolution, 1770–1804. Une histoire de représentation*. Paris: Honoré Champion, 1997.

Jourdan, Annie. *Napoléon: Héros, Imperator, Mécène*. Paris: Aubier, 1998.

Jourdan, Annie, 'Images de Napoléon – un *imperator* en quête de légitimité'. *Modern & Contemporary France*, 8 (2000): 433–44.

Kabbani, Rana. *Imperial Fictions. Europe's Myths of Orient*. London: Macmillan, 1986.

Kaiser, Thomas, 'The Evil Empire? The Debate on Turkish Despotism in Eighteenth-Century French Political Culture', *Journal of Modern History*, 72 (2000): 6–34.

Kale, Steven. *French Salons: High Society and Political Sociability from the Old Regime to the Revolution of 1848*. Baltimore: Johns Hopkins University Press, 2004.

Kaplan, Nira, 'Virtuous Competition among Citizens: Emulation in Politics and Pedagogy during the French Revolution', *Eighteenth-Century Studies*, 36 (2003): 241–8.

Khoury, Rene, 'Le mariage musulman du général Abdallah Menou', *Egyptian Historical Review*, 25 (1978): 65–93.

King, Norman, and Hoffman, Etienne, 'Les lettres de Benjamin Constant à Sieyès', *Annales Benjamin Constant*, 3 (1983): 89–110.

Knapton, Ernest John, 'A Contemporary Impression of Napoleon Bonaparte in 1797', *French Historical Studies*, 1 (1960): 476–81.

Knapton, Ernest John. *Empress Josephine*. Cambridge, Mass.: Harvard University Press, 1963.

Lacour-Gayet, G. *Talleyrand, 1754–1838* 4 vols. Paris: Payot, 1928–34.

La Jonquière, C. de. *L 'Expédition d'Egypte (1798–1801)*. 5 vols. Paris: Charles-Lavauzelle, 1899–1907.

Landrieux, Jean. *Mémoires de l'adjutant-général Jean Landrieux*. Paris: Albert Savine, 1893.

Laplanche, J., and Pontalis, J.-B. (eds). *The Language of Psycho-Analysis*. New York: Norton, 1973.

Larrey, Dominique-Jean. *Relation historique et chirurgical de l'expédition de l'armée d'Orient, en Egypt et en Syrie*. Paris: Demonville et Soeurs, 1803.

Las Cases, Emmanuel de. *Le Mémorial de Sainte-Hélène*. Critical edition by Marcel Dunan. 2 vols. Paris: Flammarion, 1983.

Lassius, Yves. *L'Egypte, une aventure savante*. Paris: Fayard, 1998.

Laugier, Jérome-Roland. *Les Cahiers du capitaine Laugier. De la guerre et de l'anarchie*. Aix: Remondet-Aubin, 1893.

Laulan, Robert, 'La chère a l'Ecole militaire au temps de Bonaparte', *Revue de l'Institut Napoléon*, 70 (1959): 18–23.

Laulan, Robert, 'Pourquoi et comment on entrait à l'Ecole royale militaire de Paris', *Revue d'Histoire Moderne et Contemporaine*, 4 (1957): 141–50.

Laurens, Henry. *Les Origines Intellectuelles de l'Expédition d'Egypte. L'Orientalisme Islamisant en France (1698–1798)*. Istanbul, Paris: Isis, 1987.

Laurens, Henry (ed.). *Kléber en Egypte, 1798–1800*. 3 vols. Paris: Éd. Simbad, 1988.

Laurens, Henry. *L'expédition d'Egypte, 1798–1801*. Paris: Editions du Seuil, 1997.

Laurens, Henry (ed.). *Campagnes d'Egypte et de Syrie*. Paris: Impr. nationale, 1998.

Laus de Boissy, Louis de. *Bonaparte au Caire, ou mémoires sur l'expédition de ce général en Egypte*. Paris: Prault, 1799.

Lavalette, Antoine-Marie Chamans, Comte de. *Mémoires et souvenirs du comte de Lavalette*. Paris: Mercure de France, 1994.

'Le dix-huit Brumaire. Extrait des mémoires du maréchal Jourdan', *Carnet historique et littéraire*, 7 (1901): 161–72.

Leclercq, Jean-Yves, 'Le mythe de Bonaparte sous le Directoire (1796–1799)', (Mémoire de Maîtrise, Université de Paris I, 1991).

Lecomte, L. Henry. *Napoléon et l'Empire racontés par le théâtre, 1797–1899.* Paris: Jules Raux, 1900.

Ledoux, Eugène, Bonaparte à Besançon', *Mémories de l'Académie des sciences, belles-lettres et arts de Besançon* (1900): 272–83.

Leijendecker, Marcel, 'Un amour inconnu de Bonaparte', *Revue des études napoléoniennes*, 36 (1933): 52–5.

Leith, James A., 'Youth Heroes of the French Revolution', *Proceedings of the Consortium on Revolutionary Europe* (1986), pp. 127–37.

Leith, James A., 'Nationalism and the Fine Arts in France, 1750–1789,' *Studies on Voltaire in the Eighteenth Century*, 89 (1972): 919–37.

Lenchère, chevalier de, 'Journal des campagnes de 1768 & 1769 en Corse par le chevalier de Lenchère', *Bulletin de la Société des sciences historiques et naturelles de la Corse* (July 1889): 383–474.

Lentz, Thierry. *Le 18-Brumaire. Les coups d'Etat de Napoléon Bonaparte.* Paris: Jean Picollec, 1997.

Lentz, Thierry. *Le Grand Consulat, 1799–1804.* Paris: Fayard, 1999.

Letteron, L. (ed.). *Pièces et documents divers pour servir à l'histoire de la Corse pendant les années 1790–1791.* 3 vols. Bastia: Ollagnier, 1884, 1891 and 1894.

Letteron, L. (ed.), 'Opérations militaires de la réduction de la Corse du 1er au 25 mai 1769, par M. de Guibert, major général de l'armée commandée par M. le comte de Vaux, lieutenant général des armées du roi', *Bulletin de la Société des sciences historiques et naturelles de la Corse* (1913): 27–43.

Lever, Maurice. *Sade. A Biography.* New York: 1993.

Lombard de Langres, Vincent (dit A. Grégoire). *Le dix-huit brumaire, ou tableau des événements qui ont amené à cette journée.* Paris: Garnery, an VIII.

Lucas, Colin, 'The Rules of the Game in Local Politics under the Directory', *French Historical Studies*, 16 (1989): 345–71.

Lucas, Colin (ed.). *Rewriting the French Revolution.* Oxford: Clarendon Press, 1991.

Lucas, Colin, 'The Theory and Practice of Denunciation in the French Revolution', *Journal of Modern History*, 68 (1996): 768–85.

Lyons, Martyn. *France under the Directory.* Cambridge: CUP, 1975.

Macaluso, Leonard, 'The Political Lives of Antoine Christophe Saliceti' (PhD, University of Kentucky, 1972).

Mainardi, Patricia, 'Assuring the Empire of the Future: The 1798 Fête de la Liberté', *Art Journal*, 48 (1989): 155–63.

Malus de Mitry, Etienne-Louis. *L'Agenda de Malus. Souvenirs de l'expédition d'Egypte, 1798–1801.* Paris: Champion, 1892.

Marbot, Jean-Baptiste. *Mémoires du général baron de Marbot*. 3 vols. Paris: Plon-Nourrit, 1891.

Marcaggi, J. B. *La Genèse de Napoléon, sa formation intellectuelle et morale jusqu'au siège de Toulon*. Paris: Perrin, 1902.

Marchi, Gian Paolo, and Marini, Paola (eds). *1797 Bonaparte a Verona*. Venice: Marsilio, 1997.

Marin-Muracciole, Madeleine-Rose. *L'honneur des femmes en Corse du XIIIe siècle à nos jours*. Paris: Cujas, 1964.

Markham, Felix. *Napoleon*. London: Weidenfeld & Nicolson, 1963.

Marmont, Auguste-Frédéric-Louis Wiesse de. *Mémoires du maréchal Marmont, duc de Raguse, de 1792 à 1841*. 9 vols. Paris: Perrotin, 1857.

Marsot, Afaf Lufti al-Sayyid, 'L'Expédition d'Egypte et le débat sur la modernité', *Egypte/Monde Arabe*, 1 (1999): 47–54.

Martin, Andy. *Napoleon the Novelist*. London: Polity, 2000.

Martin, Jean-Clément (ed.). *La Contre-Révolution en Europe, XVIIIe-XIXe siècle: réalités politiques et sociales, résonances culturelles et idéologiques*. Rennes: Presses Universitaires de Rennes, 2001.

Martin, Jean-Clément, 'Les mots de la violence: les guerres révolutionnaires', in Audoin-Rouzeau, Becker, et al. (eds), *La violence de guerre*, pp. 27–42.

Martin, Marc. *Les origines de la presse militaire en France de la fin de l'Ancien régime à la Révolution (1770–1799)*. Vincennes: Service historique de l'Armée, 1975.

Martin, Pierre-Dominique. *Histoire de l'expédition française en Egypte*. 2 vols. Paris: J.-M. Eberhart, 1815.

Martineau, Gilbert. *Lucien Bonaparte: Prince de Canino*. Paris: France-Empire, 1989.

Martinet, Johannes Florentius, *Journal physico-médical des eaux de Plombières*. Remiremont: E. Dubiez, 1798.

Masséna, André. *Mémoires d'André Masséna, duc de Rivoli, prince d'Essling*. 7 vols. Paris: Jean de Bonnot, 1966.

Masson, Frédéric. *Le Départment des Affaires Etrangers pendant la Révolution, 1787–1804*. Paris: 1887.

Masson, Frédéric and Biagi, Guido. *Napoléon Inconnu, papiers inédits (1769–1793)*. 2 vols. Paris: Ollendorff, 1895.

Masson, Frédéric. *Napoléon et sa famille*. Volume 1 (1769–1802). Paris: Albin Michel, 1897.

Masson, Frédéric, and Biagi, Guido. *Napoléon, manuscrits inédits, 1786–1791*. Paris: Société d'éditions littéraires et artistiques, 1907.

Masson, Frédéric. *Napoléon dans sa jeunesse: 1769–1793*. Paris: Société d'Editions littéraires et artistiques, 1907.

Masson, Frédéric. *Madame Bonaparte, 1796–1804*. Paris: Ollendorff, 1920.

Mauguin, George, 'Saliceti et l'arrestation de Bonaparte à Nice', *Revue des études napoléoniennes*, 39 (1934): 261–3.

Mavidal, M. J., and Laurent, M. E. (eds). *Archives parlementaires de 1787 à 1860: recueil complet des débats législatifs et politiques des Chambres françaises*. Première série, 1787 à 1799. 49 vols. Paris: P. Dupont, 1894.

Mayeur de Saint-Paul, François-Marie. *Tableau du nouveau Palais-Royal*. 2 vols. Paris: Maradan, 1788.

McClellan, Andrew. *Inventing the Louvre. Art, Politics, and the Origins of the Modern Museum in Eighteenth-Century Paris*. Cambridge: CUP, 1994.

McClellan, George B. *Venice and Bonaparte*. Princeton: Princeton University Press, 1931.

McErlean, J. M. P. *Napoleon and Pozzo di Borgo in Corsica and After, 1764–1821: Not Quite a Vendetta*. Lewiston: Edwin Mellen Press, 1996.

McErlean, J. M. P., 'Scholarships for the Bonapartes: The Political Background', *Napoleonic Alliance Gazette*, 4 (2003): 21–4.

McGrew, Roderick E. *Paul I of Russia*. Oxford: Clarendon Press, 1992.

McLynn, Frank. *Napoleon*. London: Jonathan Cape, 1997.

McPhee, Peter. *The French Revolution, 1789–1799*. Oxford: OUP, 2002.

Mercier, Louis-Sébastien. *Tableau de Paris*, in *Paris le jour, Paris la nuit*. Paris: Bouquin, 1990.

Migliorini, Luigi Mascili. *Le mythe du héros. France et Italie après la chute de Napoléon*, trans. Laurent Vallance. Paris: Nouveau Monde, 2002.

Migliorini, Luigi Mascilli. *Napoléon*, trans. Jean-Michel Gardair. Paris: Perrin, 2004.

Millet, Pierre. *Le chasseur Pierre Millet. Souvenirs de la campagne d'Egypte (1798–1801)*. Paris: Emile-Paul, 1903.

Millon, Charles. *Histoire des descentes qui ont eu lieu en Angleterre, Ecosse, Irlande et isles adjacentes*. Paris: L. Prudhomme, 1798.

Miot, André-François, Comte de Mélito. *Mémoires du Comte de Miot de Mélito*. 3 vols. Paris: Michel Levy, 1873.

Miot, Jacques-François. *Mémoires pour servir à l'histoire des expéditions en Egypte et en Syrie pendants les années VI, VII et VIII de la République française*. Paris: Demonsville, 1804.

Mirtil, Marcel. *Napoléon d'Ajaccio*. Paris: Siboney, 1947.

Mitchell, H., 'Vendemiaire, a Revaluation', *Journal of Modern History*, 30 (1958): 191–202.

Moiret, Joseph-Marie. *Memoirs of Napoleon's Egyptian Expedition, 1798–1801 by Captain Joseph-Marie Moiret*, trans. and ed. Rosemary Brindle. London: Greenhill, 2001.

Mollaret, H., and Brossollet, J., 'A propos des "Pestiférés de Jaffa" de A. J. Gros', *Jaarboek van het Koninklijk Museum voor schoone kunsten* (1968): 263–308.

Monestier, Louis. *Compte rendu des opérations des commissaires civils en-voyés en Corse par l'un d'eux, avec des observations propres à faire connaître la situation de ce département au 1er avril 1792 (15 juin–17 septembre)*. Paris: Imp. Nationale, n.d.

Montholon, Charles. *Récits de la captivité de l'empereur Napoléon à Sainte-Hélène*. 2 vols. Paris: Paulin, 1847.

Morand, Charles-Antoine. *Lettres sur l'expédition d'Egypte*. Paris: La Vouivre, 1998.

Moreh, Shmuel, 'Napoleon and the French Impact on Egyptian Society in the Eyes of Al-Jabarti', in Bierman (ed.), *Napoleon in Egypt*, pp. 77–98.

Mori, Jennifer, 'The British Government and the Bourbon Restoration: The Occupation of Toulon, 1793', *Historical Journal*, 40 (1997): 699–719.

Muir, Rory. *Tactics and the Experience of Battle in the Age of Napoleon*. New Haven and London: Yale University Press, 2000.

Murray, Stephen O., and Roscoe, Will. *Islamic Homosexualities: Culture, History, and Literature*. New York: 1997.

Napoléon, de l'histoire à la légende. Actes du colloque des 30 novembre et le 1er décembre 1999. Paris: In Forma, 2000.

Napoléon Buonaparte lieutenant d'artillerie, documents inédits sur mes premiers faits d'armes en 1793. Paris: Corréard, 1821.

Nasica, Tommaso. *Mémoires sur l'enfance et la jeunesse de Napoléon Ier jusqu'à l'age de vingt-trois ans*. Paris: P. Dupont, 1865.

Nicolas, Nicholas Harris (ed.). *The Dispatches and Letters of Vice Admiral Lord Viscount Nelson*. 7 vols. London: H. Colburn, 1845–6.

Niello Sargy, Jean Gabrielle de. *Mémoires sur l'expédition d'Egypte*. Paris: Vernarel et Tenon, 1825.

Nora, Pierre (ed.). *Realms of Memory: Rethinking the French Past*, trans. Arthur Goldhammer. 3 vols. New York: Columbia University Press, 1996–8.

Norry, Charles. *Relation de l'expédition d'Egypte*. Paris: Charles Pougens, an VII.

Norwich, John Julius. *Venice*. London: Allen Lane, 1983.

Oates, Stephen B (ed.). *Biograpy as High Adventure: Life-Writers Speak on their Art*. Amherst: University of Massachusetts, 1986.

O'Brien, David. *After the Revolution: Antoine-Jean Gros, Painting and Propaganda under Napoleon*. University Park, Penn.: Pennsylvania State University Press, 2006.

Ollivier, Albert. *Le Dix-huit brumaire*. Paris: Gallimard, 1959.

'Opinion de Du Pont (de Nemours) sur Bonaparte, en l'an IV', *Révolution française*, 35 (1898), 376 (6 March 1796).

Ouvrard, G.-J. *Mémoires de G.-J. Ouvrard sur sa vie et ses diverses opérations financières*. 3 vols. Paris: Moutardier, 1826–7.

Ozouf, Mona. *Festivals and the French Revolution*, trans. Alan Sheridan. Cambridge, Mass.: Harvard University Press, 1988.

Ozouf, Mona, 'The Pantheon', in Nora (ed.), *Realms of Memory*, pp. 325–46.

Pallain, George. *Correspondance diplomatique de Talleyrand. Le ministère Talleyrand sous le Directoire.* Paris: E. Plon, Nourrit et Cie, 1891.

Panzac, Daniel. *La peste dans l'empire ottoman, 1700–1850.* Louvain: Peeters, 1985.

Parès, A-Jacques, 'Relation inédite sur la fusillade du Champ de Mars à Toulon', *Var historique et géographique*, 50 (1932): 420–36.

Parker, Harold, 'The Formation of Napoleon's Personality: An Exploratory Essay', *French Historical Studies*, 7 (1971): 6–26.

Parker, Harold, 'Napoleon's Youth and Rise to Power', in Dwyer (ed.), *Napoleon and Europe*, pp. 25–42.

Paroy, Jean-Philippe-Gui Le Gentil. *Mémoires du comte de Paroy: souvenirs d'un défenseur de la famille royale pendant la Révolution (1789–1797).* Paris: Plon, 1895.

Pelleport, Pierre de. *Souvenirs militaires et intimes du général Vte de Pelleport.* 2 vols. Paris: Didier & Co., 1857.

[Peltier, Jean-Gabriel]. *Examen de la campagne de Buonaparte en Italie par un témoin oculaire.* Paris: Le Normant, 1814.

Perelli, Louis-Antoine. *Lettres de Pascal Paoli.* 4 vols. Bastia: Ollagnier, 1886–99.

Perrot, Jean-Claude, and Woolf, Stuart. *State and Statistics in France, 1789–1815.* New York: Harwood, 1984.

Petiet, Auguste. *Mémoires du général Auguste Petiet, hussard de l'Empire. Souvenirs historiques, militaires et particuliers, 1784–1815.* Paris: S.P.M., 1996.

Peyrou, E. *L'Expédition de Sardaigne. Le Lieutenant-Colonel Bonaparte à la Maddalena (1792–1793).* Paris: Charles-Lavauzelle, 1912.

Phillips, Roderick. *Family Breakdown in Late Eighteenth-Century France: Divorces in Rouen, 1792–1803.* Oxford: Clarendon Press, 1980.

Pietro, Dominique di. *Voyage historique en Egypte pendant les campagnes des généraux Bonaparte, Kléber et Menou.* Paris: L'Huillier, 1818.

Pietromarchi, Antonello. *Lucien Bonaparte. Prince romain.* Paris: Perrin, 1980.

Pinaud, Pierre-François. *Cambacérès.* Paris: Perrin, 1996.

Pingaud, Albert. *La domination française dans l'Italie du Nord (1796–1805). Bonaparte, président de la République italienne.* 2 vols. Paris: Perrin, 1914.

Pingué, Danièle, 'Les "néo-jacobins" franc-comtois et le 18 Brumaire', in Jessenne (ed.), *Brumaire dans l'histoire*, pp. 31–41.

Piussi, Anna, 'Images of Egypt during the French Expedition (1798–1801): Sketches of a Historical Colony' (PhD, St. Antony's College, Oxford, 1992).

Pommereul, François-Réné-Jean de. *Campagne du général Buonaparte en Italie pendant les années IVe et Ve de la République française.* Paris: Plassan, 1797.

Pommier, Edouard, 'Idéologie et Musée à l'époque de la Révolution', in Vovelle (ed.), *Les images de la Révolution française*, pp. 57–78.

Pommier, Edouard, 'La saisie des oeuvres d'art', *Revue du Souvenir napoléonienne*, 408 (1996): 30–43.

Pommier, Edouard. *L'art de la liberté. Doctrines et débats de la Révolution Française.* Paris: Gallimard, 1991.

Pommier, Edouard, 'L'invention du monument aux Grands Hommes (XVIIIe siècle)', in *Entretiens de la Garenne Lemot. Le culte des Grands Hommes au XVIIIe siècle. Actes du Colloque 3 au 5 octobre 1996.* Nantes: Institut Universitaire de France, 1998, pp. 8–23.

Pomponi, François, 'Sentiments révolutionnaires et esprit de parti en Corse au temps de la Révolution', in *Problèmes d'Histoire de la Corse*, pp. 147–78.

Pomponi, François, 'Pouvoir civil, pouvoir militaire et régime d'exception dans les "régions" périphériques au temps du Consulat', *Annales historiques de la Révolution Française*, 2 (2003): 147–69.

Pons, Zénon. *Mémoires pour servir à l'histoire de la ville de Toulon, en 1793.* Paris: C. J. Trouvé, 1825.

Pontécoulant, L. G. le Doulcet, Comte de. *Souvenirs historiques et parlementaires.* 4 vols. Paris: Levy, 1861–5.

Poupé, Edmond (ed.). *Lettres et correspondance de Barras et de Fréron en mission dans le Midi.* Draguignan: 1910.

Précis historique de la Révolution du 13 vendémiaire et de celles qui l'ont causé. Paris: chez tous les marchands de nouveautés, 1796.

Précis historique et circonstancié des événemens qui ont précédés et suivis la journée du 13 vendémiaire. Paris: Marquant, 1796.

Prendergast, Christopher. *Napoleon and History Painting: Antoine-Jean Gros's La Bataille d'Eylau.* Oxford: OUP, 1997.

Prévost, Arthur-Emile. *Le Collège et les premiers maîtres de Napoléon. Les Minimes de Brienne.* Troyes: J.-L. Paton, 1915.

Problèmes d'Histoire de la Corse (de l'Ancien régime à 1815). Actes de colloque d'Ajaccio. Paris: Société des Etudes Robespierristes, Société d'Histoire Moderne, 1971.

Procès-verbal de la séance du Conseil des Cinq-cents tenue à Saint-Cloud le 19 brumaire an VIII. Saint-Cloud: Imprimerie nationale, n.d.

Puget, Hilarion-Paul-François, Marquis de Barbentane. *Mémoires du lieutenant-général Puget-Barbantane.* Paris: Pichon-Béchet, 1827.

Rao, Anna Maria, 'Les républicains démocrates italiens et le Dìrectoire', in Bourdin and Gainot (eds), *La République directoriale*, ii. pp. 1057–90.

Rao, Anna Maria (ed.). *Folle Controrivoluzionarie. Le insorgenze populari nell'Italia giacobine e napoleonica*. Rome: Carocci, 1999.

Rao, Anna Maria, 'Révolution et Contre-Révolution pendant le Triennio italien (1796–1799)', in Martin (ed.), *La Contre-Révolution en Europe*, pp. 233–40.

Raymond, André, 'Les Egyptiens et les Lumières pendant l'expédition française', in Bret (ed.), *L'expédition d'Egypte*, pp. 103–17.

Réal, Pierre-François. *Essai sur les journées des treize et quatorze Vendémiaire*. Paris: chez l'auteur, 1795.

Reinhard, Marcel. *Avec Bonaparte en Italie d'après les lettres inédites de son aide de camp Joseph Sulkowski*. Paris: Hachette, 1946.

Rémusat, Claire-Elisabeth. *Mémoires de madame de Rémusat, 1802–1808*. 3 vols. Paris: Calmann Lévy, 1880.

Reybaud, Louis (ed.). *Histoire scientifique et militaire de l'expédition française en Egypte*. 10 vols. Paris: A.-J. Dénain, 1830–6.

Rodger, A. B. *The War of the Second Coalition, 1798 to 1801. A Strategic Commentary*. Oxford: Clarendon Press, 1964.

Rodger, N. A. M. *The Command of the Ocean. A Naval History of Britain, 1649–1815*. London: Allen Lane, 2004.

Roederer, Pierre-Louis. *Oeuvres du Comte P.-L. Roederer*. 8 vols. Paris: Firmin-Didot, 1853–9.

Roederer, Pierre-Louis. *Autour de Bonaparte. Journal du comte P.-L. Roederer*. Paris: H. Daragon, 1909.

Roederer, Pierre-Louis. *Mémoires sur la Révolution, le Consulat et l'Empire*. Paris: Plon, 1942.

Roguet, François. *Mémoires militaires du lieutenant général Cte Roguet*. 4 vols. Paris: J. Dumaine, 1862.

Roider, Karl. *Baron Thugut and Austria's Response to the French Revolution*. Princeton, NJ: Princeton University Press, 1987.

Romagnani, Gian Paolo, 'Dalle "Pasque veronese" ai moti agrari del Piemonte', in Rao (ed.), *Folle Controrivoluzionare*, pp. 89–122.

Romain, Félix de. *Souvenirs d'un officier royaliste*. 2 vols. Paris: Egron, 1829.

Rose, J. Holland, 'The Despatches of Colonel Thomas Graham on the Italian Campaign of 1796–1797', *English Historical Review*, 53 (1899): 111–24.

Rosenberg, Martin, 'Raphael's Transfiguration and Napoleon's Cultural Politics', *Eighteenth-Century Studies*, 19 (1985–6), 180–205.

Ross, Steven T., 'The Military Strategy of the Directory: The Campaigns of 1799', *French Historical Studies*, 5 (1967): 170–87.

Ross, Steven T. *Quest for Victory. French Military Strategy, 1792–1799*. South Brunswick: A. S. Barnes, 1973.

Rothenberg, Gunther E. *The Art of Warfare in the Age of Napoleon*. Bloomington: Indiana University Press, 1978.

Rothenberg, Gunther E., 'The Origins, Causes, and Extension of the Wars of the French Revolution and Napoleon', *Journal of Interdisciplinary History*, 18 (1988): 771–93.

Roux, Christine. *Les 'Makis' de la résistance Corse, 1772–1778*. Paris: Editions France-Empire, 1984.

Roux, Georges. *Monsieur de Buonaparte*. Paris: Fayard, 1964.

Roy, Stéphane, 'Le retentissement de Brumaire en image: rupture ou continuité?', in Jessenne (ed.), iii. *Brumaire dans l'histoire*, pp. 581–93.

Rudé, George. *The Crowd in the French Revolution*. Oxford: OUP, 1959.

Said, Edward W. *Orientalism*. London: Penguin, 1995, first published in 1979.

Saintine, X.-B. (ed.). *Histoire de l'expédition française en Egypte*. 3 vols. Paris: Gagniard, 1830.

Salgues, Jacques-Barthélemy. *Mémoires pour servir à l'histoire de la France sous le gouvernement de Napoléon Buonaparte et pendant l'absence de la maison de Bourbon*, 9 vols. Paris: Fayolle, 1814–26.

Salomon, Xavier F., and Woodward, Christopher, 'How England first saw Bonaparte', *Apollo*, 162 (2005): 52–8.

Samarati, Luigi (ed.). *Napoleone e la Lombardia nel Triennio Giacobino (1796–1799)*. Lodi: Archivio storico lodigiano, 1997.

Savage, Gary, 'Favier's Heirs: The French Revolution and the *Secret du Roi*', *Historical Journal*, 41 (1998): 225–58.

Savary, Anne-Jean-Marie. *Mémoires du duc de Rovigo, pour servir à l'histoire de l'empereur Napoléon*. 8 vols. Paris: A. Bossange, 1829.

Savoy, Bénédicte. *Patrimoine annexé. Les biens culturels saisis par La France en Allemagne autour de 1800*. 2 vols. Paris: Editions de la Maison des sciences de l'homme, 2003.

Sayag-Boyer, Emmanuelle, 'La liberté en Italie, d'après les Archives de l'Armée d'Italie: Vérité et apparence d'un aspect de la campagne de Bonaparte (1796–1797)', *Revue du Souvenir napoléonienne*, 408 (1996): 44–49.

Schama, Simon. *Patriots and Liberators. Revolution in the Netherlands, 1730–1815*. London: Fontana, 1992.

Schechter, Ronald, 'Gothic Thermidor: The *Bals des victimes*, the Fantastic, and the Production of Historical Knowledge in Post-Terror France', *Representations*, 61 (1998): 78–94.

Schofield, Philip, 'British Politicians and French Arms: The Ideological War of 1793–1795', *History*, 77 (1992): 183–201.

Schom, Alan. *Napoleon Bonaparte*. London: HarperCollins, 1997.

Schroder, Anne L. 'Going Public against the Academy in 1784: Mme de Genlis Speaks out on Gender Bias', *Eighteenth-Century Studies*, 32 (1999): 3756–82.

Schroeder, Paul W. *The Transformation of European Politics*. Oxford: OUP, 1994.

Schur, Nathan. *Napoleon in the Holy Land*. London: Greenhill Books, 1999.

Scott, Samuel F., *The Response of the Royal Army to the French Revolution: The Role and Development of the Line Army, 1783–93*. Oxford: Clarendon Press, 1978.

Scott, S. F., 'The French Revolution and the Professionalization of the French Officer Corps', in Janowitz and van Doorn (eds), *On Military Ideology*, pp. 8–18.

Scotti Douglas, Vittorio (ed.), *L'Europa Scopre Napoleone 1793–1804*. 2 vols. Alessandria: Edizioni dell'Orso, 1999, pp. 577–88.

Scotti Douglas, Vittorio, 'The Italian Anti-Napoleonic Insurgencies', in *L'Europa Scopre Napoleone*, ii. pp. 577–88.

Ségur, Philippe-Paul, Comte de. *Histoire et mémoires*, 7 vols, Paris: Firmon-Didot, 1877.

Semelin, Jacques, 'In Consideration of Massacres', *Journal of Genocide Research*, 3 (2001): 377–89.

Sepinwall, Alyssa Goldstein. *The abbé Grégoire and the French Revolution. The Making of Modern Universalism*. Berkeley, Cal.: University of California Press, 2005.

Serna, Pierre, 'Le Directoire ... Un non lieu de mémoire à revisiter', in Bourdin and Gainot (eds), *La République directoriale*, i. pp. 37–63.

Serna, Pierre, 'Refaire l'Histoire, écrire l'Histoire ou comment raconter le 18 Brumaire entre 1800 et 1802', *Cahiers d'histoire. Revue d'histoire critique*, 77 (1999): 101–20.

Shapiro, Barry M., 'Self-Sacrifice, Self-Interest, or Self-Defense? The Constituent Assembly and the "Self-Denying Ordinance" of May 1791', *French Historical Studies*, 25 (2002): 625–56.

Siegfried, Susan Locke. *The Art of Louis-Leopold Boilly: Modern Life in Napoleonic France*. New Haven: Yale University Press, 1995.

Silvani, Sébastien. *Deux compagnons de Napoléon. Les frères Bonelli de Bocognano*. Paris: Chiron, 1932.

Simms, Brendan, 'Britain and Napoleon', in Dwyer (ed.), *Napoleon and Europe*, pp. 189–203.

Skalkowski, Adam (ed.). *Les Polonais en Egypte, 1798–1801*. Paris: Grasset, 1910.

Smets, Josef, 'Le Rhin, frontière naturelle de la France: genèse d'une idée a l'époque révolutionnaire, 1789–1799', *Annales historiques de la Révolution Française* 1998 (314): 675–98.

Smith, Jay M. *The Culture of Merit: Nobility, Royal Service, and the Making of Absolute Monarchy in France, 1600–1789*. Ann Arbor: University of Michigan Press, 1996.

Soboul, Albert, 'Témoignage sur le général Bonaparte en l'an IV', *Annales historiques de la Révolution Française*, 27 (1955): 380–1.

Solé, Robert. *Les Savants de Bonaparte*. Paris: Seuil, 1998.

Sorel, Albert. *L'Europe et la Révolution française*. 8 vols. Paris: Plon, 1893–1904.

Sorel, Albert. *Bonaparte et Hoche en 1797*. Paris: Plon, 1896.

'Souvenirs du comte Le Couteulx de Canteleu,' in *Mémoires sur les journées révolutionnaires et les coups d'Etat*. 2 vols. Paris: Firmon-Didot, 1875.

Spang, Rebecca L., 'The Frivolous French: "Liberty of Pleasure" and the End of Luxury', in Brown and Miller (eds), *Taking Liberties*, pp. 110–25.

Staël-Holstein, Germaine de. *Considérations sur la Révolution française*. Paris: Tallandier, 1983.

Stendhal, *The Charterhouse of Parma*, trans. Robert Andrew Parker. New York: Modern Library, 1999.

Stendhal, *Napoléon*. Paris: Stock, 1998.

Stewart, Robert G., 'The Portraits of Henry Benbridge', *American Art Journal*, 2 (1970): 58–71.

Sur Bonaparte, conversations entre un soldat, un royaliste et un rentier, np, nd.

Sutherland, D.M.G. *The French Revolution and Empire: The Quest for a Civic Order*. Oxford: Blackwell, 2003.

Symcox, Geoffrey, 'The Geopolitics of the Egyptian Expedition, 1797–1798', in Bierman (ed.), *Napoleon in Egypt*, pp. 13–31.

Tackett, Timothy. *Religion, Revolution, and Regional Culture in Eighteenth-Century France. The Ecclesiastical Oath of 1791*. Princeton, NJ: Princeton University Press, 1986.

Tackett, Timothy. *When the King took Flight*. Cambridge, Mass.: Harvard University Press, 2003.

Tackett, Timothy, 'Collective Panic in the Early French Revolution, 1789–1791: A Comparative Perspective', *French History*, 17 (2003): 149–71.

Tardieu, P. F. *Notice historique des descentes qui ont été faites dans les Isles Britanniques, depuis Guillaume-le-Conquérant jusqu'à l'an VI de la République française*. Paris: Imprimerie de Crapelet, 1798.

Thibaudeau, Antoine-Claire. *Mémoires sur la Convention et le Directoire*. 2 vols. Paris: Baudouin, 1824.

Thibaudeau, Antoine-Claire. *Mémoires de A.-C. Thibaudeau*. Paris: Plon, 1913.

Thiébault, Paul. *Mémoires du général baron Thiébault*. 3 vols. Paris: Plon, 1894–5.

Thompson, J.M. *The French Revolution*. Oxford: Basil Blackwell, 1955.

Thompson, J.M. *Napoleon Bonaparte: His Rise and Fall*. Oxford: Basil Blackwell, 1958.

Thrasher, Peter Adam. *Pasquale Paoli. An Enlightened Hero, 1725–1807*. London: Constable, 1970.

Thurman, Louis-George. *Capitaine Thurman. Bonaparte en Egypte*. Paris: Emile Paul, 1902.

Tourtier-Bonazzi, Chantal de (ed.). *Napoléon. Lettres d'amour à Joséphine*. Paris: Fayard, 1981.

Traer, James F. *Marriage and the Family in Eighteenth-Century France*. Ithaca, NT: Cornell University Press, 1980.

Traits caractéristiques de la jeunesse de Bonaparte et réfutation des différentes anecdotes qui ont été publiées a ce sujet. Leipzig: Chez Hinrichs, 1802.

Tulard, Jean (ed.). *Napoléon Bonaparte. Oeuvres littéraires et écrits militaires*. 3 vols. Paris: Bibliothèque des Introuvables, 2001.

Tulard, Jean, 'Le recrutement de la Légion de police de Paris sous la Convention thermidorienne et le Directoire', *Annales historiques de la Révolution Française*, 36 (1964): 38–64.

Tulard, Jean, 'Robespierre vu par Napoléon', in *Actes du colloque Robespierre*, Paris: Société des Etudes Robespierristes, 1967, pp. 36–8.

Tulard, Jean (ed.). *Bibliographie critique des mémoires sur le Consulat et l'Empire*. Geneva: Droz, 1971.

Tulard, Jean. *Napoléon ou le Mythe du Sauveur*. Paris: Fayard, 1977.

Tulard, Jean (ed.), *Dictionnaire Napoléon*. Paris: Fayard, 1989.

Tulard, Jean, and Garros, Louis. *Itinéraire de Napoléon au jour le jour, 1769–1821*. Paris: Tallandier, 1992.

Tulard, Jean. *Le 18 Brumaire: Comment terminer une révolution*. Paris: Perrin, 1999.

Tulard, Jean. *Les Thermidoriens*. Paris: Fayard, 2005.

Turk, Niqula ibn Yusuf al. *Histoire de l'expédition des Français en Egypte*. Paris, 1839.

Turner, Marta, 'The Treaty of Tolentino and French Art Confiscations', *Risorgimento. European Review for Italian Modern History*, 2 (1981): 5–12.

Vandal, Albert. *L'avènement de Bonaparte*. 2 vols. Paris: Plon, 1903–7.

Vaublanc, Vincent-Marie Viennot de. *Mémoires sur la Révolution de France et recherches sur les causes qui ont amené la Révolution de 1789 et celles qui l'ont suivie*. 4 vols. Paris: G.-A. Dentu, 1833.

Vecchiato, Francesco, 'La resistenza antigiacobina e le Pasque Veronesi'', in Marchi and Manni (eds), *1797 Bonaparte a Verona*, pp. 180–200.

Versini, Xavier. *M. de Buonaparte ou le livre inachevé*. Paris: Albatros, 1977.

Victoires, conquêtes, désastres et guerres civiles des français de 1792 à 1815 par une société des militaires et de gens de lettres. 29 vols. Paris: Panckouke, 1817–1828.

Vigo-Roussillon, François. *Journal de Campagne (1793–1837)*. Paris: France-Empire, 1981.

Villani, Pasquale, 'Agenti e diplomatici francesi in Italia (1789–1795). Un giacobino a Genova: Jean Tilly', *Società e storia*, 65 (1994): 529–58.

Villiers du Terrage, Edouard de. *Journal et Souvenirs sur l'Expédition d'Egypte (1798–1801)*. Paris: Plon, 1899.

Vincent, Edgar. *Nelson: Love & Fame*. New Haven, Conn.: Yale University Press, 2003.

Volney, Constantin François de Chasseboeuf, Comte de. *Les Ruines*. Paris: Slatkine, 1979.

Volney, Constantin François de Chasseboeuf, Comte de. *Précis de l'Etat de la Corse*. Nucariu: Cismonte è Pumonti Edizione, 1989.

Vovelle, Michel (ed.). *Les images de la Révolution française*. Paris: Publications de la Sorbonne, 1988.

Vovelle, Michel, 'Naissance et formation du mythe napoléonien en Italie durant le trienno. Les leçons de l'image', in Samarati (ed.), *Napoleone e la Lombardia*, pp. 18–43.

Vovelle, Michel. *Les Républiques-soeurs sous le regard de la Grande Nation, 1795–1803. De l'Italie aux portes de l'Empire ottoman, l'impact du modèle républicain français*. Paris: L'Harmattan, 2000.

Wilkinson, Spenser. *The Rise of General Bonaparte*. Oxford: OUP, 1930.

Wilson, Stephen. *Feuding, Conflict and Banditry in Nineteenth-Century Corsica*. Cambridge: CUP, 1988.

Woloch, Isser, *Jacobin Legacy; The Democratic Movement under the Directory*. Princeton, NJ: Princeton University Press, 1970.

Woloch, Isser, 'Réflexions sur les réactions à brumaire dans les milieux républicains provinciaux', in Bertaud et al. (ed.), *Mélanges Michel Vovelle*, pp. 309–18.

Woloch, Isser. *Napoleon and his Collaborators: The Making of a Dictatorship*. New York: Norton, 2001.

Young, Arthur. *Travels in France*. London: George Bell, 1889.

Zaghi, Carlo. *L'Italia di Napoleone dalla Cisalpina al Regno*. Turin: UTET, 1986.

Zins, Ronald (ed.), *Journal de voyage du général Desaix, Suisse et Italie (1797)*. Paris: Horace Cardon, 2000.

Zivy, Henry. *Le Treize Vendémiaire an IV*. Paris: Felix Alcan, 1898.

Acknowledgements

This book is the product of the innumerable detailed studies that have come before it. Like all historians, I stand upon the shoulders of all those who have preceded me in an attempt to see a little further. Just as importantly, though, a number of contemporary readers were generous enough to give of their time to read part or all of the manuscript, picking up mistakes and inconsistencies, and helping me clarify my arguments. For this, my deepest thanks go to Robert Aldrich, Saliha Belmessous, Michael Broers, Hilary Carey, Stephen Clay, John Davis, William Doyle, Steven Englund (who did not see me as a rival, even though he was writing his own biography of Napoleon), Alexander Grab (who generously welcomed me to Israel and took the time to show me around Jaffa), Wayne Hanley, Peter Hempenstall (who helped guide me through the minefield that is biography), Martyn Lyons, Laura Mason, Robert McGregor, Peter McPhee, Isabelle Merle, Rory Muir, David O'Brien and Michael Sibalis. I am greatly indebted to them all, even if the conclusions and the end product do not necessarily concur with their views. This book is also the product of conversations I have had with a number of people over the years – Andrew Fitzmaurice, Henry Laurens, Peter Loewenberg and Robert Morrissey, among others, and most of all my friend and colleague, Therese Davis, who was always there when I needed to bounce ideas around. A special thanks to Andrea Low, whose keen eye for detail proved invaluable. Afaf Lufti al-Sayyid Marsot kindly answered my questions on Egyptian society, as did David Parrott on military etiquette during the *ancien régime*, and David Bell on the relationship between noble officers and the French monarchy. Hélène Jaccomard helped with some of the more difficult translations from French into English. In Paris, Martha Zuber's encouragement and support was always welcome. I am also fortunate to have good friends there who look after me as though I were one of the family, making my stays all the more pleasant: Marie-Noël and Cyril Malapert (never an empty glass in his company), and their adorable, noisy and delightfully cheeky children; and Marie-Françoise Dufief and Laurent Peyron.

Institutional support has also been invaluable. My appreciation goes to the Australian Academy of the Humanities for a Fellowship grant, and to the University of Newcastle for funding that, over the years, helped pay for the stints in Paris. Anne Taylor at the University of Newcastle's inter-library loan service invariably found what I was looking for, no matter how obscure the request. I was touched by the generosity of the people I met in Italy: my thanks to Anna Sbampato and Valentina Zenti for making my stay in Verona a memorable one. Marcello Marconi kindly showed me some of the battlefields of the Veneto. My gratitude goes to my agent, Bill Hamilton, for taking this book out of indifferent hands and placing it in much more capable ones. This was my first experience with a trade publisher and I found them more demanding than a scholarly press. Rosemary Davidson took the subject to heart, and made me rewrite and rethink large sections of the manuscript. Antonia Till did a superb job copy-editing a first draft. And then, while Rosemary was on extended leave, the project was handed over to Michael Fishwick, whose copy-editors, Kate Johnson and Anna Hervé, undertook an exhaustive reading, suggesting changes to style, pace and structure. They have all contributed to making this a far better book than it originally was. Parts of this book were published in two articles in *French History*. I am grateful to the editor of the journal, Malcolm Crook, as well as the anonymous readers for their observations.

Index

godfather, 25; temperament, 29–30, 34–5, 38, 42, 49–50, 207–8, 303; reading, 29, 44–6, 164, 517; nickname, 30; enters military, 31–2; appearance, 31, 48, 158, 166–7, 197–8, 207, 267, 472; enters *Ecole militaire*, 33–5; Corsican identity and hatred of French, 35–7, 46, 49, 62–6, 78, 82, 122; admiration for Paoli, 35–7, 69–71, 74–5, 98, 122, 515; relationship with father, 36, 38–41; relationship with mother, 41, 190, 239; takes responsibility for family affairs, 42, 46–8, 51–2, 101, 178; graduates from *Ecole militaire*, 42; posting to Valence, 42–3; social debut, 43; relationships with women, 42–3, 161, 189; life in Paris, 47; loss of virginity, 47–8; posting to Auxonne, 48–9; health, 48, 69, 167, 281, 296, 314, 475; financial affairs, 48, 128, 145, 164, 178; starts to discuss politics, 49; military education, 49–50, 196; early experiences of Revolution, 50–1; involvement in Corsican politics, 59–61, 64–6, 69, 71–5, 79, 82, 88, 90–1, 95, 120–2, 516; adopts French identity, 62–5, 125; certificates of citizenship, 72, 77, 92; cooling of relations with Paoli, 74–5, 78, 91–2, 105–6, 108, 113; politicization, 76, 79, 81–2, 98; returns to Auxonne, 77–8; returns to Valence, 78–9; swears oaths of allegiance, 80–1; elected to Corsican National Guard, 82–8, 125; and Easter Sunday 'insurrection', 88–92, 96–8, 110, 116, 125, 177, 515; arrogance, 90; attitude to Revolution, 95, 98; promoted to captain, 98; witnesses victims of Tuileries attack, 99–101, 229; participates in invasion of Sardinia, 108–12; considers going to India, 108; life threatened, 110, 112–13; and rift with Paoli, 113, 116–17, 119–22, 124–5, 131; takes French side, 116, 119, 123–5; deplores execution of king, 123; increased political acumen, 125–6, 159, 309–10, 327–9; exiled from Corsica, 128–30; and siege of Avignon, 130–1; and siege of Toulon, 135–8, 140, 144–5, 182, 229; military reputation established and strengthened, 144–5, 271, 351, 449; promoted to brigadier-general, 145; organizes defence of Provence, 145–6; summoned before Convention, 146–7; and Italian campaign, 146, 148–50, 154–7, 161, 164, 168, 179–80, 182; plans Piedmont campaign, 148–9, 156; mission to Genoa,

151–2, 154; arrested, 154–5, 158–9, 516; posting to Vendée, 157, 163–4, 167, 169, 516; lack of ideals, 158–9; relationship with Désirée (Eugénie), 159–63, 165, 187, 189; relationship with Joseph, 160–1, 241, 377; melancholy, 165–6; plans to enter Turkish service, 168–70; role in suppressing Vendémiaire insurrection, 173–6, 182, 215, 271, 305, 516; and charge of firing on crowd, 174–5, 177; narcissism, 176; appointed to command Army of Interior, 177–80, 187; promoted to general of division, 177; acquires air of grandeur, 178–9; appointed to command Army of Italy, 180–3, 195–7; meets Josephine, 186–7; marriage, 188–91, 195; other marriage proposals, 189; Italian proclamation, 200–1; disapproval of looting, 203; exaggerates enemy casualties, 205; freedom of action and relations with Directory, 208–9, 215–18, 227, 246, 254–5, 265–8, 273–4, 281–4, 289, 291–3, 303, 314–15, 515; and crossing of bridge at Lodi, 211–17; acquires sense of destiny, 215–16; entry into Milan, 219–23, 276; preoccupation with Josephine, 223–4, 238–45, 258, 263–4, 517; indifference to bloodshed, 229; orders art seizures, 235–8; morbidity, 241; takes fight to allies, 247; rebirth at Arcola, 249–50; myth of invincibility, 250–1, 415; changes in relationship with Josephine, 263–5, 302–3, 326–7, 353; marginalizes commissaires, 265–8; invades Papal States, 273–4; religious politics, 274–7; opinion of Italians, 278–9; and Italian politics, 277–82, 286–7, 289–91, 293, 311; and defeat of Austria and peace negotiations, 282–5, 291–2, 314–20; forms court at Mombello, 296–8, 301; impact of Italian campaign, 302–3; founds newspapers, 306–10, 478; and Fructidor coup, 311–14, 468; lack of long-term objectives, 317; appointed to command Army of England, 320–1; public appearances in Paris, 322–4, 345–6, 477–8; considers possibility of coup, 328–9, 349; and expedition against England, 334–6; plans Egyptian expedition, 338–47; fascination with Orient, 340–2; interest in sciences and election to Institute, 345–7; conquest of Malta, 356–9; Islamic policy, 359, 378, 441; issues proclamation to Egyptian people, 367; changed by Josephine's infidelity, 377–8, 422;

A NOTE ON THE AUTHOR

Philip Dwyer studied in Perth (Australia), Berlin and Paris, where he was a student of France's pre-eminent Napoleonic scholar, Jean Tulard. He has published widely on the Revolutionary and Napoleonic eras, and is the editor of *Napoleon and Europe*, the author of *Talleyrand*, and has co-edited *Napoleon and His Empire: Europe, 1804–1814*. He is currently Senior Lecturer in Modern European History at the University of Newcastle, Australia, and is working on the second volume of his biography of Napoleon.

A NOTE ON THE TYPE

The text of this book is set in Linotype Stempel Garamond, a version of Garamond adapted and first used by the Stempel foundry in 1924. It's one of several versions of Garamond based on the designs of Claude Garamond. It is thought that Garamond based his font on Bembo, cut in 1495 by Francesco Griffo in collaboration with the Italian printer Aldus Manutius. Garamond types were first used in books printed in Paris around 1532. Many of the present-day versions of this type are based on the *Typi Academiae* of Jean Jannon cut in Sedan in 1615.

Claude Garamond was born in Paris in 1480. He learned how to cut type from his father and by the age of fifteen he was able to fashion steel punches the size of a pica with great precision. At the age of sixty he was commissioned by King Francis I to design a Greek alphabet; for this he was given the honourable title of royal type founder. He died in 1561.

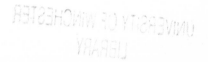